Methods and Models of Operations Research

PRENTICE-HALL INTERNATIONAL SERIES IN MANAGEMENT

Baumol *Economic Theory and Operations Analysis*
Churchman *Prediction and Optimal Decision: Philosophical Issues of a Science of Values*
Clarkson *The Theory of Consumer Demand: A Critical Appraisal*
Greenlaw, Herron, and Rawdon *Business Simulation in Industrial and University Education*
Holt, Modigliani, Muth, and Simon *Planning Production, Inventories, and Work Force*
Kaufmann *Methods and Models of Operations Research*
Miller and Starr *Executive Decisions and Operations Research*
Muth and Thompson *Industrial Scheduling*
Pfiffner and Sherwood *Administrative Organization*

PRENTICE-HALL, INC.
PRENTICE-HALL INTERNATIONAL, INC., UNITED KINGDOM AND EIRE
PRENTICE-HALL OF CANADA, LTD., CANADA
J. H. DE BUSSY, LTD., HOLLAND AND FLEMISH-SPEAKING BELGIUM
DUNOD PRESS, FRANCE
MARUZEN COMPANY, LTD., FAR EAST
C. BERTELSMANN VERLAG, WEST GERMANY AND AUSTRIA
HERRERO HERMANOS, SUCS., SPAIN AND LATIN AMERICA

Methods and Models of Operations Research

Arnold Kaufmann

Professeur a l'Institut Polytechnique de Grenoble
Conseilleur Scientifique a la Compagnie des Machines Bull

Translated by *Scripta Technica, Inc.*

Prentice-Hall, Inc.
Englewood Cliffs, N.J.

PRENTICE-HALL INTERNATIONAL, INC., *London*
PRENTICE-HALL OF AUSTRALIA, PTY., LTD., *Sydney*
PRENTICE-HALL OF CANADA, LTD., *Toronto*
PRENTICE-HALL FRANCE, S.A.R.L., *Paris*
PRENTICE-HALL OF JAPAN, INC., *Tokyo*
PRENTICE-HALL DE MEXICO, S.A., *Mexico City*

Originally published as *Méthodes et Modelès de la Recherche Opérationnelle.* ©—1959 by Dunod, Paris.

Second printing...... January, 1964

Library of Congress Catalog Card Number: 63-17410

Printed in the United States of America—C57940

Foreword

"And the science which knows to what end each thing must be done is the most authoritative of the sciences, and more authoritative than any ancillary science; and this end is the good of that thing, and in general the supreme good in the whole of nature."

(Aristotle, Metaphysics, Book I, 2)

Operations research claims to say how, but does not say to what end. This "end" will remain the ultimate question for men to ask themselves, and it is certainly not logic that will provide the answer.

***

This book is not a work of political economy or econometrics; neither is it a book on statistical methods or probability theory. Its aim is far more modest. Many engineers, management consultants, accounting experts, etc. have not been able to devote sufficient time to mathematical studies. It is with these people in mind that the author has provided a book which, while it makes use of mathematics, avoids over-complicated and often useless developments—useless, that is, except for those who intend to become economic engineers or operations research analysts. For the latter, this book will offer little, because we believe that a good analyst should have far more background in mathematics than is required to understand this book. The perfect analyst must be a statistician, a well-informed economist, and a man of experience. Does this mean that nobody else should be interested in operations research? We do not think so, because the procedures of this discipline will develop only to the degree to which it becomes generally accepted by executives in top management, no matter what their areas of special responsibility.

Actually, as we see it, there should be some kind of communication between the engineers, managers, and accountants, on the one hand, and the analysts on the other. This implies a common language and mutual understanding. Other specialists are also interested in this new discipline: mathematical engineers and programmers of electronic computers. They too, in order to develop the methods of numerical calculation, need to familiarize themselves with the methods and models of operations research.

Adapted to the mathematical level of both groups, concerned with factors currently utilized in industry for the examination and analysis of economic or management phenomena: these characteristics describe the present work.

No doubt there are some who will consider our concept of operations research a bit arbitrary. Actually, we place it in the class of artificial phenomena, i.e., those created by man to serve him: the field of structures, of machines, of products.

We ask our readers to bear with us for the inevitable imperfections in this work, and also for not having explored in detail the subjects of sequential problems, game theory, dynamic programming, and information theory, which would have required another book. This book presents the reader with models derived directly from, or associated with, only the more practical problems; the explanation of these problems will, it is hoped, inspire him to go on to the study of new and fruitful theories.

We wish, finally, to thank our good friend, Professor Reeb, of the Faculté des Sciences of the University of Grenoble, whose encouragement was invaluable; R. Cruon, former student at the Ecole Polytechnique, now Ingénieur Militaire des Poudres; and P. Simionesco, Ingénieur de l'Ecole Nationale Supérieure de l'Aéronautique.

This book is divided into two parts.

For Part One, no mathematical background is needed beyond what is taught in the first year of our second-degree classes. We have deferred to Part Two all the mathematical developments, the difficult proofs, and the complicated calculations. At the end of some of the sections in Part One, a number is given which refers the reader to the section in Part Two where he will find those developments whose understanding requires more advanced studies in mathematics. In closing, we might note that a brief summary of matrix calculations, probability concepts, the concepts of statistics, and symbolic calculus is presented at the beginning of Part Two.

A. K.

***

Contents

Part II

Mathematical Developments

Tables

Methods and Models of Operations Research

Introduction*

Operations research was christened in the cradle Mars built for it. But, although it was born in 1937, at a time when the storms were gathering over our world, its real origins reach far back in time. Let us briefly scan the principal stages of its history before going on to analyze its characteristics and explain its amazing growth.

***

As a beginning, let us accept a simple definition: Operations research is the scientific approach to decisions.

It might be said that to decide is the nature of man, for decision implies a conscious choice among several possible solutions. While this is the diametric opposite of instinct and reflex, it is nevertheless quite often dictated, to a greater or lesser degree, by intuition—that mental apprehension of the truth which finds in the data of experience what rational method seeks in applying a chain of reasoning to knowledge.

The great strategists, like the great businessmen, have for the most part been intuitive men; but it would seem that the day is past when the "Chief" could find within himself all the data needed for his decisions. The "Experience-Intuition" approach is fast giving way to one of "Information-Reasoning." This evolution has come about in two stages: first came the recourse to statistical information; then, the application of scientific reasoning.

While statistical method is a very ancient means of treating information,** its analytical techniques and the breadth of the data collected are recent developments. Despite its present-day shortcomings, statistics endows information with an objectivity it would otherwise lack. Only numbers make it possible at the same time to define and limit the object, to measure phenomena quantitatively, and even to distinguish qualitative aspects, provided always that appropriate criteria have been defined and selected.

---

*Translator's Note: The Introduction and author's Foreword are translated from the original French edition.

**See our preface to the work of R. Dumas: L'Entreprise et la Statistique ("Business and Statistics") (Dunod: Paris, 1954).

Today, businessmen have an increasing need for information. A man who heads an enterprise of complex structure and expanding dimensions cannot efficiently control his organization without the aid of copious, swift, and analytical information. But the moment that economic growth deprives the head of an enterprise of direct and personal contact with all aspects of his operation, it becomes vitally important, in order to avoid any personal bias which might have dangerous consequences, that the information gathered for him by others be "depersonalized." In other words, it must be expressed in incontestable, objective figures.

In this connection, statistical research is the first aspect of rational management; the second appears at the point where scientific reasoning replaces intuition and rough calculation. This new stage is operations research. The first manifestations of it can be found in certain studies in econometrics, which for some thirty years has made great progress (thanks to its discovery of models) in analyzing economic phenomena within a strictly defined frame of reference, by means of mathematics or statistics.

The risks of war, and the conduct of military operations, provided operations research with favorable conditions for development. Doubtless, one could describe the mission entrusted to Archimedes by Hiero, King of Syracuse, of finding a way to fend off the attack of the Roman ships, as one of the first military problems in operations research. But operations research did not really come into its own until after the start of World War II.* The substantial results it produced then were made possible by the conjunction of two essential factors:

—first, the requirements of defense, which demanded effective protection while maintaining a "cost-is-no-object" attitude towards high research expenses;

—second, the progress already achieved: in mathematics, which provided new analytical procedures for research workers; and in the field of high-speed computers, which are essential when the number of variables in a problem becomes very great.

***

Although operations research has continued to grow and develop since that time, it has not yet reached maturity. It is still too early to decide whether it should be categorized as science or as methodology. And yet one thing is certain: it already enjoys

---

*Utilization of radar in anti-aircraft defense; bomber flight programming to obtain the maximum ground destruction; calculation of the optimum size for seagoing convoys so as to reduce torpedo risks to a minimum, etc.

complete autonomy. In the world of science or technology, a discipline can claim a separate identity only when it answers a real need and comprises a body of principles that are not limited by excessive specialization. On this last count, we may note that a number of operations research procedures can be used to solve problems that are organically very different from one another. In every case, the situation presents (a) one or more objectives to be achieved for optimum conditions, and (b) constraints, i.e. limiting conditions that are imposed. And yet we notice very often that problems of different natures arise under analogous conditions. In other words, the essential identity is replaced by an analogy among the solution procedures. Hence we can say that, in operations research, there is no such thing as a specifically military or specifically economic problem. What we have are problems of certain types, which although they may arise in the most widely diverse fields, lend themselves to certain types of solutions. This same state of affairs can be found, furthermore, in disciplines closely allied with operations research: no statistical method, for example, is restricted to use in such-and-such an area. To specialize the methods of operations research would therefore mean compromising its opportunities for growth, which require, on the contrary, precisely this polyvalence.

Taking as a pretext the expanding, and highly promising, state of operations research at the present time, some people resist defining it, as if precise definition would necessarily cause it to harden into a mold. Without accepting the inverse notion that the choice of term can, of itself, confer boundless riches, it seems to us a sound move to propose a definition. As we see it, operations research is "the body of methods which makes possible a rational determination of the most efficient or economical solution in policy-decision problems concerning the management of an economic or human phenomenon, drawing upon statistical-mathematical procedures which sometimes require the use of high-speed computers. These methods are based upon a prior analysis of the relationships among the technical and psychological factors in the phenomenon's structure, which is achieved by recourse to the various appropriate scientific disciplines.*"

Of course, by choosing this way of stating it, we are considering solely the help our discipline can provide in making decisions.

---

*This is, save for certain modifications in form, the definition we suggested in 1957 in our opening lecture to the Course in Mechanographic Studies at the National Conservatory of Arts and Trades (Paris, 1958). By mechanographic machine we mean any device or process used to perform manual or intellectual work in the area of recording and calculation.

However, we are dealing here with a methodology whose useful potential must not be limited exclusively to the domain of action. Research, of whatever nature, can and should make use of it. If we wish to indicate in this definition the general applicability of operations research, we have only to include as its aim the explanation of a particular phenomenon. This is one of the concerns with which we shall deal when we come to discuss terminology.

Recherche opérationnelle is the French translation of the British term "operational research" and the American version, "operations research." The Anglo-American term "operation" designates both military activities and the understanding of a phenomenon for purposes of action. While the first meaning has entered into French terminology, the second does fall a bit harshly on the Gallic ear. Therefore, we would be tempted to suggest another term: rational computation*, which suggests both calculation and scientific rigor, and hence would have the advantage of covering both corporate management studies and research in pure theory.

***

Rather than dwell on this question of terms—which doubtless would be excessive purism, although precision in language is often the first condition of rigorous thinking—let us now ask what advantages might derive from the widespread adoption of our discipline. As we see it, there are two objectives: to encourage practical application, and to develop a particular state of mind.

If one is convinced, as we are, of the need for placing business economics** on a sound numerical and rational basis, it is essential to encourage the use of rigorous procedures. Contrary to the beliefs of some people, operations research does not always require the use of very advanced mathematics, which would make it the prerogative of large organizations alone, or of those that could afford to call in specialists. It includes a number of simple forms whose usage could well be more widely adopted in the field of moderate-sized business. In every case, it brings an analytical and integrating view to the study of problems.

---

*This is the term under which we intend subsequently to explore the problems of business management.

**For our views on business economics, see particularly La Normalisation Comptable au Service de l'Entreprise, de la Science, et de la Nation ("Accounts Standardization in the Service of the Corporation, Science, and the Nation") Goals and problems; French and foreign solutions. (Dunod: Paris, 1951).

But the spread of operations research also has the advantage of encouraging research in business economics, whose development is, we believe, the essential condition for a renaissance in economic thought and science. For the analysis of the phenomena of production and exchange at the level of the enterprise, then at the level of economic sectors, is the only thing that will enable us to grasp the reality and nature of these phenomena, whose features often are lost or blurred in the overall economy.*

As we have demonstrated in our teaching and in our work since 1945, the development of research in business economics implies several conditions:

—first, abundant documentation, which statistics cannot provide in the old form of partial and occasional samplings; it must be found within the organization itself, by means of standard bookkeeping methods, which greatly facilitate the gathering and handling of numerical data;

—second, an opportunity for fruitful discussion: first of all, within the organization itself, among engineers, salesmen, market specialists, administration and management experts; and then, among the research workers and the economic policy-makers.

—lastly, approaches and research methods that make it possible to exploit the collected information so as to solve the problems posed both by management and by the scientific study of economic phenomena.

The remarkable progress achieved on the first two points during the last fifteen years indicates that it is now time to attack the third. In fact, it is undeniable that, under the influence of various factors, the documentation is piling up and an eagerness for discussion is widely felt. It remains now to provide the methods needed. That is the aim of this book.

***

It is worth noting that the phases of M. Kaufmann's training in operations research reflect somewhat the growth pattern of the discipline itself. Assigned during the last years of the war to an American operations research service, our colleague, at war's end, pursued his studies in that field. He now holds the position of mathematical engineer in a major French company manufacturing electronic machines, where his great scientific learning is invaluable. Called upon as he is to solve numerous practical problems in operations research, M. Kaufmann has acquired an experience in depth which, it seems to us, gives him particular

---

*See Note ** on preceding page.

qualifications to be the author of the first work on this discipline to be written and edited directly in French. We believe he has produced a work in no way lacking originality and of considerable usefulness.

Another contributing factor to this success must be emphasized. Experience has shown repeatedly that the best book is the one whose subject matter has been taught before it is ever committed to paper, because the lecture hall is the true test bench of scientific and technical literature. Our colleague has already proved his pedagogical prowess as an expository writer in the many courses he has taught, particularly those he now gives to the mathematical engineering students at the University of Grenoble, the students at the Faculté des Sciences at Toulouse, the auditors of the Swiss Automation Association in a course sponsored by the University of Geneva, and the job-trainees at the Center for Study of Industrial Problems at Lille.

It is therefore with the fullest confidence that we present M. Kaufmann's work on Methods and Models of Operations Research, certain as we are that it will greatly further the development of business economics.

André A.-Brunet
Professor
at the National Conservatory of Arts and Trades
and at the Institute of Political Studies
of the University of Paris.

PART I

METHODS AND MODELS

Chapter **1**

General observations and remarks

Section 1

INTRODUCTION

Before we describe a number of mathematical models employed in operations research, and before explaining the methods that are generally used with these models to reach meaningful conclusions, we shall try to establish the real nature of our subject and the area in which our concerns will lie.

In writing this book, we did not have in mind presenting a complete course in operations research; we placed ourself in the position of an "applied" mathematician who wishes to describe the mathematical tools of physics, without pretending to be a physicist. The situation is the same here: the author makes no pretensions to a work of economic research on the grand scale nor does he intend to lecture management engineers. As the title of the book indicates, we are concerned with presenting methods and models; it is left to the individual reader to make use of them or not. We might have called this book "Applied Mathematics of Management," but those who still do not accept mathematics as a working tool would have been mislead as to the elementary character of the book.

Section 2

NATURAL PHENOMENA AND ARTIFICIAL PHENOMENA

The physical sciences emerged when it became possible to evaluate, first on a qualitative, and then on a quantitative basis, the phenomena of nature. The first attempts of the ancients in this direction were made solely with the aim of unearthing facts that would confirm metaphysical or cosmological hypotheses. Like geometry, physics was found exciting because it served no other purpose than the elevation of thought. In the eighteenth century the first utilitarian achievements of experimental physics appeared; then came mathematical physics, whose models and apparent laws made possible an almost perfect analysis and prediction of a vast number of natural phenomena. A very similar pattern of development has taken place in our knowledge and use of another science—that of artificial phenomena, those phenomena that owe their existence to the application of man's genius. Is the word "artificial" preferable to the word "economic?" Would it not be better to speak of "management phenomena?" At the risk of some criticism, we shall use the expression "management phenomena" whenever we are speaking of active wholes (ensembles) consisting of men, machines, and products, in either their concrete or abstract forms.

Although physics did not become a practical science until the eighteenth century, the science of management phenomena—which in certain of its aspects is called "economics"—did not have meaningful utility until the twentieth. We should not like there to be any confusion as to the word "utility." To us, this word means that theory has made possible certain technological or organic achievements in human society. Long before our time, and even before Adam Smith or Quesnay, political economy was a philosophical subject for certain men who, almost without exception, centered their attention on its qualitative aspects. It was the growth of the mathematical sciences that permitted a development in economics similar to that of physics; and it was this development that made possible our knowledge of structures and of laws.

Operations research is not, in itself, a science, but rather a scientific attitude towards management phenomena—unfortunately we are afflicted today with the habit of using a single word to represent both the method of observing facts and the facts themselves, precisely as happened with physics and the science of physics. However, this question of semantics is not of major interest to us: all we seek is clarity as to what we are talking about. Another word, "econometrics," is used to represent the entire body of knowledge which relates to the quantitative aspects of management phenomena. When one speaks to an economist about operations research, he will state, quite accurately, that we are just discovering what people like himself have been studying for at least a hundred years. Then why use this phrase "operations research" which has little difference of meaning? This issue is hardly worth arguing. One fact is unquestionable: reasonable men have changed their attitude towards management or economic phenomena; instead of being satisfied with intuition or qualitative deduction, they now demand a quantitative description of the facts. In order to make a decision, they want to have a formal or probabilistic knowledge of events, a knowledge that will very often be derived from statistical measurements. This is the origin of the definition—not a bad one, at that—of operations research as the scientific approach to decisions.

Since we shall be referring to management phenomena, let us here present a few concrete examples:

- —the total set of operations involved in assembly-line manufacture of a product;
- —variations in the level of inventory;
- —the distribution of rolling-stock in a railroad system;
- —the management of funds;
- —a problem of strategy;
- —sales promotion decisions;
- —the economic implications of a product mix;
- —the development of a waiting line;
- —organizing a sea convoy in wartime;
- —the planning of agricultural production;
- —the location of a factory.

These examples indicate the variety of things that can be studied in operations research. In each example there are structures, machines, or products, combined with the activities of man. The borderlines between the economic and the physical areas are not always very clearly defined—economics and technology are often closely linked; for example: the manufacture of a chemical product on an industrial scale poses both technological and economic problems, and may also pose problems that are physiological, psychological, or social in nature. The concept of economic function, which will be developed subsequently, provides some illumination of the borderlines among the various arbitrary fields.

Section 3

MEASUREMENT AND THE MATHEMATICAL MODEL

Two equally fruitful avenues are available to the physicist in his research: one is based on measurement and experiment; the other is based on mathematics. The same holds true for those interested in management phenomena. The methodology of physical measurements is better established than that of economics. Basically, this is because one can repeat a physical experiment many times under identical conditions and arrive fairly easily at an objective measurement, as well as a calculation of the maximum experimental error. In the management situation, it is rarely possible to carry out experiments, due to the high cost. Is it conceivable to arrange at will the traffic load on a highway, or to calculate the selling price of an item made by machines of a new type that has never been used before in production? Therefore we must content ourselves with statistical measurements, obtained by observing a great number of cases; analysis of such statistics allows us to discover functional relationships or theoretical distributions. Starting from such analyses, we construct a mathematical model: this is nothing more than a set of functions and probability distributions which, when the measured values of the variables and parameters are introduced, satisfies all the relationships, for all possible cases or for a very large number of them.

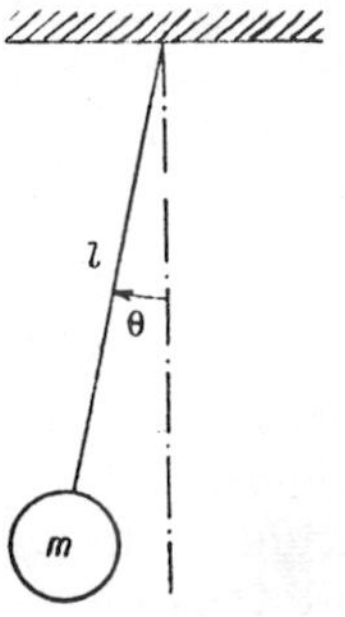

Fig. 3.1

We have no intention of presenting here a course in statistics,* but we must emphasize the importance of statistical measurements. For example, to cite a mean without specifying the standard deviation, or to give the measurements drawn from a sample without specifying the conditions under which the sample was obtained, can be very misleading. Hence a preliminary study of statistics is essential, and measurements must always be accompanied by the necessary information as to the circumstances which they were made.

When a physicist looks at a pendulum, such as the one in Fig. 3.1, he can immediately associate its behavior, once it has been set in oscillation, with a differential equation:

$$ml^2 \frac{d^2\theta}{dt^2} + mgl\theta = 0, \qquad 3.1$$

or, to simplify:

$$\frac{d^2\theta}{dt^2} + \frac{g}{l}\,\theta = 0. \qquad 3.2$$

Equation (3.2) is the mathematical model of the phenomenon which occurs when the pendulum is displaced by a very slight angle from its equilibrium position and allowed to swing freely. From this model, the physicist can derive a law: the uniform period (isochronism) of oscillations;

$$T = 2\pi \sqrt{\frac{l}{g}}; \qquad 3.3$$

and he can also use this model for other measurements.

---

*On this point, the reader may consult Dumas, L'Entreprise et la Statistique ("Business Statistics") (Dunod: Paris, 1954).

By carrying out another experiment with an electrical circuit (Fig. 3.2), and proceeding to describe the phenomenon by an equation, one obtains, if q equals the instantaneous value of the charge on the plates of capacitor C:

$$L\frac{d^2q}{dt^2} + \frac{q}{C} = 0, \qquad 3.4$$

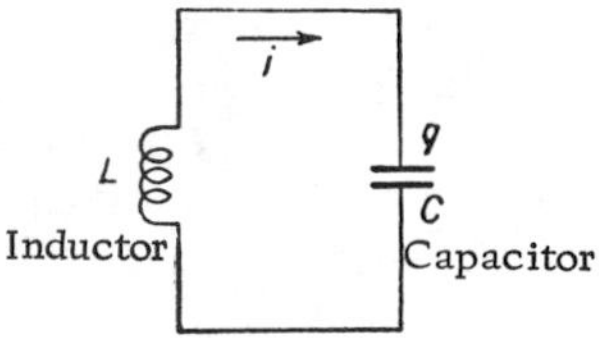

Fig. 3.2

or

$$\frac{d^2q}{dt^2} + \frac{q}{LC} = 0. \qquad 3.5$$

Equation (3.5) is the mathematical model of this electrical phenomenon, from which the physicist can derive a law: that of the uniform periodicity of the electrical oscillations produced:

$$T = 2\pi\sqrt{LC}. \qquad 3.6$$

A comparison of Equations (3.2) and (3.5), and then laws (3.3) and (3.6)—replacing l with L, g with 1/C, and θ with q—shows that they are the same. Thus, we find that one and the same model may apply to completely different phenomena. It is easy, then, to appreciate the importance in physics of having a number of such models to serve as guides for new research.

If we may philosophize a bit, we might point out that analogy is playing and will continue to play an increasingly important role in research, since by employing it we can take into account the ever-growing heritage of preceding discoveries.

It is possible to operate in the same way on a management phenomenon; having constructed a representative mathematical model, we will often find it very similar to one derived from a phenomenon involving entirely different entities.

For example, an observer measures the intervals at which vehicles arrive at a customs checkpoint and the length of time they are stopped there. After a fairly large number of observations, he notes that the average arrival rate every day from 2 to 4 p.m. is constant, that the average customs check time is also constant, and that it is possible to predict the average length of the waiting line (queue). Knowing the mathematical description of this situation, he will construct the following model:

$$\frac{d}{dt}p_n(t) = \lambda\, p_{n-1}(t) + \mu\, p_{n+1}(t) - (\lambda + \mu)\, p_n(t), \quad n > 0 \qquad 3.7$$

$$\frac{d}{dt} p_0(t) = -\lambda p_0(t) + \mu p_1(t), \qquad 3.8$$

where λ is the average arrival rate, and μ, the average customs check time; $p_n(t)$ is the probability that at time t there is a waiting line of n cars, including the car which is being serviced.

Assuming that he knows how to solve such equations, which are not, after all, excessively complicated, he will find that the average number of cars in the waiting line, including the one now going through the checkpoint, is

$$\bar{n} = \frac{\lambda}{\mu - \lambda}. \qquad 3.9$$

Thus, for example, if the average rate of arrival is 12 cars per hour, and the average check time is 16 cars per hour, the value of n, which is the mathematical expectation of the number of cars in line or going through the checkpoint, will be 3. Of course, this information alone is insufficient, since one would also wish to know the probabilities of a waiting line of zero length, or of length one, two, three, or x cars. The reader will already have realized how useful such a model can be in predicting what will happen under analogous circumstances.

Suppose now that our observer goes to a telephone switchboard and measures the intervals between calls, and the time a certain line is busy. He will quickly see that this phenomenon is governed by the same equations as the preceding one. The same mathematical model is applicable to both.

We have thus obtained models which describe management phenomena of the most diverse kinds; some of them are simple and contain few variables. In these instances we can analyze the problem very easily for some values of the variables. For others, very large calculating machines are needed, because the calculations are complicated or very numerous.

We will distinguish two basic kinds of models: first, formal or deterministic models; and second, probabilistic models.

In the first group, the variables are linked by functional relationships; in the second group, a given dimensional value is associated with a probability, and such dimensional values are called random variables. Queuing or waiting-line problems, for which we have just provided a very sketchy example, are described by a probabilistic model. The pendulum and oscillating circuit problems, on the contrary, have a deterministic model. In physics as well as in operations research, one finds both types of models. Some models are valid for physics and for management: for example, in the theory of equipment wear, a physical model of the phenomenon can be constructed and used.

Section 4

OBJECTIVES, CONSTRAINTS, ECONOMIC FUNCTION*

There is a fundamental distinction between natural and artificial phenomena. With natural phenomena, the "purpose" is entirely unknown to us, and research is limited to a description of causes and effects. With artificial phenomena, there is almost always a purpose, a goal, or a body of objectives which one plans to achieve. Every organization has a purpose; the motives behind this purpose may be moral, material, or a complex combination of factors. The description of this purpose takes explicit form when one defines the objectives to be attained. For example:

—in an industrial problem: to reach a certain production rate in a given time, to meet certain qualitative specifications for the product, to capture a given share of the market.

*Since the word objective has many shades of meaning, we think it important to examine it carefully.

For many authors, objective and economic function are synonyms. And in this case, to state that "there can be one objective, and only one, to be optimized," must mean that "there can exist only one economic function to be optimized, and no more."

Other authors take objective and goal to be achieved as synonyms. In this case, one can conceive of a problem with several objectives; for example: to equal or better a given output, not to exceed a certain investment level, not to exceed a given percentage of overhead. These objectives are actually constraints.

Unfortunately, opinion on this point is sharply divided, and, contrary to what we have done in our opening explanations, we shall employ the following definitions from now on:

By objective we shall indicate the goal to be achieved, the goal to be bettered, or the limit not to be exceeded (as the case may be); and note that there can be several objectives.

By constraint we shall indicate a limitation over which we have, or do not have, control (as the case may be).

The objectives and the constraints taken together constitute the mathematical restrictions.

As for economic function, it is the function to be optimized, which represents the value associated with the system or the operation. This function is always unique; i.e., there can be only one.

We should point out that, in certain problems, the economic function can be an objective, which is then unique. For example, an industrialist may take his own profit as his sole objective. In this case, the other limitations are only constraints.

—in a military problem: to occupy a certain portion of territory, to destroy certain designated installations.

Almost always, the purpose or the body of objectives can be fixed or attained only if prior consideration has been given to the price or the sacrifice that is acceptable as the cost of carrying out the operation. According to the nature of the problem, this price or sacrifice will arise in the form of an economic function or a function of the cost of operations that is to be "optimized," which is to say rendered maximal or minimal as the case may be. An industrialist will wish to achieve his production objectives while maximizing the economic function that represents his annual profit. A general will wish to achieve the military objectives that have been assigned to him, while minimizing the cost of operations function, which will represent, in this case, loss of life and matériel.

Hence, logically, every organization or operation must have an economic function; and, since we propose to seek the optimum of that function, it must be unique. We shall now state this observation in the form of a principle:

"In every organization or operation, one may encounter or prescribe several objectives that are to be achieved, surpassed, or not exceeded; but there can be only one economic function to be optimized in relation to that organization or operation."

It is regrettable to hear the heads of companies state their production problems in some such way as this: "I should like to boost my sales volume to the maximum, while cutting my annual manufacturing costs and my rate of investment for the next year to a minimum." A correct statement of the problem might be this: "I should like to reach or surpass such-and-such a sales volume, not exceed my fixed investment rate, and cut my manufacturing costs to the minimum." A problem stated this way is understandable, and can be solved. The first statement has no real meaning.*

Therefore, let us repeat: a management phenomenon may contain several objectives, but one, and only one, economic function to be optimized.

This economic function may be evaluated, according to circumstances, in dollars, in time, in distance, etc. Thus, we might be well advised to use another name for this function, since the function may sometimes relate to activities that cannot be classified as economic phenomena (military operations, for example).

---

*This is not to deny the propriety, in certain special cases, of simultaneously optimizing several economic functions, each of them relevant to a system or operation, or to the total property of many individuals, each taken separately (Pareto's optimality). Cf., for example, Ref. [G-22], page 49. (see Bibliography).

Evaluation function, or value function, would probably be the most suitable term. However, we shall conform to a habit acquired by operations research specialists and use the expression economic function for the industrial field, which is the principal concern of this book.

We should point out again that the objective can be the economic function itself. For example, to go back to the problem of the waiting line, we can attempt to discover what value must be assigned to μ in order to achieve a minimum total figure for the cost of customs services (wages) plus whatever value may be assigned to the waiting time of the drivers who pass through the check point.

Now let us present some specific examples in which an economic function appears. The first concerns the analysis of an economic series in a manufacturing process.

Let c_s be the cost of stocking one piece or part for one unit of time; c_l, the total set-up cost for one lot (a lot is defined as the number of units produced in a single production run); n, the number of pieces or parts in a lot; T, the duration of the production run; and θ, the supply period during which N pieces or parts are produced. Then, the total cost for the period θ can be expressed as:

$$\Gamma(n) = \frac{N}{n} c_l + \tfrac{1}{2}\, \theta\, n\, c_s \,. \qquad 4.1$$

The problem will then be expressed as follows: Produce N pieces or parts in the time θ (objective to attain), in lots of n pieces or parts, in such a way that the total cost Γ (n) is a minimum (economic function), with costs c_s and c_l known.

This minimum will occur for:

$$n = n_0 = \sqrt{2 \frac{N}{\theta} \frac{c_l}{c_s}}\,; \qquad 4.2$$

the cost value is therefore:

$$\Gamma = \Gamma_0 = \sqrt{2 N \theta c_l c_s}\,. \qquad 4.3$$

A manufacturer sells 5 products, whose unit selling prices are c_1, c_2, c_3, c_4, and c_5. Manufacture and inventory are subject to restrictions (constraints); it is desired to attain a maximum value for the volume of business as a whole (economic function):

$$\Gamma = c_1 x_1 + c_2 x_2 + c_3 x_3 + c_4 x_4 + c_5 x_5\,, \qquad 4.4$$

where x_1, x_2, x_3, x_4, and x_5 are the quantities of each product to be manufactured, with the factory output as a whole subject to the restrictions or constraints.

Another example has to do with the replacement, one by one or all at once, of machines now in service. If c_1 is the unit cost of replacement all at once, c_2 is the unit cost of one-by-one replacement, and N_0 is the initial number of new machines put into service at the beginning of each period, then the cost per unit of time will be:

$$\gamma(t) = \frac{N_0 c_1}{t} + \frac{c_2 r(t)}{t}, \qquad 4.5$$

where r(t) is the function that gives the total number of replacements up to time t. The objective is to arrange the replacement, singly or all at once, of the N_0 machines so as to maintain a constant number in operation at all times. The economic function to be optimized is the cost per unit time γ (t). This function is a minimum (as we shall show in Section 50) for an interval t_0, or period of general replacement, corresponding to equality between the cost of the rate of variation $r'(t)$ and the average cost.

It is equally interesting to see how the constraints may appear in a simple, practical problem.

A man intends to manufacture two products, P_1 and P_2. The first is sold at a unit profit of 100 francs, the second at a unit profit of 50 francs. If x_1 and x_2 are the quantities of each manufactured per day, the total daily profit will be:

$$B = 100\,x_1 + 50\,x_2 \text{ (economic function).} \qquad 4.6$$

The products are subjected during their manufacture to a certain treatment that lasts 5 seconds for P_1 and 1 second for P_2. This is done by means of a single machine which is in operation 24 hours a day (or 86,400 seconds). One restriction would then be:

$$5x_1 + x_2 \leq 86{,}400 \text{ (first constraint).} \qquad 4.7$$

The products must be held in inventory for 24 hours before delivery to the customers. The unit volume is 0.02 cubic meter for P_1, and 0.03 cubic meter for P_2; the warehouse capacity is only 1,000 cubic meters, which gives us another limitation:

$$0.02\,x_1 + 0.03\,x_2 \leq 1{,}000 \text{ (second constraint).} \qquad 4.8$$

Thus, the total daily profit is limited by the capacity of the machine and by the available warehouse space.

In other problems for which probabilistic models have been constructed, the constraints appear in the form of probability values to be surpassed or not to be exceeded. Thus, we could specify that the probability that a plane wishing to land at an airport would not have to circle and wait for a runway must be higher than 0.99.

Section 5

POLICIES

In certain problems, it is extremely difficult to evaluate some parameters; in fact, these parameters may be purely subjective. For example, in calculating a total inventory cost, the value assigned to the impossibility of supplying a requested item—the unit cost of a shortage—is very hard to determine. Under these conditions, the determination of the optimum value of the economic function would have only theoretical significance. In cases like this, we can proceed as follows: determine the optimum value of the economic function for certain arbitrary values of the parameter; often, we may even construct a family of curves giving the value of the economic function as related to the most important variable, with each curve corresponding to one arbitrary value of the parameter. The results corresponding to each of the curves constitute what is called a policy. The following is an example.

A large department store delivers customers' purchases in trucks whose daily delivery capacity and hourly cost, including personnel and overhead, are known. The problem is to determine the number of trucks that the store should own in order to minimize delivery costs. Further, we know that every purchase must be delivered within a certain time, either by company truck or by an outside delivery service that charges considerably more than it costs the store to make the delivery in its own trucks. The number of parcels to be delivered each day varies in a random manner. The same applies to the number of parcels loaded on any one truck. For the problem to be meaningful, it is necessary to set a deadline for delivery. Then, it is possible to study the total cost of deliveries as a function of the number of trucks in service. For policy P_1, the delivery deadline will correspond to a maximum of 24 hours after the day of purchase; for policy P_2, a delay of 48 hours; for P_3, a delay of 3 days; etc. It is all but impossible to assign a numerical value to the effect of an increase in delivery delay on the loyalty of customers. Management will pattern its policy on those of the competition, or choose one of its own. But, for any choice, it can determine the best number of trucks to assign to delivery service. If it chooses policy P_1 while its competitors have adopted P_2, it may well find out just how much of a sacrifice it has agreed to make.

Policies can sometimes refer to several different parameters; special graphic procedures can then be used to study and justify a choice.

Without wishing to push the analogy too far, the situation of the operations research analyst, as compared to that of the manager or executive, is similar to that of a ship's navigator, who advises the captain as to what course to chart to accomplish the objectives of the voyage, taking into account the ship's capabilities, the elements, and events foreseen or unforeseen. There are several ways to navigate, there are several possible policies; for each of them, the navigator tries to work out the minimum cost for the voyage.

Section 6

BASIC CONCEPTS

With every advance or forward step in the physical sciences, new concepts have been born; thanks to these, physicists or engineers can exchange accurate information about phenomena, define methods of measurement, and state laws of almost universal meaning. For example, the mechanical concepts of energy, momentum, moment of inertia, and natural frequency, and the electrical concepts of impedance, resonant frequency, etc. are basic concepts that play a fundamental role in the mathematical models of physics. The discovery of these concepts comes about step by step, and not without error and transformation.

The same thing holds good in our field. We know a certain number of these basic concepts, i.e. concepts that play a fundamental part in many management phenomena, but we are still far from the richness of expression of physics. Operations research has as one of its goals the discovery of such concepts: this is the means by which we will gain insight into problems and be able more readily to give quantitative expression to our aims. The problem of vehicular traffic in a city, for example, has made little or no progress towards solution because we still have no clear idea of what dimensions are characteristic of urban traffic, and also because we do not know what economic function describes it.

Let us look, just for example, at a few of the typical dimensions that play an essential role in some important problems.

In a waiting line problem, the basic dimension is the intensity of traffic:

$$\psi = \frac{\lambda}{\mu}, \qquad 6.1$$

where λ is the average rate of arrival and μ is the average rate of flow through the checkpoint. In the theory of inventory, the basic dimension is the rate of allowable shortages or service level:

$$\varrho = \frac{c_p}{c_p + c_s}, \qquad 6.2$$

where c_s is the cost of storing one piece or part and c_p is the value assigned to the lack of that piece or part. In the same way, we find an important variable in the theory of replacements:

$$p_c(t) = -\frac{n'(t)}{n(t)}, \tag{6.3}$$

where n(t) is the number of machines still operative at time t. This dimension, called the damage rate, plays a basic role in replacement theory.

In every model or theory, there are one or more particularly significant dimensions: it is important to recognize them or to define them; they will be the most important parameters or variables.

As in physics, the discovery of basic concepts in the model makes it possible to explain a phenomenon more clearly, and to relate it to others.

Section 7

SUB-OPTIMIZATION

To demonstrate the danger, which is often inevitable, that lies in attempting to find an optimum in a problem that is too restricted, i.e. not inclusive enough, let us consider the problem of inventory.

Sales management generally wishes to have a wide variety of products, highly diversified and ready for delivery on very short notice to prevent the loss of sales. The economic function, logically, is the volume of sales, and inventories should be analyzed, in the opinion of this branch of management, with an eye to optimizing this sales volume.

Production management, on the contrary, seeks an intensive program involving very little product variety, and allowing considerable savings through mass production. The economic function that interests management here is the unit cost of its product. Very large inventories will result from optimization of the unit cost of the product.

Financial management would like to see inventory handled so as to cut investment costs to a minimum.

Personnel would like to lower employee turnover, improve the working conditions and the security of the workers. It is possible to give objective meaning to these intentions, and to translate them into a function to be optimized, which can also involve inventory because of limited assets.

The warehouse manager has still another point of view. As he sees it, the best possible inventory policy is the one that will give the lowest ratio of warehouse personnel salaries to inventory value, unless he prefers to optimize ease of handling.

And so we see that in one single company, five distinct economic functions can be considered as paramount, and that the inventory policy affects many departments.

It is because we do not yet know how to construct the general mathematical model, the most general model of a business enterprise, that we regretfully limit ourselves to constructing models for a part of the activity. When we achieve a sub-optimization, we must carefully examine the effects of the solution we have chosen on the other parts of the whole. The best solution from the point of view of production can be extremely dangerous from the point of view of the comptroller.

For example, there is an increasing tendency not to consider the problem of inventory as separate from that of production.*

There is another form of sub-optimization, which occurs when too short an interval has been chosen to define the economic function: for example, when we attempt to minimize the unit cost of the product over weekly, or, still worse, daily intervals (the latter is to be dismissed a priori in certain cases). The production optimum considered over the whole year may be quite different from the sum of the optima week by week, and, much more so, day by day. It very often happens that rapid changes in demand, in technology, or in supply require weekly or monthly planning. In such cases, it is important, and sometimes unavoidable, to proceed by successive optimizations.

One should not dismiss in advance the idea of sub-optimization; it allows us to define the structure of a part of the whole, to discover basic concepts, and to find relationships to the other parts. Almost always, it gives one a better grasp of the more general problem.

Moreover, isn't it wiser to deal first with partial problems when an analyst approaches the study of an organization's functioning for the first time?

Section 8

THE DESCRIPTION INTERVAL

The time interval during which the phenomenon is observed and described by the model is very important. For example, in a queuing or delay phenomenon, the measurement of the average rate of arrival can produce markedly different results according to whether it is taken for ten minutes, an hour, or six hours. This is due to the fact that we are dealing with a phenomenon that is

---

*See, for example, the article by J. Lesourne, "La Régulation Simultanée de la Production et des Stocks" ("Simultaneous Regulation of Production and Inventory"), Revue de Recherche Opérationnelle, Vol. 1, No. 2, 1st quarter 1957.

variable in time. It is very rare, furthermore, for a system to be really permanent. Therefore it is important to make sure, by means of measurements taken over varying time intervals, that the fluctuations are properly described.

Quite often, the phenomenon is quasi-periodic, and one can select the period (a simple example of this would be an economic series): the choice that is made can be most important. In inventory management and replacement decisions, one must take the complete cycle into account.

In some cases, one is lead to study transitional states of the system.

Figs. 8.1 through 8.4 show what we mean by stationary, nonstationary, permanent, or constant phenomena. A phenomenon is stationary if its formal representation or its law of probability does not depend on the initial instant such as t', t'', or t'''. It is permanent if the phenomenon reproduces itself identically in equal time intervals.

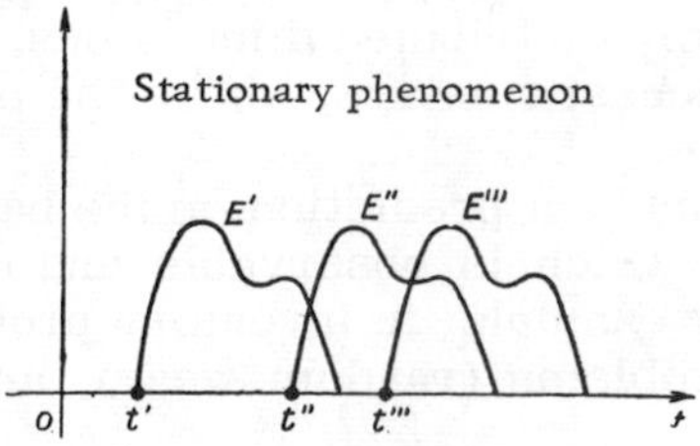

Fig. 8.1

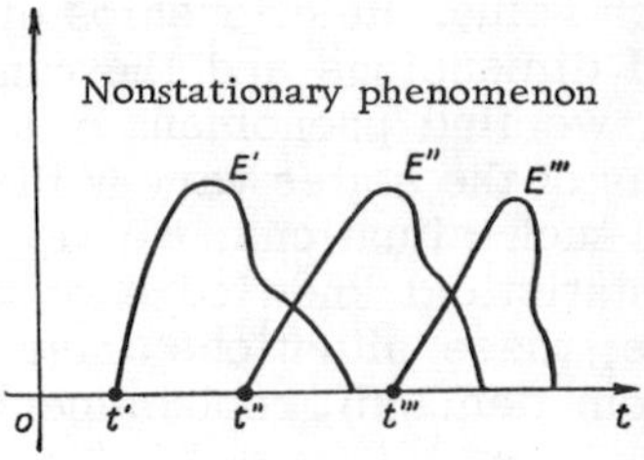

Fig. 8.2

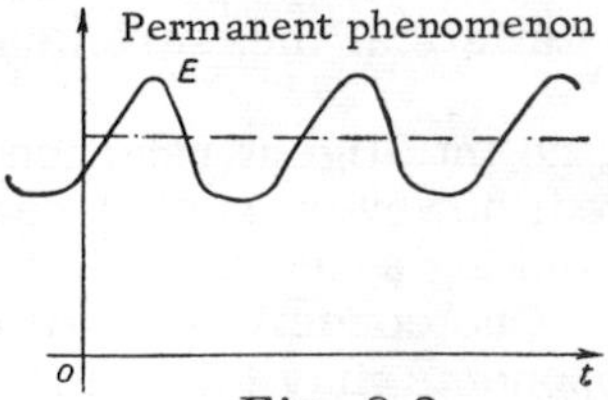

Fig. 8.3

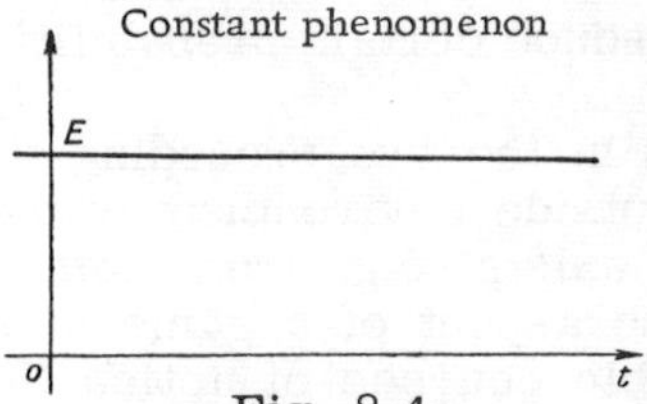

Fig. 8.4

Section 9

GENERAL ASPECT OF PROBLEMS

To analyze the structure of situations and then predict by means of scientific method: this might be a definition of operations research. Situations may be briefly classified as follows:

A) The structures are described by dimensions that are known with certainty, and the future can therefore be treated as determined. If the structures are very simple, then simple recourse to logic and experience makes it possible to choose the solution (or solutions) appropriate to the objectives, and to optimize the given economic function. If the structures are more complicated, the known dimensions can:

—form linear relationships: for example, those found in linear programs;

—involve relationships of rank order: for example, those found in priority problems;

—form systems which should be examined with respect to their combinatorial aspects: for example, planning problems;

—constitute sequential relationships, in which each state determines the following state.

Man exists in a determined universe.

B) Each decision is associated with a series of random states: certain dimensions are determined, others are random, i.e. having values depending on chance, but we know the probability distribution of each value. Relationships of all kinds can exist among the determined dimensions and the randomly distributed dimensions. Very often, we find phenomena of a stochastic nature, where the probabilities of the states vary with time.

In such situations, we try to make a prediction on the basis of our statistical knowledge of that which is observable and measurable; these situations arise, for example, in inventory problems (random demand), replacement problems (random wear), and the like.

Man exists in a universe governed by chance, but he can deduce certain probabilities from statistical measurement.

C) In the two preceding situations, no intelligent reaction from the outside environment was considered; however, such a reaction often exists, e.g. from competitors. Making a decision then takes on the aspect of a game of strategy. One conceives of all of the possible courses of action that the opponents may take, and associates each with a value or probability. A decision can then be considered as a strategy.

Man has an intelligent competitor.

D) One has some knowledge of the structures, but the probabilities of future events associated with one's decisions are unknown. One considers nature as an opponent, and step by step one looks for the most favorable outcome. Here scientific method fails, and is often replaced by intuition.

Man lives in an unknown universe.

We could not close this first chapter without recalling the prodigious work accomplished by John von Neumann, founder of the game theory of strategy, and his disciples in the application of mathematics to the analysis of economic and social phenomena. While we cannot thoroughly explore these matters here, since it would demand extensive discussion of certain developments that would carry us quite far from our subject, we do earnestly advise the reader to consult von Neumann's work and that of his successors. There the reader will find the scientific bases for the theory of the behavior of intelligent beings when dealing with nature or with one another.

Chapter **2**

Linear programs

Section 10

INTRODUCTION

Among the forms of mathematical models encountered in economic or management phenomena, linear programs occupy a very important place. In physics, linear systems have a similar importance, both because our knowledge is often, unfortunately, too limited to allow us to go any further, and because of a certain facility with which one can define concepts in these systems.

In this chapter, we shall not attempt a complete presentation of the theory of linear programming; our aim will be to explain, with the use of simple examples and illustrative cases, what linear programs consist of and how they arise. We shall avoid all theoretical questions; however, for those interested in mathematical developments, Chapter VII presents the methods of calculation that are used, some of which are basic and already classic.

We can define in a few lines what we mean by linear programming. An economic or management phenomenon involves a number of variables that are meaningful only when they are positive or null (some say "non-negative"). These variables are linked with one another by linear relationships and form a system of equations or inequations; these are the objectives or the constraints of the phenomenon. Of necessity, one adopts a linear function z of these variables, which will constitute the economic function that is to be maximized or minimized, as the case may be. These ideas will become clearer to the reader with the help of the first two of the following examples.

Section 11

CHARACTERISTICS OF LINEAR PROGRAMS

To begin with, let us clarify the distinctive structure of linear programs.

To manufacture two products, P_1 and P_2, they must be processed by three machines, M_1, M_2, and M_3, one after the other but in any order. The unit times for the operation of each machine on each product are given in the table below. Here, for example, we find that it takes 7 minutes for product P_1 to be processed by machine M_2. We assume that there is no wasted time while a machine waits for a product to emerge from another operation. We can assume this, since the order in which the operations are performed makes no difference.

	M_1	M_2	M_3
P_1	11 min.	7 min.	6 min.
P_2	9 min.	12 min.	16 min.

The hours that each machine will be available for operation during the month are as follows:

165 hours = 9,900 minutes for machine M_1,
140 hours = 8,400 minutes for machine M_2,
160 hours = 9,600 minutes for machine M_3.

Product P_1 yields a unit profit of 900 francs, and product P_2 yields a unit profit of 1,000 francs.

Under these conditions, how much of product P_1 and product P_2 should be manufactured each month in order to maximize total profit?

Profit in this case is the economic function we wish to render maximum; let us call x_1 the number of units of product P_1, and x_2 the number of units of P_2. Then:

$z = 900x_1 + 1{,}000x_2$ the function to be maximized with the condition $x_1 \geq 0$, $x_2 \geq 0$. 11.1

The constraints are:

$11x_1 + 9x_2 \leq 9{,}900$ for machine M_1 11.2
$7x_1 + 12x_2 \leq 8{,}400$ for machine M_2 11.3
$6x_1 + 16x_2 \leq 9{,}600$ for machine M_3 11.4

There is an infinity of possible solutions; among them is one or more for which z is maximum. All our readers know how to draw a straight line in a plane when the equation for the line is given. In Fig. 11.1, we draw the following straight lines:

$$\Delta_1 : 11x_1 + 9x_2 = 9{,}900, \qquad 11.5$$
$$\Delta_2 : 7x_1 + 12x_2 = 8{,}400, \qquad 11.6$$
$$\Delta_3 : 6x_1 + 16x_2 = 9{,}600. \qquad 11.7$$

A possible solution must lie in the unshaded portion (in the first quadrant, formed by the Ox_1 and Ox_2 axes) in order to satisfy the constraints [(11.2), (11.3), and (11.4)]. Let us consider, for example, the solution $x_1 = 450$, $x_2 = 100$ (point A_5), which gives us:

$$z = 900 \times 450 + 1000 \times 100 = 505{,}000 \text{ F.} \qquad 11.8$$

It is obvious that this is not the maximum, since if we move in the direction of the arrow we increase x_1 and x_2, and hence z, while continuing to meet the requirements of the constraints.

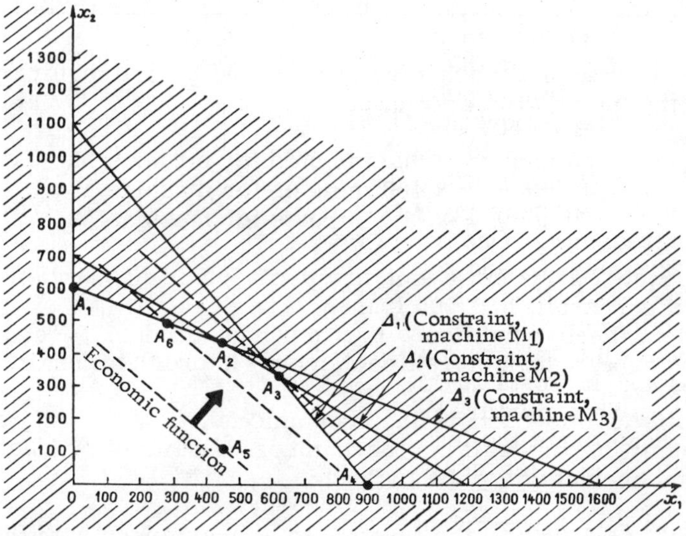

Fig. 11.1

In the same way, if we consider the solution $x_1 = 266$, $x_2 = 500$ (point A_6 lying on line Δ_3), we obtain:

$$z = 900 \times 266 + 1000 \times 500 = 739{,}400 \text{ F.} \qquad 11.9$$

This point A_6 lies on the perimeter of the polygon; we shall see that this is still not the optimum choice.

Let us use a dotted line to represent the function (11.1) for a particular value of z. Since the coefficients 900 and 1,000 are invariant, this line will remain parallel to itself when the value of z is changed. The greater z is, the further away the line will move from the origin, and vice versa.*

When we shift the line corresponding to z, we note that at point A_3, where the line Δ_1 and Δ_2 intersect, we obtain the highest value for z; thus:

$$z_{max} = 900 \times 626 + 1000 \times 334 = 897{,}400 \text{ F.} \quad 11.10$$

It will be observed that the maximum must always correspond to one of the vertices of the polygon, that is, to A_1, A_2, A_3, or A_4; we have just seen that, in this example, point A_3 is the one we must choose.

The solution $x_1 = 626$, $x_2 = 344$, which yields the maximum, corresponds to the full use of machines M_1 and M_2, with machine M_3 on standby for a time equal to:

$$9600 - (6 \times 626 + 16 \times 334) = 500 \text{ mn.} \quad 11.11$$

An examination of Fig. 11.1 will make it readily understandable why we necessarily have one partially idle machine in the solution that yields the optimum. The three machines would all be fully used only if the three lines representing the constraints intersected at a single point.

Let us now study another problem with a similar structure.

Our objective is to find an economical feed for livestock. It must contain 4 kinds of nutrient ingredients, A, B, C, and D. The feed industry already produces two feeds, M and N, which contain these ingredients. One kilogram of feed M contains 100 grams of A, 100 grams of C, and 200 grams of D; a kilogram of feed N contains 100 grams of B, 200 grams of C, and 100 grams of D.

The minimum daily requirement per head (animal) is: 0.4 kilogram of A, 0.6 kilogram of B, 2 kilograms of C, and 1.7 kilogram of D. Feed M costs 10 francs per kilo, and feed N costs 4 francs per kilo. What mixture of feeds M and N should be supplied per day per head to get the least expensive feed blend?

First of all, let us draw up a table summarizing our data:

	M	N	Amount
A	0.1	0	0.4
B	0	0.1	0.6
C	0.1	0.2	2
D	0.2	0.1	1.7
Costs	10	4	

*If the line for the equation $ax + by = c$ is drawn, the distance from the origin to the line is proportional to c. More precisely, $d = \left| \frac{c}{\sqrt{a^2 + b^2}} \right|$.

Now let us denote as x_1 and x_2 the quantities of feed M and feed N, respectively, to be supplied per day per head. The economic function is the total cost of feed per day per head, or:

$$z = 10\,x_1 + 4\,x_2 . \tag{11.12}$$

The objectives to be attained are:

$0.1\,x_1 \geqslant 0.4$		$x_1 \geqslant 4$	11.13
$0.1\,x_2 \geqslant 0.6$	or	$x_2 \geqslant 6$	11.14
$0.1\,x_1 + 0.2\,x_2 \geqslant 2$		$x_1 + 2\,x_2 \geqslant 20$	11.15
$0.2\,x_1 + 0.1\,x_2 \geqslant 1.7$		$2x_1 + x_2 \geqslant 17.$	11.16

Now let us construct Fig. 11.2.

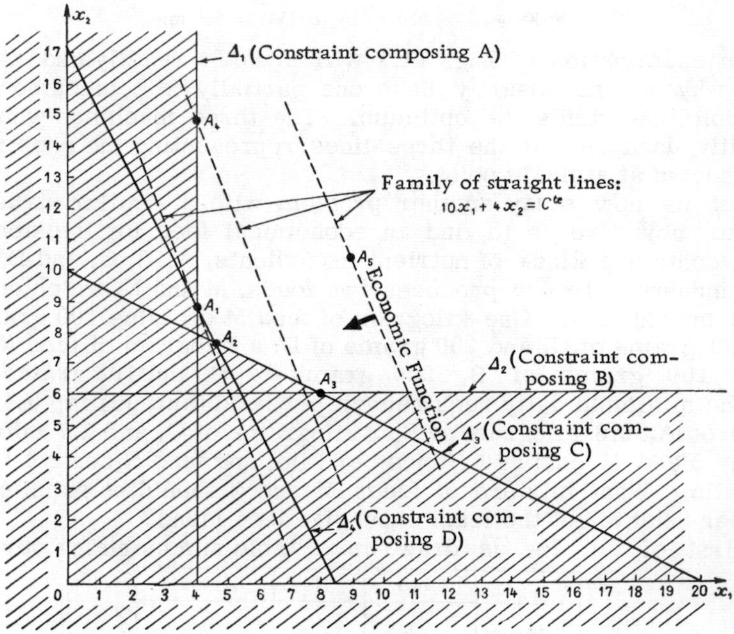

Fig. 11.2

As in the preceding problem, there are an infinite number of possible solutions. To find the optimum solution, the one that corresponds to a minimum value for z, we shall draw the four lines:

$$\Delta_1 \quad : \quad x_1 = 4 \tag{11.17}$$
$$\Delta_2 \quad : \quad x_2 = 6 \tag{11.18}$$
$$\Delta_3 \quad : \quad x_1 + 2x_2 = 20 \tag{11.19}$$
$$\Delta_4 \quad : \quad 2x_1 + x_2 = 17 . \tag{11.20}$$

A possible solution will be found in the unshaded portion. Let us consider, for example, the solution $x_1 = 9.5$, $x_2 = 10.5$ (point A_5). This gives us:

$$z = 10 \times 9.5 + 4 \times 10.5 = 137 \text{ F}. \qquad 11.21$$

Obviously, this is not the point corresponding to the minimum. In the same way the solution $x_1 = 4$, $x_2 = 15$ (point A_4) does not correspond to the minimum we are seeking. If we draw the family of lines $10x_1 + 4x_2 = z$, we see readily that point A_1, with the coordinates $x_1 = 4$, $x_2 = 9$, is the one for which z is minimum. Actually, the smaller z is, the closer the line will be to the origin, and vice versa. Here again, we observe that the minimum must of necessity correspond to one of the vertices of the polygon, either A_1, A_2, or A_3. We have seen that it was A_1. Hence the minimum value for z is:

$$z = 10 \times 4 + 4 \times 9 = 76 \text{ F}. \qquad 11.22$$

By using this mixture, we have obtained precisely the required quantities of components A and D; there is an excess of 0.3 kilo of B, and an excess of 0.2 kilo of C. It will be noted that point A_2 provides a solution in which z is very close to the minimum.*

Section 12

GENERAL FORM OF LINEAR PROGRAMS

1. General explanation. — 2. The case of inequations.

1. General explanation.

The two very simple problems for which the reader easily found the optimum of the economic function are examples of a general class of problems that frequently arise in management systems and in political economy. The mathematical models for such problems are called linear programs. The word linear means that all the relationships involve variables of the first degree. We shall present these relationships in their most general form.

An economic or management phenomenon involves a certain number of variables that are meaningful only when they are positive or null. These variables are linked together by linear relationships that are independent of one another and form a system of equations or of inequations; these are the objectives or the constraints of the phenomenon. We also choose a linear function z of these variables which constitutes the economic function. We then set about finding the maximum or the minimum for this function, according to the circumstances, while still satisfying the objectives and constraints.

---

*See part Two, Sections 57 to 67.

In mathematical language, we describe models of this kind in the following manner:

Let there be N variables, $x_1, x_2, \ldots, x_N$, which we shall call activities, and which shall be positive or null: $x_1 \geq 0$, $x_2 \geq 0, \ldots, x_N \geq 0$. We write a linear function

$$z = c_1 x_1 + c_2 x_2 + \ldots + c_N x_N \qquad 12.1$$

in which each of the coefficients c may be positive, negative, or null. For example, the coefficients $c_1, c_2, \ldots, c_N$ may be unit costs, and the variables may be the corresponding numbers of units; in this case, z would be the total cost.

The variables must satisfy M equations or inequations which constitute the mathematical constraints.

Let us consider first the case in which there are M equations making up a linear system which can be written:

$$\begin{aligned} a_{11} x_1 + a_{12} x_2 + \ldots + a_{1N} x_N &= b_1 \\ a_{21} x_1 + a_{22} x_2 + \ldots + a_{2N} x_N &= b_2 \\ \ldots\ldots\ldots\ldots \quad & \ldots\ldots\ldots \\ a_{M1} x_1 + a_{M2} x_2 + \ldots + a_{MN} x_N &= b_M . \end{aligned} \qquad 12.2$$

in which the coefficients a and b may be positive, negative, or null. Given the fact that the system (12.2) is made up of linear equations, assumed to be independent: the number of equations (M) must be less than the number of variables (N) for there to exist a set of variables that satisfy the equations (12.2); thus, M < N.

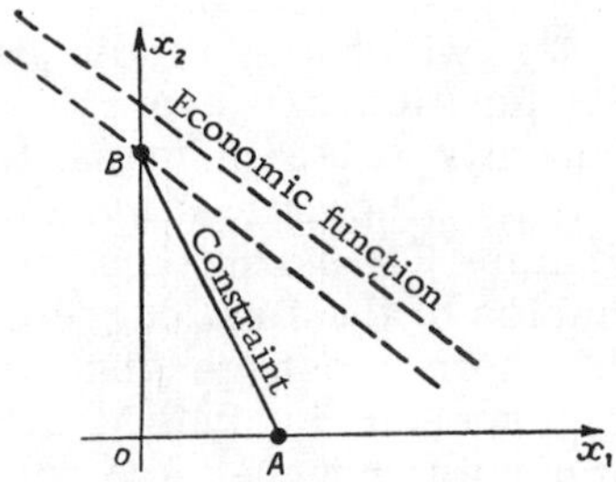

Fig. 12.1

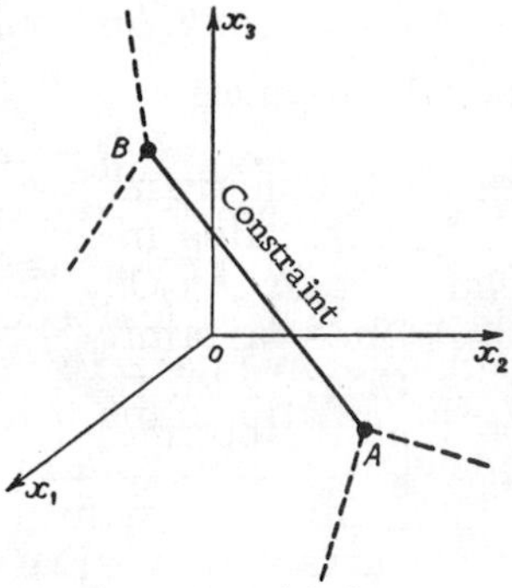

Fig. 12.2

The problem can be stated as follows: for which values of $x_1, x_2, \ldots, x_N$ is the function z optimized (maximum or minimum, as the case may be)?

Mathematicians are able to discuss, and, if necessary, to solve such a problem numerically. The reader interested in mathematics will find in Part Two of this book the methods of calculation employed. We shall limit ourselves here to a study of these structures with a minimum of mathematical impedimenta, while clearly establishing some of their fundamental properties.

Let us therefore investigate the structure of linear programs, making use of simple geometry, and beginning with the case of 2 variables and 1 equation, then going on to 3 variables with 1 or 2 equations, then 3, . . . , n variables.

Let us take the program:

$$z = c_1 x_1 + c_2 x_2 \qquad x_1 \geqslant 0, \quad x_2 \geqslant 0 \qquad 12.3$$
(economic function),

$$a_{11} x_1 + a_{12} x_2 = b_1 \quad \text{(constraint)}. \qquad 12.4$$

In Fig. 12.1, a single constraint and the economic function are shown. In view of the general condition $x_{11} \geq 0$, $x_2 \geq 0$, all solutions must lie in the first quadrant, along the line AB. Obviously, the maximum and minimum must be B and A, since these points correspond to the greatest and the smallest distances from the line representing the economic function to the origin. Hence, the optimum is either $x_1 = a$, $x_2 = 0$ or $x_1 = 0$, $x_2 = b$, where a and b are the coordinates of A and B; the solution corresponding to the optimum must necessarily include a null variable* if a solution exists. This is a point to remember.

Let us now take the program:

$$z = c_1 x_1 + c_2 x_2 + c_3 x_3 . \qquad x_1 \geqslant 0, \; x_2 \geqslant 0, \; x_3 \geqslant 0 . \qquad 12.5$$
(economic function)

$$\begin{aligned} a_{11} x_1 + a_{12} x_2 + a_{13} x_3 &= b_1 . \\ a_{21} x_1 + a_{22} x_2 + a_{23} x_3 &= b_2 . \end{aligned} \qquad 12.6$$
(constraints).

Since each constraint represents a plane, the two constraints define a line that lies in the first octant, cutting two at most of the three planes x_1Ox_2, x_2Ox_3, x_3Ox_1 at points A and B. The economic function defines a family of planes parallel to one another; it is clear, then (Fig. 12.2), that the optimum will be at A or B; it should be noted that the optimum will always lie at a point where at least one of the variables is null.

Let us proceed to the program:

$$z = c_1 x_1 + c_2 x_2 + c_3 x_3 . \qquad x_1 \geqslant 0. \; x_2 \geqslant 0. \; x_3 \geqslant 0 . \qquad 12.7$$
(economic function)

---

*The reader will note that it is possible to conceive of cases having configurations different from Fig. 12.1, in which, among other things, the line of constraint might not lie in the first quadrant; in such cases, there would be no solution to the problem.

$$a_{11} x_1 + a_{12} x_2 + a_{13} x_3 = b_1 , \qquad 12.8$$
(constraint).

We see in Fig. 12.3 that the single constraint corresponds to a plane that cuts the trihedron of reference to form the triangle ABC (if that triangle is in the first octant). The optimum must lie at A, B, or C. Hence, in the case of three variables and one constraint, the optimum will correspond to a solution in which at least 3-1 = 2 variables are null.

Let us now return to the general case where we shall consider N variables and M constraints (12.1 and 12.2), and in which M is necessarily less than N. Every solution corresponding to the optimum must lie at one of the vertices of the convex polyhedron formed by all the constraints and the planes of reference. We are no longer necessarily in 3-dimensional space: although we cannot easily represent such a figure, the properties are still valid. Hence, any solution for the system of constraints, if it is to correspond to the optimum, must fulfill the necessary condition: contain at least N - M null variables. A solution that fulfills such a condition is called a basic solution.

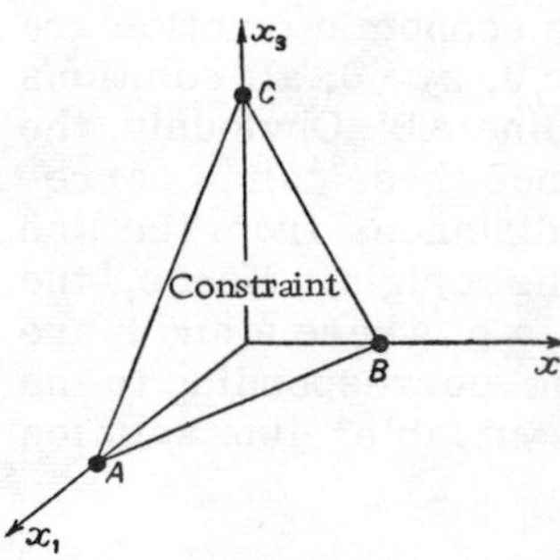

Fig. 12.3

We can point out at once that, in the case where the plane (hyper-plane is the preferred term) representing the economic function is parallel to one of the faces or edges (in n-dimensional space) of the convex polyhedron formed by the constraints, we have a degenerate case in which the optimum is no longer a point, but an edge or a face.

We shall now present an idea of the difficulties encountered in finding the optimum in a linear program. Assuming that we can readily construct a basic solution (although this is not always the case), how many basic solutions are there in a program with N variables and M constraints? Let us consider a few numbers:

Number of variables	Number of constraints	Number of basic solutions
2	1	2
3	1	3
3	2	3
4	1	4
4	2	6
4	3	4
5	1	5
5	2	10
5	3	10
5	4	5

The numbers of basic solutions given above are maximum limits, since they include basic solutions that must be eliminated as containing negative values for the variables.

It can be shown that the number of basic solutions has as its upper limit the number of combinations* of N objects taken M at a time. This number very quickly becomes astronomical; for example: when N = 17 and M = 8, it is 24,310; when N = 21 and M = 11, it is 352,716; if N = 50 and M = 14, it is a number of 11 digits; for N = 100 and M = 38, it is a number of 26 digits. Obviously, there is no question of trying all of the basic solutions to find the one that corresponds to the optimum; fortunately, a method of calculation developed by G. B. Dantzig makes it possible to find the optimum by means of a series of iterations.**

The principle of the Dantzig method is as follows: having obtained a first basic solution, we then find a neighboring basic solution for which the value of the economic function will increase (or decrease, if our objective is a minimum), considering only those basic solutions in which all variables have nonnegative values. This operation is repeated until one no longer finds any increase or decrease; at that point the optimum has been found. It is certain that the optimum will be found in a finite number of steps, because the form of the geometric figure is a convex polyhedron.

2. The case of inequations.

Now that we have considered the case of equations, let us examine the case of inequations. Every linear program containing inequations can be reduced to a program containing only equations, by the introduction of supplementary variables known as slack variables. For example, let us take the program***:

$$[\text{MAX}]\ z = 5x_1 - 2x_2 + 3x_3. \quad x_1 \geqslant 0.\ x_2 \geqslant 0.\ x_3 \geqslant 0. \qquad 12.9$$

$$\begin{aligned} x_1 - 4x_2 + 3x_3 &\leqslant 8. \\ x_1 \qquad + 2x_3 &\leqslant 9. \\ 2x_1 + 5x_2 - x_3 &\leqslant 11. \\ x_1 + x_2 + 7x_3 &\leqslant 3. \end{aligned} \qquad 12.10$$

---

*Thus $C_M^N = \dfrac{N!}{M!(N-M)!}$, where $N! = 1 \cdot 2 \cdot 3 \cdot 4 \cdot \ldots (N-1)N$.

**The method is explained in the second part of this book, Sections 57 to 67.

***When the symbol [MAX] or [MIN] is written before a function, this indicates that we intend to find the maximum or minimum of that function. We shall write max z or min z to indicate the maximum or minimum itself.

We introduce 4 new nonnegative variables: x_4, x_5, x_6, and x_7, so as to transform the inequations into equations:

$$\begin{aligned} x_1 - 4x_2 + 3x_3 + x_4 &= 8, \\ x_1 \qquad + 2x_3 + x_5 &= 9, \\ 2x_1 + 5x_2 - x_3 + x_6 &= 11, \\ x_1 + x_2 + 7x_3 + x_7 &= 3. \end{aligned} \qquad 12.11$$

Thus, we must obtain an optimum solution for a program with 7 variables and 4 equations.

The x_4, x_5, x_6, and x_7 variables represent margins or slacks that appear in each constraint.

A program such as*:

$$[\text{MIN}]\ z = 3x_1 - 2x_2 + x_3 - x_4, \qquad x_1, x_2, x_3, x_4 \geq 0 \qquad 12.12$$

$$\begin{aligned} x_1 + 5x_2 - x_3 + x_4 &\geq 2, \\ x_1 - 2x_2 + 4x_3 + 8x_4 &\geq 4, \end{aligned} \qquad 12.13$$

would be transformed to yield the equations:

$$\begin{aligned} x_1 + 5x_2 - x_3 + x_4 - x_5 &= 2, \\ x_1 - 2x_2 + 4x_3 + 8x_4 - x_6 &= 4. \end{aligned} \qquad 12.14$$

The variables x_5 and x_6 must also be nonnegative: $x_5, x_6 \geq 0$.

Contrary to what one might think at first, it is often easier to calculate a program made up of inequations than one made up of equations, even though the number of variables is considerably greater. This is due to the fact that we can quite simply obtain one basic solution immediately by setting, for example (in equations 12.11): $x_1 = x_2 = x_3 = 0$, $x_4 = 8$, $x_5 = 9$, $x_6 = 11$, $x_7 = 3$; in this case, $z = 0$ as we begin our search for the maximum. If a minimum is required, it is still possible to use this procedure by changing the variables,** or by introducing new variables known as artificial variables.

Section 13

STUDY OF A MONTHLY PRODUCTION PLAN

We have three rolling mills, A, B, and C. We plan to manufacture, as cheaply as possible, 14 classes of plate, of the following

---

*Same as footnote three on preceding page.

**See Part Two, Sections 57 to 67, for further explanations and numerical examples with solutions.

thicknesses: 5/10, 6/10, 8/10, 10/10; 12/10, 14/10, 16/10, 18/10, 20/10, 22/10, 24/10, 26/10, 28/10, and 30/10. We know the cost per ton of each class of plate in each of the mills. We also know the output in tons per hour for each plate thickness, the capacity of each mill, and the production forecasts. The capacities and the forecasts are given for one month.

Table 13.1 presents:

—the cost per ton c_{ij} of plate j in mill i (in francs);

—the output d_{ij} of plate j in mill i (in tons per hour);

—the production p_j planned for plate j (in tons);

—the upper limit b_j of time available in mill i (in hours).

The problem is to find the minimum total monthly production cost.

Table 13.2 presents the linear program for the model of the problem. The mathematical constraints involve 14 equations, 3 inequations, and 31 variables. By introducing 3 slack variables, λ_A, λ_B, and λ_C, to represent the unused capacity, we obtain a system of 17 equations and 34 variables. All basic solutions must contain at least 34 - 17 =14 null variables.

Simply by examination of Table 13.1, some interesting intuitive conclusions are immediately apparent. First of all, mill A has the lowest costs and yields the highest hourly output; thus, we should assign the largest possible number of tons in our plan to this mill. The 600-hour limitation on the capacity of mill A means that considerable work will have to be assigned to mills B and C. This is the point at which difficulties arise and we begin to appreciate that intuition, like rule-of-thumb reasoning, is simply not adequate to determine how the extra work should be assigned. Calculation becomes indispensable. For this example, calculations were performed according to Dantzig's method, or rather according to a variation of that method (see Chapter VII). A Gamma-type magnetic-drum computer was used. The computation took 10 minutes and required 21 iterations. Done by hand, it would have taken a good man several months.

The optimum program is shown at the bottom of Table 13.2. Intuition would certainly not have dictated an assignment of 4,212 tons of 5/10 plate to mill B, where the cost is highest (10,422 francs), or an assignment of 3,811 tons of 12/10 plate to mill C.

If we compare a common program solution, worked out by intuition or on the basis of experience, with the optimum program, we find that the latter provides a saving of 6%. Even if the difference had been slighter, it would have been very important to know the optimum.

Table 13.1

Product		5/10	6/10	8/10	10/10	12/10	14/10	16/10	18/10	20/10	22/10	24/10	26/10	28/10	30/10	Capacity in hrs
(1)	A	5,454 F	5,095 F	6,025 F	6,025 F	4,600 F	4,125 F	4,125 F	3,958 F	3,980 F	4,175 F	4,430 F	4,430 F			600 h
(2)	B	10,422 F	9,637 F	9,333 F	8,620 F	8,540 F	8,500 F	8,440 F	8,420 F	8,380 F	8,310 F	8,310 F	8,270 F	8,270 F	8,270 F	600 h
(3)	C				12,430 F	11,010 F	10,400 F	10,150 F	10,150 F							400 h
Planned production		5,000 t	2,200 t	5,100 t	5,000 t	4,200 t	3,000 t	2,000 t	1,300 t	750 t	500 t	500 t	250 t	100 t	100 t	

A	20.7	23.8	40	40	30	40	40	45.3	44.5	38.7	36	36		
B	7.2	8.6	9.3	11.5	11.8	12	12.2	12.3	12.5	12.8	12.8	13	13	13
C				9	12	14	15	15						

(Output, tons per hr)

788	2,200	5,100	5,000	389	3,000	2,000	1,300	750	500	500	250		
4212	0	0	0	0	0	0	0	0	0	0	0	100	100
			0	3811	0	0	0						

Assignments according to the optimum (rounded to the ton)
Minimum total cost = 199,822,700 F. Unused capacity: A = B = 0; C = 82.5h.

Table 13.2

Mathematical Constraints

$$\frac{x_{11}}{20.7} + \frac{x_{12}}{23.8} + \frac{x_{13}}{40} + \frac{x_{14}}{40} + \frac{x_{15}}{30} + \frac{x_{16}}{40} + \frac{x_{17}}{40} + \frac{x_{18}}{45.3} + \frac{x_{19}}{44.5} + \frac{x_{1\cdot 10}}{38.7} + \frac{x_{1\cdot 11}}{36} + \frac{x_{1\cdot 12}}{36} \leqslant 600$$

$$\frac{x_{21}}{7.2} + \frac{x_{22}}{8.6} + \frac{x_{23}}{9.3} + \frac{x_{24}}{11.5} + \frac{x_{25}}{11.8} + \frac{x_{26}}{12} + \frac{x_{27}}{12.2} + \frac{x_{28}}{12.3} + \frac{x_{29}}{12.5} + \frac{x_{2\cdot 10}}{12.8} + \frac{x_{2\cdot 11}}{12.8} + \frac{x_{2\cdot 12}}{13} + \frac{x_{2\cdot 13}}{13} + \frac{x_{2\cdot 14}}{13} \leqslant 600$$

$$\frac{x_{34}}{9} + \frac{x_{35}}{12} + \frac{x_{36}}{14} + \frac{x_{37}}{15} + \frac{x_{38}}{15} \leqslant 400$$

$$x_{11} + x_{21} = 5{,}000$$
$$x_{12} + x_{22} = 2{,}200$$
$$x_{13} + x_{23} = 5{,}100$$
$$x_{14} + x_{24} + x_{34} = 5{,}000$$
$$x_{15} + x_{25} + x_{35} = 4{,}200$$
$$x_{16} + x_{26} + x_{36} = 3{,}000$$
$$x_{17} + x_{27} + x_{37} = 2{,}000$$
$$x_{18} + x_{28} + x_{38} = 1{,}300$$
$$x_{19} + x_{29} = 750$$
$$x_{1\cdot 10} + x_{2\cdot 10} = 500$$
$$x_{1\cdot 11} + x_{2\cdot 11} = 500$$
$$x_{1\cdot 12} + x_{2\cdot 12} = 250$$
$$x_{2\cdot 13} = 100$$
$$x_{2\cdot 14} = 100 .$$

31 variables
17 equations or inequations

Economic function

$$\begin{aligned} z = {} & 5{,}454\, x_{11} + 5{,}095\, x_{12} + 6{,}025\, x_{13} + 6{,}025\, x_{14} + 4{,}600\, x_{15} + 4{,}125\, x_{16} + 4{,}125\, x_{17} + 3{,}958\, x_{18} + 3{,}980\, x_{19} + 4{,}175\, x_{1\cdot 10} \\ & + 4{,}430\, x_{1\cdot 11} + 4{,}430\, x_{1\cdot 12} + 10{,}422\, x_{21} + 9{,}637\, x_{22} + 9{,}333\, x_{23} + 8{,}620\, x_{24} + 8{,}540\, x_{25} + 8{,}500\, x_{26} + 8{,}440\, x_{27} + 8{,}420\, x_{28} \\ & + 8{,}380\, x_{29} + 8{,}310\, x_{2\cdot 10} + 8{,}310\, x_{2\cdot 11} + 8{,}270\, x_{2\cdot 12} + 8{,}270\, x_{3\cdot 13} + 8{,}270\, x_{2\cdot 14} + 12{,}430\, x_{34} + 11{,}010\, x_{35} \\ & + 10{,}400\, x_{36} + 10{,}150\, x_{37} + 10{,}150\, x_{38}. \end{aligned}$$

The optimum

$$z = 199{,}822{,}700 \text{ francs} .$$

Section 14

ADAPTING PRODUCTION TO DEMAND*

1. General explanation.—2. The economic function.—
3. The mathematical constraints.—4. Final linear program.

1. General explanation.

In order to keep production from corresponding exactly to sales when the latter are variable and seasonal—which would require considerable expenses in overtime—as well as to avoid the very high inventory expenses that would follow if production were held at a constant rate, we wish to prepare the production schedule to cover a whole year.

We shall take as our economic function the minimization of the total annual cost of manufacture.

To simplify matters, let us assume that we are dealing with a certain number of items for which we have been able to find a common measure of evaluation or standard unit, to use a current management term. We shall distinguish between the case of a "fixed system," in which the inventory at the end of the year is the same as it was at the beginning, and a "transitory system," where these two inventory figures differ.

We shall assume:

p_i = normal production (no overtime) during month i;

x_i = production at time-and-a-quarter rates (from 40 to 48 hours) in month i;

y_i = production at time-and-a-half rates (over 48 hours) in month i;

s = inventory at the outset;

s′ = closing inventory.

These values are given in standard units.

The x_i and y_i values are the unknowns in the problem, with the s and s′ values being either known or unknown, according to the case. All the p_i values, however, are known.

We shall further assume that:

P = unit cost of production at ordinary wage rates;

Q = unit cost of production at time-and-a-quarter rates;

R = unit cost of production at time-and-a-half rates;

S = unit cost of inventory for one production unit carried for month;

V_i = sales forecast for month i.

---

*This example was inspired by an article by A. Seigneurin: "Régulation de Production dans une Industrie à Vente Saisonnière" ("Regulation of Production in a Seasonal-Sales Industry"), Revue de Recherche Opérationnelle, Vol. 1, No. 2, 1st quarter 1957.

2. The economic function.

It is the total annual cost of manufacture which we wish to minimize. This includes the cost of production C_1 and the cost of inventory C_2. For the first figure, we have*:

$$C_1 = \sum_{j=1}^{12} (Pp_j + Qx_j + Ry_j). \qquad 14.1$$

For C_2, we assume the regularity of production and of sales for each month. Hence we have, for each month, an average inventory, which is the mean of the beginning and the final inventories. We see that the average inventory for month i is represented by the following expression:

$$\begin{aligned} s_i &= \tfrac{1}{2}\left[s + \sum_{j=1}^{i}(p_j + x_j + y_j - V_j) + s + \sum_{j=1}^{i-1}(p_j + x_j + y_j - V_j)\right] \\ &= s + \sum_{j=1}^{i-1}(p_j + x_j + y_j - V_j) + \tfrac{1}{2}(p_i + x_i + y_i - V_i). \end{aligned} \qquad 14.2$$

Fig. 14.1 illustrates what the average inventory represents. For the benefit of those who may find the mathematical expressions unfamiliar, we shall expand the formula (14.2).

---

*For those of our readers who have forgotten the meaning of the symbol Σ, we cite a few examples:

$$\sum_{i=1}^{4} c_i x_i = c_1 x_1 + c_2 x_2 + c_3 x_3 + c_4 x_4,$$

or, in other words: the sum of all the terms like $c_i x_i$ when i varies from 1 to 4 by integral values, or i = 1, 2, 3, 4.

Another example:

$$\sum_{i=1}^{3}(p_j + x_j + y_j - V_j) = p_1 + x_1 + y_1 - V_1 + p_2 + x_2 + y_2 - V_2 + p_3 + x_3 + y_3 - V_3$$

$$\sum_{j=1}^{n}(p_j + x_j + y_j - V_j) = p_1 + x_1 + y_1 - V_1 + p_2 + x_2 + y_2 - V_2 + p_3 + x_3 + y_3 - V_3 + \dots \dots + p_n + x_n + y_n - V_n.$$

It should be noted that the symbol used as an index for the addition does not enter into the final result.

$$\sum_{i=1}^{5} a_i = \sum_{j=1}^{5} a_j = \sum_{\alpha=1}^{5} a_\alpha = \sum_{\Delta=1}^{5} a_\Delta = a_1 + a_2 + a_3 + a_4 + a_5$$

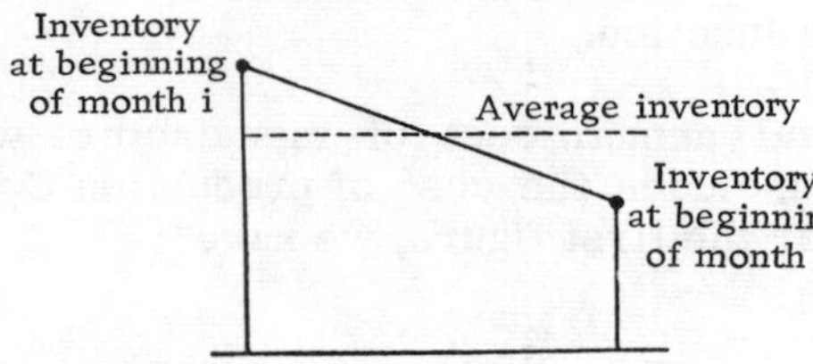

Fig. 14.1

Average inventory for the first month:

$$s_1 = s + \tfrac{1}{2}(p_1 + x_1 + y_1 - V_1) \tag{14.3}$$

Average inventory for the second month:

$$s_2 = s + p_1 + x_1 + y_1 - V_1 + \tfrac{1}{2}(p_2 + x_2 + y_2 - V_2) \tag{14.4}$$

Average inventory for the third month:

$$s_3 = s + p_1 + p_2 + x_1 + x_2 + y_1 + y_2 - V_1 - V_2 + \tfrac{1}{2}(p_3 + x_3 + y_3 - V_3) \tag{14.5}$$

Average inventory for the 12th month:

$$s_{12} = s + \sum_{j=1}^{11}(p_j + x_j + y_j - V_j) + \tfrac{1}{2}(p_{12} + x_{12} + y_{12} - V_{12}). \tag{14.6}$$

Finally, the annual cost of inventory will be:

$$C_2 = S\left[12s + \sum_{j=1}^{12}(12.5 - j)(p_j - V_j) + \sum_{j=1}^{12}(12.5 - j)(x_j + y_j)\right]. \tag{14.7}$$

Collecting the known factors in one group and the unknowns in the other, the total cost can be written thus:

$$\begin{aligned} C = {} & 12Ss + \sum_{j=1}^{12}[Pp_j + S(12.5 - j)(p_j - V_j)] \\ & + \sum_{j=1}^{12}[Q + (12.5 - j)S]x_j + \sum_{j=1}^{12}[R + (12.5 - j)S]y_j. \end{aligned} \tag{14.8}$$

Let us assume:

$$a = \sum_{j=1}^{12}[Pp_j + S(12.5 - j)(p_j - V_j)], \tag{14.9}$$

$$\beta_j = Q + (12.5 - j)S, \tag{14.10}$$

$$\gamma_j = R + (12.5 - j)S. \tag{14.11}$$

Thus we have:

$$C = 12\,S\,s + \alpha + \sum_{j=1}^{12} \beta_j\, x_j + \sum_{j=1}^{12} \gamma_j\, y_j\,. \qquad 14.12$$

The quantity α is known, and the economic function to be minimized will be:

$$\begin{aligned} \Gamma = 12\,S\,s + \beta_1 x_1 + \beta_2 x_2 + \dots + \beta_{12} x_{12} \\ + \gamma_1 y_1 + \gamma_2 y_2 + \dots + \gamma_{12} y_{12}\,. \end{aligned} \qquad 14.13$$

3. The mathematical constraints.

These are of two kinds: commercial and social.

Commercial constraints.—We shall write that every month the inventory is either positive or null:

$$s + \sum_{j=1}^{i} (p_j + x_j + y_j) \geqslant \sum_{j=1}^{i} V_j \qquad \text{(month i):} \qquad 14.14$$

this is applicable to the first 11 months of the year.

$$s + \sum_{j=1}^{12} (p_j + x_j + y_j) = s' + \sum_{j=1}^{12} V_j \text{ (12th month).} \quad s' \geqslant 0\,. \qquad 14.15$$

In the case of a fixed system, $s = s'$.

Social constraints.—The x_i values are limited to 20% of the p_i values (weekly work-hours beyond 40 and up to 48). We assume that the y_i values are limited to 15% of the p_i values (i.e. no work week may exceed 54 hours). This gives us:

$$x_i \leqslant 0.2\, p_i\,. \qquad 14.16$$
$$y_i \leqslant 0.15\, p_i\,. \qquad 14.17$$

4. Final linear program.

Economic function:

$$\Gamma = 12\,S\,s + \sum_{j=1}^{12} (\beta_j\, x_j + \gamma_j\, y_j)\,. \qquad 14.18$$

Mathematical constraints:

$$s + \sum_{j=1}^{i} (x_j + y_j) \geqslant \sum_{j=1}^{i} (V_j - p_j) \qquad i = 1.\,2. \dots 11 \quad (s \geqslant 0) \qquad 14.19$$

$$s - s' + \sum_{j=1}^{12} (x_j + y_j) = \sum_{j=1}^{12} (V_j - p_j) \qquad (s \geqslant 0, s' \geqslant 0) \qquad 14.20$$

$$0 \leqslant x_i \leqslant 0.2\, p_i \qquad i = 1.\,2, \dots, 12 \qquad 14.21$$

$$0 \leqslant y_i \leqslant 0.15\, p_i \qquad i = 1.\,2, \dots, 12\,. \qquad 14.22$$

If we note that in a fixed system s = s′ is unknown, while in a transitory system s and s′ are different but known, we see that we have, according to the case, 24 or 25 variables to consider. Neglecting the inequations showing that the variables are nonnegative, we have 36 constraints, comprising 35 inequations and 1 equation.

Mr. Seigneurin conceived the idea of using cumulative variables,

$$X_i = x_1 + x_2 + \dots + x_i\,, \quad Y_i = y_1 + y_2 + \dots + y_i; \qquad \begin{matrix}14.23\\14.24\end{matrix}$$

which allowed him to simplify his calculations considerably. He pointed out in his article that an actual application of this program produced a saving of 40 million francs a year, while the cost of the study and the calculation amounted to only a small fraction of that sum.

Section 15

CHOICE OF ENERGY SOURCES IN ELECTRICAL POWER GENERATION*

For an enterprise like Électricité de France, working out a production plan consists in minimizing an economic function that includes the total cost of investments plus the operating expenses adjusted by the market interest rate, while at the same time satisfying consumer power demand. Satisfying this demand involves meeting specified conditions for the following three dimensions:

—guaranteed power—average hourly consumption during the heavy business hours in wintertime, in megawatts (Mw), i.e., thousands of kilowatts;

—peak power—average hourly consumption during the four daily peak hours of the same wintertime business days, in Mw;

—the annual power consumption, in gigawatt-hours (Gwh), i.e., millions of kilowatt-hours.

---

*See: R. Gibrat, "Le Problème Général des Plans de Production d'Énergie Électrique et les Usines Marémotrices" ("The General Problem of Electrical Power Generation Plans and Tidal Power Plants"), Électricité de France Document, November 1955. G. Massé, Nouvelle Revue d'Économie Contemporaine (Feb., 1955). E. Ventura, "Un Exemple de Recherche Opérationnelle: la Détermination d'un Plan Optimum de Production d'Énergie Électrique par la Théorie des Programmes Linéaires" ("An Example of Operations Research: Determining an Optimum Plan for Electrical Power Generation by Means of the Theory of Linear Programming"), SOFRO Document, 1956.

To satisfy consumer demand, one can utilize various types of power plants:

—steam (thermal),
—hydroelectric (river-current, reservoir, dam, etc.),
—tidal-power,
—nuclear power.

We assume, to simplify matters, that all plants of a given type constitute a homogeneous series—in other words, show the same characteristics. This will give us the steam-plant series, the hydroelectric series, etc. For the typical plant in each series (series i for example), we shall define:

a_i - guaranteed power,
b_i - peak power,
c_i - total annual power,
d_i - investment cost,
f_i - annual operating expenses,
x_i - number of plants* of the series-i type.

We then construct the following basic hypothesis: the quantities a_i, b_i, c_i, d_i, and f_i are constants. This hypothesis is practically acceptable. Further, let us define:

A - total guaranteed power (for the entire system comprising all the plants, no matter what their type),
B - peak power output (for the entire system),
C - total annual power output.

A production plan must meet the following three conditions or constraints:

$$a_1 x_1 + a_2 x_2 + \dots + a_n x_n \geqslant A \qquad 15.1$$
$$b_1 x_1 + b_2 x_2 + \dots + b_n x_n \geqslant B \qquad 15.2$$
$$c_1 x_1 + c_2 x_2 + \dots + c_n x_n \geqslant C. \qquad 15.3$$

To these technical constraints we shall add a fourth financial constraint: let D be the ceiling on investment expenditures. This will give us:

$$d_1 x_1 + d_2 x_2 + \dots + d_n x_n \leqslant D. \qquad 15.4$$

Lastly, by introducing the slack variables x_a, x_b, x_c, and x_d, the inequations from (15.1) - (15.4) can be written:

$$\begin{aligned} a_1 x_1 + a_2 x_2 + \dots + a_n x_n - x_a &= A \\ b_1 x_1 + b_2 x_2 + \dots + b_n x_n - x_b &= B \\ c_1 x_1 + c_2 x_2 + \dots + c_n x_n - x_c &= C \\ d_1 x_1 + d_2 x_2 + \dots + d_n x_n + x_d &= D \end{aligned} \qquad 15.5$$

*We can relate the plants by a unit of output in megawatts, and an actual plant will embody a given number of such units.

The economic function will include:
—the initial investments:

$$d_1 x_1 + d_2 x_2 + \dots + d_n x_n \; ; \qquad 15.6$$

—the annual cost of installation maintenance, which will bring into play a coefficient of capitalization k. If e_i denotes the annual maintenance cost for a plant in series i, we obtain for the total maintenance cost:

$$k(e_1 x_1 + e_2 x_2 + \dots + e_n x_n) \; ; \qquad 15.7$$

—the annual cost of coal for the steam plants. We shall adopt the index 1 to represent these plants; let us call c'_1 the annual power supplied by a steam plant, and p_0 the cost of coal per thermal kilowatt-hour produced. We note that actually c'_1 will differ from c_1 because the steam plant does not operate for the total number of hours per year that its guaranteed power output would allow. Hence the annual cost of coal will be $kp_0 c'_1 x_1$.

In fact, we choose c_1 in such a way that*:

$$c_1 x_1 = c_1 x_1 - x_c \qquad 15.8$$

where x_c is the margin of power saved each year in steam. Hence:

$$c'_1 x_1 = C - c_2 x_2 - c_3 x_3 - \dots - c_n x_n \, . \qquad 15.9$$

Therefore, the economic function will be:

$$z = \sum_{i=1}^{n} d_i x_i + k \sum_{i=1}^{n} e_i x_i + k p_0 C - k p_0 \sum_{i=2}^{n} c_i x_i . \qquad 15.10$$

The annual operating costs f_i will then be represented by:

$$f_1 = e_1, \quad f_2 = e_2 - p_0 c_2, \quad \dots, \quad f_n = c_n - p_0 c_n \, . \qquad 15.11$$

Let us now define:

$$g_1 = d_1 + k f_1, \quad g_2 = d_2 + k f_2, \quad \dots, \quad g_n = d_n + k f_n \, . \qquad 15.12$$

The economic function will then be written:

$$z = g_1 x_1 + g_2 x_2 + \dots + g_n x_n + k p_0 C \, . \qquad 15.13$$

---

*The c'_1/c_1 ratio is called the rate of steam utilization for the year.

Taking:

$$z' = z - k\,p_e\,C; \qquad 15.14$$

we will then attempt to find the minimum value of:

$$z' = g_1 x_1 + g_2 x_2 + \dots + g_n x_n; \qquad 15.15$$

while the n variables must satisfy the 4 constraints (15.5):

$$\begin{aligned} a_1 x_1 + a_2 x_2 + \dots + a_n x_n - x_a &= A \\ b_1 x_1 + b_2 x_2 + \dots + b_n x_n - x_b &= B \\ c_1 x_1 + c_2 x_2 + \dots + c_n x_n - x_c &= C \\ d_1 x_1 + d_2 x_2 + \dots + d_n x_n + x_d &= D\,. \end{aligned} \qquad 15.16$$

The linear program (15.15 and 15.16) contains n+4 variables; a possible solution, in order to be optimum, must contain at least n null variables. Thus, since there are only 4 constraints, an optimum solution can contain at most 4 means of production. This fact, which is not intuitive, is very important indeed; it shows that by adopting a fifth constraint (as, for example, a social constraint), we can find an optimum that can contain an extra non-null variable, which means an extra means of production.

To make the problem practical, let us use some actual figures. In 1955, the French Parliament set these goals:

A (guaranteed power) 1,692 Mw
B (peak power) 2,307 Mw
C (annual power output) 7,200 Gwh

and as a constraint:

D (investment ceiling): an arbitrary sum (a value of D constitutes a policy).

Table 15.1

	a_i	b_i	c_i	d_i in millions of francs	g_i
1. - Steam plant	1	1.15	7	97	136
2. - River-current plant	1	1.10	12.6	420	56
3. - Reservoir plant	1	1.20	1.3	130	101
4. - Dam plant	1	3	7.35	310	104
5. - Tidal-power plant	1	2.13	5.47	213	79

Table 15.1 gives the specifications for the 5 types of plant. If, in addition, we have the following data:

—interest rate: 8%, or k = 12.5

—cost of fuel for 1 thermal kwh: 3 francs. We obtain the sum of 270 billion francs as the value of kp_0C.

The linear program to be optimized is then:

$$z = 136\,x_1 + 56\,x_2 + 101\,x_3 + 104\,x_4 + 79\,x_5$$

$$\begin{aligned} x_1 + x_2 + x_3 + x_4 + x_5 - x_a &= 1{,}692. \\ 1.15\,x_1 + 1.10\,x_2 + 1.2\,x_3 + 3\,x_4 + 2.13\,x_5 - x_b &= 2{,}307 \\ 7\,x_1 + 12.6\,x_2 + 1.3\,x_3 + 7.35\,x_4 + 5.47\,x_5 - x_c &= 7{,}200 \\ 97\,x_1 + 420\,x_2 + 130\,x_3 + 310\,x_4 + 213\,x_5 + x_d &= D \end{aligned} \qquad 15.17$$

Let us select as a possible basic solution the one that corresponds to:

$$x_2 = x_3 = x_4 = x_5 = x_b = 0, \qquad 15.18$$

or, in other words, a solution where only steam power is used, and in which the total peak power load is met. This yields:

$$x_1 = 2{,}006, \quad x_a = 314, \quad x_c = 6{,}842, \quad x_d = D - 194{,}582. \qquad 15.19$$

It appears that such a solution requires an investment that must exceed 195 billion francs (rounding off 194,582).

With a solution in which:

$$x_1 = x_3 = x_4 = x_5 = x_b = 0 \qquad 15.20$$

we would obtain:

$$x_2 = 2097, \quad x_a = 405, \quad x_c = 19{,}222, \quad x_d = D - 880{,}740 \qquad 15.21$$

in which case D must be greater than 881 billion francs (rounded off).

It is possible to make a comparative study of all the basic solutions. There are, at the most, 126 basic solutions in this program (we do well to emphasize "at the most," since among these 126 solutions, some will contain negative values of the variables and must be discarded). The basic solutions can include one, two, three, or four types of active plants.

The reader will find, in the works of Massé and Gibrat as well as in the article by Ventura, a very complete and particularly interesting discussion of this problem.*

Using an electronic computer, or even by paper-and-pencil calculations, we can study the variation in the optimum of z for different values of D, and examine, for each of these values, which kinds of plants should be used.

---

*See Bibliography: C-53 and C-59.

The considerations treated in this section make it possible to solve the basic problem of the theory of plans. This problem can be stated as follows: What modifications can we make, either in the objectives of a plan or in the costs of the various types of plants available for the formulation of a plan, in order that the optimum solution may keep its structure?

Section 16

EXAMPLE OF TWO COMPLEMENTARY PROBLEMS. THE CONCEPT OF DUALITY.

We shall first of all present an example of an important property of linear programs, and then we shall discuss this property in its most general terms. This approach permits a less abstract presentation.

Let us go back to the problem stated in Section 11. A farm animal must consume, every day, at least 0.4 kilogram of ingredient A; 0.6 kilogram of ingredient B; 2 kilograms of ingredient C, and 1.7 kilogram of ingredient D. Feed M costs 10 francs per kilo, while feed N costs 4 francs per kilo. What quantities of M and N should be supplied per head per day to get the cheapest feed?

Referring back to the complete statement of the problem given in Section 11, we obtain the following linear program:

$$[\text{MIN}]\ f = 10\,y_1 + 4\,y_2, \qquad 16.1$$

$$0.1\,y_1 \geqslant 0.4,$$

$$0.1\,y_2 \geqslant 0.6, \qquad y_1,\ y_2 \geqslant 0 \qquad 16.2$$

$$0.1\,y_1 + 0.2\,y_2 \geqslant 2,$$

$$0.2\,y_1 + 0.1\,y_2 \geqslant 1.7.$$

We have already seen that the minimum value for f will correspond to the solution:

$$y_1 = 4, \quad y_2 = 9. \text{ For these values, } f = 76. \qquad 16.3$$

The following table sums up the statement of the problem.

	M	N	Prescribed quantities
A	0.1	0	0.4
B	0	0.1	0.6
C	0.1	0.2	2
D	0.2	0.1	1.7
cost	10	4	

16.4

Now let us consider the problem of someone competing with the distributor of feeds M and N. This competitor sells the A, B, C, and D ingredients of the feed. He knows that his sales, per day and per head, equal the prescribed quantities. What he wants to know is the unit price at which he should sell his feed ingredients so as to achieve the maximum profit. His economic function, therefore, is:

$$[\text{MAX}]\, g = 0.4\, x_1 + 0.6\, x_2 + 2\, x_3 + 1.7\, x_4. \qquad 16.5$$

But, on the other hand, he does not want to charge higher prices than his competitors, and so he imposes these constraints on himself:

$$\begin{aligned} 0.1\, x_1 + 0.1\, x_3 + 0.2\, x_4 &\leq 10 \\ 0.1\, x_2 + 0.2\, x_3 + 0.1\, x_4 &\leq 4 \end{aligned} \qquad x_1, x_2, x_3, x_4 \geq 0\,. \qquad 16.6$$

If we now find the maximum for g, we will obtain as our solution:*

$$x_1 = 20, \quad x_2 = 0, \quad x_3 = 0, \quad x_4 = 40, \; g = 76. \qquad 16.7$$

Thus, the competitor knows that his maximum profit will correspond to the unit prices (16.7).

Now we shall draw up a table showing the data for the program (16.5, 16.6):

	A	B	C	D	cost
M	0.1	0	0.1	0.2	10
N	0	0.1	0.2	0.1	4
Prescribed quantities	0.4	0.6	2	1.7	

16.8

Program (16.5, 16.6) corresponds to program (16.1, 16.2); in program (16.5, 16.6) the data have been reversed, as can be seen from an examination of tables (16.4) and (16.8). A very important property is connected with this reversal of data:

$$\max g = \min f = 76\,. \qquad 16.9$$

This property, which is clearly shown in our example, is a general one. Without going into the mathematical developments, we shall state this general property, called duality, as follows:

---

*The reader interested in these calculations will find several methods discussed in Chapter VII of Part Two.

The programs

$$[\text{MAX}]\, g = \sum_{j=1}^{n} c_j x_j , \qquad \text{and} \qquad [\text{MIN}]\, f = \sum_{i=1}^{m} b_i y_i , \qquad 16.10$$

$$\sum_{j=1}^{n} a_{ij} x_j \leqslant b_i , \qquad \sum_{i=1}^{m} a_{ji} y_i \geqslant c_j . \qquad 16.11$$

$$i = 1, 2, \ldots, m \qquad\qquad j = 1, 2, \ldots, n$$

which correspond by duality, are such that:

$$\max g = \min f . \qquad 16.12$$

Thus, the search for the optimum of a program can be replaced by a search for the optimum of the dual program.

Duality is a very important concept, in relation both to the economic concepts with which it is connected and to the special methods of calculation that derive from it. It is always of interest to examine what the dual of a program may represent.*

Section 17

TRANSPORTATION PROBLEMS**

1. General explanation.—2. A variation.—
3. Approximation method.—4. An example.—5. Other methods.

1. General explanation.

Before examining the general form of certain kinds of linear programs concerning transportation problems, we shall present a simple example. Since the calculations required for transportation problems are very elementary, we shall describe them fully from the outset.

In three plants, A, B, and C, we have a certain tonnage of a product: 100, 120, and 120 tons, respectively. The product is to be delivered to 5 warehouses, 1, 2, 3, 4, and 5, each of which must receive its quota: 40, 50, 70, 90, and 90 tons, respectively. Fig. 17 is a diagram of the transportation involved.

---

*See Part Two, Section 66.

**We shall dwell particularly on linear programs of transportation because their solution requires no complicated mathematical methods.

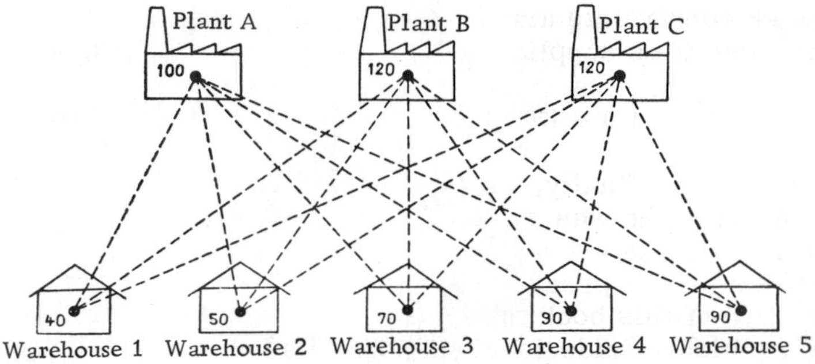

Fig. 17.1

The transportation cost for a given unit of the product is shown in Table 17.1. For example, the cost of transportation from plant B to warehouse 4 is 5. The problem is to work out a transportation plan such that the total cost of moving the 340 tons will be minimized.

Table 17.1

	(1)	(2)	(3)	(4)	(5)	
(A)	4	1	2	6	9	100
(B)	6	4	3	5	7	120
(C)	5	2	6	4	8	120
	40	50	70	90	90	

To begin, we can show that such a problem constitutes a linear program containing 15 variables and 7 independent equations. We shall number the variables in such a way that they will correspond to the rows and the columns of Table 17.1.
Economic function:

$$
\begin{aligned}
[\text{MIN}]\ z = 4\,x_{11} + x_{12} + 2\,x_{13} + 6\,x_{14} + 9\,x_{15} \\
+ 6\,x_{21} + 4\,x_{22} + 3\,x_{23} + 5\,x_{24} + 7\,x_{25} \\
+ 5\,x_{31} + 2\,x_{32} + 6x_{33} + 4x_{34} + 8x_{35}\,.
\end{aligned}
\qquad 17.1
$$

Constraints:

$$
\begin{aligned}
x_{11} + x_{12} + x_{13} + x_{14} + x_{15} &= 100 \\
x_{21} + x_{22} + x_{23} + x_{24} + x_{25} &= 120 \\
x_{31} + x_{32} + x_{33} + x_{34} + x_{35} &= 120 \\
x_{11} + x_{21} + x_{31} &= 40 \\
x_{12} + x_{22} + x_{32} &= 50 \\
x_{13} + x_{23} + x_{33} &= 70 \\
x_{14} + x_{24} + x_{34} &= 90 \\
x_{15} + x_{25} + x_{35} &= 90
\end{aligned}
\qquad 17.2
$$

But these 8 constraints are not independent, because we have:
Total quantities supplied = Total quantities received:

$$100 + 120 + 120 = 40 + 50 + 70 + 90 + 90 = 340\,. \qquad 17.3$$

Thus we have, finally, not 8 independent constraints, but only 7. If we recall what was stated in Section 12, a basic solution will contain N - M = 15 - 7 = 8 null variables. We can determine the optimum for such a program by means of the algorithms described in Part Two of this book; however, the particular structure of this kind of problem yields to a special method that is very simple in principle and can be understood and applied readily by a person who has not been trained in advanced mathematics. We owe this very elegant method, known as the stepping-stone method, to the American mathematician G. Dantzig. We shall present it now by means of an example.

Let us construct a basic solution using a very simple rule, known as the north-west corner rule. We start in the north-west corner (upper left) of the distribution table (Table 17.2). Where the first row intersects the first column, we enter the smallest

Table 17.2

	(1)	(2)	(3)	(4)	(5)	
(*A*)	40	50	10			100
(*B*)			60	60		120
(*C*)				30	90	120
	40	50	70	90	90	

of the two numbers representing supply (100) and demand (40); in this case, 40. We complete the first row (the first column, in another example) until exhaustion of supply has been achieved (or fulfillment of demand, in another example). In this way we obtain:

$$x_{11} = 40, \quad x_{12} = 50, \quad x_{13} = 10, \quad x_{14} = x_{15} = 0\,. \qquad 17.4$$

Next, we fulfill the demand in the third column, and then exhaust the supply in the second row, which will give us:

$$x_{21} = x_{22} = 0, \quad x_{23} = 60, \quad x_{24} = 60, \quad x_{25} = 0\,. \qquad 17.5$$

Now, let us fulfill the demand in the fourth column, and, finally, exhaust the supply in the third row, giving us:

$$x_{31} = x_{32} = x_{33} = 0, \quad x_{34} = 30, \quad x_{35} = 90\,. \qquad 17.6$$

We have thus arrived at our basic solution. We can now calculate the total cost:

$$z = (40)(4) + (50)(1) + (10)(2) + (60)(3) + (60)(5) + (30)(4) + (90)(8)$$
$$= 1550. \qquad 17.7$$

Starting from this solution, we shall now search for a new one that will correspond to a lower total cost, but will still contain at least 8 null variables.

Table 17.3

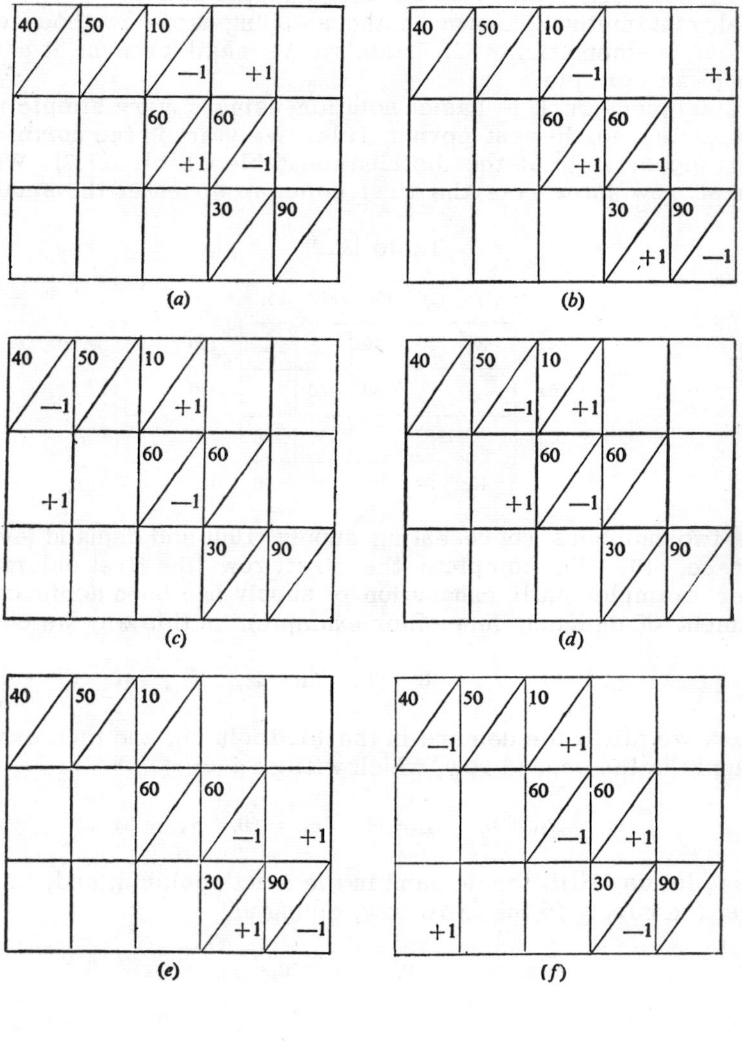

Table 17.3 (continued)

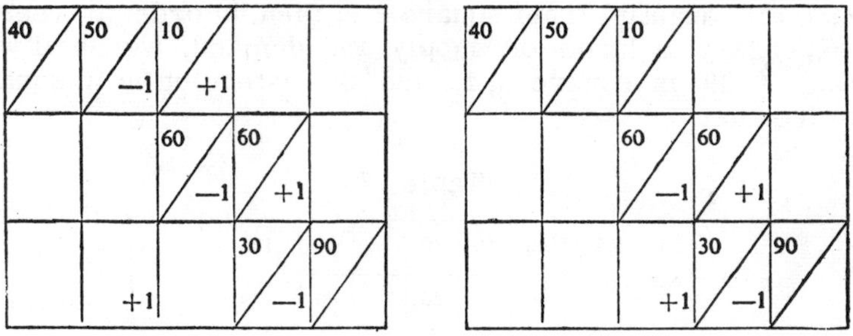

(*g*) (*h*)

In order to arrive at a more profitable solution, let us assume that we assign one unit to square 1,4 (first row, fourth column, table 17.3a); this means that we must take one unit out of square 1,3, add one unit to square 2,3, and lastly take one unit out of square 2,4. This circular transfer of a unit changes the total cost* by a quantity δ_{14} (square 1,4), which we can easily evaluate by consulting our table of unit costs (Table 17.1):

$$\delta_{14} = 6 - 2 + 3 - 5 = 2 \,. \qquad 17.8$$

In the same way, we evaluate similar changes for the other squares:

Table 17.3b: $\delta_{15} = 9 - 2 + 3 - 5 + 4 - 8 = 1$
Table 17.3c: $\delta_{21} = 6 - 3 + 2 - 4 = 1$
Table 17.3d: $\delta_{22} = 4 - 3 + 2 - 1 = 2$
Table 17.3e: $\delta_{25} = 7 - 5 + 4 - 8 = -2$ 17.8
Table 17.3f: $\delta_{31} = 5 - 4 + 5 - 3 + 2 - 4 = 1$
Table 17.3g: $\delta_{32} = 2 - 4 + 5 - 3 + 2 - 1 = 1$
Table 17.3h: $\delta_{33} = 6 - 4 + 5 - 3 = 4$.

The name "stepping-stone" comes from the arrangement of the path taken in the calculations, moving from one square of the table to another.

Now, let us determine which exchange lowers the cost; for this, δ must be negative, which is the case for $\delta_{25} = -2$. But, instead of shifting just one unit, let us shift as many units as we possibly can. To do so, we choose among the stepping-stones that square which corresponds to the smallest quantity where there is an entry of

---

*The δ_{ij} quantities represent the unit variations when a shift is made from one base to another; they constitute the marginal unit costs.

-1. Table 17.3e shows us that this will be square 2,4, which contains the number 60. We shall now shift 60 into square 2,5, subtracting this quantity from square 2,4; then, in order to reestablish the necessary balance of supply and demand, we shall write 90 instead of 30 in square 3,4, and 30 instead of 90 in square 3,5. This gives us:

Table 17.4

40	50	10			100
		60		60	120
			90	30	120
40	50	70	90	90	

The corresponding cost is:

$$z=(40)(4)+(50)(1)+(10)(2)+(60)(3)+(60)(7)+(90)(4)+(30)(8)=1430 \qquad 17.9$$

(a predictable result, since we know that the exchange of one unit cuts the total cost by 2, and that therefore the exchange of 60 units will cut it by 120).

We shall repeat, for this new solution, the preceding set of calculations. Examining Table 17.4 we observe:

Table 17.5

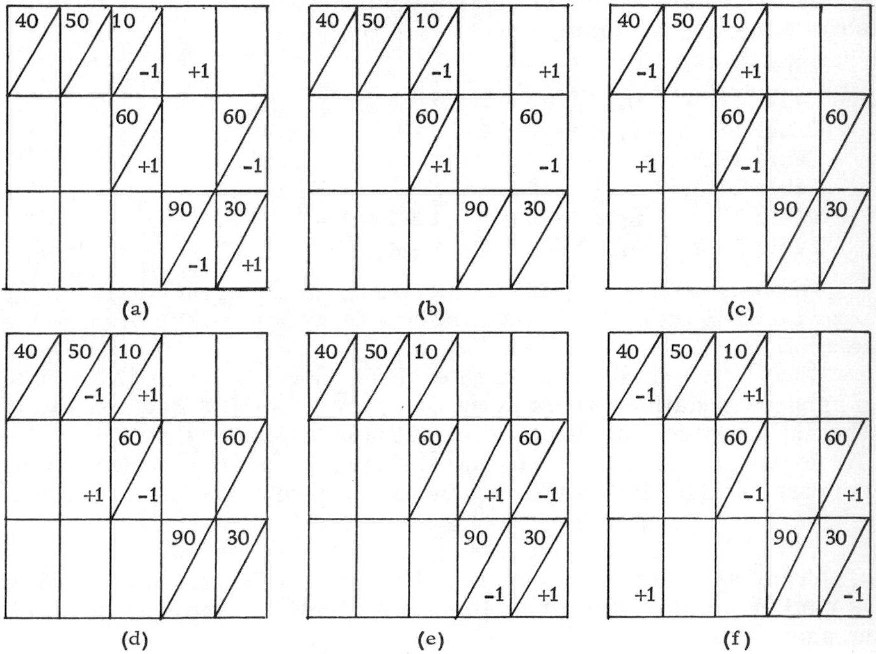

Table 17.5 (continued)

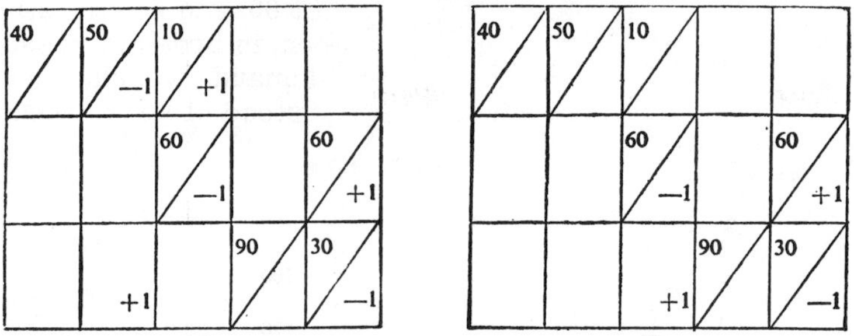

(g) (h)

$$\text{Table 17.5a:}\quad \delta_{14} = 6 - 2 + 3 - 7 + 8 - 4 = 4$$
$$\text{Table 17.5b:}\quad \delta_{15} = 9 - 2 + 3 - 7 = 3$$
$$\text{Table 17.5c:}\quad \delta_{21} = 6 - 3 + 2 - 4 = 1$$
$$\text{Table 17.5d:}\quad \delta_{22} = 4 - 3 + 2 - 1 = 2$$
$$\text{Table 17.5e:}\quad \delta_{24} = 5 - 7 + 8 - 4 = 2 \qquad 17.10$$
$$\text{Table 17.5f:}\quad \delta_{31} = 5 - 8 + 7 - 3 + 2 - 4 = -1$$
$$\text{Table 17.5g:}\quad \delta_{32} = 2 - 8 + 7 - 3 + 2 - 1 = -1$$
$$\text{Table 17.5h:}\quad \delta_{33} = 6 - 8 + 7 - 3 = 2.$$

We now have a choice between δ_{31} and δ_{32} which both yield $\delta = -1$. Just for example, let us use δ_{31}. We take a number of units equal to the smallest number to be found in the squares of Table 17.5f where there is an entry of -1.

Table 17.6

10	50	40			100
		30		90	120
30			90		120
40	50	40	80	90	

Then we shift 30 units, beginning with square 3,1. This gives the solution shown in Table 17.6, for which we have:

$$z=(10)(4)+(50)(1)+(40)(2)+(30)(3)+(90)(7)+(30)(5)+(90)(4)=1400. \qquad 17.11$$

(a predictable result, since the exchange diminished the cost by $30 \times 1 = 30$).

Let us repeat the operation still another time, but without developing the tables:

$$\begin{aligned}
\delta_{14} &= 6 - 4 + 5 - 4 = 3\\
\delta_{15} &= 9 - 2 + 3 - 7 = 3\\
\delta_{21} &= 6 - 3 + 2 - 4 = 1\\
\delta_{22} &= 4 - 3 + 2 - 1 = 2\\
\delta_{24} &= 5 - 3 + 2 - 4 + 5 - 4 = 1\\
\delta_{32} &= 2 - 5 + 4 - 1 = 0\\
\delta_{33} &= 6 - 5 + 4 - 2 = 3\\
\delta_{35} &= 8 - 5 + 4 - 2 + 3 - 7 = 1\,.
\end{aligned} \tag{17.12}$$

No exchange can lower the cost, because all values of δ are positive; we conclude then that it is impossible to obtain a better solution; on the other hand, there is an equivalent solution, because there is a null δ. An exchange with δ_{32} will give the solution found in Table 17.7:

Table 17.7

40	20	40		
		30		90
	30		90	

This solution yields the same value* for z.

$$z=(40)(4)+(20)(1)+(40)(2)+(30)(3)+(90)(7)+(30)(2)+(90)(4)=1400\,. \tag{17.13}$$

The reader will have gained from this example a specific knowledge of the nature of this kind of problem, and we can now proceed to a more general formulation of transportation problems.

A linear transportation problem consists of determining a diagram of transportation from m given origins, each of which provides a quantity a_i of supplies ($i = 1, 2, \ldots, m$), to n destinations, each of which must receive some quantity b_j of supplies ($j = 1, 2, \ldots, n$), in such a way that the total cost of transportation will be a minimum, where the known unit cost of transportation between an origin i and a destination j is found among the $m \times n$ values:

$$c_{ij} \quad \begin{matrix} i = 1, 2, \ldots, m \\ j = 1, 2, \ldots, n\,. \end{matrix} \quad c_{ij} \geqslant 0\,. \tag{17.14}$$

*In actuality, there is in this case an infinite number of solutions corresponding to the optimum, if quantities less than 30 are assigned to square 3,2. But these would no longer be basic solutions.

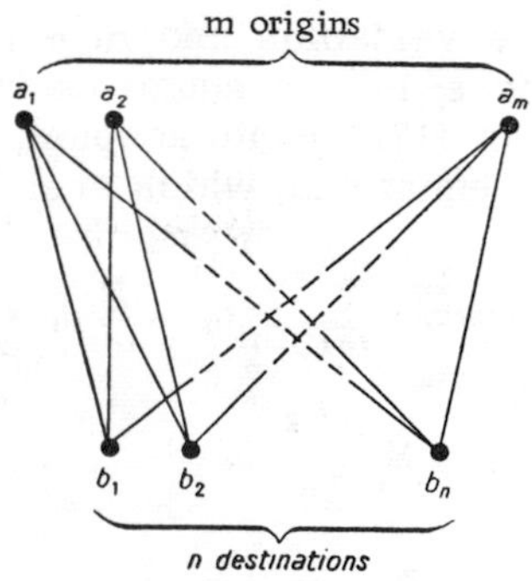

FIG. 17.2.

It is assumed here that the total demand equals the total supply:

$$\sum_{i=1}^{m} a_i = \sum_{j=1}^{n} b_j \qquad a_i > 0 \, , \; b_j > 0 \, . \tag{17.15}$$

If this were not the case, i.e. if the total supply were greater than the total demand, we could provide a fictitious additional destination, which would again give us equation (17.15).

If we denote as x_{ij} the quantity transported from origin i to destination j, the table formed by the x_{ij} coefficient (i = 1, 2, . . . , m; j = 1, 2, . . . , n) is called the flow matrix or transportation diagram. We see then that the problem constitutes a linear program with a particular structure.

$$[\text{MIN}]\; z = \sum_{i=1}^{m} \sum_{j=1}^{n} c_{ij} \, x_{ij} \quad (^1) \qquad x_{ij} \geqslant 0 \tag{17.16}$$

$$\sum_{j=1}^{n} x_{ij} = a_i \qquad i = 1, 2, \ldots, m. \tag{17.17}$$

$$\sum_{i=1}^{m} x_{ij} = b_j \qquad j = 1, 2, \ldots, n \, , \tag{17.18}$$

$$\sum_{i=1}^{m} a_i = \sum_{j=1}^{n} b_j \, . \tag{17.19}$$

---

*The sign of double summation can easily be understood:

$$\begin{aligned}\sum_{i=1}^{3} \sum_{j=1}^{4} c_{ij} \, x_{ij} &= \sum_{i=1}^{3} (c_{i1} \, x_{i1} + c_{i2} \, x_{i2} + c_{i3} \, x_{i3} + c_{i4} \, x_{i4}) \\ &= c_{11} \, x_{11} + c_{12} \, x_{12} + c_{13} \, x_{13} + c_{14} \, x_{14} \\ &\qquad + c_{21} \, x_{21} + c_{22} \, x_{22} + c_{23} \, x_{23} + c_{24} \, x_{24} \\ &\qquad + c_{31} \, x_{31} + c_{32} \, x_{32} + c_{33} \, x_{33} + c_{34} \, x_{34} \, .\end{aligned}$$

This yields m × n variables and m + n equations (17.17 and 17.18). However, these m + n equations are not independent, in view of (17.19); taking (17.19) into account, it is easy to construct m + n - 1 independent equations, which are:

$$1 \text{ equation}: \sum_{i=1}^{m} \sum_{j=1}^{n} x_{ij} = \sum_{i=1}^{m} a_i = \sum_{j=1}^{n} b_j, \qquad 17.20$$

$$(m - 1) \text{ equations}: \sum_{j=1}^{n} x_{ij} = a_i \qquad i = 1, 2, \ldots, m - 1; \qquad 17.21$$

$$(n - 1) \text{ equations}: \sum_{i=1}^{m} x_{ij} = b_j \qquad j = 1, 2, \ldots, n - 1. \qquad 17.22$$

A basic solution will therefore contain at least:

$$N - M = nm - (m + n - 1) = (m - 1)(n - 1) \qquad 17.23$$

null variables.*

There are methods other than the stepping-stone for solving transportation problems, as well as variations of this method. We shall now examine a few of these.

2. A variation.

It is often advantageous, when there are several possible exchanges that will reduce total costs, to choose not the one that gives the largest unit decrease but the one that yields the greatest total, or overall, decrease. An example will demonstrate this.

Let us consider the transportation problem given in Table 17.8.

Table 17.8

						Origins
	10	20	5	9	10	90
	2	10	8	30	6	40
	1	20	7	10	4	80
Destinations	30	50	40	60	30	

*If a solution contains more than (m - 1) (n - 1) null variables, the stepping-stone method should be followed to evaluate all of the marginal costs, by arbitrarily employing one or more zeros, according to need, in the stepping-stone path; under no circumstances can an entry be made that involves the transportation of a negative quantity. Sometimes the calculations become highly complicated.

We shall use the basic solution obtained by starting from the north-west corner.

Table 17.9

30	50	10			90	
		30	10		40	z = 2510
			50	30	80	
30	50	40	60	30		

Now we calculate:

$$\begin{aligned}
\delta_{14} &= 9 - 5 + 8 - 30 = -18 \\
\delta_{15} &= 10 - 5 + 8 - 30 + 10 - 4 = -11 \\
\delta_{21} &= 2 - 8 + 5 - 10 = -11 \\
\delta_{22} &= 10 - 8 + 5 - 20 = -13 \\
\delta_{25} &= 6 - 30 + 10 - 4 = -18 \\
\delta_{31} &= 1 - 10 + 30 - 8 + 5 - 10 = 8 \\
\delta_{32} &= 20 - 10 + 30 - 8 + 5 - 20 = 17 \\
\delta_{33} &= 7 - 10 + 30 - 8 = 19.
\end{aligned} \qquad 17.24$$

For each negative variation, which is to say for δ_{14}, δ_{15}, δ_{21}, δ_{22}, and δ_{25}, we shall work out the largest possible shift compatible with the values given for the origins and destinations. We then obtain:

For

$\delta_{14} = -18$ we can move 10 units, or a difference of -180
$\delta_{15} = -11$ we can move 10 units, or a difference of -110
$\delta_{21} = -11$ we can move 30 units, or a difference of -330 17.25
$\delta_{22} = -13$ we can move 30 units, or a difference of -390
$\delta_{25} = -18$ we can move 10 units, or a difference of -180

Thus, it is δ_{22} that yields the greatest difference; we obtain:

Table 17.10

30	20	40			90	
	30		10		40	$z = 2120$
			50	30	80	
30	50	40	60	30		

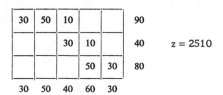

This approach sometimes allows a more rapid determination of the optimum value, but it requires calculation of each variation, and, if one considers the amount of analysis, the advantage does not always lie with this approach.

We might point out, for those who have some mathematical training, that the first method consists in optimizing by performing iterations in relation to the greatest slope, while the variant refers these iterations to the greatest difference (iterating in terms of the rate of variation or the differential).

We shall leave it to the reader to work out the optimum value for the program of Table 17.8, which is: $z = 1500$. This result can also be achieved by means of the approximation method, which we shall now describe.

3. Approximation method.

A method devised by Houthakker* makes it possible to improve a solution very rapidly, although without any certainty of reaching the optimum.

We shall define, first of all, the concept of the mutually preferable output. An output x_{ij} from an origin i to a destination j is mutually preferable if j is the cheapest destination for i, and if i is the cheapest origin for j. This mutually preferable output is characterized by the fact that its unit transportation cost must be the lowest in its row and in its column. We then place the maximum allowable outputs in the corresponding squares, and go on to the next table obtained by eliminating the rows and columns already satisfied. We repeat these operations until a solution is obtained. When one has been found, we check, by means of the stepping-stone method, to see whether or not the optimum has been achieved; if not, we then improve our solution by means of the stepping-stone method.

So far as we know, Houthakker's method cannot be analytically justified; it is justifiable only under the intuitive notion that mutually preferable outputs have a higher probability of lying within the optimum solution.

4. An example.

Returning to the example given in Table 17.8, let us find the M. P. (mutually preferable outputs). A quick scanning of the cost matrix (Table 17.11), shows that these are $c_{31} = 1$ and $c_{13} = 5$. We

*See H. S. Houthakker, "On the Numerical Solution of the Transportation Problem", J.O.R.S.A., May, 1955, Vol. 3, No. 2, pp. 210-214.

Table 17.11

	(1)	(2)	(3)	(4)	(5)	
(1)	10	20	(5)	9	10	90
(2)	2	10	8	30	6	40
(3)	(1)	20	7	10	4	80
	30	50	40	60	30	

shall therefore place the highest possible output in each of these squares. This will give us (Table 17.12):

$$x_{31} = 30, \quad \text{hence} \quad x_{11} = 0, \; x_{21} = 0$$
$$x_{13} = 40, \quad \text{hence} \quad x_{23} = 0, \; x_{33} = 0. \qquad 17.26$$

Table 17.12

0		40			90
0		0			40
30		0			80
30	50	40	60	30	

Let us eliminate columns (1) and (3) from the table of costs. We shall then seek the M.P. outputs in the sub-table (Table 17.13a): these are the outputs corresponding to $c_{14} = 9$ and $c_{35} = 4$. Adjusting the corresponding outputs (Table 17.13):

Table 17.13

	(2)	(4)	(5)	
(1)	20	(9)	10	50
(2)	10	30	6	40
(3)	20	10	(4)	50
	50	60	30	

(*a*)

0	0	40	50	0	90
0		0		0	40
30		0		30	80
30	50	40	60	30	

(*b*)

$$x_{14} = 50 \quad \text{hence} \quad x_{12} = x_{15} = 0$$
$$x_{35} = 30 \quad \text{hence} \quad x_{25} = 0. \qquad 17.27$$

Continuing with the remaining sub-table (Table 17.14a), the M.P. outputs here are: $c_{22} = 10$, $c_{34} = 10$ which gives us Table 17.14b, where we have

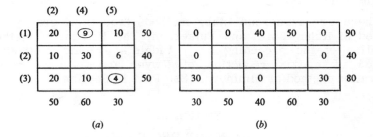

$$x_{22} = 40 \quad \text{and} \quad x_{24} = 0$$
$$x_{34} = 10 \quad \text{and} \quad x_{32} = 10 \qquad 17.28$$

The program in Table 17.15 is, in this particularly favorable example, the optimum program, and we can check this by means of the stepping-stone method. We obtain min z = 1500.

Table 17.14

	(2)	(4)	
(2)	(10)	30	40
(3)	20	(10)	20
	50	10	

0	0	40	50	0	90
0	40	0	0	0	40
30	10	0	10	30	80
30	50	40	60	30	

Table 17.15

		40	50		90
	40				40
30	10		10	30	80
30	50	40	60	30	

In other problems we might reach a possible solution that would then have to be optimized by means of the stepping-stone method.

The approximation method may be helpful for large programs; that is, in which the number of origins and destinations is fairly great.

5. Other methods.

There are numerous other methods (see Bibliography): The method of Kuhn, Ford, and Fulkerson; The Friedmann method (a variation of the preceding one); Vidale's graphic method; The method of matrix reduction of Dwyer and Galler; The star-separation method of Zimmern. (See Part II, Section 68.)

Section 18

ASSIGNMENT PROBLEMS

1. General explanation.—2. The Hungarian method.— 3.—Finding a maximum

1. General explanation.

The assignment problem is a special case of the transportation problem; it is, in fact, the simplest of all the linear programs.

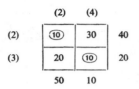

Assume that n workers are to be assigned to n tasks; worker i can do job j at a cost of c_{ij}, and can do only one such job. Let x_{ij} be an element located in row i and column j of a table containing only the numbers 1 or 0 where the sum of each row and of each column is 1. The problem is to find the minimum sum of all the $x_{ij}c_{ij}$ products. (See Tables 18.1a and 18.1b.)

Table 18.1

c_{ij}

8	7	(5)	3	4
5	(4)	4	2	3
8	2	7	4	(4)
(5)	6	5	4	4
8	3	7	(9)	4

(a)

x_{ij}

0	0	1	0	0
0	1	0	0	0
0	0	0	0	1
1	0	0	0	0
0	0	0	1	0

(b)

$z = 5+4+4+5+9$
$= 27$

A solution is shown in Table 18.1b; it corresponds to the numbers circled in Table 18.1a. Adding up these numbers, we find z = 27. There are 5×4×3×2×1 = 120 possible solutions. One of these corresponds to the minimum z, which is what we are looking for.

The mathematical formulation is the following:*

Economic function: $$[\text{MIN}]\ z = \sum_{i=1}^{n} \sum_{j=1}^{n} x_{ij}\, c_{ij} \qquad c_{ij} \geq 0 \qquad 18.1$$

Constraints: $$\sum_{i=1}^{n} x_{ij} = \sum_{j=1}^{n} x_{ij} = 1, \text{ where } x_{ij}^2 = x_{ij}. \qquad i, j = 1, 2, \ldots, n. \qquad 18.2$$

The expression $x^2_{ij} = x_{ij}$ is a convenient way of indicating that x_{ij} can have no values other than 0 or 1.**

---

*In order to remove this formula from the realm of the abstract, here again is a concrete example of the double summation:

$$\sum_{i=1}^{3} \sum_{j=1}^{3} x_{ij}\, c_{ij} = \sum_{j=1}^{3} (x_{1j}\, c_{1j} + x_{2j}\, c_{2j} + x_{3j}\, c_{3j})$$
$$= x_{11}\, c_{11} + x_{12}\, c_{12} + x_{13}\, c_{13}$$
$$+ x_{21}\, c_{21} + x_{22}\, c_{22} + x_{23}\, c_{23}$$
$$+ x_{31}\, c_{31} + x_{32}\, c_{32} + x_{33}\, c_{33}.$$

These Σ signs, despite their somewhat forbidding aspect, express a very simple operation.

**Because of this relationship, assignment problems cannot, from a purely theoretical point of view, be classed as linear programs. But they are a very closely related form.

Before describing the principal method of resolving such problems, let us look at an actual example of an assignment problem.

The problem concerns an air transport network owned by a large international company. It is proposed to find the best way to assign crews to planes in order to cut crew transportation costs to a minimum.

Let us first define what we might call the problem of crews between cities. Say that 2 cities, A and B, are joined by a direct scheduled air route (A-to-B and B-to-A). We shall assume that, every day, 3 planes leave A for B, and these will be called flights 1, 2, and 3. Let the flights from B to A be called a, b, and c. Of course we know the times of arrival and departure; the flying time between the two cities is known, uniform, and constant.

The elementary problem that arises here is the following: how can we minimize the time spent by the crews away from home (this is important financially as well as psychologically)? We know that every crewman that lives at A and takes off for B must come back to A to complete his mission; the same thing applies for every crewman that takes off from B. We can imagine several arrangements: for example, solution 1b, 2a, 3c for those leaving A; a3, b1, c2 for those leaving B. We must select the best arrangement, for example a1, 2c, b3, if this were really the best.

We shall develop a numerical example to make things clearer.

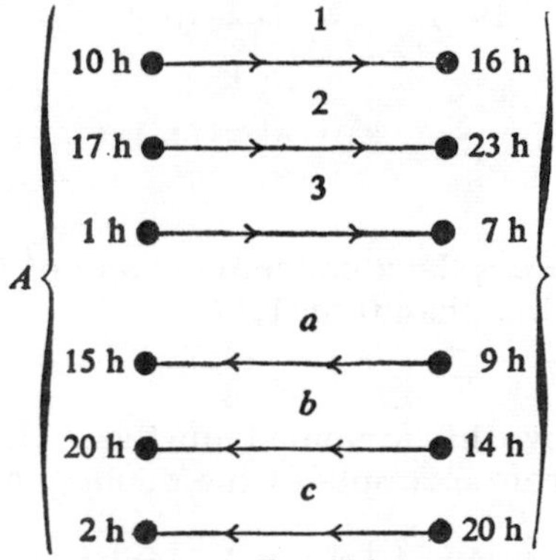

FIG. 18.1

Uniform flight time: 6 hours (actually, problems like this are expressed in minutes).

To solve the problem, we draw up Tables 18.2a and 18.2b, the first assuming that all the crews live at A, and the second assuming that all crews live at B; the numbers represent the time away from their home. All these times obviously lie between 12 and 36 hours. We assume that each crew, after arriving at its destination, will leave for home on the first available plane.

Table 18.2

(a) Crews living at A.

	a	b	c
1	29	34	16
2	22	27	33
3	14	19	25

(b) Crews living at B.

	a	b	c
1	31	26	20
2	14	33	27
3	22	17	35

(c) Shortest time intervals.

29	26	16
14	27	27
14	17	25

We then proceed to construct another table derived from these two by choosing, in each square, the smallest number in the two tables. This gives us Table 18.2c. Finally, we choose a number from a different row in each column with the intention of finding that arrangement which minimizes the sum of the three numbers. In the elementary case we are considering, this is very easy; we can form 6 distinct combinations:

$$c_{11} + c_{22} + c_{33} = 29 + 27 + 25 = 81 \text{ h}$$
$$c_{11} + c_{23} + c_{32} = 29 + 27 + 17 = 73 \text{ h}$$
$$c_{12} + c_{23} + c_{31} = 26 + 27 + 14 = 67 \text{ h}$$
$$c_{12} + c_{21} + c_{33} = 26 + 14 + 25 = 65 \text{ h} \qquad 18.3$$
$$c_{13} + c_{21} + c_{32} = 16 + 14 + 17 = 47 \text{ h} \leftarrow \text{minimum time}$$
$$c_{13} + c_{22} + c_{31} = 16 + 27 + 14 = 57 \text{ h}.$$

Thus the most favorable plan is the one that gives us 47 hours, or a2, b3, and 1c. Therefore, two crews will live at B and one at A, with their timetable set by the a2, b3, 1c arrangement.

The very simple little arithmetical problem we have just solved is an assignment problem. It was easy to solve, as we have seen, for 2 cities, 6 flights, and 3 crews. But it becomes very difficult indeed when these numbers are greater. We can see that, with m crews, it is possible to form $m(m-1)\ldots 3 \times 2 \times 1$ permutations. Consequently, with 10 crews, we would have to calculate 3,628,800 permutations, and with 20 crews, 2.4329×10^{33}, a number with 24 digits! This would take a team of good accountants, passing the task from father to son, several centuries to calculate. One can readily grasp the importance of a suitable shortcut, which we shall explain later on.

The actual problem that was studied included 13 cities, 60 connections, and 400 flights. It was agreed that each crew would come back to its point of departure. For example, in a network A, B, C, ... U, V, including junction points and feeder lines, every crew had to take a route constituting a chain link or closed circuit: ABCA - ABNCBA - MPM, etc. (Fig. 18.2).

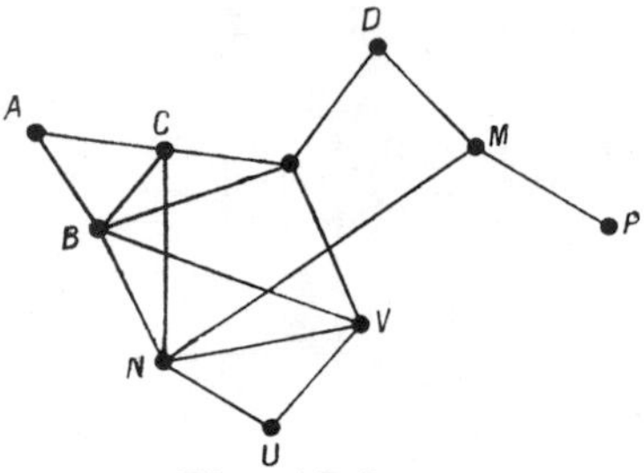

Fig. 18.2

The solution of such a system by the procedure we have used would require centuries of calculation, by hand or on an office comptometer, because it would be necessary to try every single one of the permutations!

But there is still more! The airline cannot require crews to fly if certain conditions are not met; for example:

—no crew can fly more than 8 consecutive hours;

—every crew coming off a flight must have a rest period at least twice the length of the flight time, plus a quarter of an hour;

—no crew can work more than 14 hours consecutively, counting ground time, without rest. Each airport is assigned an average length of time for ground activity.

This problem was actually studied and solved. It took 15 days to prepare the data. The solution, using an electronic computer, took an 8-hour day. The optimum solution makes it possible to save 18% over the costs arrived at by intuitive flight-planning. This saving amounted to almost 100 million francs a year.

2. The Hungarian method.

The principle of this method is simple, although certain rigorous proofs relating to it are quite subtle, and will not be given here.

There is no change in the optimal solution of an assignment problem if we increase or decrease the value of all the elements in the same row (or the same column) by a fixed quantity λ; this is obvious, because a solution can contain only one element equal to 1 for each row and column (see Table 18.1b). Such an operation decreases or increases by the value of the economic function, but does not change the optimal solution.

We shall explain this method by means of a numerical example (Table 18.3). The method involves five successive steps.

STEP I - Obtaining zeros.

From every element (number) in a column subtract a quantity equal to the smallest element in that column; in other words, form the table $c_{ij}^{(1)} = c_{ij} - \min_i c_{ij}$. This will produce at least one zero per column.

In our example (Table 18.3) we shall take away the number 7 from column (1), the number 6 from column (2), etc. This will give us Table 18.4

STEP II - Finding an optimal solution.

With the zeros from $c_{ij}^{(1)}$ try to form a zero-value solution, or, in other words, an assignment in which all the $c_{ij}^{(1)}$ elements in the solution are zeros. If this is possible, then the optimal solution has been found; if it is not, then we must go on to Step III.

To find this null solution, first consider one of the rows that has the fewest zeros; circle one of the zeros in that row, and then cross out the other zeros in the same row and the same column as the zero that has been circled. Do the same for all the rows.

Table 18.3

	(1)	(2)	(3)	(4)	(5)
(1)	12	8	7	15	4
(2)	7	9	17	14	10
(3)	9	6	12	6	7
(4)	7	6	14	6	10
(5)	9	6	12	10	6

Table 18.4

	(1)	(2)	(3)	(4)	(5)	
(1)	5	2	[0]	9	~~0~~	
(2)	[0]	3	10	8	6	×
(3)	2	~~0~~	5	~~0~~	3	× T
(4)	~~0~~	~~0~~	7	[0]	6	×
(5)	2	[0]	5	4	2	×
	×	×		×		

Table 18.5

	(1)	(2)	(3)	(4)	(5)
(1)	7	4	[0]	11	~~0~~
(2)	[0]	3	8	8	4
(3)	2	[0]	3	~~0~~	1
(4)	~~0~~	~~0~~	5	[0]	4
(5)	2	~~0~~	3	4	[0]

In our example, we started by circling $c_{21}^{(1)}$, which led us to cross out $c_{41}^{(1)}$; we then circle $c_{52}^{(1)}$, which leads us to cross out $c_{32}^{(1)}$ and $c_{42}^{(1)}$. We circle $c_{13}^{(1)}$ and cross out $c_{15}^{(1)}$; we circle $c_{44}^{(1)}$ and cross out $c_{34}^{(1)}$. This give us an incomplete assignment with all of the circled zeros. If we were to complete it by circling $c_{35}^{(1)}$, we would have an assignment plan whose total value would equal 3. Since we still have not derived an assignment plan with a total value of zero, we must go on to the next step.

STEP III - Finding a minimal group of lines and columns containing all the zeros.

Perform the following operations, step by step in sequence:
a) Mark (x) every row that contains no circled zero.
b) Mark every column that has one or more crossed-out zeros in a marked row.
c) Mark every row that has a circled zero in a marked column.
d) Repeat b) and c) until it is no longer possible to find any new marked columns or rows.

By following this procedure, it is possible to obtain a group of rows and/or columns, minimal in number, containing all the circled or crossed-out zeros.

In our procedure, we begin by marking row (3), then columns (2) and (4), then rows (4) and (5), then column (1), and lastly row (2). (See Table 18.4.)

STEP IV - (following Step III).

Draw a line through all the unmarked rows, and another line through all the marked columns. This, of necessity, gives the group of rows and/or columns, minimal in number, that contains all the zeros.

In Table (18.4), we see that the lines must be drawn through row (1) and through columns (1), (2), and (4).

STEP V - Possible shift of certain zeros.

Examine the partial (sub-) table consisting of elements that are not lined-through and take the smallest number (element) in this partial table; subtract this number in the columns not lined-through and add it in the rows that are lined-through.* It will be seen that in so doing we do not change the optimal solution of the given assignment problem.

A glance at Table 18.4 shows that the number 2 must be subtracted in columns (3) and (5), and added in row (1). This number, 2, is the smallest number in the part of the table that has not been lined-through. This will give us Table 18.5.

STEP VI - The optimal solution, or start of a new cycle.

Repeat Step II on the new table $c_{ij}^{(2)}$ produced in Step V. If an optimal solution results, the procedure is completed; if not,

---

*In effect, we are subtracting this number from the elements that are not lined-through, adding it to the elements that lie at the intersection of two lines, and leaving the rest unchanged.

continue until a Step II operation does produce an optimal solution. It is possible for this optimal solution not to be unique.

In Table 18.5, we circle $c_{21}^{(2)}$, then cross out $c_{41}^{(2)}$; we circle $c_{13}^{(2)}$, then cross out $c_{15}^{(2)}$; we circle $c_{32}^{(2)}$, then cross out $c_{34}^{(2)}$, $c_{42}^{(2)}$, and $c_{52}^{(2)}$. We circle $c_{44}^{(2)}$ and $c_{55}^{(2)}$. This produces an optimal solution; if it had not, we would then have repeated Steps II through V on $c_{ij}^{(2)}$, and so forth, until the optimum solution was finally obtained.

This optimum solution yields:

$$c_{13}^{(2)} + c_{21}^{(2)} + c_{32}^{(2)} + c_{44}^{(2)} + c_{55}^{(2)} = 0 + 0 + 0 + 0 + 0 = 0 \qquad 18.4$$

and, going back to the given problem (Table 18.3):

$$\min z = c_{13} + c_{21} + c_{32} + c_{44} + c_{55} = 7 + 7 + 6 + 6 + 6 = 32. \qquad 18.5$$

This result can be recalculated and checked. In Step I we subtracted from the z function: 7 + 6 + 7 + 6 + 4 = 30; in Step III, we subtracted 2 + 2 - 2 = 2; which, in fact adds up to 32.

3. Finding a maximum.

In some assignment problems, the idea is to find the assignment pattern that will yield the maximum for the economic function. In this case, we proceed in the following manner:

1) Determine the highest unit cost in the entire table:

$$\text{let: } c = \max_{i,j} c_{ij}; \qquad 18.6$$

2) Deduct this unit cost from each element in the table. This produces a new table, made up of zeros or negative numbers:

$$c_{ij} = c_{ij} - c\,. \qquad 18.7$$

3) Change the signs of all the c'_{ij} elements; i.e.,

$$c_{ij} = -c'_{ij} = c - c_{ij}\,, \qquad 18.8$$

Hence:

$$c_{ij} = c - c''_{ij}\,. \qquad 18.9$$

It is clear now that the maximum for the assignment problem formed with c_{ij} elements corresponds to the minimum for the problem formed with c''_{ij} elements. At this point, we proceed to find optimal solution in the table formed with c''_{ij} elements.

Note.

There are $P_n = n(n-1)(n-2)\ldots 2 \cdot 1$ possible solutions for an $n \times n$ table, which rules out a trial and error approach. The numbers quickly become very large: $P_5 = 120$, $P_6 = 720$, $P_7 = 5{,}040$, $P_8 = 40{,}320, \ldots P_{20} = 2.4329 \times 10^{23}$.

Section 19

TRAVELING SALESMAN PROBLEMS

Problems of this kind can be stated, for example, in some such manner as the following: find the lowest-cost route for a traveling salesman* who must leave a given city, stop at every city in a certain region, and then return to his starting-point.

This type of problem arises in the following management phenomena:

—deliveries
—inspection
—school bus routing
—television relays, etc.

Let us outline a very simple case: what is the lowest-cost regular route for a traveling salesman who has to stop at cities A, B, C, and D without passing twice through the same one (Fig. 19.1)? The transportation costs are shown in Table 19.1.

We can easily see that there are three possible routes:

$$\begin{aligned} ABCDA&: \quad c = 12 + 17 + 30 + 23 = 82 \\ ABDCA&: \quad c = 12 + 14 + 30 + 25 = 81 \\ ADBCA&: \quad c = 23 + 14 + 17 + 25 = 79 \leftarrow \end{aligned} \qquad 19.1$$

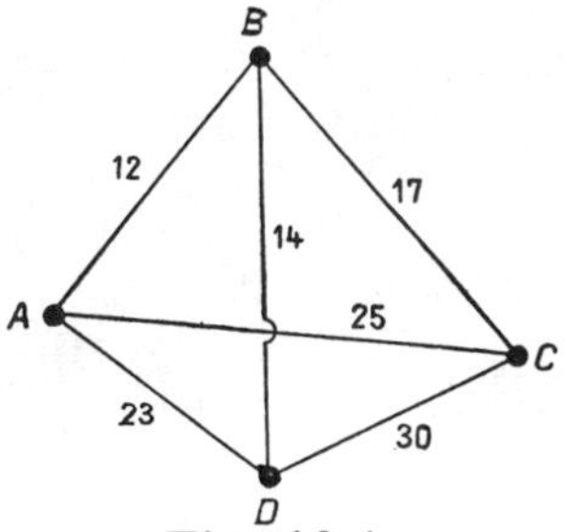

Fig. 19.1

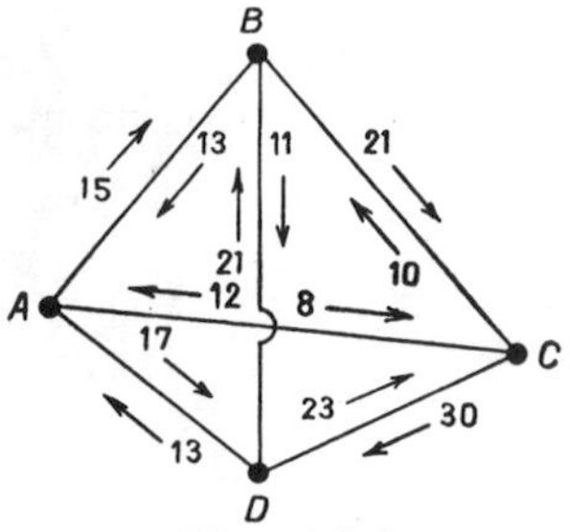

Fig. 19.2

*If travel expenses per mile are constant, then the lowest-cost route is the shortest.

Table 19.1

	A	B	C	D
A	0	12	25	23
B	12	0	17	14
C	25	17	0	30
D	23	14	30	0

Table 19.2

	A	B	C	D
A	0	15	8	17
B	13	0	21	11
C	12	10	0	30
D	13	21	23	0

Thus route ADBCA gives the lowest cost.

In some problems, the costs are not symmetrical (see Fig. 19.2 and Table 19.2); in such cases, there are twice as many routes to be examined (6 in this example):

$$\begin{aligned} ABCDA &: \; c = 15 + 21 + 30 + 13 = 79 \\ ABDCA &: \; c = 15 + 11 + 23 + 12 = 61 \\ ACBDA &: \; c = 8 + 10 + 11 + 13 = 42 \leftarrow \\ ACDBA &: \; c = 8 + 30 + 21 + 13 = 72 \\ ADBCA &: \; c = 17 + 21 + 21 + 12 = 71 \\ ADCBA &: \; c = 17 + 23 + 10 + 13 = 63\,. \end{aligned} \qquad 19.2$$

No analytical method is known for solving problems like this, and it is impossible in practice to calculate all the solutions in order to choose the best when we are dealing with a large number of cities. For example, with 12 cities there are 39,916,800 distinct routes if the cost table is asymmetrical, and 19,958,400 if it is symmetrical. One can also imagine a case in which routes must be planned within an incomplete network, i.e., where there are no connections between certain cities. In this case, the problem becomes still more complicated.

Although analytical techniques are lacking, it is possible, in certain special cases—such as those of very extended networks—to achieve a solution close to the optimum by employing a step-by-step procedure (See Part Two, Section 69).

Chapter 3

Delay (Queuing) phenomena

Section 20

INTRODUCTION

Among the diverse types of problems in which one observes a scientific attitude toward the play of chance, the problems posed by delay (queuing) phenomena merit special attention. For the theoretical study of such phenomena, we employ the concept of "stochastic" processes. These are mathematical models that involve random dimensions or variables, that is, dimensions each value of which can be associated with some probability which itself varies with time.

The waiting line (queue) is an affliction of our age. We are forced to admit that it is almost unavoidable in many cases, if we are not to adopt measures whose costs would be out of all proportion to the benefits of rapid service. When safety, or any other necessity, makes it imperative to provide a rapid service that will reduce waiting time below some fixed level, it then becomes possible to estimate the extent of the measures to be taken, as well as their cost.

This theory and its applications will be studied in a manner that reduces the necessary mathematical developments to a minimum.

Section 21

GENERAL DESCRIPTION OF DELAY PHENOMENA

1. General explanation.—2. Arrivals.—3. Length or time of service.—4. Structure of a delay phenomenon.

1. General explanation.

Waiting lines, or queues, are familiar phenomena, which we observe quite frequently in our personal activities; but they are also encountered in many economic, military, social, etc. problems. In general terms, the characteristics of a delay phenomenon are:

1—Units arrive, at regular or irregular intervals of time, at a given point called the service center. For example: the arrival of trucks at a loading station, the entry of customers into a store, the arrival of ships in a port, the arrival of work orders in a shop, etc.; all of these units will be called entries or arrivals.

2—One or more service channels or service stations (tracks, ticket windows, salesmen, etc.) are assembled at the service center. The units usually must wait for a station to be free before they can be served. The intervals of unit service time may be regular or irregular, according to the case.

The following are some examples of delay phenomena:

ENTRIES OR ARRIVALS	NATURE OF SERVICE	CHANNELS OR STATIONS
Customers	Sale of an article	Salesgirls
Ships	Unloading	Docks
Planes	Landing	Runways
Telephone calls	Conversation	Telephone circuits
Cars arriving	Customs check	Customs agents
Messages	Decoding	Decoders
Defective machines	Repairs	Mechanics
Fires	Putting out fires	Fire engines
Orders	Tailoring or repairs	Workshops
Letters	Typing	Typists

We shall be probing deeply into the structure of such phenomena, and in order to do so we shall distinguish several categories of entries and channels.

2. Entries.

Entries may be:
—separated by equal intervals of time;
—separated by unequal, but definitely known, intervals of time;
—separated by unequal intervals of time whose probabilities are known; these are then called random intervals.

3. Length or time of service.

In the same way, the service time may be:
—constant;
—variable, but known;
—random (and, therefore, with known probability).

We can also conceive of the case in which the intervals between successive arrivals and/or* the service times would be irregular and with unknown probabilities, but in such cases nothing can be predicted or estimated.

4. Structure of a delay phenomenon.

For a waiting line to occur, all that is necessary is that the entries and/or the service times form irregular intervals. A waiting line can also occur with constant entry intervals and service times if the service time is longer than the interval between entries; in this case, the waiting line will lengthen regularly and indefinitely. Such a case holds little interest for us, and so we shall exclude it from this study.

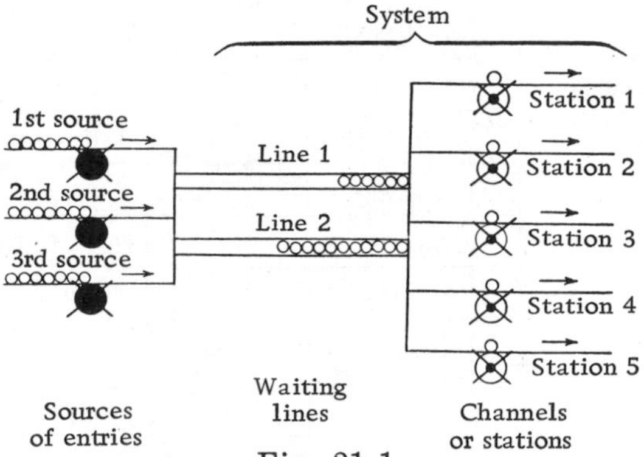

Fig. 21.1

In order to clarify the structure of delay phenomena, we have shown in Fig. 21.1 a diagram of a delay phenomenon in which there are three sources, two waiting lines, and five stations.

The waiting lines and the stations together constitute the delay system (or, briefly, system).

---

*As is the current usage, we shall employ the "and/or" symbol to indicate a coordinate conjunction corresponding to the non-exclusive "or."

One can conceive of a case with several sources of entries, each of them with a different probability distribution. For example, imagine a restaurant whose clientele consists of workers from three different plants, and in which the average number of workers arriving per minute varies according to the plant they come from. In practical cases of this type, we would replace the three sources with a single one whose probability distribution could be measured or calculated.

One can also imagine several waiting lines, in which either the arrivals take their places automatically on the shortest line or some system of priority is applied. The set of order relationships or priorities that operate on the waiting lines is called the delay discipline. Referring back to our restaurant example, we might imagine two waiting lines, one of them reserved to priority customers, of whom there would not be very many.

The units on the waiting line progress to the service stations in a time interval that may be different for each unit or each station. One must also specify how, in case there are several waiting lines, each unit chooses the station where it will be served. We might imagine, for example, that certain of the waitresses in our restaurant are faster than others and that customers in a hurry prefer these waitresses.

In Fig. 21.2 we have shown a diagram of the structure of a delay phenomenon in the general case. We shall use the following notations:

m = number of units in the total phenomenon (m can be finite or infinite);
n = number of units in the system (waiting in line or being served);
v = number of units in all the waiting lines;
j = number of units being served;
ρ = number of stations that are idle.

This gives us:

$$\begin{aligned} n &= j \quad \text{if} \quad n \leqslant S \\ &= \nu + j \quad \text{if} \quad n > S, \end{aligned} \qquad 21.1$$

where S is the number of stations.

The quantities n, v, and j will vary as a function of time in a random fashion, which means they vary by chance with a certain probability system that we propose to discover. If we call p_n the probability that there are n units in the system, the mean, or mathematical expectation, for the number of units in the system will be:

$$\bar{n} = 0\cdot p_0 + 1\cdot p_1 + 2\cdot p_2 + 3\cdot p_3 + \ldots + m\cdot p_m = \sum_{n=0}^{m} np_n \qquad 21.2$$

where m can be infinite.

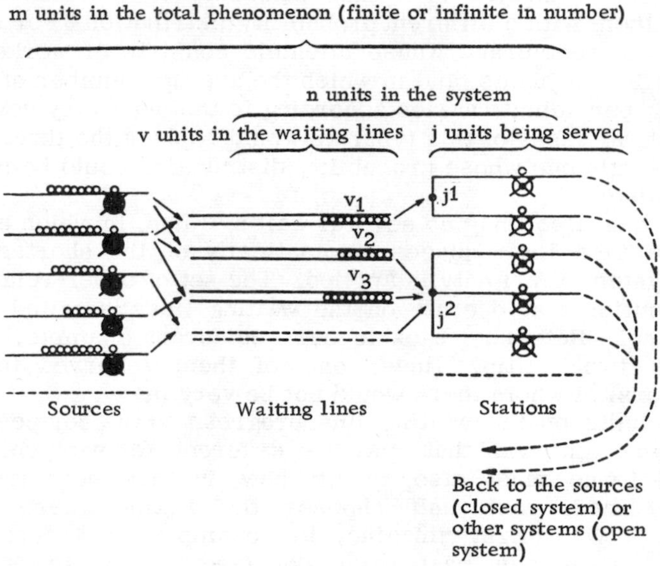

Fig. 21.2

In the case of a single waiting line and S service stations, the mean number of units in the waiting line will be:

$$\bar{\nu} = 1 \cdot p_{S+1} + 2 \cdot p_{S+2} + 3\, p_{S+3} + \ldots + (m - S)\, p_m = \sum_{n=S+1}^{m} (n - S)\, p_n \qquad 21.3$$

This formula is easy to explain: there are units waiting as soon as n becomes greater than S, or, in other words, when $n = S+1$, $n = S+2, \ldots$, and the corresponding probabilities are p_{S+1}, $p_{S+2}, \ldots$

Instead of finding the mean number of units being served, it is often of greater interest to determine the average number of idle stations. For example, we might try to find a compromise between the cost of delaying units and the cost of idle stations. Let $\bar{\varrho}$ equal the mean number of idle stations:

$$\bar{\varrho} = S\, p_0 + (S - 1)\, p_1 + \ldots + 1 \cdot p_{S-1} = \sum_{n=0}^{S} (S - n)\, p_n. \qquad 21.4$$

Among the quantities $\bar{n}$, $\bar{\nu}$ and $\bar{\varrho}$, there exists the relation:*,**

$$\bar{n} = \bar{\nu} + S - \bar{\varrho}.$$

---

*This relationship is easily demonstrated. All that is needed is some familiarity with the manipulation of the sums represented by

Section 22

THE RANDOM NATURE OF ARRIVALS OR OF SERVICE

Let us point out, first of all, that the simple statement that units arrive at random is insufficient as a characterization of these arrivals; it is essential to know the statistical description of the phenomenon and to draw from this knowledge a law of probability. This is a very important point, and we shall now explain it in some detail.

To begin with let us clarify exactly what we mean by the word chance or random. An event appears to occur in a random manner (or by chance) if the causes for its occurrence are independent and so numerous that it is impossible for us to know them all and to single out the laws that govern the occurrence of the event. For example, we cannot predict the precise timing of arrivals at a post office, the amount of gas a customer will buy when he pulls into a filling station, the number that will come up on one throw of the dice, and so on. If we can make a certain number of experiments, or if the event occurs often enough, we will be able to note the results of our tests, and to make a statistical study of the phenomenon observed.

---

the symbol Σ. We have:

$$\bar{n} = \sum_{n=0}^{m} np_n \ , \ \bar{\nu} = \sum_{n=S+1}^{m} (n - S)\, p_n \ , \ \bar{\varrho} = \sum_{n=0}^{S} (S - n)\, p_n$$

Let us calculate:

$$\begin{aligned} \bar{\nu} - \bar{\varrho} &= \sum_{n=S+1}^{m} (n - S)\, p_n - \sum_{n=0}^{S} (S - n)\, p_n \\ &= \sum_{n=S+1}^{m} (n - S)\, p_n + \sum_{n=0}^{S} (n - S)\, p_n \\ &= \sum_{n=0}^{m} (n - S)\, p_n \\ &= \sum_{n=0}^{m} n\, p_n - S \sum_{n=0}^{m} p_n \,. \end{aligned}$$

But the sum of the probabilities of all cases from $n = 0$ to $n = m$ has the value 1, and the sum $\Sigma\, np_n$ from $n = 0$ to $n = m$ has the value of $\bar{n}$; therefore:

$$\bar{\nu} - \bar{\varrho} = \bar{n} - S\,.$$

**See Part Two, Sections 72 and 73.

For example, suppose that we count the number of cars passing in one direction on a highway over a period of one minute, and that we repeat this counting procedure 100 times in succession. The first minute, we count 6 cars; the second, 9; the third, 11; the fourth, 5; and so on. We then draw up a table (Table 22.1) which shows the number of times (or frequency, f) we counted 0 cars, 1, 2, 3 . . . cars per minute. Thus (Table 22.1), we counted 10 cars per minute 9 times, 11 cars per minute 7 times, etc. This measurement gives us a quantitative representation of the phenomenon.

Table 22.1

n	f
0	0
1	0
2	1
3	3
4	5
5	10
6	12
7	14
8	15
9	12
10	9
11	7
12	5
13	3
14	2
15	1
16	1
17 or more	0

When the number of observations is large enough, we can accept the following empirical rule of behavior:

"The probability of an event, E, is, effectively, the ratio of the number, n, of cases in which E occurs, which are called favorable cases, to the total number, N, of cases observed."

In our example, what is the probability that 12 cars will go by during a period of one minute? It is:

$$Pr_{12} = \frac{5}{100} = 0.05 . \qquad 22.1$$

What would be the probability of more than 12 cars passing in one minute?

The probability of more than 12 cars: 22.2

$$= Pr_{13} + Pr_{14} + Pr_{15} + Pr_{16} + Pr_{17} + \dots$$

$$= \frac{3}{100} + \frac{2}{100} + \frac{1}{100} + \frac{1}{100} = \frac{7}{100} = 0.07$$

And that of at least 9 cars passing?

Probability of at least 9 cars: 22.3

$$= Pr_0 + Pr_1 + Pr_2 + \dots + Pr_8 + Pr_9$$

$$= \frac{1}{100} + \frac{3}{100} + \frac{5}{100} + \frac{10}{100} + \frac{12}{100} + \frac{14}{100} + \frac{15}{100} + \frac{12}{100} = \frac{72}{100} = 0.72 .$$

The concept of probability gives a practical meaning to the idea of chance. We say that a phenomenon occurs according to chance, or that it is random, when we can assign a probability to the occurrence of each event. The value of this probability may be known with more or less precision; statisticians employ procedures of progressively greater complexity in order to increase this precision.

We do not intend to give a lengthy discussion of the theory of probability or its underlying bases, but we felt it desirable to point out clearly what might be considered fundamental to the developments that will follow.

We trust that the reader will not be misled by the purposely superficial nature of the preceding remarks and will remember that the science of statistics transforms the elementary notions provided by our text into a perfectly coherent body of doctrine. In Part Two, Chapter VIII, the reader will find a mathematical exposition of the theory of delay phenomena which is based entirely on the concept of probability.

Thus, phenomena such as arrivals at a post office, gasoline demand at a filling station, or telephone calls received at a switchboard, are not necessarily governed by a single universal law. One can imagine all kinds of probability laws: there is an infinity of them. However, it has frequently been observed that the same law appears repeatedly, when certain conditions are met. These are precisely the conditions we shall meet most often in connection with the arrivals of units in delay phenomena. A statement of these conditions leads to a description which we call the Poisson process; the probability law to which it leads carries the same name: Poisson's law, and constitutes a very important special case (see Part Two, Sections 72 and 73).

Section 23

AN ALMOST GENERAL LAW OF RANDOM ARRIVALS: POISSON'S LAW

We shall now consider a series of identical events, E, which follow one another in time (for example, entries into a store, passage of cars on a highway, incoming calls at a telephone switchboard, etc). Starting from an initial instant $t = 0$, let n be the number of events that have occurred up to time t; since n is a random number, we must assign it a probability, which we shall call $p_n(t)$. The symbol $p_n(t)$ means that this probability is a function of t. Let us now state the following hypotheses:

1. The probability $p_n(t)$ depends only on the time interval t and not on the initial instant. For example, if the probability of the passage of 9 vehicles on a highway between 2:21 P.M. and 2:22 P.M. is 0.12, we will have the same probability between 1:28 and 1:29 P.M., or between 2:31 and 2:32 P.M. We say that this phenomenon is homogeneous in time, or stationary, the two expressions being synonymous.

2. We assume that two events cannot occur at the same time (for example, two customers never enter a store at precisely the same moment, two cars never pass the check point abreast). In other words, we could say that the probability of such an event is very slight (a very rare event).

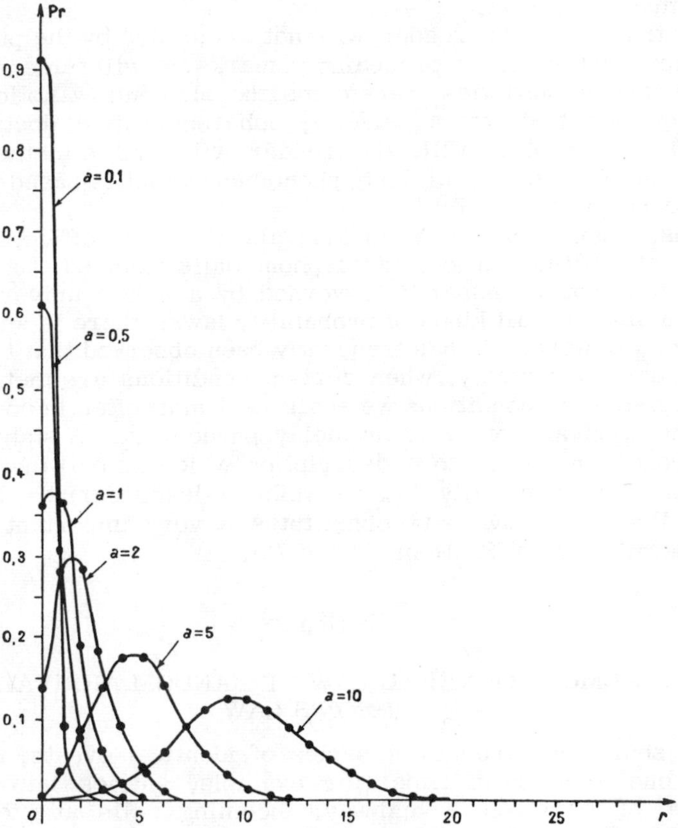

Fig. 23.1.—Graph showing the Poisson distribution for different values of a. This graph was drawn using continuous curves, although only integral values of r are significant. The points marked on the curves give the values. For greater precision, see the table in the Appendix.

3. If we consider the very small time interval Δt, chosen at any instant, the probability that an event will occur during that interval is equal to $\lambda\Delta t$; the quantity λ is called the average rate of arrival. For example, let us choose 1/10 second for Δt (or a shorter interval, if necessary, so that, effectively, there are

never two arrivals in one interval Δt. Each 1/10 second, we observe whether a car has gone by on the road; let us say: no, no, yes, no, yes, yes, no, no, no, no, no . . . and so on, every 1/10 second for an hour. Say we have logged 540 yeses and 35,460 noes. The average rate of arrival will be 9 units per minute, or 540 per hour, or 0.15 per second, depending on the time unit chosen. If the phenomenon is homogeneous in time, the probability that a car will go by during any given 1/10 second will be equal to 540/36,000 = 0.015. For 1/100 second, we have a probability of 0.0015, and so on. The constant quantity λ, related to one minute, will be 9, and the probability $\lambda \Delta t$ will be 0.0015 for a $\Delta t = 1/100$ second.

We can show (see Part Two, Section 72) that the probability $p_n(t)$ is then given by the formula:

$$p_n(t) = \frac{(\lambda t)^n e^{-\lambda t}}{n!} \qquad n = 0, 1, 2, 3, 4, \dots, \qquad 23.1$$

where e is the base of Naperian (natural) logarithms*: e = 2.71828...

n! means $n \times (n-1) \times (n-2) \dots \times 4 \times 3 \times 2 \times 1$; for example:

$$5! = 5 \times 4 \times 3 \times 2 \times 1 = 120. \qquad 23.2$$

The probability distribution:

$$f(a) = \frac{a^n\ e^{-a}}{n!} \qquad 23.3$$

is called Poisson's law. When events occur in such a way as to satisfy the three stated conditions, the phenomenon constitutes a Poisson process, whose law of probability is given by Poisson's law.

A table is included in the Appendix which gives the probabilities $p_n(t)$ for values of $a = \lambda t$ ranging from $a = 0.1$ to $a = 18$. For example, if $a = \lambda t = 8$:

$$\begin{aligned} &p_0 = 0.000,\ p_1 = 0.002,\ p_2 = 0.010,\ p_3 = 0.028,\ p_4 = 0.057,\ p_5 = 0.091,\\ &p_6 = 0.122,\ p_7 = 0.139,\ p_8 = 0.139,\ p_9 = 0.124,\ p_{10} = 0.099,\ p_{11} = 0.072,\\ &p_{12} = 0.048,\ p_{13} = 0.029,\ p_{14} = 0.016,\ p_{15} = 0.009,\ p_{16} = 0.004,\ p_{17} = 0.002,\\ &p_{18} = 0.000\ \dots \end{aligned} \qquad 23.4$$

In comparing these theoretical values with the experimentally observed values shown in Table 22.1, we note that the passage of

---

*Let us recall that Naperian logarithms have as their base, not 10, but a number called e, whose value is 2.71828. . .

cars on the highway very closely follows Poisson's law; such a case may be called a Poisson-type phenomenon.

The Poisson case is the most frequently observed because, generally, the conditions outlined above are approximately fulfilled in all phenomena involving random arrivals.

Fig. 23.1 shows graphically the probability distribution pattern given by Poisson's law for various values of $a = \lambda t$.

Let us recall that, in the case of Poisson's law, the average or mathematical expectation

$$\bar{n} = 0 \cdot p_0 + 1 \cdot p_1 + 2 \cdot p_2 + 3 \cdot p_3 + \dots + n \cdot p_n + \dots$$
$$= a = \lambda t, \qquad 23.5$$

is exactly the average number of events E observed during the interval t. Furthermore, the standard deviation is equal to $\sqrt{\lambda t}$:

$$\sigma_N = \sqrt{a} = \sqrt{\lambda t}. \qquad 23.6$$

The probability law for the time interval Θ between two successive events governed by Poisson's law is also of interest. The probability that two events will be separated by a time interval Θ greater than a given time θ is:

$$\Pr(\Theta > \theta) = e^{-\lambda\theta}. \qquad 23.7$$

The mean and the standard deviation for Θ are:

$$\bar{\theta} = \frac{1}{\lambda}, \qquad 23.8$$

$$\sigma_\Theta = \frac{1}{\lambda}. \qquad 23.9$$

This is peculiar to events that are governed by Poisson's law.

Therefore, if a stochastic phenomenon is distributed according to Poisson's law, with a rate of λ, then the intervals between the events follow the exponential law with the same rate of λ.

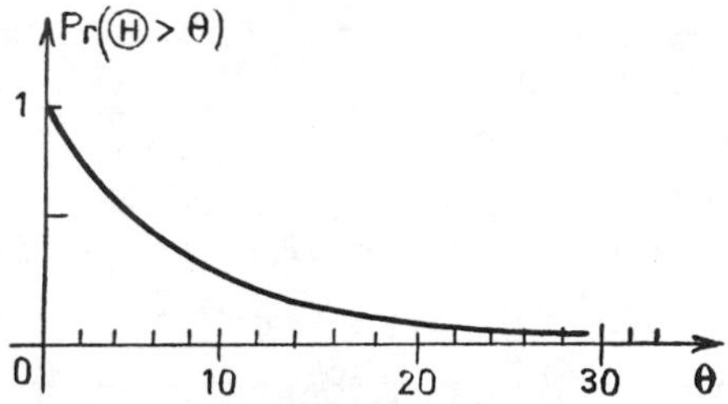

Fig. 23.2

TABLE 23.1

θ seconds	0	2	4	6	8	10	12	14	16	18	20	22	24	26	28	30
$\lambda\theta$	0	0.26	0.53	0.80	1.06	1.33	1.60	1.86	2.13	2.40	2.66	2.93	3.20	3.46	3.73	4
Pr ($\Theta > \theta$)	1	0.766	0.587	0.449	0.346	0.264	0.201	0.155	0.118	0.090	0.069	0.053	0.040	0.031	0.023	0.018

For example, when $\lambda = 8$ arrivals per minute, we obtain Table 23.1, above.

Thus, the probability of an interval greater than 10 seconds between two arrivals is 0.264, and the average interval is 60/8, or 7.5 seconds. Fig. 23.2 is the graphic representation of Table 23.1 (see Part Two, Sections 72 and 73).

Section 24

ANOTHER FREQUENTLY RANDOM DIMENSION: SERVICE TIME.

Service time may be constant, variable but determined, or, again, random. When it is random, its probability law often takes the form of an exponential curve (see Fig. 23.2). If we call μ the number of units served during a given time during which the service station is never idle, the service time Θ has as its probability law:

$$\Pr(\Theta > \theta) = e^{-\mu\theta} .$$

In certain cases, there can be some ambiguity as to which aspect constitutes the service and which the clientele. For example, at a taxi-stand where both cabs and would-be passengers arrive, there may be a waiting line of taxis or a waiting line of passengers. For the latter, the service time is the interval between the departure of the taxi one has missed and the arrival of the next. But, from the viewpoint of a waiting line of cabs, the passengers play an equivalent role.

We shall now consider a few situations, postponing their mathematical explanations to Part Two of this book. Offhand, we can imagine the various possible situations schematized in the following diagram:

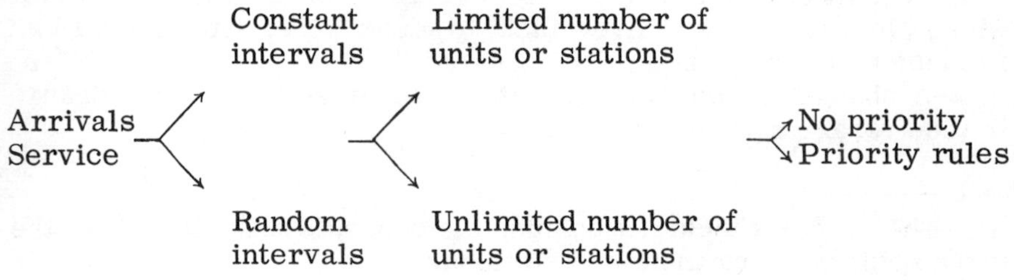

But we can also imagine cases far more complicated or varied: for example, one in which the length of a waiting line has an effect on the arrival rate or the service rate. Here we have a phenomenon equivalent to what engineers refer to as feedback, i.e. a phenomenon in which the effect (output) reacts on the cause (input). We shall limit ourselves here to a presentation of those mathematical models corresponding to the simplest and most common cases (see Part Two, Sections 72 and 73).

Section 25

DESCRIPTION OF A WAITING LINE AT A STATION—ARRIVAL RATE AND SERVICE RATE.

1. General explanation.—2. Average number of units in the line.—3. Example.—4. Average waiting time.—5. The case of uniform service (constant duration).

1. General explanation.

First, let us look at what takes place in a waiting line at a single station when arrivals follow Poisson's law and the service time intervals are distributed according to the exponential law, such as that shown in Fig. 23.2.

Anyone who intends to go to a place where he assumes he will have to wait intuitively asks himself this question: What is the probability of a waiting line of such-and-such a length? If he decides that the probability is close to 1 that there will be 20 or 25 people ahead of him in the line on a Saturday morning, he will choose another day when such a probability seems remote. In all delay phenomena, determination of the probability law p_n governing the number of units in the system is an essential calculation, on the basis of which quantitative expressions may be developed. We shall not perform such calculations as these, which the reader can find in Part Two; but we shall provide the basic formulae obtained and the conclusions that can be drawn from them.

We shall assume that the delay phenomenon is permanent* or, in other words, that the probability p_n does not vary with time. This condition is fulfilled only during a certain time interval which it will be our first task to determine. Two causes can produce a variation in p_n:

—a change in the average rate of arrivals λ, and/or a change in the average rate of service μ;

---

*The reader should not confuse the concepts associated with the two adjectives permanent and stationary.

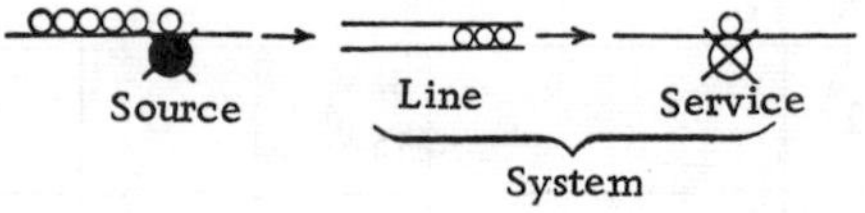

Fig. 25.1

—the transient condition that occurs between the beginning of the service operation and the instant in which the situation is stabilized. The length or duration of this transient condition is a function of λ and μ.

Thus, the measurement or the knowledge of λ and μ must be related to a time interval in which these factors can be considered constant; this time interval must also be appreciably larger than the time necessary for stabilization. For example, it would be wise to make the measurement interval a period 3 or 4 times longer than the time it takes the situation to stabilize.

Therefore, we shall consider the phenomenon as permanent; the probability p_n is then given by the formula:

$$p_n = \left(\frac{\lambda}{\mu}\right)^n \left(1 - \frac{\lambda}{\mu}\right) \qquad n = 0, 1, 2, 3, 4, \ldots \qquad 25.1$$

where $0 < \lambda/\mu < 1$.

The quantity

$$\psi = \frac{\lambda}{\mu} \qquad 25.2$$

is called the traffic intensity or utilization factor and characterizes the delay phenomenon. We can now write*:

$$p_n = \psi^n (1 - \psi) \qquad 0 < \psi < 1. \qquad 25.3$$

---

*Formula (25.3) is very easy to apply. Assume, for example, that $\psi = 2/3$; therefore $1 - \psi = 1/3$; then

$$p_0 = \left(\frac{2}{3}\right)^0 \left(\frac{1}{3}\right) = 1 \times \frac{1}{3} = \frac{1}{3}$$

$$p_1 = \left(\frac{2}{3}\right)^1 \left(\frac{1}{3}\right) = \frac{2}{3} \times \frac{1}{3} = \frac{2}{9}$$

$$p_2 = \left(\frac{2}{3}\right)^2 \left(\frac{1}{3}\right) = \frac{4}{9} \times \frac{1}{3} = \frac{4}{27}$$

Table 25.1

Ψ \ n	0	1	2	3	4	5	6	7	8
0.1	0.900	0.090	0.009	0.000					
0.2	0.800	0.160	0.032	0.006	0.001	0.000			
0.3	0.700	0.210	0.063	0.018	0.005	0.002	0.000		
0.4	0.600	0.240	0.096	0.038	0.015	0.006	0.002	0.000	
0.5	0.500	0.250	0.125	0.062	0.031	0.015	0.007	0.004	0.002
0.6	0.400	0.240	0.144	0.086	0.051	0.031	0.018	0.011	0.006
0.7	0.300	0.210	0.147	0.102	0.072	0.050	0.035	0.024	0.017
0.8	0.200	0.160	0.128	0.102	0.081	0.065	0.052	0.041	0.033
0.9	0.100	0.090	0.081	0.072	0.065	0.059	0.053	0.047	0.043

There is another convenient formula, which mathematicians call a recurrence formula:

$$p_n = \psi\, p_{n-1} \qquad n \geqslant 1 \qquad 25.4$$

with

$$p_0 = 1 - \psi . \qquad 25.4a$$

Traffic intensity must be less than 1, otherwise the waiting line would constantly grow longer.

Table 25.1 gives the values of these probabilities as a function of n and ψ. One important probability is that of no delay at all, which corresponds to n = 0; it is given by formula (25.4a).

The probability that the system will contain a number of units N less than or equal to n is given by the formula:

$$\Pr(N \leqslant n) = p_0 + p_1 + p_2 + \dots + p_n = 1 - \psi^{n+1} . \qquad 25.5$$

$$p_3 = \left(\frac{2}{3}\right)^3 \left(\frac{1}{3}\right) = \frac{8}{27} \times \frac{1}{3} = \frac{8}{81}$$

....

etc...

Formula (25.4) is even simpler:

$$p_0 = 1 - \frac{2}{3} = \frac{1}{3},\quad p_1 = \frac{2}{3}\cdot p_0 = \frac{2}{9},\quad p_2 = \frac{2}{3}\cdot p_1 = \frac{4}{27},\quad p_3 = \frac{2}{3}\cdot p_2 = \frac{8}{81},\quad \dots \text{ etc...}$$

The probability of N being greater than n is given by:

$$\begin{aligned} \Pr(N > n) &= 1 - \Pr(N \leqslant n) \\ &= 1 - (1 - \psi^{n+1}) \\ &= \psi^{n+1}. \end{aligned} \qquad 25.6$$

For example, the probability of finding more than 4 units in a system where $\psi = 0.7$ is:

$$\Pr(N > 4) = (0.7)^5 = 0.168. \qquad 25.7$$

The average number of units in the system is given by:

$$\bar{n} = 0 \cdot p_0 + 1 \cdot p_1 + 2 \cdot p_2 + 3 \cdot p_3 + \ldots + np_n + \ldots \qquad 25.8$$

This gives us:

$$\bar{n} = \frac{\psi}{1 - \psi}. \qquad 25.9$$

Hence the mathematical expectation for a traffic density of 5/6 is 5.

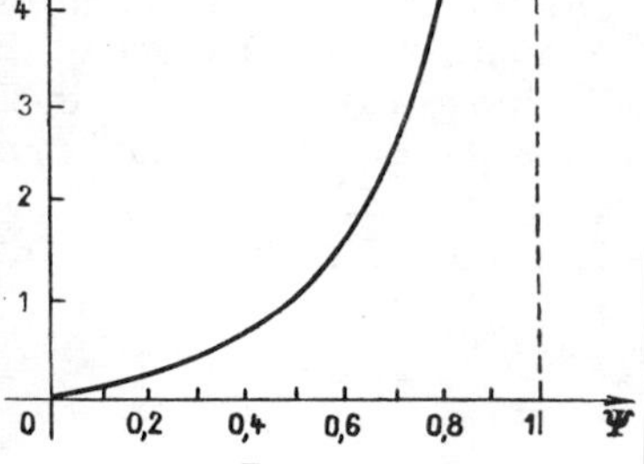

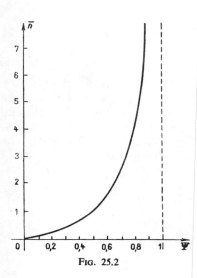

FIG. 25.2

Fig. 25.2 is a graph showing $\bar{n}$ as a function of ψ. Formula (25.9) can be used to determine the traffic intensity corresponding to a certain average number of units $\bar{n}$ in the system:

$$\psi = \frac{\bar{n}}{1 + \bar{n}}. \qquad 25.10$$

Thus, for an average $\bar{n} = 4$, we find a corresponding traffic intensity of $\psi = 4/5$.

2. Average number of units in the line.

If n is the number of units in the system, and v is the number of units in the line, we have:

$$\begin{aligned} \nu &= n && \text{if } n = 0 \\ &= n - 1 && \text{if } n > 0; \end{aligned} \qquad 25.11$$

This does not necessarily imply:

$$\bar{\nu} = \bar{n} - 1\,, \qquad 25.12$$

however:

$$\begin{aligned}\bar{\nu} &= \bar{n} - 1 + p_0 \\ &= \frac{\psi}{1-\psi} - \psi = \frac{\psi^2}{1-\psi}.\end{aligned} \qquad 25.13$$

The fact that (25.11) does not imply (25.12) is not paradoxical. We must remember that the service station is not always in use and that the average number of units receiving service is therefore not equal to 1, but to 1 - p_0.

It is interesting to develop the average value of the idle time of the service station, which we shall call $\bar{\rho}$; in the case we are studying:

$$\bar{\varrho} = \sum_{n=0}^{1} (1 - n)\, p_n = p_0 = 1 - \psi\,. \qquad 25.14$$

We can then write:

$$\bar{n} = \bar{\nu} + (1 - \bar{\varrho}) = \bar{\nu} + 1 - p_0 \qquad 25.15$$

or

$$\bar{\nu} = \bar{n} - 1 + p_0 = \bar{n} - \psi\,. \qquad 25.16$$

3. Example

Suppose 70 people per day come to a post-office window (which is open 10 hours a day). The window can serve an average of 10 people per hour. Taking Poisson's hypothesis for arrivals, and assuming that the exponential law governs the service distribution, what will be the average length of the waiting line in front of the window and the probability of a line with more than 2 people in it? We count the person who is being served as being in the line; thus, the average length of the line will correspond to $\bar{n}$.

If we take T = 1 hour, we have $\lambda = 7$, $\mu = 10$; therefore, $\psi = 0.7$. This gives us:

$$\bar{n} = \frac{0.7}{1 - 0.7} = \frac{7}{3}\,,$$

therefore, $\bar{n}$ will lie between 2 and 3.

Furthermore:

$$\Pr(N > 2) = (0.7)^3 = 0{,}343\,.$$

4. Average waiting time.

Still holding to the hypotheses we adopted earlier (Poisson arrivals, exponential service), the average time spent in the waiting line (which does not include time in service) is given by a simple formula:

$$\bar{t}_f = \frac{\bar{\nu}}{\lambda} = \frac{1}{\mu} \cdot \frac{\psi}{1 - \psi} = \frac{\bar{n}}{\mu} \qquad 25.17$$

This relation can be obtained directly if we reason as follows: in a permanent system, as many units leave as arrive, on the average; since λ units arrive per unit of time, we see that $t_f = \bar{\nu}/\lambda$.

In the example just given:

$$\mu = 10, \quad \psi = 0.7, \quad \bar{n} = \frac{7}{3}, \quad \bar{t}_f = \frac{7/3}{10} = \frac{7}{30}; \qquad 25.18$$

the average waiting time is 14 minutes.

The probability of a delay longer than a time w can also be calculated, but the formula is slightly more complicated for those without mathematical training beyond the elementary level:

$$p(> w) = \psi\, e^{-\mu w(1-\psi)}, \qquad 25.19$$

where e is the base of Naperian (natural) logarithms.

The probability for any delay is:

$$p(> 0) = 1 - p_0 = \psi. \qquad 25.19a$$

Still referring to the preceding example, let us calculate the probability of a waiting time greater than 20 minutes. We have:

$$\mu = 10, \quad \psi = 0.7, \quad w = 1/3; \qquad 25.20$$

which yields:

$$p(> w) = 0.7\, e^{-10 \times 1/3 \times 0,3} = 0.7\, e^{-1} = 0.257 \qquad 25.21$$

(A table of the function of e^x gives: $e^{-1} = 0.36788$.)

Thus, there are 25 chances out of 100 that the waiting time will exceed 20 minutes.

5. The case of uniform service (constant duration).

If the service time is uniform, i.e., if each service interval has a duration of exactly $\theta = 1/\mu$, the average waiting time in line will be:

$$\bar{t}_f^* = \frac{1}{\mu} \frac{\psi}{2(1 - \psi)}, \qquad 25.22$$

This time is half as long as the case where service is randomly distributed according to the exponential law (cf. (25.17)).

Furthermore, still postulating uniform service, the average length of the line is:

$$\bar{n}^* = \psi + \frac{\psi^2}{2(1-\psi)}. \qquad 25.23$$

One can prove that the minimum for $\bar{t}_f$ and $\bar{n}$ with respect to arbitrary service distributions occurs when the service is uniform. This agrees with the intuitive notion that regularity of service lowers waiting time. The inquisitive reader should compare these ideas with the concept of entropy as developed in thermodynamics and information theory (see Part Two, Section 74).

Section 26

THE CASE OF SERVICE RATE PROPORTIONAL TO LENGTH OF WAITING LINE

An interesting theoretical case is the one in which the average rate of service is proportional to n, or:

$$\mu_n = n\mu ; \qquad 26.1$$

while λ is independent of n (in a Poisson phenomenon, of course).

The distribution of the probability p_n units in the system is then:

$$p_n = \frac{(\lambda/\mu)^n e^{-\lambda/\mu}}{n!}, \qquad 26.2$$

which is, precisely, Poisson's law.

The average number of units in the system has the value:

$$\bar{n} = \lambda/\mu . \qquad 26.3$$

If $\psi = (\lambda/\mu) < 1$, there will never be a waiting line.

It is noteworthy that in a transient system:

$$\bar{n}(t) = \frac{\lambda}{\mu}(1 - e^{-\mu t}), \qquad 26.4$$

which shows that n will increase from 0 to λ/μ during the time it takes to establish a permanent system; if μ is small, it will take a relatively long time for the permanent system to become established.

Let us compare the distribution of p_n in the cases where $\mu_n = \mu = C$ and $\mu_n = n\mu$. Let $\lambda = 7$ and $\mu = 10$.

	n	0	1	2	3	4	5	6	7	8
(1)	$p_n\ (\mu_n = \mu)$	0.300	0.210	0.147	0.102	0.072	0.050	0.035	0.024	0.017
(2)	$p_n\ (\mu_n = n\mu)$	0.496	0.347	0.121	0.028	0.005	0.000	...	...	...

For (1), we have: $\bar{n} = \dfrac{\lambda/\mu}{1 - \lambda/\mu} = \dfrac{7}{3}$; i.e. $2 < \bar{n} < 3$ 26.5

For (2), we have: $\bar{n} = \lambda/\mu = \dfrac{7}{10}$, i.e. $0 < \bar{n} < 1$. 26.6

One can see the advantage of a system in which the service rate rises proportionally with n.

As a concrete example, consider a restaurant where the service rate is essentially proportional to the number of customers waiting for a table. Actually, it is difficult to achieve such service when the number of customers rises rapidly; the real situation corresponds to the case of a waiting line at several stations, which we shall now consider. (See Part Two, Section 75.)

Section 27

DESCRIPTION OF A WAITING LINE AT SEVERAL STATIONS

1. General explanation.—2. Erlang's formula.

1. General explanation.

In a great many interesting cases, the main question is to find out how many stations will suffice to provide service at a minimum cost, with constraints imposed in the form of probabilities that must or must not be exceeded. Also, in some cases, a unit cost is assigned to the waiting time of customers, just as one is assigned to idle service stations, and the problem then is to find the number of stations for which the total cost is minimized. To solve problems like this, we must be able to evaluate a number of factors whose formulation will be presented here without proof (the proofs will be found in Part Two).

We shall assume several hypotheses, which are the usual ones for the most frequent kinds of delay phenomena where several stations are active. When a station is free, the first customer in line is served by that station. There is no customer preference for a station. All stations have the same average rate of service μ, governed by the exponential distribution. Arrivals follow Poisson's law, and the average rate of arrivals is λ.

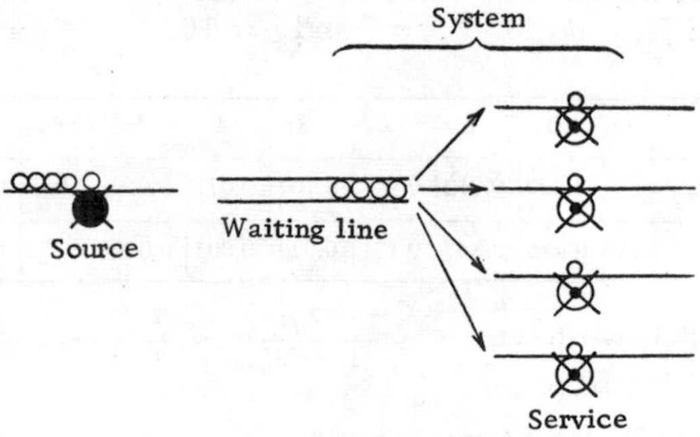

Fig. 27.1

Fig. 27.1 is a diagram of the situation. Let us denote:

S - number of stations;

v - number of units in the waiting line;

n - total number of units in the system (waiting and receiving service): $n = v + j$;

j - number of units being served in the stations ($0 \le j \le S$);

ρ - number of idle stations;

$\bar{n}$, $\bar{v}$, $\bar{j}$, and $\bar{\rho}$ - the average values of n, v, j, and ρ;

$\bar{t}_f$ - average waiting time before service.

This situation is clear-cut. So long as $j < S$, i.e., when not all stations are busy, there is no waiting line and every unit that arrives is served immediately ($v = 0$). If, on the other hand, $j = S$, a waiting line can form, and then $v \ge 0$.

In view of the stochastic nature of delay problems, whether they involve one or several stations, the important thing is to find the probability p_n that a number of units n is in the system, i.e., in the waiting line or in the process of being served. Here, again, we shall assume that we have a permanent system — one in which the probabilities p_n are independent of time.

We state:

$$\psi = \lambda/\mu \,. \tag{27.1}$$

As before, we shall call this quantity the traffic intensity per station. Notice that this time we adopt the restriction:

$$\frac{\lambda}{S\mu} < 1; \quad \text{that is:} \quad \psi < S \,, \tag{27.2}$$

otherwise the waiting line would become infinite.

The probabilities p_n are*:

$$p_n = p_0 \frac{\psi^n}{n!} \qquad 1 \leqslant n < S \qquad 27.3$$

$$p_n = p_0 \frac{\psi^n}{S!S^{n-S}} \qquad n \geqslant S \qquad 27.4$$

where

$$p_0 = \frac{1}{\dfrac{\psi^S}{S!\left(1-\dfrac{\psi}{S}\right)} + 1 + \dfrac{\psi}{1} + \dfrac{\psi^2}{2!} + \dfrac{\psi^3}{3!} + \ldots + \dfrac{\psi^{S-1}}{(S-1)!}} \qquad 27.5$$

We can also make use of the more convenient formulae which mathematicians call recurrence formulae:

$$p_n = \frac{\psi}{n} p_{n-1} \quad \text{if} \quad 1 \leqslant n < S, \qquad 27.6$$

with p_0 as given by (27.5), and

$$p_n = \frac{\psi}{S} p_{n-1} \quad \text{if} \quad n \geqslant S. \qquad 27.7$$

These formulae may seem complicated to those not accustomed to the use of mathematics or to those who have lost this facility through disuse. We shall now show how simple they are to use.

$$\text{Let} \quad \lambda = 6, \quad \mu = 2, \quad S = 4; \quad \text{then} \quad \psi = \frac{\lambda}{\mu} = \frac{6}{2} = 3. \qquad 27.8$$

Calculating p_0 by means of (27.5), we obtain:

$$p_0 = \frac{1}{\dfrac{3^4}{4!\left(1-\dfrac{3}{4}\right)} + 1 + \dfrac{3}{1} + \dfrac{3^2}{2!} + \dfrac{3^3}{3!}}$$

$$= \frac{1}{\dfrac{81}{24 \times \dfrac{1}{4}} + 1 + 3 + \dfrac{9}{2} + \dfrac{27}{6}} = \frac{2}{53} = 0.0377. \qquad 27.9$$

---

*Let us recall that n! means factorial n; that is:
$n! = n \times (n-1) \times (n-2) \times \ldots \times 3 \times 2 \times 1.$
and therefore: $5! = 5 \cdot 4 \cdot 3 \cdot 2 \cdot 1 = 120.$

Now we calculate p_1, p_2, and p_3, using (27.6):

$$p_1 = \frac{3}{1} p_0 = 0.1132\,, \tag{27.10}$$

$$p_2 = \frac{3}{2} p_1 = 0.1698\,, \tag{27.11}$$

$$p_3 = \frac{3}{3} p_2 = 0.1698\,. \tag{27.12}$$

To calculate $p_4, p_5, p_6, \ldots$, we make use of (27.7):

$$p_4 = \tfrac{3}{4} p_3 = 0.1273, \tag{27.13}$$

$$p_5 = \tfrac{3}{4} p_4 = 0.0955, \tag{27.14}$$

$$p_6 = \tfrac{3}{4} p_5 = 0.0716, \tag{27.15}$$

$$p_7 = \tfrac{3}{4} p_6 = 0.0537, \quad p_8 = 0.0403, \quad p_9 = 0.0302, \quad p_{10} = 0.0226 \tag{27.16}$$
$$p_{11} = 0.0169, \quad p_{12} = 0.0127, \quad p_{13} = 0.0095, \ldots$$

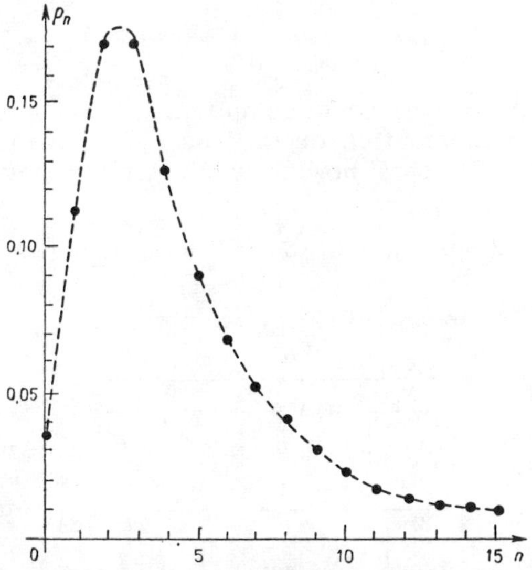

Fig. 27.2. The dotted curve was drawn to show the general appearance of the distribution; only the points corresponding to integral values of n are significant.

Fig. 27.2 shows the pattern of the distribution p_n corresponding to the numerical example we have just discussed.

A knowledge of the probabilities p_n allows us to determine the average number of units $\bar{v}$ in the waiting line. For this purpose, we shall calculate the expected value of the random variable $v = n - S$ (units waiting in line) distributed according to p_n; let:

$$\bar{\nu} = \sum_{n=S+1}^{\infty} (n - S)\, p_n . \qquad 27.17$$

Now let us apply this formula to our example.

27.18

$$\begin{aligned}\bar{\nu} &= 1.p_5 + 2.p_6 + 3.p_7 + 4.p_8 + \dots + (n-4)\,p_n + \dots \\ &= (1)\,(0.0955) + (2)\,(0.0716) + (3)\,(0.0537) + (4)\,(0.0403) + (5)\,(0.0302) \\ &\quad + (6)\,(0.0226) + (7)\,(0.0169) + (8)\,(0.0127) + (9)\,(0.0095) + \dots \\ &= 0.0955 + 0.1432 + 0.1611 + 0.1612 + 0.1510 + 0.1356 + 0.1183 + 0.1016 \\ &\quad + 0.0855 + \dots\end{aligned}$$

= 1.52 (we have carried our calculation as far as n = 20).

Formula (27.17) is not convenient, because the series that constitutes this sum converges quite slowly. It is more practical to use the following formula:

$$\bar{\nu} = \frac{\psi^{S+1}}{S \cdot S!\left(1 - \dfrac{\psi}{S}\right)^2}\, p_0 \qquad 27.19$$

Thus, in our example:

$$\bar{\nu} = \frac{3^5.}{4 \cdot 4!\left(1 - \dfrac{3}{4}\right)^2} \cdot \frac{2}{53} = 1.528. \qquad 27.20$$

Therefore, the average length of the waiting line will lie between 1 and 2.

The average number of units in the system, $\bar{n}$, is given by:

$$\bar{n} = \sum_{n=0}^{\infty} n p_n . \qquad 27.21$$

In problems of this type, one is also interested in the average number of idle stations, $\bar{\rho}$:

$$\bar{\varrho} = \sum_{n=0}^{S} (S - n)\, p_n = S - \psi \quad * \qquad 27.22$$

The averages $\bar{n}$, $\bar{v}$, and $\bar{\rho}$ are linked by the relationship:

$$\bar{n} = \bar{\nu} + S - \bar{\varrho} = \bar{\nu} + \psi . \qquad 27.23$$

---

*This formula is derived in Section 76 (Part Two).

The probability of a delay (wait) of no matter what duration, i.e. the probability of waiting, which will be written p (> 0), is simply the probability that n will be greater than or equal to S: Pr(n ≥ S), or:

$$p\,(>0) = \Pr(n \geqslant S) = \sum_{n=S}^{\infty} p_n = p_S + p_{S+1} + p_{S+2} + \dots \qquad 27.24$$

(if n ≡ S, any new unit arriving will have to wait, the more so if n = S.)

Let us calculate this probability, in our example:

$$\begin{aligned} p\,(>0) &= \Pr\,(n \geqslant 4) = p_4 + p_5 + p_6 + \dots \\ &= 0.1273 + 0.0955 + 0.0716 + 0.0537 + 0.0403 \\ &\quad + 0.0302 + 0.0226 + 0.0169 + 0.0127 \\ &\quad + 0.0095 + \dots \\ &= 0{,}50 \quad (p_n \text{ has been calculated to } n = 20). \end{aligned} \qquad 27.25$$

For this probability, there is another convenient formula:

$$p(>0) = \Pr(n \geqslant S) = \frac{\psi^S}{S!\left(1 - \dfrac{\psi}{S}\right)}\, p_0\,; \qquad 27.26$$

or, in our example:

$$p\,(>0) = \frac{3^4}{4!\left(1 - \dfrac{3}{4}\right)} \times \frac{2}{53} = 0.509\,. \qquad 27.27$$

2. Erlang's Formula.

Formula (27.26) may also be written as follows, using the expression for p_0 given by (27.5):

$$p\,(>0) = \Pr(n \geqslant S) = \frac{\dfrac{\psi^S}{S!\left(1 - \dfrac{\psi}{S}\right)}}{\dfrac{\psi^S}{S!\left(1 - \dfrac{\psi}{S}\right)} + 1 + \dfrac{\psi}{1} + \dfrac{\psi^2}{2!} + \dots + \dfrac{\psi^{S-1}}{(S-1)!}}\,; \qquad 27.28$$

This is Erlang's formula, a graph of which is shown in Fig. 27.3.

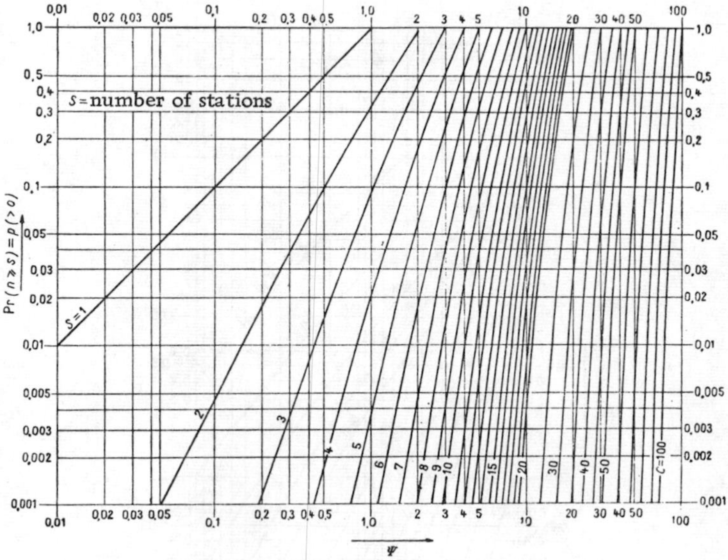

Fig. 27.3

In our example, the probability of having to wait is about 0.5.

This is of special interest when one wishes to determine the number of stations that should be set up in order to keep the probability of waiting below a given value.

Such questions arise particularly when we relate the probability of delay to a safety requirement. This is the case for aircraft waiting to land on an empty runway. For example, with given values of λ (arrival rate) and $1/\mu$ (average time required to prepare a runway for the next plane), we might seek the number of runways for which $p(>0)$ is less than 0.05. A problem of this kind can be solved simply by drawing up tables for $p(>0)$ as a function of ψ and of S.

To calculate the average time on the waiting line t_f, we need only note that in a permanent system:

$$\bar{\nu} = \lambda\, \bar{t}_f \qquad 27.29$$

hence:

$$\bar{t}_f = \frac{\bar{\nu}}{\lambda} = \frac{\psi^S}{S \cdot S!\mu\left(1 - \frac{\psi}{S}\right)^2}\, p_0 \qquad \text{If we wish to use Formula 27.19} \qquad 27.30$$

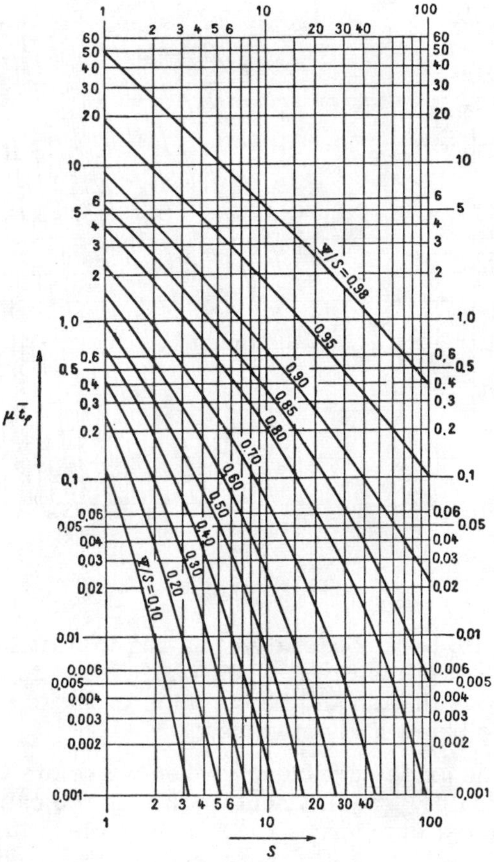

Fig. 27.4

Still referring to the preceding example:

$$\bar{t}_f = \frac{3^4}{4 \cdot 4!\, 2\left(1 - \dfrac{3}{4}\right)^2} \cdot \frac{2}{53} = 0.255 \text{ time units.} \qquad 27.31$$

If λ and μ represent rates per minute, the average delay is equal to about 15 seconds.

Fig. 27.4 presents a graph giving the values of the product $\mu \bar{t}_f$ for various values of S and ψ/S.

It is interesting to compare two cases: one with a single line before a single station whose service rate is 8, and one with a line before 4 stations, each of whose service rates is 2, both cases having $\lambda = 6$.

1 Station	4 Stations	
$\mu = 8$	$\mu = 2$	
$p_0 = 0.25$	$p_0 = 0.0377$	
$\bar{n} = 3$	$\bar{n} = 4.52$	
$\bar{\nu} = 2.25$	$\bar{\nu} = 1.52$	27.32
$p(>0) = 0.75$	$p(>0) = 0.51$	
$\bar{t}_f = 0.375$	$\bar{t}_f = 0.255$	

We can see that the arrangement ($S = 4, \mu = 2$) is far more acceptable from the customers' (arrivals') point of view than is ($S = 1, \mu = 8$). This supports our intuitive notion that for a given value of $S\mu$, $\bar{v}$, $p(>0)$ and $\bar{t}_f$ diminish with increasing values of S. It is always wise, given the same overall rate and the same cost, to use the largest possible number of stations. (See Part Two, Section 76.)

Section 28

ANALYSIS OF SOME CASES OF WAITING LINES AT SEVERAL STATIONS

1. First example.—2. Second example.

1. First example.*

In an automobile plant, a study was made of the problem of determining the optimum number of employees to be assigned to the windows of the various stock rooms from which tools and supplies are issued to workers. We shall examine one such stock room. The same analysis with different numbers, could apply to the others.

The tool room study began with a determination of the statistical characteristics of worker (customer) arrivals and of the time spent by tool room employees in issuing the requested tools (service time).

As regards arrivals, the following procedure was used: the number of workers who came to the tool room to withdraw tools was counted over a 10-minute interval, for 100 such intervals in succession. These results are tabulated in columns (1) and (2) of Table 28.1. The average value of these counts is found to be 16. In column (3) of Table 28.1, the corresponding frequencies that

---

*This study is an application of the method described to us at the Case Institute of Technology in Cleveland, Ohio (Course in Operations Research).

Table 28.1
Statistical study of the arrivals

(1) Number of arrivals per 10 min.	(2) Observed frequency	(3) Theoretical frequency (poisson's law)
5	1	0.1
6	0	0.2
7	1	0.6
8	2	1.2
9	1	2.1
10	3	3.4
11	5	4.9
12	6	6.6
13	9	8.1
14	10	9.3
15	11	9.9
16	12	9.9
17	8	9.3
18	9	8.3
19	7	6.9
20	5	5.5
21	4	4.2
22	3	3.1
23	1	2.1
24	1	1.4
25	1	0.9

Table 28.2
Statistical study of the duration of the service

(4) Time interval, seconds	(5) Cumulative observed frequency	(6) Theoretical frequency (exponential)
0	1000	1000
15	813	798
30	652	637
45	512	508
60	408	406
75	330	324
90	261	259
105	210	207
120	163	165
135	125	131
150	95	105
165	79	84
180	62	67
195	51	53
210	44	42
225	35	34
240	26	27
255	21	21
270	17	17
285	13	14
300	10	11

would be given theoretically by Poisson's law were listed. A χ^2 test* was then used to determine whether it was allowable to consider the observed frequencies as being Poisson-distributed. It was found that $\chi^2 = 12$ (degrees of freedom = 19). The probability that the hypothesis of a Poisson distribution is true is greater than 0.88. It was therefore assumed that the distribution was Poissonian. The calculation of λ, then, is very simple:

$$\lambda = \frac{16}{10} = 1.6 \text{ arrivals per minute.} \qquad 28.1$$

Another approach was used to measure service time. An electrical recording device was started at the beginning of each service interval and was stopped at its end. This device was used to record the individual durations of 1,000 service intervals. Next, the cumulative frequencies were calculated for 0, 15, 30, 45, 60, 75, . . . seconds. This is shown in columns (4) and (5) of Table 28.2. After calculation of the average value $\mu = 0.9$, by means of a table of non-cumulative frequencies drawn from columns (4) and (5), the corresponding values given by the exponential function 1,000 $e^{-\mu t}$ were entered in column (6), furnishing a theoretical distribution for purposes of comparison. A χ^2 test then yielded the $\chi^2 = 8.85$, with 19 degrees of freedom. The probability that the value hypothesis of an exponential law is true is greater than 0.97. Therefore, it was assumed that the observed distribution was exponential, the rate being:

$$\mu = 0.9 \text{ service interval per minute.} \qquad 28.2$$

Knowing λ and μ, we then calculate the traffic intensity:

$$\psi = \frac{1.6}{0.9} = 1.77 .$$

Formula (27.30) can then be used to calculate the average waiting time $\bar{t}_f$. To this end, we first calculate the value of p_o corresponding to S = 2, S = 3, S = 4 (more than 4 employees seems unreasonable, because of the cost). Using formula (27.5), we obtain for S = 2:

$$p_0 = \frac{1}{\dfrac{1.77^2}{2\left(1 - \dfrac{1.77}{2}\right)} + 1 + \dfrac{1.77}{1}} = 0.061 , \qquad 28.3$$

*The reader who has not studied statistics may refer to Chapter II — and to Dumas, L'Entreprise et la Statistique ("Business and Statistics") (Paris: Dunod, 1954).

for S = 3:

$$p_0 = \cfrac{1}{\cfrac{(1.77)^3}{3\cdot 2\left(1 - \cfrac{1.77}{3}\right)} + 1 + \cfrac{1.77}{1} + \cfrac{(1.77)^2}{2}} = 0.152\,, \qquad 28.4$$

for S = 4:

$$p_0 = \cfrac{1}{\cfrac{(1.77)^4}{4\cdot 3\cdot 2\left(1 - \cfrac{1.77}{4}\right)} + 1 + \cfrac{1.77}{1} + \cfrac{(1.77)^2}{2} + \cfrac{(1.77)^3}{3\cdot 2}} = 0.166\,. \qquad 28.5$$

Calculating the average waiting time $\bar{t}_f$, we find, for S = 2:

$$\bar{t}_f = \frac{(1.77)^2}{2\cdot 2\cdot 0.9\left(1 - \frac{1.77}{2}\right)^2} \times 0.061 = 4.00\,, \qquad 28.6$$

for S = 3:

$$\bar{t}_f = \frac{(1.77^3)}{3\cdot 3\cdot 2\cdot 0.9\left(1 - \frac{1.77}{3}\right)^2} \times 0.152 = 0.31\,, \qquad 28.7$$

for S = 4:

$$\bar{t}_f = \frac{(1.77)^4}{4\cdot 4\cdot 3\cdot 2\cdot 0.9\left(1 - \frac{1.77}{4}\right)^2} \times 0.166 = 0.06\,. \qquad 28.8$$

Let us determine the average number of arrivals in an 8-hour day:

$$\lambda \times 60 \times 8 = 1.6 \times 60 \times 8 = 768. \qquad 28.9$$

This number of arrivals, with an average service time of $1/\mu$, gives us:

$$\frac{768}{\mu} = \frac{768}{0.9} = 853 \text{ minutes of service per day.}$$
$$= 14\text{ h } 13\text{ mn} = 14.21\text{ h} \qquad 28.10*$$

---

*We should recall here what was said in Section 23: if a stochastic phenomenon is Poissonian and has a rate μ, the intervals between events will follow the exponential law, with the same rate μ. The reciprocal also holds true.

Thus we would have for

$$\left.\begin{array}{l} \text{2 employees: } 2 \times 8 - 14.21 = 16 - 14.21 = 1.79 \text{ idle hours per day;} \\ \text{3 employees: } 3 \times 8 - 14.21 = 24 - 14.21 = 9.79 \text{ idle hours per day;} \\ \text{4 employees: } 4 \times 8 - 14.21 = 32 - 14.21 = 17.79 \text{ idle hours per day.} \end{array}\right\} \quad 28.11$$

And now let us examine the amount of time lost each day caused by waiting at the tool room:

$$\begin{array}{ll} S = 2 & 768 \times 4 = 3072 \text{ mn} = 51.2 \text{ h} \\ S = 3 & 768 \times 0.31 = 238 \text{ mn} = 3.96 \text{ h} \\ S = 4 & 768 \times 0.06 = 46 \text{ mn} = 0.76 \text{ h.} \end{array} \quad 28.12$$

If the gross hourly cost of an attendant's time is 300 francs, and that of a worker's is 600 francs, the total cost of the wasted time will come to:

$$\begin{array}{ll} S = 2 & \Gamma_2 = 1.79 \times 300 + 51.2 \times 600 = 31{,}257 \text{ fr.} \\ S = 3 & \Gamma_3 = 9.79 \times 300 + 3.96 \times 600 = 5{,}313 \text{ fr.} \leftarrow \\ S = 4 & \Gamma_4 = 17.79 \times 300 + 0.76 \times 600 = 5{,}793 \text{ fr.} \end{array} \quad 28.13$$

The optimum number of attendants to assign to this tool room is 3. A rule-of-thumb calculation, which failed to take into account the random nature of the phenomenon and the different costs for workers and tool room attendants, might have led to adoption of $S = 2$, which is the closest number to the traffic intensity of $\psi = 1.77$. As a result of that decision, the tool room would have operated at a loss of about 26,000 francs a day.

It is useful to construct graphs for $\bar{v}$, $p(> 0)$, and $\bar{t}_f$ as functions of ψ and of S. From these, it is quite easy to determine the cost Γ_S. Curves of $\Gamma_S(\psi)$ can be constructed from which we can read directly the optimum value as well as the sensitivity of the field around the optimum, for given costs of tool room attendants and workers. It is important to know this sensitivity; for example, the values developed in (28.13) show that there is a slight difference between solutions $S = 3$ and $S = 4$; it is not illogical to choose $S = 4$; but $S = 5$ would result in about 7,800 francs. For the gross hourly cost of 300 francs (attendants) and 750 francs (workers), we would find $\Gamma_3 = \Gamma_4$.

This study was extended to all of the supply and equipment stockrooms in the plant, and made it possible to reduce the cost of waiting lines considerably.

To find Γ_S we can also use the formula:

$$\Gamma_S = (c_1 \bar{\nu} + c_2 \bar{\varrho})T \quad \text{(see also: 31.5)} \qquad 28.14$$

This formula can be reduced to the one just used (28.13) by means of the relations (27.30) and (27.22):

$$\Gamma_s = [c_1 \lambda \bar{t}_f + c_2 (S - \psi)]\, T. \qquad 28.15$$

2. Second example.

How many runways should there be at an airport to insure a probability of less than 0.1 that a plane wishing to land will have to wait for a free runway?

A statistical study of arrivals showed that we could assume the Poisson hypothesis for arrivals. Measurements showed that $\lambda = 27$ arrivals per hour. The time during which a runway is in service is exponentially distributed with an average of 2 minutes, or $\mu = 30$.

We can then calculate the probabilities $p(>0)$ for $S = 2$, $S = 3$, and $S = 4$ (with the value of ψ given as $27/30 = 0.9$, it is highly probable that more than one runway will be needed). Using Erlang's formula (27.28), we find:

$$S = 2 \quad p(>0) = \frac{\dfrac{(0.9)^2}{2!\left(1 - \dfrac{0.9}{2}\right)}}{\dfrac{(0.9)^2}{2!\left(1 - \dfrac{0.9}{2}\right)} + 1 + 0.9} = 0.278, \qquad 28.16$$

$$S = 3 \quad p(>0) = \frac{\dfrac{(0.9)^3}{3!\left(1 - \dfrac{0.9}{3}\right)}}{\dfrac{(0.9)^3}{3!\left(1 - \dfrac{0.9}{3}\right)} + 1 + 0.9 + \dfrac{(0.9)^2}{2}} = 0.070, \qquad 28.17$$

$$S = 4 \quad p(>0) = \frac{\dfrac{(0.9)^4}{4!\left(1 - \dfrac{0.9}{4}\right)}}{\dfrac{(0.9)^4}{4!\left(1 - \dfrac{0.9}{4}\right)} + 1 + 0.9 + \dfrac{(0.9)^2}{2} + \dfrac{(0.9)^3}{3!}} = 0.014 \qquad 28.18$$

The reader can check these values against the graph of Erlang's formula given in Fig. 27.3 (page 99).

We see that 3 runways are needed to achieve a probability of 0.1.

Let us now calculate the average delay time for S = 3, using formulas (27.5) and 27.30):

$$p_0 = \frac{1}{\dfrac{(0.9)^3}{3!\left(1 - \dfrac{0.9}{3}\right)} + 1 + 0.9 + \dfrac{(0.9)^2}{2}} = 0.403 \qquad 28.19$$

$$\bar{t}_f = \frac{(0.9)^3}{3 \cdot 3!30\left(1 - \dfrac{0.9}{3}\right)^2} \cdot 0.403 = 0.001108 \text{ h} = 0.0665 \text{ mn.} \qquad 28.20$$

This same evaluation can be obtained approximately from the graph given in Fig. 27.4 on page 96.

The average number of planes waiting will be:

$$\bar{\nu} = \lambda\, \bar{t}_f = 27 \times 0.001108 = 0.03\,. \qquad 28.21$$

The waiting time $\bar{t}_f$ is quite within acceptable limits.

In a problem such as this, other restricting factors may often be introduced, such as limits on the traffic in the approach lanes, installation costs, and so on.

We have intentionally simplified the problem and assumed that the distribution of the service times (plane landings) was exponential. Actually, we noted that this distribution was usually of another and slightly different type: the Erlang distribution (also known as the Type III Pearson distribution):

$$f_k(t) = \frac{(k\mu)^k\, e^{-k\mu t}\, t^{k-1}}{(k-1)!} \quad \text{(probable density)} \qquad 28.22$$

$$k = 1, 2, 3, 4, \ldots$$

This distribution becomes an exponential distribution for k = 1 and gives a constant service time for $k \to \infty$. (See Part Two, Section 76).

Section 29

THE CASE OF A SINGLE STATION AND A LIMITED NUMBER OF CUSTOMERS

1. General explanation.—2. First case.—2. Second case.

1. General explanation

To present a realistic example, we shall consider a shop in which m identical machines are used, each operating independently of the others. Machine breakdowns occur in a random Poisson pattern, at the rate of λ for each one. One mechanic is available to repair them, constituting the single station through which any ailing machine must pass. The lengths of repair times are distributed according to the exponential law, with a rate μ. The situation is schematized in Fig. 29.1.

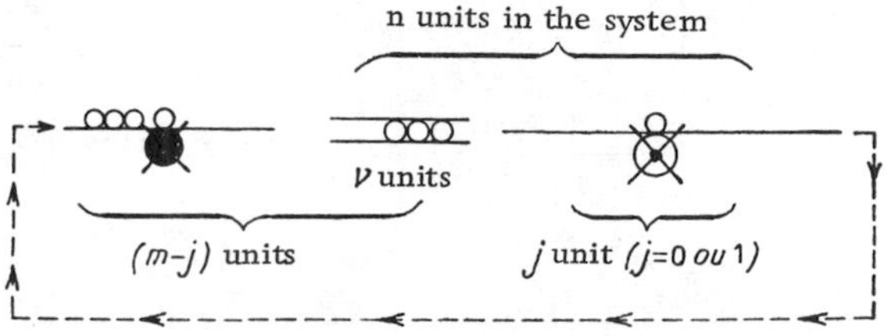

Fig. 29.1

Thus, we can describe this group of machines, as far as repair processes are concerned, by two constants: λ and μ. We can also reason along the following lines: if a machine is operating in good order at time t, the probability that it will require repairs (servicing by the mechanic) during the interval Δt that immediately follows t is $\lambda \Delta t$, plus negligible terms when $\Delta t \to 0$; if, at time t, this same machine is undergoing repairs, the probability that the repairs will be completed during the immediately following period Δt is $\mu \Delta t$, plus negligible terms when $\Delta t \to 0$.

For a reliable machine, λ is small and μ relatively large; in other words, breakdowns are rare, and repairs do not take long. The traffic intensity:

$$\psi = \frac{\lambda}{\mu} \tag{29.1}$$

in such an application is called the service factor or maintenance factor. In general, we disregard any value of $\psi \geq 1$, because this indicates a congestion phenomenon (which we shall discuss later).

Of course, if the foregoing hypotheses (Poisson's law and the exponential law) are to provide an accurate description, we must have a statistically homogeneous machine population, or, in the simplest case, a population of technologically identical machines.

In the case we are studying, n is the number of machines in the system (either undergoing repairs or broken down and awaiting repair). Either of the two following situations is possible: if $1 \leq n \leq m$, then there is one machine undergoing repairs, and $n - 1$ machines are awaiting repair. If $n = 0$, all the machines are operating and the mechanic is idle.

Our first concern, in this problem as in any problem concerned with a delay phenomenon, is to find the probability p_n that there will be n units in the system.

This probability is provided by the formula:

$$p_n = \frac{m!}{(m-n)!}\psi^n p_0, \qquad 29.2$$

where

$$p_0 = \frac{1}{1+\sum_{n=1}^{m}\frac{m!\,\psi^n}{(m-n)!}} \quad \text{and} \quad \sum_{n=0}^{m} p_n = 1; \qquad 29.3$$

or, using the recurrence formula which facilitates calculations:

$$p_n = (m-n+1)\,\psi\, p_{n-1} \qquad 1 \leqslant n \leqslant m. \qquad 29.4$$

The average number of units in the line is:

$$\bar{\nu} = \sum_{n=2}^{m}(n-1)\,p_n = m - \frac{1+\psi}{\psi}(1-p_0). \qquad 29.4$$

The other significant dimensions are:

$$p(>0) = \sum_{n=1}^{m} p_n = 1 - p_0, \qquad 29.5$$

$$\bar{t}_f = \frac{\bar{\nu}}{\lambda(m-\bar{n})} = \frac{1}{\mu}\left(\frac{m}{1-p_0} - \frac{1+\psi}{\psi}\right). \qquad 29.6$$

We shall examine two cases, one dealing with machines having a good maintenance factor ($\psi = 0.1$), and the other with machines having a very poor maintenance factor, $\psi = 2$. In practice, we disregard situations in which $\psi \geq 1$, because of the phenomenon of congestion: in such cases, there is a very high probability that all the machines are waiting. Under those circumstances, we would be forced to increase the number of mechanics.

2. First case: $\psi = 0.1$, m = 6.

We begin by calculating p_0:

$$p_0 = \qquad 29.7$$

$$\frac{1}{1+6!\left[\frac{0.1}{5!}+\frac{(0.1)^2}{4!}+\frac{(0.1)^3}{3!}+\frac{(0.1)^4}{2!}+\frac{(0.1)^5}{1!}+\frac{(0.1)^6}{0!}\right]}$$

$$= \frac{1}{1+[0.6+0.3+0.12+0.036+0.0072+0.00072]}$$

$$= \frac{1}{2.0639} = 0.484.$$

Next, we determine p_n, n = 1, 2, 3, 4, 5, 6, obtaining the following table:

Table 29.1

Number of machines out of service n	0	1	2	3	4	5	6
Number of machines awaiting repair v	0	0	1	2	3	4	5
p_n	0.484	0.290	0.145	0.058	0.017	0.003	0.000

3. Second case: ψ = 2, m = 6.

$$p_0 = \frac{1}{1 + 6!\left[\frac{2}{5!} + \frac{2^2}{4!} + \frac{2^3}{3!} + \frac{2^4}{2!} + \frac{2^5}{1!} + \frac{2^6}{0!}\right]} \qquad 29.9^*$$

$$= \frac{1}{75{,}973}.$$

Table 29.2

Number of machines out of service n	0	1	2	3	4	5	6
Number of machines awaiting repair v	0	0	1	2	3	4	5
p_n	$\frac{1}{75{,}973}$	$\frac{12}{75{,}973}$	0.001	0.012	0.075	0.303	0.606
	$\simeq 0$	$\simeq 0$					

Obviously, a single mechanic cannot handle the job.

And now, using formulas (29.4), (29.5), and (29.6), we find

$$\begin{array}{ll} \psi = 0.1 & \psi = 2 \\ \hline \bar{\nu} = 0.324 & \bar{\nu} = 4.5 \\ p(>0) = 0.516 & p(>0) = \dfrac{75972}{75973} = 0.999\ \dots\ (!!\dots) \end{array} \qquad 29.11$$

---

*By definition, 0! = 1. This definition can be justified, for example, by the fact that it makes the formula n! = (n +1)!/(n+1) applicable to the case of n = 0.

Assuming that $1/\mu = 4$ machines per hour:

$\bar{t}_f = 2.51$ hours $\qquad$ $\bar{t}_f = 18$ hours (!!!...)

At this point, it is apparent that we are dealing with a congestion phenomenon. (See Part Two, Section 77.)

Section 30

THE CASE OF SEVERAL STATIONS WITH A LIMITED NUMBER OF CUSTOMERS

This situation is merely a generalization of the first one. By using a realistic example with m machines (customers) and S mechanics (stations), and with the hypothesis that S is smaller than m, we can define the phenomenon as follows: if $1 \leq n \leq S$, there are $S - n$ idle mechanics (n machines are being repaired and none is wating for repair); if $S \leq n \leq m$, there are S machines being repaired, and $n - S$ are waiting for repair. The situation is shown in Fig. 30.1.

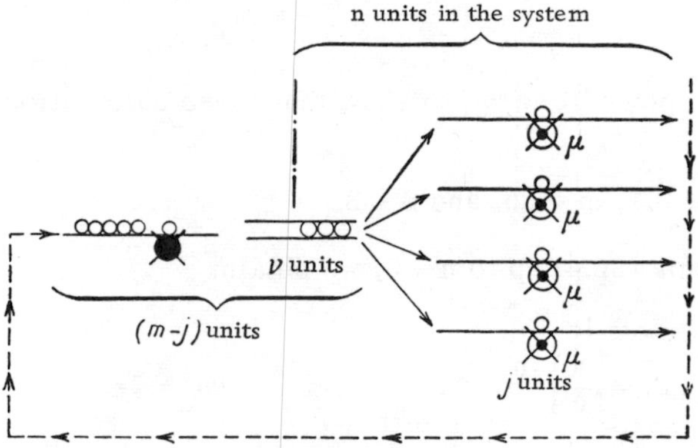

Fig. 30.1

The considerations set forth in Section 29 apply here again. A low value for the maintenance factor ψ corresponds to reliable machines. We can allow $\psi \geq 1$ without any danger of congestion, which would occur when $\psi \geq S$.

Keeping the same hypotheses (Poisson, exponential, permanent system), we find this time that:

$$0 \leqslant n \leqslant S, \quad p_n = C_n^m \psi^n p_0, \text{where } C_n^m = \frac{m!}{(m-n)!\, n!} \qquad 30.1$$

$$S \leqslant n \leqslant m, \qquad p_n = \frac{n!}{S!\,S^{n-S}}\, C_n^m\, \psi^n p_0\,, \tag{30.2}$$

with

$$\sum_{n=0}^{m} p_n = 1\,. \tag{30.2a}$$

We can abandon these formulas, which will be too complicated for some, and rely instead on a recurrence formula.

Let α_n denote the quotient:

$$\alpha_n = \frac{p_n}{p_0}. \tag{30.3}$$

From $n = 0$ to $n = S - 1$, we may calculate α_n by means of the formula:

$$\alpha_n = \frac{m - n + 1}{n}\,\psi\,\alpha_{n-1}\;, \quad \text{avec } \alpha_0 = 1\,. \tag{30.4}$$

Continuing from $n = S$ to $n = m$, we use the formula:

$$\alpha_n = \frac{m - n + 1}{S}\,\psi\,\alpha_{n-1}\,. \tag{30.5}$$

An example will serve to show that these calculations are very simple:

Let: $\psi = 0.1$, $m = 20$, and $S = 3$.

Using formula (30.4) up to $n = 3$, we obtain:

$$\begin{aligned}
\alpha_0 &= 1;\\
\alpha_1 &= \frac{20 - 0}{0 + 1} \times 0.1 \times 1 = \frac{20}{1} \times 0.1 = 2;\\
\alpha_2 &= \frac{20 - 1}{1 + 1} \times 0.1 \times 2 = 1.9;\\
\alpha_3 &= \frac{20 - 2}{2 + 1} \times 0.1 \times 1.9 = 1.14.
\end{aligned} \tag{30.6}$$

Then, using (30.5) for $n = 4$ to $n = 20$, we obtain:

$$\begin{aligned}
\alpha_4 &= \frac{20 - 3}{3} \times 0.1 \times 1.14 = 0.646;\\
\alpha_5 &= \frac{20 - 4}{3} \times 0.1 \times 0.646 = 0.3445;
\end{aligned}$$

$$\begin{aligned}
a_6 &= \frac{20-5}{3} \times 0.1 \times 0.3445 = 0.17227; \\
a_7 &= \frac{20-6}{3} \times 0.1 \times 0.17227 = 0.08039; \\
a_8 &= \frac{20-7}{3} \times 0.1 \times 0.08039 = 0.03483; \\
a_9 &= \frac{20-8}{3} \times 0.1 \times 0.03483 = 0.01393; \\
a_{10} &= 0.00511, \quad a_{11} = 0.00170, \\
a_{12} &= 0.00051, \quad a_{13} = 0.00013 \\
a_{14}, &\, a_{15}, a_{16}, \ldots, a_{20} \quad \text{are less than} \quad 0.0001.
\end{aligned} \tag{30.7}$$

Now, starting from the relationship:

$$p_0 = 1 - \sum_{n=1}^{m} p_n , \tag{30.8}$$

we can write:

$$1 = \frac{1}{p_0} - \sum_{n=1}^{m} \frac{p_n}{p_0} = \frac{1}{p_0} - \sum_{n=1}^{m} a_n ; \tag{30.9}$$

which yields:

$$p_0 = \frac{1}{1 + \sum_{n=1}^{m} a_n} \tag{30.10}$$

This gives us:

$$\begin{aligned}
\sum_{n=1}^{m} a_n &= 2 + 1.9 + 1.14 + 0.646 + 0.3445 + 0.17227 + 0.08039 + 0.03483 \\
&\quad + 0.01393 + 0.00511 + 0.00170 + 0.00051 + 0.00013 + \ldots \\
&= 6.3394
\end{aligned} \tag{30.11}$$

Therefore we find:

$$p_0 = \frac{1}{1 + 6.3394} = 0.13625 . \tag{30.12}$$

which yields:

$$\begin{aligned}
p_1 &= a_1 p_0 = 2 \times 0.13625 = 0.27250, \\
p_2 &= a_2 p_0 = 1.9 \times 0.13625 = 0.25888 \ldots \text{etc...};
\end{aligned} \tag{30.13}$$

Table 30.1 shows the probabilities for these various conditions. If we compare Tables 29.1 and 30.1, we observe that, with essentially equal numbers of machines per mechanic (6 and 6-2/3), the situation is clearly better in the case of 20 machines and 3 mechanics. Once again we reach the conclusion developed in the case of an unlimited number of customers: the situation always improves, given a fixed overall service rate μS, as the number of stations is increased.

Table 30.1

$m = 20$, $S = 3$, $\psi = 0.1$

n	Machines under repair j	Machines waiting ν	Idle mechanics ϱ	p_n
0	0	0	3	0.13625
1	1	0	2	0.27250
2	2	0	1	0.25888
3	3	0	0	0.15533
4	3	1	0	0.08802
5	3	2	0	0.04694
6	3	3	0	0.02347
7	3	4	0	0.01095
8	3	5	0	0.00475
9	3	6	0	0.00190
10	3	7	0	0.00070
11	3	8	0	0.00023
12	3	9	0	0.00007

In a maintenance and repair problem with random delay, such as the one studied in this section, we can define two coefficients:

$$k_1 = \frac{\bar{\nu}}{m} \quad \frac{\text{average number of machines waiting (in the line)}}{\text{total number of machines}}. \qquad 30.14$$

The coefficient k_1 is called the coefficient of unavailability for machines.

$$k_2 = \frac{\bar{\rho}}{S} = \frac{\text{average number of idle mechanics}}{\text{number of mechanics}}. \qquad 30.15$$

The coefficient k_2 is called the coefficient of idleness for mechanics.

The values of $\overline{v}$, $\overline{\rho}$, and $\overline{n}$ are obtained by formulas (21.2), (21.3), and (21.4):

$$\overline{\nu} = \sum_{n=S+1}^{m} (n - S)\, p_n\,, \qquad 30.16$$

$$\overline{\varrho} = \sum_{n=0}^{S} (S - n)\, p_n\,, \qquad 30.17$$

$$\overline{n} = S + \overline{\nu} - \overline{\varrho} = S + \underbrace{\sum_{n=S+1}^{m} (n - S) p_n}_{\overline{\nu}} - \underbrace{\sum_{n=0}^{S} (S - n) p_n}_{\overline{\varrho}}\,. \qquad 30.18$$

In our example, S = 3, m = 20;

$$\overline{\nu} = \sum_{n=4}^{20} (n - 3) p_n = p_4 + 2p_5 + 3p_6 + \ldots + 17p_{20} = 0.339 \qquad 30.19$$

$$\overline{\varrho} = \sum_{n=0}^{3} (3 - n) p_n = 3p_0 + 2p_1 + p_2 = 1.213\,. \qquad 30.20$$

From this we find:

$$\bar{n} = 3 + 0.339 - 1.213 = 2.126\,, \qquad 30.21$$

and then:

$$k_1 = \frac{0{,}339}{20} = 0.0169\,, \qquad 30.22$$

$$k_2 = \frac{1.213}{3} = 0.404\,. \qquad 30.23$$

Let us compare these results with the case in which S = 1 and m = 6, the value of $\psi = 0.1$ remaining unchanged.

We found in (29.11) that: v = 0.324. Therefore:

$$\overline{\varrho} = \sum_{n=0}^{1} (1 - n) p_n = p_0 = 0.484 \text{ (see Table 29.1)} \qquad 30.24$$

$$\overline{n} = 1 + \overline{\nu} - \overline{\varrho} = 1 + 0.324 - 0.484 = 0.840\,, \qquad 30.25$$

$$k_1 = \frac{0{,}324}{6} = 0.0540\,, \qquad 30.26$$

$$k_2 = \frac{0.484}{1} = 0.484\,. \qquad 30.27$$

Examining (30.22, 30.23) and (30.26, 30.27), we see how much better the situation is for (S = 3, m = 20, $\psi = 0.1$) as compared with (S = 1, m = 6, $\psi = 0.1$).

The probability of a delay is given by:

$$p(>0) = \Pr(N \geqslant S) = \sum_{n=S}^{m} p_n .$$

In our example:

$$\begin{aligned} p(>0) &= \sum_{n=3}^{20} p_n = 1 - \sum_{n=0}^{2} p_n \\ &= 1 - (0.13625 + 0.27250 + 0.25888) \\ &= 1 - 0.66763 = 0.33237. \end{aligned} \qquad 30.28$$

The average waiting time in line is:

$$\bar{t}_f = \frac{\bar{\nu}}{\lambda(m - \bar{n})} = \frac{1}{\lambda(m - \bar{n})} \sum_{n=S+1}^{m} (n - S)p_n . \qquad 30.29$$

Using these same examples, and assuming that $\mu = 1/5$, or 5 hours to repair each machine, we will have:

$$S = 3, \quad m = 20, \quad \bar{t}_f = \frac{0.339}{1.727 \times \frac{1}{5}} = 0.981 \text{ h, or about 59 minutes} \qquad 30.30$$

$$S = 1, \quad m = 6, \quad \bar{t}_f = \frac{0.324}{0.516 \times \frac{1}{5}} = 3.14 \text{ h, or about 188 minutes} \qquad 30.31^*$$

→

Section 31

THE ECONOMIC ASPECT OF DELAY PHENOMENA

1. General explanation.—2. Example.

1. General explanation.

The selection of an economic function in a management phenomenon is arbitarary and must correspond to the objectives of the person who makes the selection. In general, the economic function in a delay phenomenon is taken to be the total cost of the clients' waiting time and the stations' idle time, or, more precisely, the mathematical expectation of expenses caused by delays (waiting idleness) to both clients and stations.

---

*See Part Two, Section 78.

If S is the number of stations in parallel, and m the number of clients (which can be infinite), the average number of clients waiting in line will be:

$$\bar{\nu} = \sum_{n=S}^{m} (n - S) p_n \,; \qquad 31.1$$

the average number of idle stations is:

$$\bar{\varrho} = \sum_{n=0}^{S} (S - n) p_n \,. \qquad 31.2$$

Taking a time interval T during which we will determine the average total cost Γ of delay, the average time lost by clients is expressed as:

$$\bar{\nu} T, \qquad 31.3$$

and the average idle time lost by the stations is expressed as:

$$\bar{\varrho} T. \qquad 31.4$$

Let c_1 equal the cost of a unit of time for the client and c_2 the cost of a unit of time for the station. Then, the total cost will be:

$$\Gamma(S) = (c_1 \bar{\nu} + c_2 \bar{\varrho})\, T = T[c_1 \sum_{n=S+1}^{m} (n - S) p_n + c_2 \sum_{n=0}^{S} (S - n) p_n] \,. \qquad 31.5$$

S is usually the variable, but, in some cases, control can be exercised over the value of m.

If the costs c_1 and c_2 are constant during interval T, we may also calculate the total cost per unit of time:

$$\gamma(S) = \frac{\Gamma(S)}{T} = c_1 \sum_{n=S+1}^{m} (n - S) p_n + c_2 \sum_{n=0}^{S} (S - n) p_n \,. \qquad 31.6$$

This total cost per unit of time is often the factor which one hopes to minimize.

In some problems, the economic function may involve values proportional to $\bar{n}$ or to $\bar{p}$ (> w), or, again, may take the form of a nonlinear function of various other basic factors considered in the theory of delay phenomena.

In addition to the economic function, one sometimes sets various objectives or constraints.

The optimum solution is usually determined by the numerical calculation of λ (S) for various values of S. In certain cases, we can make use of special formulas.

As an example of the use of the general formula (31.6), we shall obtain the optimum solution for the problem stated in Section 30 (a waiting line with a limited number of customers and several stations, m machines, and S mechanics).

2. Example.

In the stated problem we had: $\psi = 0.1$, $m = 20$. Let us assume that the time unit is one hour, and that the hourly cost of machine downtime is 18,000 francs, while a mechanic is paid 600 francs per hour. Under these conditions, what is the optimum number of mechanics?

Using formula (31.6), we find that the total hourly cost will vary with S. Table 31.1 gives the values of p_n for S = 3, 4, 5, 6, and 7 (we know by experience that S must not be less than 3 or more than 7). Table 31.2 gives the $\lambda(S)$ values. We observe that the minimum lies at S = 5.

Given the small value of ψ, it may be noted that the value of the minimum would not change significantly even if m were much larger.

Table 31.1

S	p_0	p_1	p_2	p_3	p_4	p_5	p_6	p_7	p_8	p_9
3	0.136	0.272	0.258	0.155	0.088	0.047	0.023	0.011	0.005	0.002
4	0.146	0.292	0.278	0.166	0.071	0.028	0.010	0.003	0.001	0.000
5	0.148	0.296	0.281	0.168	0.071	0.022	0.006	0.001	0.000	...
6	0.148	0.297	0.282	0.169	0.072	0.023	0.006	0.001	...	...
7	0.148	0.297	0.282	0.169	0.072	0.023	0.006	0.001	...	...

Table 31.2

S	$\sum_{n=S+1}^{20}(n-S)\,p_n$	$\sum_{n=0}^{S}(S-n)\,p_n$	$c_1\sum_{n=S+1}^{20}(n-S)p_n + c_2\sum_{n=0}^{S}(S-n)p_n$
3	0.34	1.21	$18{,}000\times 0.34 + 600\times 1.21 = 6{,}846$ fr
4	0.06	2.18	$18{,}000\times 0.06 + 600\times 2.18 = 2{,}388$ fr
5	0.01	3.17	$18{,}000\times 0.01 + 600\times 3.17 = 2{,}082$ fr ←
6	negligible	4.17	$600\times 4.17 = 2{,}502$ fr
7	negligible	5.16	$600\times 5.16 = 3{,}096$ fr

Section 32

THE USE OF SIMULATION PROCEDURES

1. The Monte Carlo method (simulation on an artificial sample).— 2. Direct simulation (on real data).—3. Artificial sample of arrivals of service times.—4. Use of a simulation device (Description of "Queuiac").

Delay phenomena can be studied by the use of simulation methods, of which the three principal ones are:

— the method of indirect simulation (Monte Carlo)

— the method of direct simulation

(These first two methods often require the use of an electronic computer.)

— the use of a special simulation device, i.e. a device whose design is based on a given mathematical model, thus making it possible to physically reconstruct a management phenomenon.

1. The Monte Carlo method (simulation on an artificial sample).

This method can be described by means of an example. We wish to find the optimum number of delivery trucks for a parcel service. Each day, packages arrive at the loading center. If we try to provide enough trucks and personnel to make it almost certain that every package will be delivered within 24 hours of its arrival at the loading center, our expenses will certainly be high, as will the waste of resources. If, on the contrary, the number of trucks is set too low, we will lose business because of delays in delivery, or else we will have to allocate overtime for both personnel and trucks, which could prove quite costly. Therefore, what we shall try to find is the number of trucks that will minimize the overall cost figure.

To solve such a problem, we must first know the daily operating cost for a delivery truck (both fixed and variable costs). Let us take 6,000 francs for this cost. We must also know the cost of a delay in delivery of 1 day, 2 days, etc. But this cost is hard to calculate. Despite this difficulty, the cost of such a delay can often be estimated by means of a survey of the customers.

In the problem to be analyzed here, we shall consider two policies: the first, p_1, corresponds to delivery the day after the parcel is taken in at the shipping window; the second, p_2, corresponds to an extra day of delay beyond the first policy. In the case of P_1, we have assumed that deliveries will be made five days a week, Monday through Friday; the shipping windows will be open on Saturdays and closed Sundays. Parcels turned in on Saturday are treated as if they were turned in on Monday, without counting any delay of the week-end. Under policy P_2, deliveries are made Monday through Friday, with the shipping windows open on Saturday, but any parcels left over from Friday are delivered on Saturday on an overtime basis. The cost per overtime hour is 2,500 francs.

Of course, these hypotheses have purposely been simplified, but the demonstration of the method will serve to point out the possibilities of systems which are even closer to real situations. The complexity of a more detailed study would simply involve an increase in numerical calculations; this, however, should present no difficulty where an electronic computer is available.

We have supposed, in our example, that the statistics supplied by the parcel service provided the following averages and standard deviations for one week:

Table 32.1

Day	Monday	Tuesday	Wednesday	Thursday	Friday
Average	7,800	6,400	5,500	7,000	5,000
Standard deviation	800	700	600	750	500

The statistical study also revealed that we can safely assume that the number of parcels to be delivered is random and follows a Gaussian law.

Furthermore, for the same period, the average number of parcels delivered by one truck during an 8-hour day is 80, with a standard deviation of 15; the number of parcels loaded per truck and per day also follows a Gaussian law.

We shall use the Monte Carlo method, or simulation on an artificial sample taken from a table of random numbers (see Tables 32.2 and 32.3).

Let us begin with a brief examination of artificial sampling.

Table 32.2 presents 500 numbers between 0 and 99,999, the particular numbers having been selected at random by an electronic computer, with every precaution taken to make sure that any number would have the same probability of being chosen, $p = 1/10$. Using these numbers, we draw up a new table of random numbers, which this time are stated in standard deviation units for a Gaussian distribution: these numbers have a zero average and a standard deviation of 1, if we take a large enough sample. To obtain these numbers in Gaussian standard deviation units, we utilize the transformation indicated in Fig. 32.1. For every "random number" we substitute a value in standard deviation units. For example, according to the cumulative Gauss distribution, the deviation of 0

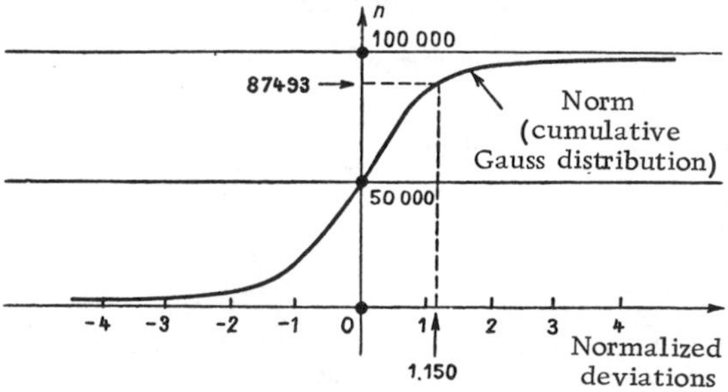

Fig. 32.1

corresponds to the number 0.5 (or 50,000); the number 0.87493 (or 87,493) corresponds to a deviation of 1.150. Numbers from 00000 to 49,999 will have negative deviations, while numbers from 50,001 to 99,999 will have positive deviations. The random number table can thus be converted to a table of deviations corresponding to the Gaussian distribution (or any other distribution). In this way we derive a table of normalized deviations drawn at random (Table 32.3).

Table 32.2

List of 500 random numbers between 0 and 99,999.

22719	92549	10907	35994	63461	83659	24494	53825	97047	79069
17618	88357	52487	79816	74600	50436	88823	19806	33960	30928
25267	35973	80231	60039	50253	63457	97444	13799	35853	03149
88594	69428	66934	27705	51262	63941	77660	66418	84755	29197
60482	33679	03078	08047	39891	34068	81957	02985	83113	36981
30753	19458	02849	30366	83892	80912	91335	41703	79401	97251
60551	24788	35764	57453	06341	10178	91896	70819	46440	98356
35612	09972	98891	92625	70599	95484	34858	13499	28966	88287
43713	18448	45922	55179	18442	31186	91047	37949	76542	79361
73998	97374	66685	06639	34590	17935	79544	15475	74765	11199
14971	68806	49122	16124	61905	22047	17229	46703	39727	16753
78976	48382	25242	97656	51686	15537	73857	35398	91783	92825
37868	82946	73732	63230	85306	56988	15570	98029	42208	00190
01666	48114	95183	02628	05355	97627	74554	91267	31240	34723
56638	70054	19427	24811	37164	71641	50515	88231	99539	75745
43973	07496	17405	08966	65989	68017	56975	94080	93689	98889
05540	72301	36504	00187	90375	22891	22205	27777	84803	39220
95141	07885	94399	41145	50210	92423	13303	09621	94153	18691
75954	68499	42308	38387	52163	64563	02843	45577	93125	25294
97905	05301	98496	20682	68082	68537	70220	78282	02396	10002

Table 32.2 (Cont'd)

23458	57782	67537	38813	00377	93873	97813	10039	25457	28716
03954	14799	63187	46191	12805	50502	08810	19572	48024	58206
52251	06804	85959	20974	73104	15009	25486	09306	24721	04187
62361	59105	39338	59358	69193	15586	57695	89518	59788	04215
54954	90337	99346	60442	90933	58323	83183	90041	44236	90815
70773	03331	84228	01405	61494	72064	24713	39851	01431	60841
68702	08331	08923	83173	67081	87472	47980	08802	95495	78745
39599	33465	96705	41458	34670	55385	25484	71068	15155	85371
54958	34935	16858	16523	54262	63310	50348	53457	39440	80411
98124	08864	36485	78766	52802	56315	43523	06513	50899	86432
43099	88373	80091	35058	35755	47556	98602	71744	70442	92312
88667	44515	80435	17140	32588	98708	93010	98590	23656	85664
87009	95736	76930	71090	27143	95229	24799	02313	17436	20273
70581	40618	16631	54178	44737	02544	81368	08078	46740	52583
03723	25551	03816	97612	99833	06779	47619	12901	60179	23780
49943	30139	07932	29267	01934	19584	13356	35803	90284	97565
71559	30728	83499	65977	37442	72526	53123	99948	59762	19952
75500	16143	79028	81790	57747	87972	54981	10079	17490	15215
59894	59543	13668	27197	51979	38403	23989	38549	82968	53300
29757	26942	08736	15184	73650	51130	59160	89866	06030	88929
87650	08162	90596	70312	84462	07653	80962	96692	07030	62470
84094	70059	86833	23531	31749	23930	04763	89322	67576	38627
92101	17194	06003	99847	12781	38729	88072	92589	61828	36504
26641	99088	65294	37138	75881	12627	19461	69536	64419	82106
04920	91233	46959	14735	15153	28306	76351	28109	86078	45234
25417	97570	91045	09929	75140	43926	90282	99088	93605	03547
98874	96989	84371	87624	74090	71983	62424	62130	44470	74725
82127	82000	84618	58572	56716	79862	59896	50702	31938	18336
26311	59516	98602	47197	31139	27631	64619	01504	77617	30219
76176	03499	17999	84361	63898	97861	63620	23931	87903	91566

(From a Rand Corporation Table)

Table 32.3

Normal random deviations$_{n \to \infty}$: $\lim_{n \to \infty} n = 0$,

.202–	1.303–	.671–	.140–	.018–	1.565	.284–	.622–	2.073	.481
.420	1.103–	.176	1.099	.092–	.482–	.543	.218–	1.683–	2.836
2.417	1.181	.168–	.238–	.560	1.847–	.061–	.578	.513	2.014
.260	.580–	.539	.955	1.128–	.730	.979	1.812	.195	1.322–
.353–	.151–	1.592–	1.213–	.189	1.014–	.678–	.412–	.165	.101
2.555–	.712–	.567	.085–	1.792	1.116	.252	1.676–	.121	.346
.666	.149–	1.359	.760–	.214	.446	.682	.584	.126–	.662–
.077	.526	.783–	1.950–	.854	.084	.552	.757–	1.108–	.578
1.365–	.027–	.251–	.273–	.494	.022–	.383	1.253–	.728–	.194
1.833	.154–	1.804	.414–	.103	.759	.054	.504–	.066	1.647

Table 32.3 (Cont'd)

Sequence chosen for parcel numbers

.308	2.537	1.220	1.250–	.371–	1.210–	.906	.604–	1.361–	.519–
.768	.132	1.464	.428–	.182	1.792–	.864	.483	1.799–	.349–
.957–	.265	.724	.055	.885	.379–	.694	1.448–	.672–	.209
.094–	.957–	.373–	.792–	.086	.134–	1.493	.210–	1.830	.109–
.148	.539–	.397	.362	.245–	1.194	.746–	.242	.197	1.375
.661–	.654–	.379–	.759–	.804	.282	1.317–	.219–	.318–	.580–
1.231	.337–	.125–	1.373–	.535–	.119	.775	.254–	.598	1.200
1.117–	.871–	.187–	.543–	.421	.311	.493	.574	.145–	2.332–
.551	.335	1.746–	.235	1.455	.251	1.024	.062	.009	.676
.743	1.076	.766	.052–	1.194	.517	.401–	1.292	.280–	.540
.329–	.277	1.736	.175	.401–	.665	.479	1.322	.072	.867–
1.264–	.970	.639–	.761–	.502–	1.559–	.249	.119	.065–	.812–
2.092–	1.610	1.423–	1.071–	.642	.759–	2.276–	.133	.976–	1.506
1.447–	.154	1.464	.032	.1076–	.327	.378–	.055	.521–	1.400–
.018	.533	.558	.593	.737–	.189	1.876–	.140–	1.380–	.303–
1.445–	1.357	1.657–	.837–	1.417–	.548	.423–	.398	.167	.147
.002	1.537	.113	1.008–	1.080	.772–	.368–	.290–	2.146	.539–
.576	1.201–	.108–	.334	.659	1.192	.119	1.861	.856	.018–
.108	.385–	.228	.166	1.169–	1.099	.914–	.462–	1.132	.266–
.233	1.043–	.852	.746–	.046	.395	.735	1.526–	1.065	1.450

Sequence chosen for truckloads

1.239–	.155	.090	1.130	2.623	.811	1.372–	.647	.858	.740–
.928–	.802	.043–	.463–	.985	.395–	.386	.465	.372–	.278–
.670–	.821–	1.092–	1.062	.601	2.509	1.557–	.814–	.220–	.019–
.643	1.339	1.287	.446	.042–	.593	.366	.640	.850–	.847
2.503	.162–	1.125	1.241–	2.226	1.063	.085	.016	.786	.766–
.895	2.238–	1.711	.640	.067–	.088–	.031–	1.184	1.550	.417
.070–	1.367–	.659–	1.025–	.475	0.59	.792–	.468	.284	.185–
.891	.903–	.213–	1.847	.223	1.640–	.772–	.324	.013–	1.757
1.170	.340–	.295–	.451	1.081	1.073–	.073	.477–	.397	1.282–
.130	.205	.665	.306	.790	.851–	.935	.502–	.650	.254
.591	1.342–	1.194	1.428	1.470–	1.202–	.450–	.668–	.212	1.161
.487–	.792–	1.453	1.465–	.390	.796	2.186–	.461	.848	.236–
1.048–	2.550–	.241–	.109–	1.385–	.066–	2.523–	1.270	.914	.157–
.984	.357	.563	1.177–	.371	.624–	.614–	.566	1.292	.776
1.217	.976	1.516–	.737–	.018	.768–	.712	1.001–	.012	.456–
1.008–	.849–	1.272–	.903	1.192–	2.081–	.157	.708	2.132–	.297–
.596–	.219–	.726–	.417–	.214–	.625	.699–	.276	1.505	.672
.315–	.999–	1.788	.592	.640	.677	.965–	1.066	1.189–	.657
1.441–	1.171	.192–	.315–	1.714	1.131	.001–	.342–	.039	1.486
.413	.269–	.602	.085	.848–	.207–	.396	2.358–	.045–	.087–

(Extract from a Rand Corporation Table)

— Negative numbers are not preceded, but followed, by the (—) sign. A number less than 1, such as 0,832, is written in the American manner: e.g. .832.

Using this table of random deviations, from which we have arbitrarily drawn two lots of 30 numbers (the boxed sequences in Table 32.3) we shall now proceed to reconstitute the random pattern of the number of parcels to be delivered and of the truck loads. Thus, we have constructed, for a period of 6 weeks (or, to be more precise, for an artificial sample of 6 weeks), a table of the number of parcels to be delivered and a table of the number of parcels that can be delivered by truck.

Table 32.4

Number of parcels to be delivered

Day \ Week	S_1	S_2	S_3	S_4	S_5	S_6
Monday	8,046	9,830	8,776	6,800	7,503	6,832
Tuesday	6,938	6,492	7,425	6,100	6,527	5,146
Wednesday	4,926	5,659	5,066	5,533	6,031	5,273
Thursday	6,929	6,282	6,720	6,406	7,065	6,899
Friday	5,074	4,730	5,199	4,819	4,877	5,597

The numbers for S_6, for example, were established by starting with the normalized random sequence:

$$\begin{array}{lcl} -1.210 & & 6{,}832 = 7{,}800 - 1.210 \times 800 \\ -1.792 & & 5{,}146 = 6{,}400 - 1.792 \times 700 \\ -0.379 & \text{as follows:} & 5{,}273 = 5{,}500 - 0.379 \times 600 \\ -0.137 & & 6{,}899 = 7{,}000 - 0.134 \times 750 \\ 1.194 & & 5{,}597 = 5{,}000 + 1.194 \times 500 \end{array} \quad (32.1)$$

In a like manner, the number of parcels that can be delivered per day was obtained by means of 6 sequences of random numbers, taking into account the average of 80 and standard deviation of 15 parcels per truck. As an example, for 70 trucks the average should be:

$$70 \times 80 = 5{,}600$$

and the standard deviation should be:

$$\sqrt{70} \times 15 = 125.3\,.$$

(see formula (54.36) in Section 54).

Using this sequence of random numbers, we have obtained the 6 tables in Table 32.5, corresponding to the use of 110, 100, 90, 80, 70, and 60 trucks, each for a period of 6 weeks.

Table 32.5

110 trucks $m = 8800$ $\sigma = 157$

Week / Day	S_1	S_2	S_3	S_4	S_5	S_6
Monday	8,606	8,824	8,814	8,977	9,212	8,927
Tuesday	8,654	8,926	8,793	8,727	8,955	8,738
Wednesday	8,695	8,671	8,629	8,967	8,894	9,194
Thursday	8,901	9,010	9,002	8,870	8,793	8,893
Friday	9,193	8,775	8,977	8,605	9,149	8,967

100 trucks $m = 8000$ $\sigma = 150$

Week / Day	S_1	S_2	S_3	S_4	S_5	S_6
Monday	7,814	8,023	8,013	8,169	8,394	8,122
Tuesday	7,861	8,120	7,994	7,931	8,148	7,941
Wednesday	7,900	7,877	7,836	8,159	8,090	8,376
Thursday	8,096	8,201	8,193	8,067	7,994	8,089
Friday	8,376	7,976	8,169	7,814	8,334	8,159

90 trucks $m = 7200$ $\sigma = 142$

Week / Day	S_1	S_2	S_3	S_4	S_5	S_6
Monday	7,024	7,222	7,213	7,360	7,572	7,315
Tuesday	7,068	7,314	7,194	7,134	7,340	7,144
Wednesday	7,105	7,084	7,045	7,351	7,285	7,556
Thursday	7,291	7,390	7,383	7,263	7,194	7,284
Friday	7,556	7,177	7,360	7,024	7,516	7,351

Table 32.5 (Cont'd)

80 trucks $m = 6400$ $\sigma = 134$

Day \ Week	S_1	S_2	S_3	S_4	S_5	S_6
Monday	6,234	6,421	6,412	6,551	6,752	6,509
Tuesday	6,276	6,507	6,394	6,338	6,532	6,347
Wednesday	6,310	6,290	6,254	6,542	6,481	6,736
Thursday	6,486	6,579	6,572	6,460	6,394	6,479
Friday	6,736	6,378	6,551	6,234	6,698	6,542

70 trucks $m = 5600$ $\sigma = 125$

Day \ Week	S_1	S_2	S_3	S_4	S_5	S_6
Monday	5,445	5,620	5,611	5,742	5,929	5,702
Tuesday	5,484	5,701	5,595	5,542	5,724	5,550
Wednesday	5,516	5,497	5,463	5,733	5,675	5,915
Thursday	5,681	5,768	5,761	5,656	5,595	5,674
Friday	5,914	5,580	5,741	5,444	5,879	5,733

60 trucks $m = 4800$ $\sigma = 116$

Day \ Week	S_1	S_2	S_3	S_4	S_5	S_6
Monday	4656	4818	4810	4931	5105	4894
Tuesday	4693	4893	4795	4746	4914	4754
Wednesday	4722	4705	4673	4923	4870	5091
Thursday	4875	4955	4949	4852	4795	4869
Friday	5091	4781	4931	4656	5057	4923

The random sequences that were used to construct Tables 32.4 and 32.5 are different and independent, which implies (as a working hypothesis) that the delivery rate is independent of the arrival rate.

A study of the statistics obtained by accountants makes it possible to verify this hypothesis. (If this hypothesis were not fully realized and a certain correlation were found between the two rates, it would be possible to construct parallel normalized random sequences by drawing them from distributions having the given correlation.) Finally, the 12 sequences of 5 random numbers used for the two tables were subjected to likelihood tests (Student's t test for the average, and Fisher's F test for the standard deviation). For, even though these numbers were taken from a carefully constructed table, it is best to eliminate any very unlikely sequences in such a limited example as the present one. Even so, such an elimination was not found to be necessary.

Table 32.6

(1) Number of trucks in line	(2) Day	(3) Number of parcels to deliver	(4) Delivery capacity (parcels)	(5) Parcel carry-over	(6) Number of over-time hours	
	Monday	8,776	8,814			
	Tuesday	7,425	8,793			
110	Wednesday	5,066	8,629			
	Thursday	6,720	9,002			
	Friday	5,199	8,977			
	Monday	8,776	8,013	763	76	
	Tuesday	7,425	7,994			
100	Wednesday	5,066	7,836			total : 76 h.
	Thursday	6,720	8,193			
	Friday	5,199	8,169			
	Monday	8,776	7,213	1,563	156	
	Tuesday	7,425	7,194	231	23	
90	Wednesday	5,066	7,045			total : 179 h
	Thursday	6,720	7,383			
	Friday	5,199	7,360			

Table 32.6 (Cont'd)

80	Monday	8,776	6,412	2,364	236	total 339 h.
	Tuesday	7,425	6,384	1,031	103	
	Wednesday	5,066	6,254			
	Thursday	6,720	6,572			
	Friday	5,199	6,551			
70	Monday	8,776	5,611	3,165	316	total : 592 h.
	Tuesday	7,425	5,595	1,830	183	
	Wednesday	5,066	5,463			
	Thursday	6,720	5,761	959	93	
	Friday	5,199	5,741			

Having constructed the tables that will serve as the artificial sample, we calculate, for different numbers of trucks, the weekly balance of overtime hours for each of the samples. For example, using S_3 and policy P_1, we obtain Table 32.6.

Columns (3) and (4) can be read directly from the random tables (Tables 32.4 and 32.5).

The number of overtime hours is calculated with reference to the delivery capacity for the day under consideration. Thus, the delivery rate in parcels per hour which is applied in each respective case is that given by Table 32.5, divided by 8.

Thus, for 70 trucks, the number of parcels still remaining for delivery at the close of an average Tuesday was 1,830; the delivery rate for that day was 79.93, and hence the hourly delivery rate would be 79.93/8 = 9.99. Therefore,

$$\text{number of overtime hours: } \frac{1{,}830}{9.99} = 183. \qquad 32.2$$

Table 32.7

Number of trucks	110	100	90	80	70
Total cost (trucks and over-time hours) in thousands of francs	660	638	629.5	649.5	716

Table 32.8

(1)	(2)	(3)	(4)	(5)	(6)	(7)	(8)	
Number of trucks in line	Day	Number of parcels (by the day)	Number of parcels to deliver	Delivery capacity	Carry-over	Number of parcels to be delivered in over-time hours	Number of over-time hours	
90	Monday	8,776	8,776	7,213	1,563			total : 0 h.
	Tuesday	7,425	8,988	7,194	1,794			
	Wednesday	5,066	6,860	7,045				
	Thursday	6,720	6,720	7,383				
	Friday	5,199	5,199	7,360				
80	Monday	8,776	8,776	6,412	2,364			total : 98 h.
	Tuesday	7,425	9,789	6,394	3,395			
	Wednesday	5,066	8,461	6,254	2,207			
	Thursday	6,720	8,927	6,572	2,355			
	Friday	5,199	7,554	6,551	1,003	1,003	98	
70	Monday	8,776	8,776	5,611	3,165			total : 490 h.
	Tuesday	7,425	10,590	5,595	4,995			
	Wednesday	5,066	10,061	5,463	4,598			
	Thursday	6,720	11,318	5,761	5,557			
	Friday	5,199	10,756	5,741	5,015	5,015	490	
60	Monday	8,776	8,776	4,810	3,966			total : 888 h.
	Tuesday	7,425	11,391	4,795	6,596			
	Wednesday	5,066	9739 + 1923	4,673	5,066	1,923	197	
	Thursday	6,720	11,669 + 117	4,949	6,720	117	11	
	Friday	5,199	11,919	4,931	6,988	6,988	680	

If we rate overtime hours at 2,500 francs, the budget for S_3 would be given by Table 32.7 (costs given in daily averages)

Hence, for S_3, the optimum number of trucks, among those we have considered, would be 90.

For the same week, if policy P_2, is followed, we obtain Table 32.8.

Overtime hours are required, on the one hand, the leftover from Friday to be delivered on Saturday, and, on the other hand, every time an evening's leftover pushes the next day's load beyond the delivery capacity. We have shown in column (7) the number of parcels to be delivered during overtime for each day. The budget for S_3 under policy P_2 then works out as shown in Table 32.9 (costs are given in daily averages).

Table 32.9

Number of trucks	90	80	70	60
Total cost (trucks and over-time hours) in thousands of francs	540	529	665	804

Grouping together the results for all 6 weeks, we obtain (in thousands of francs):

Table 32.10—Policy P_1

Week \ Number of trucks	110	100	90	80	70	60
S_1	660	612	592.5	628.5	689.5	761.5
S_2	710	690	670	650	702	801
S_3	660	638	629.5	649.5	716	808.5
S_4	660	600	540	492.5	536.5	634.5
S_5	660	600	540	549	625	722.5
S_6	660	600	540	517	536	616.5
Total	4010	3740	3512	3486.5	3805	4344.5
Average	668	623	585	581	634	724

Table 32.11—Policy P_2

Week \ Number of trucks	100	90	80	70	60
S_1	600	540	480	603.5	735
S_2	600	540	521	662.5	803.5
S_3	600	540	529	665	804
S_4	600	540	480	499	646
S_5	600	540	480	572.5	706
S_6	600	540	480	477.5	614
Total	3600	3240	2970	3480	4308.5
Average	600	540	495	580	718

Representative points have been plotted on the graph in Fig. 32.2.

This problem was studied more thoroughly by taking 20 weeks, which made it possible to compare the results with actual operating figures for a corresponding period of the preceding year; furthermore, calculations were made for all the points corresponding to 70, 71, 72, 73, . . . , 88, 89, 90 trucks. This study produced the curves of Fig. 32.2, which reveal:

— optimum for policy P_1 : 85,
— optimum for policy P_2 : 80.

Several remarks should be made at this point. Let us recall that we assumed that the averages and standard deviations were constant over the entire year; in reality, the problem proved to be seasonal, and the more thorough study covered several different periods of the year. This resulted in families of curves which showed the optimum decision for each policy, P_1, P_2, etc., for each seasonal period.

One might think that a knowledge of the averages would suffice for the resolution of such a problem; however, this would be to overlook the critical role played by the standard deviation. The artificial method of sampling, as developed here, is specifically designed to take these standard deviations into account.

In a real problem, the volume of calculations can be considerable. Consequently, if we wish to approximate the real conditions very closely, the use of an electronic computer can become practically indispensable.

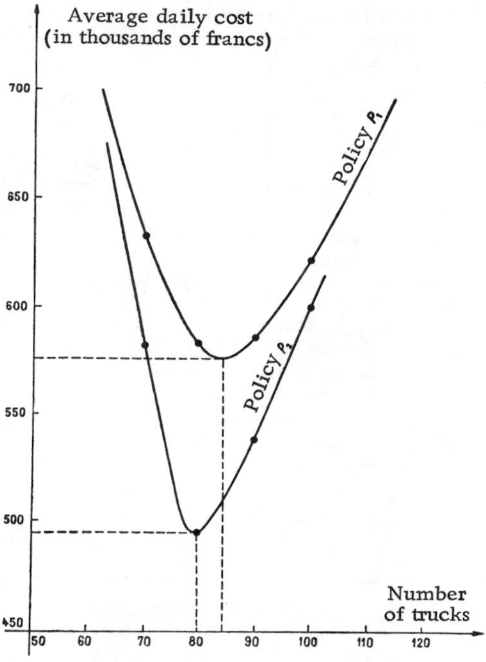

Fig. 32.2

2. Direct simulation (on real data).

As a beginning, we shall use a graphic method to study a delay phenomenon consisting of one line and one station. The intervals between arrivals and the service times were measured for 20 consecutive units. (Of course, this number of observations would be grossly inadequate in practice; it has been used here only to avoid over-lengthy calculations.) A statistical analysis showed that the distribution of arrivals followed Poisson's law, while that of the service times was not exponential. The observed data are recorded in Table 32.12. Using these data, one can draw up the diagram shown in Fig. 32.3, whose construction is fairly self-evident. This diagram makes it easy to find the average delay time spent in the system and the average waiting time in line; it also makes it possible to determine the average values $\bar{n}$, $\bar{v}$, and $\bar{\rho}$.

The average delay time in the system can be figured roughly by taking the sum of the individual delay times and dividing this result by 20; this gives us:

$$\bar{t}_s = \frac{57.8}{20} = 2.89 \text{ time units.} \tag{32.5}$$

Table 32.12

Units	Intervals between arrivals
a	
	3.4
b	
	1.8
c	
	4.2
d	
	0.6
e	
	3.1
f	
	4.5
g	
	0.3
h	
	1.7
i	
	2.2
j	
	2.2
k	
	0.2
l	
	0.6
m	
	1.0
n	
	0.2
o	
	0.7
p	
	1.1
q	
	2.7
r	
	3.4
s	
	0.6
t	
	7.8

Total : 42.3
Average: 2.11

Units	Service times
a	0.2
b	4.0
c	0.1
d	0.8
e	2.2
f	6.7
g	0.7
h	0.5
i	0.4
j	0.2
k	0.4
l	1.4
m	0.2
n	0.1
o	3.4
p	1.4
q	2.2
r	2.9
s	2.5
t	2.8

Total : 33.1
Average: 1.65

Similarly, for the average waiting time on line we obtain:

$$\bar{t}_f = \frac{24,7}{20} = 1.23 \text{ time units.} \qquad 32.6$$

The total idle time of the station is:

$$T_{\text{idle}} = 9.2 \text{ time units.} \qquad 32.7$$

The rate of idleness in relation to the total time:

$$K = \frac{T_{\text{idle}}}{T_{total}} = \frac{9.2}{42.3} \simeq 0.22\,. \tag{32.8}$$

To calculate the probabilities p_0, p_1, p_2, p_3, we shall compute the ratios:

$$\frac{T_i}{T_{total}}, \qquad i = 0, 1, 2, 3, \tag{32.9}$$

where T_i is the total time during which there are i units in the system. We then assume that:

$$p_i = \frac{T_i}{T_{total}}\,. \tag{32.10}$$

This mode of procedure is not rigorous, but it is fully adequate for practical purposes.

We find:

$$\begin{aligned} T_0 &= 9.2 \\ T_1 &= 14.8 \\ T_2 &= 12.2 \\ T_3 &= 6.1 \\ \hline T &= 42.3. \end{aligned} \tag{32.11}$$

This gives us:

$$\begin{aligned} p_0 &= \frac{T_0}{T} = 0.22 \\ p_1 &= \frac{T_1}{T} = 0.35 \\ p_2 &= \frac{T_2}{T} = 0.29 \\ p_3 &= \frac{T_3}{T} = 0.14\,. \end{aligned} \tag{32.12}$$

Based on these calculations, we obtain:

$$\bar{n} = \sum_{n=0}^{3} n p_n = 1 \times 0.35 + 2 \times 0.29 + 3 \times 0.14 = 1.35\,. \tag{32.13}$$

$$\bar{\nu} = \sum_{n=1}^{3} (n - 1) p_n = 0.58 \tag{32.14}$$

$$\bar{\varrho} = \sum_{n=0}^{1} (1 - n) p_n = p_0 = 0.22\,. \tag{32.15}$$

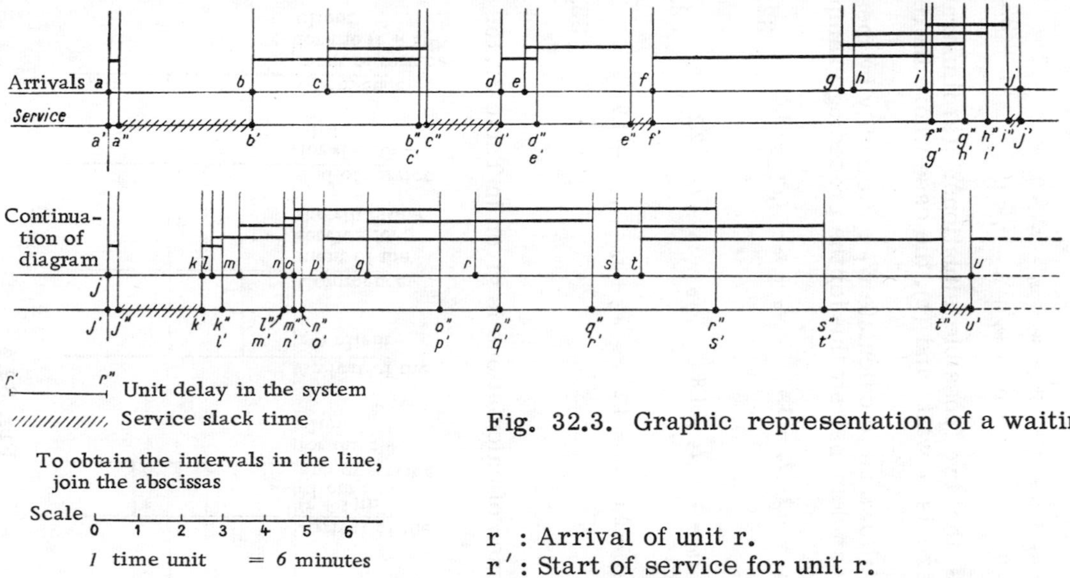

Fig. 32.3. Graphic representation of a waiting line at one station.

r : Arrival of unit r.
r′ : Start of service for unit r.
r″ : End of service for unit r.
t_r = Time interval between arrival of unit r and that of unit r+1.
s_r = Service time for unit r.
w_r = Waiting time on line for unit r.
$w_r + s_r$ = Delay time in the system for unit r.

For this method to have validity, it must be applied to a larger sample—for example, one hundred units. The example given above was intended to illustrate the method and serve as an introduction to the more general explanation that follows here.

Let:

t_r = time interval between arrival of unit r and arrival of unit r+1;

s_r = service time for unit r;

w_r = waiting time on line for unit r.

Then:

$$w_{r+1} = w_r + s_r - t_r \quad \text{if} \quad w_r + s_r - t_r > 0$$
$$= 0 \quad \text{if} \quad w_r + s_r - t_r \leqslant 0. \qquad 32.16$$

Fig. 32.4 shows the two possible situations: (a) illustrates the case where there is a wait, and (b), the case where there is no wait.

Formula (32.16) allows us to calculate w_r quite easily by means of recurrence. We can demonstrate this for the preceding example:

$$w_a = 0, \quad s_a = 0.2, \quad t_a = 3.4 \quad w_a + s_a - t_a = -3.2$$
$$\text{therefore } w_b = 0. \qquad 32.17$$

$$w_b = 0, \quad s_b = 4. \quad t_b = 1.8 \quad w_b + s_b - t_b = 2.2$$
$$\text{therefore } w_c = 2.2 \qquad 32.18$$

$$w_c = 2.2, \quad s_c = 0.1, \quad t_c = 4.2 \quad w_c + s_c - t_c = -1.9$$
$$\text{therefore } w_d = 0 \qquad 32.19$$

etc...

The complete series of calculations is given in Table 32.13.

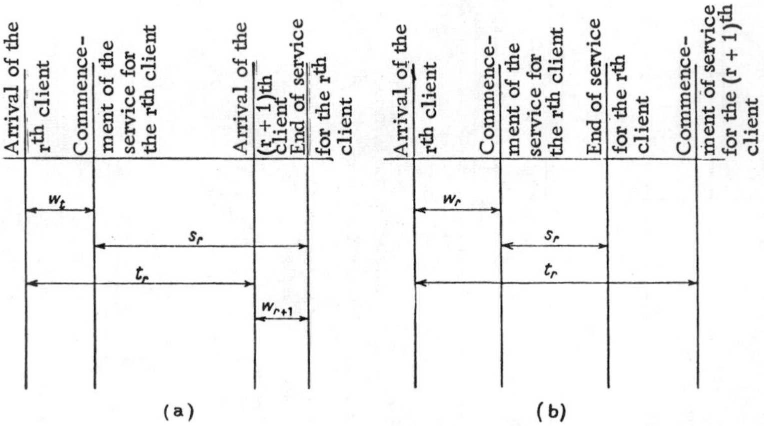

Fig. 32.4

Table 32.13

	w_α	s_α	t_α	$w_\alpha + s_\alpha - t_\alpha$	$w_{\alpha+1}$	$w_\alpha + s_\alpha$
a	0	0.2	3.4	—3.2	0	0.2
b	0	4.0	1.8	2.2	2.2	4.0
c	2.2	0.1	4.2	—1.9	0	2.3
d	0	0.8	0.6	0.2	0.2	0.8
e	0.2	2.2	3.1	—0.7	0	2.4
f	0	6.7	4.5	2.2	2.2	6.7
g	2.2	0.7	0.3	2.6	2.6	2.9
h	2.6	0.5	1.7	1.4	1.4	3.1
i	1.4	0.4	2.2	—0.4	0	1.8
j	0	0.2	2.2	—2.0	0	0.2
k	0	0.4	0.2	0.2	0.2	0.4
l	0.2	1.4	0.6	1.0	1.0	1.6
m	1.0	0.2	1.0	0.2	0.2	1.2
n	0.2	0.1	0.2	0.1	0.1	0.3
o	0.1	3.4	0.7	2.8	2.8	3.5
p	2.8	1.4	1.1	3.1	3.1	4.2
q	3.1	2.2	2.7	2.6	2.6	5.3
r	2.6	2.9	3.4	2.1	2.1	5.5
s	2.1	2.5	0.6	4.0	4.0	4.6
t	4.0	2.8	7.8	—1.0	0	6.8
Total:	24.7				Total:	57.8

This table allows us to determine the average delay time in the system and the average waiting time on the line (32.5 and 32.6). To obtain the average number of units in the system or in the line, we can prepare a diagram such as that shown in Fig. 32.3, or a corresponding table such as Table 32.14. In the latter table, events are described with reference to a theoretical clock whose

Table 32.14

(1) 0,1 t	(2) Arrivals	(3) Units in the system	(4) Units in line	(5) Departures
0	1	1	0	
1		1	0	
2		0	0	1
3		0	0	
4		0	0	
5		0	0	
6		0	0	
7		0	0	
30		0	0	
31		0	0	
32		0	0	
33		0	0	
34	1	1	0	
35		1	0	
36		1	0	
37		1	0	
50		1	0	
51		1	0	
52	1	2	1	
53		2	1	
54		2	1	
55		2	1	
71		2	1	
72		2	1	
73		2	1	
74		1	0	1
75		0	0	1
76		0	0	
77		0	0	
78		0	0	
93		0	0	
94	1	1	0	
95		1	0	
96		1	0	
97		1	0	
98		1	0	
99		1	0	
100	1	2	1	
101		2	1	
102		1	0	1
103		1	0	
104		1	0	
124		0	0	1
125		0	0	
126		0	0	
127		0	0	
128		0	0	
129		0	0	
130		0	0	
131	1	1	0	
132		1	0	

time intervals are tenths of the selected unit of time. Arrivals and departures are recorded in columns (2) and (5), and we sum the numbers in columns (3) and (4).

This type of calculation is of special interest in the study of interconnected (cascaded) systems: the departures from one system are then considered as the arrivals at the next. Also, a procedure of this kind makes it possible to study the transient condition of a delay phenomenon, where the analytical method would be too complicated.

3. Artificial sample of arrivals or service.

To set up an artificial sample of arrival intervals or service times, we begin by using statistical measurements to construct a histogram (see Part Two, Section 54) of the intervals (θ) between arrivals (or service times). Suppose that we have measured 1,000 such intervals, and that the frequencies (n) are as shown in Table 32.15, with the time intervals stated in arbitrary units.

Table 32.15

(1)	(2)	(3)	(4)
θ	n	$\Pr\{(\theta-1) < \Theta < \theta\}$	$\Pr\{0 < \Theta < \theta\}$
1	186	0.186	0.186
2	171	0.171	0.357
3	160	0.160	0.517
4	132	0.132	0.649
5	113	0.113	0.762
6	90	0.090	0.852
7	53	0.053	0.905
8	31	0.031	0.936
9	28	0.028	0.964
10	18	0.018	0.982
11	13	0.013	0.995
12	5	0.005	1.000
$\geqslant 13$	0	0	1

We estimate that:

$$\Pr[(\theta - 1) < \Theta < \theta] = \frac{n}{1000}. \qquad 32.20$$

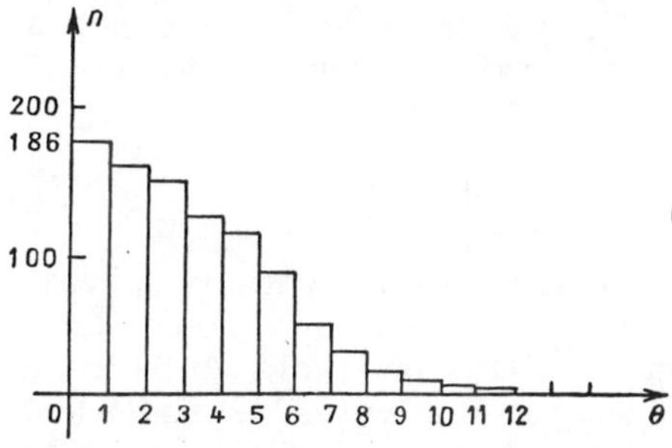

Fig. 32.5

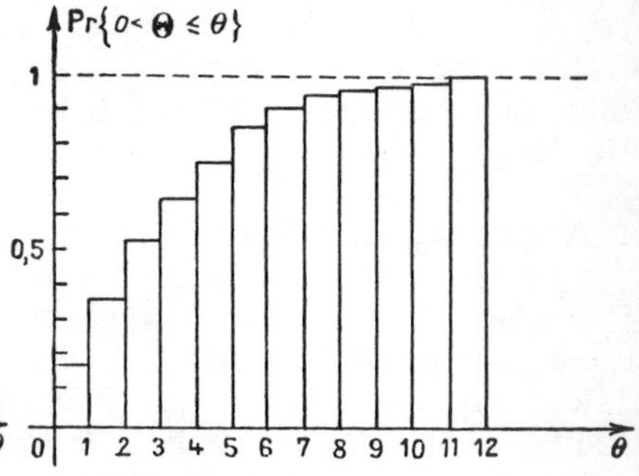

Fig. 32.6

which will give us column (3) of Table 32.15; then, accumulating the column (3) values in column (4), we will obtain the breakdown shown in Fig. 32.6.

Table 32.16

N	
$000 \leqslant N < 186$	1
$186 \leqslant N < 357$	2
$357 \leqslant N < 517$	3
$517 \leqslant N < 649$	4
$649 \leqslant N < 762$	5
$762 \leqslant N < 852$	6
$852 \leqslant N < 905$	7
$905 \leqslant N < 936$	8
$936 \leqslant N < 964$	9
$964 \leqslant N < 982$	10
$982 \leqslant N < 995$	11
$995 \leqslant N < 1000$	12

Next, we construct a table similar to Table 32.16. Selecting a random series of 20 3-digit numbers from Table 32.2, we establish a series of 20 values for θ, constituting an artificial sample of arrivals. In our example, a check of the sample by means of a

Table 32.17

N	θ
070	1
675	5
618	4
644	4
860	7
936	9
444	3
319	2
776	6
879	7

N	θ
624	4
386	3
365	3
821	6
452	3
035	1
747	5
183	1
302	2
915	8

significance test (Student and Fisher) showed that the sample was acceptable.

The choice of the class interval for the histogram is very important: it must be small enough.

Table 32.17 shows how our artificial sample was obtained. The numbers N are random numbers taken from the table in this section.

4. Use of a simulation device (Description of "Queuiac").*

We shall present a brief description of a simulation device constructed at Johns Hopkins University, in the United States, and known as the "Queuiac." This device makes it possible to study quite complex delay phenomena which form systems of parallel or series networks. One can introduce arbitrary distributions for arrivals or service intervals, different queue disciplines, and various relationships that might exist between the rate of service and the number of units waiting, etc. With this device, there is no need to perform statistical analyses of distributions; rather, one has only to observe the intervals of the real phenomenon, record them on a perforated tape, and feed this into the simulator. The

*See: P. F. Dunn, C. D. Flagle, and P. A. Nicks "The Queuiac: An Electromechanical Analog for the Simulation of Waiting Line Problems," J.O.R.S.A., Vol. 4, No. 6, December 1956, pp. 649-662.

signals representing arrivals are sent into the recording unit, where the presence of an arrival is indicated by a little light. In the same way, signals relating to service intervals are fed into the recorder, which then determines the number of units in the waiting line at any given moment. Associated with the recorder is an interval counter; thus the data can be converted directly into probabilities. The sum of the np_n's yields the average length of the waiting line.

Many recording units, each one associated with a counter, can be linked in series or parallel formation to reconstitute a complicated network of delay systems.

The recording unit consists of a luminous waiting line and a priority selector. (Readers interested in the electronic details of the device will find them in the article cited above.)

The tape reader is a Type 1-A Western Union transmitter, which reads pulses from the perforated tape. The tape speed is continuously variable. Information is sent directly to the recording units. The tapes are perforated directly according to the sample of time intervals for arrivals or service that are actually observed. One can also produce artificial samples of intervals by the Monte Carlo method, and thus introduce any desired distribution at will.

The "Queuiac" makes it possible to simulate delay phenomena that are impossible to analyze, and, in particular, to study transient systems.

Section 33

EXAMPLE OF A COMPLETE STUDY OF A DELAY PHENOMENON*

1. General explanation.—2. Occupancy rate of a slip.—3. Calculation of waiting lines for the case of uninterrupted 3-shift operation. 4. Calculation of waiting lines for the case of 3-shift operation with week-ends off.—5. Calculation of waiting lines for the case of 2-shift operation.—6. Total monthly cost of operation.—7. Total annual cost of operation.—8. Conclusions.

1. General explanation.

A mining company must necessarily be concerned with the cost of transporting its heavy ores, and a major item in this transportation cost is the charge for ship's time spent in port for loading

*Taken from an essay by M. E. Ventura, Director of the Sociéte de'Etudes Pratiques de Recherche Opérationelle ("Society for Practical Studies in Operations Research"). See bulletin S.E.D.E.I.S. (205 Boulevard St. Germain, Paris), Study No. 691, 1-2-58.

and unloading ("lay days"). The problem is to find loading methods that will minimize the total of the following costs:

a) annual amortization and operating costs for loading installations;
b) wages for personnel employed in loading;
c) freight rates, corrected for any delay beyond the standard "lay days" (average length of the ship's stay fixed for each port) or, on the other hand, for rebates due to time saved.

Insofar as cost a) is concerned, the choice lies between two possible installations (4,000 or 6,000 tons per hour). For b), the choice lies between 3 crews if the port works on a round-the-clock (3-shift) basis, or 2 if work is not continuous. The week-end off may or may not apply. In any case, there will be heavy overtime rates to take into account. For c), the rate is calculated by adding to the cost of transport at sea the cost of time lost during the stay in port.

The length of stay in port is random. It depends on the size of the cargo shipped, the speed of loading, and the congestion of the port. The applicable probability distribution for service times is difficult to determine. We shall return to it later.

Arrivals of ships in port (to take on cargo) follow Poisson's law. However, the rate of arrivals, λ, is seasonal, with more ships docking in summer than in winter.

The service time, $1/\mu$, is the time it takes to load if service at the slip is continuous. If there are periods during which no work is done (at night, for example), there may be interruptions in the work of loading cargo. Hence the total service time will include:

— duration of actual service;
— delay time during loading;
— time waiting for the slip to be free.

It was found that the total service time, s, could be determined correctly by means of the formula:

$$s = s_0 + k \frac{L}{v}, \qquad 33.1$$

where s_0 = total idle time (casting ballast, docking, make-ready);
L = gross tonnage of the ship we are considering;
v = speed of loading.

Therefore, if we know the statistical distribution by gross tonnage, of the ships putting in at this port to take on cargo, we can

We quote this study almost in its entirety because of its great practical interest and because of the high quality of the analytical explanation given by the Director of the S.E.P.R.O.

deduce from these data the service time for each case (v = 4,000 tons/hour; v = 6,000 tons/hour).

2. Occupancy rate of a slip.

If λ is the average rate of arrivals and μ is the average rate of service, the traffic intensity, $\psi = \lambda/\mu$, will be called the occupancy

Table 33.1

Number of units in the system	Dockside conditions	Probability p_n	
		4,000 t/h installations	6,000 t/h installations
0	0 ship at dockside, 0 waiting	0.580	0.640
1	1 " " , 0 " "	0.303	0.277
2	1 " " , 1 " "	0.087	0.067
3	1 " " , 2 " "	0.022	0.013
4	1 " " , 3 " "	0.006	0.002
5	1 " " , 4 " "	0.002	0.000
6	1 " " , 5 " "	0.000	0.000

Table 33.2

Length of stay	4,000 t/h installations	6,000 t/h installations
$0 < T < 24$ h	0.942	0.982
24 h $< T < 48$ h	0.056	0.018
48 h $< T < 72$ h	0.002	0.000
72 h $< T$	0.000	0.000

rate of a slip. We shall call the complementary quantity, $1 - \psi$, the vacancy rate.

3. Calculation of waiting lines for the case of uninterrupted 3-shift operation.

Here, for example, are the results obtained in the case of a dock working 3 shifts, with 32 ships arriving per month, and under the verified hypothesis of a stationary and permanent system. As would be expected, the waiting lines are not as long for an installation that can handle 6,000 tons per hour as they are for one that has a capacity of 4,000 tons. The slip will be busy 36% of the time, instead of 42% ($p(>0) = 1 - p_o$).

By means of tables similar to Table 33.1 for various rates of arrival, we can determine the probability of a length of stay (delay + service time) of less than 24 hours, 24 to 48 hours, 48 to 72 hours, and so on.

For 32 ships a month, this method produces Table 33.2, which allows us to calculate the extra cost for exceeding the lay days, taking into account the cost per day's delay after an allowance of 24 hours.

4. Calculation of waiting lines for the case of 3-shift operation with week-ends off.

The classical theory, which was applied to the case of round-the-clock work, must be modified to fit the hypothesis of non-continuous work. Take the case where the only break is the Sunday holiday; in this case Sunday is a day when no ship can be served or sail from the port. The result will be a bottleneck on Monday morning, which must be absorbed little by little during the rest of the week. We must study the phenomenon as a transient system, and consider the probabilities $p_n(t)$ and the values of $n(t)$. Obviously, we will find that $\bar{n}(t)$ is higher at the beginning of the week. Tables 33.3 and 33.4, developed for work stoppages of 24 or 32 hours, show the evolution of $p_n(t)$ for periods separated by 9.5 hours, starting at 7 o'clock Monday morning, for a loading speed of 4,000 tons/hour. The probabilities $p_n(t)$ for a speed of 6,000 tons/hour have also been calculated, in the same manner.

Thus we are dealing with a periodic phenomenon, whose period is the week. The mean probabilities $\tilde{p}_n$ were calculated and are listed in Table 33.5. It can be seen that $p(> 0)$ ranges from 0.42 with round-the-clock service to 0.498 with a break of 24 hours, and to 0.539 with a break of 32 hours, for a rate of 4,000 tons/hour. For $v = 6,000$ tons/hour, the range varies from 0.36 to 0.431 and 0.503.

Table 33.3

ν = 4 000 t/h 24-h interruption

$p_n(t)$ / n	1	2	3	4	5	6	7	8	9		Week-end
0	0.199	0.339	0.426	0.480	0.514	0.536	0.550	0.560	0.567	...	0.580
1	0.317	0.310	0.305	0.303	0.303	0.303	0.303	0.303	0.303	...	0.303
2	0.255	0.192	0.154	0.132	0.117	0.108	0.102	0.098	0.095	...	0.087
3	0.140	0.097	0.070	0.054	0.043	0.036	0.031	0.028	0.026	...	0.022
4	0.060	0.041	0.029	0.022	0.016	0.012	0.010	0.008	0.007	...	0.006
5	0.021	0.015	0.011	0.007	0.005	0.004	0.003	0.002	0.002	...	0.002
6	0.006	0.005	0.004	0.002	0.002	0.001	0.001			...	0.000
7	0.002	0.001	0.001							...	0.000

Table 33.4

n ν = 4 000 t/h 32-h interruption

$p_n(t)$ / n	1	2	3	4	5	6	7	8	9		Week-end
0	0.140	0.271	0.367	0.434	0.481	0.514	0.535	0.550	0.560	....	0.580
1	0.273	0.289	0.294	0.297	0.300	0.301	0.301	0.301	0.302	....	0.303
2	0.266	0.213	0.173	0.147	0.129	0.116				....	0.087
3	0.176	0.125	0.092	0.070	0.054	0.042				....	0.022
4	0.088	0.061	0.044	0.031	0.022	0.017				....	0.006
5	0.036	0.025	0.018	0.014	0.010	0.007				....	0.002
6	0.013	0.010	0.008	0.005	0.004	0.003				....	0.000
7	0.005	0.004	0.003	0.001	0.001	0.000				....	0.000

On the basis of these data, Table 33.5a was drawn up, similar to Table 33.2 and still using 32 ships, but with the hypothesis of a weekly 24-hour work stoppage.

The conclusion was that the week-end break proved very expensive, and that it would be better to pay overtime, even at the rate of 50%.

Table 33.5

n	$\tilde{p}_n$			
	$v = 4\,000$ t/h		$v = 6\,000$ t/h	
	24-h wait	32-h wait	24-h wait	32-h wait
0	0.502	0.461	0.569	0.497
1	0.305	0.296	0.286	0.282
2	0.122	0.128	0.098	0.110
3	0.046	0.070	0.032	0.044
4	0.017	0.027	0.011	0.019
5	0.006	0.011	0.003	0.006
6	0.002	0.005	0.001	0.002
7	0.000	0.000	0.000	0.000

Table 33.5a

Length of stay	$v = 4,000$ t/h	$v = 6,000$ t/h
$0 < T < 24$ h	0.808	0.894
24 h $< T <$ 48 h	0.174	0.103
48 h $< T <$ 72 h	0.017	0.003
72 h $< T$	0.001	0.000

5. Calculation of waiting lines for the case of 2-shift operation.

Still assuming that the ship arrival rate is the same both day and night, a 2-shift dock necessarily leads to some congestion in the mornings, due to the arrival of several ships that cannot be served during the night. Little by little, the effect of the congestion will disappear. This means that we must consider that the probabilities $p_n(t)$ change during the day; then we must calculate the mean daily probabilities, $\tilde{p}_n$, and from these derive the probabilities of a stay of 0 to 24 hours, 24 to 48 hours, etc. Such calculations are more complicated and require the use of an electronic computer. The results are shown in Tables 33.6 and 33.7.

Table 33.6
With $v = 4,000$ t/h

n	$p_n(t)$			
	At the beginning of the first shift	At the beginning of the second shift	At the beginning of the third shift	Daily average
0	0.432	0.508	0.539	0.497
1	0.341	0.313	0.306	0.318
2	0.151	0.121	0.108	0.126
3	0.052	0.040	0.033	0.041
4	0.017	0.013	0.010	0.013
5	0.005	0.004	0.003	0.004
6	0.002	0.001	0.001	0.001

Table 33.7
With $v = 6,000$ t/h

n	$p_n(t)$			
	At the beginning of the first shift	At the beginning of the second shift	At the beginning of the third shift	Daily average
0	0.413	0.529	0.579	0.507
1	0.345	0.301	0.288	0.311
2	0.159	0.114	0.092	0.122
3	0.057	0.038	0.028	0.041
4	0.018	0.013	0.009	0.013
5	0.006	0.004	0.003	0.004
6	0.002	0.001	0.001	0.002

It can be seen that p_0 rises, from morning to night, from 0.43 to 0.54, and that the average occupancy rate is 50.3% for $v = 4,000$ tons/hour. For $v = 6,000$ tons/hour, p_0 ranges from 0.41 to 0.58, with a longer stop at night.

These data provide the basis for Table 33.8.

Table 33.8

Length of stay	$\nu = 4,000$ t/h	$\nu = 6,000$ t/h
$0 < T < 24$ h	0.815	0.818
$24\text{ h} < T < 48$ h	0.166	0.163
$48\text{ h} < T < 72$ h	0.017	0.019
$72\text{ h} < T$	0.001	0.000

6. Total monthly cost of operation.

The total cost for personnel, equipment, and ship's time of stay is easily calculated: the first two are known, and the stay time is evaluated on the basis of the probabilities just given. This calculation was made for several different average monthly ship-arrival rates. The results are shown in Fig. 33.1.

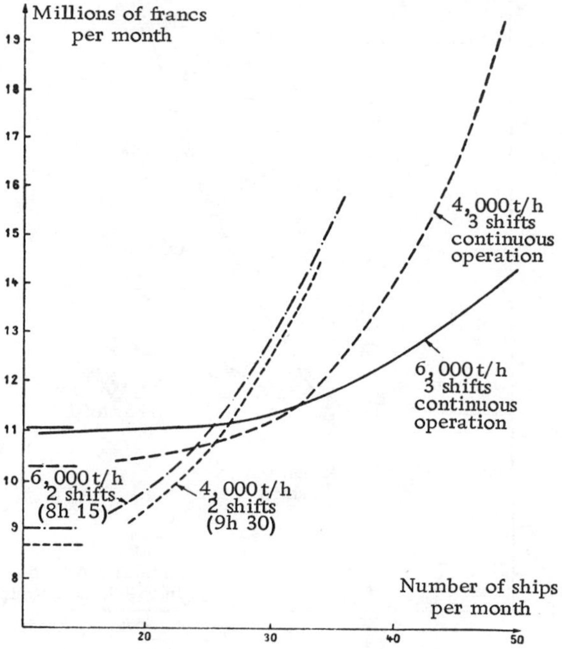

Fig. 33.1

a) Choice of loading rate.

Below 5,000,000 tons, a 4,000-ton/hr installation is more profitable. At about 5,000,000 tons, there is not much difference between the two. Above 5,000,000 tons, the 6,000-ton/hour installation is more profitable. We can also compute the actual costs for the output period.

b) Choice of work plan.

The 2-shift plan is preferable, no matter what loading speed we choose, if the number of ships to be handled is less than 25; the 3-shift system should be adopted if more than 25 ships are expected.

We can observe the following results:

For a 4,000-ton/hour installation, it becomes profitable to convert from a 2-shift to a 3-shift operation when the annual activity reaches 4,300,000 tons. For a 6,000-ton/hour installation, this point occurs at 4,500,000 tons. Failing to observe this rule, and if the activity is 6,000,000 tons, the loss would be about 46 million francs a year with a 4,000-ton/hour installation, or about 52 million francs a year with a 6,000-ton/hour installation.

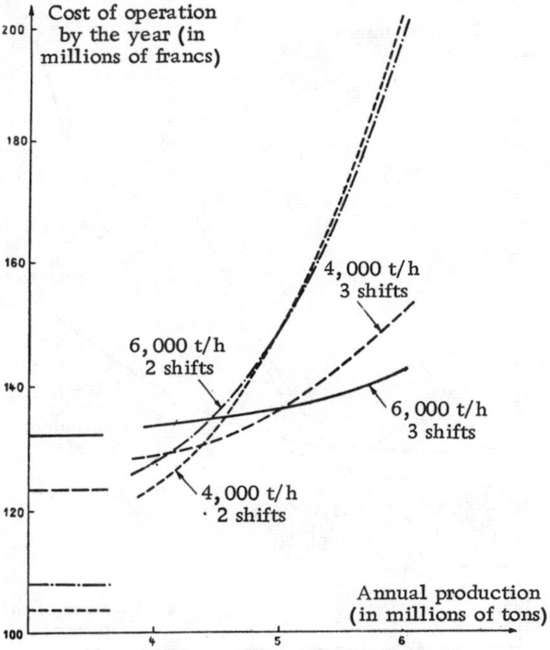

Fig. 33.2

8. Conclusions.

a) The differences between the total operating costs for 4,000- and 6,000-ton/hour installations are slight.

b) On the other hand, costs are very sensitive to the choice of work plan. Night and week-end breaks should be avoided.

c) Changing any of the unit costs requires that new curves be plotted; these, however, are fairly simple to obtain on the basis of the old ones and by means of a simple geometrical construction. The set of networks and curves makes it possible to cope with many real situations, and provides valuable information.

This was the advice that the mining company received:

1st. Choose a 6,000-ton/hour installation if activity will exceed 6,000,000 tons after the first few shakedown years;

2nd. Put on 3 shifts (this poses a social problem);

3rd. Start with a 2-shift operation, and convert to 3 shifts as soon as the activity is clearly over 4,000,000 tons;

4th. Restudy these conclusions whenever new developments evolve in the basic parameters.

This type of study made it possible for the company to see its position clearly, to orient itself, and to determine important changeover thresholds; it constitutes a notable example of the rational approach to decisions.

Chapter **4**

Inventory problems

Section 34

INTRODUCTION

1. General remarks.—2. General characteristics of inventory problems.—3. Graphic representation.—4. Replenishment.—5. Lead-time for replenishment.

1. General remarks.

Supplying materials and equipment for manufacturing, production filling customer requests, and maintaining adequate stocks of spare parts—these operations pose extremely varied problems. It is difficult to arrive at any consistent or logical classification of inventory problems. However, we can make a good start by recognizing the nature of the demand, which may be:

—determined (predictable with some degree of precision);
—stochastic, but statistically stable;
—stochastic, but statistically unstable (seasonal)
—unknown.

The constraints that appear in inventory problems may be:
—interactions among the various products;
—limitations of means (volume, weight, operating time, available funds, etc.).

In every case, it is possible to define an economic function to be optimized; when the demand is random, this function will frequently take the form of an expected value of total cost.

2. General characteristics of inventory problems.

In view of the great variety of inventory problems encountered in industry and other fields, we shall limit ourselves to a review of the principal ones, from which some simple concepts can be derived.

Inventory problems appear in the form of delay (queuing) phenomena of a very special type. Instead of assuming, as we did in Chapter III, that units arrive or are served one by one, we shall now assume that both arrivals and service are concerned with groups of units. These phenomena can be studied by means of concepts; however, in certain (fairly common) cases, the statistical measures exhibit very little variance and we can assign deterministic models to the phenomena.

Every inventory problem involves:

1—a demand for certain articles, which generally is random and a function of time, but which also can be known and determined;

2—the existence of an inventory of these articles to meet the demand, the inventory becoming exhausted and requiring replenishment or replacement. Replenishment may be continuous, periodic, or performed at any given intervals.

3—the costs associated with these operations—investment, depreciation, insurance, sundry risks, warehouse space, etc.—not forgetting the cost assigned more or less arbitrarily to a shortage, which plays an essential role in certain problems: these costs make it possible to develop an economic function to be optimized.

4—the objectives to be achieved, subject to the constraints arising from the very nature of the problem.

All of these factors will be illustrated in the various cases examined below.

3. Graphic representation.

To describe an inventory problem, it is convenient to use the representation shown in Fig. 34.1, where the initial inventory is S_i, the final inventory is S_f, and the interval θ separates the points in time at which we measure S_i and S_f. Usually, demand is randomly distributed, and it is shown on the graph as a step function. It is convenient to replace this pattern with a straight line or a curve that will provide a more workable analytical description of the demand.

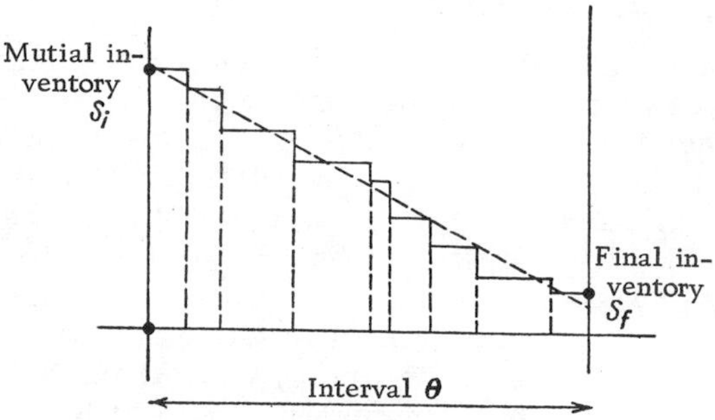

Fig. 34.1

4. Replenishment.

Let us assume that the time interval between the replenishment order and receipt of the new supply is zero. We can then distinguish two principal methods of elementary inventory management. The first, shown in Fig. 34.2, is called the periodic system or Type I management. A period of time, T, is specified at the end of which replenishment is regularly accomplished. This method has a drawback in that there is a risk of running out of stock, which can prove costly; but it also has the advantage of being automatic. The second method, shown in Fig. 34.3, might be called the relaxation system, by analogy with physical phenomena of the same nature. We shall call it Type II management: the quantity replenished is constant, but the intervals, T_1, T_2, T_3, . . . , are not equal. Here there is no risk of running out of stock, and administration of the method is usually less costly; however, this method is less easily systematized than the first.

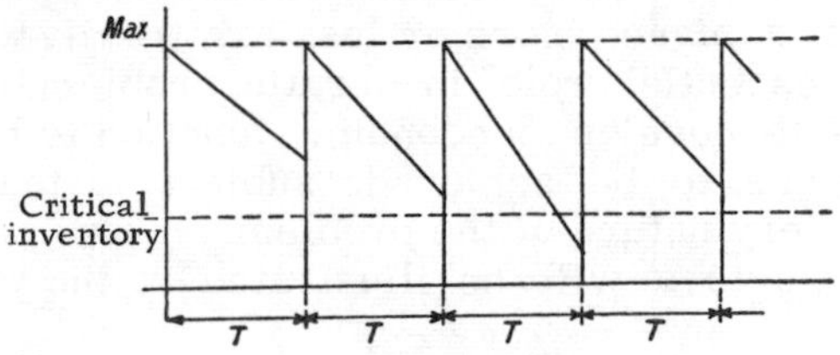

Fig. 34.2

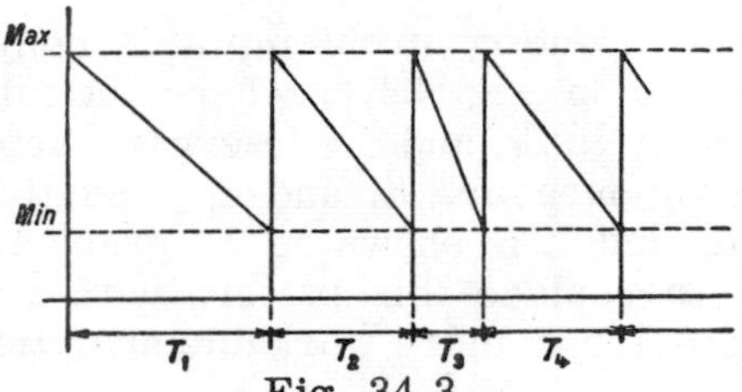

Fig. 34.3

5. Lead-time for replenishment.

Let us assume now that the lead-time for replenishment (the time that elapses between placement of the order and receipt of the stock) is independent of the size of the order; in other words, assume that it is constant, and that its duration is τ. We shall compare what happens under one system with what happens under the other. In the first system (Fig. 34.4), the date on which the order is placed is known, and the quantity to be ordered is found by extrapolating the amount demanded during the preceding interval $T - \tau$; in some cases, τ will be greater than T. In the second system, on the other hand, the quantity to be ordered is constant, but the date on which the order is placed is unknown and must be determined by extrapolation. Sometimes this is not accurate enough (see interval T_3, Fig. 34.5, for example); in some cases $\tau \geq T_i$. Generally, the probability distribution of demand is known. Sometimes, the lead-time is proportional to, or a function of the size of the order, which further complicates the problem of inventory management.

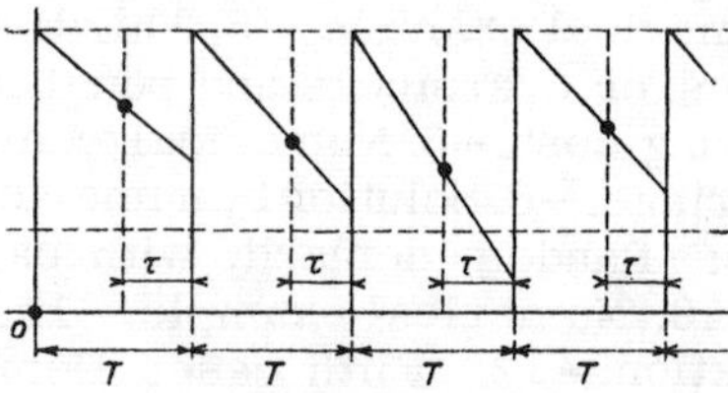

Fig. 34.4

A method very often used for inventory management consists of placing a constant replenishment order the moment the inventory level reaches a critical value, or reorder level.*

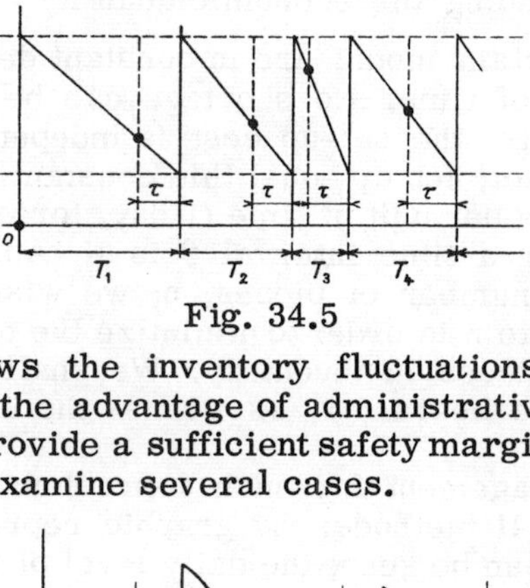

Fig. 34.5

Fig. 34.6 shows the inventory fluctuations for such a case. This method has the advantage of administrative convenience, but does not always provide a sufficient safety margin against shortage.

We shall now examine several cases.

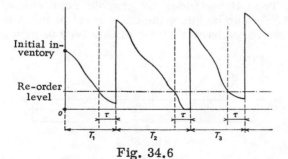

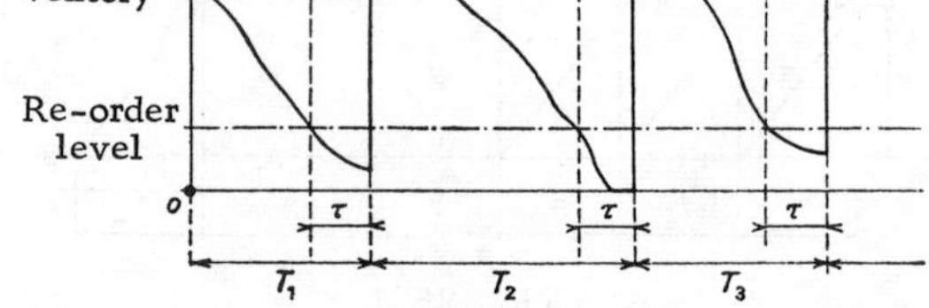

Fig. 34.6

*The English and Americans call this method the "Two-Bin System," or sometimes the "s,S policy," meaning replenishment of a quantity S when the level s is reached.

Section 35

STUDY OF SIMPLE CASES—PROPORTIONAL COSTS

1. First case: Finding an economic quantity'' or ''lot size.''—2. Numerical example.—3. Second case: Finding the ''economic quantity'' while taking the cost of shortage into account.—4. Numerical example.—5. Third case: Random demand with losses on overstocks and penalties for shortage, neglecting carrying cost.—6. Numerical example.—7. Finding the cost of a shortage.—8. Solution by numerical calculation.—9. Fourth case: Random demand, with carrying cost and shortage cost.—10. Numerical example.—11. Solution by numerical calculation.—12. Fifth case: Demand known, with carrying cost proportional to cost of production or purchase price.-13. Numerical example.

We shall begin by examining several cases involving proportional costs.

1. First case: Finding an ''economic quantity'' or ''lot''.

Units of a certain model are in constant demand at a rate of h pieces per unit of time. No shortage can be allowed. The units are stocked in lots; the set-up cost is independent of the number of pieces in the lot; let c_l equal this constant cost. The carrying cost for one piece per unit of time (1 day, for example) is c_s. The total demand over a time interval θ is N. Assuming that all lots contain an equal number of pieces, n, we wish to find what value must be assigned to n in order to minimize the total cost for set-up and carrying N pieces in inventory. We shall also determine the number of lots to be run, r, as well as the inventory replenishment period, T.

Inventory management for such a problem will fall under both Type I and Type II methods; its graphic representation is shown in Fig. 35.1. As can be seen, the daily level of inventory is a saw-tooth function, very characteristic of this type of problem.

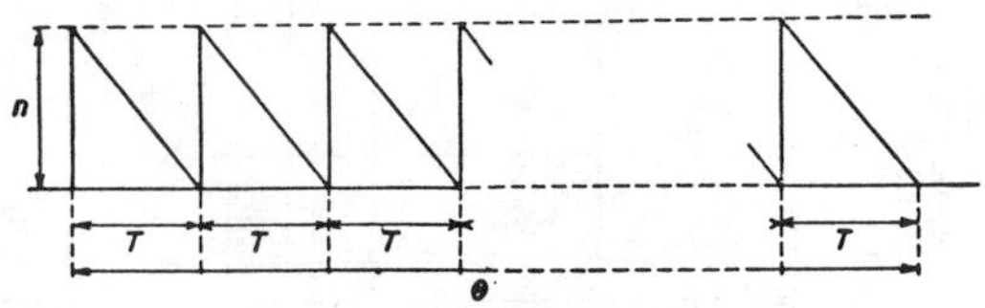

Fig. 35.1

The mean inventory level during a period T is n/2 (see Fig. 35.2). Carrying cost during that interval is $1/2 n c_s T$. Thus the total cost for one lot is:

$$c_l + \tfrac{1}{2} n T c_s . \tag{35.1}$$

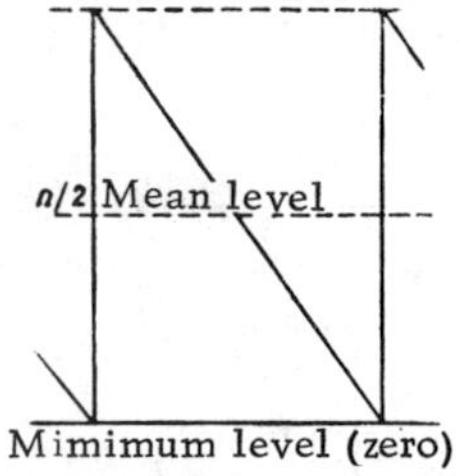

Fig. 35.2

Furthermore, we have:

$$n = h\,T \qquad 35.2$$

and

$$r = \frac{N}{n} = \frac{\theta}{T}. \qquad 35.3$$

The total cost for the time interval θ is;

$$\begin{aligned} \Gamma &= \left(c_l + \frac{nT}{2}\,c_s\right) r \\ &= \left(c_l + \frac{nT}{2}\,c_s\right) \frac{N}{n} \\ &= \frac{Nc_l}{n} + \frac{NT}{2}\,c_s \\ &= \frac{Nc_l}{n} + \frac{\theta c_s}{2}\,n. \end{aligned} \qquad 35.4$$

Thus we have been able to express Γ as a function of the variable quantity n; the other dimensions, N, θ, c_l and c_s, are known.

$$\Gamma(n) = \frac{Nc_l}{n} + \frac{\theta c_s}{2}\,n. \qquad 35.5$$

If we call $\Gamma_l = \frac{Nc_l}{n}$ the total set-up cost, 35.6

and

$\Gamma_s = \frac{1}{2}\,\theta\, c_s n$ the total carrying cost, 35.7

we see that Γ_l is inversely proportional to n, whereas Γ_s is proportional to n.

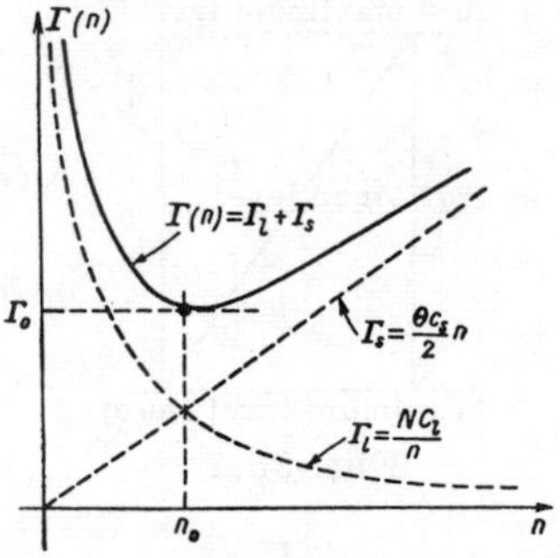

Fig. 35.3

If we plot the variations of Γ_l and Γ_s on a graph (Fig. 35.3), we see that the sum $\Gamma(n) = \Gamma_l + \Gamma_s$ must have a minimum value for a certain value of n.

Now, we know that the minimum of the sum of two variables whose product is constant occurs when these variables are equal; this is the case here:

$$\Gamma_l \,.\, \Gamma_s = \tfrac{1}{2} N \theta c_l c_s = C^{te}. \tag{35.8}$$

Thus, the minimum of $\Gamma_l + \Gamma_s$ occurs for

$$\Gamma_l = \Gamma_s, \tag{35.9}$$

or again:

$$\frac{Nc_l}{n} = \frac{\theta c_s}{2} n; \tag{35.9a}$$

thus

$$n = n_o = \sqrt{2 \frac{N}{\theta} \frac{c_l}{c_s}}; \tag{35.10}$$

this is the "economic quantity" we were to find.

A first conclusion can already be drawn: "the minimum of the economic function for inventory management occurs when the total set-up cost is equal to the total carrying cost."

Substituting (35.10) into (35.3), we obtain:

$$T = T_o = \sqrt{2 \frac{\theta}{N} \frac{c_l}{c_s}} = \frac{\theta}{N} n_o \tag{35.11}$$

and

$$\Gamma_o = \Gamma(n_o) = \sqrt{2 N \theta c_l c_s}\,. \tag{35.12}$$

Fig. 35.4 presents a graphic representation of the function $\Gamma(n)$. This curve is very important: it shows the sensitivity of the variation of n and $\Gamma(n)$ in the neighborhood of n_0. It is evident that if c_s is large, a variation of n in the region near n_0 will produce important variations in the total cost.

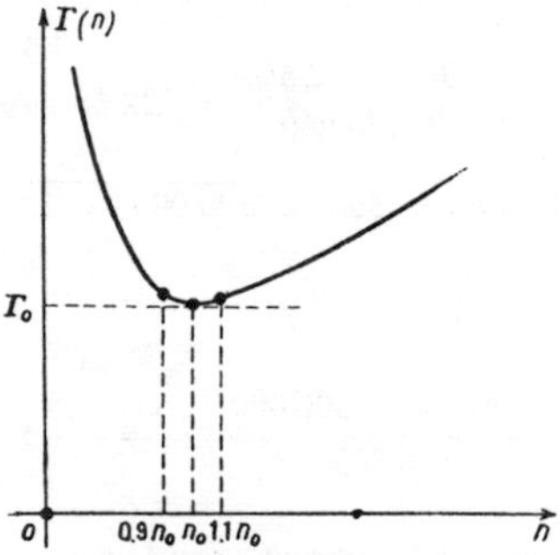

Fig. 35.4

It is helpful to adopt a standard of sensitivity, i.e., a way of recognizing whether or not the choice of a value close to n_0 will involve a large change in $\Gamma(n)$. For this standard, we can average the variation of $\Gamma(n)$ when determined for n_0 - 10% n_0 and for n_0 + 10% n_0, or;*

$$\delta\Gamma = \tfrac{1}{2}\,[\Gamma(0.9\,n_0) + \Gamma(1.1\,n_0) - 2\,\Gamma(n_0)] \qquad 35.13$$

or again:

$$\frac{\delta\Gamma}{\Gamma_0} = \frac{1}{2}\left(\frac{\Gamma(0.9\,n_0) + \Gamma(1.1\,n_0)}{\Gamma_0}\right) - 1\,. \qquad 35.14$$

2. Numerical example.

A manufacturer of automobile accessories receives an order for 120,000 dashboards to be delivered within a year. At what rate should he replenish his inventory if he cannot allow any delay in

---

*We have avoided introducing the concept of derivatives and of differential equations; the variation in the neighborhood of the minimum will be given by the differential

$$d\Gamma = \Gamma' dn = (\tfrac{1}{2}\theta c_s - \frac{N c_l}{n^2})\,dn\,.$$

This shows that sensitivity increases linearly with c_s, and diminishes linearly with c_l.

his deliveries? The automobile manufacturer's demand is constant; the costs are:

$c_s = 3.50$ francs per unit per day, $c_l = 300{,}000$ francs.

This gives us:

$$n_0 = \sqrt{2\,\frac{120{,}000 \times 300{,}000}{360 \times 3.5}} = 7{,}559\,, \qquad 35.15$$

$$T_0 = \frac{360 \times 7{,}559}{120{,}000} = 22.68 \text{ days} \qquad 35.16$$

$$\Gamma_0 = \sqrt{2 \times 120{,}000 \times 360 \times 300{,}000 \times 3.5} = 9{,}525{,}000 \text{ F} \qquad 35.17$$

Let us examine the sensitivity:

$$\Gamma(7559 - 756) = \frac{120{,}000 \times 300{,}000}{6{,}803} + \frac{360 \times 3.5}{2} \times 6803 = 9{,}578{,}000 \text{ F} \qquad 35.18$$

$$\Gamma(7559 + 756) = \frac{120{,}000 \times 300{,}000}{8{,}315} + \frac{360 \times 3.5}{2} \times 8{,}315 = 9{,}568{,}000 \text{ F} \qquad 35.19$$

The relative variation is then:

$$\frac{\delta\Gamma}{\Gamma_0} = \tfrac{1}{2}\left(\frac{9{,}578{,}000 + 9{,}568{,}000}{9{,}525{,}000}\right) - 1 = 0.005 \text{ (approx.)} \qquad 35.20$$

Here we see that a variation of 10% in the value of n_0 causes a variation of about 5% in the total cost; hence the sensitivity is not very great.

3. Second case: Finding the "economic quantity" while taking the cost of shortage into account.

If, in the preceding case, we allow a shortage and arbitrarily assign to it a cost c_p per unit of time, the mathematical model of inventory management will be modified, and its graphic representation will take the form shown in Fig. 35.5.

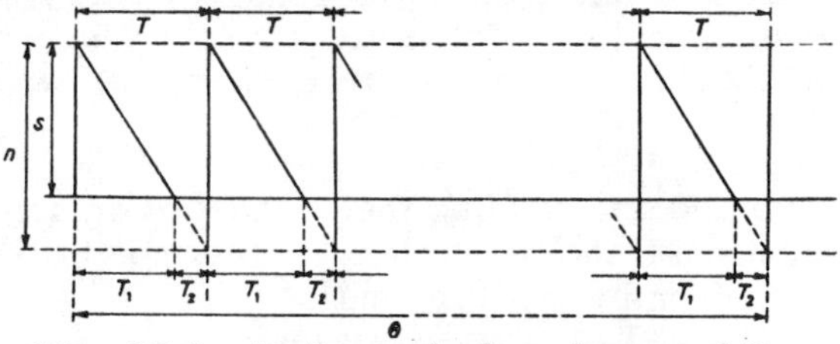

Fig. 35.5. At the end of each period T, we begin a new lot n, for the purpose of, on the one hand, supplying the demand $s' = n - s$ which could not be met during T_2, and, on the other hand, building up the inventory, s.

During an interval T_1 in each period T, the daily inventory level is adequate to meet the demand; then, during an interval T_2, there is a shortage, and the backlog is delivered as soon as the next lot goes into inventory.

Let s be the maximum stock level. It is easy to derive the following relations from Fig. 35.5:

$$\frac{T_1}{T} = \frac{s}{n}, \qquad \frac{T_2}{T} = \frac{n-s}{n}; \tag{35.21, 35.22}$$

or again

$$T_1 = \frac{s}{n}\,T, \qquad T_2 = \frac{n-s}{n}\,T. \tag{35.23, 35.24}$$

Thus we have:

—carrying cost for one lot: $\frac{1}{2}\, s\, T_1\, c_s$, 35.25

—set-up cost of a lot: c_l, 35.26

—cost of shortage for one lot: $\frac{1}{2}\,(n-s)\, T_2\, c_p$, 35.27

The total cost will be:

$$\Gamma(n, s) = [\tfrac{1}{2}\, s\, T_1\, c_s + c_l + \tfrac{1}{2}\,(n-s)\, T_2\, c_p]\, r\,; \tag{35.28}$$

where r is the number of lots:

$$r = \frac{N}{n} = \frac{\theta}{T}. \tag{35.29}$$

The symbol Γ (n,s) indicates that the total cost depends on both n and s.

Substituting relations (35.21) and (35.22) into (35.28), we obtain:

$$\Gamma(n, s) = \frac{s^2 \theta c_s}{2n} + \frac{N}{n}\, c_l + \frac{(n-s)^2 \theta}{2n}\, c_p\,. \tag{35.30}$$

The minimum of this function of two variables, n and s, occurs for:*

---

*To calculate this minimum, we take the partial derivatives and equate them to zero.

$$\frac{\partial \Gamma}{\partial n} = -\frac{s^2 \theta c_s}{2n^2} - \frac{N}{n^2}\, c_l + \left(1 - \frac{s^2}{n^2}\right) \frac{\theta}{2}\, c_p = 0,$$

$$\frac{\partial \Gamma}{\partial s} = \frac{s\theta}{n}\, c_s - \frac{(n-s)}{n}\, \theta\, c_p = 0.$$

$$n = n_0 = \sqrt{2\frac{N}{\theta}\frac{c_l}{c_s}\sqrt{\frac{c_s + c_p}{c_p}}}, \tag{35.31}$$

$$s = s_0 = \sqrt{2\frac{N}{\theta}\frac{c_l}{c_s}\sqrt{\frac{c_p}{c_s + c_p}}} = n_0\frac{c_p}{c_s + c_p}. \tag{35.32}$$

The quantity

$$\varrho = \frac{c_p}{c_s + c_p}, \tag{35.33}$$

is called the shortage rate or scarcity rate. This quantity plays an essential role in inventory problems when shortages or out-of-stock conditions are allowed. In this problem, we see that the quantities n_0 and s_0 must be chosen so that:

$$\frac{s_0}{n_0} = \varrho.* \tag{35.34}$$

---

*Simplifying, we obtain:

$$s = n\frac{c_p}{c_p + c_s} \quad \text{et} \quad n^2 c_p - (c_s + c_p)s^2 = \frac{2 c_l N}{\theta}$$

from which (35.31) and (35.32) follow. By calculating the second partial derivatives we prove that the conditions

$$\left(\frac{\partial^2 r}{\partial n \partial s}\right)^2 - \frac{\partial^2 r}{\partial n^2}\frac{\partial^2 r}{\partial s^2} < 0, \quad \frac{\partial^2 r}{\partial n^2} > 0, \quad \frac{\partial^2 r}{\partial s^2} > 0$$

are satisfied for $n = n_0$ and $s = s_0$, which shows that we definitely have obtained a minimum.

*This is equivalent to writing, according to (35.23):

$$\frac{T_1}{T} = \frac{s_0}{n_0} = \varrho \quad \text{or:} \quad \frac{T_2}{T} = 1 - \varrho.$$

To say that we accept a shortage rate equal to ρ is to say that we allow shortages to occur $1 - \rho$ times (in percentage) during interval T. In terms of probabilities, we are saying that the probability of a shôrtage is equal to $1 - \rho$, or:

$$1 - \varrho = \frac{c_0}{c_0 + c_p}, \text{ or again: } c_p = \frac{1-\alpha}{\alpha} c_s$$

which gives us a subjective estimate of c_p starting with $\alpha = 1 - \rho$, the probability of a shortage.

We may note that the shortage rate, ρ, is always between 0 and 1. We can readily see that ρ is very small if $c_p \ll c_s$ and that ρ tends toward 1 when $c_p \gg c_s$. To assume an infinitely large c_p amounts to disallowing any possibility of a shortage.

From expressions (35.31) and (35.32), we obtain:

$$T_0 = \sqrt{2 \frac{\theta}{N} \frac{c_l}{c_s}} \sqrt{\frac{c_s + c_p}{c_p}}, \qquad 35.35$$

$$\Gamma_0 = \sqrt{2 N \theta c_s c_l} \sqrt{\frac{c_p}{c_s + c_p}}. \qquad 35.36$$

From these we find:

$$n_0 = \frac{(n_0 \text{ with } \varrho = 1)}{\sqrt{\varrho}}, \quad s_0 = (n_0 \text{ with } \varrho = 1).\sqrt{\varrho}, \qquad \begin{cases} 35.37 \\ 35.38 \end{cases}$$

$$T_0 = \frac{(T_0 \text{ with } \varrho = 1)}{\sqrt{\varrho}}, \quad \Gamma_0 = (\Gamma_0 \text{ with } \varrho = 1).\sqrt{\varrho}. \qquad \begin{cases} 35.39 \\ 35.40 \end{cases}$$

This shows that if we allow a rate $\rho < 1$, n_0 and T_0 will increase and s_0 and Γ_0 decrease; for a given value of ρ, the economic quantities n_0 and s_0 will be chosen so as to respect the ratio of (35.34).

4. Numerical example.

In the preceding example, let us assume that the shortage cost is:

$$c_p = 10\, c_s = 35 \text{ fr. per unit per day.} \qquad 35.41$$

In this case:

$$\varrho = \frac{10 c_s}{c_s + 10 c_s} = \frac{10}{11} = 0.909, \qquad 35.42$$

$$\sqrt{\varrho} = 0.953. \qquad 35.43$$

The economic quantities, then, are:

$$n_0 = \frac{7{,}560}{0.953} = 7{,}930, \quad s_0 = 7{,}930 \times 0.909 = 7{,}210. \qquad \begin{cases} 35.44 \\ 35.45 \end{cases}$$

$$T_0 = \frac{22.7}{0.953} = 24 \text{ days}, \qquad 35.46$$

$$\Gamma_0 = 9{,}525{,}000 \times 0.953 = 9{,}077{,}000 \text{ fr.} \qquad 35.47$$

5. Third case: Random demand with losses on overstocks and penalties for shortage, neglecting carrying cost.

We shall assume now that the demand r for a time interval T is random, and that we know the distribution p(r) of the probability of a demand equal to r. If r is less than the inventory, s, the left-over pieces will be sold at a unit loss of c_1; if r is greater than s, there will have to be a special order for the backlog pieces, and the extra cost will represent a unit loss of c_2. If the carrying cost is negligible by comparison with c_1 or c_2, the interval T no longer has any effect, and we can then say that the management policy is independent of time.

Such a case arises, for example, when spare parts are manufactured at the same time as finished assemblies. If too many spare parts are produced, the excess must be sold at a considerable loss. If too few are produced, the lacking parts will have to be ordered at a higher unit cost (spare parts for aircraft typically fall under this case).

Let us call s the number of pieces to be placed in stock. Two mutually exclusive situations are possible:

(1): $r \leq s$: the stock will cover the demand, and a quantity equal to s - r will have to be sold at a unit loss of c_1;

(2): $r > s$: there is a shortage, and r - s pieces must be specially ordered or specially made, at a unit loss of c_2.

The demand r is unknown, but, since we know the distribution p(r), we can evaluate the mathematical expectation of the expenditures:*

$$\Gamma(s) = c_1 \sum_{r=0}^{s} (s - r)\, p(r) + c_2 \sum_{r=s+1}^{\infty} (r - s)\, p(r). \qquad 35.48$$

We can make this formula less abstract for readers not very familiar with mathematical symbols; for example, if s = 5, we obtain:

$$\begin{aligned}\Gamma(5) = c_1 [5\,p(0) + 4\,p(1) + 3\,p(2) + 2\,p(3) + p(4)] \\ + c_2 [p(6) + 2\,p(7) + 3\,p(8) + 4\,p(9) + \dots].\end{aligned} \qquad 35.49$$

It can be shown** that the minimum of $\Gamma(s)$ occurs for a value of s_0 such that:

$$p(r \leqslant s_0 - 1) < \varrho < p(r \leqslant s_0), \qquad 35.50$$

where

$$\varrho = \frac{c_2}{c_1 + c_2}, \qquad 35.50a$$

$$p(r \leqslant s_0) = p(0) + p(1) + p(2) + \dots + p(s_0). \qquad 35.51$$

---

*We have deliberately assumed that the economic function in this problem was just this mathematical expectation.

**See Part Two, Section 83.

The comparison between ρ and the cumulative distribution $p(r \leq s)$ immediately gives us s_0, and hence $\Gamma(s_0) = \Gamma_{min}$.

We observe that if s_0 is such that:

$$p(r \leqslant s_0 - 1) < \varrho = p(r \leqslant s_0)\,; \tag{35.52}$$

this means that:

$$\Gamma(s_0 + 1) = \Gamma(s_0)\,; \tag{35.53}$$

and then the optimum will correspond to either s_0 or $s_0 + 1$. The same holds true if:

$$p(r \leqslant s_0 - 1) = \varrho < p(r \leqslant s_0)\,; \tag{35.54}$$

that means that:

$$\Gamma(s_0 - 1) = \Gamma(s_0)\,; \tag{35.55}$$

therefore the optimum corresponds to s_0 - or s_0.

6. Numerical example

$$c_1 = 50 \text{ fr}, \tag{35.56}$$

$$c_2 = 20\,c_1 = 1{,}000 \text{ fr}, \tag{35.57}$$

$$\varrho = \frac{1000}{50 + 1000} = 0.952\,; \tag{35.57a}$$

The distribution is given in Table 35.1.

Table 35.1

s	r	p(r)	$p(r \leq s)$
0	0	0.900	0.900
1	1	0.050	0.950
2	2	0.020	0.970
3	3	0.010	0.980
4	4	0.010	0.990
5	5	0.010	1
6 or more	6	0	1

Thus:

$$p(r \leqslant 1) < 0.952 < p(r \leqslant 2), \tag{35.58}$$

i.e.:

$$0{,}950 < 0.952 < 0.970. \tag{35.59}$$

Thus the optimum occurs for s = 2, for which the corresponding value is:

$$\begin{aligned} \Gamma(2) &= c_1 \sum_{r=0}^{2}(2 - r)\, p(r) + c_2 \sum_{r=3}^{\infty}(r - 2)\, p(r) \\ &= 50\,[(2)\,(0.900) + (1)\,(0.050)] \\ &\qquad + 1{,}000[(1)\,(0.010) + (2)\,(0.010) + (3)\,(0.010)] \\ &= 152.5 \text{ fr}. \end{aligned} \tag{35.60}$$

7. Finding the cost of a shortage.

If we wish to determine what value must be assigned to shortages in order that the optimum inventory will be s_0, we shall once again use condition (35.50). Let us take the preceding numerical example and try to find the unit cost c_2 such that s_0 will equal 3:

$$p(r \leqslant s_0 - 1) < \frac{c_2}{c_1 + c_2} < p(r \leqslant s_0), \tag{35.61}$$

let

$$p(r \leqslant 2) < \frac{c_2}{50 + c_2} < p(r \leqslant 3), \tag{35.62}$$

$$0.970 < \frac{c_2}{50 + c_2} < 0.980, \tag{35.63}$$

$$1{,}620 \text{ F} < c_2 < 2{,}450 \text{ fr}. \tag{35.64}$$

8. Solution by numerical calculation.

Referring again to the mathematical expectation of the cost (35.48):

$$\Gamma(s) = c_1 \sum_{r=o}^{s} (s - r)\, p(r) + c_2 \sum_{r=s+1}^{\infty} (r - s)\, p(r), \tag{35.65}$$

let us evaluate $\Gamma(s)$ for s = 0, 1, 2, 3, 4, 5, 6, . . . , with $c_1 = 50$ and $c_2 = 1{,}000$.

$$\begin{aligned} \Gamma(0) &= 1000\,[(1)\,(0.050) + (2)\,(0.020) + (3)\,(0.010) + (4)\,(0.010) + \\ &\qquad + (5)\,(0.010)] \\ &= 210 \text{ fr}, \end{aligned}$$

$$\begin{aligned} \Gamma(1) &= 50 \times (1)\,(0.900) + 1000\,[(1)\,(0.020) + (2)\,(0.010) + (3)\,(0.010) \\ &\qquad + (4)\,(0.010)] \\ &= 155 \text{ fr}, \end{aligned}$$

$$\Gamma(2) = 50\,[(2)\,(0.900) + (1)\,(0.050)] + 1000\,[(1)\,(0.010) + (2)\,(0.010) + (3)\,(0.010)] = \boxed{152.50\ \text{fr}},$$

$$\Gamma(3) = 50\,[(3)\,(0.900) + (2)\,(0.050) + (1)\,(0.020)] + 1000\,[(1)\,(0.010) + (2)\,(0.010)] = 171\ \text{fr},$$

$$\Gamma(4) = 50\,[(4)\,(0{,}900) + (3)\,(0{,}050) + (2)\,(0{,}020) + (1)\,(0.010)] + 1000\,[(1)\,(0.010)] = 200\ \text{fr},$$

$$\Gamma(5) = 50\,[(5)\,(0.900) + (4)\,(0.050) + (3)\,(0.020) + (2)\,(0.010) + (1)\,(0.010)] = 239.50\ \text{fr}.$$

35.66

This result corresponds to a shortage cost $c_2 = 1000$; we may calculate $\Gamma(s)$ for $c_2 = 500$, $c_2 = 750$, $c_2 = 1000$, $c_2 = 1250$, $c_2 = 1500$, $c_2 = 1750$, $c_2 = 2000$;

For example, for $c_2 = 500$ fr:

$$\Gamma(0) = 500\,[(1)\,(0.050) + (2)\,(0.020) + (3)\,(0.010) + (4)\,(0.010) + (5)\,(0.010)] = 105\ \text{fr},$$

$$\Gamma(1) = 50 \times (1)\,(0.900) + 500\,[(1)\,(0.020) + (2)\,(0.010) + (3)\,(0.010) + (4)\,(0.010)] = \boxed{100\ \text{fr}},$$

$\Gamma(2) = 122.50$ fr, $\Gamma(3) = 156$ fr,
$\Gamma(4) = 195$ fr, $\Gamma(5) = 239.50$ fr.

35.67

For $c_2 = 750$ fr:

$\Gamma(0) = 157.50$ fr, $\Gamma(1) = \boxed{127.50\ \text{fr}}$, $\Gamma(2) = 137.50$ fr
$\Gamma(3) = 163.50$ fr, $\Gamma(4) = 197.50$ fr, $\Gamma(5) = 239.50$ fr 35.68

For $c_2 = 1000$ fr:

$\Gamma(0) = 210$ fr, $\Gamma(1) = 155$ fr, $\Gamma(2) = \boxed{152.50\ \text{fr}}$,
$\Gamma(3) = 171$ fr, $\Gamma(4) = 200$ fr, $\Gamma(5) = 239.50$ fr 35.69

For $c_2 = 1250$ fr:

$\Gamma(0) = 262.50$ fr, $\Gamma(1) = 182.50$ fr, $\Gamma(2) = \boxed{167.50\ \text{fr}}$.
$\Gamma(3) = 178.50$ fr, $\Gamma(4) = 202.50$ fr, $\Gamma(5) = 239.50$ fr 35.70

For $c_2 = 1500$ fr:

$\Gamma(0) = 315$ fr, $\Gamma(1) = 210$ fr, $\Gamma(2) = \boxed{182.50\ \text{fr}}$.
$\Gamma(3) = 186$ fr, $\Gamma(4) = 205$ fr, $\Gamma(5) = 239.50$ fr, 35.71

For c_2 = 1750 fr:

$$\Gamma(0) = 367.50 \text{ fr}, \quad \Gamma(1) = 237.50 \text{ fr}, \quad \Gamma(2) = 197.50 \text{ fr},$$
$$\Gamma(3) = \boxed{193.50 \text{ fr}}, \quad \Gamma(4) = 207.50 \text{ fr}, \quad \Gamma(5) = 239.50 \text{ fr}. \qquad 35.72$$

For c_2 = 2000 fr:

$$\Gamma(0) = 420 \text{ fr}, \quad \Gamma(1) = 265 \text{ fr}, \quad \Gamma(2) = 212.50 \text{ fr},$$
$$\Gamma(3) = \boxed{201 \text{ fr}}, \quad \Gamma(4) = 210 \text{ fr}, \quad \Gamma(5) = 239.50 \text{ fr}.$$

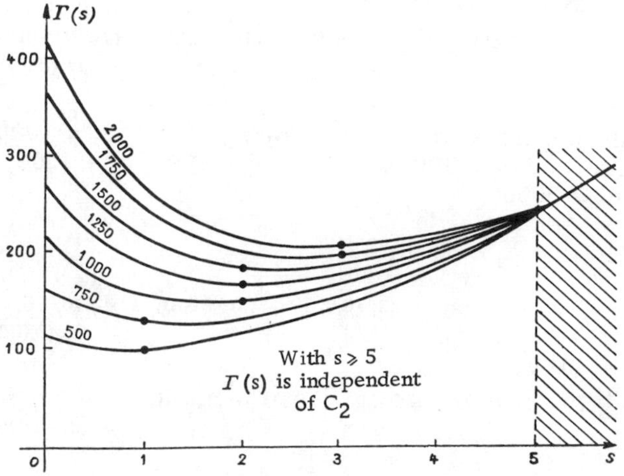

Fig. 35.6

Shown in Fig. 35.6 are the $\Gamma(s)$ values for different c_2 values (we have plotted the curves using the points with abscissae 0, 1, 2, 3, 4, 5); the minima are indicated. Such curves allow us to study the effect of shortages on the optimal inventory plan.

9. Fourth case—Random demand, with carrying cost and shortage cost.

Assume that demand during a certain time interval T is random, with $p(r)$ being the probability that the total demand is r during the interval T. The demand is discontinuous, but in practice we can assume that its rate is constant (see Fig. 35.7). The pieces do not lose value during the interval T, but the storage cost per unit of time plus the interest on the capital they represent is evaluated as c_s (cost per piece per unit of time). We assume that a shortage (out-of-stock) of one piece causes a loss of c_p per unit of time.

This inventory situation corresponds to Fig. 35.7. If the total demand is less than the inventory ($s \geq r$), the situation is represented by (a). If demand is greater than inventory ($s < r$), the situation is represented by (b).

Such a case is described in the following simple example.

A large factory makes cranes, and has several regional warehouses. Certain spare parts are very costly but must be readily available to customers at the warehouses, because the cranes cannot be kept idle for any appreciable time as the result of repair part shortages. We shall consider one of these parts, and find out how large a stock of this particular part should be kept in inventory at the warehouses to minimize both the carrying costs (including revenue lost on the tied-up capital) and the cost of shortages (loss of a customer, loan of another crane, etc.).

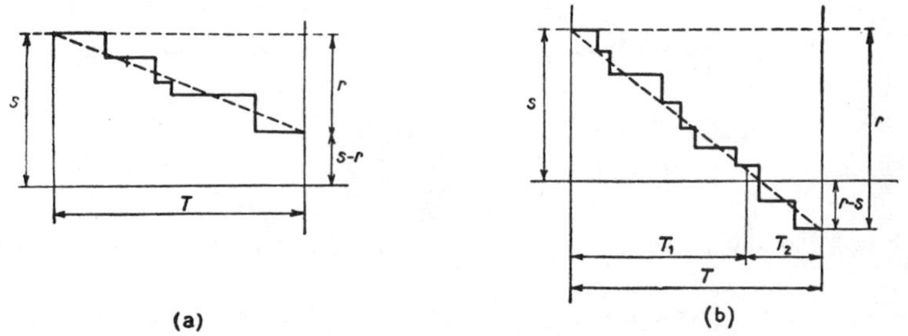

Fig. 35.7

Assuming that the inventory level variation can be represented by a straight line (Fig. 35.7), we have:

1—Average inventory corresponding to situation (a):

$$s_a = \tfrac{1}{2}[s + (s - r)] = s - \tfrac{1}{2}r, \tag{35.73}$$

2—Average inventory corresponding to situation (b):

$$\bar{s}_b = \tfrac{1}{2}s\frac{T_1}{T} = \tfrac{1}{2}\frac{s^2}{r}, \tag{35.74}$$

3—Average shortage in situation (b):

$$\bar{p}_b = \tfrac{1}{2}(r - s)\frac{T_2}{T} = \tfrac{1}{2}\frac{(r - s)^2}{r}. \tag{35.75}$$

The mathematical expectation for the total inventory cost will be:

$$\Gamma(s) = c_s\sum_{r=0}^{s}\left(s - \frac{r}{2}\right)p(r) + c_s\sum_{r=s+1}^{\infty}\tfrac{1}{2}\frac{s^2}{r}p(r) + c_p\sum_{r=s+1}^{\infty}\tfrac{1}{2}\frac{(r - s)^2}{r}p(r). \tag{35.76}$$

Now let us apply this formula to a specific case, assuming that s = 5. We have:

$$\Gamma(5) = c_s \left[5\,p(0) + \frac{9}{2}p(1) + 4\,p(2) + \frac{7}{2}p(3) + 3p(4) + \frac{5}{2}p(5)\right] + c_s\left[\frac{25}{12}\,p(6) + \frac{25}{14}\,p(7) + \frac{25}{16}\,p(8) + \ldots\right] + c_p\left[\frac{1}{12}\,p(6) + \frac{4}{14}\,p(7) + \frac{9}{16}\,p(8) + \ldots\right] \qquad 35.77$$

It can be demonstrated (see Part Two, Section 83) that the minimum of Γs occurs for a value of s_o such that:

$$L(s_o - 1) < \varrho < L(s_o), \quad \text{où} \quad \varrho = \frac{c_p}{c_s + c_p} \qquad 35.78$$

and

$$L(s_o) = p(r \leqslant s_o) + (s_o + \tfrac{1}{2}) \sum_{r=s_o+1}^{\infty} \frac{p(r)}{r}\,. \qquad 35.79$$

The probability $p(r \leq s)$ is, by definition, the cumulative probability:

$$p\,(r \leqslant s) = p\,(0) + p\,(1) + p\,(2) + \ldots + p\,(s)\,. \qquad 35.80$$

We may note that

$$\varrho = L\,(s_o) \qquad 35.81$$

implies that s_o or $s_o + 1$ corresponds to the optimum; while

$$\varrho = L\,(s_o - 1) \qquad 35.82$$

implies that s_o or $s_o - 1$ corresponds to the optimum.

The comparison between ρ and the distribution L(s) immediately gives us s_o, and hence $\Gamma(s_o) = \Gamma_{min}$.

10. Numerical example.

Let c_s = 100,000 francs, and $c_p = 20\,c_s$ = 2,000,000 francs. 35.83

We shall now calculate L(s) for the different values of s.

For s = 3, we have:

$$[L(2) = 0.8625] < \left(\varrho = \frac{20}{21} = 0.9524\right) < [L(3) = 0.9575]\,. \qquad 35.84$$

The optimum inventory level is therefore equal to 3.

The corresponding cost is equal to:

$$\begin{aligned}\Gamma(3) &= 0.1\ [(3)\ (0.1) + (2.5)\ (0.2) + (2)\ (0.2) + (1.5)\ (0.3)] \\ &\quad + 0.1\ [(1.125)\ (0.1) + (0.9)\ (0.1)] + 2[(0.125)\ (0.1) + (0.4)\ (0.1)] \\ &= 0.29 \text{ million.}\end{aligned} \qquad 35.85$$

Table 35.2

s	r	$p(r)$	$\frac{p(r)}{r}$	$\sum_{r=s+1}^{\infty} \frac{p(r)}{r}$	$(s+\frac{1}{2}) \sum_{r=s+1}^{\infty} \frac{p(r)}{r}$	$p(r \leqslant s)$	$L(s) = p(r \leqslant s) + (s+\frac{1}{2}) \sum_{r=s+1}^{\infty} \frac{p(r)}{r}$.
0	0	0.1	∞	0.445	0.2225	0.1	0.3225
1	1	0.2	0.200	0.245	0.3675	0.3	0.6675
2	2	0.2	0.100	0.145	0.3625	0.5	0.8625
3	3	0.3	0.100	0.045	0.1575	0.8	0.9575
4	4	0.1	0.025	0.020	0.0900	0.9	0.9900
5	5	0.1	0.020	0.000	0.0000	1	1
>5	>5	0	0.000	0.000	0.0000	1	1

11. Solution by numerical calculation.

We shall calculate the general expression of the cost $\Gamma(s)$ for $s = 0, 1, 2, 3, 4, 5, 6, \ldots$

$$\Gamma(0) = c_p \sum_{r=1}^{\infty} \tfrac{1}{2}\, r\, p(r)$$
$$= 2\,[(0.5)\,(0.2) + (1)\,(0.2) + (1.5)\,(0.3) + (2)\,(0.1) + (2.5)\,(0.1)]$$
$$= 2{,}4 \text{ million fr.}$$

$$\Gamma(1) = c_s \sum_{r=0}^{1}\left(1 - \frac{r}{2}\right)p(r) + c_s \sum_{r=2}^{\infty} \frac{1}{2}\frac{1}{r}\,p(r) + c_p \sum_{r=2}^{\infty} \frac{1}{2}\frac{(r-1)^2}{r}\,p(r)$$
$$= 0.1\,[(1)\,(0.1) + (0.5)\,(0.2)]$$
$$+ 0.1\,[(0.25)\,(0.2) + (0.166)\,(0.3) + (0.125)\,(0.1) + (0.1)\,(0.1)]$$
$$+ 2\,[(0.25)\,(0.2) + (0.666)\,(0.3) + (1.125)\,(0.1) + (1.6)\,(0.1)]$$
$$= 1.07 \text{ million fr.}$$

$$\Gamma(2) = c_s \sum_{r=0}^{2}\left(2 - \frac{r}{2}\right) p(r) + c_s \sum_{r=3}^{\infty} \frac{1}{2}\frac{4}{r}\, p(r) + c_p \sum_{r=3}^{\infty} \frac{1}{2}\frac{(r-2)^2}{r}\, p(r)$$
$$= 0.1\,[(2)\,(0.1) + (1.5)\,(0.2) + (1)\,(0.2)]$$
$$+ 0.1\,[(0.666)\,(0.3) + (0.5)\,(0.1) + (0.4)\,(0.1)]$$
$$+ 2\,[(0.166)\,(0.3) + (0.5)\,(0.1) + (0.9)\,(0.1)]$$
$$= 0.48 \text{ million fr.}$$

$$\Gamma(3) = c_s \sum_{r=0}^{3}\left(3-\frac{r}{2}\right)p(r) + c_s \sum_{r=4}^{\infty}\frac{1}{2}\frac{9}{r}p(r) + c_p \sum_{r=4}^{\infty}\frac{1}{2}\frac{(r-3)^2}{r}p(r)$$

$$= 0.1\,[(3)(0.1) + (2.5)(0.2) + (2)(0.2) + (1.5)(0.3)]$$

$$+ 0.1\,[(1.125)(0.1) + (0.9)(0.1)]$$

$$+ 2\,[(0.125)(0.1) + (0.4)(0.1)]$$

$$= \boxed{0.29 \text{ million fr.}}$$

$$\Gamma(4) = c_s \sum_{r=0}^{4}\left(4-\frac{r}{2}\right)p(r) + c_s \sum_{r=5}^{\infty}\frac{1}{2}\frac{16}{r}p(r) + c_p \sum_{r=5}^{\infty}\frac{1}{2}\frac{(r-4)^2}{r}p(r) \quad 35.86$$

$$= 0.1\,[(4)(0.1) + (3.5)(0.2) + (3)(0.2) + (2.5)(0.3) + (2)(0.1)]$$

$$+ 0.1\,[(1.6)(0.1)] + 2\,[(0.1)(0.1)]$$

$$= 0.30 \text{ million fr.}$$

$$\Gamma(5) = c_s \sum_{r=0}^{5}\left(5-\frac{r}{2}\right)p(r) + c_s \sum_{r=6}^{\infty}\frac{1}{2}\frac{25}{r}p(r) + c_p \sum_{r=6}^{\infty}\frac{(r-5)^2}{2r}p(r)$$

$$= 0.1\,[(5)(0.1) + (4.5)(0.2) + (4)(0.2) + (3.5)(0.3) + (3)(0.1) + (2.5)(0.1)]$$

$$= 0.38 \text{ million fr.}$$

We find, of course, that the optimum occurs for s = 3. Fig. 35.8 is a graph of the variation in the cost $\Gamma(s)$.

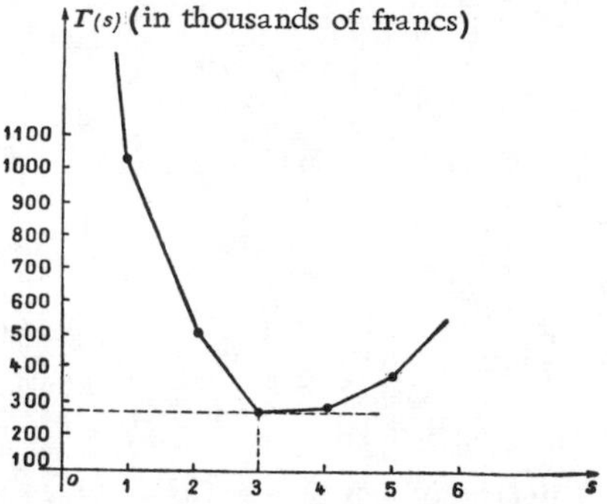

Fig. 35.8

12. Fifth case: Demand known, with carrying cost proportional to cost of production or purchase price.

We shall now place ourselves in a situation similar to that of our first case ("Finding an economic quantity or lot size"), but this time we introduce the cost price or the selling price of the parts, this cost being proportional to the cost price of a lot.

The inventory level will be represented by Fig. 35.1. Let:

N = number of parts for period θ;

n = number of parts in a lot sufficient for an interval T;

c_a = selling price or cost price of a part (not including the fixed cost of a lot);
c_b = fixed cost of a lot;
α = coefficient of proportionality between the carrying cost per part per unit of time and the value $c_a + c_b/n$;
r = number of lots produced during period θ.
The total cost is then:

$$\begin{aligned}\Gamma(n) &= [nc_a + c_b + \tfrac{1}{2}\,\alpha T\,(nc_a + c_b)]\,r \\ &= [nc_a + \tfrac{1}{2}\,(\alpha T)\,nc_a + c_b + \tfrac{1}{2}\,\alpha T\,c_b]\,r.\end{aligned} \qquad 35.87$$

But:

$$\frac{T}{\theta} = \frac{n}{N} \qquad 35.88$$

and

$$r = \frac{N}{n}; \qquad 35.88a$$

therefore:

$$\Gamma(n) = \underbrace{Nc_a + \frac{\alpha}{2}\,\theta c_b}_{\text{quantity independent of n}} + n\,\frac{\alpha\theta}{2}\,c_a + \frac{Nc_b}{n}. \qquad 35.89$$

The minimum of $\Gamma(n)$ corresponds to the minimum of

$$n\,\frac{\alpha\theta}{2}\,c_a + \frac{Nc_b}{n},$$

which occurs when:

$$n\,\frac{\alpha\theta}{2}\,c_a = \frac{Nc_b}{n}. \qquad 35.90$$

i.e.,

$$n = n_0 = \sqrt{\frac{2N}{\alpha\theta}\,\frac{c_b}{c_a}}, \qquad 35.91$$

$$T_0 = \sqrt{2\,\frac{\theta}{N\alpha}\,\frac{c_b}{c_a}}, \qquad 35.92$$

and

$$\Gamma_0 = \sqrt{2N\theta\alpha c_a c_b} + Nc_a + \tfrac{1}{2}\,\theta\alpha c_b. \qquad 35.93$$

13. Numerical example.

$c_a = 1{,}000$ fr, $c_b = 50{,}000$ fr, $N = 75{,}000$, $\theta = 360$ days, $\alpha = 0.3 \cdot 10^{-3}$. 35.94

Then:

$$n_0 = \sqrt{\frac{2 \times 75{,}000 \times 50{,}000}{360 \times 1{,}000 \times 0.3{\cdot}10^{-3}}} = 8{,}333, \qquad 35.95$$

$$T_0 = \frac{360 \times 8{,}333}{75{,}000} = 40 \text{ days},$$ 35.96

$$\Gamma_0 = \sqrt{2 \times 75{,}000 \times 360 \times 0.3 \times 10^{-3} \times 1{,}000 \times 50{,}000} + 75{,}000 \times 1{,}000 + \tfrac{1}{2} \times 360 \times 0.3\ 10^{-3} \times 50{,}000$$ 35.97

$$= 75{,}903{,}000 \text{ fr.}$$

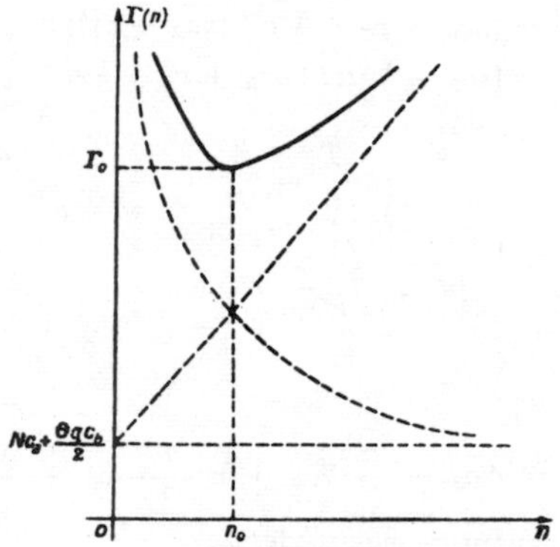

Fig. 35.9

The curve representing $\Gamma(n)$ is the same as that in Fig. 35.3, but it is shifted by a quantity equal to $Nc_a + 1/2\,(\theta\,\alpha)\,c_b$ (Fig. 35.9). (See Part Two, Section 83.)

Section 36

CALCULATING DEMAND PROBABILITIES

1. General explanation.—2. Example.—3. Calculating the $p_1(r)$ distribution when $p_2(r)$ is known.

1. General explanation.

Suppose that statistical measurements have given us the distribution of probabilities $p_1(r)$ for demand r during an interval T; it is useful to be able to develop the probability distribution $p_2(r)$ for the interval 2T then $p_3(r)$ for the interval 3T, or $p_n(r)$ for the interval nT.

We can begin by showing how to calculate $p_2(r)$ from $p_1(r)$, and from this proceed to $p_n(r)$.

By virtue of the principles of compound probabilities and of total probabilities (see Part Two, Section 53), we have:

$$p_2(0) = p_1(0) \,.\, p_1(0) = p^2(0)$$

$$p_2(1) = p_1(0) \,.\, p_1(1) + p_1(1) \,.\, p_1(0) = 2\, p_1(0) \,.\, p_1(1)$$

$$\begin{aligned} p_2(2) &= p_1(0) \,.\, p_1(2) + p_1(1) \,.\, p_1(1) + p_1(2) \,.\, p_1(0) \\ &= 2p_1(0) \,.\, p_1(2) + p_1^2(1) \end{aligned}$$

$$\begin{aligned} p_2(3) &= p_1(0) \,.\, p_1(3) + p_1(1) \,.\, p_1(2) + p_1(2) \,.\, p_1(1) + p_1(3) \,.\, p_1(0) \\ &= 2\, p_1(0)\, p_1(3) + 2\, p_1(1)\, p_1(2) \end{aligned} \qquad 36.1$$

$$\begin{aligned} p_2(4) &= p_1(0)\, p_1(4) + p_1(1)\, p_1(3) + p_1(2)\, p_1(2) + p_1(3)\, p_1(1) \\ &\qquad + p_1(4)\, p_1(0) \\ &= 2\, p_1(0)\, p_1(4) + 2\, p_1(1)\, p_1(3) + p_1^2(2). \end{aligned}$$

$$p_2(5) = 2\, p_1(0)\, p_1(5) + 2\, p_1(1)\, p_1(4) + 2\, p_1(2)\, p_1(3)$$

$$p_2(6) = 2\, p_1(0)\, p_1(6) + 2\, p_1(1)\, p_1(5) + 2\, p_1(2)\, p_1(4) + p_1^2(3),$$

etc. The law of formation is obvious:

$$p_2(r) = \sum_{k=0}^{r} p_1(r - k).p_1(k). \qquad 36.2$$

The distribution $p_2(r)$ once calculated, we can move on to the distribution $p_3(r)$:

$$\begin{aligned} p_3(0) &= p_1(0) \,.\, p_2(0) \\ &= p_1^3(0). \end{aligned}$$

$$\begin{aligned} p_3(1) &= p_1(0) \,.\, p_2(1) + p_1(1) \,.\, p_2(0) \\ &= 3\, p_1^2(0)\, p_1(1) \end{aligned} \qquad 36.3$$

$$\begin{aligned} p_3(2) &= p_1(0)\, p_2(2) + p_1(1)\, p_2(1) + p_1(2)\, p_2(0) \\ &= 3\, p_1^2(0)\, p_1(2) + 3\, p_1(0)\, p_1^2(1) \end{aligned}$$

$$\begin{aligned} p_3(3) &= p_1(0)\, p_2(3) + p_1(1)\, p_2(2) + p_1(2)\, p_2(1) + p_1(3)\, p_2(0) \\ &= 3\, p_1^2(0)\, p_1(3) + 6\, p_1(0)\, p_1(1)\, p_1(2) + p_1^3(1) \end{aligned}$$

etc.

More generally:

$$p_n(r) = \sum_{k=0}^{r} p_{n-m}(r - k).p_m(k) = \sum_{k=0}^{r} p_m(r - k).p_{n-m}(k) \qquad 36.4$$

$$1 < m < n \text{ (positive wholes).}$$

2. Example.

We shall take the probability distribution p(r) given in Table 35.2 as $p_1(r)$, and calculate $p_2(r)$ by means of formulas (36.1).

It is of interest to compare the cost of inventory based on a period T with that for a period of 2T. Let us return to Table 35.2, but this time putting $p_2(r)$ in place of $p_1(r)$.

Table 36.1

r	0	1	2	3	4	5	6	7	8	9	10	>10
$p_1(r)$	0.1	0.2	0.2	0.3	0.1	0.1	0	—	—	—	—	—
$p_2(r)$	0.01	0.04	0.08	0.14	0.18	0.18	0.17	0.10	0.07	0.02	0.01	0

We have:

$$[L(5) = 0.9297] < (\varrho = 0.9524) < [L(6) = 0.9703]. \qquad 36.5$$

The optimum inventory level is 6. The reader should not conclude from this that whenever we double the period, we must necessarily double the inventory; this is evident if we take $\rho = 0.9$, in which case:

for a period T: $[L(2) = 0.8625] < (\varrho = 0.9) < [L(3) = 0.9575]$ 36.6

for a period 2T: $[L(4) = 0.8572] < (\varrho = 0.9) < [L(5) = 0.9297]$ 36.7

With $\rho = 0.9$, we note that the optimum for period T occurs when $s = 3$, while for a period of 2T it occurs when $s = 5$.

Table 36.2

s	r	$p(r)$	$\frac{p(r)}{r}$	$\sum_{r=s+1}^{\infty} \frac{p(r)}{r}$	$(s+\frac{1}{2}) \sum_{r=s+1}^{\infty} \frac{p(r)}{r}$	$p(r \leqslant s)$	$L(s) = p(r \leqslant s) + (s+\frac{1}{2}) \sum_{r=s+1}^{\infty} \frac{p(r)}{r}$
0	0	0.01	-	0.2621	0.1310	0.01	0.1410
1	1	0.04	0.0400	0.2221	0.3331	0.05	0.3831
2	2	0.08	0.0400	0.1821	0.4552	0.13	0.5852
3	3	0.14	0.0466	0.1355	0.4742	0.27	0.7442
4	4	0.18	0.0450	0.0905	0.4072	0.45	0.8572
5	5	0.18	0.0360	0.0545	0.2997	0.63	0.9297
6	6	0.17	0.0283	0.0262	0.1703	0.80	0.9703
7	7	0.10	0.0143	0.0119	0.0892	0.90	0.9892
8	8	0.07	0.0087	0.0032	0.0272	0.97	0.9972
9	9	0.02	0.0022	0.0010	0.0095	0.99	0.9995
10	10	0.01	0.0010	0	0	1	1
>10	>10	0	0	0	0	1	1

Returning to the example in which $\rho = 0.9524$, we shall now calculate $\Gamma_2(6)$; we obtain:

$$\Gamma_2(6) = c_s \sum_{r=0}^{6}\left(6-\frac{r}{2}\right)p(r) + c_s \sum_{r=7}^{\infty} \frac{1}{2}\,\frac{36}{r}\,p(r) + c_p \sum_{r=7}^{\infty} \frac{1}{2}\,\frac{(r-6)^2}{r}\,p(r)\,.$$

$$= 0.1\,[(6)(0.01) + (5.5)(0.04) + (5)(0.08) + (4.5)(0.14) + (4)(0.18) + (3.5)(0.18) + (3)(0.17)] + 0.1\,[(2.571)(0.10) + (2.25)(0.07) + (2)(0.02) + (1.8)(0.01)] + 2\,[(0.071)(0.10) + (0.25)(0.07) + (0.5)(0.02) + (0.8)(0.01)] \qquad 36.8$$

$$= 0.45 \text{ million fr.}$$

Let us suppose that the period T is equal to a month, and that the costs c_S and c_p are monthly costs; the annual costs for policies T and 2T can then be compared:

$$12\,\Gamma_1(3) = 12 \times 0.29 = 3.48 \text{ million fr}; \qquad 36.9$$

$$6\,\Gamma_2(6) = 6 \times 0.45 = 2.70 \text{ million fr.} \qquad 36.10$$

A more complete analysis would show that the function $\Gamma(T,s)$ has a minimum for a value of T_0 and a value of s_0 which constitute the economic period and inventory level. In general, the determination of T_0 and s_0 is done by means of numerical calculation. The minimum values for $\Gamma(T,s)$, given as a function of kT, k = 1, 2, 3, 4, 5, . . . , produce a graph whose appearance is similar to that shown in Fig. 36.1. (See Part Two, Section 84.)

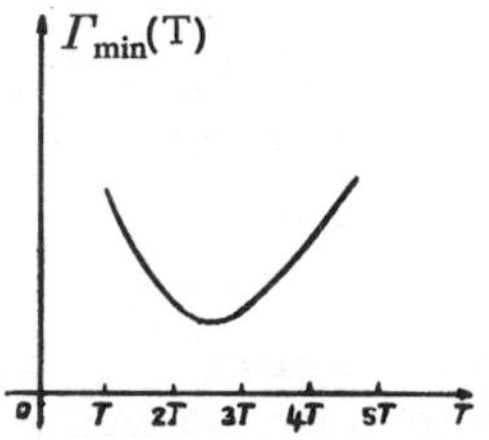

Fig. 36.1

3. Calculating the $p_1(r)$ distribution when $p_2(r)$ is known.

In some cases, we require the distribution for an interval of a month when, for example, we know the distribution for 2 months. Considering formulas (36.1), we see that:

$$p_1(0) = \sqrt{p_2(0)},$$

$$p_1(1) = \frac{p_2(1)}{2p_1(0)},$$

$$p_1(2) = \frac{p_2(2)}{2p_1(0)} - \frac{p_1^2(1)}{2p_1(0)},$$

$$p_1(3) = \frac{p_2(3)}{2p_1(0)} - \frac{p_1(2).p_1(1)}{p_1(0)},$$

$$p_1(4) = \frac{p_2(4)}{2p_1(0)} - \frac{p_1(3).p_1(1)}{p_1(0)} - \frac{p_1^2(2)}{2p_1(0)} \qquad 36.11$$

$$p_1(5) = \frac{p_2(5)}{2p_1(0)} - \frac{p_1(4).p_1(1)}{p_1(0)} - \frac{p_1(3)p_1(2)}{p_1(0)} \ldots \text{etc} \ldots$$

... the rule governing this construction is obvious.

These recurrence formulas make it easy to calculate $p_1(r)$ from $p_2(r)$.

An important (and unfortunately frequent) error occurs when it is assumed that the probability $p_1(r)$ is equal to $p_2 2r)$. Taking as an example the $p_1(r)$ and $p_2(r)$ distributions given in Table 36.1, we see that, if the probability of a demand level r = 6 is 0.17 for 2 months, the probability of a demand level r = 3 for 1 month is not 0.17 but 0.3.

There are cases when it is possible to apply the same distribution to intervals of T, 2T, ..., nT, but with different averages and different standard deviations. This is the case, for example, with a Gaussian distribution or a Poisson distribution (see Section 53).

Section 37

DELAYS BETWEEN ORDERS AND DELIVERIES

1. General explanation.—2. Example.—3. The minimum-level or two-bin method.—4. Simulation: Dynamic stock accounting.

1. General explanation.

Let us consider a time interval θ divided into n equal periods T, and let us assume that the delay between the placement of an order for supplies and the receipt of the supplies is equal to θ. At the beginning of each period T, orders are placed so that delivery will be made n periods later. We have determined the distribution p(r) for a demand level r covering the interval θ. The problem that now arises is the following: what quantity, q_i, should be ordered n periods before period i so that the total cost for that period will be minimum?

To simplify this analysis, we shall adopt the hypothesis that the q_i quantities for the n - 1 periods that precede period n are known, and have been ordered regularly; we shall simply attempt to find the optimum quantity q_n. Let us select a case we have already studied, the case of random demand with overstock losses and penalties for shortage (neglecting carrying costs). Let c_1 be the unit loss for overstocks, c_2 the unit cost for understocks. The problem will be formulated as follows, setting:

s_o = initial inventory (start of the first period),
s_i = inventory at the end of period i,
r_i = demand for period i,
q_i = replenishment order for period i.

Then:

$$\begin{aligned} s_1 &= s_0 - r_1 + q_1\,, \\ s_2 &= s_1 - r_2 + q_2\,, \\ s_3 &= s_2 - r_3 + q_3\,, \\ &\ldots\ldots \\ s_i &= s_{i-1} - r_i + q_i\,, \\ &\ldots\ldots \\ s_n &= s_{n-1} - r_n + q_n\,, \end{aligned} \qquad 37.1$$

from which we can easily obtain:

$$s_n = s_0 + q_1 + q_2 + \ldots + q_n - (r_1 + r_2 + \ldots + r_n)\,. \qquad 37.2$$

Let us set:

$$s = s_0 + q_1 + q_2 + \ldots + q_n\,. \qquad 37.3$$

$$r = r_1 + r_2 + \ldots + r_n\,. \qquad 37.4$$

Therefore:

$$s_n = s - r\,. \qquad 37.5$$

and this quantity will be positive or negative, depending on whether $s > r$ or $s < r$, respectively.

The mathematical expectation of the total cost for time interval $\theta = nT$ is, according to (35.48),*

$$\Gamma(s) = c_1 \sum_{s=0}^{s} (s-r)p(r) + c_2 \sum_{r=s+1}^{\infty} (r-s)p(r)\,. \qquad 37.6$$

The minimum of (37.6) occurs, as we have seen (35.50), for a value of s* such that:

---

*where $\Gamma(s) = c_1 \int_0 (s-r)f(r)dr + c_2 \int_s^{\infty} (r-s)\,f(r)dr$

if the random variable r is continuous.

$$p(r \leqslant s^* - 1) < \varrho < p(r \leqslant s^*), \qquad 37.7$$

where

$$\varrho = \frac{c_2}{c_1 + c_2} \qquad 37.8$$

The optimum stock s* having been determined, and the quantities $q_1, q_2, \ldots, q_{n-1}$ being given, we have:

$$q_n = s^* - s_0 - (q_1 + q_2 + \ldots + q_{n-1}). \qquad 37.9$$

2. Example.

A regional warehouse for a factory receives stock replenishment supplies of a certain article every month; the number of articles received is a multiple of 100. During the first five months of the year, replenishments were:

$$q_1 = 100,\ q_2 = 200,\ q_3 = 200,\ q_4 = 200,\ q_5 = 300. \qquad 37.10$$

The initial stock, s_0, is equal to 100.

The distribution of demand r, calculated for a period of 6 months, is shown in Table 37.1. The lead-time between the order for supplies and delivery to the warehouse is 6 months. The unit cost for overstocks is 1,500 francs, and the unit cost for a shortage is 18,000 francs. What quantity, q_6, should be ordered for the 6th month?

First of all, let us calculate the shortage rate:

$$\varrho = \frac{18{,}000}{1{,}500 + 18{,}000} = \frac{12}{13} = 0.923. \qquad 37.11$$

From (37.7), the economic stock level for a period of 6 months will be:

$$[p(r < 1200)] < 0.923 < [p(r < 1300)]. \qquad 37.12$$

Thus, the optimum stock for 6 months will be:

$$s^* = 1300. \qquad 37.13$$

From this, we obtain:

$$\begin{aligned} q_6 &= s^* - s_0 - (q_1 + q_2 + q_3 + q_4 + q_5) \\ &= 1300 - 100 - (100 + 200 + 200 + 200 + 300) \qquad 37.14 \\ &= 200. \end{aligned}$$

The same problem can be set up with a carrying cost of c_s and a shortage cost of c_p, both costs being per piece per unit of time.

Once again we determine the economic stock level, s*, by means of (35.78):

$$L(s^* - 1) < \varrho < L(s^*), \quad 37.15$$

where

$$L(s) = p(r \leqslant s) + (s + \tfrac{1}{2}) \sum_{r=s+1}^{\infty} \frac{p(r)}{r}. \quad 37.16$$

Table 37.1

r	p(r)	p(r ≤ s)
0	0.000	0.000
100	0.002	0.002
200	0.008	0.010
300	0.022	0.032
400	0.046	0.078
500	0.078	0.156
600	0.109	0.265
700	0.131	0.396
800	0.138	0.534
900	0.129	0.663
1000	0.108	0.771
1100	0.082	0.853
1200	0.057	0.910
1300	0.037	0.947
1400	0.022	0.969
1500	0.012	0.981
1600	0.007	0.988
1700	0.004	0.992
1800	0.002	0.994
1900	0.001	0.995
2000	0.001	0.996
> 2000	0.004	1

Again, we find:

$$q_n = s^* - s_0 - (q_1 + q_2 + \ldots + q_{n-1})\,. \qquad 37.17$$

Since the quantity q_n has been determined, we then calculate the quantity q_{n+1} such that:

$$q_{n+1} = s^* - s_1 - (q_2 + q_3 + \ldots + q_n); \qquad 37.18$$

(if the p(r) distribution is invariant when the time interval θ is shifted, the optimum quantity s* will not vary).

And so on, in a like manner:

$$q_{n+2} = s^* - s_2 - (q_3 + q_4 + - \ldots + q_{n+1}) \qquad 37.19$$

This makes it possible to order the optimum quantities in sufficient time.

3. The minimum-level or two-bin method.

Suppose that the total demand for a period θ is N, the carrying cost per part per day is c_s, and the set-up cost for a replenishment is c_l. As we saw in Section 35, the total cost for the time interval θ is given by (35.5), if we assume that the delay in replenishment is negligible:

$$\Gamma(n) = \frac{Nc_l}{n} + \frac{\theta c_s}{2} n. \qquad 37.20$$

Now let us adopt the hypothesis that the delay in replenishment stock delivery is essentially constant, and let τ equal this delay. We will also suppose that demand is random, and that two warehouses (whether physically distinct or not) are used to store the inventory. When the first warehouse is out of stock, we draw upon the second and immediately place a replenishment order for n units, which will be delivered within the interval τ. While waiting for the order to arrive, the second warehouse supplies the needed parts and constitutes a cushion against shortages. We can also approach this system of inventory management by introducing a minimum reorder level, m; when the stock reaches this level, an order is placed for n parts.

The given dimensions are θ, τ, N, c_s, and c_l, with the notations used in Section 35. We propose to determine m and n such that the inventory cost for the period θ will be a minimum.

One approximate method consists of assuming that the average demand rate is constant, so that the quantity n_o (which represents the optimum value without introducing m) is:

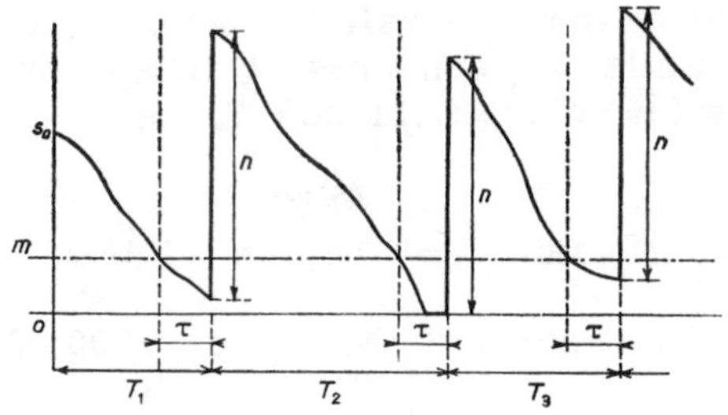

Fig. 37.1

$$n_0 = \sqrt{\frac{2N}{\theta}\frac{c_l}{c_s}} \qquad 37.21$$

and hence:

$$T_0 = \sqrt{2\frac{\theta}{N}\frac{c_l}{c_s}} \qquad 37.22$$

and

$$\Gamma_0 = \sqrt{2N\theta c_l c_s} \qquad 37.23$$

(formulas (35.10), (35.11), and (35.12).

If τ is the average lead-time between order and delivery (with a small standard deviation), we shall determine the probability distribution of demand during this time interval. Let $f_\tau(y)$ be the probability of a demand for y pieces during interval τ, and

$$F_\tau(y) = \Pr(Y \leqslant y) \qquad 37.24$$

the cumulative probability.

Let us impose the condition, for example, that the probability of running out of stock must be less than or equal to the value α $(0 \leq \alpha < 1)$. We should have:

$$1 - F_\tau(y) = \alpha . \qquad 37.25$$

This makes it possible, knowing α and the probability distribution of $F_\tau(y)$, to determine for what value $y = m$ equation (37.25) is satisfied; we thereby obtain the level m corresponding to the given condition.

The method described so far is only approximate, because it forces us to assume separate working hypotheses for the stocks in each of the bins (warehouses). A more accurate analytical method has been developed by Whitin* and by Vazsonyi;* however, the calculations can be performed without restrictive hypotheses by

*See Bibliography, refs. E2 and E30.

the Monte Carlo method, as will be demonstrated in an example later on. Meanwhile, we can present an approximate numerical calculation using formulas (37.21) to (37.25).

Let:

$$\theta = 360\,\text{j}, \qquad \tau = 7\,\text{j}, \qquad N = 120{,}000, \tag{37.26}$$

$c_s = 3.5$ fr per unit per day, $c_l = 300{,}000$ fr.

We have already found (see (35.15)-(35.17)) that:

$$n_0 = 7{,}559, \qquad T_0 = 22{,}68\,\text{j}, \qquad \Gamma_0 = 9{,}525\,000\ \text{F}. \tag{37.27}$$

Now let us suppose that the demand distribution is Gaussian, with mean $\bar{y} = (120{,}000/360) \times 7 = 2{,}333$ for one week, and standard deviation $\sigma = 170$.

For a normalized Gauss distribution ($\bar{x} = 0, \sigma = 1$), let us take $\alpha = 0.06$; we should then have:

$$P(x) = 0.94\,. \tag{37.28}$$

Examination of a table of the Gauss distribution (see Appendix) will show that:

$$P(1.57) = 0.94\,. \tag{37.29}$$

If $\bar{y}$ is the mean demand for 7 days, and m the reorder level:

$$\begin{aligned} m &= \bar{y} + x.\sigma \\ &= 2333 + (1.57)(170) \\ &= 2333 + 267 = 2600\,. \end{aligned} \tag{37.30}$$

The quantity $x\sigma = 267$ is called the safety stock.

Thus, by placing an order for 7,559 parts each time the stock level reaches 2,600 units, the probability of running out of stock will be less than 0.6.

This approximate method generally yields a total cost which is quite close to the true optimum and allows us to calculate the minimum reorder level, taking into account the assumptions we have made in connection with shortages. In practice, the delay τ is a random variable, and, since analytical study becomes too complicated, it is often preferable to determine the optimum by simulation.

4. Simulation: Dynamic stock accounting.

We can quite readily simulate this stock management problem by means of the probability distributions obtained from statistical data of daily demand. We will use tables of random numbers or deviations.

Suppose that we have observed a mean daily demand of 333 pieces, with a standard deviation of 64, and that we have proven, by means of a significance test, that the distribution is normal. Using a series of random normalized Gaussian deviations (see Table 32.3), we can establish a random series of demands. Table 37.2 presents such a series, obtained by means of the formula:

$$A = \bar{a} + \varepsilon\,\sigma_A\,, \qquad 37.31$$

where A = value of the random demand,
$\bar{a}$ = mean of A,
σ_A = standard deviation of A,
ϵ = the random deviation taken from the table.

In this numerical example, we obtain:

$$A = 333 + \varepsilon\,64\,. \qquad 37.32$$

Table 37.2

ε	—1.445	1.357	—1.657	—0.837	—1.417	0.548	—0.423	0.398
A	241	419	227	280	243	368	306	358
	0.167	0.147	0.002	1.537	0.113	—1.008	1.080	—0.772
	343	342	333	431	340	264	402	284
	—0.368	—0.290	2.146	—0.539	0.576	—1.201	—1.672	0.334
	310	315	470	299	370	257	226	354
	0.659	1.192	0.119	1.361	0.856	—0.018	0.108	—0.385
	375	409	340	420	387	332	340	309
	0.228	0.166	—1.169	1.099	—0.914	—0.462	1.312	—0.266
	347	343	259	403	275	303	417	316
	0.233	—1.043	0.852	—0.746	...	...	...	
	348	267	387	286	...	...	...	

Let us adopt the hypothesis that lead-times are random, and follow Poisson's law, with a mean of 7 days. It is equally easy to construct a series of numbers following this law with a mean of 7. For this purpose, we utilize a table whose probabilities correspond to a cumulative Poisson's law with a mean of 7.* The results obtained are shown in Table 37.3, in which we have calculated the average intervals.

Table 37.3

r	0	1	2	3	4	5	6
$P(r)$	0	0.001	0.008	0.030	0.082	0.173	0.301
$1000\,\dfrac{P(r)+P(r+1)}{2}$	0	4	19	56	127	237	

r	6	7	8	9	10	11	12
$P(r)$	0.301	0.450	0.599	0.730	0.831	0.902	0.947
$1000\,\dfrac{P(r)+P(r+1)}{2}$	375	524	664	780	866	924	

r	12	13	14	15	16	17	⩾18
$P(r)$	0.947	0.973	0.988	0.995	0.998	0.999	1
$1000\,\dfrac{P(r)+P(r+1)}{2}$	960	980	993	996	998	999	1000

Taking a series of 3-digit random numbers in Table 32.2, we shall allow a lead-time of 1 day for every number between 0 and 4, 2 days for every number between 4 and 19, 3 days between 19 and 56,..., 9 days between 664 and 780,..., 17 days between 998 and 999, etc. (if the 3-digit number equals the upper limit of the interval, we take the larger delay). Of course, the Poisson distribution obtained by this method is an approximate one, but it is suitable to the use for which it is intended. This gives us a random series of lead-times as shown in Table 37.4

Table 37.4

Random number	252	739	227	176	604	307	605	356
Lead time	6	9	5	5	8	6	8	6
	437	885	149	...	...	...		
	7	11	5	...	...	...		

---

*For example, see the table in the Appendix which gives the complementary probabilities.

We are now ready to simulate the behavior of our inventory, using Table 37.5. We have assumed an initial stock of 4,700, and production-line replenishment in lots of 7,500.

Table 37.5

Day	Demand	Cumulative demand	Stock	
0	0	0	4700	
1	241	241	4459	
2	419	660	4040	
3	227	887	3813	
4	280	1167	3533	
5	243	1410	3290	
6	368	1778	2922	
7	306	2084	2616	
8	358	2442	2258	Order ↑
9	343	2785	1915	
10	342	3127	1573	
11	333	3460	1240	6 days
12	431	3891	809	
13	340	4231	469	↓
14	264	4495	7705	Receipt
15	402	402	7303	7500 + 205
16	284	686	7019	7705
17	310	996	6709	
18	315	1311	6394	
19	470	1781	5924	
20	299	2080	5625	
21	370	2450	5255	

Table 37.5 (continued)

Day	Demand	Cumulative demand	Stock	
22	257	2707	4998	
23	226	2933	4772	
24	354	3287	4418	
25	375	3662	4043	
26	409	4071	3634	
27	340	4411	3294	
28	420	4831	2874	
29	387	5218	2487	↑
30	332	5550	2155	
31	340	5890	1815	
32	309	6199	1506	
33	347	6546	1159	9 days
34	343	6889	816	
35	259	7148	557	
36	403	7551	154	
37	275	7826	—121	← Shortage
38	303	8129	7076	↓
39	417	417	6659	7500 — 424
40	316	733	6343	7076
41	348	1081	5995	
42	267	1348	5628	
...	...	...	...	

We shall leave it to the reader to finish these calculations; the procedure to be followed is evident. At each step in the calculations, we determine the inventory cost, including (if desired) the shortage cost for each out-of-stock. It can readily be seen how, in this way, one can find the minimum cost by varying n, m, or the mean value of τ (the quantity τ is generally random). It is also possible to study the effect of a change in the other parameters. Furthermore, it is easy to introduce seasonal variations into such a simulation. Procedures like this are obviously not feasible in practice unless an electronic computer of adequate size is available. What we have described amounts, in fact, to simulating stock accounting by varying those parameters subject to our influence. We have suggested that such evaluations obtained by simulation of inventory problems, and of management problems generally, might be called dynamic accounting.

Section 38

NON-PROPORTIONAL COSTS (STEP-WISE VARIATIONS)*

1. First case: Two unit selling prices depending upon quantity.— 2. Numerical examples.—3. Second case: Three unit selling prices depending upon quantity.—4. Example.

We can conceive of many inventory problems in which costs are not proportional; here we shall consider only the case in which the unit selling price is a function of the quantity purchased, varying in a discontinuous fashion (i.e., in steps or jumps). For example, we have a unit selling price c_1 for a quantity $0<n<a$; c_2 for $a \leq n < b$; etc.

1. First case: Two unit selling prices depending upon quantity.

Referring back to the 5th case in Section 35, let us now assume that the unit selling price is variable and equal to:

$$c_1 \quad \text{if } 0 < n < a$$
$$c_2 \quad \text{if } a \leqslant n < \infty .$$

Once again using the expression of the cost given in (35.89), we find this time:

$$\Gamma_1(n) = Nc_1 + \frac{Nc_b}{n} + \frac{\theta c_b a}{2} + \frac{\theta n c_1 a}{2} \quad \text{if} \quad 0 < n < a \qquad 38.1$$

$$\Gamma_2(n) = Nc_2 + \frac{Nc_b}{n} + \frac{\theta c_b a}{2} + \frac{\theta n c_2 a}{2} \quad \text{if} \quad a \leqslant n < \infty \qquad 38.2$$

---

*If the distribution $p(r)$ varies, we must re-calculate s^* for each replenishment period (non-stationary phenomenon).

In Fig. 38.1, we have constructed the curve:

$$\Gamma(n) = \Gamma_1(n) \quad 0 < n < a$$
$$= \Gamma_2(n) \quad a \leqslant n < \infty \tag{38.3}$$

We see immediately that, if $n_{1,0}$ corresponds to the minimum of $\Gamma_1(n)$ and $n_{2,0}$ to the minimum of $\Gamma_2(n)$, and assuming $c_2 < c_1$, the $\Gamma(n)$ curve will show a discontinuity (Fig. 38.1), and the minimum of $\Gamma(n)$ will depend on the respective positions of $n_{1,0}$, $n_{2,0}$, and a.

The various situations that can exist are shown in Figs. 38.2a, b, c and d.

(1) If $a > n_{2,0}$ and $\Gamma_2(a) > \Gamma_1(n_{1,0})$
(Fig. 38.2a) 38.4

then:

$$\min \Gamma(n) = \Gamma_1(n_{1,0}) .$$

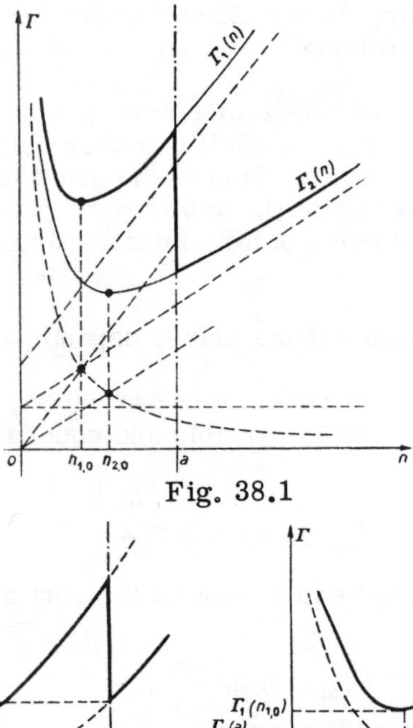

Fig. 38.1

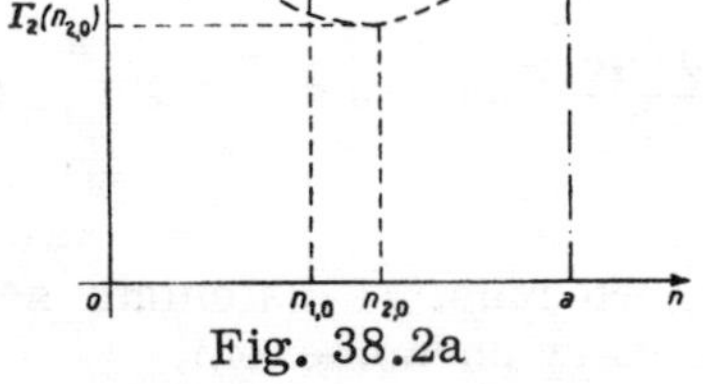

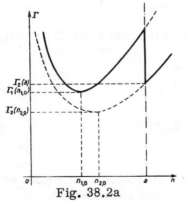

Fig. 38.2a

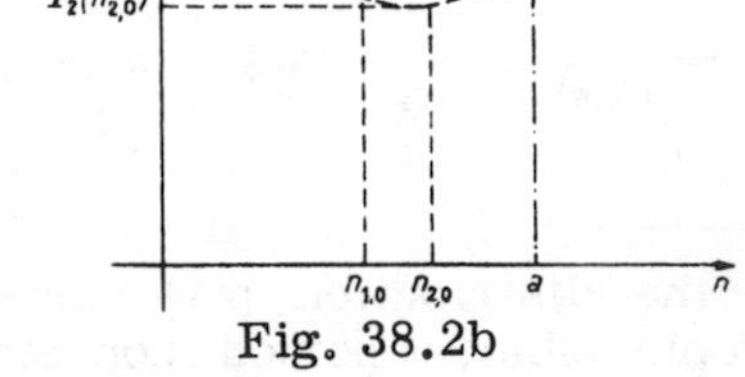

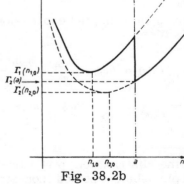

Fig. 38.2b

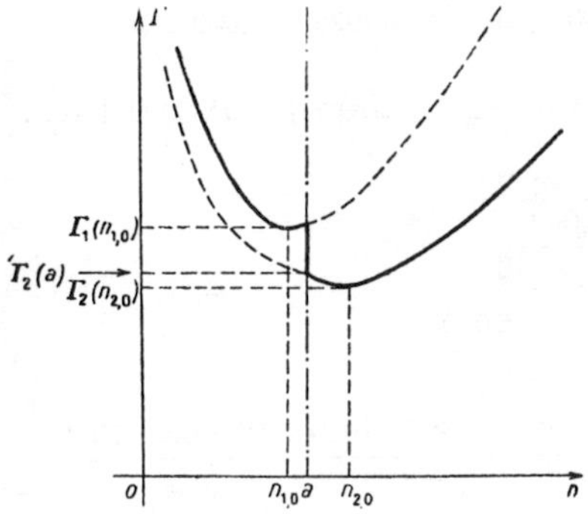

Fig. 38.2c

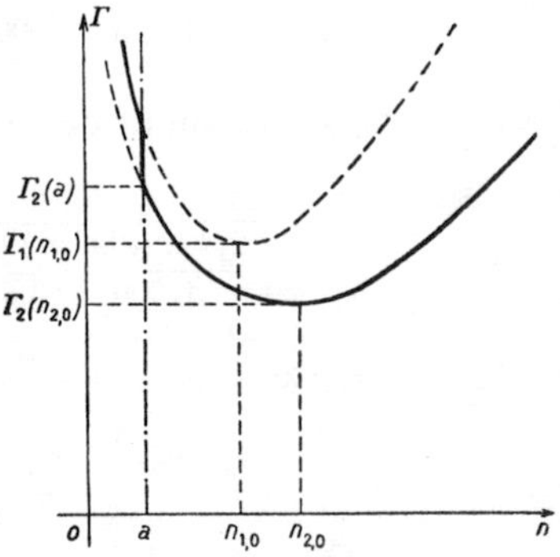

Fig. 38.2d

(2) If $a > n_{2,0}$, and $\Gamma_2(a) < \Gamma_1(n_{1,0})$

(Fig. 38.2b) 38.5

then:

$$\min \Gamma(n) = \Gamma_2(a)\,.$$

(3) If $a < n_{2,0}$

(Figs. 38.2c and d) 38.6

then:

$$\min \Gamma(n) = \Gamma_2(n_{2,0})\,.$$

Thus the first quantity to be calculated is $n_{2,0}$, which will then be compared with a. Next, we will calculate, according to the case, $\Gamma_1(n_{1,0})$, $\Gamma_2(a)$, and $\Gamma_2(n_{2,0})$.

2. Numerical examples.

First example—Let:

$$c_1 = 1\,000 \quad 0 < n < 500 \quad \text{and} \quad c_2 = 925 \quad 500 \leqslant n\,,$$
$$c_b = 35\,000, \quad N = 2\,400, \quad \theta = 360, \quad \alpha = 0{,}6.10^{-3}. \qquad 38.7$$

Using (35.91), we find:

$$n_{2,0} = \sqrt{\frac{2 \times 2\,400 \times 35\,000}{360 \times 925 \times 0{,}6 \times 10^{-3}}} = 917, \qquad 38.8$$

since $a < n_{2,0}$: the economic order quantity is 917.

Second example—Referring to the preceding example, let us change the intervals:

$$c_1 = 1{,}000 \quad 0 < n < 1{,}000 \quad \text{et} \quad c_2 = 925 \quad 1{,}000 \leqslant n. \tag{38.9}$$

Since $a > n_{2,0}$, we must calculate $n_{1,0}$, then $\Gamma_2(a)$ and $\Gamma_1(n_{1,0})$.

$$n_{1,0} = \sqrt{\frac{2 \times 2{,}400 \times 35{,}000}{360 \times 1{,}000 \times 0.6 \times 10^{-3}}} = 882. \tag{38.10}$$

$$\begin{aligned}\Gamma_2(a) &= (2{,}400 \times 925) + \frac{2{,}400 \times 35{,}000}{1{,}000} \\ &\quad + \frac{360 \times 35000 \times 0.6 \times 10^{-3}}{2} + \frac{360 \times 1000 \times 925 \times 0.6 \times 10^{-3}}{2} \\ &= 2{,}407{,}680 \text{ F}.\end{aligned} \tag{38.11}$$

$$\begin{aligned}\Gamma_1(n_{1,0}) &= (2{,}400 \times 1{,}000) + \frac{2{,}400 \times 35{,}000}{882} \\ &\quad + \frac{360 \times 35000 \times 0.6 \times 10^{-3}}{2} + \frac{360 \times 882 \times 1000 \times 0.6 \times 10^{-3}}{2} \\ &= 2{,}594{,}280 \text{ F}.\end{aligned} \tag{38.12}$$

Thus:

$$\Gamma_2(a) < \Gamma_1(n_{1,0}) \tag{38.13}$$

and the optimum of $\Gamma(n)$ corresponds to

$$n = a = 1{,}000, \quad c_2 = 925 \text{ F}. \tag{38.14}$$

Third example

$$c_1 = 1{,}000 \quad 0 < n < 4{,}000, \text{ and } c_2 = 925 \quad 4{,}000 \leqslant n. \tag{38.15}$$

Thus we have $a > n_{2,0}$.

Let us calculate $\Gamma_2(a)$, where $a = 4{,}000$:

$$\begin{aligned}\Gamma_2(a) &= (2{,}400 \times 925) + \frac{2{,}400 \times 35{,}000}{4{,}000} \\ &\quad + \frac{360 \times 35000 \times 0.6 \times 10^{-3}}{2} + \frac{360 \times 4000 \times 925 \times 0.6 \times 10^{-3}}{2} \\ &= 2{,}644{,}380 \text{ F}.\end{aligned} \tag{38.16}$$

Thus:

$$\Gamma_2(a) > \Gamma_1(n_{1,0}) \tag{38.17}$$

and the optimum of $\Gamma(n)$ corresponds to $n = n_{1,0} = 882$, $c_1 = 1{,}000$.

3. Second case—Three unit selling prices depending upon quantity.

Let the purchase prices be:

$$\begin{aligned} &c_1 \text{ if } 0 < n < a \\ &c_2 \text{ if } a \leqslant n < b \\ &c_3 \text{ if } b \leqslant n \end{aligned} \qquad 38.18$$

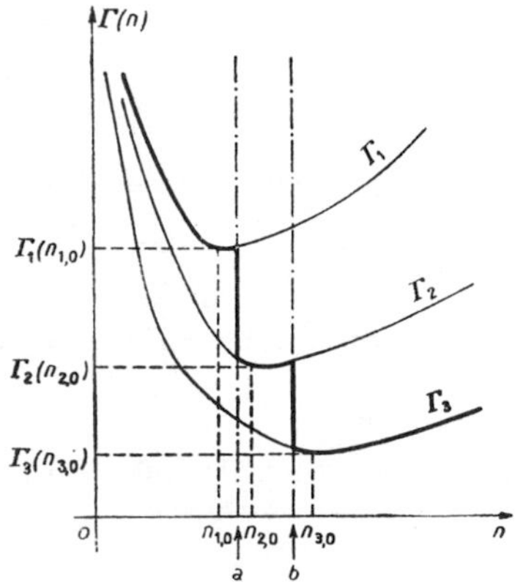

FIG. 38.3

The function $\Gamma(n)$ will have the shape shown in Fig. 38.3, where there are obviously two discontinuities.

The calculation is performed in the following way:

(1) Calculate $n_{3,0}$. If it is greater than b, the economic order quantity is $n_{3,0}$.

(2) If $n_{3,0} < b$, calculate $n_{2,0}$. Since $n_{3,0} < b$, then necessarily $n_{2,0} < b$. As a consequence, we have: $n_{2,0} < a$ or $n_{2,0} > a$.

a) If $n_{3,0} < b$ and $a \leq n_{2,0} < b$, compare $\Gamma_2(n_{2,0})$ with $\Gamma_3(b)$. The smaller of these quantities will be the economic order quantity.

b) If $n_{3,0} < b$ and $n_{2,0} < a$, calculate $n_{1,0}$, which will necessarily satisfy the inequality $n_{1,0} < a$. In this case, compare $\Gamma_1(n_{1,0})$, $\Gamma_2(a)$, and $\Gamma_3(b)$ to determine the economic order quantity.

4. Example.

Once again let us use the preceding example with the costs:

$$\begin{aligned} &c_1 = 1\,000 \text{ fr} && 0 < n < 500 \\ &c_2 = 925 \text{ fr} && 500 \leqslant n < 4\,000 \\ &c_3 = 850 \text{ fr} && 4\,000 \leqslant n\,. \end{aligned} \qquad 38.19$$

(1) Calculating $n_{3,0}$, we obtain 956. Therefore, we note:

$$n_{3,0} < (b = 4\,000)\,. \qquad 38.20$$

(2) Calculating $n_{2,0}$, we obtain 917. We now have

$$(a = 500) < n_{2,0} < (b = 4\,000)\,. \qquad 38.21$$

We then determine the value of $\Gamma_2(n_{2,0})$ and $\Gamma_3(b)$:

$$\Gamma_2(n_{2,0}) = 2\,407\,000 \text{ fr} \qquad 38.22$$

and

$$\Gamma_3(b) = 2\,432\,200 \text{ fr.} \qquad 38.23$$

Since $\Gamma_2(n_{2,0}) < \Gamma_3(b)$, the economic order quantity is:

$$n_{2,0} = 917\,. \qquad 38.24$$

Just for practice, let us study the case:

$$\begin{aligned} c_1 &= 1\,000 \text{ fr} & 0 &< n < 1\,000 \\ c_2 &= 925 \text{ fr} & 1\,000 &\leqslant n < 4\,000 \\ c_3 &= 850 \text{ fr.} & 4\,000 &\leqslant n \end{aligned} \qquad 38.25$$

where $n_{2,0} < (a = 1{,}000)$.

The reader will find in Part Two a study of the general case in which any number of discontinuities in the unit prices can exist. There we present a number of developments which utilize more advanced mathematical techniques. (See Part Two, Section 85.)

Chapter 5

Deterioration, replacement, and maintenance of equipment

Section 39

INTRODUCTION

Deciding on a policy of equipment replacement as against one of continued maintenance of equipment is generally a delicate matter. Guidelines drawn from broad experience can sometimes produce acceptable results, but very often intuition can lead to mistaken estimates. Mathematics, and probabilistic techniques in particular, allow us to calculate such estimates very accurately and easily. One is certainly struck by the simplicity of such calculations.

In this chapter, we shall make an effort to keep our explanations elementary, but we shall also provide enough development to satisfy the reader's curiosity.

There are profound analogies among industrial problems of stochastic deterioration and replacement, mathematical biology, and electrical power systems and their formal analogs; the same equations (known as the Volterra equations) constitute models common to them all. In Part Two of this book (Chapter X), these equations will be studied and will be the object of major developments.

The elements of the theory of deterioration and replacement which will be explained further on will perhaps give the reader a better understanding of equipment life.

Section 40

REPLACEMENT OF EQUIPMENT IN THE CASE OF NON-STOCHASTIC-DETERIORATION

Take an item of equipment whose value at the time of purchase is A, and which, by reason of deterioration, is the object of predictable maintenance and repair expenses. Let us assume that we know the cost of installation, maintenance, and repair, C_1, C_2, $C_3, \ldots$, to be carried out at the beginning of the first, second, third, ..., periods. Let us assume that these periods are equal (years, or months, for example). If the equipment is regularly replaced at the end of n periods, the total gross price after r replacements will be:

$$\Gamma = (A + C_1 + C_2 + \ldots + C_n)_1 + (A + C_1 + C_2 + \ldots + C_n)_2 + \ldots \\ \ldots + (A + C_1 + C_2 + \ldots + C_n)_r. \quad 40.1$$

If the quantities A and C are not constant and vary with time, we will have:

$$\Gamma = (A_1 + C_{11} + C_{12} + \ldots + C_{1n}) + (A_2 + C_{21} + C_{22} + \ldots + C_{2n}) + \\ \ldots + (A_r + C_{r1} + C_{r2} + \ldots + C_{rn}) \quad 40.2$$

or again, using the algebraic sum symbol;

$$\Gamma = \sum_{i=1}^{r} [A_i + \sum_{j=1}^{n} C_{ij}] \quad 40.3$$

where the elementary costs A_i and C_{ij} refer to replacement i.

The cost per period will then be:

$$\gamma = \frac{1}{nr} \Gamma = \frac{1}{nr} \sum_{i=1}^{r} [A_i + \sum_{j=1}^{n} C_{ij}]. \quad 40.4$$

Now let us imagine a certain number of items of equipment that are equivalent insofar as their use is concerned but have different replacement frequencies and costs. It will be noted that the respective costs per period, $\gamma_1, \gamma_2, \gamma_3, \ldots$, may be unequal and it may be worthwhile to find the lowest mean cost.

Table 40.1

Equipment	$A + C_1$	C_2	C_3	C_4	C_5
a	3,500,000 fr	200,000 fr	/	/	/
b	4,200,000 fr	150,000 fr	350,000 fr	/	/
c	5,200,000 fr	130,000 fr	370,000 fr	500,000 fr	/
d	7,000,000 fr	100,000 fr	280,000 fr	400,000 fr	700,000 fr

Table 40.1 gives an example in which there is a choice among 4 items of equipment whose use is equivalent. The purchase price A and the cost C_1 have been lumped together, because they both relate to the same period (the first). It is easy now to calculate the costs per period:

$$
\begin{aligned}
r = 2 \quad & \gamma_a = \tfrac{1}{2}[3{,}500\,000 + 200{,}000] = 1{,}850{,}000 \text{ fr} \\
r = 3 \quad & \gamma_b = \tfrac{1}{3}[4{,}200\,000 + 150{,}000 + 350{,}000] = 1{,}566{,}000 \text{ fr} \\
r = 4 \quad & \gamma_c = \tfrac{1}{4}[5{,}200\,000 + 130{,}000 + 370{,}000 + 500{,}000] = \boxed{1{,}525\,000 \text{ fr}} \\
r = 5 \quad & \gamma_d = \tfrac{1}{5}[7{,}000\,000 + 100{,}000 + 280{,}000 + 400{,}000 + 700{,}000] \\
& \quad = 1{,}696{,}000 \text{ fr}.
\end{aligned}
\tag{40.5}
$$

These calculations show that the γ_C solution, calling for replacement of the equipment every 4 years, is the most advantageous.

This type of problem does not call for analytical study, and we have had to postpone to Part Two our study of a slightly different problem, which requires more advanced mathematics. The latter concerns an item of equipment with purchase price A_0 which loses value in a continuous fashion as it ages, while the cost of repairs and maintenance increases almost continuously with age. The problem is to find out at what point the equipment should be sold so as to keep the cost per unit of time at a minimum. A typical example is that of the second-hand car.

The expression of cost would appear as follows:

Let A_0 be the purchase price, and let $A_0\varphi(t)$ be the value of the equipment when resold after a time t. Let $\psi(t)$ be the cumulative cost of repairs and maintenance during t; then:

$$\Gamma(t) = A_0 - A_0\varphi(t) + \psi(t) \tag{40.6}$$

and the mean cost of utilization (per unit of time) will be

$$\gamma(t) = \frac{\Gamma(t)}{t} = \frac{1}{t}[A_0 - A_0\varphi(t) + \psi(t)]. \tag{40.7}$$

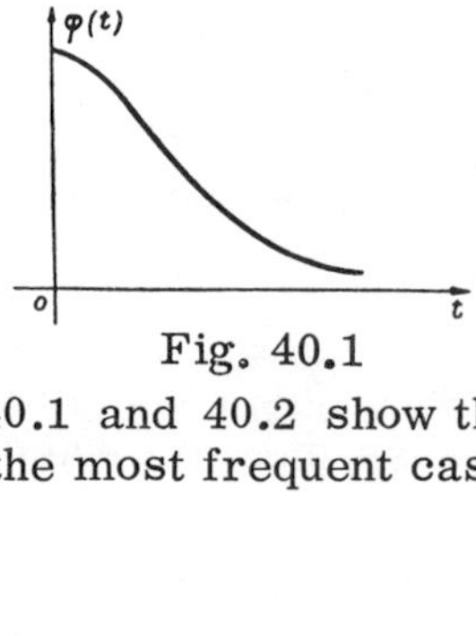

Fig. 40.1

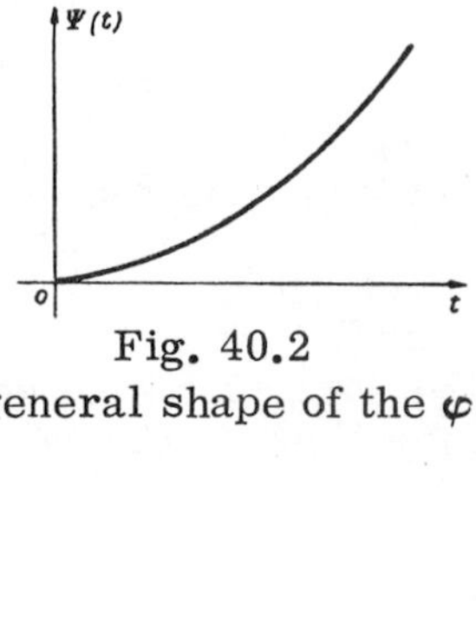

Fig. 40.2

Figs. 40.1 and 40.2 show the general shape of the $\varphi(t)$ and $\psi(t)$ curves in the most frequent cases.

The problem here is to find the minimum for $\gamma(t)$, which is readily obtained by taking the derivative of this function. One finds that the minimum of $\gamma(t)$ occurs for a value $t = t_0$ such that:

$$\gamma(t_0) = \frac{\Gamma(t_0 + \tau) - \Gamma(t_0)}{\tau} \qquad 40.8$$

for a sufficiently small τ.

The $\gamma(t)$ function has the shape shown in Fig. 40.3. From the mathematical results, one can draw the following rule of decision: "To obtain a minimum mean utilization cost, γ, replace the equipment as soon as the rate of variation of the cost:

$$\frac{\Gamma(t + \tau) - \Gamma(t)}{\tau} \qquad 40.9$$

exceeds $\gamma(t)$."

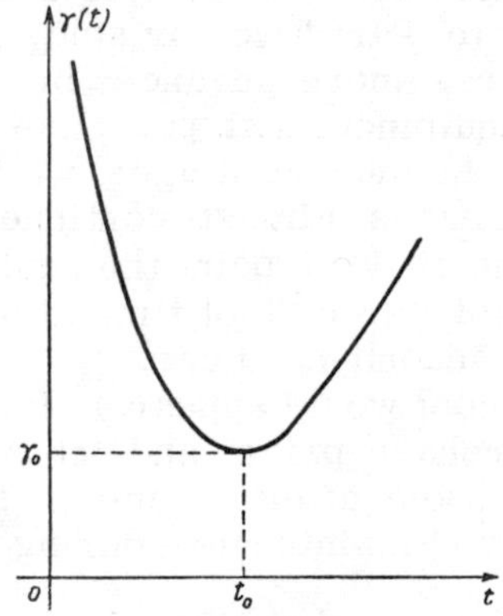

Fig. 40.3

In practice, $\gamma(t)$ can be evaluated numerically for reasonable intervals of time (e.g., monthly, for automobiles). (See Part Two, Section 90.)

Section 41

CONVERTING COSTS

1. General explanation.—2. Optimum replacement time.

1. General explanation.

Let there be 3 items of equipment, E_1, E_2, and E_3. The first was bought for 2,200,000 fr cash. The second cost 900,000 fr cash, but requires a further expenditure of 600,000 fr at the beginning of the next year, and 700,000 fr at the end of the third year. The third machine cost 1,400,000 fr, and requires annual expenditures of 100,000 and 700,000 fr. In all three cases, the total cost is the same; but, because of the interest on the money—which we shall assume is 10%—the real costs differ.

$$\text{1st machine:}\quad 2{,}200{,}000 \text{ fr}, \tag{41.1}$$

$$\text{2nd machine:}\quad 900{,}000 + \frac{600{,}000}{1.1} + \frac{700{,}000}{(1.1)^2} = 2{,}023{,}970 \text{ fr}, \tag{41.2}$$

$$\text{3rd machine:}\quad 1{,}400{,}000 + \frac{100{,}000}{1.1} + \frac{700{,}000}{(1.1)^2} = 2{,}069{,}430 \text{ fr}. \tag{41.3}$$

The second machine is the least expensive if the interest rate is taken into account. One can also compare two machines that last different lengths of time. For example:

Equipment \ Year	1	2	3	4	5	6
1	1,000,000	200,000	400,000			
2	1,700,000	100,000	200,000	300,000	400,000	500,000

41.4

We find, still using the same interest rate:

$$1)\quad 1{,}000{,}000 + \frac{200{,}000}{1.1} + \frac{400{,}000}{(1.1)^2} = 1{,}512{,}000 \text{ fr} \tag{41.5}$$

$$2)\quad 1{,}700{,}000 + \frac{100{,}000}{1.1} + \frac{200{,}000}{(1.1)^2} + \frac{300{,}000}{(1.1)^3} + \frac{400{,}000}{(1.1)^4} + \frac{500{,}000}{(1.1)^5} = 2{,}765{,}000 \text{ fr (rounded off)} \tag{41.6}$$

Per year, we have:

$$1):\ 504{,}000 \text{ fr} \qquad 2):\ 461{,}000 \text{ fr}; \tag{41.7}$$

It is apparent from these figures, that machine 2 is the less expensive. But, if it is remembered that another machine of the same kind must be bought when this type-1 machine is worn out, one finds:

$$1)\quad 1{,}000{,}000 + \frac{200{,}000}{1.1} + \frac{400{,}000}{(1.1)^2} + \frac{1{,}000{,}000}{(1.1)^3} + \frac{200{,}000}{(1.1)^4} + \frac{400{,}000}{(1.1)^5} = 2{,}647{,}000 \text{ fr (rounded off)} \tag{41.8}$$

or 441,000 fr per year.

Finally, we see that over a period of 6 years, machine 1 is the more advantageous investment.

What these very elementary examples have brought out is the importance of the way in which the cost is defined.

2. Optimum replacement time.

Let there be a series of equal periods numbered 1, 2, 3, 4, . . . , and corresponding maintenance costs, C_1, C_2, C_3, C_4, . . . We assume that these costs increase in a monotone fashion (that is, $C_2 > C_1$, $C_3 > C_2$, . . . , $C_{n+1} > C_n$ for any n), and that the charges are paid at the beginning of the corresponding period. With the initial expenditure A and the interest rate r, the cost—when the equipment is replaced after n periods—will be:

$$\Gamma_n = \left[A + C_1 + \frac{C_2}{1+r} + \frac{C_3}{(1+r)^2} + \dots + \frac{C_n}{(1+r)^{n-1}}\right] + \left[\frac{A}{(1+r)^n} + \frac{C_1}{(1+r)^n} + \frac{C_2}{(1+r)^{n+1}} + \dots + \frac{C_n}{(1+r)^{2n-1}}\right] + \dots\dots \qquad 41.9$$

which can be written:

$$\Gamma_n = \left[A + \sum_{i=1}^{n} \frac{C_i}{(1+r)^{i-1}}\right] + \frac{1}{(1+r)^n}\left[A + \sum_{i=1}^{n} \frac{C_i}{(1+r)^{i-1}}\right] + \frac{1}{(1+r)^{2n}}\left[A + \sum_{i=1}^{n} \frac{C_i}{(1+r)^{i-1}}\right] + \dots, \qquad 41.10$$

and finally:

$$\Gamma_n = \frac{A + \sum_{i=1}^{n} \frac{C_i}{(1+r)^{i-1}}}{1 - \frac{1}{(1+r)^n}} = \frac{A + \sum_{i=1}^{n} a^{i-1} c_i}{1 - a^n} \qquad 41.11$$

where

$$a = \frac{1}{1+r}. \qquad 41.12$$

This sum represents the amount that must be available at the beginning of these periods to replace the equipment every n periods (n years, for example) during an infinite time.

It can be shown (see Part Two, Section 91) that the minimum of (41.11) is obtained by means of the following rule: "Do not replace equipment until the cost of the next period is greater than the weighted average of expenditures already made." That is to say, in effect: replace when

$$C_{n+1} > \frac{A + C_1 + C_2\,a + \dots + C_n\,a^{n-1}}{1 + a + a^2 + \dots + a^{n-1}} \qquad 41.13$$

To illustrate the use of this rule by a practical example, we shall take a new case:

Let:

$A_0 = 1{,}000{,}000$ fr, with the C_i values given in column (2) of Table 41.1; we have taken:

$$r = 6\,\%, \qquad \text{Therefore,} \qquad a = \frac{1}{1.06} = 0.943. \qquad 41.14$$

This table brings out the property we referred to earlier. The minimum occurs for $\Gamma_9 = 257{,}000$ F. It will be seen that, for $i = 10$:

$$C_{10} > \frac{A + \sum_{i=1}^{10} c_i\,a^{i-1}}{\sum_{i=1}^{10} a^{i-1}}, \qquad \text{i.e.} \qquad 300 > 260. \qquad 41.15$$

Table 41.1

(1) Year	(2) C_i in thousands of fr.	(3) a^{i-1}	(4) $C_1 a^{i-1}$	(5) $A+\Sigma C_i a^{i-1}$	(6) Σa^{i-1}	(7) $\frac{A+\Sigma C_i a^{i-1}}{\Sigma a^{i-1}}$
1	50	1	50	1,050	1	1050
2	60	0.943	56,6	1,106	1.943	568
3	70	0.890	62,3	1,168	2.833	412
4	90	0.840	75,6	1,244	3.673	339
5	120	0.792	95	1,323	4.465	296
6	150	0.747	112	1,435	5.212	281
7	180	0.705	127	1,562	5.917	264
8	210	0.665	139	1,701	6.582	258
9	240	0.627	150	1,851	7.209	257 ←
10	300	0.592	177	2,028	7.801	260
11	400	0.558	223	2,251	8.359	269
12	500	0.527	263	2,514	8.886	283

Section 42

COST CALCULATIONS INVOLVING RESALE PRICE AND INTEREST RATE

Equipment is often resold after a certain period of use and taking the interest rate into account. We shall now study the case in which we deal with discrete values (i.e., where variations occur by jumps).

Let A_0 be the purchase price of the equipment, and R_1 the maintenance and repair costs paid at the end of the first year. If the equipment is sold at the end of the first year, at a loss of P_1, and if the interest rate is r, the cost of the equipment per year will be:

$$\Gamma_1 = A_0(1 + r) + R_1 - (A_0 - P_1) = A_0 r + R_1 + P_1. \qquad 42.1$$

Suppose that we keep the equipment another year. The interest will then apply to the value as of the beginning of the year, or:

$$(A_0 - P_1)r\ ; \qquad 42.2$$

The expenditures represented by R_1 will have become

$$R_1 r. \qquad 42.3$$

Therefore, if R_2 and P_2 are values analogous to the preceding ones but referring to the second year, the cost for the second year plus the first year will be:

$$\begin{aligned} \Gamma_2 &= \Gamma_1 + (A_0 - P_1)r + R_1 r + R_2 + P_2 \\ &= A_0 r + R_1 + P_1 + (A_0 - P_1)r + R_1 r + R_2 + P_2 \\ &= 2A_0 r + R_1(1 + r) + P_1(1 - r) + R_2 + P_2. \end{aligned} \qquad 42.4$$

For a third year, we would have:

$$\begin{aligned} \Gamma_3 &= \Gamma_2 + (A_0 - P_1 - P_2)r + R_1(1 + r)r + R_2 r + R_3 + P_3 \\ &= 3A_0 r + R_1(1 + r)^2 + P_1(1 - 2r) + R_2(1 + r) + P_2(1 - r) + R_3 + P_3. \end{aligned} \qquad 42.5$$

and so on:

$$\begin{aligned} \Gamma_n &= nA_0 r + R_1(1 + r)^{n-1} + R_2(1 + r)^{n-2} + \dots + R_{n-1}(1 + r) + R_n \\ &\quad + P_1[1 - (n - 1)r] + P_2[1 - (n - 2)r] + \dots + \\ &\quad + P_{n-1}(1 - r) + P_n \\ &= nA_0 r + \sum_{i=1}^{n} R_i(1 + r)^{n-i} + \sum_{i=1}^{n} P_i[1 - (n - i)r]. \end{aligned} \qquad 42.6$$

The average cost per year, for a machine kept n years, will be:

$$\gamma_n = \frac{\Gamma_n}{n} = A_0 r + \frac{1}{n} \sum_{=1}^{n} R_i(1 + r)^{n-i} + \frac{1}{n} \sum_{i=1}^{n} P_i[1 - (n - i)r]. \qquad 42.7$$

As will be noted, γ_n includes a factor $A_0 r$ which is independent of n and another, more complicated in form, which depends on n.

The function γ_n may possess one optimum or several, or may constantly increase or decrease, depending on the values of R_i and P_i.

The following numerical example illustrates the case in which γ_n has a single minimum:

$$\begin{array}{ll} A_0 = 700{,}000 \text{ fr} & r = 10\% \\ R_1 = 30{,}000 \text{ fr} & P_1 = 150{,}000 \text{ fr} \\ R_2 = 50{,}000 \text{ fr} & P_2 = 100{,}000 \text{ fr} \\ R_3 = 70{,}000 \text{ fr} & P_3 = 100{,}000 \text{ fr} \\ R_4 = 100{,}000 \text{ fr} & P_4 = 50{,}000 \text{ fr} \\ R_5 = 120{,}000 \text{ fr} & P_5 = 50{,}000 \text{ fr}. \end{array} \qquad 42.8$$

This gives us (in thousands of francs):

$$\begin{aligned} \gamma_1 &= 70 + 30 + 150 = 250 \\ \gamma_2 &= 70 + \tfrac{1}{2}[(30)(1.1) + (150)(0.9) + 50 + 100] = 229 \\ \gamma_3 &= 70 + \tfrac{1}{3}[(30)(1.21) + (150)(0.8) + (50)(1.1) + (100)(0.9) + 70 + 100] = 227.1 \\ \gamma_4 &= 70 + \tfrac{1}{4}[(30)(1.33) + (150)(0,7) + (50)(1.21) + (100)(0.8) + (70)(1.1) + (100)(0.9) + 100 + 50] = \boxed{220.6} \\ \gamma_5 &= 70 + \tfrac{1}{5}[(30)(1.46) + (150)(0.6) + (50)(1.33) + (100)(0.7) + (70)(1.21) + (100)(0.8) + (100)(1.1) + (50)(0.9) + 120 + 50] = 222. \end{aligned} \qquad 42.9$$

We might compare these results with those obtained when the interest rate is not considered:

$$\begin{aligned} \gamma_1 &= 30 + 150 = 180 \\ \gamma_2 &= \tfrac{1}{2}[30 + 150 + 50 + 100] = \boxed{165} \\ \gamma_3 &= \tfrac{1}{3}[30 + 150 + 50 + 100 + 70 + 100] = 166.6 \\ \gamma_4 &= \tfrac{1}{4}[30 + 150 + 50 + 100 + 70 + 100 + 100 + 50] = \boxed{162{,}5} \\ \gamma_5 &= \tfrac{1}{5}[30 + 150 + 50 + 100 + 70 + 100 + 100 + 50 + 120 + 50] = 164 \end{aligned} \qquad 42.10$$

It will be noted that here we have two minima, with γ_4 as the minimum minimorum. (See Part Two, Section 91.)

Section 43

STOCHASTIC DETERIORATION—EQUIPMENT SURVIVAL CURVE

1. General explanation.—2. Probability of failure.—
3. Terminology.—4. Operating limit.

1. General explanation.

By way of introduction, let us take a classic example: Suppose that we simultaneously light 100,000 light bulbs, and that we record afterwards, at equal operating intervals, the number of bulbs still lit. The result is shown in Table 43.1.

Table 43.1

Elapsed time t	Survivors n(t)	Casualties n(t−1)−n(t)
0	100,000	
1	100,000	0
2	99,000	1,000
3	98,000	1,000
4	97,000	1,000
5	96,000	1,000
6	93,000	3,000
7	87,000	6,000
8	77,000	10,000
9	63,000	14,000
10	48,000	15,000
11	32,000	16,000
12	18,000	14,000
13	10,000	8,000
14	6,000	4,000
15	3,000	3,000
16	2,000	1,000
17	1,000	1,000
18	0	1,000
⩾ 19	0	0

Let us call n(t) the number of surviving bulbs at time t (the time relating to an arbitrary unit), with n(0) = 100,000. From Table 43.1, we can construct a curve (Fig. 43.1) by joining the points corresponding to the following values:

$$\nu(t) = \frac{n(t)}{n(0)} \qquad 0 \leqslant \nu(t) \leqslant 1 . \tag{43.1}$$

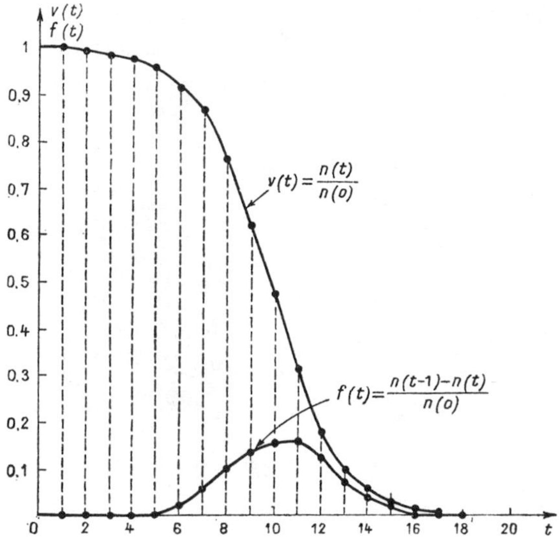

Fig. 43.1

This curve gives the ratio between the number of surviving bulbs at any given moment and the number of bulbs originally placed in service.

We shall assume that the 100,000 bulbs constitute a perfectly homogeneous population from the probability point of view; this means that each bulb has, a priori, the same probability as any other bulb in the same lot of still being in operation at time t.

In view of the size of the population on which measurements were based, we can assume that the probability of survival after age t for each bulb is:

$$\Pr(T \geqslant t) = \nu(t) = \frac{n(t)}{n(0)} . \tag{43.2}$$

For example, according to Table 43.1:

$$\Pr(T \geqslant 5) = \frac{96{,}000}{100{,}000} = 0.96 , \tag{43.3}$$

$$\Pr(T \geqslant 13) = \frac{10{,}000}{100{,}000} = 0.10 . \tag{43.4}$$

The function v(t), as defined by (43.2), is called the survival function of a piece of equipment, and is evaluated from a population or a sample considered representative of the entire population.

We also define the complementary probability:

$$\Pr(T < t) = j(t) = 1 - v(t) \tag{43.5}$$

where j(t) is the distribution function of the random variable T, representing the operating life of the equipment.

The probability distribution corresponding to (43.5), i.e., the probability that a bulb burns out within an interval falling between t - 1 and t, will be:

$$p_t = \Pr[(t-1) \leqslant T < t] = \frac{n(t-1) - n(t)}{n(0)}. \tag{43.6}$$

The f(t) curve which passes through the points

$$\frac{n(t-1) - n(t)}{n(0)}$$

has been shown in Fig. 43.1.

For example, still referring to Table 43.1:

$$\Pr(3 \leqslant T < 4) = 0.01, \tag{43.7}$$

$$\Pr(11 \leqslant T < 12) = 0.14. \tag{43.8}$$

2. Probability of failure.

We give the name probability of failure (breakdown) to the conditional probability that an item of equipment, after having survived to the age of t - 1, will fail (or break down) in the interval between t-1 and t. Denoting this conditional probability as $p_c(t)$, we can write:

$$\Pr(t-1 \leqslant T < t) = \Pr(T \geqslant t-1) . p_c(t) \tag{43.9}$$

which means: the a priori probability of failure in the interval between t - 1 and t is equal to the probability that there will be no failure between 0 and t - 1, multiplied by the conditional probability, $p_c(t)$, that there will be a failure during the interval between t - 1 and t. Thus:

$$p_c(t) = \frac{\Pr(t-1 \leqslant T < t)}{\Pr(T \geqslant t-1)}, \tag{43.10}$$

but:

$$\Pr(t-1 \leqslant T < t) = \frac{n(t-1) - n(t)}{n(0)}, \tag{43.11}$$

and

$$\Pr(T \geqslant t-1) = \frac{n(t-1)}{n(0)}, \tag{43.12}$$

Table 43.2

(1) t	(2) Survivors n(t)	(3) $n(t-1) - n(t)$	(4) $\frac{n(t-1)-n(t)}{n(0)}$	(5) $p_c(t) = \frac{n(t-1)-n(t)}{n(t-1)}$
0	100,000			
1	100,000	0	0	0
2	99,000	1,000	0.01	0.0100
3	98,000	1,000	0.01	0.0101
4	97,000	1,000	0.01	0.0102
5	96,000	1,000	0.01	0.0103
6	93,000	3,000	0.03	0.0312
7	87,000	6,000	0.06	0.0645
8	77,000	10,000	0.10	0.1149
9	63,000	14,000	0.14	0.1818
10	48,000	15,000	0.15	0.2381
11	32,000	16,000	0.16	0.3333
12	18,000	14,000	0.14	0.4375
13	10,000	8,000	0.08	0.4444
14	6,000	4,000	0.04	0.4000
15	3,000	3,000	0.03	0.5000
16	2,000	1,000	0.01	0.3333
17	1,000	1,000	0.01	0.5000
18	0	1,000	0.01	1
> 18	0	0	0	no more survivors

Therefore:

$$p_c(t) = \frac{n(t-1) - n(t)}{n(t-1)} = 1 - \frac{n(t)}{n(t-1)}. \qquad 43.13$$

For example, and still making use of Table 43.1, we see that

$$p_c(t = 12) = 1 - \frac{n(12)}{n(11)} = 1 - \frac{18{,}000}{32{,}000} = 1 - 0.5625 = 0.4375. \qquad 43.14$$

Table 43.2 gives the values of $p_c(t)$ corresponding to $n(t)$.

The probability of failure is an important characteristic. It gives a measure of the risk involved in keeping in service an item of equipment that has been in operation for a time t.

3. Terminology.

What we refer to as the age of an item of equipment is the interval that elapses between the time it goes into service and the instant, t, under consideration. It should be noted that the time and age factors can be replaced in certain problems by hours of operation (for aircraft engines), by kilometers (for automobiles), or by actions (number of landings for a plane, number of actuations for a relay, etc.). To simplify our language, we shall use the time dimension in the following analyses. If necessary, a conversion can be made by analogy.

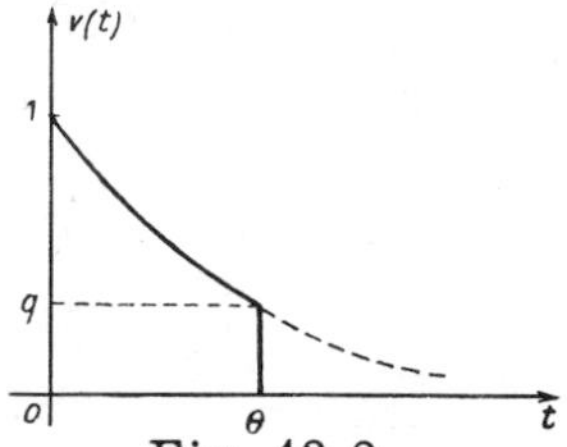

Fig. 43.2

4. Operating limit.

A management policy often requires that equipment placed in service be retired or downgraded upon expiration of a time, θ, called the operating limit or retirement age. In this case, the survival curve at time θ shows a discontinuity (Fig. 43.2). (See Part Two, Section 92.)

Section 44

MEAN AND STANDARD DEVIATION OF THE AGE AT WHICH FAILURE OCCURS

1. General explanation.—2. Case involving the introduction of an operating limit.

1. General explanation.

Let T be the random variable corresponding to the age at which failure occurs: the probability of failure in the interval between t - 1 and t will then be, according to (43.6):

$$p_t = \Pr(t - 1 \leqslant T < t) = \frac{n(t-1) - n(t)}{n(0)}. \qquad 44.1$$

The average age at failure will be the mean value of the random variable T:

$$\bar{t} = \sum_{t=1}^{\infty} t\, p_t. \qquad 44.2$$

For example, consulting Table 43.2, we see that:

$$\begin{aligned}\bar{t} = {} & (1)(0) + (2)(0.01) + (3)(0.01) + (4)(0.01) + (5)(0.01) + (6)(0.03) \\ & + (7)(0.06) + (8)(0.10) + (9)(0.14) + (10)(0.15) \\ & + (11)(0.16) + (12)(0.14) + (13)(0.08) + (14)(0.04) \\ & + (15)(0.03) + (16)(0.01) + (17)(0.01) + (18)(0.01) \\ = {} & 10.30.\end{aligned} \qquad 44.3$$

Thus the average age at failure is 10.30.

To calculate the variance of T, we shall use the formula:

$$\sigma_T^2 = \sum_{t=1}^{\infty} (t - \bar{t})^2 p_t, \qquad 44.4$$

or the following equivalent:

$$\sigma_T^2 = \left(\sum_{t=1}^{\infty} t^2 p_t\right) - (\bar{t})^2. \qquad 44.5$$

These formulas are well known.*

Still using the same example, we can calculate σ_T^2; to begin, we have:

$$\begin{aligned}\sum_{t=1}^{\infty} t^2 p_t = {} & (1)(0) + (4)(0.01) + (9)(0.01) + (16)(0.01) + (25)(0.01) \\ & + (36)(0.03) + (49)(0.06) + (64)(0.10) \\ & + (81)(0.14) + (100)(0.15) + (121)(0.16) \\ & + (144)(0.14) + (169)(0.08) + (196)(0.04) \\ & + (225)(0.03) + (256)(0.01) + (289)(0.01) \\ & + (324)(0.01) \\ = {} & 113.62.\end{aligned} \qquad 44.6$$

Thus:

$$\sigma_T^2 = 113.62 - (10.3)^2 = 7.53, \qquad 44.7$$

from which we obtain the standard deviation:

$$\sigma_T = \sqrt{7.53} = 2.74 \qquad 44.8$$

---

*These equations are to be found in the mathematical review given at the beginning of Part Two.

2. Case involving the introduction of an operating limit.

Returning to Table 43.2, suppose that the equipment must be retired at the age t = 13. We must then modify our table as follows:

t	$n(t)$	$n(t-1) - n(t)$	$\frac{n(t-1) - n(t)}{n(0)}$
12	18,000	14,000	0.14
13	0	18,000	0.18
> 13	0	0	0

44.9

Of course, the mean age and the standard deviation are also changed:

$$\bar{t} = \sum_{t=1}^{13} t\,p_t = (1)(0) + (2)(0.01) + (3)(0.01) + (4)(0.01) + (5)(0.01) + (6)(0.03) + (7)(0.06) + (8)(0.10) + (9)(0.14) + (10)(0.15) + (11)(0.16) + (12)(0.14) + (13)(0.18) = 10.08 \qquad 44.10$$

$$\sum_{t=1}^{13} t^2 p_t = (1)(0) + (4)(0.01) + (9)(0.01) + (16)(0.01) + (25)(0.01) + (36)(0.03) + (49)(0.06) + (64)(0.10) + (81)(0.14) + (100)(0.15) + (121)(0.16) + (144)(0.14) + (169)(0.18) = 107.24 \qquad 44.11$$

$$\sigma_T^2 = 107.24 - (10.08)^2 = 5.64 \qquad 44.12$$

and

$$\sigma_T = \sqrt{5.64} = 2.37 \qquad 44.13$$

It is evident that t and σT decrease when we lower the retirement age. (See Part Two, Section 93.)

Section 45

PROBABILITY OF CONSUMPTION

Let us assume that a new item of equipment is part of an assembly and that it is replaced whenever a breakdown occurs or when the operating limit is reached. Our problem is to find the probability, $p_m(t)$, that there will be m replacements of the initial item of equipment by new equipment during the interval between 0 and t. We shall use the term consumption for the number of pieces of equipment replaced during that time interval.

The probability, $p_o(t)$, of zero consumption, meaning no replacements (m = 0), is obviously v(t):

$$p_0(t) = v(t) = \frac{n(t)}{n(0)}. \qquad 45.1$$

We should recall that v(t) represents the probability of an equipment life greater than or equal to t, that is, the probability that the equipment initially installed has operated without failure during a time t.

To calculate $p_1(t)$, we shall write that there is one, and only one, failure (or replacement because of operating limit) during the interval between 0 and t. This means that a replacement is required at some instant, u, falling between 0 and t; then, no failure between u and t. Now, the probability that there will be a failure (or that the operating limit will be reached) between the ages of u - 1 and u is f(u), or:

$$f(t) = \frac{n(t-1) - n(t)}{n(0)}. \qquad 45.2$$

On the other hand, the probability that the equipment installed as a replacement at time u will operate without failure between u and t is v(t - u). The probability that both of these conditions will be fulfilled, according to the theorem of compound probabilities (see Part Two, Section 53), is equal to the product of the two separate probabilities, or:

$$v(t-u) \,.\, f(u) = \frac{n(t-u)}{n(0)} \cdot \frac{n(u-1) - n(u)}{n(0)}. \qquad 45.3$$

Now, we must consider all the possibilities for failure of the first item of equipment installed at various times u falling between 0 and t, and then add the corresponding probabilities, according to the theorem of total probabilities:

$$p_1(t) = \sum_{u=1}^{t} v(t-u) \,.\, f(u) \qquad 45.4$$

where

$$v(t-u) = \frac{n(t-u)}{n(0)} \quad \text{and} \quad f(u) = \frac{n(u-1) - n(u)}{n(0)}. \qquad 45.5 \quad 45.6$$

More generally, there is a relation giving $p_m(t)$ as a function of $p_{m-1}(t)$. For m items of equipment to be consumed between 0 and t, it is necessary and sufficient that there be a replacement (due to failure or expiration of operating limit) at any instant u between 0 and t, and that (m - 1) items of equipment then be consumed between u and t. Thus:

$$p_m(t) = \sum_{u=1}^{t} p_{m-1}(t-u) \, . \, f(u), \qquad \text{with } p_m(0) = 0. \qquad 45.7 \quad 45.7a$$

Therefore, starting with $p_o(t)$, we shall successively calculate $p_1(t)$, $p_2(t)$, $p_3(t)$, ... etc.; that is:

$$\begin{aligned} p_1(t) &= \sum_{u=1}^{t} v(t-u) \, . \, f(u) \\ p_2(t) &= \sum_{u=1}^{t} p_1(t-u) \, . \, f(u) \\ p_3(t) &= \sum_{u=1}^{t} p_2(t-u) \, . \, f(u) \\ &\ldots\ldots \\ p_m(t) &= \sum_{u=1}^{t} p_{m-1}(t-u) \, . \, f(u) \\ &\ldots\ldots \end{aligned} \qquad 45.8$$

For example, using Table 43.2, we shall calculate $p_1(t)$, taking n(t) from column (2) and f(t) from column (4), or:

$$v(t) = \frac{n(t)}{n(0)} \qquad 45.9$$

and

$$f(t) = \frac{n(t-1) - n(t)}{n(0)}, \qquad 45.10$$

which gives us:

$$\begin{aligned} p_1(1) &= \sum_{u=1}^{1} v(1-u) \cdot f(u) = v(1-1) \, . \, f(1) = v(0) \, . \, f(1) = (1)(0) \\ &= 0 \end{aligned} \qquad 45.11$$

$$\begin{aligned} p_1(2) &= \sum_{u=1}^{2} v(2-u) \, . \, f(u) = v(2-1) \, . \, f(1) + v(2-2) \, . \, f(2) \\ &= v(1) \, . \, f(1) + v(0) \, . \, f(2) \\ &= (1) \, . \, (0) + (1) \, . \, (0.01) \\ &= 0.01 \end{aligned} \qquad 45.12$$

$$\begin{aligned} p_1(3) &= \sum_{u=1}^{3} v(3-u) \, . \, f(u) \\ &= v(3-1) \, . \, f(1) + v(3-2) \, . \, f(2) + v(3-3) \, . \, f(3) \\ &= v(2) \, . \, f(1) + v(1) \, . \, f(2) + v(0) \, . \, f(3) \\ &= (0.99) \, . \, (0) + (1) \, . \, (0.01) + (1) \, . \, (0.01) \\ &= 0.02 \end{aligned} \qquad 45.13$$

$$\begin{aligned} p_1(4) &= \sum_{u=1}^{4} v(4-u).f(u) \\ &= v(3).f(1) + v(2).f(2) + v(1).f(3) + v(0).f(4) \\ &= (0.98).(0) + (0.99)(0.01) + (1).(0.01) + (1).(0.01) \\ &= 0.0299 \end{aligned} \tag{45.14}$$

$$\begin{aligned} p_1(5) &= \sum_{u=1}^{5} v(5-u).f(u) \\ &= v(4).f(1) + v(3).f(2) + v(2).(f3) + v(1).f(4) + v(0).f(5) \\ &= (0.97)(0) + (0.98).(0.01) + (0.99).(0.01) + (1)(0.01) + (1).(0.01) \\ &= 0.0397 \end{aligned} \tag{45.15}$$

$$\begin{aligned} p\,(6) &= \sum_{u=1}^{6} v(6-u).f(u) \\ &= v(5).f(1) + v(4).f(2) + v(3).f(3) + v(2).f(4) + v(1).f(5) \\ &\qquad + v(0).f(6) \\ &= (0.96).(0) + (0.97).(0.01) + (0.98).(0.01) + (0.99).(0.01) \\ &\qquad + (1).(0,01) + (1).(0.03) \\ &= 0.0694 \end{aligned} \tag{45.16}$$

$$\begin{aligned} p_1(7) &= \sum_{u=1}^{7} v(7-u).f(u) \\ &= v(6).f(1) + v(5).f(2) + v(4).f(3) + v(3).f(4) + v(2).f(5) \\ &\qquad + v(1).f(6) + v(0).f(7) \\ &= (0.93)(0) + (0.96).(0.01) + (0.97).(0.01) + (0.98).(0.01) \\ &\qquad + (0.99).(0.01) + (1).(0.03) + (1).(0.06) \\ &= 0.1290 \end{aligned} \tag{45.17}$$

and so:

$$\begin{array}{lll} p_1(8) = 0.2481, & p_1(9) = 0.3661, & p_1(10) = 0.5122 \\ p_1(11) = 0.6656, & p_1(12) = 0.7957, & p_1(13) = 0.8611 \\ p_1(14) = 0.8797, & p_1(15) = 0.8796, & p_1(16) = 0.8445 \\ p_1(17) = 0.7931, & p_1(18) = 0.7227, & p_1(19) = 0.6253 \\ p_1(20) = 0.5168, & p_1(21) = 0.4064, & p_1(22) = 0.3038 \\ p_1(23) = 0.2158, & p_1(24) = 0.1464, & p_1(25) = 0.0962 \\ p_1(26) = 0.0612, & p_1(27) = 0.0374, & p_1(28) = 0.0220 \\ p_1(29) = 0.0120, & \ldots\ldots & \end{array} \tag{45.18}$$

The probabilities $p_1(t)$ having been calculated, we go on to probabilities $p_2(t)$, then $p_3(t)$, etc. We shall not bother with calculations which can be made with a desk calculator. For example:

$$\begin{aligned} p_2(5) &= \sum_{u=1}^{5} p_1(5-u).f(u) \\ &= p_1(4).f(1) + p_1(3).f(2) + p_1(2).f(3) + p_1(1).f(4) + p_1(0).f(5) \\ &= (0.0299.(0) + (0.02).(0.01) + (0.01).(0.01) + (0).(0.01) + (0)(0.01) \\ &= 0.0003 \end{aligned} \tag{45.19}$$

$$
\begin{aligned}
p_2(11) &= \sum_{u=1}^{11} p_1(11-u).f(u) \\
&= p_1(10).f(1) + p_1(9).f(2) + p_1(8).f(3) \\
&\qquad + p_1(7).f(4) + p_1(6).f(5) + p_1(5).f(6) \\
&\qquad\qquad + p_1(4).f(7) + p_1(3).f(8) + p_1(2).f(9) \\
&\qquad\qquad\qquad + p_1(1).f(10) + p_1(0).f(11). \qquad 45.19 \\
&= (0.5122)\,(0) + (0.3661)\,(0.01) + \\
&\qquad + (0.2481)(0.01) + (0.1290)(0.01) + (0.0694)\,(0.01) \\
&\qquad + (0.0397)\,(0.03) + (0.0299)\,(0.06) + (0.02)\,(0.10) \\
&\qquad\qquad + (0.01)(0.14) + (0.01)(0.15) + (0)\,(0.16) \\
&= 0.0145.
\end{aligned}
$$

By hypothesis, we should have:

$$p_0(t) + p_1(t) + p_2(t) \ldots + p_n(t) + \ldots = 1. \qquad 45.20$$

i.e.,

$$\sum_{i=0}^{\infty} p_i(t) = 1, \qquad 45.21$$

since the probability that the consumption at time t will be either zero or some positive value is equal to 1.

An analytical study of such a case is demonstrated in Part Two, Section 95. There it is shown, in particular, that in the case where the function v(t) is exponential:

$$v(t) = e^{-\lambda_0 t}, \qquad 45.22$$

the probability distribution $p_m(t)$ is a Poisson distribution:

$$p_m(t) = \frac{(\lambda_0 t)^m e^{-\lambda_0 t}}{m!}. \qquad 45.23$$

One figure of special interest is the mean value $\overline{m}$ of the consumption at time t, or mean consumption. We have:

$$\overline{m}(t) = \sum_{m=0}^{\infty} m\, p_m(t). \qquad 45.24$$

For example, in the case of Poisson's law (45.16), we obtain:

$$\overline{m}(t) = \lambda_0 t. \qquad 45.25$$

In this important case, the consumption rate is constant and equal to λ_0.

Let us take a numerical example relating to this Poisson case:

$$\lambda_0 = 10^{-3} \text{ hours} \ , \quad t = 10^4 \text{ hours} \ . \qquad 45.26$$

What is the probability that we shall have to make 5 replacements?

We have:

$$\lambda_0 t = 10^{-3} \ . \ 10^4 = 10 \qquad 45.27$$

$$p_5(10^4) = \frac{10^5 \, e^{-10}}{5!} = 0.0378 \ . \qquad 45.28$$

The mean consumption, according to what we have just written in (45.25), will be:

$$\overline{m}(10^4) = 10 \ . \qquad 45.29$$

Furthermore, in a Poisson distribution:

$$\sigma_M^2 = \lambda_0 t \ . \qquad 45.30$$

Thus, in our example, the standard deviation of the consumption will be:

$$\sigma_M = \sqrt{10} \ . \qquad 45.31$$

Certain probabilities are important:

Probability of consumption less than or equal to m during a time t:

$$\Pr(M \leqslant m) = \sum_{r=1}^{m} p_r(t) \ . \qquad 45.32$$
from 0 to t.

Probability of consumption greater than m during a time t:

$$\Pr(M > m) = \sum_{r=m+1}^{\infty} p_r(t) \ . \qquad 45.33$$
from 0 to t

The values for a Poisson distribution are given in a table in the Appendix. (See Part Two, Section 95.)

Section 46

CASE OF USED EQUIPMENT

1. General explanation.—2. Degree of deterioration.

1. General explanation.

In the foregoing, we have assumed that the equipment was initially new. Now let us suppose that the equipment has an age, a, when it is initially placed in service. The survival function is no longer v(t), but $v_a(t)$. We shall now determine this function: it is the conditional probability that an item of equipment having reached age a without failure will continue to operate without failure for a time t; that is, will survive to the age of a + t. The a priori probability of this eventuality, from the definition of v(t), is:

$$v(t + a) \tag{46.1}$$

and, from the theorem of compound probabilities:

$$v(t + a) = v(a).v_a(t), \tag{46.2}$$

or

$$v_a(t) = \frac{v(t + a)}{v(a)}. \tag{46.3}$$

Thus, the survival curve for an item of equipment initially having some degree of deterioration (having already been used up to age a) is obtained by displacing the survival curve for new equipment to the left by an amount a and then multiplying the ordinates of the curve thus obtained by 1/2(a). Fig. 46.1 illustrates how to obtain v(t+a), and from it, $v_a(t)$.

As a numerical example, Table 46.1 gives the survival curve values for an item of equipment having been used previously for a time t = 7, based on the survival curve for new equipment given in Fig. 43.1.

We should not be surprised to find that the probability $v_a(t)$ is higher than the probability v(t) for some values of t. Fig. 46.2 shows a v(t) curve for which $v_a(t)$ is greater than v(t) for a certain value of a (and even for several values), regardless of what value t may have. This is not paradoxical. It depends solely on the nature of the function v(t). In practice, this case arises only when the survival curve falls very rapidly for small values of t, and when a is a value of t at which the v(t) curve has a sufficiently small slope.

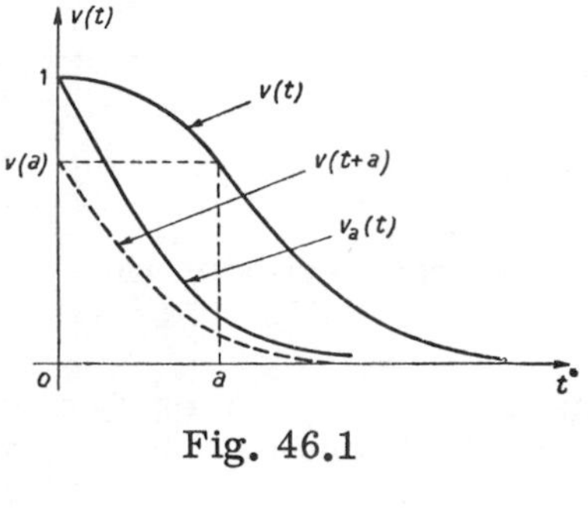

Fig. 46.1

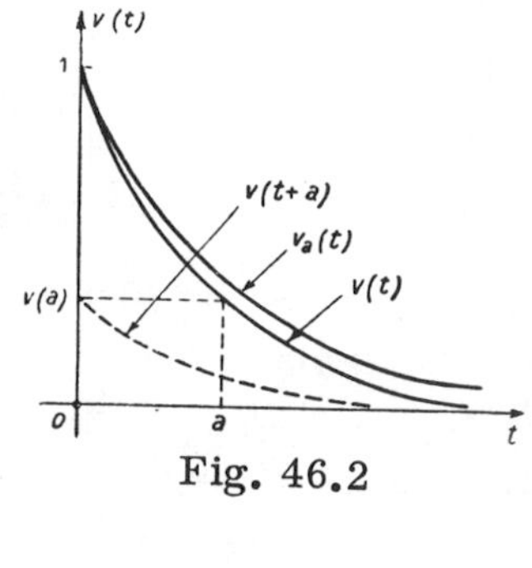

Fig. 46.2

There is a certain survival curve that possesses the following property:

$$v_a(t) = v(t) \tag{46.4}$$

whatever value a may have; this is the exponential curve (see Section 96):

$$v(t) = e^{-\lambda_0 t}\ .^* \tag{46.5}$$

To calculate the probability $p_m(t)$ that there will have been m replacements at the time the original equipment wears out, we

Table 46.1

Time t	$v(t)$	$v(t+7)$	$v_7(t) = \dfrac{v(t+7)}{v(7)}$
0	1	0.87	1
1	1	0.77	0.884
2	0.99	0.63	0.723
3	0.98	0.48	0.552
4	0.97	0.32	0.368
5	0.96	0.18	0.207
6	0.93	0.10	0.115
7	0.87	0.06	0.069
8	0.77	0.03	0.034
9	0.63	0.02	0.023
10	0.48	0.01	0.011
11	0.32	0	0
12	0.18	0	0
13	0.10	—	—
14	0.06	—	—
15	0.03	—	—
16	0.02	—	—
17	0.01	—	—
>17	0	—	—

shall once again make use of formulas (45.4) and (45.7), after we have modified them to take into account the state of the original equipment.

$$p_1(t) = \sum_{u=1}^{t} v(t-u).f_a(u), \qquad 46.6$$

where $$f_a(t) = v_a(t-1) - v_a(t)$$

$$m > 1,\ p_m(t) = \sum_{u=1}^{t} p_{m-1}(t-u)\, f(u), \qquad 46.7$$

where $$f(t) = v(t-1) - v(t)$$

In the case where all the equipment is used and has the same initial amount of wear:

$$p_1(t) = \sum_{u=1}^{t} v_a(t-u).f_a(u), \qquad 46.8$$

$$m > 1, \quad p_m(t) = \sum_{u=1}^{t} p_{m-1}(t-u).f_a(u). \qquad 46.9$$

2. Degree of wear

The probability:

$$u(a) = 1 - v(a), \qquad 46.10$$

is often called "degree of wear," and is expressed as a percentage. Thus, a piece of equipment 90 percent worn has a 10 percent survival probability. (See Part Two, Section 96.)

Section 47

SUPPLY RATE

1. General explanation.—2. Numerical example.

1. General explanation.

Let there be N_0 new equipments put into service at time $t = 0$. If $v(t)$ is the survival function of this equipment, then at time t the number of equipments remaining in operation, if no replacements have been made, will be:

$$n(t) = N_0\, v(t). \qquad 47.1$$

We now propose to replace, or better to supply, additional equipments in sufficient quantities so that the number in service will follow a law, f(t), which we shall call the utilization function. Fig. 47.1 provides an example of a utilization curve; such curves, of course, are arbitrarily set for each problem.

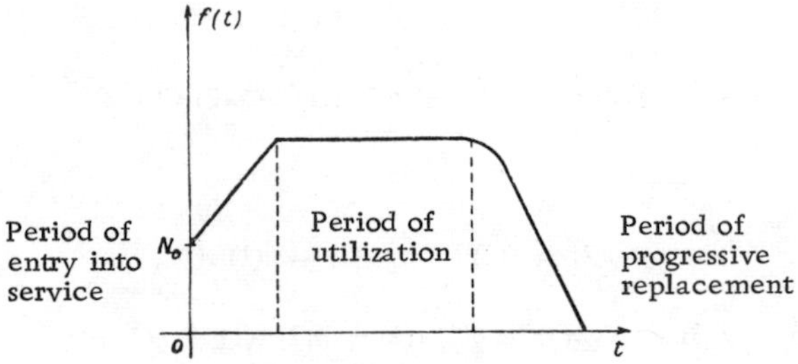

Fig. 47.1

If r(u) is the number of equipments replaced up to time u, the quantity

$$\varrho(u) = r(u) - r(u-1) \qquad (u > 1) \tag{47.2}$$

gives the number of equipments replaced during the interval between u - 1 and u. The function:

$$\varrho(t) \tag{47.3}$$

is called the supply rate.

The number of resupplied equipments surviving to some future time t will be:

$$\varrho(u) \,.\, v(t-u) = [r(u) - r(u-1)]\, v(t-u)\,. \tag{47.4}$$

The number of equipments in service at time t is the sum of such survivals for each interval of time between u = 1 and u = t plus the survivors of the N_0 equipments that were put into service at the outset and which have followed the same survival law. Thus, the total number of equipments in operation at time t will be:

$$f(t) = N_0\, v(t) + \sum_{u=1}^{t} \varrho(u).v(t-u)\,. \tag{47.5}$$

This formula allows us to calculate $\rho(t)$ step by step. To start with, we have:

$$f(0) = N_0\,. \tag{47.6}$$

We now proceed to calculate first $\rho(1)$, then $\rho(2)$, $\rho(3)$, ...:

$$f(1) = N_0\, v(1) + \varrho(1)\, v(0) = N_0\, v(1) + \varrho(1), \qquad 47.7$$

therefore:

$$\varrho(1) = f(1) - N_0\, v(1)\,, \qquad 47.8$$

$$f(2) = N_0\, v(2) + \varrho(1)\, v(1) + \varrho(2)\, v(0)\,, \qquad 47.9$$

therefore:

$$\varrho(2) = f(2) - N_0\, v(2) - \varrho(1)\, v(1)\,, \qquad 47.10$$

$$f(3) = N_0\, v(3) + \varrho(1)\, v(2) + \varrho(2)\, v(1) + \varrho(3)\, v(0)\,, \qquad 47.11$$

therefore:

$$\varrho(3) = f(3) - N_0\, v(3) - \varrho(1)\, v(2) - \varrho(2)\, v(1)\,, \qquad 47.12$$

......

$$f(t) = N_0\, v(t) + [\sum_{u=1}^{t-1} \varrho(u)\, v(t-u)] + \varrho(t)\, v(0) \qquad t > 1 \qquad 47.13$$

therefore:

$$\varrho(t) = f(t) - N_0\, v(t) - \sum_{u=1}^{t-1} \varrho(u)\, v(t-u) \qquad t > 1 \qquad 47.14$$

which gives $\rho(t)$ for t = 1, 2, 3, 4, 5, ...

2. Numerical example.

Referring to Table 47.1, let us take the data in columns (1), (2), and (3). Since $N_0 = 0$, formula (47.14) can be written:

$$\varrho(t) = f(t) - \sum_{u=1}^{t-1} \varrho(u)\, v(t-u)\,, \qquad t > 1\,. \qquad 47.15$$

Then, writing $\rho(t)$ for $\frac{\rho(t)}{10{,}000}$ and f(t) for $\frac{f(t)}{10{,}000}$ (simply to abbreviate the notation), we obtain:

$$\begin{aligned} \varrho(1) &= f(1) = 0.170 \\ \varrho(2) &= f(2) - \varrho(1).v(1) = 0.330 - (0.170).(0.98) = 0.164 \\ \varrho(3) &= f(3) - \varrho(1).v(2) - \varrho(2).v(1) \\ &= 0.500 - (0.170)\,(0.91) - (0.164)\,(0.98) \\ &= 0.184 \end{aligned} \qquad 47.16$$

$$\varrho(4) = f(4) - \varrho(1)\, v(3) - \varrho(2).v(2) - \varrho(3).v(1)$$
$$= 0.670 - (0.170)\,(0.81) - (0.164)\,(0.91) - (0.184)\,(0.98)$$
$$= 0.203$$

$$\varrho(5) = f(5) - \varrho(1).v(4) - \varrho(2).v(3) - \varrho(3).v(2) - \varrho(4).v(1)$$
$$= 0.830 - (0.170)\,(0.69) - (0.164)\,(0.81) - (0.184)\,(0.91) - (0.203)(0.98$$
$$= 0.214$$

$$\varrho(6) = f(6) - \varrho(1).v(5) - \varrho(2).(4) - \varrho(3)\, v(3) - \varrho(4)\ v(2) - \varrho(5)\ v(1)$$
$$= 1 - (0.170)\,(0.56) - (0.164)\,(0.69) - (0.184)\,(0.81)$$
$$- (0.203)\,(0.91) - (0.214)\,(0.98)$$
$$= 0.248$$

$\varrho(7) = 0.106$, $\varrho(8) = 0.130$, $\varrho(9) = 0.144$ ...... etc...

Table 47.1 gives the value found for $\rho(t)$ and r(t).*

To give practical meaning to the results shown in this table, we should point out that the utilization curve shown in Fig. 47.3 has the following special characteristics:

—length of the entry-into-service period: 6 months;

—length of the utilization period: 2 years;

—length of the progressive burn-out or replacement period: 1 year and 6 months.

---

*To verify these calculations, we can check to see whether the total number r(40) of equipments successively put into service is the number actually required. To do so, we calculate the total number of units of operating time required between t = 0 and t = 40, or: $\sum_{t=0}^{40} f(t) = 348{,}100$. We then add the probable value of the total number of units of operating time for t > 40 corresponding to the number of equipments still in service at time t = 40:

$$\sum_{i=1}^{14} \overline{m}_i\, \varrho(40 - i + 1)\, v(i) = 14{,}200,$$

where $\overline{m}_i$ is the probable value of the remaining life-expectancy of an equipment that has already reached age i, and $\rho(40 - i + 1)\, v(i)$ is the number of equipments put into service at time t = 40 - i + 1 and surviving to time t = 41.

The total thus obtained, 348,100 + 14,200 = 362,300, represents the probable value of the total life-expectancy of the entire group of equipments put into service; it must be equal to the product of this number of equipments, r(40) = 57,470, times the average operating life of an equipment, $\overline{m}_0 = 6.31$. Thus we have: 57,470 × 6.31 = 362,000. The check is satisfactory, in view of the degree of precision of the calculations.

Table 47.1

This table corresponds to the curves A_2, B_2 and C of figures 47.2 and 47.3)

(1) t	(2) $v(t)$	(3) $\frac{f(t)}{10,000}$	(4) $\frac{\varrho(t)}{10,000}$	(5) $\frac{r(t)}{10,000}$	(6) Remarks
0	1	0	0	0	We take $N_0 = 0$.
1	0.98	0.17	0.170	0.170	
2	0.91	0.33	0.164	0.334	
3	0.81	0.50	0.184	0.518	
4	0.69	0.67	0.203	0.721	
5	0.56	0.83	0.214	0.935	
6	0.43	1	0.248	1.185	Beginning of the f(t) plateau
7	0.32	1	0.106	1.289	
8	0.23	1	0.130	1.417	
9	0.15	1	0.144	1.583	
10	0.10	1	0.155	1.718	
11	0.06	1	0.159	1.877	
12	0.04	1	0.161	2.038	
13	0.02	1	0.161	2.199	
14	0.01	1	0.167	2.366	
15	0	1	0.153	2.519	
16	—	1	0.157	2.676	
17	—	1	0.160	2.836	
18	—	1	0.158	2.994	
19	—	1	0.159	3.152	
20	—	1	0.160	3.313	
21	—	1	0.157	3.470	
22	—	1	0.157	3.627	
23	—	1	0.161	3.788	
24	—	1	0.159	3.947	
25	—	1	0.157	4.104	
26	—	1	0.160	4.264	
27	—	1	0.159	4.425	
28	—	1	0.158	4.581	
29	—	1	0.159	4.740	Beginning of the period of replacement
30	—	0.97	0.121	4.869	
31	—	0.95	0.138	5.007	
32	—	0.92	0.126	5.133	
33	—	0.87	0.106	5.239	
34	—	0.83	0.104	5.343	
35	—	0.77	0.086	5.429	
36	—	0.72	0.089	5.518	
37	—	0.66	0.069	5.587	
38	—	0.60	0.062	5.649	
39	—	0.54	0.054	5.703	
40	—	0.48	0.044	5.747	

etc....

Two survival curves are shown in Fig. 47.2: the bell-shaped curve, A_2, corresponds to the data in Table 47.1; curve A_1 an exponential curve. Both curves are such that, at the end of 10 months, only 10% of the equipments will survive.

The number of equipments in service during the utilization period is 10,000; furthermore, $N_0 = 0$.

We can see from curves B_1 and B_2 how sensitive the supply curve is to the shape of the survival curve.

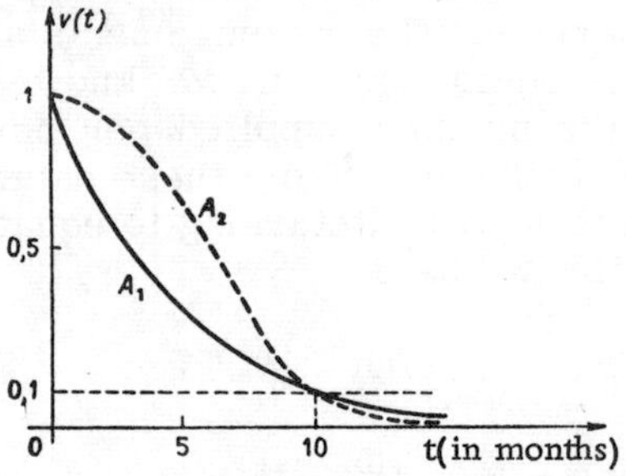

Fig. 47.2

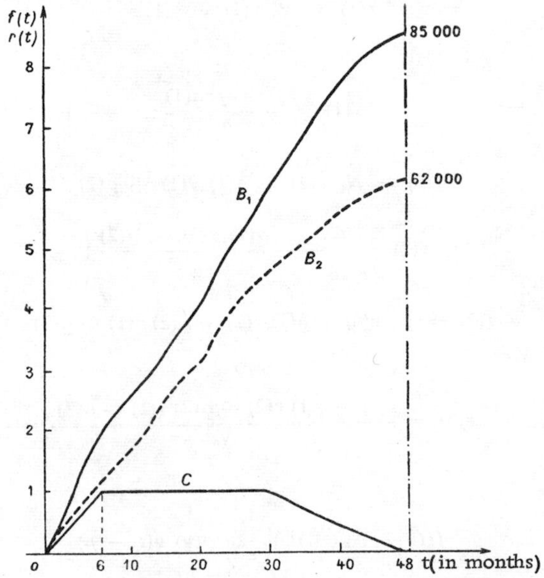

Fig. 47.3. Example of a supply diagram.
B_1—supply function corresponding to curve A_1, Fig. 47.2; B_2—supply function corresponding to curve A_2, Fig. 47.2; C—utilization function.

Curves such as those in Fig. 47.3 make it possible to schedule the exact supply quantities required for a specific equipment-utilization program which is variable in time. (See Part Two, Section 99.)

Section 48

INDIRECT DETERMINATION OF THE SURVIVAL CURVE

The v(t) curve is obtained by means of a statistical study of the equipment in service. The measurements are often taken on a sample lot of the equipment. If we know both the number in service, f(t), and the number supplied per unit of time, $\rho(t)$, we can deduce the survival curve from these data. Our knowledge of f(t) and $\rho(t)$ will give us v(t). Returning to equations (47.6), (47.7), (47.9), (47.11), (47.13), we have:

$$f(0) = N_0, \tag{48.1}$$

$$v(0) = 1, \tag{48.2}$$

$$f(1) = N_0\, v(1) + \varrho(1), \tag{48.3}$$

therefore:

$$v(1) = \frac{f(1) - \varrho(1)}{N_0}; \tag{48.4}$$

$$f(2) = N_0\, v(2) + \varrho(1)\, v(1) + \varrho(2), \tag{48.5}$$

therefore:

$$v(2) = \frac{f(2) - \varrho(1)\, v(1) - \varrho(2)}{N_0};$$

$$f(3) = N_0\, v(3) + \varrho(1)\, v(2) + \varrho(2)\, v(1) + \varrho(3), \tag{48.7}$$

therefore:

$$v(3) = \frac{f(3) - \varrho(1)\, v(2) - \varrho(2)\, v(1) - \varrho(3)}{N_0}; \tag{48.9}$$

......

$$f(t) - N_0\, v(t) + \sum_{u=1}^{t} \varrho(u)\, v(t-u) \tag{48.10}$$

therefore:

$$v(t) = \frac{f(t) - \sum_{u=1}^{t} \varrho(u)\, v(t-u)}{N_0}. \tag{48.11}$$

In this way, step by step, we can calculate v(t) by means of very simple formulas.

This method provides a particularly easy evaluation of v(t) and, in general, gives highly useful results.

Section 49

MAINTENANCE RATE*

Let us now consider the case in which the utilization function, f(t), is constant and equal to N_0. We propose now to find the rate, $\rho(t)$, that will allow us to maintain f(t) at the value N_0. After a sufficient time has elapsed, the function $\rho(t)$ will reach a limiting value, ρ^*, which we shall call the maintenance rate.

Referring back to formulas (47.8), (47.10), (47.12), and (47.14), we shall set f(t) = N_0. This gives us:

$$\begin{aligned} \varrho(1) &= N_0 [1 - \nu(1)] \\ \varrho(2) &= N_0 [1 - \nu(2)] - \varrho(1).\nu(1) \\ \varrho(3) &= N_0 [1 - \nu(3)] - \varrho(1).\nu(2) - \varrho(2).\nu(1) \\ &\ldots\ldots \\ \varrho(t) &= N_0 [1 - \nu(t)] - \sum_{u=1}^{t-1} \varrho(u).\nu(t-u)\,. \end{aligned} \tag{49.1}$$

The use of these formulas is quite easy; let us again use the example given in Table 43.1. Setting N_0 = 100,000, we obtain:

$$\begin{aligned} \varrho(1) &= 10^5 [1 - 1] = 0 \\ \varrho(2) &= 10^5 [1 - 0.99] - (0)(1) = 1{,}000 \\ \varrho(3) &= 10^5 [1 - 0.98] - (0)(0.99) - (1{,}000)(1) = 1{,}000 \\ \varrho(4) &= 10^5 [1 - 0.97] - (0)(0.98) - (1{,}000)(0.99) - (1{,}000)(1) \\ &= 1{,}010 \\ \varrho(5) &= 10^5 ([1 - 0.96] - (0)(0.97) - (1{,}000)(0.98) \\ &\qquad - (1{,}000)(0.99) - (1{,}010)(1) \\ &= 1{,}020 \\ \varrho(6) &= 10^5 [1 - 0.93] - (0)(0.96) \\ &\quad - (1{,}000)(0.97) - (1{,}000)(0.98) \\ &\quad - (1{,}010)(0.99) - (1{,}020)(1) \\ &= 3{,}030. \\ &\ldots\ldots \end{aligned} \tag{49.2}$$

Thus, we arrive at Table 49.1 (See Bibliography, ref. A-2) and the corresponding diagram (Fig. 49.1). In the reference cited, the

---

*The English word "maintenance" generally represents the sum total of the operations and supplies that make it possible to support a piece of equipment in service. This word has been in use in France since 1945, where it has acquired a slightly different meaning limiting it to supplies.

Table 49.1

t	$\varrho(t)$	$r(t)$	t	$\varrho(t)$	$r(t)$
1	0	0	21	12,047	162,167
2	1,000	1,000	22	11,706	173,873
3	1,000	2,000	23	10,820	184,693
4	1,010	3,010	24	9,697	194,390
5	1,020	4,030	25	8,700	203,090
6	3,030	7,060	26	8,288	211,378
7	6,040	13,100	27	8,413	219,791
8	10,090	23,190	28	8,862	228,653
9	14,201	37,391	29	9,529	238,176
10	15,392	52,783	30	10,100	248,276
11	16,665	69,448	31	10,413	269,196
12	15,000	84,448	32	10,507	269,196
13	9,480	93,928	33	10,348	279,544
14	6,175	100,103	34	9,999	289,543
15	6,160	106,263	35	9,636	299,179
16	5,521	111,784	36	9,079	308,258
17	7,309	119,093	37	9,220	317,478
18	9,317	128,410	38	9,271	326,749
19	10,181	138,591	39	9,447	336,196
20	11,529	150,120	40	9,669	345,865

For very large n: $\varrho \to 9{,}709$

reader will find another formula for calculating $\rho(t)$, which seemed to us to be considerably more complicated. In this same reference, the reader will find a method of calculation using the properties of matrix multiplication. (See Part Two, Section 52: The Theory of Matrices.)

It will be noted on Fig. 49.1 that the function $\rho(t)$ oscillates around a limit value of $\rho = 9{,}709$. This property is general, as the reader will discover in Part Two (Section 100), where it is demonstrated that:

$$\varrho^* = \lim_{t \to \infty} \varrho(t) = \frac{N_0}{\bar{t}}, \qquad 49.3$$

where $\bar{t}$ is the mean survival time. Thus, in our example:

$$\varrho^* = \frac{10^5}{10.3} = 9{,}709. \qquad 49.4$$

To calculate $\rho(t)$, we can also use the Monte Carlo (or simulation) method: however, this method is no easier than the application of formulas (49.1), which does not require the use of large calculators or computers.

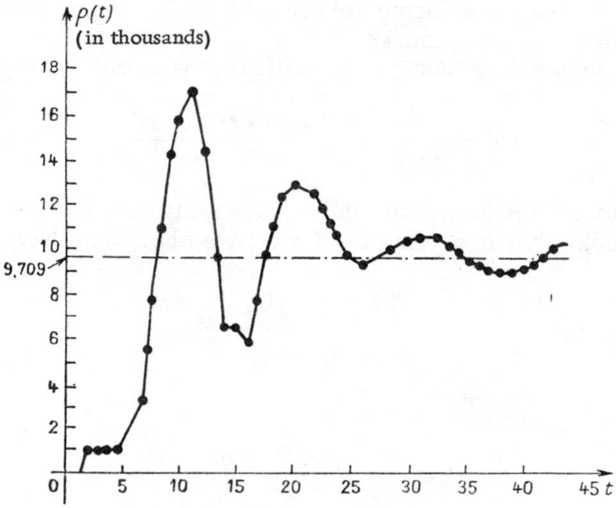

Fig. 49.1

The use of electronic computers becomes particularly helpful, and even indispensable, when the problem involves a large number of equipments that differ from both the technological and statistical points of view.

Section 50

THE ECONOMIC FUNCTION OF MAINTENANCE

In general, the unit cost of putting equipment into service in groups is lower than the unit cost of putting equipment into service piece by piece (as when equipment is replaced after breakdown or at an operating limit). Thus, it may be more profitable to replace all the equipment, old or new, at regular intervals. We shall now calculate the optimum interval corresponding to the minimum over-all cost per unit of time, under this regular group replacement policy.

Let:

c_1 = unit cost of group replacement,

c_2 = unit cost of individual replacement,

N_0 = number of new equipments put into service at the beginning of each period.

The total cost for a time interval t will be:

$$\Gamma(t) = c_1 N_0 + c_2 r(t-1), (^*) \qquad 50.1$$

---

*At the end of interval t, no individual replacements are made, since all the equipment is systematically replaced.

where r(t) is the cumulative function of replacement that assures maintenance of N_0 equipments.

The corresponding cost per unit of time will be:

$$\gamma(t) = \frac{\Gamma(t)}{t} = \frac{c_1 N_0}{t} + \frac{c_2 r(t-1)}{t}. \tag{50.2}$$

There is no difficulty in finding the minimum of this function. Let us suppose that it occurs for $t = t_0$; we shall then have:

$$\gamma(t_0 - 1) > \gamma(t_0), \tag{50.3}$$

$$\gamma(t_0 + 1) > \gamma(t_0). \tag{50.4}$$

Let us calculate $\gamma(t-1)$ et $\gamma(t+1)$:

$$\gamma(t-1) = \frac{c_1 N_0}{t-1} + \frac{c_2 r(t-2)}{t-1}, \tag{50.5}$$

$$\gamma(t+1) = \frac{c_1 N_0}{t+1} + \frac{c_2 r(t)}{t+1}. \tag{50.6}$$

Therefore:

$$\begin{aligned} \gamma(t-1) - \gamma(t) &= c_1 N_0 \left(\frac{1}{t-1} - \frac{1}{t}\right) + c_2 \left(\frac{r(t-2)}{t-1} - \frac{r(t-1)}{t}\right) \\ &= c_1 N_0 \frac{1}{t(t-1)} + c_2 \frac{t\, r(t-2) - (t-1)\, r(t-1)}{t(t-1)} \end{aligned} \tag{50.7}$$

$$\begin{aligned} \gamma(t+1) - \gamma(t) &= c_1 N_0 \left(\frac{1}{t+1} - \frac{1}{t}\right) + c_2 \left(\frac{r(t)}{t+1} - \frac{r(t-1)}{t}\right) \\ &= -c_1 N_0 \frac{1}{(t+1)t} + c_2 \frac{t\, r(t) - (t+1)\, r(t-1)}{(t+1)t}. \end{aligned} \tag{50.8}$$

If t is greater than 2, conditions (50.3) and (50.4) can then be written:

$$(t-1)\, r(t-1) - t\, r(t-2) < \frac{c_1}{c_2} N_0, \qquad \text{for (50.3)} \tag{50.9}$$

$$t\, r(t) - (t+1)\, r(t-1) > \frac{c_1}{c_2} N_0, \qquad \text{for (50.4)} \tag{50.10}$$

Let us pose:

$$S(t) = t\, r(t) - (t+1)\, r(t-1) : \tag{50.11}$$

then the condition will be written:

$$S(t-1) < \frac{c_1}{c_2} N_0 < S(t). \tag{50.12}$$

The value of t_0 which satisfies (50.12) gives the minimum.* To determine t_0 it is only necessary to calculate one S(t) table. For example, let us suppose:

$$c_1 = 2.5, \quad c_2 = 10, \quad N_0 = 100{,}000, \tag{50.13}$$

r(t) being given by table 49.1.

Let us set up table 50.1. We have:

$$\frac{c_1}{c_2} N_0 = 0.25 \times 100{,}000 = 25{,}000\ ; \tag{50.14}$$

in the table, we see that:

$$14{,}150 < 25{,}000 < 35{,}220. \tag{50.15}$$

Table 50.1

(1) t	(2) $r(t)$	(3) $t\,r(t)$	(4) $(t+1)r(t-1)$	(5) $S(t)$	(6) $\Gamma(t)$	(7) $\gamma(t)$
1	0	0	—	—	250,000	250,000
2	1,000	2,000	0	2,000	250,000	125,000
3	2,000	6,000	4,000	2,000	260,000	86,670
4	3,010	12,040	10,000	2,040	270,000	67,500
5	4,030	20,150	18,060	2,090	280,100	56,020
6	7,060	42,360	28,210	14,150	290,300	48,380
7	13,100	91,700	56,480	35,220	320,600	45,800
8	23,190	185,520	117,900	67,620	381,000	47,620
9	37,391	336,519	231,900	104,619	481,900	53,540

*In the case of a continuous r(t) function, we shall have:

$$\gamma(t) = \frac{c_1 N_0}{t} + \frac{c_2 r(t)}{t}$$

$$\frac{d\gamma}{dt} = \frac{c_2 r'(t)\,.\,t - [c_1 N_0 + c_2 r(t)]}{t^2}\ ;$$

the minimum (and it actually is a minimum) occurs for $t = t_0$, in such fashion that:

$$c_2 r'(t_0) = \frac{c_1 N_0 + c_2 r(t_0)}{t}$$

Thus, and this is remarkable, the minimum occurs for a time t_0, or period of general equipment replacement, that corresponds to equality between the cost of variation and the mean cost.

Let:

$$S(6) < 25{,}000 < S(7)\,. \tag{50.16}$$

Thus we would select t = 7, for which $\gamma(7) = 45{,}800$.

Let us set:

$$\alpha = \frac{c_1}{c_2}; \tag{50.17}$$

It is interesting to construct a curve for a given function r(t) that will show the optimum times, t_o, for different values of α (Fig. 50.1).

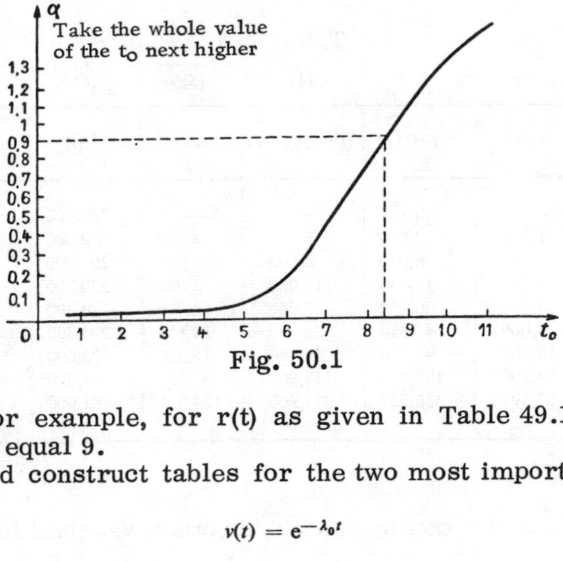

Fig. 50.1

Thus, for example, for r(t) as given in Table 49.1, if $\alpha = 0.9$, then t_o will equal 9.

We could construct tables for the two most importance cases:

$$v(t) = e^{-\lambda_0 t} \tag{50.18}$$

and

$$v(t) = e^{-\mu_0 t^2}\,. \tag{50.19}$$

We could also state the optimum time as a function of λ_o and c_1/c_2, or of μ_o and c_1/c_2. This task we shall leave to the reader.

In the work cited under ref. A-2 in the Bibliography, the reader will find various further developments: of particular interest is the comparative study of two policies, one in which group replacement takes place for an interval t satisfying inequations (50.12) and the other in which group replacement is never used.

PART II

MATHEMATICAL DEVELOPMENTS

Chapter **6**

Mathematical review

Section 51
INTRODUCTION

In this chapter we shall give only those formulas and properties that are most important in helping the reader interested in mathematical developments to follow them more readily. This very brief review will deal with:

—matrix calculations
—the concepts of probability and random variables
—statistical concepts;

and, even more briefly, with the Carson-LaPlace transformation.

In order to explain the formulas more clearly, we shall often give examples.

Section 52
MATRIX CALCULATIONS

1. General remarks.—2. Operations on matrices.

1. General remarks.

Instead of writing a system of linear algebraic equations in the form:

$$\begin{aligned} a_{11}x_1 + a_{12}x_2 + a_{13}x_3 &= b_1 \\ a_{21}x_1 + a_{22}x_2 + a_{23}x_3 &= b_2 \\ a_{31}x_1 + a_{32}x_2 + a_{33}x_3 &= b_3, \end{aligned} \qquad 52.1$$

we can present the three sets of magnitudes a_{ij}, x_i, and b_j in the form of tables or matrices:

$$\begin{bmatrix} a_{11} & a_{12} & a_{13} \\ a_{21} & a_{22} & a_{23} \\ a_{31} & a_{32} & a_{33} \end{bmatrix} \begin{Bmatrix} x_1 \\ x_2 \\ x_3 \end{Bmatrix} = \begin{Bmatrix} b_1 \\ b_2 \\ b_3 \end{Bmatrix} \qquad 52.2$$

associating with this representation a very simple rule of multiplication: take the sum of the products of the elements in row i times the elements in column j. For example:

$$a_{11}x_1 + a_{12}x_2 + a_{13}x_3 = b_1 \qquad 52.3$$

This rule can be generalized, no matter how many columns or rows there are in the matrices, provided that the number of columns in the matrix at the left is always equal to the number of rows in the matrix at the right.

Numerical example:

$$\begin{bmatrix} 5 & 0 & 3 \\ 2 & -1 & 2 \\ 4 & 8 & -3 \end{bmatrix}\begin{bmatrix} 4 & -8 \\ 0 & -15 \\ 1 & 2 \end{bmatrix} = \begin{bmatrix} (5)(4)+(0)(0)+(3)(1) & (5)(-8)+(0)(-15)+(3)(2) \\ (2)(4)+(-1)(0)+(2)(1) & (2)(-8)+(-1)(-15)+(2)(2) \\ (4)(4)+(8)(0)+(-3)(1) & (4)(-8)+(8)(-15)+(-3)(2) \end{bmatrix}$$

$$= \begin{bmatrix} 23 & -34 \\ 10 & 3 \\ 13 & -158 \end{bmatrix}. \qquad 52.4$$

We shall use the following abbreviated notation:

$$\begin{array}{l} [a] \text{ for a rectangular or square matrix,} \\ \{a\} \text{ for a column matrix,} \end{array} \qquad 52.5$$

or, when there is no possibility of confusion, simply a.

2. Operations on matrices.

Equality of two matrices: $[a] = [b]$ 52.6

Two matrices are equal if all the corresponding elements are equal.

Addition of matrices:

$$[a] + [b] = [c], \quad \text{où} \quad c_{ij} = a_{ij} + b_{ij}. \qquad 52.7$$

Example:

$$\begin{bmatrix} 2 & 3 & 1 \\ 0 & -1 & 4 \end{bmatrix} + \begin{bmatrix} 7 & 8 & 11 \\ -11 & 3 & 4 \end{bmatrix} = \begin{bmatrix} 9 & 11 & 12 \\ -11 & 2 & 8 \end{bmatrix}.$$

Multiplication by a scalar: 52.9

$$\lambda[a] = [b], \text{ where } b_{ij} = \lambda a_{ij}.$$

Example:

$$5\begin{bmatrix} 3 & 2 \\ -1 & 8 \end{bmatrix} = \begin{bmatrix} 15 & 10 \\ -5 & 40 \end{bmatrix} \qquad 52.10$$

Multiplication of one matrix by another*:

$$[a]\,[b] = [c], \qquad \text{where} \quad c_{ij} = \sum_{k=1}^{n} a_{ik}\, b_{kj}, \qquad 52.11$$

If n is the number of columns in a, then b must have n rows if multiplication is to be possible.

Null matrix: $[0]$ 52.12

A matrix in which all elements are zero.

Example:

$$\begin{bmatrix} 0 & 0 & 0 \\ 0 & 0 & 0 \end{bmatrix}. \qquad 52.13$$

Unit matrix. 52.14

A square matrix in which all the elements are zero except those along the main diagonal (the diagonal from upper left to lower right), which are 1:

$$[a] = [1] \quad \text{if} \quad \begin{aligned} a_{ij} &= 0 \qquad i \neq j \\ &= 1 \qquad i = j; \end{aligned} \qquad 52.14$$

Examples:

$$\begin{bmatrix} 1 & 0 \\ 0 & 1 \end{bmatrix}, \quad \begin{bmatrix} 1 & 0 & 0 \\ 0 & 1 & 0 \\ 0 & 0 & 1 \end{bmatrix}. \qquad 52.15$$

For every unit matrix: $[a]\,[1] = [a], \quad [1]\,[b] = [b]$.

Whole powers

$$[a]^2 = [a]\,[a]\,, \qquad [a]^n = \underbrace{[a]\,[a] \ldots [a]}_{n}\,, \qquad 52.18,\ 52.19$$

$$[a]^m\,[a]^n = [a]^n\,[a]^m = [a]^{m+n}, \qquad 52.20$$

$$([a]^m)^n = ([a]^n)^m = [a]^{mn}. \qquad 52.21$$

Inverse of a matrix:

[b] is the inverse of [a] if $[a]\,[b] = [b]\,[a] = [1]$. 52.22

We write: $[b] = [a]^{-1}$. 52.23

(See the calculation of $[a]^{-1}$ below.)

---

*Except in special cases, we have: $[a]\,[b] \neq [b]\,[a]$.

Transposed:
Matrix obtained by switching rows and columns.
We write: $[a]'$.
Example:

$$[a] = \begin{bmatrix} 3 & 2 & -5 \\ 1 & 0 & 4 \end{bmatrix}, \qquad [a]' = \begin{bmatrix} 3 & 1 \\ 2 & 0 \\ -5 & 4 \end{bmatrix}. \qquad 52.24 \quad 52.25$$

Adjunct:

Square matrix formed with the co-factors of the transposed matrix of the given square matrix.

We write: $[a]^{\Gamma}$.

Example:

$$[a] = \begin{bmatrix} 2 & 1 & 0 \\ 3 & 0 & 1 \\ -2 & 4 & 2 \end{bmatrix}, \qquad [a]' = \begin{bmatrix} 2 & 3 & -2 \\ 1 & 0 & 4 \\ 0 & 1 & 2 \end{bmatrix}, \qquad 52.26 \quad 52.27$$

$$[a]^{\Gamma} = \begin{bmatrix} +\begin{vmatrix} 0 & 4 \\ 1 & 2 \end{vmatrix} & -\begin{vmatrix} 1 & 4 \\ 0 & 2 \end{vmatrix} & +\begin{vmatrix} 1 & 0 \\ 0 & 1 \end{vmatrix} \\ -\begin{vmatrix} 3 & -2 \\ 1 & 2 \end{vmatrix} & +\begin{vmatrix} 2 & -2 \\ 0 & 2 \end{vmatrix} & -\begin{vmatrix} 2 & 3 \\ 0 & 1 \end{vmatrix} \\ +\begin{vmatrix} 3 & -2 \\ 0 & 4 \end{vmatrix} & -\begin{vmatrix} 2 & -2 \\ 1 & 4 \end{vmatrix} & +\begin{vmatrix} 2 & 3 \\ 1 & 0 \end{vmatrix} \end{bmatrix} \qquad 52.28$$

I.e.:

$$[a]^{\Gamma} = \begin{bmatrix} -4 & -2 & 1 \\ -8 & 4 & -2 \\ 12 & -10 & -3 \end{bmatrix}. \qquad 52.29$$

The inverse of a square matrix may be written:

$$[a]^{-1} = \frac{[a]^{\Gamma}}{|a|}. \qquad 52.30$$

Thus, we may calculate in the following sequence:*

$[a]'$, $[a]^{\Gamma}$, $|a|$ (derived from $|a|\,[1] = [a]\,[a]^{\Gamma}$) we finally obtain $[a]^{-1}$.

---

*Actually, easier methods of calculation are used when matrices are of a higher order.

Example:

$$[a]=\begin{bmatrix} 5 & 3 & -1 \\ 2 & 0 & 4 \\ -2 & 3 & 1 \end{bmatrix},\quad [a]'=\begin{bmatrix} 5 & 2 & -2 \\ 3 & 0 & 3 \\ -1 & 4 & 1 \end{bmatrix},\quad [a]^{\Gamma}=\begin{bmatrix} -12 & -6 & 12 \\ -10 & 3 & -22 \\ 6 & -21 & -6 \end{bmatrix} \qquad \begin{matrix} 52.32 \\ 52.33 \\ 52.34 \end{matrix}$$

$$[a]\,[a]^{\Gamma} = \begin{bmatrix} -96 & 0 & 0 \\ 0 & -96 & 0 \\ 0 & 0 & -96 \end{bmatrix}, \qquad 52.35$$

$$[a]^{-1} = \frac{1}{-96}\begin{bmatrix} -12 & -6 & 12 \\ -10 & 3 & -22 \\ 6 & -21 & -6 \end{bmatrix} = \begin{bmatrix} \frac{1}{8} & \frac{1}{16} & -\frac{1}{8} \\ \frac{5}{48} & -\frac{1}{32} & \frac{11}{48} \\ -\frac{1}{16} & \frac{7}{32} & \frac{1}{16} \end{bmatrix}. \qquad 52.36$$

Sub-matrices:
Matrices can be broken down into "sub-matrices."
Example:

$$[A] = \left[\begin{array}{c:cc} a & b & c \\ \hdashline d & e & f \\ g & h & i \end{array}\right]. \qquad 52.37$$

By posing:

$$[z_1] = a, \qquad 52.38$$

$$[z_2] = [b\ c], \qquad 52.39$$

$$[z_3] = \begin{bmatrix} d \\ g \end{bmatrix}, \qquad 52.40$$

$$[z_4] = \begin{bmatrix} e & f \\ h & i \end{bmatrix}; \qquad 52.41$$

we have:

$$[A] = \begin{bmatrix} z_1 & z_2 \\ z_3 & z_4 \end{bmatrix}. \qquad 52.42$$

Another example will demonstrate the use of sub-matrices.

Assume a system of 5 equations with 5 unknowns.

$$\left[\begin{array}{cc:ccc} a_{11} & a_{12} & a_{13} & a_{14} & a_{15} \\ a_{21} & a_{22} & a_{23} & a_{24} & a_{25} \\ \hdashline a_{31} & a_{32} & a_{33} & a_{34} & a_{35} \\ a_{41} & a_{42} & a_{43} & a_{44} & a_{45} \\ a_{51} & a_{52} & a_{53} & a_{54} & a_{55} \end{array}\right] \begin{Bmatrix} x_1 \\ x_2 \\ \cdots \\ x_3 \\ x_4 \\ x_5 \end{Bmatrix} = \begin{Bmatrix} b_1 \\ b_2 \\ \cdots \\ b_3 \\ b_4 \\ b_5 \end{Bmatrix}. \qquad 52.43$$

We pose:

$$\alpha = \begin{bmatrix} a_{11} & a_{12} \\ a_{21} & a_{22} \end{bmatrix}, \quad \beta = \begin{bmatrix} a_{13} & a_{14} & a_{15} \\ a_{23} & a_{24} & a_{25} \end{bmatrix}, \quad \gamma = \begin{bmatrix} a_{31} & a_{32} \\ a_{41} & a_{42} \\ a_{51} & a_{52} \end{bmatrix}$$ 52.44 52.45 52.46

$$\delta = \begin{bmatrix} a_{33} & a_{34} & a_{35} \\ a_{43} & a_{44} & a_{45} \\ a_{53} & a_{54} & a_{55} \end{bmatrix}, \; X_1 = \begin{Bmatrix} x_1 \\ x_2 \end{Bmatrix}, \quad X_2 = \begin{Bmatrix} x_3 \\ x_4 \\ x_5 \end{Bmatrix}, \quad B_1 = \begin{Bmatrix} b_1 \\ b_2 \end{Bmatrix}, \; B_2 = \begin{Bmatrix} b_3 \\ b_4 \\ b_5 \end{Bmatrix}.$$ 52.47 52.48 52.49 52.50 52.51

The system of equations (52.43) will then be written:

$\alpha X_1 + \beta X_2 = B_1$ where we derive: $X_1 = (\alpha - \beta\delta^{-1}\gamma)^{-1}(B_1 - \beta\delta^{-1}B_2)$ 52.52

$\gamma X_1 + \delta X_2 = B_2$ $\qquad X_2 = (\delta - \gamma\alpha^{-1}\beta)^{-1}(B_2 - \gamma\alpha^{-1}B_1),$ 52.53

which allows us to obtain the unknowns x_1, x_2, x_3, x_4, x_5 by inverting at the most (3 x 3) matrices, instead of a (5 x 5) matrix.

Section 53

THE CONCEPTS OF PROBABILITY AND RANDOM VARIABLE

Concept of probability:

The probability that an event E will occur is the ratio between the number, n, of cases in which E does occur (called favorable cases) and the total number, N, of the elementary cases, all equally possible.

$$p = \Pr(E) = \frac{n}{N}. \qquad 53.1$$

Probability of the contrary event:

$$q = 1 - p = \frac{N - n}{N}. \qquad 53.2$$

Conditional probability: 53.3

The probability that an event A will occur, if we know that event B has occurred, is called the conditional probability. It is written: $\Pr_B(A)$.

A priori probability. 53.4

As contrasted with the expression "conditional probability of event A with relation to B", the expression "a priori probability of A" so often used, instead of probability of A. In this way, we emphasize the fact that we are not concerned with the occurrence of any other event.

Compound probability: 53.5

This is the probability that both A and B will occur. It is written: Pr (A. B).

Total probability:

This is the probability that A and/or B (A alone, B alone, or A and B together) will occur. It is written:

$$\Pr(A + B) \qquad 53.6$$

Principle of compound probabilities:

$$\Pr(A \, . \, B) = \Pr(A) \, . \, \Pr_A(B) = \Pr(B) \, . \, \Pr_B(A). \qquad 53.7$$

Principle of total probabilities:

$$\Pr(A + B) = \Pr(A) + \Pr(B) - \Pr(AB). \qquad 53.8$$

If the events are mutually exclusive:

$$\Pr(A.B) = 0 \qquad 53.9$$

and

$$\Pr(A + B) = \Pr A + \Pr B. \qquad 53.10$$

Random variable:

If a variable, X, can assume the values

$$x_1, x_2, \ldots, x_n \qquad 53.11$$

with each of these values having a probability of

$$p(x_1), \, p(x_2), \ldots, p(x_n) \qquad 53.12$$

where

$$\sum_{i=1}^{n} p(x_i) = 1, \qquad 53.13$$

it is called a random variable. We write it as X, and its value as x_i.

Mathematical expectation or probable value:

This is the weighted mean value of X:

$$E(x) = x_1 p(x_1) + x_2 p(x_2) + \ldots + x_n p(x_n). \tag{53.14}$$

This may also be written $\overline{X}$ or $\overline{x}$.

Reduced random variable:

$$X' = X - \bar{x}; \tag{53.15}$$

we find:

$$E(X') = E(X - \bar{x}) = 0. \tag{53.16}$$

Function of a random variable:

If y = f(x) is a certain function, then Y = f(X) is a function of the random variable X and is, in turn, a random variable. We give the name expectation of the Y function of the random variable X to the quantity:

$$E(Y) = E[f(X)] = \sum_{i=1}^{n} f(x_i).p(x_i). \tag{53.17}$$

Variance:

$$\begin{aligned} \sigma_x^2 &= E[(X - \bar{x})^2] \\ &= (x_1 - \bar{x})^2 p(x_1) + (x_2 - \bar{x})^2 p(x_2) + \ldots + (x_n - \bar{x})^2 p(x_n). \end{aligned} \tag{53.18}$$

σ_x is called the standard deviation or the mean square deviation. Once again, we use the formula:

$$\sigma_x^2 = E(X^2) - [E(X)]^2. \tag{53.18a}$$

Probability or frequency function:

The function p(x) which assumes the discrete values $p(x_1)$, $p(x_2), \ldots, p(x_n)$ is called the probability or frequency function. We may also use the notation:

$$p(x_i) = \Pr(X = x_i). \tag{53.19}$$

Cumulative probability or distribution function:

By accumulating the values of p(x), we obtain a new function called the cumulative probability or distribution function.

$$P(x) = \Pr(X \leqslant x) = \sum_{x_i \leqslant x} p(x_i). \tag{53.20}$$

The function:

$$\Pr(X > x) = 1 - \Pr(X \leqslant x) \qquad 53.21$$

is called the complementary distribution.

The Bienaymé-Tchebycheff inequality:

This unequality gives the upper limit of the probability that a variable X will deviate (in absolute value) from its mean by a quantity equal to t times the standard deviation.

$$\Pr\left[|X - \bar{x}| \geqslant \sigma t\right] \leqslant \frac{1}{t^2} \qquad t > 1. \qquad 53.22$$

For example, the probability of a deviation greater than 10σ is less than 1/100.

If t is large, the second member of this inequality becomes very small, and the information provided by the inequality becomes very useful.

This inequality is valid for any distribution of X.

Binomial distribution:

If X assumes the integral values 0, 1, 2, 3, . . . , r with the probabilities:

$$B_r = C_n^r p^r (1 - p)^{n-r}, \quad \text{where } C_n^r = \frac{n!}{r!(n-r)!}, \qquad 53.23 \quad 53.24$$

and where n is a positive integer, the distribution is called a binomial distribution. The distribution:

$$P_r = \sum_{s=0}^{r} C_n^s p^s (1 - p)^{n-s} \qquad 53.25$$

is called the cumulative binomial distribution.

We have:

$$E(X) = np \text{ and } \sigma_x^2 = np(1 - p). \qquad 53.26 \quad 53.27$$

Poisson distribution:

If X assumes the integral values r = 0, 1, 2, 3,. . . with the probabilities:

$$p_r = \frac{a^r}{r!} e^{-a}, \qquad 53.28$$

where a is a positive parameter, the distribution is called a Poisson distribution. The corresponding cumulative distribution is:

$$P_r = \sum_{s=0}^{r} \frac{a^s}{s!} e^{-a} . \qquad 53.29$$

We have:

$$E(X) = a, \qquad \sigma_x^2 = a. \qquad 53.30 \quad 53.31$$

System of two random variables:

If X can assume values x_i with the probabilities $p(x_i)$, $i = 1, 2, \ldots, m$, and if Y can assume values y_j with the probabilities $q(y_j)$, $j = 1, 2, \ldots n$, then the simultaneous occurrence of the events E_1 and E_2, corresponding respectively to X and Y, has the compound probability p(X,Y). This will be written:

$$p(x_i, y_j) = \Pr [X = x_i, Y = y_j] \qquad 53.32$$

where

$$\sum_{i=1}^{m} \sum_{j=1}^{n} p(x_i, y_j) = 1. \qquad 53.33$$

From the distribution with two variables p(x, y) we find the function of the division of:

$$P(x, y) = \Pr [X \leqslant x, Y \leqslant y] = \sum_{x_i \leqslant x} \sum_{y_j \leqslant y} p(x_i, y_j). \qquad 53.34$$

We have

$$p(x_i, y_j) = q_{x_i}(y_j) . p(x_i) = p_{y_j}(x_i) . q(y_j), \qquad 53.35$$

where

$$p(x_i) = \Pr [X = x_i, Y < \infty], \qquad 53.36$$

$$q(y_j) = \Pr [X < \infty, Y = y_j]. \qquad 53.37$$

The mathematical expectancy of a function of two random variables:

$$E [f(X, Y)] = \sum_{i=1}^{m} \sum_{j=1}^{n} f(x_i, y_j) . \ p(x_i, y_j) , \qquad 53.38$$

$$E [X + Y] = E(X) + E(Y), \qquad 53.39$$

$$E [X . Y] = E(X) . E(Y) \qquad 53.40$$

if X and Y are independent.

Continuous distribution:

$$f(x) = \lim_{\Delta x \to 0} \frac{\Pr[x \leqslant X \leqslant x + \Delta x]}{\Delta x} \tag{53.41}$$

$$p[x \leqslant X \leqslant x + dx] = f(x)\, dx, \tag{53.42}$$

$$p[a \leqslant x \leqslant b] = \int_a^b f(x)\, dx, \tag{53.43}$$

$$p[-\infty < x < \infty] = \int_{-\infty}^{+\infty} f(x) dx = 1\,. \tag{53.44}$$

f(x) is called the probability density.

$$P(x) = \Pr(-\infty < X \leqslant x) = \int_{-\infty}^{x} f(x) dx \tag{53.45}$$

is the distribution function.

System of 2 continuous random variables:

$$f(x, y)\, dxdy = \Pr[x \leqslant X \leqslant x + dx,\, y \leqslant Y \leqslant y + dy]\,; \tag{53.46}$$

the probability density is f(x, y).

$$\begin{aligned} P(x, y) &= \int_{-\infty}^{x} \int_{-\infty}^{y} f(x, y)\, dx\, dy \\ &= \Pr[X \leqslant x, \quad Y \leqslant y] \end{aligned} \tag{53.47}$$

is the distribution function.

We have:

$$\frac{\partial^2}{\partial x \partial y}[P(x, y)] = f(x, y), \tag{53.48}$$

$$f(x, y) = p_x(y).f(x) = p_y(x).g(y); \tag{53.49}$$

where

$$f(x) = \frac{\partial}{\partial x} P(x, \infty), \tag{53.50}$$

$$g(y) = \frac{\partial}{\partial y} P(\infty, y). \tag{53.51}$$

Hence:

$$p_x(y) = \frac{f(x, y)}{f(x)}, \qquad p_y(x) = \frac{f(x, y)}{g(y)}. \tag{53.52}$$

Mathematical expectancy of a function of two continuous random variables:

$$E[h(X, Y)] = \int_{-\infty}^{\infty} \int_{-\infty}^{\infty} h(x, y)\, f(x, y)\, dx\, dy, \tag{53.54}$$

$$E(X + Y) = E(X) + E(Y), \tag{53.55}$$

$$E(X.Y) = E(X)\ .\ E(Y). \tag{53.56}$$

if the variables are independent.

Correlation coefficient:

If

$$_x^2 = E[(X - \bar{x})^2], \tag{53.57}$$

$$\sigma_y^2 = E[(Y - \bar{y})^2] \tag{53.58}$$

$$\sigma_{xy}^2 = E[(X - \bar{x})(Y - \bar{y})] \tag{53.59}$$

$$\tau = \frac{\sigma_{xy}^2}{\sigma_x . \sigma_y} \tag{53.60}$$

is called the correlation coefficient.

$$0 \leqslant |\tau| \leqslant 1. \tag{53.61}$$

This statistically characterizes the independence of X and Y.

Normal or Gaussian distribution:

If a random variable X can assume all the continuous values x in the interval $-\infty < x < \infty$ with a probability density of:

$$f(x) = \frac{1}{\sqrt{2\pi}} e^{-\frac{1}{2}x^2}, \tag{53.62}$$

its distribution is called normal or Gaussian.

The corresponding distribution function is:

$$P(x) = \Pr(X \leqslant x) = \frac{1}{\sqrt{2\pi}} \int_{-\infty}^{x} e^{-\frac{1}{2}\lambda^2} d\lambda \tag{53.63}$$

where

$$\frac{1}{\sqrt{2\pi}} \int_{-\infty}^{+\infty} e^{-\frac{1}{2}\lambda^2} d\lambda = 1 \tag{53.64}$$

We have

$$\bar{x} = E(X) = 0, \quad \sigma_X^2 = E[(X - \bar{x})^2] = 1. \qquad 53.65 \quad 53.66$$

For a non-reduced variable X′ we write:

$$\varphi(x) = \frac{1}{\sigma\sqrt{2\pi}} e^{-\frac{1}{2}\left(\frac{x-\bar{x}}{\sigma}\right)^2}, \qquad 53.67$$

$$\Phi(x) = \frac{1}{\sigma\sqrt{2\pi}} \int_{-\infty}^{x} e^{-\frac{1}{2}\left(\frac{\lambda-\bar{x}}{\sigma}\right)} d\lambda, \qquad 53.68$$

with:

$$\bar{x} = E(X'), \qquad 53.69$$

$$\sigma_{x'} = E[(X' - \bar{x})^2] = \sigma^2. \qquad 53.70$$

If X and Y are random Gaussian variables, then the random variable:

$$Z = X + Y \qquad 53.71$$

also has a Gaussian distribution, such that:

$$\bar{z} = \bar{x} + \bar{y} \qquad 53.72$$

and

$$\sigma_z^2 = \sigma_x^2 + \sigma_y^2. \qquad 53.73$$

If $X_i (i = 1, 2, \ldots, n)$ represents a set of independent random variables all having the same arbitrary distribution, the sum:

$$X = \frac{\sum_{i=1}^{n} X_i}{n} \qquad 53.74$$

approaches the normal distribution when $n \to \infty$. If each X_i (i = 1, 2, . . . , n) has a zero mean and a finite variance $\sigma_{X_i}^2$, then:

$$E(X) = 0 \text{ and } \sigma_X = \frac{1}{n}\sum_{i=1}^{n} \sigma_{X_i}. \qquad 53.75$$

Section 54

STATISTICAL CONCEPTS

Histogram:

A table showing the number of individuals falling within each interval or class; this number is called the frequency.

Before constructing a histogram, we must define:
—the limits of the group studied,
—the data or characteristics measured for each individual,
—the conditions under which the measurements were made.

Mean:

Given a population consisting of N individuals, if f_i is the frequency of the variate x_i, the mean, $\bar{x}$, is given by the formula:

$$\bar{x} = \frac{1}{N}\sum_{i=1}^{k} f_i x_i, \qquad 54.1$$

where k is the number of classes and

$$N = \sum_{i=1}^{k} f_i. \qquad 54.2$$

The term frequency is also used by some for the ratio f_i/N.

Translation of axes:

Displacement of all the variates by a given quantity, x_0:

$$x'_i = x_i - x_0 \qquad i = 1, 2, \ldots, k. \qquad 54.3$$

Deviations:

Translation by an amount equal to the mean:

$$x'_i = x_i - \bar{x} \qquad i = 1, 2, \ldots, k. \qquad 54.4$$

Fundamental property:

$$\sum_{i=1}^{k} f_i (x_i - \bar{x}) = 0. \qquad 54.5$$

Measure referred to the class interval (reduced measure).

If c is the class interval, variates are related to that interval and the mean by

$$u_i = \frac{x_i - \bar{x}}{c}; \qquad 54.6$$

Obviously, this will yield:

$$\bar{u} = 0. \qquad 54.7$$

Mean of the means.

If m measurements are taken in populations of the same nature:

$$\bar{x} = \frac{n_1 \bar{x}_1 + n_2 \bar{x}_2 + \dots + n_m \bar{x}_m}{N}.$$

Mode:

The value of x_i for which f_i is greatest.

Median.

The value of x_i (or lying between two consecutive x_i) for which

$$\text{cum}\, f = \tfrac{1}{2} N \qquad 54.8$$

where cum f means the cumulative value of f_i.

Moments:

1st moment: $$\nu_1 = \frac{1}{N} \sum_{i=1}^{k} f_i x_i = \bar{x}, \qquad 54.9$$

2nd moment: $$\nu_2 = \frac{1}{N} \sum_{i=1}^{k} f_i x_i^2, \qquad 54.10$$

rth moment: $$\nu_r = \frac{1}{N} \sum_{i=1}^{k} f_i x_i^r. \qquad 54.11$$

Moments relative to the average:

rth moment: $$\mu_{r,x} = \frac{1}{N} \sum_{i=1}^{k} f_i (x_i - \bar{x})^r, \qquad 54.12$$

$$\mu_{r,u} = \frac{1}{N} \sum_{i=1}^{k} f_i (u_i - \bar{u})^r. \qquad 54.13$$

Relations between moments μ and ν:

$$\mu_{2,x} = c^2 \mu_{2,u}\ , \quad \mu_{3,x} = c^3 \mu_{3,u}\ , \quad \mu_{4,x} = c^4 \mu_{4,u} \qquad 54.14\ \ 54.15\ \ 54.16$$

$$\mu_{2,u} = \nu_2 - \nu_1^2\ , \quad \mu_{3,u} = \nu_3 - 3\nu_2\nu_1 + 2\nu_1^3, \qquad 54.17\ \ 54.18$$

$$\mu_{4,u} = \nu_4 - 4\nu_3\nu_1 + 6\nu_2\nu_1^2 - 3\nu_1^4. \qquad 54.19$$

Variance:

Measure of the dispersion:

$$\sigma_x^2 = \mu_{2,x} = \frac{1}{N}\sum_{i=1}^{k} f_i\,(x_i - \bar{x})^2. \qquad 54.20$$

Standard deviation, or mean square deviation:

$$\sigma_x = \sqrt{\mu_{2,x}} = \sqrt{\frac{1}{N}\sum_{i=1}^{k} f_i\,(x_i - \bar{x})^2}\,. \qquad 54.21$$

Standard deviation:

$$\sigma_u = \sqrt{\mu_{2,u}} = \sqrt{\frac{1}{N}\sum_{i=1}^{k} f_i\,(u_i - \bar{u})^2}\,. \qquad 54.22$$

Invariance of σ_u:

A change in origin does not change σ_u.

$$\sigma_u^2 = \mu_{2,u} = \frac{1}{N}\sum_{i=1}^{k} f_i\,(u_i - \bar{u})^2 = \frac{1}{N}\sum_{i=1}^{k} f_i(u_i^* - \bar{u})^2 \qquad 54.23$$

where

$$u_i^* = u_i - u_0. \qquad 54.24$$

Standard units:

$$t_i = \frac{x_i - \bar{x}}{\sigma_x}. \qquad 54.25$$

Moments in standard units:

$$\alpha_r = \frac{1}{N}\sum_{i=1}^{k} f_i\,t_i^r = \frac{\mu_{r,x}}{(\sigma_x)^r}. \qquad 54.26$$

Note that α_r are pure numbers; α_3 measure of dissymetry, α_4 measure of flattening.

For curves approximating bell curves:

$$-2 < \alpha_3 < 2, \quad \alpha_4 \simeq 3, \quad \alpha_4 \geqslant \alpha_3^2 + 1. \qquad 54.27 \quad 54.28 \quad 54.29$$

Other measures of dispersion:

Quartile deviation: $Q = \frac{1}{2}(Q_3 - Q_1)$, 54.30

where

Q_3 = x value for which cum f = 3/4 N, 54.31

Q_1 = x value for which cum f = 1/4 N. 54.32

Mean deviation:

$$\overline{DM}_x = \frac{1}{N} \sum_{i=1}^{k} f_i \,|x_i - \bar{x}| \quad 54.33$$

$$\overline{DM}_u = \frac{1}{N} \sum_{i=1}^{k} f_i \,|u_i - \bar{u}| = \frac{1}{c} \overline{DM}_x. \quad 54.34$$

Random sample:

A sample from a population is considered to be drawn at random if the trials that produced the sample are independent, and if the probability distribution function of the random variable connected with each trial remains unchanged throughout the trials.

A sample is said to be of size n if it contains n individuals.

Relationship between the total population and a group of samples all having the same size.

It can be demonstrated that, given a group of random samples $x_1, x_2, x_3, \ldots, x_i$, each one of size n, having the respective means $\bar{x}_1, \bar{x}_2, \bar{x}_3, \ldots, \bar{x}_i$, and denoting:

m = mean of the unknown total population,
σ^2 = variance of the total population,
$\bar{x}$ = mean of the sample means, $\bar{x}_i$,
$\sigma^2_{\bar{x}}$ = variance of the sample mean, $\bar{x}_i$,

then:

$$\bar{x} = m \quad 54.35$$

and

$$\sigma^2_{\bar{x}} = \frac{\sigma^2}{n}. \quad 54.36$$

Estimates of m and σ_2^2:

The usual estimates of the mean, m, and the unknown theoretical variance σ^2, of an entire population, based on a sample of size n, are:

estimate of m = arithmetic mean of the values contained in the sample. 54.37

$$s^2 = \text{estimate of } \sigma^2 = \frac{\Sigma (x - \bar{x})^2}{n - 1}. \quad 54.38$$

The presence of the dênominator n - 1 instead of n constitutes compensation for bias.

Significance tests:

A sample having been taken from a population, the question arises as to whether the evaluations produced on the basis of that sample are meaningful. Significance tests provide an answer to this problem. Three of these tests are explained below: those of Pearson, Student's t, and Fisher-Snedecor.

Pearson's χ^2 ("chi square") test:

One calculates:

$$\chi^2 = \sum_{i=1}^{k} \frac{(o_i - e_i)^2}{e_i}. \quad 54.39$$

where k is the number of pairs of frequencies o_i (observed) and e_i (expected, theoretical).

Once this calculation has been performed, we find the number, ν, of independent frequencies, or degrees of freedom. In a distribution associated with a single variable, we have:

$$\nu = k - 1 \text{ (}^1\text{)}. \quad 54.40$$

For distributions of several variables, ν must be calculated. The variable χ^2 has the distribution:

---

*This holds true only if the theoretical distribution is completely independent of the observed distribution. If observed data have been used to estimate h parameters of the theoretical law, then: $\nu = k - 1 - h$.

$$f(\chi^2) = \frac{(\chi^2)^{(\frac{1}{2}\nu-1)}\ e^{-\frac{1}{2}\chi^2}}{2^{\frac{1}{2}\nu}\,\Gamma(\frac{1}{2}\nu)}. \qquad 54.41$$

where

$$\Gamma(n) = \int_0^\infty t^{n-1}\,e^{-t}\,dt \quad \text{(gamma function)} \qquad 54.42$$

If we adopt some probability as the criterion upon which a hypothesis can be accepted or rejected, a χ^2 table (see Appendix) will enable us to decide whether to accept or reject this hypothesis.

Student's t test:

This test is used for means of small samples drawn from a Gaussian population (number of individuals less than 30).

In such cases, we cannot assume the property of normality for the distribution of

$$\frac{\bar{x} - m}{s/\sqrt{n-1}}, \qquad 54.43$$

because the estimate of σ,

$$s = \sqrt{\frac{\Sigma(x - \bar{x})^2}{n-1}} \qquad 54.44$$

is too subject to large fluctuations where n is very small; therefore we calculate:

$$t = \frac{\bar{x} - m}{s}\sqrt{n-1}, \qquad 54.45$$

the distribution of which has been calculated by Student:

$$\varphi(t) = \frac{1}{\sqrt{\nu\pi}}\,\frac{\Gamma\left(\frac{\nu+1}{2}\right)}{\Gamma\left(\frac{\nu}{2}\right)\left(1+\frac{t^2}{\nu}\right)^{\frac{\nu+1}{2}}}, \qquad 54.46$$

where ν is the number of degrees of freedom defined above.

By the use of a distribution table

$$P(t) = 2\int_t^\infty \varphi(\lambda)\,d\lambda \quad \text{(see appendix)} \qquad 54.47$$

which gives the probability of obtaining an absolute value higher than t, one can accept or reject a hypothesis if a limiting probability has been established for such acceptance or rejection.

Here, we have two distinct cases:
a) deviation of a mean from its theoretical value (treated as shown above, taking $\nu = n - 1$);
b) difference between two means, $\overline{x}'$ and $\overline{x}''$.
In this latter case, we calculate:

$$t = \frac{\bar{x}' - \bar{x}''}{s_d} \sqrt{\frac{n_1 n_2}{n_1 + n_2}}, \qquad 54.48$$

where

$$s_d = \frac{1}{n_1 + n_2 - 2} \sqrt{\sum_{i=1}^{n_1} (x' - \bar{x}')^2 + \sum_{i=1}^{n_2} (x'' - \bar{x}'')^2} \qquad 54.49$$

and t is distributed as $\varphi(t)$, with:

$$\nu = n_1 + n_2 - 2. \qquad 54.50$$

Fisher-Snedecor F Test:

This test is used for standard deviations of samples taken from a Gaussian population.
Assume we have two samples, whose standard deviations are s_1, s_2:

$$s_1^2 = \frac{\Sigma(x'_i - \bar{x}')^2}{n_1 - 1}, \quad s_2^2 = \frac{\Sigma(x''_i - \bar{x}'')^2}{n_2 - 1}. \qquad \begin{matrix} 54.51 \\ 54.52 \end{matrix}$$

Fisher has shown that the distribution of

$$F = \frac{s_1^2}{s_2^2} \qquad (s_1 > s_2) \qquad 54.53$$

is:

$$\varphi(F) = \frac{\Gamma[\frac{1}{2}(\nu_1 + \nu_2)].F^{\frac{1}{2}(\nu_1 - 2)} n_1^{\frac{1}{2}\nu_1} n_2^{\frac{1}{2}\nu_2}}{\Gamma(\frac{1}{2}\nu_1)\, \Gamma(\frac{1}{2}\nu_2)\, (\nu_2 + \nu_1 F)^{\frac{1}{2}(\nu_1 + \nu_2)}} \qquad 54.54$$

where

$$\nu_1 = n_1 - 1 \quad \text{and} \quad \nu_2 = n_2 - 1. \qquad 54.55$$

(see table in the Appendix). 54.56

This test is used in the same manner as the other tests for accepting or rejecting a hypothesis.

Regression:

To find a regression curve is to determine the curve that best represents a group of points referred to a reference system. We assume that the best evaluation of the parameters of the curve is the one for which the sum of the squares of the deviations from the mean is minimum (principle of least squares).

Straight-line regression curve:

Case 1. Deviations measured for y_i.

Equation sought: $$y = mx + k; \qquad 54.57$$

Deviations: $$d_i = y_i - (mx_i + k); \qquad 54.58$$

m and n are given by:

$$m \Sigma x_i + kn = \Sigma y_i, \qquad 54.59$$

$$m \Sigma x_i^2 + k \Sigma x_i = \Sigma x_i y_i, \qquad 54.60$$

where n is the number of points.

Case 2. Deviations measured for x_i.

Equation sought: $$x = ay + b; \qquad 54.61$$

Deviations: $$d_i = x_i - (ay_i + b); \qquad 54.62$$

a and b are given by:

$$a \Sigma y_i + bn = \Sigma x_i, \qquad 54.63$$

$$a \Sigma y_i^2 + b \Sigma y_i = \Sigma x_i y_i. \qquad 54.64$$

Case 3. Deviations measured on the perpendicular erected on the straight-line regression curve.

Equation sought: $$y = \alpha x + \beta, \qquad 54.65$$

Deviations: $$d_i = \frac{y_i* - \alpha y_i^*}{\sqrt{1 + \alpha^2}}, \qquad 54.66$$

where

$$x_i^* = x_i - \bar{x} \qquad 54.67$$

and

$$y_i^* = y_i - \bar{y} \qquad 54.68$$

α and β are given by:

$$\alpha = \lambda \pm \sqrt{\lambda^2 + 1}, \qquad 54.69$$

where

$$\lambda = \frac{\sigma_y^2 - \sigma_x^2}{2\sigma_x \sigma_y}, \qquad 54.70$$

$$\beta = \bar{y} - \alpha\bar{x}. \qquad 54.71$$

Regression curves. Deviations measured for y_i.

Equations sought: $y = f(x);$ 54.72

Deviations: $d_i = y_i - f(x_i);$ 54.73

If f(x) contains m parameters, $a_1, a_2, \ldots, a_m$, these can be evaluated by means of the following m equations:

$$\sum_{i=1}^{n} \left(\frac{\partial f}{\partial a_k}\right)_i [y_i - f(x_i)] = 0 \qquad \begin{cases} k = 1, 2, \ldots, m \\ i = 1, 2, \ldots, n. \end{cases} \qquad 54.74$$

When the deviations are measured for x_i, the same method is used.

Correlation coefficient:

$$\text{Si}: \quad u_i = \frac{x_i - \bar{x}}{s_x}, \quad v_i = \frac{y_i - \bar{y}}{s_y}, \qquad \begin{matrix} 54.75 \\ 54.76 \end{matrix}$$

where s_x and s_y are the standard deviations of x_i and y_i, the mean value,

$$\frac{1}{n} \sum_{i=1}^{n} u_i v_i$$

is called the correlation coefficient:

$$r = \frac{1}{n} \sum_{i=1}^{n} \frac{(x_i - \bar{x})(y_i - \bar{y})}{s_x s_y} \qquad 54.77$$

$$0 \leqslant |r| \leqslant 1. \qquad 54.78$$

Section 55

THE CARSON-LAPLACE TRANSFORMATION*

Let h(t) be a function of the real variable t, defined for all values of t and zero for $t < 0$. We refer to the function

*The Carson-Laplace transformation method is often called operational calculus; in view of the danger of confusion, we shall avoid the use of this expression here.

$$g(s) = s \int_0^{\infty} e^{-st}\, h(t)\, dt. \qquad 55.1$$

as the Carson-Laplace transform of h(t).

In this integral, s is a real or complex variable; if s is complex, we assume that the real part c of s is greater than a given positive number c_0, and that, under these conditions, the integral 55.1) is convergent.

Symbolically, we write this as:

$$g(s) = \mathscr{L} h(t). \qquad 55.2$$

The inverse transform, known as the Mellin-Fourier transform, is:

$$h(t) = \frac{1}{2\pi j} \int_{c-j\infty}^{c+j\infty} \frac{e^{st} g(s)}{s}\, ds, \qquad (j = \sqrt{-1}) \qquad 55.3$$

where $c > c_0$ is stated above. Symbolically, this is written:

$$h(t) = \mathscr{L}^{-1} g(s). \qquad 55.4$$

COMMON THEOREMS:

1. $\mathscr{L}\Upsilon(t) = 1$ where $\Upsilon(t)$ is the unit scale function, 55.5

such that

$$\Upsilon(t) = 0 \text{ for } t < 0$$
$$= 1 \text{ for } t > 0.$$

2. If $\mathscr{L}h(t) = g(s)$, then $\mathscr{L}k\, h(t) = k\, g(s)$, 55.6 55.7

where k is a constant.

3. $\mathscr{L}[h_1(t) + h_2(t)] = \mathscr{L}h_1(t) + \mathscr{L}h_2(t) = g_1(s) + g_2(s).$ 55.8

4. If $\mathscr{L}h(t) = g(s)$: $\mathscr{L}\frac{dh}{dt} = sg(s) - sh(+0)$, 55.9

$$\mathscr{L}\frac{d^2h}{dt^2} = s^2g(s) - s^2h(+0) - sh'(+0), \qquad 55.10$$

$$\mathscr{L}\frac{d^3h}{dt^3} = s^3g(s) - s^3h(+0) - s^2h'(+0) - sh''(+0), \qquad 55.11$$

......

$$\mathscr{L}\frac{d^n h}{dt^n} = s^n g(s) - \sum_{r=0}^{n-1} h(r)(+0).s^{n-r}. \qquad 55.12$$

5. If $\mathscr{L}h(t) = g(s)$: $$\mathscr{L}\int_0^t h(u)du = \frac{g(s)}{s} \qquad 55.13$$

and

$$\mathscr{L}\underbrace{\int_0^t \int_0^\tau \dots \int_0^v}_{n \text{ times}} h(u)du \dots d\tau = \frac{g(s)}{s^n}. \qquad 55.14$$

6. If $\mathscr{L}h(t) = g(s)$: $\mathscr{L}h(kt) = g\left(\frac{s}{k}\right)$, where k is a constant. 55.15

7. If $\mathscr{L}h(t) = g(s)$: $\mathscr{L}[e^{-at}h(t)] = \frac{s}{s+a}\, g(s+a)$. 55.16

8. If g(s) has the form N(s)/D(s), where N(s) and D(s) are polynomials in s, in which the degree of N is lower than that of D, we can decompose g(s) into simple rational fractions:

$$\frac{N(s)}{D(s)} = \frac{A_m}{(s-a)^m} + \frac{A_{m-1}}{(s-a)^{m-1}} + \dots + \frac{A_1}{s-a} \qquad 55.17$$

(if a is a real root of order m)

$$+ \frac{B_n}{(s-b)^n} + \frac{B_{n-1}}{(s-b)^{n-1}} + \dots + \frac{B_1}{s-b}$$

(if b is a real root of order n)

......

$$+ \frac{H_r + K_r s}{(s^2 + \alpha s + \beta)^r} + \frac{H_{r-1} + K_{r-1}s}{(s^2 + \alpha s + \beta)^{r-1}} + \dots + \frac{H_1 + K_1 s}{(s^2 + \alpha s + \beta)}$$

(if $s^2 + \alpha s + \beta$ is a trinomial whose roots are complex.)

9. If $\mathscr{L}h(t) = g(s)$: $\mathscr{L}^{-1} e^{-s\tau} g(s) = 0$ for $t < \tau$

$$= h(t - \tau) \text{ for } t > \tau. \qquad 55.18$$

10. If $\mathscr{L}h(t) = g(s)$, with $h(t) = 0$ for $t < \tau$:

$$\mathscr{L}^{-1} e^{s\tau} g(s) = h(t + \tau). \qquad 55.19$$

11. Let there be a periodic function, with period 2a:

$$h(t) = h(t + 2a) = h(t + 4a) = \dots = h(t + 2ka) \qquad 55.20$$

then:

$$\mathscr{L}h(t) = \frac{s}{1-e^{-2sa}} \int_0^{2a} e^{-st} h_1(t)dt, \qquad 55.21$$

where $h_1(t)$ is equal to h(t) in the interval from 0 to 2a, and zero outside that interval.

12. If $g_1(s) = \mathscr{L}h_1(t), \quad g_2(s) = \mathscr{L}h_2(t),$ 55.22

then

$$\frac{g_1(s).g_2(s)}{s} = \mathscr{L}\int_0^t h_1(\tau)h_2(t-\tau)d\tau,$$

$$= \mathscr{L}\int_0^t h_1(t-\tau).h_2(\tau)d\tau. \qquad 55.23$$

We write symbolically:

$$h_1(t) * h_2(t) = \int_0^t h_1(\tau)h_2(t-\tau)d\tau; \qquad 55.24$$

this is the Borel theorem. This operation is called composition.

We also have:

$$g_1(s).g_2(s) = \mathscr{L}\frac{d}{dt}\int_0^t h_1(\tau)h_2(t-\tau)d\tau$$

$$= \mathscr{L}\left[\frac{d}{dt}\left(h_1(t) * h_2(t)\right)\right], \qquad 55.25$$

Note that:

$$h_1(t) * h_2(t) = h_2(t) * h_1(t). \qquad 55.26$$

13. If $\mathscr{L}h(t) = g(s)$: $\lim_{|s|\to\infty} g(s) = \lim_{t\to 0} h(t)$ 55.27

for any h(t) which gives meaning to the transformation.

14. If $\mathscr{L}h(t) = g(s)$: $\lim_{|s|\to 0} g(s) = \lim_{t\to\infty} h(t),$ 55.28

if certain conditions are satisfied. A sufficient condition is that g(s) be the quotient of two polynomials, N(s) and D(s), with the denominator having no root in which the real part is positive.

15. If $g(s) = \frac{N(s)}{D(s)}$ (quotient of polynomials in s):

$$\mathscr{L}^{-1} \frac{N(s)}{D(s)} = \frac{N(0)}{D(0)} + \sum_{n=1}^{m} \frac{N(s_n)}{s_n D'(s_n)} e^{s_n t} \qquad 55.29$$

where m is the number of roots.

The reader will find in the Appendix a summarized table of Carson-Laplace transforms.*

*We refer to one of our own works: Cours de Calcul opérationnelle (transformation de Carson-Laplace), by M. Denis-Papin and A. Kaufmann, Editions Albin Michel, Paris.

Chapter 7

Methods of computing linear programs

Section 56

INTRODUCTION

The basic method for finding the optimum of the economic function of a linear program is the simplex, or Dantzig, method. We shall explain this in detail. George Dantzig published his celebrated notes in 1947; since that time, he has continuously published new variations that facilitate the solution of programs with special structures. At the same time, many mathematicians and economists were hard at work deepening and developing both the theory and its applications. In France, we may cite G. T. Guilbaud; in the United States, Kuhn, Tucker, Charnes, Orden, Cooper, and Henderson. But, given the profound connection between the theory of linear programs and game theory (or the theory of games of strategy), we must not overlook the great mathematician Von Neumann and his followers.

Here we shall present only the essentials of what may be of interest to those who would like to know just how to go about calculating the optimum for a program. For further details or for a study in depth, we refer those interested to the references quoted in the Bibliography.

Section 57

GENERAL MATHEMATICAL STATEMENT OF LINEAR PROGRAMS

Let there be n + m non-negative variables satisfying m linear equations that we shall call constraints:

$$\begin{array}{l} a_{11}x_1 + a_{12}x_2 + \dots + a_{1n}x_n + a_{1n+1}x_{n+1} + \dots + a_{1,n+m}x_{n+m} = b_1 \\ a_{21}x_1 + a_{22}x_2 + \dots + a_{2n}x_n + a_{2n+1}x_{n+1} + \dots + a_{2,n+m}x_{n+m} = b_2 \\ \dots\dots\dots\dots \\ a_{m1}x_1 + a_{m2}x_2 + \dots + a_{mn}x_n + a_{mn+1}x_{n+1} + \dots + a_{m,n+m}x_{n+m} = b_m, \end{array} \qquad 57.1$$

where the coefficients $a_{ij}(i=1, 2, \ldots, n+m)$ and $b_i(i=1, 2, \ldots, m)$ are real numbers concerning which we shall make no special hypothesis.

We also adopt a linear function which constitutes the economic function:

$$z = c_1x_1 + c_2x_2 + \ldots + c_nx_n + c_{n+1}x_{n+1} + \ldots + c_{n+m}x_{n+m}, \qquad 57.2$$

where the coefficients $c_j(j = 1, 2, \ldots, n+m)$ are also real numbers concerning which we shall make no special hypothesis.

For simplicity's sake, we shall abbreviate equations (57.1) and (57.2) as follows:

$$\sum_{j=1}^{n+m} a_{ij}\, x_j = b_i \qquad i = 1,2,\ldots, m, \qquad 57.3$$

and

$$z = \sum_{j=1}^{n+m} c_j\, x_j. \qquad 57.4$$

The solution of a linear program consists of finding the values of the non-negative variables x_j that satisfy the constraints (57.3) and optimize (maximize or minimize, according to the case) the function z given by (57.4).

In some programs there are inequations in place of equations, or both together. We shall now show that one can always convert these to produce equations alone.

Let:

$$\sum_{j=1}^{n} a_{ij}\, x_j \leqslant b_i \qquad i = 1,2,\ldots, m, \qquad 57.5$$

and

$$z = \sum_{j=1}^{n} c_j\, x_j. \qquad 57.6$$

Now we introduce m new variables, $x_{n+1}, x_{n+2}, \ldots, x_{n+m}$, which we shall call "slack variables," all of them non-negative, and such that

$$\begin{aligned} a_{11}x_1 + a_{12}x_2 + \ldots + a_{1n}x_n + x_{n+1} &= b_1 \\ a_{21}x_1 + a_{22}x_2 + \ldots + a_{2n}x_n + x_{n+2} &= b_2 \\ \ldots\ldots\ldots\ldots \qquad \ldots\ldots\ldots\ldots &\quad \ldots \\ a_{m1}x_1 + a_{m2}x_2 + \ldots + a_{mn}x_n + x_{n+m} &= b_m. \end{aligned} \qquad 57.7$$

Here, we then find ourselves with a special case of (57.1), in which some of the coefficients a_{ij} are zero or equal to 1. If the signs of the inequations are opposite, we place a minus sign before the slack variables, but they will still be considered as non-negative. If we encounter a mixture of equations and inequations, we simply introduce a sufficient number of slack variables.

If we now consider N variables and M constraints, any solution that produces a maximum (or minimum) of the function z will correspond to one of the vertices of the convex polyhedron formed by the intersection of the reference N-hedron ($x_i \geq 0$) with the hyperplanes constituting the constraints.* Hence, any solution must fulfill the following necessary condition if it is to correspond to a maximum (or minimum): it must include at least N-M variables of zero value. If we set $N = n + m$ and $M = m$, the condition can also be stated as follows: the solution must include at most m positive variables, all others being zero.

It is of prime importance to point out that all polyhedrons constructed in this way are convex; the polyhedron formed by the intersection of the hyperplanes of the constraints and the reference N-hedron is convex because the intersection of two convex polyhedrons is always a convex polyhedron. Thus, we are certain, as we move from vertex to vertex increasing (or decreasing) z at each step, that we will eventually reach the maximum (or minimum) we are looking for. If this were not the case, we should not be sure of attaining the maximum maximorum (or minimum minimorum).

To avoid confusion, let us define exactly what we mean by the word "solution" in the problem that concerns us.

Solution: The set of $n + m$ quantities x_j that satisfy the system of equations (57.3).

Possible solution: The set of $n + m$ quantities x_j ($x_j \geq 0$) that satisfy the system of equations (57.3).

Possible basic solution (more briefly, a basic solution): The set of m quantities x_i ($x_i \geq 0$) and n quantities x_j ($x_j = 0$) that satisfy the system of equations (57.3).**

Optimum basic solution (more briefly, optimum solution): the basic solution that renders (57.4) optimum.

The foregoing considerations underlie the simplex method, which we shall now take up.

---

*The foregoing statement is strictly true if the maximum or minimum is obtained at one single point. Degenerate cases in which the maximum (or minimum) is obtained by all the points of a face are also possible.

**Certain authors use the expression "nondegenerate possible basis solution" to refer to the body of m quantities x_i ($x_i > 0$) and n quantities x_j ($x_j = 0$) that satisfy the constraints.

Section 58

THE SIMPLEX, OR DANTZIG, METHOD*

1. General explanation.—2. Marginal costs.—3. Example.—4. Second example.—5. Use of the variant.

1. General explanation.

Let us return to the m equations (57.3):

$$\sum_{j=1}^{n+m} a_{ij}\, x_j = b_i \qquad i = 1, 2, \dots m, \tag{58.1}$$

where the matrix a_{ij} is of order m by hypothesis.

The columns in the matrix a_{ij} and the column formed by the quantities b_i can be considered as the vectors P_j ($j = 1, 2, \dots n+m$) and P_0 in a linear m-dimensional space. We assume that in arbitrarily taking m distinct vectors P_i among the n + m vectors P_j, we achieve a system of linearly independent vectors. We shall therefore state that:

$$\sum_{j=1}^{n+m} P_j\, x_j = P_0, \quad \text{where} \quad P_j = \begin{Bmatrix} a_{1j} \\ a_{2j} \\ \vdots \\ a_{mj} \end{Bmatrix} \quad \text{and} \quad P_0 = \begin{Bmatrix} b_1 \\ b_2 \\ \vdots \\ b_m \end{Bmatrix}. \qquad 58.2\ \ 58.3\ \ 58.4$$

Since we have assumed that this system of m linear equations in n + m variables is of order m, we can now express n vectors P_j, numbered from 1 to n, and P_0 as a function of the m vectors, P_i, numbered from n + 1 to n + m, which are, by hypothesis, linearly independent.

Let us assume that we have found a basic solution whose variables are all positive, or m positive quantities x_i, numbered from n + 1 to n + m, while all the others, numbered from 1 to n, are assumed to be zero. For this basic solution, equations (57.3) and (57.4) will be reduced to:

$$\sum_{i=n+1}^{n+m} P_i\, x_i = P_0 \quad \text{and} \quad z_0 = \sum_{i=n+1}^{n+m} c_i\, x_i \tag{58.5}$$

$$x_i > 0 \quad , \quad i = n+1, n+2, \dots n+m. \tag{58.6}$$

---

*See the fundamental article by G. B. Dantzig: "Maximization of a Linear Function of Variables Subject to Linear Inequalities," in "Activity Analysis of Production and Allocation," T. C. Koopmans (ed.) (New York: Wiley, 1951), pp. 339-347.

The n other vectors P_j (j = 1, 2, . . . , n,) can, as we have just written, be expressed linearly as a function of the m vectors P_i, which will constitute, as they are generally called in the theory of linear spaces, a basis (the case in which the vectors are not linearly independent will be discussed further on.) We write:

$$P_j = \sum_{i=n+1}^{n+m} x_{ij} P_i \qquad j = 1, 2, \ldots, n. \tag{58.7}$$

The coefficients x_{ij} can be calculated by inverting the square matrix formed by the m vectors P_i, that constitute the basis.

We shall call z_j the quantities:

$$z_j = \sum_{i=n+1}^{n+m} x_{ij} c_i \qquad j = 1, 2, \ldots, n; \tag{58.8}$$

z_j is the increment of z corresponding to P_j.

Now, let one of the vectors P_j (58.7) that are not in the basis be multiplied by a positive scalar quantity θ; referring to (58.5), we will write:

$$\sum_{i=n+1}^{n+m} P_i x_i = \sum_{i=n+1}^{n+m} (x_i - \theta x_{ij}) P_i + \theta P_j = P_0 , \tag{58.9}$$

(we do not write j = 1, 2, . . . , n since the vector P_j was chosen from among the n vectors).

In the same manner, by adding $\theta(c_j - z_j)$ to both sides of (58.6), we obtain:

$$z_0 + \theta(c_j - z_j) = \sum_{i=n+1}^{n+m} (x_i - \theta x_{ij}) c_i + \theta c_j. \tag{58.10}$$

We have thus developed a new basis solution, on condition that not all x_{ij} are negative, and that $\theta \neq 0$ (if $\theta = 0$, the solution will not be changed).

If some x_{ij} are positive (at least one), we choose the positive quantity θ in such manner that;

$$\theta = \theta_0 = \min_i \frac{x_i}{x_{ij}} \tag{58.11}$$

this means that θ corresponds to the smallest value of the ratio x_i/x_{ij} among those that are positive: (i = n + 1, n + 2, . . . , n + m).

If we choose θ in this manner, all the terms

$$(x_i - \theta x_{ij}) \tag{58.12}$$

will be positive except one, which will be zero and will correspond to (58.11).

With θ thus determined and denoted as θ_0, we shall remove from the basis the vector P_i, such that $\theta_0 = x_i/x_{ij}$, since its coefficient will be cancelled out in (58.9) where it will be replaced by the vector P_j whose coefficient is θ_0. The basic solution thus obtained will therefore be distinct from the preceding one.

Lastly, let us try to increase z_0: consulting (58.10), we see that this will occur if we choose j in such a manner that:

$$c_j - z_j > 0. \tag{58.13}$$

The highest value of $c_j - z_j$ will correspond to the greatest possible increase in z_0 by this procedure; it is this value that we shall choose and which we shall use to designate the vector P_j that will become part of the basis. We may say, for convenience, that we choose the value of j corresponding to the most negative quantity of the values of $z_j - c_j$.

The result is that by choosing P_j such that $z_j - c_j$ is most negative, and by choosing the row i for which $\theta = x_i/x_{ij}$ is minimum but positive*, we can determine a transformation of the initial basic solution such as to produce the greatest possible increase in z_0. When it is no longer possible to find a single quantity $z_j - c_j$, it is no longer possible to increase z_0, and we shall thus have found the maximum of z**. An analogous line of reasoning, taking the most negative value of $c_j - z_j$, would have allowed us to diminish z_0 and find its minimum.

The number of basic solutions (m non-negative variables, that are not all zero, and n zero variables) is at most C_{n+m}^{m}; this number is very high when m and n are large. Finding an optimum solution by calculating all the basic solutions would require enormous amounts of calculation; this will convey some idea of the value of Dantzig's method of analysis by iteration.

A variation of this method consists of choosing j such that $\theta_0(c_j - z_j)$ has the largest possible value, or (which amounts to the same thing) that $\theta_0(z_j - c_j)$ has the most negative value possible. However, this procedure greatly complicates the calculations, since we must then evaluate all the quotients x_i/x_{ij} instead of calculating only the ones that correspond to column j.

2. Marginal costs.

The quantities $z_j - c_j$ or $c_j - z_j$ represent the unit variation of the economic function when the basis is changed. These quantities

---

*We shall refer to these selection conditions as the Dantzig criteria.

**We should emphasize the fact that this conclusion is linked to the property of convexity of the polyhedron formed by the constraints.

allow one to evaluate the sensitivity of the economic function about each stationary point (basic solution) and, in particular, about the optimum. In some cases, it is preferable to consider the variations:

$$\frac{x_i}{x_{ij}}(z_j - c_j) \quad \text{or} \quad \frac{x_i}{x_{ij}}(c_j - z_j)$$

corresponding to the inclusion of a vector P_j and the exclusion of a vector P_i in the basis.

In economic studies, the development of the concept of marginal cost is of great interest.

3. Example.

We shall take some very elementary examples to demonstrate how to apply the Dantzig algorithm.

Find:

$$[\text{MAX}]\, z = 3x_1 + 2x_2 + x_3 + x_4 + 5x_5 \qquad 58.14$$

with the constraints;

$$\begin{aligned} 3x_1 + x_3 - x_5 &= 3 \\ x_1 + x_2 - 3x_4 &= -12 \\ x_2 + x_3 + x_5 &= 4 \end{aligned} \qquad 58.15$$

which can be written in matrix form as:

$$\begin{bmatrix} 3 & 0 & 1 & 0 & -1 \\ 1 & 1 & 0 & -3 & 0 \\ 0 & 1 & 1 & 0 & 1 \end{bmatrix} \begin{Bmatrix} x_1 \\ x_2 \\ x_3 \\ x_4 \\ x_5 \end{Bmatrix} = \begin{Bmatrix} 3 \\ -12 \\ 4 \end{Bmatrix}. \qquad 58.16$$

$$(1) \quad (2) \quad (3) \quad (4) \quad (5)$$

Let us start with an arbitrarily chosen basic solution*:

Let

$$x_1 = 0, \quad x_2 = 0, \quad x_3 = \frac{7}{2} \quad x_4 = 4, \quad x_5 = \frac{1}{2}. \qquad 58.17$$

The value of z corresponding to this solution is.

$$z = 3(0) + 2(0) + 1\left(\frac{7}{2}\right) + 1(4) + 5\left(\frac{1}{2}\right) = 10. \qquad 58.18$$

---

*We shall show later on how to find a basic solution.

First, let us find the transformation (58.7), that is, the coefficients x_{ij} such that:

$$P_j = \sum_{i=3}^{5} x_{ij} P_i \qquad j = 1, 2; \tag{58.19}$$

this gives us the matrix equation:

$$\begin{bmatrix} 3 & 0 \\ 1 & 1 \\ 0 & 1 \end{bmatrix} = \begin{bmatrix} 1 & 0 & -1 \\ 0 & -3 & 0 \\ 1 & 0 & 1 \end{bmatrix} \begin{bmatrix} x_{31} & x_{32} \\ x_{41} & x_{42} \\ x_{51} & x_{52} \end{bmatrix}. \tag{58.20}$$

(1) (2) (3) (4) (5)

Inversion of the square matrix (58.20) immediately gives us the coefficients x_{ij}:

$$\begin{aligned} \begin{bmatrix} x_{31} & x_{32} \\ x_{41} & x_{42} \\ x_{51} & x_{52} \end{bmatrix} &= \begin{bmatrix} 1 & 0 & -1 \\ 0 & -3 & 0 \\ 1 & 0 & 1 \end{bmatrix}^{-1} \begin{bmatrix} 3 & 0 \\ 1 & 1 \\ 0 & 1 \end{bmatrix} \\ &= \begin{bmatrix} -\frac{1}{2} & 0 & \frac{1}{2} \\ 0 & -\frac{1}{3} & 0 \\ -\frac{1}{2} & 0 & \frac{1}{2} \end{bmatrix} \begin{bmatrix} 3 & 0 \\ 1 & 1 \\ 0 & 1 \end{bmatrix} = \begin{bmatrix} \frac{3}{2} & \frac{1}{2} \\ -\frac{1}{3} & -\frac{1}{3} \\ -\frac{3}{2} & \frac{1}{2} \end{bmatrix}. \end{aligned} \tag{58.21}$$

Let us now find quantities z_j yielded by relations (58.8):

$$z_j = \sum_{i=3}^{5} x_{ij} c_i \qquad j = 1, 2. \tag{58.22}$$

Thus:

$$[z_1 \quad z_2] = [1 \quad 1 \quad 5] \begin{bmatrix} \frac{3}{2} & \frac{1}{2} \\ -\frac{1}{3} & -\frac{1}{3} \\ -\frac{3}{2} & \frac{1}{2} \end{bmatrix} = \begin{bmatrix} -\frac{19}{3} & \frac{8}{3} \end{bmatrix}. \tag{58.23}$$

We then find the corresponding quantities $z_j - c_j$:

$$z_1 - c_1 = -\frac{19}{3} - 3 = -\frac{28}{3}, \qquad z_2 - c_2 = \frac{8}{3} - 2 = \frac{2}{3}. \tag{58.24}$$

We select $z_1 - c_1$ as having provided the most negative $z_j = c_j$ (evidently, this is the only negative value at this stage of the calculation.). Therefore we introduce a non-zero coefficient for the vector P_1. Next we find this coefficient; to do so, we calculate the ratios x_i/x_{ij} and select that index i for which we obtain the smallest positive value:

$$\frac{x_3}{x_{31}} = \frac{\frac{7}{2}}{\frac{3}{2}} = \frac{7}{3}, \qquad \frac{x_4}{x_{41}} = \frac{4}{-\frac{1}{3}} = -12, \qquad \frac{x_5}{x_{51}} = \frac{\frac{1}{2}}{-\frac{3}{2}} = -\frac{1}{3}. \tag{58.25}$$

Hence, we shall take $\theta_0 = x_3/x_{31} = 7/3$. This is, furthermore, the only positive value in this case.

For the new solution, we obtain:

$$x'_1 = \theta_0 = \frac{x_3}{x_{31}} = \frac{7}{3}, \qquad x'_2 = 0, \qquad x'_3 = 0$$

$$x'_4 = x_4 - \frac{x_3}{x_{31}} x_{41} = 4 - \left[\frac{7}{3}\right]\left[-\frac{1}{3}\right] = \frac{43}{9} \qquad 58.26$$

$$x'_5 = x_5 - \frac{x_3}{x_{31}} x_{51} = \frac{1}{2} - \left[\frac{7}{3}\right]\left[-\frac{3}{2}\right] = 4.$$

The new value of z will be:

$$z = 3\left(\frac{7}{3}\right) + 2(0) + 1(0) + 1\left(\frac{43}{9}\right) + 5(4) = 31 + \frac{7}{9}. \qquad 58.27$$

We can check this as follows:

$$z = z_0 + \theta_0(c_1 - z_1) = 10 + \left(\frac{7}{3}\right)\left(\frac{28}{3}\right) = 31 + \frac{7}{9}. \qquad 58.28$$

$$\begin{bmatrix} 3 & 0 & 1 & 0 & -1 \\ 1 & 1 & 0 & -3 & 0 \\ 0 & 1 & 1 & 0 & 1 \end{bmatrix} \begin{Bmatrix} \frac{7}{3} \\ 0 \\ 0 \\ \frac{43}{9} \\ 4 \end{Bmatrix} = \begin{Bmatrix} 3 \\ -12 \\ 4 \end{Bmatrix}. \qquad 58.29$$

Now let us try to find a third solution that will give a higher value of z. Let us calculate the transformation this time for vectors 2 and 3.

$$\underset{(2)\ (3)}{\begin{bmatrix} 0 & 1 \\ 1 & 0 \\ 1 & 1 \end{bmatrix}} = \underset{(1)\ (4)\ (5)}{\begin{bmatrix} 3 & 0 & -1 \\ 1 & -3 & 0 \\ 0 & 0 & 1 \end{bmatrix}} \begin{bmatrix} x_{12} & x_{13} \\ x_{42} & x_{43} \\ x_{52} & x_{53} \end{bmatrix} \qquad 58.30$$

Inversion of the matrix formed by the basis gives:

$$\begin{bmatrix} x_{12} & x_{13} \\ x_{42} & x_{43} \\ x_{52} & x_{53} \end{bmatrix} = \begin{bmatrix} \frac{1}{3} & \frac{2}{3} \\ -\frac{2}{9} & \frac{2}{9} \\ 1 & 1 \end{bmatrix}. \qquad 58.31$$

Now let us find the quantities z_j:

$$[z_2 \quad z_3] = [3 \quad 1 \quad 5] \begin{bmatrix} \frac{1}{3} & \frac{2}{3} \\ -\frac{2}{9} & \frac{2}{9} \\ 1 & 1 \end{bmatrix} = \begin{bmatrix} \frac{52}{9} & \frac{65}{9} \end{bmatrix}, \qquad 58.32$$

hence:

$$z_2 - c_2 = \frac{52}{9} - 2 = \frac{34}{9} > 0, \quad z_3 - c_3 = \frac{65}{9} - 1 = \frac{56}{9} > 0. \qquad 58.33$$

Since these two numbers are positive, it is no longer possible to increase z, and the value $z = 31 + 7/9$, for which we have

$$x_1 = \frac{7}{3}, \quad x_2 = 0, \quad x_3 = 0, \quad x_4 = \frac{43}{9}, \quad x_5 = 4. \qquad 58.33a$$

corresponds to the maximum.

We have chosen an "apple pie" example to start with, since only a single stage gave us the maximum.

4. Second example.

This time, we shall deal with inequations:

$$[\text{MAX}]z = 4x_1 + 3x_2 \qquad 58.34$$

$$x_1 \leqslant 4{,}000, \quad x_2 \leqslant 6{,}000, \quad x_1 + \tfrac{2}{3}x_2 \leqslant 6{,}000. \qquad 58.35$$

We introduce three new variables, x_3, x_4, and x_5, which constitute the slack variables:

$$\begin{aligned} x_1 + x_3 &= 4{,}000, \\ x_2 + x_4 &= 6{,}000, \\ x_1 + \tfrac{2}{3}x_2 + x_5 &= 6{,}000. \end{aligned} \qquad 58.36$$

Using the matrix form, we have:

$$\underset{(1)\ (2)\ (3)\ (4)\ (5)}{\begin{bmatrix} 1 & 0 & 1 & 0 & 0 \\ 0 & 1 & 0 & 1 & 0 \\ 1 & \frac{2}{3} & 0 & 0 & 1 \end{bmatrix}} \begin{Bmatrix} x_1 \\ x_2 \\ x_3 \\ x_4 \\ x_5 \end{Bmatrix} = \begin{Bmatrix} 4{,}000 \\ 6{,}000 \\ 6{,}000 \end{Bmatrix}. \qquad 58.37$$

One obvious basic solution is:

$$x_1 = 0,\ x_2 = 0,\ x_3 = 4{,}000,\ x_4 = 6{,}000,\ x_5 = 6{,}000 \qquad 58.38$$

which yields:

$$z_0 = 4(0) + 3(0) = 0. \qquad 58.39$$

Performing the transformation (58.7), we find:

$$\underset{(1)\ (2)}{\begin{bmatrix} 1 & 0 \\ 0 & 1 \\ 1 & \frac{2}{3} \end{bmatrix}} = \underset{(3)\ (4)\ (5)}{\begin{bmatrix} 1 & 0 & 0 \\ 0 & 1 & 0 \\ 0 & 0 & 1 \end{bmatrix}} \begin{bmatrix} x_{31} & x_{32} \\ x_{41} & x_{42} \\ x_{51} & x_{52} \end{bmatrix}. \qquad 58.40$$

Since the basis constitutes a unit matrix, the coefficients x_{ij} are given directly by the vectors P_1 and P_2:

$$\begin{bmatrix} x_{31} & x_{32} \\ x_{41} & x_{42} \\ x_{51} & x_{52} \end{bmatrix} = \begin{bmatrix} 1 & 0 \\ 0 & 1 \\ 1 & \frac{2}{3} \end{bmatrix}. \qquad 58.41$$

Let us compute z_1 and z_2:

$$[z_1 \quad z_2] = [0 \quad 0 \quad 0] \begin{bmatrix} 1 & 0 \\ 0 & 1 \\ 1 & \frac{2}{3} \end{bmatrix} = [0 \quad 0], \qquad 58.42$$

hence:

$$z_1 = 0, \qquad z_2 = 0; \qquad 58.43$$

and:

$$z_1 - c_1 = 0 - 4 = -4, \qquad z_2 - c_2 = 0 - 3 = -3. \qquad 58.44$$

Therefore we shall choose P_1, for which we have $z_1 - c_1 = -4$ (the most negative). Now let us calculate the ratios x_i/x_{ij}:

$$\frac{x_3}{x_{31}} = \frac{4{,}000}{1} = 4{,}000,\ \frac{x_4}{x_{41}} = \frac{6{,}000}{0} = \infty,\ \frac{x_5}{x_{51}} = \frac{6{,}000}{1} = 6{,}000. \qquad 58.45$$

We shall therefore select index 3, which gives the smallest positive number, and we shall take $\theta_0 = x_3/x_{31} = 4{,}000$.

The new solution will be:

$$\begin{aligned} x_1' &= \theta_0 = \frac{x_3}{x_{31}} = 4{,}000, \qquad x_2' = 0, \qquad x_3' = 0 \\ x_4' &= x_4 - \frac{x_3}{x_{31}} x_{41} = 6{,}000 - (4{,}000)(0) = 6{,}000, \\ x_5' &= x_5 - \frac{x_3}{x_{31}} x_{51} = 6{,}000 - (4{,}000)(1) = 2{,}000; \end{aligned} \qquad 58.46$$

hence:

$$z = 4(4{,}000) + 3(0) = 16{,}000. \qquad 58.47$$

We verify this through:

$$z = z_0 + \theta(c_1 - z_1) = 0 + 4{,}000(4) = 16{,}000. \qquad 58.48$$

$$\begin{bmatrix} 1 & 0 & 1 & 0 & 0 \\ 0 & 1 & 0 & 1 & 0 \\ 1 & \frac{2}{3} & 0 & 0 & 1 \end{bmatrix} \begin{Bmatrix} 4{,}000 \\ 0 \\ 0 \\ 6{,}000 \\ 2{,}000 \end{Bmatrix} = \begin{Bmatrix} 4{,}000 \\ 6{,}000 \\ 6{,}000 \end{Bmatrix}. \qquad 58.49$$

Let us go on to a new stage, attempting to transform the vectors P_2 and P_3:

$$\underset{(2)\ (3)}{\begin{bmatrix} 0 & 1 \\ 1 & 0 \\ \frac{2}{3} & 0 \end{bmatrix}} = \underset{(1)\ (4)\ (5)}{\begin{bmatrix} 1 & 0 & 0 \\ 0 & 1 & 0 \\ 1 & 0 & 1 \end{bmatrix}} \begin{bmatrix} x_{12} & x_{13} \\ x_{42} & x_{43} \\ x_{52} & x_{53} \end{bmatrix}; \qquad 58.50$$

which gives, after inversion of the square matrix:

$$\begin{bmatrix} x_{12} & x_{13} \\ x_{42} & x_{43} \\ x_{52} & x_{53} \end{bmatrix} = \begin{bmatrix} 0 & 1 \\ 1 & 0 \\ \frac{2}{3} & -1 \end{bmatrix} \qquad 58.51$$

Let us calculate z_2 and z_3:

$$[z_2 \quad z_3] = [4 \quad 0 \quad 0] \begin{bmatrix} 0 & 1 \\ 1 & 0 \\ \frac{2}{3} & -1 \end{bmatrix} = [0 \quad 4], \qquad 58.52$$

hence:

$$z_2 - c_2 = 0 - 3 = -3, \quad z_3 - c_3 = 4 - 0 = 4. \qquad 58.53$$

We shall select P_2. Next:

$$\frac{x_1}{x_{12}} = \frac{4{,}000}{0} = \infty, \quad \frac{x_4}{x_{42}} = \frac{6{,}000}{1} = 6{,}000,$$
$$\frac{x_5}{x_{52}} = \frac{2{,}000}{\frac{2}{3}} = 3{,}000. \qquad 58.54$$

Then we shall choose P_2 to take the place of P_5 in the base. The new solution will be:

$$x_1' = x_1 - \frac{x_5}{x_{52}} x_{12} = 4{,}000 - (3{,}000)(0) = 4{,}000, \quad x_2' = \frac{x_5}{x_{52}} = 3{,}000$$

$$x_3' = 0, \quad x_4' = x_4 - \frac{x_5}{x_{52}} x_{42} = 6{,}000 - (3{,}000)(1) = 3{,}000, \qquad 58.55$$

$$x_5' = 0.$$

i.e.:

$$z = 4(4{,}000) + 3(3{,}000) + 0(0) + 0(3{,}000) + 0(0) = 25{,}000. \qquad 58.56$$

Leaving the task of verification to the reader, let us seek a new solution.

$$\underset{(3)\ (5)}{\begin{bmatrix} 1 & 0 \\ 0 & 0 \\ 0 & 1 \end{bmatrix}} = \underset{(1)\ (2)\ (4)}{\begin{bmatrix} 1 & 0 & 0 \\ 0 & 1 & 1 \\ 1 & \frac{2}{3} & 0 \end{bmatrix}} \begin{bmatrix} x_{13} & x_{15} \\ x_{23} & x_{25} \\ x_{43} & x_{45} \end{bmatrix} = \begin{bmatrix} 1 & 0 & 0 \\ 0 & 1 & 1 \\ 1 & \frac{2}{3} & 0 \end{bmatrix} \begin{bmatrix} 1 & 0 \\ -\frac{3}{2} & \frac{3}{2} \\ \frac{3}{2} & -\frac{3}{2} \end{bmatrix} \qquad 58.57$$

$$[z_3 \quad z_5] = [4 \quad 3 \quad 0] \begin{bmatrix} 1 & 0 \\ -\frac{3}{2} & \frac{3}{2} \\ \frac{3}{2} & -\frac{3}{2} \end{bmatrix} = [-\tfrac{1}{2} \quad \tfrac{9}{2}], \qquad 58.58$$

$$z_3 - c_3 = -\tfrac{1}{2} - 0 = -\tfrac{1}{2}, \qquad z_5 - c_5 = \tfrac{9}{2} - 0 = \tfrac{9}{2}. \qquad 58.59$$

Then we shall select P_3.

$$\frac{x_1}{x_{13}} = \frac{4{,}000}{1} = 4{,}000, \quad \frac{x_2}{x_{23}} = \frac{3{,}000}{-\frac{3}{2}} = -2{,}000, \quad \frac{x_4}{x_{43}} = \frac{3{,}000}{\frac{3}{2}} = 2{,}000. \qquad 58.60$$

We shall choose P_4.
The new solution will be:

$$x_1' = x_1 - \frac{x_4}{x_{43}} x_{13} = 4{,}000 - (2{,}000)(1) = 2{,}000$$

$$x_2' = x_2 - \frac{x_4}{x_{43}} x_{23} = 3{,}000 - (2{,}000)(-\tfrac{3}{2}) = 6{,}000 \qquad 58.61$$

$$x_3' = \frac{x_4}{x_{43}} = 2{,}000, \quad x_4' = 0, \quad x_5' = 0.$$

i.e.:

$$z = 4(2{,}000) + 3(6{,}000) + 0(2{,}000) + 0(0) + 0(0) = 26{,}000. \qquad 58.62$$

Let us go on to a new solution:

$$\underset{(4)\ (5)}{\begin{bmatrix} 0 & 0 \\ 1 & 0 \\ 0 & 1 \end{bmatrix}} = \underset{(1)\ (2)\ (3)}{\begin{bmatrix} 1 & 0 & 1 \\ 0 & 1 & 0 \\ 1 & \frac{2}{3} & 0 \end{bmatrix}} \begin{bmatrix} x_{14} & x_{15} \\ x_{24} & x_{25} \\ x_{34} & x_{35} \end{bmatrix} = \begin{bmatrix} 1 & 0 & 1 \\ 0 & 1 & 0 \\ 1 & \frac{2}{3} & 0 \end{bmatrix} \begin{bmatrix} -\frac{2}{3} & 1 \\ 1 & 0 \\ \frac{2}{3} & -1 \end{bmatrix}, \qquad 58.63$$

$$[z_4 \quad z_5] = [4 \quad 3 \quad 0] \begin{bmatrix} -\frac{2}{3} & 1 \\ 1 & 0 \\ \frac{2}{3} & -1 \end{bmatrix} = [\tfrac{1}{3} \quad 4], \qquad 58.64$$

$$z_4 - c_4 = \tfrac{1}{3} - 0 = \tfrac{1}{3}, \qquad z_5 - c_5 = 4 - 0 = 4. \qquad 58.65$$

There is no larger negative $z_j - c_j$. z can no longer be increased so:

$$z = 26{,}000 \text{ is the maximum,} \qquad 58.66$$

with

58.67

$x_1 = 2{,}000$, $x_2 = 6{,}000$ and the deviations $x_3 = 2{,}000$, $x_4 = 0$, $x_5 = 0$.

5. Use of the variant.

Let us pick up the preceding program (58.34) and (58.35), at the point to which we had carried it at (58.44).

This time, let us calculate all the ratios x_i/x_{ij} corresponding to the indices j = 1 and j = 2.

$$\frac{x_3}{x_{31}} = \frac{4{,}000}{1} = 4\,000, \quad \frac{x_4}{x_{41}} = \frac{6{,}000}{0} = \infty, \quad \frac{x_5}{x_{51}} = \frac{6{,}000}{1} = 6{,}000 \ \text{(already calculated)} \qquad 58.68$$

$$\frac{x_3}{x_{32}} = \frac{4{,}000}{0} = \infty, \quad \frac{x_4}{x_{42}} = \frac{6{,}000}{1} = 6{,}000, \quad \frac{x_5}{x_{52}} = \frac{6{,}000}{\frac{2}{3}} = 9{,}000. \qquad 58.69$$

The smallest positive number corresponding to the index j = 1 is 4,000, and the smallest for j = 2 is 6,000. Comparing we have:

$$\frac{x_3}{x_{31}}(c_1 - z_1) = (4{,}000)\,(4) = 16{,}000,$$
$$\frac{x_4}{x_{42}}(c_2 - z_2) = (6{,}000)\,(3) = 18{,}000. \qquad 58.70$$

The greatest increase in z, 18,000, corresponds to the inclusion of vector P_2 in the basis in place of P_4. We shall therefore take $\theta_0 = x_4/x_{42} = 6{,}000$. This gives us:

$$x_1' = 0, \quad x_2' = \theta_0 = \frac{x_4}{x_{42}} = 6{,}000, \quad x_3' = x_3 - \frac{x_4}{x_{42}}\, x_{32} = 4{,}000 - (6000\,(0)$$
$$= 4{,}000 \qquad 58.71$$
$$x_4' = 0, \quad x_5' = x_5 - \frac{x_4}{x_{42}}\, x_{52} = 6{,}000 - (6{,}000)\,(\tfrac{2}{3}) = 2{,}000.$$

hence:

$$z=4(0)+3(6{,}000)+0(4{,}000)+0(0)+0(2{,}000)=18{,}000. \qquad 58.72$$

Let us go on to the next stage, calculating the transformation of vectors P_1 and P_4:

$$\underset{(1)\ (4)}{\begin{bmatrix}1 & 0\\ 0 & 1\\ 1 & 0\end{bmatrix}} = \underset{(2)\ (3)\ (5)}{\begin{bmatrix}0 & 1 & 0\\ 1 & 0 & 0\\ \frac{2}{3} & 0 & 1\end{bmatrix}} \begin{bmatrix}x_{21} & x_{24}\\ x_{31} & x_{34}\\ x_{51} & x_{54}\end{bmatrix}, \qquad 58.73$$

hence:

$$\begin{bmatrix}x_{21} & x_{24}\\ x_{31} & x_{34}\\ x_{51} & x_{54}\end{bmatrix} = \begin{bmatrix}0 & 1 & 0\\ 1 & 0 & 0\\ \frac{2}{3} & 0 & 1\end{bmatrix}^{-1} \begin{bmatrix}1 & 0\\ 0 & 1\\ 1 & 0\end{bmatrix} = \begin{bmatrix}0 & 1 & 0\\ 1 & 0 & 0\\ 0 & -\frac{2}{3} & 1\end{bmatrix} \begin{bmatrix}1 & 0\\ 0 & 1\\ 1 & 0\end{bmatrix} = \begin{bmatrix}0 & 1\\ 1 & 0\\ 1 & -\frac{2}{3}\end{bmatrix} \qquad 58.74$$

Calculating z_1 and z_4, we have:

$$[z_1 \quad z_4] = [3 \quad 0 \quad 0] \begin{bmatrix}0 & 1\\ 1 & 0\\ 1 & -\frac{2}{3}\end{bmatrix} = [0 \quad 3], \qquad 58.75$$

and

$$z_1 - c_1 = 0 - 4 = -4, \qquad z_4 - c_4 = 3 - 0 = 3. \qquad 58.76$$

We shall select P_1, for which we have a negative value. Let us calculate ratios x_i/x_{ij}:

$$\frac{x_2}{x_{21}}=\frac{6{,}000}{0}=\infty, \quad \frac{x_3}{x_{31}}=\frac{4{,}000}{1}=4{,}000, \quad \frac{x_5}{x_{51}}=\frac{2{,}000}{1}=2{,}000. \qquad 58.77$$

We shall select index 5, for which we have the smallest positive number. Hence, vector P_1 will enter the basis, while vector P_5 will leave it.

The new solution will be:

$$x'_1=\theta_0=\frac{x_5}{x_{51}} = 2{,}000, \; x'_2=x_2-\frac{x_5}{x_{51}}x_{21}=6{,}000-(2{,}000)(0)=6{,}000$$

$$x'_3=x_3-\frac{x_5}{x_{51}}x_{31} = 4{,}000-(2{,}000)(1) = 2{,}000, \quad x'_4=0, \quad x'_5=0. \qquad 58.78$$

Finally, we have the solution:

$$x_1 = 2{,}000, \quad x_2 = 6{,}000, \quad x_3 = 2{,}000, \quad x_4 = x_5 = 0, \quad z = 26{,}000. \qquad 58.79$$

This is the solution of (58.67) obtained in two stages instead of three.

This variant has the advantage of reducing the number of iterations but, on the other hand, requires calculation of all the quotients x_i/x_{ij} relative to the basis vectors. One can also combine the two methods if there is a possibility of thereby finding a means of reducing the volume of calculations.

Section 59

FINDING A POSSIBLE BASIC SOLUTION

1. General explanation.—2. Algorithm for finding a possible basic solution.—3. Example.

1. General explanation.

With the exception of the case of inequations of the type:

$$\sum_{j=1}^{n} a_{ij} x_j \leqslant b_i, \qquad 59.1$$

knowledge of a possible basic solution is not immediate (one does not know how to find a vertex of a convex polyhedron).* Dantzig has suggested a method for finding such a basic solution. We shall now present his method, as well as its demonstration.

We arbitrarily choose a basis made up of m - 1 vectors P_k and the vector P_0. Then each of the other vectors can be expressed as linear combinations of the vectors in this basis.

$$P_j = y_{0j} P_0 + y_{1j} P_1 + \dots + y_{m-1,j} P_{m-1} = \sum_{k=0}^{m-1} y_{kj} P_k . \qquad 59.2$$

First, let us demonstrate that there exists no possible basic solution if:

$$y_{0j} \leq 0 \text{ for all values of j.} \qquad 59.3$$

To prove this, let us begin by supposing, on the contrary, that there exists a possible basic solution $\lambda_1, \lambda_2, \dots, \lambda_\mu$; that is:

$$P_0 = \lambda_1 P_1 + \lambda_2 P_2 + \dots + \lambda_\mu P_\mu \qquad \lambda_j > 0 \quad j = 1, 2, \dots, \mu. \qquad 59.4$$

---

*We have seen, for example in (58.38), how to obtain a basic solution very easily in the case where we have only inequations similar to (59.1). In that example, it was enough to take $x_1 = 0$ and $x_2 = 0$.

Substituting (59.2) into (59.4), we obtain:

$$\begin{aligned} P_0 = {} & \lambda_1 [y_{01} P_0 + y_{11} P_1 + \dots + y_{m-1,1} P_{m-1}] \\ & + \lambda_2 [y_{02} P_0 + y_{12} P_1 + \dots + y_{m-1,2} P_{m-1}] \\ & + \dots \\ & + \lambda_\mu [y_{0\mu} P_0 + y_{1\mu} P_1 + \dots + y_{m-1,\mu} P_{m-1}]. \end{aligned} \quad 59.5$$

After some collection of terms and rearrangement, we have:

$$P_0[\sum_{j=1}^{\mu} \lambda_j y_{0j} - 1] + P_1[\sum_{j=1}^{\mu} \lambda_j y_{1j}] + \dots + P_{m-1}[\sum_{j=1}^{\mu} \lambda_j y_{m-1,j}] = 0 \quad 59.6$$

However, the vectors P_0, $P_1, \dots, P_{m-1}$ have been assumed linearly independent (a necessary condition for forming a basis), and therefore we must have

$$\sum_{j=1}^{\mu} \lambda_j y_{0j} - 1 = 0 \quad 59.7$$

which is impossible if we have, simultaneously, $\lambda j > 0$ and $y_{0j} \leq 0$ for all values of j.

To find a basic solution, we begin with some arbitrary values:

$$w_1, w_2, \dots, w_{m-1}, -\varrho_0, \quad 59.8$$

where

$$w_i > 0, \quad \varrho_0 > 0; \qquad i = 1, 2, \dots, m-1.$$

Let:

$$G = w_1 P_1 + w_2 P_2 + \dots + w_{m-1} P_{m-1} - \varrho_0 P_0, \quad 59.9$$

which is more conveniently written:

$$G + \varrho_0 P_0 = w_1 P_1 + w_2 P_2 + \dots + w_{m-1} P_{m-1}. \quad 59.10$$

(In what follows, ρ_0 will play a role analogous to that of z_0 in the preceding example.)

From what was said above, if a basic solution exists, there is at least one j such that $y_{0j} > 0$. Let us choose such a j.

Now we multiply (59.2) by a quantity θ and subtract the result from (59.10); this yields:

$$G + (\varrho_0 + \theta y_{0j}) P_0 = \theta P_j + (w_1 - \theta y_{1j}) P_1 + \dots + (w_{m-1} - \theta y_{m-1,j}) P_{m-1}. \quad 59.11$$

At this point, we return to the argument of Section 58, from (58.8) to (58.13). For values of θ: $0 < \theta < \theta_0$, we can construct a set of vectors, $G + \rho P_0$, each of them given by a linear combination of the vectors P_j. Since ρ plays a role analogous to that of z, we shall be interested in the highest value of ρ for which this is possible. It will be noted that:

$$\varrho = \varrho_0 + \theta y_{0j} > \varrho_0, \qquad 59.12$$

since $y_{0j} > 0$ was taken as a hypothesis.

If, in the representation of P_j in (59.2), all $y_{ij} < 0$ ($i = 1, 2, \ldots, m-1$), the coefficients of P_j in (59.11) will be positive and $\rho \to \infty$ when $\theta \to \infty$. At the same time, we see, in solving (59.2) for P_0,

$$P_0 = \left(\frac{1}{y_{0j}}\right) P_j + \left(-\frac{y_{1j}}{y_{0j}}\right) P_1 + \ldots + \left(-\frac{y_{m-1,j}}{y_{0j}}\right) P_{m-1}, \qquad 59.13$$

a possible basic solution has been obtained; that is, P_0 has been expressed as a linear combination of $P_1, P_2, \ldots, P_{m-1}$, and P_j with non-negative coefficients. If at least one $y_{ij} > 0$ ($i = 1, 2, \ldots, m-1$), the highest value of θ is given by:

$$\theta_0 = \min_i \frac{w_i}{y_{ij}}, \qquad 59.14$$

for values of i such that $y_{ij} > 0$.

By taking $\theta = \theta_0$, there is at least one coefficient of a vector P_i that cancels out, and one new vector:

$$G + \varrho_1 P_0 \qquad 59.15$$

will be formed from (59.9) which is expressed as a linear combination of exactly $m - 1$ vectors, where:

$$\varrho_1 = \varrho_0 + \theta_0 y_{0j} > \varrho_0. \qquad 59.16$$

By expressing all the vectors P as functions of the new basis, the process can be repeated, and each step will yield a higher value of ρ (or an infinite value, meaning a possible basic solution). The process must permit a conclusion in a finite number of iterations; actually, if this were not so, since there is a finite number of basic solutions, the same combination of $m - 1$ vectors P_i would appear a second time. In other words, we would have:

$$G + \varrho' P_0 = w_1' P_1 + w_2' P_2 + \ldots + w_{m-1}' P_{m-1}, \qquad 59.17$$

$$G + \varrho'' P_0 = w_1'' P_1 + w_2'' P_2 + \ldots + w_{m-1}'' P_{m-1}, \qquad 59.18$$

with $\rho'' > \rho'$. By subtracting (59.18) from (59.17), we obtain an expression which is not identically zero and gives P_0 as a function of (m - 1) vectors P_i, in contradiction of our hypothesis concerning the basis (linearly independent vectors). Hence, there are only two conditions which determine the process.

After a finte number of iterations, we have:
either:

$$y_{0j} \leqslant 0 \text{ for all } j = 1, 2, \ldots, m, \tag{59.19}$$

in which case there is no possible basic solution;
or:

$$y_{ij} \leqslant 0 \text{ for all } i = 1, 2, \ldots, m \tag{59.20}$$

in which case the desired basic solution is found by solving (59.2) for P_0, as we did for (59.13).

2. Algorithm for finding a possible basic solution.

1. Determine the coefficients y_{ij};
2. Choose arbitrary values for ρ_0 and for the m - 1 coefficients w_i of the vectors included in the basis, expressing:

$$G + \varrho_0 P_0 = \sum_{i=1}^{m-1} w_i P_i. \tag{59.21}$$

3. Select y_{0j}, which gives the vector P_j that enters into the basis;
4. Express:

$$P_j = y_{0j} P_0 + \sum_{i=1}^{m-1} y_{ij} P_i. \tag{59.22}$$

If all y_{ij} are not negative, continue; otherwise a possible basic solution has been found;

5. Select

$$\theta = \min_i (w_i/y_{ij} > 0), \tag{59.23}$$

which gives the vector P_i to be removed from the basis,

6. Form:

$$G + (\varrho_0 + \theta\, y_{0j}) P_0 = \theta P_j + \sum_{i=1}^{m-1} (w_i - \theta\, y_{ij}) P_i, \tag{59.24}$$

which yields the new solution:

$$\varrho' = \varrho_0 + \theta y_{0j}\,,\ w'_j = \theta\ ,\ w'_i = w_i - \theta y_{ij} \quad i = 1, 2, \ldots, m-1. \tag{59.25}$$

7. Repeat all these operations from the beginning until:

$$P_j = y_{0j} P_0 + \sum_{i=1}^{m-1} y_{ij} P_i \tag{59.26}$$

contains only negative y_{ij} quantities. We then have a possible basic solution:

$$\frac{1}{y_{0j}} P_j - \sum_{i=1}^{m-1} \frac{y_{ij}}{y_{0j}} P_i = P_0. \tag{59.27}$$

3. Example.

Let us find a possible basic solution for;

$$\begin{aligned} 3x_1 + x_3 - x_5 &= 3 \\ x_1 + x_2 - 3x_4 &= -12 \\ x_2 + x_3 + x_5 &= 4\,. \end{aligned} \tag{59.28}$$

Or, using matrices and numbering the vectors:

$$\underset{(1)\ (2)\ (3)\ (4)\ (5)}{\begin{bmatrix} 3 & 0 & 1 & 0 & -1 \\ 1 & 1 & 0 & -3 & 0 \\ 0 & 1 & 1 & 0 & 1 \end{bmatrix}} \begin{Bmatrix} x_1 \\ x_2 \\ x_3 \\ x_4 \\ x_5 \end{Bmatrix} = \underset{(0)}{\begin{Bmatrix} 3 \\ -12 \\ 4 \end{Bmatrix}} \tag{59.29}$$

Let us take as an arbitrary basis the (0), (1), and (3) vectors and write the corresponding quantities y_{ij}:

$$\underset{(2)\ (4)\ (5)}{\begin{bmatrix} 0 & 0 & -1 \\ 1 & -3 & 0 \\ 1 & 0 & 1 \end{bmatrix}} = \underset{(0)\ (1)\ (3)}{\begin{bmatrix} 3 & 3 & 1 \\ -12 & 1 & 0 \\ 4 & 0 & 1 \end{bmatrix}} \begin{bmatrix} y_{02} & y_{04} & y_{05} \\ y_{12} & y_{14} & y_{15} \\ y_{32} & y_{34} & y_{35} \end{bmatrix}, \tag{59.30}$$

hence:

$$\begin{aligned} \begin{bmatrix} y_{02} & y_{04} & y_{05} \\ y_{12} & y_{14} & y_{15} \\ y_{32} & y_{34} & y_{35} \end{bmatrix} &= \begin{bmatrix} 3 & 3 & 1 \\ -12 & 1 & 0 \\ 4 & 0 & 1 \end{bmatrix}^{-1} \begin{bmatrix} 0 & 0 & -1 \\ 1 & -3 & 0 \\ 1 & 0 & 1 \end{bmatrix} \\ &= \begin{bmatrix} \frac{1}{35} & -\frac{3}{35} & -\frac{1}{35} \\ \frac{12}{35} & -\frac{1}{35} & -\frac{12}{35} \\ -\frac{4}{35} & \frac{12}{35} & \frac{39}{35} \end{bmatrix} \begin{bmatrix} 0 & 0 & -1 \\ 1 & -3 & 0 \\ 1 & 0 & 1 \end{bmatrix} \\ &= \begin{bmatrix} -\frac{4}{35} & \frac{9}{35} & -\frac{2}{35} \\ -\frac{13}{35} & \frac{3}{35} & -\frac{24}{35} \\ \frac{51}{35} & -\frac{36}{35} & \frac{43}{35} \end{bmatrix} \end{aligned} \tag{59.31}$$

We start with arbitrary coefficients:

$$\varrho_0 = 2, \quad w_1 = 4, \quad w_3 = 3. \qquad 59.32$$

Then

$$G = 4P_1 + 3P_3 - 2P_0. \qquad 59.33$$

To select y_{oj}, we have:

$$y_{02} = -\frac{4}{35}, \quad y_{04} = \frac{9}{35}, \quad y_{05} = -\frac{2}{35}. \qquad 59.34$$

Thus, we shall select j = 4 (the only positive y_{oj}). We then express P_4:

$$P_4 = y_{04}P_0 + y_{14}P_1 + y_{34}P_3 = \frac{9}{35}P_0 + \frac{3}{35}P_1 - \frac{36}{35}P_3. \qquad 59.35$$

Next, we find the vector that will be replaced by P_4:

$$\frac{w_1}{y_{14}} = \frac{4}{\frac{3}{35}} = \frac{140}{3}, \quad \frac{w_3}{y_{34}} = \frac{3}{-\frac{36}{35}} = -\frac{35}{12}. \qquad 59.36$$

Therefore, we choose the vector P_1, which gives the smallest positive value. Next, we find the new coefficients:

$$G + (\varrho_0 + \theta y_{04})P_0 = \theta P_4 + (w_3 - \theta y_{34})P_3, \qquad 59.37$$

$$G + [2 + (\tfrac{140}{3})(\tfrac{9}{35})]P_0 = \frac{140}{3}P_4 + [3 - (\tfrac{140}{3})(-\tfrac{36}{35})]P_3 \qquad 59.38$$

or

$$G + 14P_0 = \frac{140}{3}P_4 + 51P_3. \qquad 59.39$$

The new coefficients are therefore:

$$\varrho_0 = 14, \quad w_3 = 51, \quad w_4 = \frac{140}{3}. \qquad 59.40$$

Taking as our new basis the vectors P_0, P_3, and P_4, we find the corresponding y_{ij}:

$$\underset{(1)\ (2)\ (5)}{\begin{bmatrix} 3 & 0 & -1 \\ 1 & 1 & 0 \\ 0 & 1 & 1 \end{bmatrix}} = \underset{(0)\ (3)\ (4)}{\begin{bmatrix} 3 & 1 & 0 \\ -12 & 0 & -3 \\ 4 & 1 & 0 \end{bmatrix}} \begin{bmatrix} y_{01} & y_{02} & y_{05} \\ y_{31} & y_{32} & y_{35} \\ y_{41} & y_{42} & y_{45} \end{bmatrix} \qquad 59.41$$

hence:

$$\begin{bmatrix} y_{01} & y_{02} & y_{05} \\ y_{31} & y_{32} & y_{35} \\ y_{41} & y_{42} & y_{45} \end{bmatrix} = \begin{bmatrix} 3 & 1 & 0 \\ -12 & 0 & -3 \\ 4 & 1 & 0 \end{bmatrix}^{-1} \begin{bmatrix} 3 & 0 & -1 \\ 1 & 1 & 0 \\ 0 & 1 & 1 \end{bmatrix}$$

$$= \begin{bmatrix} -1 & 0 & 1 \\ 4 & 0 & -3 \\ 4 & -\frac{1}{3} & -4 \end{bmatrix} \begin{bmatrix} 3 & 0 & -1 \\ 1 & 1 & 0 \\ 0 & 1 & 1 \end{bmatrix} \qquad 59.42$$

$$= \begin{bmatrix} -3 & 1 & 2 \\ 12 & -3 & -7 \\ \frac{35}{3} & -\frac{13}{3} & -8 \end{bmatrix}$$

the columns

$$\begin{matrix} 1 \\ -3 \\ -\frac{13}{3} \end{matrix} \quad \text{and} \quad \begin{matrix} 2 \\ -7 \\ -8 \end{matrix}$$

each give a solution.

To select y_{0j}, we have:

$$y_{01} = -3, \quad y_{02} = 1, \quad y_{05} = 2. \qquad 59.43$$

We shall therefore take y_{05} (we might equally well take (y_{02}). Now let us express P_5.

$$P_5 = y_{05}P_0 + y_{35}P_3 + y_{45}P_4 = 2P_0 - 7P_3 - 8P_4. \qquad 59.44$$

All y_{ij} ($i \neq 0$) are negative: therefore, we have found a solution; it remains only to write (59.44) as follows:

$$\tfrac{7}{2} P_3 + 4 P_4 + \tfrac{1}{2} P_5 = P_0, \qquad 59.45$$

giving:

$$x_1 = 0, \quad x_2 = 0, \quad x_3 = \tfrac{7}{2}, \quad x_4 = 4, \quad x_5 = \tfrac{1}{2}. \qquad 59.46$$

This is the way we obtained (58.17).

Another basic solution could have been obtained with y_{02}:

$$P_2 + 3 P_3 + \tfrac{13}{3} P_4 = P_0, \qquad 59.47$$

giving:

$$x_1 = 0, \quad x_2 = 1, \quad x_3 = 3, \quad x_4 = \tfrac{13}{3}, \quad x_5 = 0. \qquad 59.48$$

Section 60

CONDITIONS FOR THE EXISTENCE OF AN OPTIMUM OF THE ECONOMIC FUNCTION

Referring back to what was said at the beginning of Section 58, we can formulate the conditions for the existence of an optimum as follows: Let there be 3 possibilities, p_1, p_2, and p_3:

p_1: max $z = \infty$

p_2: max z is finite and was found by the present solution;

p_3: an optimum solution has not been obtained, and a higher value of z must be found.

A) If at least one $z_j - c_j < 0$, then p_1 or p_3 is true.

a) If all $x_{ij} \leq 0$, for the $z_j - c_j < 0$ columns, then p_1 is true.*

b) If some of $x_{ij} > 0$, the solution can be improved, which means that p_3 is true.

B) If all $z_j - c_j \geq 0$, then max z has been reached, and p_2 is true.

In the case of a minimum, it is only necessary to repeat this explanation replacing $z_j - c_j$ by $c_j - z_j$, and max $z = \infty$ by min $z = -\infty$.

Section 61

USE OF THE INVERSE PRODUCT FORM**

1. General explanation.—2. Example.—3. Application to the simplex method.

1. General explanation.

Let $[B_a]$ be the regular matrix corresponding to the arbitrarily chosen basis, and let $[B_b]$ be the regular matrix corresponding

---

*Actually, in this case, the coefficients of the p_i and p_j in (59.9) are positive and constitute a possible solution (which is not, however, a basic solution, since it contains m + 1 non-zero variables). The corresponding value of z is

$$z = \sum_{i=n+1}^{n+m} (x_i - \theta x_{ij}) c_i + \theta c_j,$$

in which θ can be as large as desired; the same is true for z, and consequently there is no maximum.

**It might perhaps be better to call this method: factoring the inverse. The reader is free to adopt whichever he likes.

to a new basis obtained by the inclusion of a vector P_e in place of a vector P_s removed from the basis. Let us give the vectors P_e and P_s the first position at the left in the bases B_a and B_b, in order to simplify the beginning of our presentation. To state it concretely, let there be 5 vectors forming the matrix:

$$\begin{bmatrix} 5 & 3 & 2 & 4 & 0 \\ 2 & 1 & 0 & -3 & 4 \\ 2 & 8 & 1 & 0 & 1 \end{bmatrix}. \qquad 61.1$$
$$\begin{matrix} (1) & (2) & (3) & (4) & (5) \end{matrix}$$

Now take the basis:

$$[B_a] = \begin{bmatrix} 2 & 4 & 0 \\ 0 & -3 & 4 \\ 1 & 0 & 1 \end{bmatrix}; \qquad 61.2$$
$$\begin{matrix} (3) & (4) & (5) \end{matrix}$$

replacing vector (3) by vector (2), we have:

$$[B_b] = \begin{bmatrix} 3 & 4 & 0 \\ 1 & -3 & 4 \\ 8 & 0 & 1 \end{bmatrix}. \qquad 61.3$$
$$\begin{matrix} (2) & (4) & (5) \end{matrix}$$

If we multiply $[B_b]$ by the vector $\begin{Bmatrix} 1 \\ 0 \\ 0 \end{Bmatrix}$ we obtain:

$$[B_b] \begin{Bmatrix} 1 \\ 0 \\ 0 \end{Bmatrix} = \begin{bmatrix} 3 & 4 & 0 \\ 1 & -3 & 4 \\ 8 & 0 & 1 \end{bmatrix} \begin{Bmatrix} 1 \\ 0 \\ 0 \end{Bmatrix} = \begin{Bmatrix} 3 \\ 1 \\ 8 \end{Bmatrix} = \{P_e\}; \qquad 61.4$$

but:

$$\{P_e\} = \begin{Bmatrix} 3 \\ 1 \\ 8 \end{Bmatrix} = [1] \begin{Bmatrix} 3 \\ 1 \\ 8 \end{Bmatrix} = [B_a]\,[B_a]^{-1} \begin{Bmatrix} 3 \\ 1 \\ 8 \end{Bmatrix} \qquad 61.5$$

Let us set:

$$\{X_b\} = [B_a]^{-1} \begin{Bmatrix} 3 \\ 1 \\ 8 \end{Bmatrix} = \begin{bmatrix} -\frac{3}{10} & -\frac{4}{10} & \frac{16}{10} \\ \frac{4}{10} & \frac{2}{10} & -\frac{8}{10} \\ \frac{3}{10} & \frac{4}{10} & -\frac{6}{10} \end{bmatrix} \begin{Bmatrix} 3 \\ 1 \\ 8 \end{Bmatrix} = \begin{Bmatrix} \frac{115}{10} \\ -\frac{50}{10} \\ -\frac{35}{10} \end{Bmatrix}. \qquad 61.6$$

Therefore, from (61.4)—(61.6), we have:

$$[B_b]\begin{Bmatrix}1\\0\\0\end{Bmatrix} = [B_a]\begin{Bmatrix}\frac{115}{10}\\-\frac{50}{10}\\-\frac{35}{10}\end{Bmatrix}; \qquad 61.7$$

and, since $[B_b]$ and $[B_a]$ differ only by their first vectors:

$$[B_b]\begin{bmatrix}1 & 0 & 0\\0 & 1 & 0\\0 & 0 & 1\end{bmatrix} = [B_a]\begin{bmatrix}\frac{115}{10} & 0 & 0\\-\frac{50}{10} & 1 & 0\\-\frac{35}{10} & 0 & 1\end{bmatrix}. \qquad 61.8$$

Let us set:

$$[E_b]^{-1} = \begin{bmatrix}\frac{115}{10} & 0 & 0\\-\frac{50}{10} & 1 & 0\\-\frac{35}{10} & 0 & 1\end{bmatrix} = \begin{bmatrix} & 0 & 0\\\{X_b\} & 1 & 0\\ & 0 & 1\end{bmatrix}. \qquad 61.9$$

Then we have:

$$[B_b] = [B_a]\,[E_b]^{-1}. \qquad 61.10$$

It is apparent that the property shown by formula (61.10), in which the special form of (61.9) is used, is general, no matter what the order of the basis and the position of the vector replacing a unit vector in $[E_b]^{-1}$ may be. We have presented the demonstration of (61.10) by means of a numerical case so as to avoid excessive abstraction.

By inversion of (61.10), we obtain:

$$[B_b]^{-1} = [E_b]\,[B_a]^{-1} \qquad 61.11$$

The (61.11) form is of special interest in relation to the direct form (61.10) for purposes of electronic computation as will be brought out further in Section 70.

If we change a new vector, we can also write:

$$[B_c]^{-1} = [E_c]\,[B_b]^{-1}, \qquad 61.12$$

and so forth.

For any $(m \times n)$ matrix of rank m, we can write:

$$[B_l]^{-1} = [E_l]\,[E_k]\,\ldots\,[E_c]\,[E_b]\,[B_a]^{-1}, \qquad 61.13$$

where the matrices $[E_i]$ are unit matrices in which we have replaced one column by the column $[B_{i-1}]^{-1}$ $\{P_e\}$ and inverted the square matrix thus obtained. The column must be chosen to correspond to the position of the vector $\{P_s\}$.

Therefore, if we know $[B_a]^{-1}$, we can find $[B_b]^{-1}$, $[B_c]^{-1}$. If $[B_a]$ is a matrix that can be inverted easily, the calculation of the matrices of the succeeding bases will be particularly simple. In the case where $[B_a]$ is a unit matrix, we have:

$$\begin{aligned} [B_b]^{-1} &= [E_b] \\ [B_c]^{-1} &= [E_c]\,[B_b]^{-1} = [E_c]\,[E_b] \\ [B_d]^{-1} &= [E_d]\,[B_c]^{-1} = [E_d]\,[E_c]\,[E_b] \\ &\cdots\cdots \\ [B_l]^{-1} &= [E_l]\,[E_k]\,\ldots\,[E_c]\,[E_b]\,. \end{aligned} \qquad 61.14$$

It is easy to invert a regular matrix that differs from a unit matrix by only one column. Let l be the index of the column that is not formed by a unit vector, let y_{il} represent the elements of this column, and let y_{ij} $(j \neq l)$ represent those of the other j columns. Then the elements of the inverse will be:

$$\begin{aligned} n_{il} &= -\frac{y_{il}}{y_{ll}} \qquad i \neq l \\ n_{ll} &= \frac{1}{y_{ll}} \\ n_{ij} &= 0 \qquad i \neq j,\; j \neq l \\ n_{ij} &= 1 \qquad i = j \quad j \neq l\,. \end{aligned} \qquad 61.15$$

2. Example.

$$[a] = \begin{bmatrix} 1 & 3 & 0 & 0 \\ 0 & 2 & 0 & 0 \\ 0 & -1 & 1 & 0 \\ 0 & 4 & 0 & 1 \end{bmatrix} \qquad 61.16$$

$$y_{12} = 3\,, \quad y_{22} = 2\,, \quad y_{32} = -1\,, \quad y_{42} = 4, \qquad 61.17$$

$$\begin{aligned} n_{12} &= -\frac{y_{12}}{y_{22}} = -\frac{3}{2}, \qquad & n_{22} &= \frac{1}{y_{22}} = \frac{1}{2} \\ n_{32} &= -\frac{y_{32}}{y_{22}} = \frac{1}{2}, \qquad & n_{42} &= -\frac{y_{42}}{y_{22}} = -2; \end{aligned} \qquad 61.18$$

thus:

$$[a]^{-1} = \begin{bmatrix} 1 & -\frac{3}{2} & 0 & 0 \\ 0 & \frac{1}{2} & 0 & 0 \\ 0 & \frac{1}{2} & 1 & 0 \\ 0 & -2 & 0 & 1 \end{bmatrix}. \qquad 61.19$$

3. Application to the simplex method.

Let us take a program:

$$[\text{MAX}]\ z = 3x_1 + 4x_2 + x_3 \qquad 61.20$$

$$\begin{bmatrix} 2 & 8 & -3 & 1 & 0 & 0 & 0 \\ 1 & 4 & 7 & 0 & 1 & 0 & 0 \\ 0 & 2 & 3 & 0 & 0 & 1 & 0 \\ 1 & 5 & -2 & 0 & 0 & 0 & 1 \end{bmatrix}_{(1)\,(2)\,(3)\,(4)\,(5)\,(6)\,(7)} \begin{pmatrix} x_1 \\ x_2 \\ x_3 \\ x_4 \\ x_5 \\ x_6 \\ x_7 \end{pmatrix} = \begin{pmatrix} 2 \\ 10 \\ 1 \\ 3 \end{pmatrix}, \qquad 61.21$$

One apparent solution is:

$$x_1 = 0,\ x_2 = 0,\ x_3 = 0,\ x_4 = 2,\ x_5 = 10,\ x_6 = 1,\ x_7 = 3\,. \qquad 61.22$$

giving:

$$z = 3(0) + 4(0) + 1(0) = 0\,. \qquad 61.23$$

Now we find the transformation:

$$\underset{(1)\,(2)\,(3)}{\begin{bmatrix} 2 & 8 & -3 \\ 1 & 4 & 7 \\ 0 & 2 & 3 \\ 1 & 5 & -2 \end{bmatrix}} = \underset{(4)\,(5)\,(6)\,(7)}{\begin{bmatrix} 1 & 0 & 0 & 0 \\ 0 & 1 & 0 & 0 \\ 0 & 0 & 1 & 0 \\ 0 & 0 & 0 & 1 \end{bmatrix}} \begin{bmatrix} x_{41} & x_{42} & x_{43} \\ x_{51} & x_{52} & x_{53} \\ x_{61} & x_{62} & x_{63} \\ x_{71} & x_{72} & x_{73} \end{bmatrix}. \qquad 61.24$$

Here, the basis $[B_a]$ is the unit basis: $[B_a]^{-1} = [1]$. Thus, we have:

$$\begin{bmatrix} x_{41} & x_{42} & x_{43} \\ x_{51} & x_{52} & x_{53} \\ x_{61} & x_{62} & x_{63} \\ x_{71} & x_{72} & x_{73} \end{bmatrix} = \begin{bmatrix} 2 & 8 & -3 \\ 1 & 4 & 7 \\ 0 & 2 & 3 \\ 1 & 5 & -2 \end{bmatrix}. \qquad 61.25$$

Now we calculate z_1, z_2, z_3:

$$[z_1\ \ z_2\ \ z_3] = \underset{(4)\,(5)\,(6)\,(7)}{[0\ \ 0\ \ 0\ \ 0]} \begin{bmatrix} 2 & 8 & -3 \\ 1 & 4 & 7 \\ 0 & 2 & 3 \\ 1 & 5 & -2 \end{bmatrix} = [0\ \ 0\ \ 0]; \qquad 61.26$$

hence:

$$z_1 = 0,\ \ z_2 = 0,\ \ z_3 = 0\,. \qquad 61.27$$

This gives:

$$z_1 - c_1 = 0 - 3 = -3, \quad z_2 - c_2 = 0 - 4 = -4, \quad z_3 - c_3 = 0 - 1 = -1. \qquad 61.28$$

Therefore, we choose P_2, for which we have the largest negative number, for inclusion in the basis. Next, we calculate the ratios x_i/x_{ij}:

$$\frac{x_4}{x_{42}} = \frac{2}{8} = \frac{1}{4}, \quad \frac{x_5}{x_{52}} = \frac{10}{4} = \frac{5}{2}, \quad \frac{x_6}{x_{62}} = \frac{1}{2}, \quad \frac{x_7}{x_{72}} = \frac{3}{5}. \qquad 61.29$$

We select the index 4, for which we have the smallest positive number; thus, we remove P_4 from the basis, to be replaced by P_2.

$$\begin{aligned} &x_1' = 0, \quad x_2' = \theta = \frac{x_4}{x_{42}} = \tfrac{1}{4}, \quad x_3' = 0, \\ &x_4' = 0, \quad x_5' = x_5 - \theta\, x_{52} = 10 - (\tfrac{1}{4})(4) = 9 \quad x_6' = x_6 - \theta\, x_{62} = 1 - (\tfrac{1}{4})(2) = \tfrac{1}{2} \qquad 61.30 \\ &x_7' = x_7 - \theta\, x_{72} = 3 - (\tfrac{1}{4})(5) = \tfrac{7}{4}\,; \end{aligned}$$

hence:

$$z = 3(0) + 4(\tfrac{1}{4}) + 1(0) = 1. \qquad 61.31$$

Now we verify:

$$z = z_0 + \theta\,(c_2 - z_2) = 0 + \tfrac{1}{4}[4 - 0] = 1 \qquad 61.32$$

$$\underset{(1)\,(2)\,(3)\,(4)\,(5)\,(6)\,(7)}{\begin{bmatrix} 2 & 8 & -3 & 1 & 0 & 0 & 0 \\ 1 & 4 & 7 & 0 & 1 & 0 & 0 \\ 0 & 2 & 3 & 0 & 0 & 1 & 0 \\ 1 & 5 & -2 & 0 & 0 & 0 & 1 \end{bmatrix}} \begin{Bmatrix} 0 \\ \frac{1}{4} \\ 0 \\ 0 \\ 9 \\ \frac{1}{2} \\ \frac{7}{4} \end{Bmatrix} = \begin{Bmatrix} 2 \\ 10 \\ 1 \\ 3 \end{Bmatrix}. \qquad 61.33$$

Let us proceed to the next step, which is to find the transformation of vectors P_1, P_2, and P_3.

$$\underset{(1)\,(4)\,(3)}{\begin{bmatrix} 2 & 1 & -3 \\ 1 & 0 & 7 \\ 0 & 0 & 3 \\ 1 & 0 & -2 \end{bmatrix}} = \underset{(2)\,(5)\,(6)\,(7)}{\begin{bmatrix} 8 & 0 & 0 & 0 \\ 4 & 1 & 0 & 0 \\ 2 & 0 & 1 & 0 \\ 5 & 0 & 0 & 1 \end{bmatrix}} \begin{bmatrix} x_{21} & x_{24} & x_{23} \\ x_{51} & x_{54} & x_{53} \\ x_{61} & x_{64} & x_{63} \\ x_{71} & x_{74} & x_{73} \end{bmatrix}. \qquad 61.34$$

To invert the matrix formed by the vectors, P_2, P_5, P_6, P_7, we shall use the product form (one might also invert it directly, since it has the requisite special form):

$$[B_a]^{-1}\{P_e\} = [1]\begin{Bmatrix}8\\4\\2\\5\end{Bmatrix} = \begin{Bmatrix}8\\4\\2\\5\end{Bmatrix}, \qquad 61.35$$

$$[E_b]^{-1} = \begin{bmatrix}8&0&0&0\\4&1&0&0\\2&0&1&0\\5&0&0&1\end{bmatrix}, [E_b] = \begin{bmatrix}\frac{1}{8}&0&0&0\\-\frac{1}{2}&1&0&0\\-\frac{1}{4}&0&1&0\\-\frac{5}{8}&0&0&1\end{bmatrix}, [B_b]^{-1} = \begin{bmatrix}\frac{1}{8}&0&0&0\\-\frac{1}{2}&1&0&0\\-\frac{1}{4}&0&1&0\\-\frac{5}{8}&0&0&1\end{bmatrix}. \qquad \begin{matrix}61.36\\61.37\\61.38\end{matrix}$$

This gives:

$$\begin{bmatrix}x_{21}&x_{24}&x_{23}\\x_{51}&x_{54}&x_{53}\\x_{61}&x_{64}&x_{63}\\x_{71}&x_{74}&x_{73}\end{bmatrix} = \begin{bmatrix}\frac{1}{8}&0&0&0\\-\frac{1}{4}&1&0&0\\-\frac{1}{2}&0&1&0\\-\frac{5}{8}&0&0&1\end{bmatrix}\begin{bmatrix}2&1&-3\\1&0&7\\0&0&3\\1&0&-2\end{bmatrix} = \begin{bmatrix}\frac{1}{4}&\frac{1}{8}&-\frac{3}{8}\\0&-\frac{1}{2}&\frac{17}{2}\\-\frac{1}{2}&-\frac{1}{4}&\frac{15}{4}\\-\frac{1}{4}&-\frac{5}{8}&-\frac{1}{8}\end{bmatrix} \qquad 61.39$$

Now we calculate z_1, z_4, z_3:

$$[z_1 \quad z_4 \quad z_3] = \underset{(2)\ (5)\ (6)\ (7)}{[4 \quad 0 \quad 0 \quad 0]}\begin{bmatrix}\frac{1}{4}&\frac{1}{8}&-\frac{3}{8}\\0&-\frac{1}{2}&\frac{17}{2}\\-\frac{1}{2}&-\frac{1}{4}&\frac{15}{4}\\-\frac{1}{4}&-\frac{5}{8}&-\frac{1}{8}\end{bmatrix} = [1 \ \tfrac{1}{2} \ -\tfrac{3}{2}]; \qquad 61.40$$

hence

$$z_1 - c_1 = 1 - 3 = -2, \quad z_4 - c_4 = \tfrac{1}{2} - 0 = \tfrac{1}{2}, \quad z_3 - c_3 = -\tfrac{3}{2} - 1 = -\tfrac{5}{2}. \qquad 61.41$$

The most negative value corresponds to index 3, hence we introduce into the basic, vector P_3. Let us calculate the ratios x_i/x_{ij}:

$$\frac{x_2}{x_{23}} = \frac{\frac{1}{4}}{-\frac{3}{8}} = -\frac{2}{3}; \quad \frac{x_5}{x_{53}} = \frac{9}{\frac{17}{2}} = \frac{18}{17};$$

$$\frac{x_6}{x_{63}} = \frac{\frac{1}{2}}{\frac{15}{4}} = \frac{2}{15}; \quad \frac{x_7}{x_{73}} = \frac{\frac{7}{4}}{-\frac{1}{8}} = -14. \qquad 61.42$$

The smallest positive is 2/15, hence we shall eliminate P_6. We obtain:

$$x_1' = 0, \qquad x_2' = x_2 - \theta\, x_{23}, \qquad x_3' = \theta = \frac{x_6}{x_{63}} = \frac{2}{15}$$
$$= \tfrac{1}{4} - (\tfrac{2}{15})(-\tfrac{3}{8})$$
$$= \frac{3}{10}$$

$$x_4' = 0, \qquad x_5' = x_5 - \theta\, x_{53}, \qquad x_6' = 0, \tag{61.43}$$
$$= 9 - (\tfrac{2}{15})(\tfrac{17}{2})$$
$$= \tfrac{118}{1}$$
$$x_7' = x_7 - \theta\, x_{73}$$
$$= \tfrac{7}{4} - (\tfrac{2}{15})(-\tfrac{1}{8}) = \tfrac{53}{30}$$

hence:

$$z = 3(0) + 4(-\tfrac{3}{10}) + 1(\tfrac{2}{15}) = \tfrac{4}{3}\,. \tag{61.44}$$

Now we verify:

$$\begin{aligned} z &= z_0 + \theta(c_3 - z_3) \\ &= 1 + \tfrac{2}{15}[1 - (-\tfrac{3}{2})] \\ &= \tfrac{4}{3}\,. \end{aligned} \qquad \begin{bmatrix} 2 & 8 & -3 & 1 & 0 & 0 & 0 \\ 1 & 4 & 7 & 0 & 1 & 0 & 0 \\ 0 & 2 & 3 & 0 & 0 & 1 & 0 \\ 1 & 5 & -2 & 0 & 0 & 0 & 1 \\ (1) & (2) & (3) & (4) & (5) & (6) & (7) \end{bmatrix} \begin{Bmatrix} 0 \\ \frac{3}{10} \\ \frac{2}{15} \\ 0 \\ \frac{118}{15} \\ 0 \\ \frac{53}{30} \end{Bmatrix} = \begin{Bmatrix} 2 \\ 10 \\ 1 \\ 3 \end{Bmatrix}. \qquad \begin{matrix} 61.45 \\ 61.46 \end{matrix}$$

Let us pass to the next step; let us find the transformation of vectors $P_1\ P_4\ P_6$:

$$\underset{(1)\ (4)\ (6)}{\begin{bmatrix} 2 & 1 & 0 \\ 1 & 0 & 0 \\ 0 & 0 & 1 \\ 1 & 0 & 0 \end{bmatrix}} = \underset{2)\ (5)\ (3)\ (7)}{\begin{bmatrix} 8 & 0 & -3 & 0 \\ 4 & 1 & 7 & 0 \\ 2 & 0 & 3 & 0 \\ 5 & 0 & -2 & 1 \end{bmatrix}} \begin{bmatrix} x_{21} & x_{24} & x_{26} \\ x_{51} & x_{54} & x_{56} \\ x_{31} & x_{34} & x_{36} \\ x_{71} & x_{74} & x_{76} \end{bmatrix}. \tag{61.47}$$

To invert the matrix formed with vectors P_2, P_5, P_3, P_7, we use the product form.

$$[B_b]^{-1}\{P_e\} = \begin{bmatrix} \frac{1}{8} & 0 & 0 & 0 \\ -\frac{1}{2} & 1 & 0 & 0 \\ -\frac{1}{4} & 0 & 1 & 0 \\ -\frac{5}{8} & 0 & 0 & 1 \end{bmatrix} \begin{Bmatrix} -3 \\ 7 \\ 3 \\ -2 \end{Bmatrix} = \begin{Bmatrix} -\frac{3}{8} \\ \frac{17}{2} \\ \frac{15}{4} \\ -\frac{1}{8} \end{Bmatrix}, \tag{61.48}$$

$$[E_c]^{-1} = \begin{bmatrix} 1 & 0 & -\frac{3}{8} & 0 \\ 0 & 1 & \frac{17}{2} & 0 \\ 0 & 0 & \frac{15}{4} & 0 \\ 0 & 0 & -\frac{1}{8} & 1 \end{bmatrix}, \qquad [E_c] = \begin{bmatrix} 1 & 0 & \frac{1}{10} & 0 \\ 0 & 1 & -\frac{34}{15} & 0 \\ 0 & 0 & \frac{4}{15} & 0 \\ 0 & 0 & \frac{1}{30} & 1 \end{bmatrix} \qquad \begin{matrix} 61.49 \\ 61.50 \end{matrix}$$

$$[B_c]^{-1} = [E_c][E_b] = \begin{bmatrix} 1 & 0 & \frac{1}{10} & 0 \\ 0 & 1 & -\frac{34}{15} & 0 \\ 0 & 0 & \frac{4}{15} & 0 \\ 0 & 0 & \frac{1}{30} & 1 \end{bmatrix} \begin{bmatrix} \frac{1}{8} & 0 & 0 & 0 \\ -\frac{1}{2} & 1 & 0 & 0 \\ -\frac{1}{4} & 0 & 1 & 0 \\ -\frac{5}{8} & 0 & 0 & 1 \end{bmatrix} = \begin{bmatrix} \frac{1}{10} & 0 & \frac{1}{10} & 0 \\ \frac{1}{15} & 1 & -\frac{34}{15} & 0 \\ -\frac{1}{15} & 0 & \frac{4}{15} & 0 \\ -\frac{19}{30} & 0 & \frac{1}{30} & 1 \end{bmatrix}. \qquad 61.51$$

Thus:

$$\begin{bmatrix} x_{21} & x_{24} & x_{26} \\ x_{51} & x_{54} & x_{56} \\ x_{31} & x_{34} & x_{36} \\ x_{71} & x_{74} & x_{76} \end{bmatrix} = \begin{bmatrix} \frac{1}{10} & 0 & \frac{1}{10} & 0 \\ \frac{1}{15} & 1 & -\frac{34}{15} & 0 \\ -\frac{1}{15} & 0 & \frac{4}{15} & 0 \\ -\frac{19}{30} & 0 & \frac{1}{30} & 1 \end{bmatrix} \begin{bmatrix} 2 & 1 & 0 \\ 1 & 0 & 0 \\ 0 & 0 & 1 \\ 1 & 0 & 0 \end{bmatrix} = \begin{bmatrix} \frac{1}{5} & \frac{1}{10} & \frac{1}{10} \\ \frac{17}{15} & \frac{1}{15} & -\frac{34}{15} \\ -\frac{2}{15} & -\frac{1}{15} & \frac{4}{15} \\ -\frac{4}{15} & -\frac{19}{30} & \frac{1}{30} \end{bmatrix}. \qquad 61.52$$

Now we calculate z_1, z_4, z_6.

$$[z_1 \;\; z_4 \;\; z_6] = \underset{(2)\;(4)\;(3)\;(7)}{[4 \;\; 0 \;\; 1 \;\; 0]} \begin{bmatrix} \frac{1}{5} & \frac{1}{10} & \frac{1}{10} \\ \frac{17}{15} & \frac{1}{15} & -\frac{34}{15} \\ -\frac{2}{15} & -\frac{1}{15} & \frac{4}{15} \\ -\frac{4}{15} & -\frac{19}{30} & \frac{1}{30} \end{bmatrix} = [\tfrac{2}{3} \;\; \tfrac{1}{3} \;\; \tfrac{2}{3}]; \qquad 61.53$$

hence

$$z_1 = \tfrac{2}{3}, \qquad z_4 = \tfrac{1}{3}, \qquad z_6 = \tfrac{2}{3}, \qquad 61.54$$

and

$$z_1 - c_1 = \tfrac{2}{3} - 3 = -\tfrac{7}{3}, \qquad z_4 - c_4 = \tfrac{1}{3} - 0 = \tfrac{1}{3}, \qquad z_6 - c_6 = \tfrac{2}{3} - 0 = \tfrac{2}{3}. \qquad 61.55$$

Therefore we introduce vector P_1 into the basis.

The reader can continue these calculations for practice.

The principle of this variant (see Section 70) is particularly useful when the simplex method of calculation is used with the aid of an electronic computer. This variant was developed by Dantzig and Orchard-Hays.*

---

*See, for example: G. B. Dantzig and W. Orchard-Hays, "The Product Form for the Inverse in the Simplex Method," Mathematical Tables and Other Aids to Computation, VIII, No. 46, April 1954, pp. 63-67.

Section 62

DEGENERACY

Let us return to expressions (57.3), (57.4), and (58.2). Let:

$$\sum_{j=1}^{n+m} a_{ij}\, x_j = b_i, \qquad z = \sum_{j=1}^{n+m} c_j\, x_j \quad \text{et} \quad \sum_{j=1}^{n+m} P_j\, x_j = P_0. \qquad \begin{matrix} 62.1 \\ 62.2 \end{matrix}$$

$$i = 1, 2, \ldots, m \qquad 62.3$$

If the m equations (62.1) are not linearly independent, we say that we have degeneracy. In this case, we can form $1 < m$ new linearly independent equations to replace equations (62.1).

Another case of degeneracy can occur if the vectors representing columns of the matrix of coefficients are not linearly independent; at a certain point in computation, this involves the presence of a quantity $\theta_0 = \min/i\ (x_i/x_{ij}) = 0$, and it is no longer possible to increase (or decrease, as the case may be) the value of the function. We say that this is a cyclical degeneracy. It can occur at the beginning of computation, or even after several iterations.*

Furthermore, it is possible that P_0 may be a linear combination of p ($p < m$) vectors chosen among the P_i; this is another case of degeneracy. This kind of degeneracy can be avoided by modifying slightly the values of the components of P_0. This method is employed particularly in transportation problems. It is also possible to increase the number of P_j vectors, by means of a certain number of unit vectors V_i, with the corresponding c_i in z being chosen very small in relation to the others. By replacing V_i with $-V_i$, if need be, a possible solution can be obtained. The rank of the linear system in this case is $k = m$.

In linear programs corresponding to actual economic phenomena, the presence of degeneracy is a rare occurence; for lack of space in this book, we refer the interested reader to several works on the subject.*

---

*See the following references: A. Charnes, "Optimality and Degeneracy in Linear Programming," Econometrica, Vol. 20 (1950), No. 2, pp. 160-170. E. M. L. Beale, "Cycling in the Dual Simplex Algorithm," Naval Research Logistics Quarterly, Vol. 2 (1954), pp. 269-275. A. J. Hoffman, Cycling in the Simplex Algorithm (National Bureau of Standards Report), December 16, 1953.

Section 63

METHOD OF SUBMATRICES*

1. General explanation.—2. Variant.—3. The case of equations.—4. Example.

1. General explanation.

A purely algebraic method, using a breakdown into submatrices, will be our next object of inquiry.

First of all, we shall show how to find a maximum in the case of finding an optimum with any kind of equations whatever.

The relations (57.5) and (57.6) can be written, after the introduction of slack variables as:

$$\begin{bmatrix} a_{11} & a_{12} & \dots & a_{1n} & 1 & 0 & \dots & 0 \\ a_{21} & a_{22} & \dots & a_{2n} & 0 & 1 & \dots & 0 \\ \dots\dots & & \dots\dots & & & & & \dots\dots \\ a_{m1} & a_{m2} & \dots & a_{mn} & 0 & 0 & \dots & 1 \\ -c_1 & -c_2 & \dots & -c_n & 0 & 0 & \dots & 0 \end{bmatrix} \begin{Bmatrix} x_1 \\ x_2 \\ \vdots \\ x_n \\ x_{n+1} \\ \vdots \\ x_{n+m} \end{Bmatrix} = \begin{Bmatrix} b_1 \\ b_2 \\ \vdots \\ b_m \\ -z \end{Bmatrix} \qquad 63.1$$

Let us adopt the hypothesis that all the quantities b_j ($j = 1, 2, \dots, m$) are positive. We have changed the sign of z for reasons of convenience, which will become apparent later on.

We can divide this into submatrices as follows:

$$\left[\begin{array}{c|cccccccc} a_{11} & a_{12} & \dots & a_{1n} & 1 & 0 & \dots & 0 \\ \hline a_{21} & a_{22} & \dots & a_{2n} & 0 & 1 & \dots & 0 \\ \dots\dots & \dots\dots & \dots & \dots\dots & & & & \dots\dots \\ a_{m1} & a_{m2} & \dots & a_{mn} & 0 & 0 & \dots & \\ -c_1 & -c_2 & \dots & -c_n & 0 & 0 & \dots & 0 \end{array}\right] \begin{Bmatrix} x_1 \\ \hline x_2 \\ \vdots \\ x_n \\ x_{n+1} \\ \vdots \\ x_{n+m} \end{Bmatrix} = \begin{Bmatrix} b_1 \\ \hline b_2 \\ \vdots \\ b_m \\ -z \end{Bmatrix} \qquad 63.2$$

Let us take:

$$\alpha_1 = a_{11}, \qquad 63.3$$

$$\alpha_2 = [a_{12} \ \dots \ a_{1n} \ \ 1 \ 0 \ \dots \ 0], \qquad 63.4$$

---

*This method was inspired by the work of Dantzig, Orden, Charnes, Cooper, and Henderson on the one hand, and that of Gabriel Kron on the other.

$$a_3 = \begin{bmatrix} a_{21} \\ \vdots \\ a_{m1} \\ -c_1 \end{bmatrix}, \quad a_4 = \begin{bmatrix} a_{22} & \dots & a_{2n} & 0 & 1 & \dots & 0 \\ \dots & & & & & & \\ \dots & & & & & & \\ a_{m2} & \dots & a_{mn} & 0 & 0 & \dots & 1 \\ -c_2 & \dots & -c_n & 0 & 0 & \dots & 0 \end{bmatrix} \qquad \begin{matrix} 63.5 \\ 63.6 \end{matrix}$$

$$\lambda_1 = x_1, \quad \lambda_2 = \begin{Bmatrix} x_2 \\ \vdots \\ x_n \\ x_{n+1} \\ \vdots \\ x_{n+m} \end{Bmatrix}, \quad \mu_1 = b_1, \quad \mu_2 = \begin{Bmatrix} b_2 \\ \vdots \\ b_m \\ -z \end{Bmatrix} \qquad \begin{matrix} 63.7 \\ 63.8 \\ 63.9 \\ 63.10 \end{matrix}$$

Then, the system of equations (63.1) can be written:

$$a_1 \lambda_1 + a_2 \lambda_2 = \mu_1, \qquad 63.11$$

$$a_3 \lambda_1 + a_4 \lambda_2 = \mu_2. \qquad 63.12$$

We propose to transform equations (63.11) and (63.12) in such a manner that the new system will take the form:

$$\lambda_1 + a_2' \lambda_2 = \mu_1' \qquad 63.13$$

$$a_4' \lambda_2 = \mu_2'; \qquad 63.14$$

this in order that the set of solutions to (63.11), (63.12) will remain unchanged in the transformation that leads to (63.13), (63.14). Note that this amounts to replacing the first column in (63.1) by:

$$\begin{bmatrix} 1 \\ 0 \\ \vdots \\ 0 \\ 0 \end{bmatrix}. \qquad 63.15$$

If we remove λ from (63.11), we obtain:

$$\lambda_1 = a_1^{-1} \mu_1 - a_1^{-1} a_2 \lambda_2. \qquad 63.16$$

Substituting (63.16) into (63.12), we obtain:

$$a_3 a_1^{-1} \mu_1 - a_3 a_1^{-1} a_2 \lambda_2 + a_4 \lambda_2 = \mu_2, \qquad 63.17$$

or

$$(a_4 - a_3 a_1^{-1} a_2) \lambda_2 = \mu_2 - a_3 a_1^{-1} \mu_1. \qquad 63.18$$

The system (63.11), (63.12) thus becomes:

$$\lambda_1 + \alpha_1^{-1} \alpha_2 \lambda_2 = \alpha_1^{-1} \mu_1, \tag{63.19}$$

$$(\alpha_4 - \alpha_3 \alpha_1^{-1} \alpha_2) \lambda_2 = \mu_2 - \alpha_3 \alpha_1^{-1} \mu_1; \tag{63.20}$$

this is the desired new form. Identifying (63.19), (63.20) with (63.13), (63.14), we obtain:

$\alpha_1' = 1,$ 63.21 $\quad \alpha_2' = \alpha_1^{-1} \alpha_2,$ 63.22 $\quad \mu_1' = \alpha_1^{-1} \mu_1,$ 63.23

$\alpha_3' = 0,$ 63.24 $\quad \alpha_4' = \alpha_4 - \alpha_3 \alpha_1^{-1} \alpha_2,$ 63.25 $\quad \mu_2' = \mu_2 - \alpha_3 \alpha_1^{-1} \mu_1,$ 63.26

To avoid tedious explanations, we shall now demonstrate this method by an example. Returning to (58.34), (58.35), after the introduction of the slack variables (58.36), we write:

$$\left[\begin{array}{c|cccc} 1 & 0 & 1 & 0 & 0 \\ \hline 0 & 1 & 0 & 1 & 0 \\ 1 & \frac{2}{3} & 0 & 0 & 1 \\ -4 & -3 & 0 & 0 & 0 \end{array}\right] \begin{Bmatrix} x_1 \\ \text{--} \\ x_2 \\ x_3 \\ x_4 \\ x_5 \end{Bmatrix} = \begin{Bmatrix} 4{,}000 \\ \text{---} \\ 6{,}000 \\ 6{,}000 \\ -z \end{Bmatrix}. \tag{63.27}$$
$$\begin{array}{ccccc} (1) & (2) & (3) & (4) & (5) \end{array}$$

Now we apply the Dantzig criteria given in Section 58. We choose the first column, which contains, in the bottom row, the most negative quantity (the choice is limited to columns (1) and (2), since the other columns relate to the unit matrix; thus, we exclude them from our field of choice.) So we choose column (1-), in which we find (-4). Next, we compute the quotients:

$$\frac{4{,}000}{1} = 4{,}000, \qquad \frac{6{,}000}{0} = \infty, \qquad \frac{6{,}000}{1} = 6{,}000. \tag{63.28}$$

We choose the element in the first row, for which we have found the smallest positive quantity (4,000).

Then we divide into submatrices as shown in (63.27); this gives us:

$$\alpha_1' = 1, \tag{63.29}$$

$$\alpha_2' = \alpha_1^{-1} \alpha_2 = [1]\,[0\ 1\ 0\ 0] = [0\ 1\ 0\ 0], \tag{63.30}$$

$$\alpha_3' = \begin{bmatrix} 0 \\ 0 \\ 0 \end{bmatrix}, \tag{63.31}$$

$$\alpha'_4=\alpha_4-\alpha_3\,\alpha_1^{-1}\,\alpha_2=\begin{bmatrix}1&0&1&0\\ \frac{2}{3}&0&0&1\\ -3&0&0&0\end{bmatrix}-\begin{bmatrix}0\\ 1\\ -4\end{bmatrix}[0\ 1\ 0\ 0]$$

$$=\begin{bmatrix}1&0&1&0\\ \frac{2}{3}&-1&0&1\\ -3&4&0&0\end{bmatrix} \qquad 63.32$$

$$\mu'_1=\alpha_1^{-1}\,\mu_1=4{,}000, \qquad 63.33$$

$$\mu'_2=\mu_2-\alpha_3\,\alpha_1^{-1}\mu_1=\begin{bmatrix}6{,}000\\ 6{,}000\\ -z\end{bmatrix}-\begin{bmatrix}0\\ 1\\ -4\end{bmatrix}[4{,}000]$$

$$=\begin{bmatrix}6{,}000\\ 6{,}000\\ -z\end{bmatrix}-\begin{bmatrix}0\\ 4{,}000\\ -16{,}000\end{bmatrix} \qquad 63.34$$

$$=\begin{bmatrix}6{,}000\\ 2{,}000\\ -z+16{,}000\end{bmatrix}.$$

Which gives:

$$\begin{matrix}\\ \\ \rightarrow\\ \\ \end{matrix}\begin{bmatrix}1&0&1&0&0\\ 0&1&0&1&0\\ 0&\frac{2}{3}&-1&0&1\\ 0&-3&4&0&0\end{bmatrix}\begin{Bmatrix}x_1\\ x_2\\ x_3\\ x_4\\ x_5\end{Bmatrix}=\begin{Bmatrix}4{,}000\\ 6{,}000\\ 2{,}000\\ -z+16{,}000\end{Bmatrix}. \qquad 63.35$$
$$\qquad\uparrow$$

This time, in conformity with the Dantzig criterion, we select the second column and the third line. Let us perform permutations to place them in the first column and in the first line:

$$\left[\begin{array}{c|cccc}\frac{2}{3}&0&-1&0&1\\ \hline 1&0&0&1&0\\ 0&1&1&0&0\\ -3&0&4&0&0\end{array}\right]\begin{Bmatrix}x_2\\ --\\ x_1\\ x_3\\ x_4\\ x_5\end{Bmatrix}=\begin{Bmatrix}2{,}000\\ ------\\ 6{,}000\\ 4{,}000\\ -z+16{,}000\end{Bmatrix}. \qquad 63.36$$

This gives:

$$\alpha'_1=1, \qquad 63.37$$

$$\alpha'_2=\alpha_1^{-1}\,\alpha_2=\frac{3}{2}\,[0\ -1\ 0\ 1]=\Big[0\ -\frac{3}{2}\ \ 0\ \ \frac{3}{2}, \qquad 63.38$$

$$\alpha'_3=\begin{bmatrix}0\\ 0\\ 0\end{bmatrix}, \qquad 63.39$$

$$\alpha_4' = \alpha_4 - \alpha_3\,\alpha_1^{-1}\alpha_2 = \begin{bmatrix} 0 & 0 & 1 & 0 \\ 1 & 1 & 0 & 0 \\ 0 & 4 & 0 & 0 \end{bmatrix} - \frac{3}{2}\begin{bmatrix} 1 \\ 0 \\ -3 \end{bmatrix}[0\ \ -1\ \ 0\ \ 1],$$

$$= \begin{bmatrix} 0 & \frac{3}{2} & 1 & -\frac{3}{2} \\ 1 & 1 & 0 & 0 \\ 0 & -\frac{1}{2} & 0 & \frac{9}{2} \end{bmatrix}, \qquad 63.40$$

$$\mu_1' = \alpha_1^{-1}\mu_1 = \frac{3}{2}\cdot 2{,}000 = 3{,}000, \qquad 63.41$$

$$\mu_2' = \mu_2 -- \alpha_3\alpha_1^{-1}\mu_1$$

$$= \begin{bmatrix} 6{,}000 \\ 4{,}000 \\ -z + 16{,}000 \end{bmatrix} - \begin{bmatrix} 3{,}000 \\ 0 \\ -9{,}000 \end{bmatrix} = \left\{ \begin{matrix} 3{,}000 \\ 4{,}000 \\ -z + 25{,}000 \end{matrix} \right\} \qquad 63.42$$

which gives:

$$\rightarrow \begin{bmatrix} 1 & 0 & -\frac{3}{2} & 0 & \frac{3}{2} \\ 0 & 0 & \frac{3}{2} & 1 & -\frac{3}{2} \\ 0 & 1 & 1 & 0 & 0 \\ 0 & 0 & \underset{\uparrow}{-\frac{1}{2}} & 0 & \frac{9}{2} \end{bmatrix} \left\{ \begin{matrix} x_2 \\ x_1 \\ x_3 \\ x_4 \\ x_5 \end{matrix} \right\} = \left\{ \begin{matrix} 3{,}000 \\ 3{,}000 \\ 4{,}000 \\ -z + 25{,}000 \end{matrix} \right\}. \qquad 63.43$$

This time let us select the third column and the second line.

$$\left[\begin{array}{c|cccc} \frac{3}{2} & 0 & 0 & 1 & -\frac{3}{2} \\ \hline -\frac{3}{2} & 0 & 1 & 0 & \frac{3}{2} \\ 1 & 1 & 0 & 0 & 0 \\ -\frac{1}{2} & 0 & 0 & 0 & \frac{9}{2} \end{array} \right] \left\{ \begin{array}{c} x_3 \\ \hline x_1 \\ x_2 \\ x_4 \\ x_5 \end{array} \right\} = \left\{ \begin{array}{r} 3{,}000 \\ \hline 3{,}000 \\ 4{,}000 \\ -z + 25{,}000 \end{array} \right\}. \qquad 63.44$$

Let us not give the details of the computation any more:

$$\alpha_1' = 1, \quad 63.45 \qquad \alpha_2' = [0\ \ 0\ \ \tfrac{2}{3}\ \ -1], \quad 63.46$$

$$\alpha_3' = \begin{bmatrix} 0 \\ 0 \\ 0 \end{bmatrix}, \quad 63.47 \qquad \alpha_4' = \begin{bmatrix} 0 & 1 & 1 & 0 \\ 1 & 0 & -\frac{2}{3} & 1 \\ 0 & 0 & \frac{1}{3} & 4 \end{bmatrix}. \quad 63.48$$

$$\mu_1' = 2000, \quad 63.49 \qquad \mu_2' = \begin{bmatrix} 6{,}000 \\ 2{,}000 \\ -z + 26{,}000 \end{bmatrix}. \quad 63.50$$

Which gives:

$$\begin{bmatrix} 1 & 0 & 0 & \frac{2}{3} & -1 \\ 0 & 0 & 1 & 1 & 0 \\ 0 & 1 & 0 & -\frac{2}{3} & 1 \\ 0 & 0 & 0 & \frac{1}{3} & 4 \end{bmatrix} \begin{Bmatrix} x_3 \\ x_1 \\ x_2 \\ x_4 \\ x_5 \end{Bmatrix} = \begin{Bmatrix} 2{,}000 \\ 6{,}000 \\ 2{,}000 \\ -z + 26{,}000 \end{Bmatrix} . \qquad 63.51$$

There are no more negative numbers in the last row, and thus we have reached the maximum. The solution is obvious; in order to state it, let us transpose the columns and rows back into their original order:

$$\begin{bmatrix} 0 & 0 & 1 & -\frac{2}{3} & -1 \\ 0 & 1 & 0 & 1 & 0 \\ 1 & 0 & 0 & \frac{2}{3} & 1 \\ 0 & 0 & 0 & \frac{1}{3} & 4 \end{bmatrix} \begin{Bmatrix} x_1 \\ x_2 \\ x_3 \\ x_4 \\ x_5 \end{Bmatrix} = \begin{Bmatrix} 2{,}000 \\ 6{,}000 \\ 2{,}000 \\ -z + 26{,}000 \end{Bmatrix} \qquad 63.52$$

We have:

$$x_1 = 2{,}000,\ x_2 = 6{,}000,\ x_3 = 2{,}000,\ x_4 = 0,\ x_5 = 0;\ z = 26{,}000. \qquad 63.52a$$

Before going on to equations, we should point out that in the case of a minimum we would take z rather than -z in the column of the second member, and in the bottom row, c_i rather than $-c_i$. Consequently, the signs of the coefficients a_{ij} will be changed, as will the Dantzig criteria (see Section 64).

2. Variant.

To obtain, in the first column of the rectangular matrix on which we perform the transformation, the values:

$$\begin{matrix} 1 \\ 0 \\ 0 \\ \\ 0 \end{matrix} , \qquad 63.53$$

we can avoid the computations indicated by formulas (63.21)-(63.26) simply as follows (the explanations will be given by means of an example). Returning to (63.36), we multiply the first row by the inverse of 2/3, or 3/2. This gives:

$$\begin{bmatrix} 1 & 0 & -\frac{3}{2} & 0 & \frac{3}{2} \\ 1 & 0 & 0 & 1 & 0 \\ 0 & 1 & 1 & 0 & 0 \\ -3 & 0 & 4 & 0 & 0 \end{bmatrix} \begin{Bmatrix} x_2 \\ x_1 \\ x_3 \\ x_4 \\ x_5 \end{Bmatrix} = \begin{Bmatrix} 3{,}000 \\ 6{,}000 \\ 4{,}000 \\ -z + 16{,}000 \end{Bmatrix} \qquad 63.54$$

Now we multiply the first row by -1 and add it to the second row; then we multiply the first row by 3 and add this to the fourth line; this yields:

$$\begin{array}{r} \\ \rightarrow \\ \\ \\ \end{array}\left[\begin{array}{ccccc} 1 & 0 & -\frac{3}{2} & 0 & \frac{3}{2} \\ 0 & 0 & \frac{3}{2} & 1 & -\frac{3}{2} \\ 0 & 1 & 1 & 0 & 0 \\ 0 & 0 & \underset{\uparrow}{-\frac{1}{2}} & 0 & \frac{9}{2} \end{array}\right] \begin{Bmatrix} x_2 \\ x_1 \\ x_3 \\ x_4 \\ x_5 \end{Bmatrix} = \begin{Bmatrix} 3{,}000 \\ 3{,}000 \\ 4{,}000 \\ -z + 25{,}000 \end{Bmatrix} \qquad 63.55$$

And thus we find exactly (63.43).

Using this same procedure, we shall now try to obtain the third column the values:

$$\begin{matrix} 0 \\ 1 \\ 0 \\ 0 \end{matrix} \qquad 63.56$$

We multiply the second row by the inverse of 3/2, or 2/3, and then we obtain zeros in this row by means of suitable multiplication and the addition of certain other lines. We can very quickly obtain (63.51). This procedure is much faster than the preceding one, and is used in the Charnes, Cooper, and Henderson table presented in Section 65.

3. The case of equations.

We proceed as follows:

1. The economic function is transformed by the addition of m variables whose coefficients are equal, very large, and negative; in this way, we know that the solution corresponding to the maximum will contain none of these variables.

2. These variables which are called artificial variables, are added to the constraints, as in the case of inequations, but we know that these variables will be zero for the maximum.

3. The remaining procedure is the same for inequations.

4. Example.

Let us take:

$$\begin{aligned} 3x_1 + x_3 - x_5 &= 3 \\ x_1 + x_2 - 3x_4 &= -12 \\ x_2 + x_3 + x_5 &= 4\,. \\ [\text{MAX}]\ z = 3x_1 + 2x_2 &+ x_3 + x_4 + 5x_5. \end{aligned} \qquad 63.57$$

With the addition of the artificial variables, this becomes:

$$\begin{aligned} 3x_1 + x_3 - x_5 \quad + x_6 &= 3 \\ x_1 + x_2 - 3x_4 - x_7 &= -12 \\ x_2 + x_3 + x_5 \quad + x_8 &= 4. \end{aligned} \qquad 63.58$$

It will be noted that the artificial variables are given the sign corresponding to that of the second member. Thus, in our example, we begin with the solution: $x_6 = 3$, $x_7 = 12$, $x_8 = 4$, the others being zero.

$$z = 3x_1 + 2x_2 + x_3 + x_4 + 5x_5 - Mx_6 - Mx_7 - Mx_8, \qquad 63.58a$$

where M is a very large and arbitrary quantity (as we shall see, there is no point in assigning a value to M).

This gives us:

$$\begin{bmatrix} 3 & 0 & 1 & 0 & -1 & 1 & 0 & 0 \\ -1 & -1 & 0 & 3 & 0 & 0 & 1 & 0 \\ 0 & 1 & 1 & 0 & 1 & 0 & 0 & 1 \\ -3 & -2 & -1 & -1 & -5 & M & M & M \end{bmatrix} \begin{Bmatrix} x_1 \\ x_2 \\ x_3 \\ x_4 \\ x_5 \\ x_6 \\ x_7 \\ x_8 \end{Bmatrix} = \begin{Bmatrix} 3 \\ 12 \\ 4 \\ -z \end{Bmatrix}, \qquad 63.59$$

or, by shifting the square matrix:

$$\left[\begin{array}{ccc|ccccc} 1 & 0 & 0 & 3 & 0 & 1 & 0 & -1 \\ 0 & 1 & 0 & -1 & -1 & 0 & 3 & 0 \\ 0 & 0 & 1 & 0 & 1 & 1 & 0 & 1 \\ \hline M & M & M & -3 & -2 & -1 & -1 & -5 \end{array}\right] \begin{Bmatrix} x_6 \\ x_7 \\ x_8 \\ \hline x_1 \\ x_2 \\ x_3 \\ x_4 \\ x_5 \end{Bmatrix} = \begin{Bmatrix} 3 \\ 12 \\ 4 \\ \hline -z \end{Bmatrix}. \qquad 63.60$$

Using formulas (63.21) - (63.26), which are valid no matter what the division of the submatrices, we obtain:

$$\rightarrow \begin{bmatrix} 1 & 0 & 0 & 3 & 0 & 1 & 0 & -1 \\ 0 & 1 & 0 & -1 & -1 & 0 & 3 & 0 \\ 0 & 0 & 1 & 0 & 1 & 1 & 0 & 1 \\ 0 & 0 & 0 & -2M-3 & -2 & -2M-1 & \underset{\uparrow}{-3M-1} & -5 \end{bmatrix} \begin{Bmatrix} x_6 \\ x_7 \\ x_8 \\ x_1 \\ x_2 \\ x_3 \\ x_4 \\ x_5 \end{Bmatrix} = \begin{Bmatrix} 3 \\ 12 \\ 4 \\ -z - 19M \end{Bmatrix}. \qquad 63.61$$

This result can be obtained directly (as can easily be shown) by placing zeros below the unit matrix and adding to each $-c_i$ the quantity $-(a_{1i} + a_{2i} + \ldots + a_{mi})M$, and to $-z$ the quantity $-M(b_1 + b_2 + \ldots + b_m)$.

Now we choose the seventh column (the most negative of the $-c_i$, taking into account, of course, the $-M$).

$$\left[\begin{array}{c|ccccccc} 3 & 1 & 0 & -1 & -1 & 0 & 0 & 0 \\ \hline 0 & 0 & 0 & 3 & 0 & 1 & 1 & -1 \\ 0 & 0 & 1 & 0 & 1 & 1 & 0 & 1 \\ 3M-1 & 0 & 0 & -2M-3 & -2 & -2M-1 & 0 & 5 \end{array}\right] \left(\begin{array}{c} x_4 \\ \hline x_7 \\ x_8 \\ x_1 \\ x_2 \\ x_3 \\ x_6 \\ x_5 \end{array}\right) = \left\{\begin{array}{c} 12 \\ \hline 3 \\ 4 \\ -z-19M \end{array}\right\}. \tag{63.62}$$

The transformation gives:

$$\rightarrow \begin{bmatrix} 1 & \frac{1}{3} & 0 & -\frac{1}{3} & -\frac{1}{3} & 0 & 0 & 0 \\ 0 & 0 & 0 & 3 & 0 & 1 & 1 & -1 \\ 0 & 0 & 1 & 0 & 1 & 1 & 0 & 1 \\ 0 & M+\frac{1}{3} & 0 & -3M-\frac{10}{3} & -M-\frac{7}{3} & -2M-1 & 0 & -5 \end{bmatrix} \left\{\begin{array}{c} x_4 \\ x_7 \\ x_8 \\ x_1 \\ x_2 \\ x_3 \\ x_6 \\ x_5 \end{array}\right\} = \left\{\begin{array}{c} 4 \\ 3 \\ 4 \\ -z-7M+4 \end{array}\right\} \tag{63.63}$$
$$\qquad\qquad\qquad\uparrow$$

$$\left[\begin{array}{c|ccccccc} 3 & 0 & 0 & 0 & 0 & 1 & 1 & -1 \\ \hline -\frac{1}{3} & \frac{1}{3} & 0 & 1 & -\frac{1}{3} & 0 & 0 & 0 \\ 0 & 0 & 1 & 0 & 1 & 1 & 0 & 1 \\ -3M-\frac{10}{3} & M+\frac{1}{3} & 0 & 0 & -M-\frac{7}{3} & -2M-1 & 0 & -5 \end{array}\right] \left\{\begin{array}{c} x_1 \\ x_7 \\ x_8 \\ x_4 \\ x_2 \\ x_3 \\ x_6 \\ x_5 \end{array}\right\} = \left\{\begin{array}{c} 3 \\ \hline 4 \\ 4 \\ -z-7M+4 \end{array}\right\} \tag{63.64}$$

The transformation gives:

$$\rightarrow \begin{bmatrix} 1 & 0 & 0 & 0 & 0 & \frac{1}{3} & \frac{1}{3} & -\frac{1}{3} \\ 0 & \frac{1}{3} & 0 & 1 & -\frac{1}{3} & \frac{1}{9} & - & -\frac{1}{9} \\ 0 & 0 & 1 & 0 & 1 & 1 & 0 & 1 \\ 0 & M+\frac{1}{3} & 0 & 0 & -M-\frac{7}{3} & -M+\frac{1}{9} & M+\frac{10}{9} & -M-\frac{55}{9} \end{bmatrix} \left\{\begin{array}{c} x_1 \\ x_7 \\ x_8 \\ x_4 \\ x_2 \\ x_3 \\ x_6 \\ x_5 \end{array}\right\} = \left\{\begin{array}{c} 1 \\ \frac{13}{3} \\ 4 \\ -z-4M+\frac{2}{3} \end{array}\right\} \tag{63.65}$$
$$\qquad\qquad\qquad\qquad\qquad\qquad\uparrow$$

$$\left[\begin{array}{c|cccccccc} 1 & 0 & 1 & 0 & 1 & 1 & 0 & 0 \\ \hline -\frac{1}{9} & \frac{1}{3} & 0 & 1 & -\frac{1}{3} & \frac{1}{9} & \frac{1}{9} & 0 \\ -\frac{1}{3} & 0 & 0 & 0 & 0 & \frac{1}{3} & \frac{1}{3} & 1 \\ -M-\frac{55}{9} & M+\frac{1}{3} & 0 & 0 & -M-\frac{7}{3} & -M+\frac{1}{9} & M+\frac{10}{9} & 0 \end{array}\right]\begin{pmatrix} x_5 \\ x_7 \\ x_8 \\ x_4 \\ x_2 \\ x_3 \\ x_6 \\ x_1 \end{pmatrix}=\begin{Bmatrix} 4 \\ \frac{13}{3} \\ 1 \\ -z-4M+\frac{22}{3} \end{Bmatrix}. \qquad 63.66$$

The transformation gives:

$$\begin{bmatrix} 1 & 0 & 1 & 0 & 1 & 1 & 0 & 0 \\ 0 & \frac{1}{3} & \frac{1}{9} & 1 & -\frac{2}{9} & \frac{2}{9} & \frac{1}{9} & 0 \\ 0 & 0 & \frac{1}{3} & 0 & \frac{1}{3} & \frac{2}{3} & \frac{1}{3} & 1 \\ 0 & M+\frac{1}{3} & M+\frac{55}{9} & 0 & \frac{34}{9} & \frac{56}{9} & M+\frac{10}{9} & 0 \end{bmatrix}\begin{pmatrix} x_5 \\ x_7 \\ x_8 \\ x_4 \\ x_2 \\ x_3 \\ x_6 \\ x_1 \end{pmatrix}=\begin{Bmatrix} 4 \\ \frac{43}{9} \\ \frac{7}{3} \\ -z+\frac{286}{9} \end{Bmatrix}. \qquad 63.67$$

The solution is:

$$x_1=\tfrac{7}{3},\quad x_2=0,\quad x_3=0,\quad x_4=\tfrac{43}{9},\quad x_5=4,\quad x_6=0,\quad x_7=0,\quad x_8=0. \qquad 63.68$$

We find the same result as in (58.33a).

Section 64

FINDING A MINIMUM

1. The Dantzig method.—2. Submatrix method.— 3. Another method.—4. The case of equations.

1. The Dantzig method.

We proceed as in Section 58, except that j must be chosen so that $c_j - z_j$ is as negative as possible.

Example:

$$[\text{MIN}]\ z = 15x_1 + 33x_2 \qquad 64.1$$

with the constraints:

$$\begin{aligned} 3x_1 + 2x_2 &\geqslant 6 \\ 6x_1 + x_2 &\geqslant 6 \qquad x_i \geqslant 0. \\ x_2 &\geqslant 1 \end{aligned} \qquad 64.2$$

With the slack variables, we shall write:

$$[\text{MIN}] \quad z = 15x_1 + 33x_2 \qquad 64.3$$

$$\begin{aligned} 3x_1 + 2x_2 - x_3 &= 6 \\ 6x_1 + x_2 - x_4 &= 6 \\ x_2 - x_5 &= 1 \end{aligned} \qquad x_i \geq 0. \qquad 64.4$$

Let us start with an arbitrary solution:

$$x_1 = \tfrac{2}{3},\ x_2 = 2, x_3 = 0,\ x_4 = 0,\ x_5 = 1, z = 15(\tfrac{2}{3}) + 33(2) = 76. \qquad 64.5$$

We have:

$$\underset{(1)\ (2)\ (3)\ (4)\ (5)}{\begin{bmatrix} 3 & 2 & -1 & 0 & 0 \\ 6 & 1 & 0 & -1 & 0 \\ 0 & 1 & 0 & 0 & -1 \end{bmatrix}} \begin{pmatrix} x_1 \\ x_2 \\ x_3 \\ x_4 \\ x_5 \end{pmatrix} = \begin{pmatrix} 6 \\ 6 \\ 1 \end{pmatrix}, \qquad 64.6$$

$$\underset{(3)\ (4)}{\begin{bmatrix} -1 & 0 \\ 0 & -1 \\ 0 & 0 \end{bmatrix}} = \underset{(1)(2)(5)}{\begin{bmatrix} 3 & 2 & 0 \\ 6 & 1 & 0 \\ 0 & 1 & -1 \end{bmatrix}} \begin{bmatrix} x_{13} & x_{14} \\ x_{23} & x_{24} \\ x_{53} & x_{54} \end{bmatrix} = \begin{bmatrix} 3 & 2 & 0 \\ 6 & 1 & 0 \\ 0 & 1 & -1 \end{bmatrix} \begin{bmatrix} \frac{1}{9} & -\frac{2}{9} \\ -\frac{2}{3} & \frac{1}{3} \\ -\frac{2}{3} & \frac{1}{3} \end{bmatrix}, \qquad 64.7$$

$$[z_3 \quad z_4] = [15 \quad 33 \quad 0] \begin{bmatrix} \frac{1}{9} & -\frac{2}{9} \\ -\frac{2}{3} & \frac{1}{3} \\ -\frac{2}{3} & \frac{1}{3} \end{bmatrix} = [-\tfrac{61}{3} \quad \tfrac{23}{3}], \qquad 64.8$$

$$c_3 - z_3 = 0 - (-\tfrac{61}{3}) = \tfrac{61}{3}, \qquad c_4 - z_4 = 0 - (\tfrac{23}{3}) = -\tfrac{23}{3}. \qquad 64.9$$

Thus we select j = 4.

$$\begin{aligned} x'_1 &= x_1 - \frac{x_5}{x_{54}} x_{14} = \tfrac{2}{3} - 3\left(-\tfrac{2}{9}\right) = \tfrac{4}{3}, \\ x'_2 &= x_2 - \frac{x_5}{x_{54}} x_{24} = 2 - 3\left(\tfrac{1}{3}\right) = 1 \\ x'_3 &= 0, \quad x'_4 = \frac{x_5}{x_{54}} = 3, \quad x'_5 = 0. \end{aligned} \qquad 64.10$$

$$z = 15\,(\tfrac{4}{3}) + 33(1) + 0(0) + 0(3) + 0(0) = 53. \qquad 64.11$$

Verification:

$$\begin{bmatrix} 3 & 2 & -1 & 0 & 0 \\ 6 & 1 & 0 & -1 & 0 \\ 0 & 1 & 0 & 0 & -1 \end{bmatrix} \begin{pmatrix} \frac{4}{3} \\ 1 \\ 0 \\ 3 \\ 0 \end{pmatrix} = \begin{pmatrix} 6 \\ 6 \\ 1 \end{pmatrix}. \qquad 64.12$$

$$z = z_0 + \theta(c_4 - z_4) = 76 + 3(-\tfrac{23}{3}) = 76 - 23 = 53. \qquad 64.13$$

Search for a new solution

$$\begin{bmatrix} -1 & 0 \\ 0 & 0 \\ 0 & -1 \end{bmatrix} = \begin{bmatrix} 3 & 2 & 0 \\ 6 & 1 & -1 \\ 0 & 1 & 0 \end{bmatrix} \begin{bmatrix} x_{13} & x_{15} \\ x_{23} & x_{25} \\ x_{43} & x_{45} \end{bmatrix} = \begin{bmatrix} 3 & 2 & 0 \\ 6 & 1 & -1 \\ 0 & 1 & 0 \end{bmatrix} \begin{bmatrix} -\frac{1}{3} & \frac{2}{3} \\ 0 & -1 \\ -2 & 3 \end{bmatrix} \qquad 64.14$$

(3) (5) (1) (2) (4)

$$[z_3 \quad z_5] = [15 \quad 33 \quad 0] \begin{bmatrix} -\frac{1}{3} & \frac{2}{3} \\ 0 & -1 \\ -2 & 3 \end{bmatrix} = [-5 \quad -23], \qquad 64.15$$

$$c_3 - z_3 = 0 - (-5) = 5, \quad c_5 - z_5 = 0 - (-23) = 23. \qquad 64.16$$

There is no more $c_j - z_j$ negative, the value $z = 53$ is the minimum.

2. Submatrix method.

There are several ways of using this method. First, let us study the case of inequations.

The search for a minimum can be transformed into a search for a maximum, simply by transforming the variables. Remember that in the submatrix method, we must start from a $z = 0$ solution, which cannot be a basic solution in finding a minimum. In other words, we must transform the inequations and the economic function in such manner that the origin of the new reference (n-hedron) will lie upon the convex polyhedron formed by the hyperplanes, and that this new reference will contain, in its positive portion, at least one vertex of the polyhedron if the program has a solution. This is achieved by transforming the variables as follows:

$$x_k = x_{ok} - x'_k \qquad 64.17$$

where x_{ok} are suitable constants.

One can, except in special cases, take all the x_{ok} constants as equal to a single constant α, so that the new inequations, with their signs changed, make possible a basic solution made up of the slack variables.

Example.

Returning to (64.1) and (64.2):

$$[\text{MIN}]\ z = 15x_1 + 33x_2 \qquad 64.18$$

with the constraints:

$$\begin{aligned} 3x_1 + 2x_2 &\geq 6 \\ 6x_1 + x_2 &\geq 6 \qquad x_i \geq 0. \\ x_2 &\geq 1 \end{aligned} \qquad 64.19$$

Now let us find a quantity α such that, when $x_i = \alpha - x_i{}'$ is substituted into (64.19), these inequations will hold for $x_1{}' = x_2{}' = 0$.

$$\begin{aligned} 3(\alpha - x_1{}') + 2(\alpha - x_2{}') &\geqslant 6 \\ 6(\alpha - x_1{}') + (\alpha - x_2{}') &\geqslant 6 \\ \alpha - x_2{}' &\geqslant 1. \end{aligned} \qquad 64.20$$

This yields:

$$\alpha > \tfrac{6}{5}, \quad \alpha > \tfrac{6}{7}, \quad \alpha > 1. \qquad 64.21$$

Let us take $\alpha = 2$, which satisfies all the inequalities. The minimum we are seeking becomes:

$$[\text{MIN}]\ z = 96 - 15x_1{}' - 33x_2{}' \qquad 64.22$$

with the constraints*:

$$\begin{aligned} 3x_1{}' + 2x_2{}' &\leqslant 4 \\ 6x_1{}' + x_2{}' &\leqslant 8 \\ x_2{}' &\leqslant 1. \end{aligned} \qquad 64.23$$

In place of this minimum, we shall now search for a maximum:

$$[\text{MAX}]\ z' = 15x_1{}' + 33x_2{}', \qquad 64.23\text{a}$$

with the same constraints as above (64.23).

This yields:

$$\begin{array}{c} \\ \\ \rightarrow \\ \\ \end{array}\begin{bmatrix} 3 & 2 & 1 & 0 & 0 \\ 6 & 1 & 0 & 1 & 0 \\ 0 & 1 & 0 & 0 & 1 \\ -15 & -33 & 0 & 0 & 0 \end{bmatrix} \begin{Bmatrix} x_1{}' \\ x_2{}' \\ x_3{}' \\ x_4{}' \\ x_5{}' \end{Bmatrix} = \begin{Bmatrix} 4 \\ 8 \\ 1 \\ -z' \end{Bmatrix}, \qquad 64.24$$
$$\qquad\qquad \uparrow \text{ (under column 2)}$$

$$\left[\begin{array}{c|cccc} 1 & 0 & 0 & 0 & 1 \\ \hline 1 & 6 & 0 & 1 & 0 \\ 2 & 3 & 1 & 0 & 0 \\ -33 & -15 & 0 & 0 & 0 \end{array}\right] \begin{Bmatrix} x_2{}' \\ x_1{}' \\ x_3{}' \\ x_4{}' \\ x_5{}' \end{Bmatrix} = \begin{Bmatrix} 1 \\ 8 \\ 4 \\ -z' \end{Bmatrix}, \qquad 64.25$$

---

*To these constraints it would be well to add: $x_1' \leq 2$ and $x_2' \leq 2$, so that $x_1 \geq 0$ and $x_2 \geq 0$. However, in this example chosen expressly for its great simplicity, the first inequation implies that x_1' and x_2' are less than or equal to 2; we have therefore omitted the constraints $x_1' \leq 2$ and $x_2' \leq 2$, but this should by no means be taken as a general rule.

$$\rightarrow\begin{bmatrix}1 & 0 & 0 & 0 & 1\\ 0 & 6 & 0 & 1 & -1\\ 0 & 3 & 1 & 0 & -2\\ 0 & -15 & 0 & 0 & 33\end{bmatrix}\begin{Bmatrix}x_2'\\ x_1'\\ x_3'\\ x_4'\\ x_5'\end{Bmatrix}=\begin{Bmatrix}1\\ 7\\ 2\\ -z'+33\end{Bmatrix}, \qquad \uparrow \tag{64.26}$$

$$\left[\begin{array}{c|cccc}3 & 0 & 1 & 0 & -2\\ \hline 6 & 0 & 0 & 1 & -1\\ 0 & 1 & 0 & 0 & 1\\ -15 & 0 & 0 & 0 & 33\end{array}\right]\begin{Bmatrix}x_1'\\ x_2'\\ x_3'\\ x_4'\\ x_5'\end{Bmatrix}=\begin{Bmatrix}2\\ 7\\ 1\\ -z'+33\end{Bmatrix}, \tag{64.27}$$

$$\begin{bmatrix}1 & 0 & \frac{1}{3} & 0 & -\frac{2}{3}\\ 0 & 0 & -2 & 1 & 3\\ 0 & 1 & 0 & 0 & 1\\ 0 & 0 & \underbrace{5}_{+} & 0 & \underbrace{3}_{+}\end{bmatrix}\begin{Bmatrix}x_1'\\ x_2'\\ x_3'\\ x_4'\\ x_5'\end{Bmatrix}=\begin{Bmatrix}\frac{2}{3}\\ 3\\ 1\\ -z'+43\end{Bmatrix} \tag{64.28}$$

Therefore, the optimum solution is:

$$x_1' = \frac{2}{3},\quad x_2' = 1,\quad x_3' = 0,\quad x_4' = 3,\quad x_5' = 0,\quad z' = 43; \tag{64.29}$$

which gives:

$$x_1 = \frac{4}{3},\quad x_2 = 1,\quad z = 53, \tag{64.30}$$

a result which is already known (64.13).

3. Another method.

In addition to the m slack variables, one may add m other artificial variables (or complementary variables), giving them a + sign and introducing them into the economic function with very large positive coefficients, so as to make sure that these complementary variables will not appear in the solution corresponding to the minimum. Thus, the program:

$$[\text{MIN}]\ z = 15x_1 + 33x_2 \tag{64.31}$$

with the constraints:

$$\begin{aligned}3x_1 + 2x_2 &\geq 6\\ 6x_1 + x_2 &\geq 6 \qquad x_i \geq 0,\\ x_2 &\geq 1\end{aligned} \tag{64.32}$$

will become:

$$[\text{MIN}]\ z = 15x_1 + 33x_2 + Mx_6 + Mx_7 + Mx_8 \tag{64.33}$$

with the constraints:

$$\begin{aligned} 3x_1 + 2x_2 - x_3 + x_6 &= 6 \\ 6x_1 + x_2 - x_4 + x_7 &= 6 \\ x_2 - x_5 + x_8 &= 1\,. \end{aligned} \qquad 64.34$$

We are thus brought back to the search for a minimum for the case of equations, which we shall discuss below. In the case of (64.33) and (64.34), we start from the solution $x_i = 0$, $i = 1, 2, 3, 4, 5$, $x_6 = 6$, $x_7 = 6$, $x_8 = 1$, which gives us a unit starting basis and makes it possible to apply the submatrix method.

4. The Case of equations.

We shall treat linear systems as we did (63.57), adding an artificial basis whose coefficients M in the economic function are very large.

Example:

$$[\text{MIN}]\ z = 3x_1 - x_2 + x_3 + x_4 \qquad 64.35$$

with the constraints:

$$\begin{aligned} -3x_1 + 5x_2 - 2x_3 + x_4 &= 1 \\ 4x_1 - x_2 + x_4 &= 4 \\ x_1 + 2x_2 + 8x_3 - 4x_4 &= 8. \end{aligned} \qquad 64.36$$

We shall take:

$$[\text{MIN}]\ z = 3x_1 - x_2 + x_3 + x_4 + Mx_5 + Mx_6 + Mx_7 \qquad 64.37$$

$$\begin{aligned} -3x_1 + 5x_2 - 2x_3 + x_4 + x_5 &= 1 \\ 4x_1 - x_2 + x_4 + x_6 &= 4 \\ x_1 + 2x_2 + 8x_3 - 4x_4 + x_7 &= 8. \end{aligned} \qquad 64.38$$

Now we set:

$$\left[\begin{array}{ccc|cccc} 1 & 0 & 0 & -3 & 5 & -2 & 1 \\ 0 & 1 & 0 & 4 & -1 & 0 & 1 \\ 0 & 0 & 1 & 1 & 2 & 8 & -4 \\ \hline M & M & M & 3 & -1 & 1 & 1 \end{array}\right] \begin{Bmatrix} x_5 \\ x_6 \\ x_7 \\ x_1 \\ x_2 \\ x_3 \\ x_4 \end{Bmatrix} = \begin{Bmatrix} 1 \\ 4 \\ 8 \\ z \end{Bmatrix}, \qquad 64.39$$

from which we obtain:

$$\rightarrow\begin{bmatrix} 1 & 0 & 0 & -3 & 5 & -2 & 1 \\ 0 & 1 & 0 & 4 & -1 & 0 & 1 \\ 0 & 0 & 1 & 1 & 2 & 8 & -4 \\ 0 & 0 & 0 & -2M+3 & -6M-1 & -6M+1 & 2M+1 \end{bmatrix} \begin{Bmatrix} x_5 \\ x_6 \\ x_7 \\ x_1 \\ x_2 \\ x_3 \\ x_4 \end{Bmatrix} = \begin{Bmatrix} 1 \\ 4 \\ 8 \\ z-13M \end{Bmatrix} \quad 64.40$$

$$\uparrow \text{ (under column } -6M-1\text{)}$$

Here we proceed just as we did for (63.57), except that the selection of columns is made by taking the largest negative number among the coefficients of M in the economic function. Thus, we shall select in (64.40) the vector with index 2 in the first row.

We shall leave the remaining calculations to the reader. One obtains, finally:

$$x_1 = 1.298,\ x_2 = 1.194,\ x_3 = 0.539,\ x_4 = 0,\ x_5 = x_6 = x_7 = 0$$
$$\min z = 3.2402. \quad 64.41$$

Section 65

THE CHARNES, COOPER, AND HENDERSON TABLE

Let us consider the matrix equations (63.21) - (63.26), writing them with the system of index symbols used for (63.2); thus, if r is the index of the row that has been transposed to appear in the first row, and if j is the index of the column transposed to appear in the first column:*

	In place of:	We shall write:	
65.1	$a_1' = 1$	$x'_r = 1$	
65.2	$a'_2 = a_1^{-1} a_2$	$x'_{rl} = \dfrac{x_{rl}}{x_{rj}}$	$l \neq j$
65.3	$a_3' = 0$	$x'_{ij} = 0$	$i \neq r$

*The coefficients a_{ij} are written x_{ij} in this section, so as to follow the notation of the authors of the table.

	In place of:	We shall write:
65.4	$\alpha'_4 = \alpha_4 - \alpha_3 \alpha_1^{-1} \alpha_2$	$x'_{il} = x_{il} - \left(\frac{x_{rl}}{x_{rj}}\right) x_{ij}$ $i \neq r$ et $l \neq j$ $z'_j - c'_j = 0$ $z'_l - c'_l = (z_l - c_l) - \left(\frac{x_{rl}}{x_{rj}}\right)(z_j - c_j)$ $l \neq j$
65.5	$\mu'_1 = \alpha_1^{-1} \mu_1$	$b'_r = \frac{b_r}{x_{rj}}$
65.6	$\mu'_2 = \mu_2 - \alpha_3 \alpha_1^{-1} \mu_1$	$b'_i = b_i - \left(\frac{x_{rl}}{x_{rj}}\right) b_r \quad i \neq r$ $-z' = -\left[z - \frac{x_{rl}}{x_{rj}}(z_r - c_r)\right]$

These relations can be written in a more condensed manner as follows, letting:

$$x_{r0} = b_r, \qquad x_{i0} = b_i. \qquad \begin{matrix} 65.7 \\ 65.8 \end{matrix}$$

Thus, with row r and row j chosen:

$$x'_{rl} = \frac{x_{rl}}{x_{rj}} \qquad l = 0, 1, 2, \ldots, n+m, \qquad 65.9$$

$$x'_{il} = x_{il} - \left(\frac{x_{rl}}{x_{rj}}\right) x_{ij} \qquad i \neq r \qquad l = 0, 1, 2, \ldots, n+m, \qquad 65.10$$

$$z'_l - c'_l = (z_l - c_l) - \left(\frac{x_{rl}}{x_{rj}}\right)(z_j - c_j) \qquad l = 0, 1, 2, \ldots, n+m, \qquad 65.11$$

$$z' = z - \frac{x_{rl}}{x_{rj}}(z_r - c_r). \qquad 65.12$$

Charnes, Cooper, and Henderson suggested a table for easy computation which is justified by relations (65.7) - (65.12), above. In this table, the rows are no longer numbered in their arbitrary, 1, 2, 3, 4 order, but in numbers corresponding to the basis vectors (see Table 65.1, where as an example we have used four equations in six variables.) The quantities x_{il} ($i = 7, 8, 9, 10$; $l = 1, 2, 3, 4, 5,$

6) are the coefficients a_{ij} corresponding to the four equations. Starting with this table, one forms a new one, which is obtained by means of relations (65.7) - (65.12).

It will be convenient to show the mechanics of this computation by means of an example. We choose the one given in the Operations Research course at the Case Institute of Technology (Cleveland, Ohio).*

Table 65.1

c_j			0	0	0	0	c_1	c_2	c_3	c_4	c_5	c_6
	Vectors	P_0	P_7	P_8	P_9	P_{10}	P_1	P_2	P_3	P_4	P_5	P_6
	P_7	x_{70}	1	0	0	0	x_{71}	x_{72}	x_{73}	x_{74}	x_{75}	x_{76}
	P_8	x_{80}	0	1	0	0	x_{81}	x_{82}	x_{83}	x_{84}	x_{85}	x_{86}
	P_9	x_{90}	0	0	1	0	x_{91}	x_{92}	x_{93}	x_{94}	x_{95}	x_{96}
	P_{10}	$x_{10.0}$	0	0	0	1	$x_{10.1}$	$x_{10.2}$	$x_{10.3}$	$x_{10.4}$	$x_{10.5}$	$x_{10.6}$
	z_j											
	$z_j - c_j$											

Let us take the following linear program:

$$\begin{aligned} 0.01x_1 + 0.01x_2 + 0.01x_3 + 0.03x_4 + 0.03x_5 + 0.03x_6 &\leqslant 850, \\ 0.02x_1 + 0.05x_4 &\leqslant 700, \\ 0.02x_2 + 0.05x_5 &\leqslant 100, \\ 0.03x_3 + 0.08x_6 &\leqslant 900. \end{aligned} \qquad 65.13$$

$$[\text{MAX}]\ z = 0.40x_1 + 0.28x_2 + 0.32x_3 + 0.72x_4 + 0.64x_5 + 0.60x_6. \qquad 65.14$$

After introducing the four slack variables x_7, x_8, x_9, x_{10}, these data will be introduced in Table 65.2. We shall employ the term vector, which is very useful and is altogether justified by the geometric consideration relating to the linear spaces in which the convex polyhedrons of the linear programs are embedded.

---

*"A Short Course of Operations Research," Case Institute of Technology. This example is also used in the Introduction to Operations Research, by Churchman, Ackoff, and Arnoff.

We begin with Table 65.2, and we use the Dantzig criteria to select the vectors P_4 and P_8; the vector P_8 will enter the basis, and the vector P_8 will leave. We must now calculate the new coefficients x_{ij} of Table 65.3, which will follow Table 65.2. We obtain:

$$x'_{70} = x_{70} - \frac{x_{80}}{x_{84}} x_{74} = 850 - \frac{700}{0.05} 0.03 = 430\,,$$

$$x'_{77} = x_{77} - \frac{x_{87}}{x_{84}} x_{74} = 1 - 0 = 1,$$

$$x'_{78} = x_{78} - \frac{x_{88}}{x_{84}} x_{74} = 0 - \frac{1}{0.05} 0.03 = -0.6\,,$$

$$x'_{79} = x_{79} - \frac{x_{89}}{x_{84}} x_{74} = 0 - 0 = 0,$$

etc...

$$x'_{40} = \frac{x_{80}}{x_{84}} = \frac{700}{0.05} = 14{,}000,$$

$$x'_{47} = \frac{x_{87}}{x_{84}} = \frac{0}{0.05} = 0, \qquad 65.15$$

$$x'_{48} = \frac{x_{88}}{x_{84}} = \frac{1}{0.05} = 20.$$

etc...

$$z'_7 - c'_7 = (z_7 - c_7) - \frac{x_{87}}{x_{84}}(z_4 - c_4) = 0 - \frac{0}{0.05} \times (-0.72) = 0$$

$$z'_8 - c'_8 = (z_8 - c_8) - \frac{x_{88}}{x_{84}}(z_4 - c_4) = 0 - \left(\frac{1}{0.05}\right)(-0.72) = 14.4 \ldots \text{etc}$$

Table 65.2

	c_j						0.40	0.28	0.32	0.72	0.64	0.60
	Vectors	P_0	P_7	P_8	P_9	P_{10}	P_1	P_2	P_3	P_4	P_5	P_6
	P_7	850	1				0.01	0.01	0.01	0.03	0.03	0.03
→	P_8	700		1			0.02			[5]		
	P_9	100			1			0.02			0.05	
	P_{10}	900				1			0.03			0.08
	z_j						0	0	0	0	0	0
	$z_j - c_j$						—0.40	—0.28	—0.32	—0.72	—0.64	—0.60
										↑		

Table 65.3

	c_j						0.40	0.28	0.32	0.72	0.64	0.60
		Vectors	P_0	P_7	P_8	P_9	P_{10}	P_1	P_2	P_3	P_4	P_5	P_6
		P_7	430	1	−0.6			−0.002	0.01	0.01		0.03	0.03
	0.72	P_4	14,000		20			0.4			1		
→		P_9	100			1			0.02			[0.05]	
		P_{10}	900				1			0.03			0.08
		z_j	10,080		14.4			0.288			0.72		
		$z_j - c_j$	10,080		14.4			−0.112	−0.28	−0.32		−0.64	−0.60
												↑	

Thus we obtain Table 65.3. Figure 65.1, shows schematically* how a new table is obtained from the old. Tables 65.4 to 8 and the rest give succesive results.

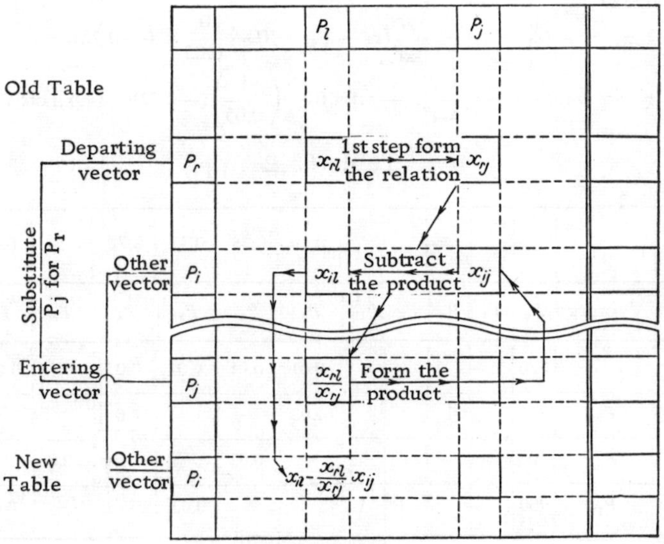

Fig. 65.1

---

*This scheme is given in the course of the Case Institute of Technology.

Table 65.4

c_j							0.40	0.28	0.32	0.72	0.64	0.60
	Vectors	P_0	P_7	P_8	P_9	P_{10}	P_1	P_2	P_3	P_4	P_5	P_6
	P_7	370	1	–0.6	–0.6		–0.002	–0.002	0.01			0.03
0.72	P_4	14,000		20			0.4			1		
0.64	P_5	2,000			20			0.4			1	
→	P_{10}	900				1			0.03			**0.08**
	$z_j - c_j$	11,360		14.4	12.8		–0.112	–0.024	–0.32			–0.60
												↑

Table 65.5

c_j							0.40	0.28	0.32	0.72	0.64	0.60
	Vectors	P_0	P_7	P_8	P_9	P_{10}	P_1	P_2	P_3	P_4	P_5	P_6
	P_7	32.5	1	–0.6	–0.6	–3/8	–0.002	–0.002	–1/800			
← 0.72	P_4	14,000		20			**0.4**			1		
0.64	P_5	2,000			20			0.4			1	
0.60	P_6	11,250				12.5			3/8			1
	$z_j - c_j$	18,110		14.4	12,8	7.5	–0.112	–0.024	–0.095			
							↑					

Table 65.6

c_j							0.40	0.28	0.32	0.72	0.64	0.60
	Vectors	P_0	P_7	P_8	P_9	P_{10}	P_1	P_2	P_3	P_4	P_5	P_6
	P_2	102.5	1	–0.5	–0.6	–3/8		–0.002	–1/800	0.005		
0.40	P_1	35,000		50			1			2.5		
0.64	P_5	2,000			20			0,4			1	
→ 0.60	P_6	11,250				100/8		**3/8**				1
	$z_j - c_j$	22,030		20	12.8	7.5		–0.024	–0.095	0.28		
									↑			

Table 65.7

c_j							0.40	0.28	0.32	0.72	0.64	0.60
	Vectors	P_0	P_7	P_8	P_9	P_{10}	P_1	P_2	P_3	P_4	P_5	P_6
	P_7	140	1	−1/2	−0.6	−1/3		−0.002		0.005		1/300
0.40	P_1	35,000		50			1			2.5		
→ 0.64	P_5	2,000			20			[0.4]			1	
0.32	P_3	30,000				100/3			1			8/3
	$z_j - c_j$	24,800		20	12.8	32/3		−0.024		0.28		0.253
								↑				

Table 65.8

c_j							0.40	0.28	0.32	0.72	0.64	0.60
	Vectors	P_0	P_7	P_8	P_9	P_{10}	P_1	P_2	P_3	P_4	P_5	P_6
	P_7	150	1	-0.5	-0.5	−1/3				1/200	1/200	1/300
0.40	P_1	35,000		50			1			5/2		
0.28	P_2	5,000			50			1			5/2	
0.32	P_3	30,000				100/3			1			8/3
	$z_j - c_j$	25,000		20	14	32/3				0.28	0.06	0.253

Table 65.8 is the final table, since all the z_j - c_j are positive. The optimum solution is:

$$x_1 = 35{,}000,\ x_2 = 5{,}000,\ x_3 = 30{,}000,\ x_4 = x_5 = x_6 = 0$$
$$x_7 = 150,\ x_8 = x_9 = x_{10} = 0\,. \qquad 65.16$$
$$\max z = 25{,}000\,.$$

The Charnes, Cooper, and Henderson table is equally readily used in the case of equations: we simply add artificial vectors, the coefficients of whose variables are quantities, M, that are very large — positive or negative, as required — in the economic function. Then one proceeds as in the submatrix method, of which the table is a different presentation.

Section 66

PROPERTIES OF DUALITY

1. General explanation.—2. First example.— 3. Second example.—4. Third example.

1. General explanation.

In Section 16 we illustrated the property of duality by means of a simple example. We shall now discuss this very important question in more detail, without, however, going into its proof, whose difficulty is far too great for the scope of this elementary book.*

The programs:

I

$$[\text{MAX}]\, g = \sum_{j=1}^{n} c_j x_j \qquad [\text{MAX}]\, g = \{c\}'\{x\} \qquad 66.1$$

$$\sum_{j=1}^{n} a_{ij} x_j \leqslant b_i \quad \text{or in matrix style:} \quad [a]\{x\} \leqslant \{b\} \qquad 66.2$$

$$i = 1, 2, \ldots, m$$

and

II

$$[\text{MIN}]\, f = \sum_{i=1}^{m} b_i y_i \qquad [\text{MIN}]\, f = \{b\}'\{y\} \qquad 66.3$$

$$\sum_{i=1}^{m} a_{ij} y_i \geqslant c_j \quad \text{or in matrix style:} \quad [a]'\{y\} \geqslant \{c\} \qquad 66.4$$

$$j = 1, 2, \ldots, n$$

are called duals of each other, and possess the following properties:

1. $\max g = \min f.$

2. Let us designate the marginal costs $z_j - c_j \geq 0$ of the programs at their optimum value as follows

$$g_k - c_k \text{ for program I} \qquad 66.5$$
$$-(f_k - b_k) \text{ for program II.} \qquad 66.6$$

---

*See bibliography: refs. C-3 and C-4, for example.

Now let us number, from 1 to n, the effective variables of I: $x_1, x_2, \ldots, x_n$; and from n + 1 to n + m the slack variables: $x_{n+1}, x_{n+2}, \ldots, x_{n+m}$. For program II, however, let us number the effective variables from n + 1 to n + m, or y_{n+1}, $y_{n+2}, \ldots, y_{n+m}$, and the slack variables from 1 to n, or $y_1, y_2, \ldots, y_n$. The only purpose of this numbering system is to facilitate the explanation.

The marginal costs of I will provide the solution for II, and the marginal costs of II will provide the solution for I.

Thus:

$$g_k - c_k = y_k \qquad y_k \geqslant 0 \qquad k = n+1,\, n+2, \ldots, n+m. \tag{66.7}$$

$$b_k - f_k = x_k \qquad x_k \geqslant 0 \qquad k = 1, 2, \ldots n. \tag{66.8}$$

2. First example.

Let us take the programs:

$$[\text{MAX}]\, g = 4x_1 + 3x_2 \qquad\qquad [\text{MAX}]\, g = 4x_1 + 3x_2 \tag{66.9}$$

$$\begin{array}{rcr} x_1 \leqslant 4{,}000 & \text{i.e., by adding the} & x_1 + x_3 = 4{,}000 \\ x_2 \leqslant 6{,}000 & \text{deviation variables} & x_2 + x_4 = 6{,}000 \\ x_1 + \frac{2}{3} x_2 \leqslant 6{,}000 & & x_1 + \frac{2}{3} x_2 + x_3 = 6{,}000 \end{array} \tag{66.10}$$

and

$$[\text{MIN}]\, f = 4{,}000\, y_3 + 6{,}000\, y_4 + 6{,}000\, y_2 \tag{66.11}$$

$$\begin{array}{rcr} y_3 + y_3 \geqslant 4 & \text{i.e., by adding the} & -y_1 + y_3 = 4 \\ y_4 + \frac{2}{3} y_5 \geqslant 3 & \text{deviation variables} & -y_2 + y_4 + \frac{2}{3} y_5 = 3, \end{array} \tag{66.12}$$

that we will write by means of matrices to make concrete the expressions:

$$[\text{MAX}]\, g = [4 \quad 3] \begin{Bmatrix} x_1 \\ x_2 \end{Bmatrix}, \tag{66.13}$$

$$\begin{bmatrix} 1 & 0 & 1 & 0 & 0 \\ 0 & 1 & 0 & 1 & 0 \\ 1 & \frac{2}{3} & 0 & 0 & 1 \end{bmatrix} \begin{Bmatrix} x_1 \\ x_2 \\ x_3 \\ x_4 \\ x_5 \end{Bmatrix} = \begin{Bmatrix} 4{,}000 \\ 6{,}000 \\ 6{,}000 \end{Bmatrix}. \tag{66.14}$$

and

$$[\text{MIN}]\, f = [4{,}000 \;\; 6{,}000 \;\; 6{,}000] \begin{Bmatrix} y_3 \\ y_4 \\ y_5 \end{Bmatrix}, \tag{66.15}$$

$$\begin{bmatrix} -1 & 0 & 1 & 0 & 1 \\ 0 & -1 & 0 & 1 & \frac{2}{3} \end{bmatrix} \begin{Bmatrix} y_1 \\ y_2 \\ y_3 \\ y_4 \\ y_5 \end{Bmatrix} = \begin{Bmatrix} 4 \\ 3 \end{Bmatrix}. \qquad 66.16$$

We have seen in section 58 that the optimum of the program (66.13, 14) was, according to (58.65, 6, and 7):

$$\begin{gathered} \max g = 26{,}000, \quad x_1 = 2{,}000, \quad x_2 = 6{,}000, \quad x_3 = 2{,}000 \\ g_4 - c_4 = \tfrac{1}{3}, \quad g_5 - c_5 = 4. \end{gathered} \qquad 66.17$$

From this it results that the optimum of this program is:

$$\begin{gathered} \min f = 26.000, \quad y_4 = \tfrac{1}{3}, \quad y_5 = 4 \\ b_1 - f_1 = 2{,}000, \quad b_2 - f_2 = 6{,}000, \quad b_3 - f_3 = 2\,000. \end{gathered} \qquad 66.18$$

3. Second example.

The dual of program (65.13, 14) is:

$$[\text{MIN}]\; f = 850\, y_7 + 700\, y_8 + 100\, y_9 + 900\, y_{10} \qquad 66.19$$

$$\begin{aligned} 0.01\, y_7 + 0.02\, y_8 &\geqslant 0.40 \\ 0.01\, y_7 + 0.02\, y_9 &\geqslant 0.28 \\ 0.01\, y_7 + 0.03\, y_{10} &\geqslant 0.32 \\ 0.03\, y_7 + 0.05\, y_8 &\geqslant 0.72 \\ 0.03\, y_7 + 0.05\, y_9 &\geqslant 0.64 \\ 0.03\, y_7 + 0.08\, y_{10} &\geqslant 0.60 \end{aligned} \qquad 66.20$$

and according to table 65.8, we can write:

$$\begin{gathered} \min f = 25{,}000, \quad y_7 = 0, \quad y_8 = 20, \quad y_9 = 14, \quad y_{10} = 32/3, \\ b_1 - f_1 = 35{,}000, \quad b_2 - f_2 = 5{,}000, \quad b_3 - f_3 = 30{,}000, \quad b_4 - f_4 = 0 \\ b_5 - f_5 = 0, \quad b_6 - f_6 = 0. \end{gathered} \qquad 66.21$$

4. Third example.

Let us take (64.1, 2) again:

$$[\text{MIN}]\; f = 15\, y_1 + 33\, y_2 \qquad 66.22$$

$$\begin{aligned} 3\, y_1 + 2\, y_2 &\geqslant 6 \\ 6\, y_1 + y_2 &\geqslant 6 \\ y_2 &\geqslant 1 \end{aligned} \quad \text{or, after the addition of the deviation variables} \quad \begin{bmatrix} 3 & 2 & -1 & 0 & 0 \\ 6 & 1 & 0 & -1 & 0 \\ 0 & 1 & 0 & 0 & -1 \end{bmatrix} \begin{Bmatrix} y_1 \\ y_2 \\ y_3 \\ y_4 \\ y_5 \end{Bmatrix} = \begin{Bmatrix} 6 \\ 6 \\ 1 \end{Bmatrix}. \qquad 66.23$$

The dual is:

$$[\text{MAX}]\ g = 6x_3 + 6x_4 + x_5 \qquad [\text{MAX}]\ g = 6x_3 + 6x_4 + x_5 \tag{66.24}$$

$$\begin{matrix} 3x_3 + 6x_4 \leqslant 15 \\ 2x_3 + x_4 + x_5 \leqslant 33 \end{matrix} \quad \text{ou} \quad \begin{bmatrix} 1 & 0 & 3 & 6 & 0 \\ 0 & 1 & 2 & 1 & 1 \end{bmatrix} \begin{Bmatrix} x_1 \\ x_2 \\ x_3 \\ x_4 \\ x_5 \end{Bmatrix} = \begin{Bmatrix} 15 \\ 33 \end{Bmatrix}. \tag{66.25}$$

The solution of (66.22, 23) is:

$$\begin{matrix} \min f = 53 & y_1 = 2, \quad y_2 = 1 \\ & b_3 - f_3 = 5, \quad b_4 - f_4 = 0, \quad b_5 - f_5 = 23. \end{matrix} \tag{66.26}$$

The solution of (66.24, 25) is:

$$\begin{matrix} \max g = 53 & x_3 = 5, \quad x_4 = 0, \quad x_5 = 23 \\ & g_1 - c_1 = 2, \quad g_2 - c_2 = 1. \end{matrix} \tag{66.27}$$

These properties enable one to transform a search for a minimum into a search for a maximum, or vice versa; and this can make computation much simpler. They make possible the choice between two programs of the one with fewer rows, which reduces the volume of calculations; they also make it possible to check the accuracy of computations by calculating the economic function of the dual. Furthermore, the property of duality of linear programs has made it possible to prove some important theoretical properties in the theory of linear programs and in that of games of strategy.

Section 67

CONVERSION OF EQUALITIES INTO INEQUALITIES.

To compute certain linear programs, or to demonstrate certain properties, one must convert equalities into inequalities. Let:

$$[\text{MIN}]\ f = \sum_{i=1}^{m} b_i\, y_i, \tag{67.1}$$

$$\sum_{i=1}^{m} a_{ij}\, y_i = c_j, \quad j = 1, 2, \ldots, n. \qquad m > n \tag{67.2}$$

The n equalities (67.2) can be replaced by the following 2n inequalities:

$$\sum_{i=1}^{m} a_{ij}\, y_i \geqslant c_j \qquad j = 1, 2, \ldots, n, \tag{67.3}$$

$$-\sum_{i=1}^{m} a_{ij}\, y_i \geqslant -c_j \qquad j = 1, 2, \ldots, n. \tag{67.4}$$

Let:

$$[\text{MIN}]\, f = b_1 y_1 + b_2 y_2 + \ldots + b_m y_m \tag{67.5}$$

$$\begin{bmatrix} a_{11} & a_{12} & \cdots & \cdots & a_{1m} \\ -a_{11} & -a_{12} & \cdots & \cdots & -a_{1m} \\ a_{21} & a_{22} & \cdots & \cdots & a_{2m} \\ -a_{21} & -a_{22} & \cdots & \cdots & -a_{2m} \\ \cdots & \cdots & \cdots & \cdots & \cdots \\ \cdots & \cdots & \cdots & \cdots & \cdots \\ a_{n1} & a_{n2} & \cdots & \cdots & a_{nm} \\ -a_{n1} & -a_{n2} & \cdots & \cdots & -a_{nm} \end{bmatrix} \begin{Bmatrix} y_1 \\ y_2 \\ \vdots \\ y_m \end{Bmatrix} \geqslant \begin{Bmatrix} c_1 \\ -c_1 \\ c_2 \\ -c_2 \\ \vdots \\ c_n \\ -c_n \end{Bmatrix}. \tag{67.6}$$

We shall have to deal with the dual of this problem:

$$[\text{MAX}]\, g = c_1 x_1^+ - c_1 x_1^- + c_2 x_2^+ - c_2 x_2^- + \ldots + c_n x_n^+ - c_n x_n^- .$$

$$\begin{bmatrix} a_{11} & -a_{11} & a_{21} & -a_{21} & \cdots & a_{n1} & -a_{n1} \\ a_{12} & -a_{12} & a_{22} & -a_{22} & \cdots & a_{n2} & -a_{n2} \\ \cdots & \cdots & \cdots & \cdots & \cdots & \cdots & \cdots \\ \cdots & \cdots & \cdots & \cdots & \cdots & \cdots & \cdots \\ a_{1m} & -a_{1m} & a_{2m} & -a_{2m} & \cdots & a_{nm} & -a_{nm} \end{bmatrix} \begin{Bmatrix} x_1^+ \\ x_1^- \\ x_2^+ \\ x_2^- \\ \vdots \\ x_n^+ \\ x_n^- \end{Bmatrix} \leqslant \begin{Bmatrix} b_1 \\ b_2 \\ \vdots \\ b_m \end{Bmatrix} \tag{67.7}$$

The meaning of the + or - signs written above and to the right of the variables is obvious. It will be noted that $x_j^+ \geq 0$, $x_j^- \geq 0$, but the same does not necessarily hold true for $x_j = x_j^+ - x_j^-$. The usefulness of this arrangement will be brought out in the next section.

Section 68

MATHEMATICAL ANALYSIS OF THE TRANSPORTATION PROBLEM

We return to equations (17.16) - (17.19):

$$[\text{MIN}]\, z = \sum_{i=1}^{m} \sum_{j=1}^{n} c_{ij}\, x_{ij} \qquad x_{ij} \geqslant 0, \tag{68.1}$$

$$\sum_{j=1}^{n} x_{ij} = a_i \qquad i = 1, 2, \ldots, m, \tag{68.2}$$

$$\sum_{i=1}^{m} x_{ij} = b_j \qquad j = 1, 2, \ldots, n, \tag{68.3}$$

$$\sum_{i=1}^{m} a_i = \sum_{i=1}^{n} b_j. \tag{68.4}$$

The m + n equations (68.2) and (68.3) can be replaced by the following 2(m + n) inequations:

$$\sum_{j=1}^{n} x_{ij} \geqslant a_i, \qquad -\sum_{j=1}^{n} x_{ij} \geqslant -a_i \tag{68.5}$$

$$\sum_{i=1}^{m} x_{ij} \geqslant b_j, \qquad -\sum_{i=1}^{m} x_{ij} \geqslant -b_j. \tag{68.6}$$

The 2 (m + n) inequations (68.5) and (68.6) can be grouped together in a single matrix:

$$\overbrace{\underbrace{}_{n}\quad\underbrace{}_{n}\quad\cdots\quad\underbrace{}_{n}}^{mn}$$

$$\left[\begin{array}{cccccccccccc|ccccc}
1 & 1 & \ldots & 1 & 1 & 0 & 0 & \ldots & \ldots & \ldots & \ldots & & \ldots & \ldots & \ldots & \ldots & 0 \\
-1 & -1 & \ldots & -1 & -1 & 0 & 0 & \ldots & \ldots & \ldots & \ldots & & \ldots & \ldots & \ldots & \ldots & 0 \\
0 & 0 & \ldots & 0 & 0 & 1 & 1 & \ldots & 1 & 1 & \ldots & & \ldots & \ldots & \ldots & \ldots & 0 \\
0 & 0 & \ldots & 0 & 0 & -1 & -1 & \ldots & -1 & -1 & \ldots & & \ldots & \ldots & \ldots & \ldots & 0 \\
\ldots & & & & & & & & & & & & & & & & \\
\ldots & & & & & & & & & & & & 2m & & & & \\
0 & \ldots & \ldots & \ldots & \ldots & \ldots & \ldots & \ldots & \ldots & \ldots & \ldots & & 1 & 1 & \ldots & 1 & 1 \\
0 & \ldots & \ldots & \ldots & \ldots & \ldots & \ldots & \ldots & \ldots & \ldots & \ldots & & -1 & -1 & \ldots & -1 & -1 \\
1 & 0 & \ldots & \ldots & 0 & 0 & 1 & 0 & \ldots & 0 & 1 & 0 & \ldots & \ldots & \ldots & \ldots & 0 \\
-1 & 0 & \ldots & \ldots & 0 & 0 & -1 & 0 & \ldots & 0 & -1 & 0 & \ldots & \ldots & \ldots & \ldots & 0 \\
0 & 1 & \ldots & \ldots & 0 & 0 & 0 & 1 & \ldots & 0 & 0 & 1 & \ldots & \ldots & \ldots & \ldots & 0 \\
0 & -1 & \ldots & \ldots & 0 & 0 & 0 & -1 & \ldots & 0 & 0 & -1 & \ldots & \ldots & \ldots & \ldots & 0 \\
\ldots & & & & & & & & & & & & & & & & \\
 & & & & & & & & & & & & 2n & & & & \\
0 & \ldots & \ldots & 0 & 1 & 0 & 0 & \ldots & \ldots & 1 & 0 & 0 & \ldots & \ldots & \ldots & \ldots & 1 \\
0 & \ldots & \ldots & 0 & -1 & 0 & 0 & \ldots & \ldots & -1 & 0 & 0 & \ldots & \ldots & \ldots & \ldots & -1
\end{array}\right]
\begin{Bmatrix} x_{11} \\ x_{12} \\ \vdots \\ x_{1n} \\ x_{21} \\ x_{22} \\ \vdots \\ x_{2n} \\ \vdots \\ x_{m1} \\ x_{m2} \\ \vdots \\ x_{mn} \end{Bmatrix}
\geqslant
\begin{Bmatrix} a_1 \\ -a_1 \\ a_2 \\ -a_2 \\ \vdots \\ a_m \\ -a_m \\ b_1 \\ -b_1 \\ b_2 \\ -b_2 \\ \vdots \\ b_n \\ -b_n \end{Bmatrix} \tag{68.7}$$

which we shall write as:

$$[A]\{X\} \geqslant \{B\}. \tag{68.8}$$

These constraints will be associated with the economic function:

$$[\text{MIN}]\, f = \{C\}'\{X\}, \qquad 68.9$$

where

$$\{C\}' = [c_{11}\, c_{12} \ldots c_{1n}\, c_{21}\, c_{22} \ldots c_{2n} \ldots c_{m1}\, c_{m2} \ldots c_{mn}]. \qquad 68.10$$

Now let us consider the dual problem:

$$[A]'\{Y\} \leqslant \{C\}, \qquad 68.11$$

$$[\text{MAX}]\, g = \{B\}'\{Y\}, \qquad 68.12$$

where

$$\{Y\}' = [\, u_1^+\, u_1^-\, u_2^+\, u_2^- \;\ldots\; u_m^+\, u_m^-\, v_1^+\, v_1^-\, v_2^+\, v_2^- \;\ldots\; v_n^+\, v_n^- \,] \qquad 68.13$$

the meaning of the + or - signs being obvious.

Equation (68.12) can also be written:

$$\begin{aligned}[\text{MAX}]\, g &= \sum_{i=1}^{m} (u_i^+ - u_i^-)\, a_i + \sum_{j=1}^{n} (v_j^+ - v_j^-)\, b_j \\ &= \sum_{i=1}^{m} u_i\, a_i + \sum_{j=1}^{n} v_j\, b_j\end{aligned} \qquad 68.14$$

where

$$u_i = u_i^+ - u_i^-, \qquad v_j = v_j^+ - v_j^- \qquad 68.15$$

$$i = 1, 2, \ldots, m \qquad j = 1, 2, \ldots, n. \qquad 68.16$$

Remember that $u_i^+ \geq 0$, $u_i^- \geq 0$, $v_j^+ \geq 0$, and $v_j^- \geq 0$, but that this does not any longer apply to u_i and v_j, because the differences do not necessarily yield positive quantities.

The inequations of (68.11), in turn, can be written:

$$\begin{aligned} &(u_1^+ - u_1^-) + (v_1^+ - v_1^-) \leqslant c_{11}, \\ &\qquad\vdots \\ &(u_i^+ - u_i^-) + (v_j^+ - v_j^-) \leqslant c_{ij}, \\ &\qquad\vdots \\ &(u_m^+ - u_m^-) + (v_n^+ \ldots v_n^-) \leqslant c_{mn}\,; \end{aligned} \qquad 68.17$$

or, again:

$$u_i + v_j \leqslant c_{ij} \qquad i = 1, 2, \ldots, m, \quad j = 1, 2, \ldots, n. \qquad 68.18$$

Since there are m + n - 1 variables associated with a basis, there are m + n - 1 equations such that:

$$u_i + v_j = c_{ij}, \qquad 68.19$$

to determine the m quantities u_i and the n quantities v_j.

Now we will use the stepping-stone method, described in Section 17. In (17.8), we calculate, for example, δ_{15} corresponding to an x_{ij} which is not associated with the basis.

$$\begin{aligned}\delta_{15} &= c_{15} - c_{13} + c_{23} - c_{24} + c_{34} - c_{35} \\ &= c_{15} - u_1 - v_3 + u_2 + v_3 - u_2 - v_4 + u_3 + v_4 - u_3 - v_5 \\ &= c_{15} - u_1 - v_5.\end{aligned} \qquad 68.20$$

It will be seen that this property is general, and that one can find the value of the variation of z corresponding to a unit increase in the zero variable x_{ij} (outside the basis), i.e., the unit marginal cost, by means of the formula:

$$\delta_{ij} = c_{ij} - u_i - v_j. \qquad 68.21$$

We can avoid working out the steps and the somewhat lengthy computations that are involved in this operation. For example, to calculate (17.8), it is necessary to first determine u_i and v_j, which can be done by taking the 7 equations relative to the c_{ij} in the squares corresponding to the basis.

Suppose we have to find the m + n = 8 variables:

$$u_1, u_2, u_3, v_1, v_2, v_3, v_4, v_5. \qquad 68.22$$

$$\begin{aligned}u_1 + v_1 &= 4 \\ u_1 + v_2 &= 1 \\ u_1 + v_3 &= 2 \\ u_2 + v_3 &= 3 \\ u_2 + v_4 &= 5 \\ u_3 + v_4 &= 4 \\ u_3 + v_5 &= 8\end{aligned} \qquad 68.23$$

Since we have m + n - 1 = 3 + 5 - 1 = 7 equations, and m + n = 8 variables, we shall set one of the variables arbitrarily equal to zero say $u_i = 0$; then we have:

$$u_1 = 0,\ u_2 = 1,\ u_3 = 0,\ v_1 = 4,\ v_2 = 1,\ v_3 = 2,\ v_4 = 4,\ v_5 = 8. \qquad 68.24$$

Thus, we find once again:

$$\begin{array}{lll} \text{For } x_{14} \text{ a variation} & \delta_{14} = c_{14} - u_1 - v_4 = 6 - 0 - 4 = 2 \\ x_{15} \text{ a variation} & \delta_{15} = c_{15} - u_1 - v_5 = 9 - 0 - 8 = 1 \\ x_{21} \text{ a variation} & \delta_{21} = c_{21} - u_2 - v_1 = 6 - 1 - 4 = 1 \\ x_{22} \text{ a variation} & \delta_{22} = c_{22} - u_2 - v_2 = 4 - 1 - 1 = 2 \\ x_{25} \text{ a variation} & \delta_{25} = c_{25} - u_2 - v_5 = 7 - 1 - 8 = -2 \\ x_{31} \text{ a variation} & \delta_{31} = c_{31} - u_3 - v_1 = 5 - 0 - 4 = 1 \\ x_{32} \text{ a variation} & \delta_{32} = c_{32} - u_3 - v_2 = 2 - 0 - 1 = 1 \\ x_{33} \text{ a variation} & \delta_{33} = c_{33} - u_3 - v_3 = 6 - 0 - 2 = 4 \end{array} \qquad 68.25$$

This can constitute a variation of the stepping-stone method. All we need do is compute u_i and v_j for each new basis by means of equations (68.19).

Section 69

MATHEMATICAL ANALYSIS OF THE "TRAVELING SALESMAN" PROBLEM

The "traveling salesman" can be formulated as follows: find a permutation $P(1, i_2, i_3, \ldots, i_n)$ of the integers from 1 to n that minimizes the quantity:

$$z = c_{1i_2} + c_{i_2i_3} + \ldots + c_{i_n1} \qquad 69.1$$

where

$$c_{\alpha\beta}, \qquad \alpha = 1, i_2, i_3, \ldots, i_n; \qquad \beta = i_2, i_3, \ldots, i_n, 1 \qquad 69.2$$

are real numbers (negative costs are conceivable).

If:

$c_{\alpha\beta} \neq c_{\beta\alpha}$ the matrix is nonsymmetrical; there are $(n-1)!$ possible permutations. 69.3

$c_{\alpha\beta} = c_{\beta\alpha}$ the matrix is symmetrical; there are $1/2\,(n-1)!$ possible permutations. 69.4

The problem can be stated in another way: find a cyclical permutation matrix [X] such that the trace* of the matrix [X] [D] is minimum, with [D] being the matrix of costs.

$$\mathrm{Tr}\,[X]\,[D] \text{ minimum.} \qquad 69.5$$

---

*Let us recall that the "trace" of a square matrix is the sum of the terms of its principal diagonal.

Table 69.1
Cyclical permutation matrix

	1			
			1	
				1
		1		
1				

Table 69.2
Non-cyclical permutation matrix

	1			
1				
				1
		1		
			1	

Tables 69.1 and 69.2 show the special characteristic of a cyclical permutation matrix: it cannot be divided by partition at the principal diagonal, whether or not one forms cyclical permutation submatrices. In Table 69.2, one can form cyclical permutation submatrices, which means that this matrix itself is not one of cyclical permutation.

We regret to state that there is, at present, no analytical method that makes it possible, in the general case, to find the minimum solution of a traveling salesman problem, other than by trying all the permutations, whose number quickly becomes astronomical: for example, with symmetrical unit costs:

10 cities: 181,940 cycles,
20 cities: a number of 19 digits.

Even the fastest electronic computer would never complete such a task.

In a report to the Operations Research Seminar at the University of Paris, M. Kreweras pointed out: "Even in cases where the costs are uniform, in which case we naturally minimize the length of a closed circuit (let us call this minimum L), it is easy to show that the minimum circuit is not that of the convex polygon possible, nor that of the maximum enclosed area; the method that consists of starting at any arbitrary point and moving on to the closest one, and so on, does not give us L. The method of dividing the region into two parts and searching for an L in each of them is just as disappointing; the method of improving the length by operating with limited regions having arbitrary closed contours also fails to yield results."

Some methods have given partial results (improved the economic function in some cases, but with no assurance that the minimum has been found); but a general method has yet to be devised.*

---

*See G. Dantzig, R. Fulkerson, and E. Johnson, "Solution of a Large-Scale Traveling Salesman Problem," J.O.R.S.A., No. 4, November, 1954; M. Flood, "The Traveling Salesman Problem," J.O.R.S.A., Vol. 4, No. 1, January, 1956.

Section 70

USE OF ELECTRONIC COMPUTERS

1. Description of operations on a GAMMA magnetic drum computer.—2. Data preparation.—3. Data recording.—4. Summary of the algorithm.—5. Distribution of numbers in the drum memory.—6. Sequence of operations.—7. Examples.

1. Description of operations on a GAMMA magnetic drum computer.*

To make the most of the possibilities offered by electronic computers, one is lead to utilize a variant of the simplex method usually called the inverse product form (see Section 61), and to operate with an adapted algorithm; we shall describe this method in such fashion that it can readily be associated with a flow diagram and a machine program.

Take the linear program**

$$[\text{MAX}]\ z = \sum_{i=1}^{n} c_i x_i \qquad x_i \geqslant 0, \tag{70.1}$$

$$\sum_{i=1}^{n} a_{ij}\ x_i = b_j \qquad j = 1, 2, \ldots, m, \qquad b_j \geqslant 0. \tag{70.2}$$

We now introduce the artificial variables x_j, $j = n + 1, n + 2, \ldots, n + m$, which gives us:

$$[\text{MAX}]\ z = \sum_{i=1}^{n} c_i x_i - M \sum_{j=1}^{m} x_{n+j} \qquad x_k \geqslant 0 \quad k = 1, 2, \ldots, n + m, \tag{70.3}$$

$$\sum_{i=1}^{n} a_{ij} x_i + x_{n+j} = b_j \qquad j = 1, 2, \ldots, m\,; \tag{70.4}$$

where M is a quantity we make arbitrarily large. We limit the number of artificial variables introduced strictly to that required to provide a unitary starting basis.

---

*We are particularly grateful to M. de Bournonville, Ingénieur des Mines, and to M. Havelka, both of the Compagnie des Machines Bull, for their invaluable assistance in preparing this section.

**This discussion will be stated with reference to systems of equations. However, the reader should find no difficulty in making the transition to the cases of systems containing inequations.

We shall use $\mathscr{A}$ to denote the elements of the matrix formed as follows:

$$[\mathscr{A}] = \begin{bmatrix} c_1 & c_2 & \dots & c_n & 0 & 0 & \dots & 0 \\ a_{11} & a_{12} & \dots & a_{1n} & 1 & 0 & \dots & 0 \\ a_{21} & a_{22} & \dots & a_{2n} & 0 & 1 & \dots & 0 \\ \dots & & & & & & & \\ \dots & & & & & & & \\ a_{m1} & a_{m2} & \dots & a_{mn} & 0 & 0 & \dots & 1 \end{bmatrix}. \qquad 70.5$$

This matrix comprises the coefficients of the economic function (the first row), then the m × n matrix of the coefficients a_{ij}, and the m × n unit matrix. The first row will not contain the coefficient (-M); we shall bring in these coefficients later on (70.12), in the calculation of $z_j - c_j$. Thus, in the initial basic solution that will be chosen (70.7), the economic function z will be equal to 0. Therefore we can write:

$$\begin{bmatrix} c_1 & c_2 & \dots & c_n & 0 & 0 & \dots & 0 \\ a_{11} & a_{12} & \dots & a_{1n} & 1 & 0 & \dots & 0 \\ a_{21} & a_{22} & \dots & a_{2n} & 0 & 1 & \dots & 0 \\ \dots & & & & & & & \\ \dots & & & & & & & \\ a_{m1} & a_{m2} & \dots & a_{mn} & 0 & 0 & \dots & 1 \end{bmatrix} \begin{Bmatrix} x_1 \\ x_2 \\ \vdots \\ x_n \\ x_{n+1} \\ x_{n+2} \\ \vdots \\ x_{n+m} \end{Bmatrix} = \begin{Bmatrix} z \\ b_1 \\ b_2 \\ \vdots \\ b_m \end{Bmatrix} \qquad 70.6$$

Or, in a condensed form using symbols whose correspondence is obvious, we can write:

$$[\mathscr{A}]\{x\} = \{\beta\}. \qquad 70.6a$$

In this system, an initial basic solution is given by:

$$x_{n+1} = b_1, \quad x_{n+2} = b_2, \quad \dots, x_{n+m} = b_m, \quad z = 0; \qquad 70.7$$

that is, by the second member of (70.6), where we have made z = 0.

We can also write equations (70.6a) in the following form:

$$\begin{Bmatrix} -z \\ x_{n+1} \\ x_{n+2} \\ \vdots \\ x_{n+m} \end{Bmatrix} = \begin{Bmatrix} 0 \\ b_1 \\ b_2 \\ \vdots \\ b_m \end{Bmatrix}. \qquad 70.7a$$

Note that by adding (-z) to the vector solution, we have enlarged the base by one row and one column. Let $[B_a]$ be the m × m unit basis:

$$[B_a] = \underbrace{\begin{bmatrix} 1 & 0 & \dots & 0 \\ 0 & 1 & \dots & 0 \\ \dots & \dots & \dots & \dots \\ 0 & 0 & \dots & 1 \end{bmatrix}}_{m} m\,; \qquad 70.8$$

we shall call $[\mathscr{B}_a]$ the (m + 1) × (m + 1) unit basis:

$$[\mathscr{B}_a] = \underbrace{\begin{bmatrix} 1 & 0 & \dots & 0 \\ 0 & 1 & \dots & 0 \\ \dots & \dots & \dots & \dots \\ 0 & 0 & \dots & 1 \end{bmatrix}}_{m+1} m+1\,. \qquad 70.9$$

Similarly, we shall call $[\mathscr{B}_b]$, $[\mathscr{B}_c]$, ... the (m + 1) × (m + 1) bases of the iterations which will follow. Each of these basis matrices can be decomposed into "the inverse product form," as we did in Section 61. We can then write:

$$\begin{aligned} &[\mathscr{B}_b]^{-1} = [\mathscr{E}_b]\,[\mathscr{B}_a]^{-1} = [\mathscr{E}_b]\,[1] = [\mathscr{E}_b] \\ &[\mathscr{B}_c]^{-1} = [\mathscr{E}_c]\,[\mathscr{B}_b]^{-1} = [\mathscr{E}_c]\,[\mathscr{E}_b] \\ &\dots\dots \\ &[\mathscr{B}_T]^{-1} = [\mathscr{E}_T]\,[\mathscr{E}_{T-1}] \dots [\mathscr{E}_c]\,[\mathscr{E}_b]\,, \\ &\dots\dots \end{aligned} \qquad 70.10$$

but each matrix $[\mathscr{E}]$ will be an (m + 1) × (m + 1) matrix formed by an (m + 1) × (m + 1) unit matrix in which one of the columns is replaced by a column of coefficients, as was shown in Section 61 (see (61.15)); in this case, however, each column thus introduced has (m + 1) elements and is incorporated in matrix (70.5).

As was seen in Section 61, to obtain a new basis we must post-multiply a given basis (the first in the order of these operations being (70.9) by $[\mathscr{E}]^{-1}$ corresponding to the chosen new basis.

In selecting the most negative $z_j - c_j$ (the Dantzig criteria), we shall make use of the formula:*

$$[z_j] = [c_j]\,[B_a]^{-1}\,[P_j]\,. \qquad 70.11$$

If we replace $[B_a]^{-1}$ by $[\mathscr{B}_a]^{-1}$, $[P_j]$ by $[\mathscr{A}]$, and $[c_i]$ by the first row of $[f_i]$ of the initial basis $[B_a]$, while making the first coefficient of $[f_i]$ negative, we obtain $[z_j - c_j]$ directly in place of $[z_j]$.

---

*Referring back to (58.7) and (58.8): $[x_{ij}] = [P_i]^{-1}\,[P_j]$, $[z_j] = [c_i]\,[x_{ij}]$.

This vector (row) $[f_i]$ will always have the form $[-1, 0, 0, \ldots, 0]$; in practice, we take advantage of the fact that we can assure that a particular variable will be eliminated from the basis first by artificially assigning the value -M to a particular coefficient in $[f_i]$. Of course, as soon as this variable is eliminated, the corresponding coefficient in $[f_i]$ will be returned to its normal value, which is 0. The example given a bit further on ((70.17) and (70.18)) will clarify this procedure.

The formula becomes:

$$[z_j - c_j] = [f_i]\,[\mathscr{B}_a]^{-1}\,[\mathscr{A}]. \qquad 70.12$$

If we begin with the unit basis containing the artificial variables* (which necessarily must all be eliminated), the vector $[f_i]$ will, in the first iteration, become:

$$[f_i] = [-1 \; -M \; -M \; \ldots \; -M] \qquad 70.13$$

and the $[z_j - c_j]$ vector will, in turn, become:

$$[z_j - c_j] = [-1 \; -M \; -M \; \ldots \; -M]\,[\mathscr{B}_a]^{-1}\,[\mathscr{A}]. \qquad 70.14$$

In the subsequent steps of the calculation, the (-M) quantities must disappear, one after the other, from $[f_i]$ as new vectors are introduced into the basis. Thus, we shall know $z_j - c_j$ for every iteration by means of (70.14), in which we will have progressively replaced the (-M) quantities by zeros with each successive iteration. Of course, the Dantzig criterion concerning $z_j - c_j$ will apply only to the indices j which are not in the basis. In practice, this selection is not difficult, as we shall show in an example. To obtain the x_i/x_{ij} values, we need only compute the x_i corresponding to the elements that are not all zero in the solution, by means of the successive products which we shall now describe.

If $\{\beta_a\}$ is the first vector constituting a solution corresponding to the second member of (70.6), we take as the vectors constituting the successive solutions:

$$\{\beta_a\} = \begin{Bmatrix} 0 \\ b_1 \\ b_2 \\ \\ b_m \end{Bmatrix}$$

*As noted in an earlier reference, (-M) will appear with the artificial variables, and zero with the slack variables.

$$\begin{aligned}\{\beta_b\} &= [\mathscr{E}_b]\{\beta_a\}\\ \{\beta_c\} &= [\mathscr{E}_c]\{\beta_b\}\\ &\cdots\cdots\cdots\cdots\\ \{\beta_T\} &= [\mathscr{E}_T]\{\beta_{T-1}\}\\ &\cdots\cdots\cdots\cdots\end{aligned} \qquad 70.15$$

Similarly, if we call $\{p_j\}$ the vector of index j that enters the basis, we shall have, successively:

$$\{\mathscr{P}_a\} = \{p_j\}$$

$$\{\mathscr{P}_b\} = [\mathscr{E}_b]\{p_j\}$$

entering the basis at the 2nd iteration.

$$\{\mathscr{P}_c\} = [\mathscr{E}_c][\mathscr{E}_b]\{p_j\} \qquad 70.16$$

entering the basis at the 3rd iteration.

....

$$\{\mathscr{P}_T\} = [\mathscr{E}_T][\mathscr{E}_{T-1}]\cdots[\mathscr{E}_c][\mathscr{E}_b]\{p_j\}$$

entering the basis at the 7th iteration.

....

The vectors $\{\mathscr{P}_a\}$, $\{\mathscr{P}_b\}$, $\{\mathscr{P}_c\}$, ... $\{\mathscr{P}_T\}$, ... will provide the x_{ij} for each j chosen at each iteration. The x_i/x_{ij} quotients will thus be obtained by taking the corresponding quotients, element by element (except for the first row, given the manner in which these vectors were constructed). In this fashion we find the vector to be removed at each step.

When seeking a minimum rather than a maximum, we would take the most negative of the $c_j - z_j$ quantities, which amounts to changing the signs of the $z_j - x_j$.

As we pointed out at the beginning of this section, this procedure is particularly helpful in electronic computation because it reduces sharply the number of numerical elements to be placed in the memory. In fact, all that need be placed in the memory is the zeros, and eventually the ones, of the unit matrix; matrix multiplications are reduced to only the essential operations.

Let us again consider the example of (58.14), (58.15), which we have already treated in Sections 58, 62, and 63; this will permit the reader to compare all the variations on the simplex method as applied to one example. Here, of course, the problem is not one of simplifying manual calculation, but of saving space in the memory and in reducing calculation time to a minimum.

Let:

$$[\text{MAX}]\ z = 3x_1 + 2x_2 + x_3 + x_4 + 5x_5, \qquad 70.17$$

$$\begin{aligned}3x_1 + x_3 - x_5 &= 3,\\ x_1 + x_2 - 3x_4 &= -12,\\ x_2 + x_3 + x_5 &= 4.\end{aligned} \qquad 70.18$$

Changing the signs of the second equation in (70.18) and introducing the artificial variables x_6, x_7, and x_8, we can write:*

$$\begin{bmatrix} 3 & 2 & 1 & 1 & 5 & 0 & 0 & 0 \\ 3 & 0 & 1 & 0 & -1 & 1 & 0 & 0 \\ -1 & -1 & 0 & 3 & 0 & 0 & 1 & 0 \\ 0 & 1 & 1 & 0 & 1 & 0 & 0 & 1 \end{bmatrix} \begin{Bmatrix} x_1 \\ x_2 \\ x_3 \\ x_4 \\ x_5 \\ x_6 \\ x_7 \\ x_8 \end{Bmatrix} = \begin{Bmatrix} z \\ 3 \\ 12 \\ 4 \end{Bmatrix}. \quad 70.19$$

First iteration

The initial vector solution is:

$$\begin{Bmatrix} z \\ x_6 \\ x_7 \\ x_8 \end{Bmatrix} = \begin{Bmatrix} 0 \\ 3 \\ 12 \\ 4 \end{Bmatrix}. \quad 70.20$$

The first basis is:

$$[\mathscr{B}_a] = \begin{bmatrix} 1 & 0 & 0 & 0 \\ 0 & 1 & 0 & 0 \\ 0 & 0 & 1 & 0 \\ 0 & 0 & 0 & 1 \end{bmatrix} \quad 70.21$$

and its inverse:

$$[\mathscr{B}_a]^{-1} = \begin{bmatrix} 1 & 0 & 0 & 0 \\ 0 & 1 & 0 & 0 \\ 0 & 0 & 1 & 0 \\ 0 & 0 & 0 & 1 \end{bmatrix}. \quad 70.22$$

The calculation of $z_j - c_j$ is given by:

$$[z_j - c_j] = [-1 \ -M \ -M \ -M] \begin{bmatrix} 1 & 0 & 0 & 0 \\ 0 & 1 & 0 & 0 \\ 0 & 0 & 1 & 0 \\ 0 & 0 & 0 & 1 \end{bmatrix} \begin{bmatrix} \overset{(1)}{3} & \overset{(2)}{2} & \overset{(3)}{1} & \overset{(4)}{1} & \overset{(5)}{5} & \overset{(6)}{0} & \overset{(7)}{0} & \overset{(8)}{0} \\ 3 & 0 & 1 & 0 & -1 & 1 & 0 & 0 \\ -1 & -1 & 0 & 3 & 0 & 0 & 1 & 0 \\ 0 & 1 & 1 & 0 & 1 & 0 & 0 & 1 \end{bmatrix} \quad 70.23$$

$$= [\underbrace{\overset{(1)}{-2M-3}, \ \overset{(2)}{-2}, \ \overset{(3)}{-2M-1}, \ \overset{(4)}{-3M-1}, \ \overset{(5)}{-5}}_{\text{outside the basis}}, \ \overset{(6)}{-M}, \ \overset{(7)}{-M}, \ \overset{(8)}{-M}].$$

---

*This arrangement has been chosen to agree with the description of the machine program that will follow.

The choice will turn on the $z_j - c_j$ that are not in the basis; thus we will take $j = 4$, which yields the most negative $z_j - c_j$ (remembering that $-M$ is arbitrarily very large). Therefore:

$$\{\beta_a\} = \begin{Bmatrix} 0 \\ 3 \\ 12 \\ 4 \end{Bmatrix}, \quad \{\mathscr{P}_a\} = [\mathscr{B}_a]^{-1}\begin{Bmatrix} 1 \\ 0 \\ 3 \\ 0 \end{Bmatrix} = [1]\begin{Bmatrix} 1 \\ 0 \\ 3 \\ 0 \end{Bmatrix} = \begin{Bmatrix} 1 \\ 0 \\ 3 \\ 0 \end{Bmatrix}. \qquad 70.24$$

Thus:

$$\frac{x_6}{x_{64}} = \frac{3}{0} = \infty, \quad \frac{x_7}{x_{74}} = \frac{12}{3} = 4, \quad \frac{x_8}{x_{84}} = \frac{4}{0} = \infty. \qquad 70.26$$

Therefore vector 7 will leave the basis.

For the rest of the computation, we must evaluate the matrix:

$$[\mathscr{E}_b]^{-1} = \begin{bmatrix} 1 & 0 & 1 & 0 \\ 0 & 1 & 0 & 0 \\ 0 & 0 & 3 & 0 \\ 0 & 0 & 0 & 1 \end{bmatrix}, \qquad 70.27 \qquad [\mathscr{E}_b] = \begin{bmatrix} 1 & 0 & -\frac{1}{3} & 0 \\ 0 & 1 & 0 & 0 \\ 0 & 0 & \frac{1}{3} & 0 \\ 0 & 0 & 0 & 1 \end{bmatrix}. \qquad 70.28$$

Second iteration

$$[z_j - c_j] = [-1 \;\; -M \quad 0 \;\; -M] \begin{bmatrix} 1 & 0 & -\frac{1}{3} & 0 \\ 0 & 1 & 0 & 0 \\ 0 & 0 & \frac{1}{3} & 0 \\ 0 & 0 & 0 & 1 \end{bmatrix} \begin{bmatrix} 3 & 2 & 1 & 1 & 5 & 0 & 0 & 0 \\ 3 & 0 & 1 & 0 & -1 & 1 & 0 & 0 \\ -1 & -1 & 0 & 3 & 0 & 0 & 1 & 0 \\ 0 & 1 & 1 & 0 & 1 & 0 & 0 & 1 \end{bmatrix} \qquad 70.29$$

70.29 (1) (2) (3) (4) (5) (6) (7) (8)

$$= \left[-3M - \tfrac{10}{3},\; -M - \tfrac{7}{3},\; -2M - 1,\; 0,\; -5,\; -M,\; \tfrac{1}{3},\; -M\right]$$

We bring into the basis vector 1, for which we have the most negative value of $z_j - c_j$ (we do not consider vectors 4, 6, and 8, which are in the basis).

$$\{\beta_b\} = [\mathscr{E}_b]\{\beta_a\} = \begin{bmatrix} 1 & 0 & -\frac{1}{3} & 0 \\ 0 & 1 & 0 & 0 \\ 0 & 0 & \frac{1}{3} & 0 \\ 0 & 0 & 0 & 1 \end{bmatrix} \begin{Bmatrix} 0 \\ 3 \\ 12 \\ 4 \end{Bmatrix} = \begin{Bmatrix} -4 \\ 3 \\ 4 \\ 4 \end{Bmatrix}, \qquad 70.30$$

$$\{\mathscr{P}_b\} = [\mathscr{B}_b]^{-1}\{\mathscr{P}_{(1)}\} = [\mathscr{E}_b]^{-1}\{\mathscr{P}_{(1)}\} = \begin{bmatrix} 1 & 0 & -\frac{1}{3} & 0 \\ 0 & 1 & 0 & 0 \\ 0 & 0 & \frac{1}{3} & 0 \\ 0 & 0 & 0 & 1 \end{bmatrix} \begin{Bmatrix} 3 \\ 3 \\ -1 \\ 0 \end{Bmatrix} = \begin{Bmatrix} \frac{10}{3} \\ 3 \\ -\frac{1}{3} \\ 0 \end{Bmatrix}. \qquad 70.31$$

$$\frac{x_6}{x_{61}} = \frac{3}{3} = 1, \quad \frac{x_4}{x_{41}} = \frac{4}{-\frac{1}{3}} = -12, \quad \frac{x_8}{x_{81}} = \frac{4}{0} = \infty. \qquad 70.32$$

Vector 6 will leave the basis.

To continue the computation, we evaluate the matrix $[\mathscr{E}_c]$:

$$[\mathscr{E}_c]^{-1} = \begin{bmatrix} 1 & \frac{10}{3} & 0 & 1 \\ 0 & 3 & 0 & 0 \\ 0 & -\frac{1}{3} & 1 & 0 \\ 0 & 0 & 0 & 1 \end{bmatrix}, \quad 70.33 \qquad [\mathscr{E}_c] = \begin{bmatrix} 1 & -\frac{10}{9} & 0 & 0 \\ 0 & \frac{1}{3} & 0 & 0 \\ 0 & \frac{1}{9} & 1 & 0 \\ 0 & 0 & 0 & 1 \end{bmatrix}. \quad 70.34$$

Third iteration

$$[z_j - c_j] = [-1 \quad 0 \quad 0 - M]\,[\mathscr{E}_c]\,[\mathscr{E}_b]\,[\mathscr{A}]$$

$$= [-1 \quad 0 \quad 0 \quad -M] \begin{bmatrix} 1 & -\frac{10}{9} & 0 & 0 \\ 0 & \frac{1}{3} & 0 & 0 \\ 0 & \frac{1}{9} & 1 & 0 \\ 0 & 0 & 0 & 1 \end{bmatrix} \begin{bmatrix} 1 & 0 & -\frac{1}{3} & 0 \\ 0 & 1 & 0 & 0 \\ 0 & 0 & \frac{1}{3} & 0 \\ 0 & 0 & 0 & 1 \end{bmatrix} \begin{bmatrix} 3 & 2 & 1 & 1 & 5 & 0 & 0 & 0 \\ 3 & 0 & 1 & 0 & -1 & 1 & 0 & 0 \\ -1 & -1 & 0 & 3 & 0 & 0 & 1 & 0 \\ 0 & 1 & 1 & 0 & 1 & 0 & 0 & 1 \end{bmatrix} \quad 70.35$$

$$\begin{matrix} & (1) & (2) & (3) & (4) & (5) & (6) & (7) & (8) \\ = [& 0, & -M - \frac{7}{3}, & -M + \frac{1}{9}, & 0, & -M - \frac{55}{9}, & \frac{10}{9}, & \frac{1}{3}, & -M]. \end{matrix}$$

We bring into the basis vector 5, for which we have the most negative value of $z_j - c_j$ (there are several $-M$ values, but $-M-55/9$ is more negative than any other value outside the basis).

$$\{\beta_c\} = [\mathscr{E}_c]\,\{\beta_b\} = \begin{bmatrix} 1 & -\frac{10}{9} & 0 & 0 \\ 0 & \frac{1}{3} & 0 & 0 \\ 0 & \frac{1}{9} & 1 & 0 \\ 0 & 0 & 0 & 1 \end{bmatrix} \begin{Bmatrix} -4 \\ 3 \\ 4 \\ 4 \end{Bmatrix} = \begin{Bmatrix} -\frac{22}{3} \\ 1 \\ \frac{13}{3} \\ 4 \end{Bmatrix}. \quad 70.36$$

$$\{\mathscr{P}_c\} = [\mathscr{B}_c]^{-1}\,\{\mathscr{P}_{(5)}\} = [\mathscr{E}_c]\,[\mathscr{E}_b] \begin{Bmatrix} 5 \\ -1 \\ 0 \\ 1 \end{Bmatrix} = \begin{Bmatrix} \frac{55}{9} \\ -\frac{1}{3} \\ -\frac{1}{9} \\ 1 \end{Bmatrix} \quad 70.37$$

$$\frac{x_4}{x_{45}} = \frac{1}{-\frac{1}{3}} = -3, \qquad \frac{x_1}{x_{15}} = \frac{}{-\frac{1}{3}} = -13, \qquad \frac{x_8}{x_{85}} = \frac{4}{1} = 4. \quad 70.38$$

Therefore we remove vector 8.

To continue the computation evaluate $[\mathscr{E}_d]$:

$$[\mathscr{E}_d]^{-1} = \begin{bmatrix} 1 & 0 & 0 & \frac{55}{9} \\ 0 & 1 & 0 & -\frac{1}{3} \\ 0 & 0 & 1 & -\frac{1}{9} \\ 0 & 0 & 0 & 1 \end{bmatrix}, \quad 70.39 \qquad [\mathscr{E}_d] = \begin{bmatrix} 1 & 0 & 0 & -\frac{55}{9} \\ 0 & 1 & 0 & \frac{1}{3} \\ 0 & 0 & 1 & \frac{1}{9} \\ 0 & 0 & 0 & 1 \end{bmatrix}. \quad 70.40$$

Fourth iteration

$$[z_j - c_j] = [-1 \quad 0 \quad 0 \quad 0]\,[\mathscr{E}_d]\,[\mathscr{E}_c]\,[\mathscr{E}_b]\,[\mathscr{A}]$$

$$\begin{matrix} & (1) & (2) & (3) & (4) & (5) & (6) & (7) & (8) \\ = [& 0, & \frac{34}{9}, & \frac{56}{9}, & 0, & 0, & \frac{10}{9}, & \frac{1}{3}, & \frac{55}{9}]; \end{matrix} \quad 70.41$$

since there are no more negative $z_j - c_j$, we have attained the maximum.

Calculating the optimum solution, we obtain:

$$\{\beta_d\}=[\mathscr{E}_d]\{\beta_c\} = \begin{bmatrix} 1 & 0 & 0 & -\frac{58}{9} \\ 0 & 1 & 0 & \frac{1}{3} \\ 0 & 0 & 1 & \frac{1}{9} \\ 0 & 0 & 0 & 1 \end{bmatrix} \begin{Bmatrix} -\frac{22}{3} \\ 1 \\ \frac{13}{3} \\ 4 \end{Bmatrix} = \begin{Bmatrix} -31-\frac{7}{9} \\ \frac{7}{3} \\ \frac{43}{9} \\ 4 \end{Bmatrix}. \qquad 70.42$$

Hence:

$$z = 31 + \tfrac{7}{9},\ x_1 = \tfrac{7}{3},\ x_4 = \tfrac{43}{9},\ x_5 = 4, \text{ the other } x_i \text{ being zero.} \qquad 70.43$$

The marginal costs are given by (70.41).

We shall now describe in detail the use of this algorithm with an electronic computer. For this presentation we have chosen the type GAMMA electronic computer with magnetic drum memory (Gamma-E.T.), made in France by the Compagnie des Machines Bull. This computer may be considered typical of the medium-size computers found in the research departments of large corporations as well as in mathematical laboratories, universities, and other organizations that engage in scientific calculation.

The GAMMA-E.T. computer comprises three major units:

1. The input-output unit, which receives the input data and prints out the results. This unit consists of a standard punched card tabulator and line printer. Data are introduced at the rate of 150 80-column cards per minute, and results are printed out at the rate of 150 lines per minute.

2. The arithmetic unit, which can perform the 4 operations to 12 decimal places. This unit has 71 rapid store memory banks which can store not only the input data and intermediate results but also the portion of the program in process.

3. The memory. This unit consists of a high-capacity magnetic drum that can record more than 16,000 numbers of 12 decimal places.

A program read into the drum from punched cards permits automatic control of the entire computer.

2. Data preparation.

Data are presented in the form of a table containing the coefficients of the equations and inequations, including the second members and the coefficients of the economic function. This table requires considerable preparation before it is put into the form of punched cards.

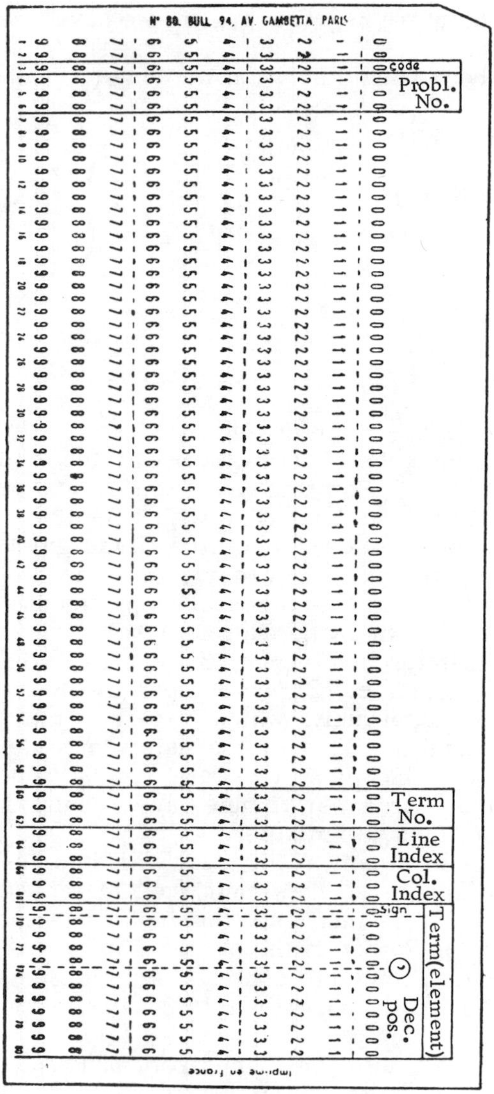

Fig. 70.1

a) The second members of the equations and inequations must be made positive; actually, this second member is to serve as a basic solution by the addition of artificial variables.

b) The inequations must be transformed into equations by the addition of slack variables.

c) Artificial variables must be added so as to obtain a basic solution formed by the second members.

The artificial variables must tend to be eliminated first in the computation. If all the artificial variables cannot be eliminated, the system is insoluble. The values of the artificial variables that are not eliminated enable one to know the deviations in the unsatisfied equations.

We may note that a basic solution can be formed by using the slack variables of the relations that contain a "less than or equal to" sign, because the coefficient of each of these variables is equal to 1; this makes it possible to reduce correspondingly the number of artificial variables to be introduced.

In the algorithm to be used, zero coefficients will be assigned to the slack variables and artificial variables.

d) Sequence numbers must be assigned to the equations and inequations (row indices) and to the real, slack, and artificial variables (column indices).

3. Data recording.

Data are recorded one datum to a card. One card is made for each non-zero coefficient of the first members; one card is made for each second member, whether or not it is zero.

The data-recording area of the card is divided into 4 zones (see Fig. 70.1) (columns 1-6 are used only for auxiliary purposes and columns 7-57 are not utilized):

Zone 1 (5 columns): sequence number ("term number") of the card (0 to 99,999).

Zone 2 (3 columns): row index of the matrix element (1 to 999).

Zone 3 (3 columns): column index of the matrix element (1 to 999).

Zone 4 (12 columns): coefficient: 1 column for its sign and 11 columns for its value; the decimal point is located after the 4th digit. If a coefficient is greater than 10,000, all the coefficients of the equation are divided by a suitable power of 10.

4. Summary of the algorithm.

The calculation is iterative*, and the chain of calculations for iteration T can be summed up as follows.

---

*Mathematical engineers and programmers habitually use the word iteration for what is generally a step in the algorithm. The word iteration has a narrower meaning for mathematicians. We trust the reader will pardon us for accepting this abuse of terminology, which is so widely adopted.

On the one hand, we have the coefficients of the $[\mathscr{A}]$ and $\{\beta\}$ matrices, and, on the other, the vector $\{\beta_{T-1}\}$ which is the solution to the preceding iteration. We also have the $[\mathscr{E}_a]$, $[\mathscr{E}_b]$, . . . , $[\mathscr{E}_{T-1}]$ matrices of the past iterations.

If the artificial variables have not been eliminated, we create an artificial vector, $[f_i]$, giving the position of these variables, so that the machine can assign priority to the non-artificial variables.

We compute:

$$[f_i]\,[\mathscr{B}_T]^{-1} = [\mathscr{E}_{T-1}]\,[\mathscr{E}_{T-2}]\ldots[\mathscr{E}_a] \qquad 70.44$$

and

$$[d_j] = [z_j - c_j] = [f_i]\,[\mathscr{B}_T]^{-1}\,[\mathscr{A}]. \qquad 70.45$$

We find the index corresponding to the most negative element of $[d_j]$. Let that index be s. Now we compute the vectors:

$$\{\mathscr{P}_s\} = [\mathscr{E}_{T-1}]\,[\mathscr{E}_{T-2}]\ldots[\mathscr{E}_a]\,\{p_s\} \qquad 70.46$$

and the x_i/x_{ij} quotients that are given by $\{\mathscr{P}_s\}$ and $[\mathscr{B}_{T-1}]$.

We select the i index for which x_i/x_{ij} has the smallest positive value; let this index be r.

We compute $[\mathscr{E}_T]$ as the inverse of the unit matrix in which the r column has been replaced by $\{\mathscr{P}_s\}$. The inversion formula can be reduced to $1/y_{rs}$ if r = s and $-y_{is}/y_{rs}$ if $i \neq s$ (see (61.15)), denoting as y_{ij} the elements of $[\mathscr{E}_T]$, the other elements being those of the unit mátrix.

Finally, we obtain the new solution vector from the product:

$$\{\beta_T\} = [\mathscr{E}_T]\,\{\beta_{T-1}\}, \qquad 70.47$$

and, if necessary, proceed to another iteration.

We would point out that at the end of the calculation, the marginal costs are given by the elements of the $[d_j]$ vector of the last iteration, and the value of the variables of the dual corresponding to the optimum are given by the $[f_i]\,[\mathscr{B}_T]^{-1}$ vector of this last iteration.

5. Distribution of numbers in the drum memory.

The drum memory is divided into 6 major zones whose dimensions may be varied to suit the problem to be solved (see Fig. 70.2):

Zone 1: this zone holds the elements of the $[\mathscr{A}]$ matrix.

Zone 2: this zone holds the elements of the second member (those in column $\{\beta\}$).

Zone 3: this zone holds the solution vector $\{\beta_T\}$, each successive new $\{\beta_T\}$ taking the place of the preceding vector $\{\beta_{T-1}\}$.

Zone 4: this is an operating zone which holds the following intermediate results:

$$[f_i],\ [f_i][\mathscr{B}_T]^{-1},\ \{\mathscr{P}_s\};$$

Zone 5: this zone holds the meaningful colums of the successive $[\mathscr{E}_T]$ matrices; all these columns must be retained in memory.

Zone 6: this zone holds the program, which contains slightly more than 2,000 instructions (at 3 instructions per location, this comprises slightly less than 700 locations).

MEMORY ZONES

ZONE 1	ZONE 2	ZONE 3	ZONE 4	ZONE 5	ZONE 6
$\mathscr{A}$	β	$\beta_a, \beta_b \dots \beta_T$	$f_i \to f_i \mathscr{B}_a^{-1} \to \mathscr{P}_T$	$\mathscr{E}_a, \mathscr{E}_b, \dots \mathscr{E}_T$	Program

Fig. 70.2

6. Sequence of operations.

The sequence of operations performed by the machine is summarized in Fig. 70.3. This sequence can be broken down into 13 phases, which we shall now describe in detail.

1. Reading and arrangement of the elements of $[\mathscr{A}]$ and $\{\beta\}$. The program orders the reading of cards containing the elements of $[\mathscr{A}]$, then of the $\{\beta\}$ cards. The data read are arranged in order in zones 1 and 2; during this operation, the coefficients are changed into "numeration with floating decimal point."* This numeration makes it possible to maintain a constant number of significant digits (in this case, 11) throughout the computation.

---

*We say that a number is expressed in "numeration with floating decimal point" when it is represented by a mantissa and an exponent. The mantissa may (for example) involve 11 meaningful digits. The exponent is equal to that power of 10 which, multiplied by the mantissa, gives the value of the number considered. For example: 1.25 can be written: 0.125×10^1 or 125 (mantissa) and 1 (exponent).

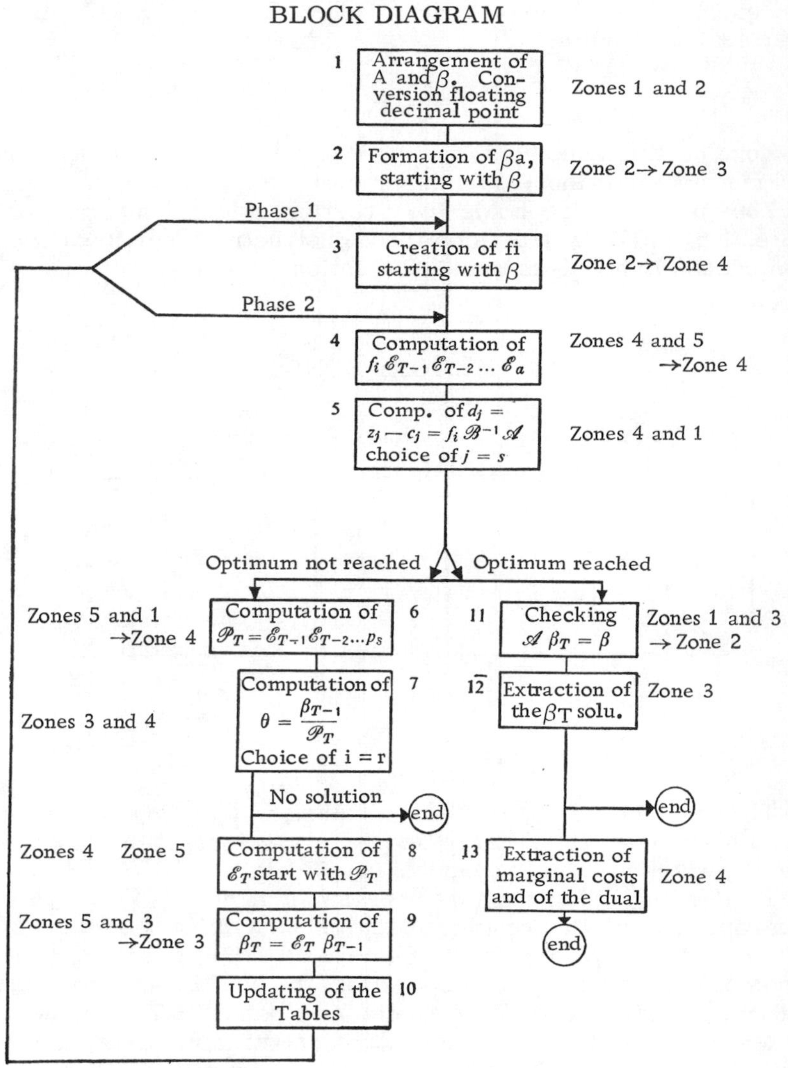

Fig. 70.3

2. Transfer of $\{\beta\}$ into $\{\beta_T\}$. The first solution is formed by the second member; the machine therefore transfers $\{\beta\}$ to $\{\beta_T\}$ (transfer of zone 2 into zone 3) to set up the first solution vector.

3. Creation of the artificial vector $[f_i]$. This phase is the first in the iterative part of the program. It is skipped over automatically by the machine when all the artificial variables have been

eliminated; from that point on, the $[f_i]$ vector will always have the form [-1 0 0 ... 0]. The iterations that eliminate the artificial variables constitute phase 1 of the computation. The succeeding iterations constitute phase 2. The artificial variables are distinguished at the outset by the special indices assigned to the elements of $\{\beta\}$. As the artificial variables are eliminated, these indices are erased in $\{\beta\}$. Creation of the $[f_i]$ vector consists of forming a vector in zone 4 made up of a 0 for every $\{\beta\}$ element lacking a special index, and a very large negative number for every $\{\beta\}$ element that carries the special index. By this means, in the later calculation of $[d_j]$, the artificial variables will have priority of selection.

4. Computation of $[f_i][\mathscr{B}_T]^{-1}$. The $[f_i]$ vector is multiplied successively by all the $[\mathscr{E}_T]$ square matrices in the order of decreasing indices. During each matrix multiplication, one single element is modified; the successive results are placed in zone 4. The $[\mathscr{E}_T]$ matrices are taken from zone 5.

5. Computation of $[d_j]$. This vector is obtained by post-multiplying $[f_i][\mathscr{B}_T]^{-1}$ by $[\mathscr{A}]$. The $[f_i][\mathscr{B}_T]^{-1}$ vector is taken from zone 4, while the $[\mathscr{A}]$ is taken from zone 1. The machine calculates the elements of the successive $[d_j]$ and retains only the elements which satisfy the following two conditions:

a) the element is negative and less than any of the corresponding elements previously calculated;

b) the element corresponds neither to an artificial variable nor to a variable relative to the basis.

If no element of $[d_{ij}]$ is negative, the optimum has been reached and the machine goes on to operation 11, which will be described below. Otherwise the machine proceeds to operation 6:

6. Computation of $\{\mathscr{P}_s\}$. The index corresponding to the highest negative value found in $[d_j]$ is taken as index s. $\{\mathscr{P}_s\}$ is calculated by pre-multiplying $\{p_s\}$ by the successive $[\mathscr{E}_T$ matrices. Note that these successive products are easy to calculate in view of the special nature of the $[\mathscr{E}_T]$ matrices. The machine selects the $[p_s]$ vector in zone 1 and places it in zone 4. The successive products are formed in zone 4 after taking the $\{p_s\}$ matrices from zone 5.

7. Computation of $\theta = x_i/x_{ij}$. The calculation is performed using $\{\beta_{T-1}\}$ read in zone 3 and $\{\mathscr{P}_s\}$ read in zone 4.

The problem is to select the row for which x_i/x_{ij} is the smallest positive number. This row index will be called r from now on. If there is no x_i/x_{ij} that is positive, the system has no solution, and the machine stops after printing a special signal. If there are positive values for x_i/x_{ij}, the machine prints the value of the chosen pivot-point as well as the r and s indices.

8. Computation of $\mathscr{E}_{T'}]$. The $[\mathscr{E}\ ]$ matrix is calculated from the $\{\mathscr{P}_s\}$ stored in zone 4; this is then placed in zone 5, following the

earlier matrices of this same type. It is sufficient to store these matrices in zone 5 in the form of a column, with an indication of its position in the unit matrix. As can be seen, zone 5 is the only variable capacity zone, and the machine will eventually announce that zone 5 is full and that it is approaching zone 6, which contains the program. When zone 5 is full, it is necessary to perform a re-inversion, which makes it possible, knowing the variables that must be found in the basis, to reduce the number of $[\mathscr{E}_T]$ matrices to the minimum.

9. Computation of $\{\beta_T\}$. This is done by pre-multiplication of $\{\beta_{T-1}\}$ stored in zone 3 by $[\mathscr{E}_T]$ stored in zone 5. The result of the calculation takes its position in zone 3, in place of $\{\beta_{T-1}\}$. Simultaneously, the value of the economic function is calculated and printed by the machine.

10. Updating of the tables. This phase of the computation permits the revision of the various tables contained in the drum: table of artificial variables, table of variables contained in the basis, etc. It also permits the determination as to whether all the artificial variables have been eliminated, and thus whether or not the machine should return to phase 3 or 4.

These 10 initial phases end the iterative part of the computation. The phases described below are performed only at the end, once the optimum has been reached.

11. Checking. The final $\{\beta_T\}$ solution found in zone 3 is carried over into the system (this solution is introduced without its first element, which, as we know, represents the economic function). In practice, this is achieved by a post-multiplication of $\{\beta_T\}$ by $[\mathscr{A}]$ which is taken from zone 1. The result is compared with $\{\beta\}$ as read in zone 2. If the system of equations or inequations checks out, the machine prints "correct" and goes on to the next phase. Otherwise, the machine prints the index of the equation, the value of the first member, and the value of the second member and then stops.

12. Extraction of solution. The machine prints the final $\{\beta_T\}$ stored in zone 3. The economic function is printed first and is followed by the values of the variables specified by the indices.

13. Extraction of marginal costs (finding the optimum solution of the dual problem). This phase is performed only when it is desired to know the marginal costs, and hence the optimum solution of the dual. These numbers are contained in the $[d_j]$ vector of the last iteration, and are readily obtained.

The 13 phases which we have just described are carried out automatically by the machine, without any intervention on the part of the operator. The result obtained gives the indices and the values of the successive pivot-points, as well as the value of the economic function in each iteration. At the end, the printed answer includes the optimum value of the economic function and the values of the non-zero variables of the given system of equations or inequations, as well as the non-zero slack variables.

7. Examples.

The reader will probably be interested in a statement of some concrete results achieved by the use of the GAMMA-E.T. We shall outline here the results of three different problems, one quite small, one medium, and the third of quite respectable dimensions. It is possible to provide approximate formulas relating the number of variables, the number of constraints, and the number of iterations; however, this last number has such great influence on the calculation time and is so dependent on the quantity of zeros occurring in the given matrix that such formulas do not provide any exact idea of the calculation time required. Here, then are three examples:

a) A production problem (our example from Section 13):
—number of variables: $n = 34$, of which 3 are slack variables.
—number of constraints: $m = 17$, of which 3 are inequations.
—number of non-zero elements in the matrix: $\nu = 93$.
—number of iterations: $k = 21$.
—calculation time including introduction of data and extraction of results: $T = 10$ minutes.

b) An investment problem:
$n = 88$, including 12 slack variables
$m = 43$, including 12 inequations
$\nu = 345$
$k = 95$
$T = 3$ hours and 30 minutes.

c) A problem in inventory and production:
$n = 159$, including 1 slack variable
$m = 63$, including 1 inequation;
$\nu = 618$
$k = 187$
$T = 10$ hours.

Chapter **8**

Theory of delay (Queuing) phenomena

Section 71

INTRODUCTION

Waiting lines (queues) are stochastic phenomena for which we shall establish, in the course of this chapter, the equations of state that are used in the calculation of a number of different average dimensions. These equations were first presented about thirty years ago by the Danish engineer Erlang, in connection with the problem of telephone communications. They are generalized by means of so-called birth and death equations which allow us to describe a great many stationary cases in transient or permanent systems.

This subject might properly deserve a major work by itself, if only to describe the cases which display complicated structures and on which recent work has been done. We shall regretfully limit ourselves to the equations of state of the most frequently encountered phenomena, but we shall deal with this aspect of the subject in considerable depth.

For lack of space, we shall merely touch on the study of conditions of priority, the concept of impatience, network systems, and cases with non-Poisson arrivals and service times, in the hope that growing curiosity will lead the reader to consult the many works dealing with these questions, whose study is extremely rewarding.

Section 72

THE CONCEPT OF THE STOCHASTIC PROCESS—MARKOV CHAINS—THE POISSON PROCESS

1. Markov chains.—2. Example.—3. The Poisson process.

A "stochastic process"* is a process in which changes of state, related by laws of probability, succeed one another at

---

*Stochastic comes from the Greek στόκοζ, which means "goal to be achieved." στόκασιζ means "assumption" or "conjecture."

random or determined intervals. This is also called a "random process."

We shall now review briefly what we mean by a "Markov chain," and discuss more fully the Poisson process.

1. Markov chains.

Let us consider a group of possible independent results, E_1, E_2, ... (finite or infinite in number); with each result we associate a probability, p_k. The probability of a sequence of results is defined by the multiplicative property:

$$\Pr\{E_{j_0}, E_{j_1}, \ldots, E_{j_n}\} = p_{j_0} \cdot p_{j_1} \cdots p_{j_n}. \quad 72.1$$

In the "Markov chain" theory, we consider the simplest generalization (72.1), which consists of making the result of each trial depend on the result of the immediately preceding trial, and only on that result.

As a consequence, we associate with each (E_j, E_k) pair the conditional probability p_{jk}. That is to say: if E_j occurs, the probability that E_k will also occur is p_{jk}. It is also necessary to introduce the probability a_j of the result E_j of the initial trial. Thus, for the probability of a sequence of 2, 3, 4... trials, we obtain:

$$\Pr\{(E_j, E_k)\} = a_j\, p_{jk}, \quad 72.2$$

$$\Pr\{(E_j, E_k, E_r)\} = a_j\, p_{jk}\, p_{kr}, \quad 72.3$$

$$\Pr\{(E_j, E_k, E_r, E_s)\} = a_j\, p_{jk}\, p_{kr}\, p_{rs}; \quad 72.4$$

and more generally:

$$\Pr\{(E_{j_0}, E_{j_1}, \ldots, E_{j_n})\} = a_{j_0}, p_{j_0 j_1}, p_{j_1 j_2}, \ldots, p_{j_{n-2} j_{n-1}} \cdot p_{j_{n-1} j_n}, \quad 72.5$$

where the initial trial is numbered zero and the second trial is numbered 1.

Another terminology is frequently used. Instead of saying: the kth trial has E_k as its result, we say: at time k, the system is in state E_k. The conditional probability p_{jk} is then called the transition probability $E_j \rightarrow E_k$ (from state E_j to state E_k).

A στοχαστικής was a person adept at the art of divination, or predicting a future event. Bernoulli, in 1713, published his "Ars conjectandis," and in that work he speaks of the "ars conjectandis sive stochastice," the art of conjecture, or of stochastics.

Transition probabilities are usually represented in the form of a square matrix:

$$[P] = \begin{bmatrix} p_{11} & p_{12} & p_{13} & \cdots \\ p_{21} & p_{22} & p_{23} & \cdots \\ p_{31} & p_{32} & p_{33} & \cdots \\ \vdots & \vdots & \vdots & \end{bmatrix}. \qquad 72.6$$

This is called a transition probability matrix, or a stochastic matrix; it may be finite or infinite; all its elements are obviously non-negative, and all the elements of any given row add up to 1.

Every Markov chain is wholly defined by its stochastic matrix [P] and the initial distribution, a_k.

To sum up: "A series of trials with possible results E_1, E_2, ... will be called a 'Markov chain' if the probabilities for the sequences are defined by (72.5) as a function of an initial probability distribution a_k for the E_k states at time 0, and of the conditional probabilities p_{jk} of E_k when E_j has occurred in the preceding trial."

2. Example.

Take three "wheels of fortune" each of them divided into three unequal sectors marked A, B, and C (see Fig. 72.1). Make a random choice of one of the wheels, and spin it. If A comes up, you spin wheel A again; if B comes up, your second play is on B; if C comes up, your second play is on wheel C; and so on for the following plays. The sectors form given angles (see Fig. 72.1); with these angles in some arbitrary unit, we have:*

$$\begin{aligned} a_1 &= \tfrac{1}{3}(\alpha_1 + \alpha_2 + \alpha_3) & \qquad & \alpha_1 + \beta_1 + \gamma_1 = 1 \qquad 72.7 \\ a_2 &= \tfrac{1}{3}(\beta_1 + \beta_2 + \beta_3) & \text{with} \qquad & \alpha_2 + \beta_2 + \gamma_2 = 1 \\ a_3 &= \tfrac{1}{3}(\gamma_1 + \gamma_2 + \gamma_3) & \qquad & \alpha_3 + \beta_3 + \gamma_3 = 1. \qquad 72.8 \end{aligned}$$

The matrix of transition probabilities is:

$$[P] = \begin{bmatrix} p_{11} & p_{12} & p_{13} \\ p_{21} & p_{22} & p_{23} \\ p_{31} & p_{32} & p_{33} \end{bmatrix} = \begin{bmatrix} \alpha_1 & \beta_1 & \gamma_1 \\ \alpha_2 & \beta_2 & \gamma_2 \\ \alpha_3 & \beta_3 & \gamma_3 \end{bmatrix}. \qquad 72.9$$

---

*The first trial consists of choosing one of the wheels by lot and spinning it; the result is designated by the number 1, 2, or 3 corresponding to the letter A, B, or C of the sector in which the wheel stops. In the succeeding trials, there is no more drawing of lots, since the wheel to be used is designated by the result of the preceding trial.

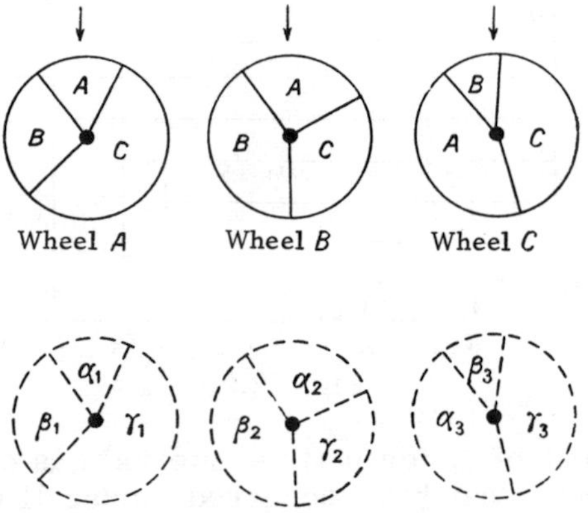

Fig. 72.1.

The probability of obtaining the sequence ABCAC is:

$$p = a_1 . p_{12} . p_{23} . p_{31} . p_{13} = \tfrac{1}{3} (\alpha_1 + \alpha_2 + \alpha_3)\, \beta_1\, \gamma_2\, \alpha_3\, \gamma_1. \qquad 72.10$$

The probability of obtaining B at the second trial is:

$$\begin{aligned} p &= \Pr(A, B) + \Pr(B, B) + \Pr(C, B) \\ &= a_1 p_{12} + a_2 p_{22} + a_3 p_{32} \qquad 72.11 \\ &= \tfrac{1}{3} [(\alpha_1 + \alpha_2 + \alpha_3)\beta_1 + (\beta_1 + \beta_2 + \beta_3)\beta_2 + (\gamma_1 + \gamma_2 + \gamma_3)\beta_3]. \end{aligned}$$

3. The Poisson process.

Consider a series of events E resulting from the repetition of the same experiment and occurring consecutively. The number, n, of events that occur in the time interval t is a random variable which we shall call N; the probability that $N = n$ we shall call $p_n(t)$. We shall adopt the following hypotheses:

1. $p_n(t)$ depends only upon the time interval, and does not depend on the initial instant (homogeneity in time, also called stationarity in time);
2. The probability that event E will occur more than once in the time interval dt is infinitesimally small in relation to dt;
3. The probability that E will occur once in the infinitesimal time interval dt is proportional to dt, and is written λdt.

The random variable N is such that:

1. N remains constant when E does not occur;
2. N increases by 1 when E occurs;
3. N is initially zero.

This random variable, N, is therefore a function of t which can assume the values 0, 1, 2, 3, . . . , n, . . . ; at random instants t_1, t_2, t_3, . . . , t_n, . . . it jumps abruptly from 0 to 1, from 1 to 2, . . . (Fig. 72.2).

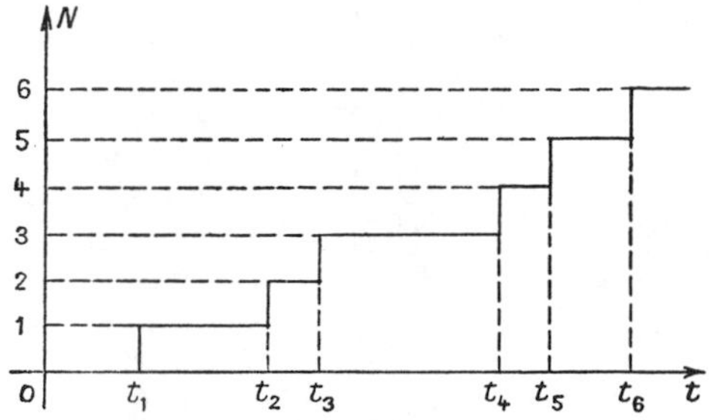

Fig. 72.2.

The increment of N for a time interval t is equal to the number, n, of events that have occurred during that interval. If we know the value, $N(t_o)$, of N(t) at the instant t_o, its value, $N(t_o + \tau) = N(t_o) + n$ at the instant $t_o + \tau$ is random. The increment n has the following properties:

—its probability is $p_n(\tau)$;

—it is independent of the values of N(t) prior to t_o.

Therefore, if the value of $N(t_o)$ is known, the future of N(t) depends solely on the law of probability governing the increment n of N(t) after $N(t_o)$. At no time is it possible to predict with certainty what N(t) will be later on: chance enters into the result at every instant.

The random function N(t) therefore defines a Poisson process, and constitutes an example of a Markov chain. It is wholly defined by the probability $p_n(t)$, and we shall now show that $p_n(t)$ obeys "Poisson's law."

$$p_n(t) = \frac{(\lambda t)^n e^{-\lambda t}}{n!} \qquad n = 0, 1, 2, 3, \ldots . \qquad 72.12$$

From what has been said about $p_n(t)$, the principal part of $p_1(\Delta t)$ is $\lambda \Delta t$

$$p_1(\Delta t) = \lambda \Delta t + O_1(\Delta t) \, (^*) \quad . \qquad 72.13$$

Furthermore, the probability that E will occur 0 times or 1 time in the interval Δt is equal to:

$$p_0(\Delta t) + p_1(\Delta t) \quad , \qquad 72.14$$

since the two eventualities are mutually exclusive.

---

*The $O_i(\Delta t)$, i = 1, 2, 3, 4, 5, which will be used as symbols are infinitesimally small in relation to Δt.

But:

$$p_0(\Delta t) + p_1(\Delta t) + p_2(\Delta t) + p_3(\Delta t) + \dots = 1, \qquad 72.15$$

or again:

$$1 - p_0(\Delta t) - p_1(\Delta t) = p_2(\Delta t) + p_3(\Delta t) + \dots . \qquad 72.16$$

This represents the probability that E will occur more than once in the interval Δt; it is infinitesimally small, hypothetically, in relation to Δt. Since the sum $p_2(\Delta t) + p_3(\Delta t) + \dots$ is infinitesimally small in relation to Δt, we can say with all the more assurance that the same holds true for all the positive numbers, $p_2(\Delta t)$, $p_3(\Delta t)$, etc.

Now let us examine the nature of the distribution $p_n(t)$, $n = 0, 1, 2, 3 \dots$ To have E occur precisely n times during the interval $t + \Delta t$, there are the following mutually exclusive possibilities:

E occurs n times in the interval t, 0 times in the interval Δt;
E occurs n - 1 times in the interval t, once in the interval Δt;
E occurs n - 2 times in the interval t, twice in the interval Δt;

....

As a result, we have:

$$p_n(t + \Delta t) = p_n(t).p_0(\Delta t) + p_{n-1}(t).p_1(\Delta t) + O_3(\Delta t). \qquad 72.17$$

But:

$$p_1(\Delta t) = \lambda \Delta t + O_1(\Delta t) \text{ and following (72.16)}: \qquad 72.18$$

$$\begin{aligned} p_0(\Delta t) &= 1 - p_1(\Delta t) - O_2(\Delta t) \\ &= 1 - \lambda\,\Delta t - O_2(\Delta t). \end{aligned} \qquad 72.19$$

Therefore we have:

$$p_n(t + \Delta t) = p_n(t).[1 - \lambda \Delta t] + p_{n-1}(t).\lambda \Delta t + O_4(\Delta t); \qquad 72.20$$

or:

$$p_n(t + \Delta t) - p_n(t) = [p_{n-1}(t) - p_n(t)]\lambda \Delta t + O_4(\Delta t). \qquad 72.21$$

I.e., finally:

$$\frac{1}{\lambda} p_n'(t) = p_{n-1}(t) - p_n(t) \qquad n = 1, 2, 3, \dots . \qquad 72.22$$

But this equation does not hold for n = 0, which requires some special investigation. We have:

$$\begin{aligned} p_0(t + \Delta t) &= p_0(t) \,.\, p_0(\Delta t) \\ &= p_0(t)\,[1 - \lambda\,\Delta t - O_5(\Delta t)] \end{aligned} \qquad 72.23$$

Thus:

$$p_0(t + \Delta t) - p_0(t) = -p_0(t)\,\lambda\,\Delta t - O_5(\Delta t); \qquad 72.24$$

which permits us to write:

$$p'_0(t) = -\lambda p_0(t). \qquad 72.25$$

At the beginning of the interval t, we have:

$$p_0(0) = 1 \qquad 72.26$$

and

$$p_n(0) = 0 \qquad n \neq 0. \qquad 72.27$$

Condition (72.26) carried over into the general solution of equation (72.25) gives:

$$p_0(t) = e^{-\lambda t}. \qquad 72.28$$

To find the solution of differential equation (72.22) for all the values of n = 1, 2, 3, ..., taking into account initial conditions (72.27), it is convenient to use the Carson-Laplace transformation:*

$$g(s) = s\int_0^\infty e^{-st}\,h(t)\,dt, \text{ where } h(t) = 0 \quad \text{for} \quad t < 0. \qquad 72.29$$
$$= \mathscr{L}\,h(t).$$

Let us set:

$$P_n(s) = \mathscr{L}\,p_n(t) \qquad n = 0, 1, 2, 3, \ldots . \qquad 72.30$$

With conditions (72.26), equations (72.22) and (72.25) become:

$$P_n = \frac{\lambda}{\lambda + s} P_{n-1}, \qquad 72.31$$

$$P_0 = \frac{s}{\lambda + s}. \qquad 72.32$$

Thus by recurrence:

$$P_0 = \frac{s}{\lambda+s}, \quad P_1 = \frac{\lambda s}{(\lambda+s)^2}, \quad P_2 = \frac{\lambda^2 s}{(\lambda+s)^3}, \ldots, \quad P_n = \frac{\lambda^n s}{(\lambda+s)^{n+1}}, \ldots \qquad 72.33$$

---

*The Carson-Laplace (or Laplace) transformation is particularly useful for analyzing phenomena in which unilateral distributions appear.

We obtain, finally:

$$p_n(t) = \mathscr{L}^{-1} P_n(s) = \lambda^n \mathscr{L}^{-1} \frac{s}{(\lambda+s)^{n+1}} = \frac{(\lambda t)^n e^{-\lambda t}}{n!} \qquad 72.34$$

$$n = 0, 1, 2, 3, \ldots .$$

The variable N is therefore distributed according to Poisson's law.

$$f_n(a) = \frac{a^n e^{-a}}{n!}, \qquad n = 0, 1, 2, 3, \ldots . \qquad 72.35$$

Remember that the Poisson distribution given in (72.35) has the following properties:

$$\text{mean:} \qquad \bar{n} = a , \qquad 72.36$$

$$\text{variance:} \qquad \sigma_N^2 = a . \qquad 72.37$$

Thus, the mean number of events E during the interval t is λt, and the quantity λ may be called the average or mean rate of occurrence of E.

Section 73

EXPONENTIAL DISTRIBUTION OF INTERVALS BETWEEN TWO EVENTS

Let us consider a Poisson process, and try to find the law of probability governing the intervals that separate two successive events. We wish to find the probability density of the random variable Θ representing these intervals; let $f(\theta)$ be this function.

We begin by finding the probability $f(\theta)d(\theta)$ that if an event E has just occurred, no event will occur in the interval θ that immediately follows it, and that an event will occur in the interval $\Delta\theta$ that immediately follows θ.

The probability that no event will occur during the time θ is:

$$p_0(\theta) = \frac{(\lambda\theta)_0 e^{-\lambda\theta}}{0!} = e^{-\lambda\theta} \qquad 73.1$$

The probability that no event will occur during the interval $\Delta\theta$ is:

$$p_0(\Delta\theta) = e^{-\lambda\Delta\theta}. \qquad 73.2$$

The probability that at least one event will occur in the interval $\Delta\theta$ is:

$$1 - p_0(\Delta\theta) = 1 - e^{-\lambda\Delta\theta}. \qquad 73.3$$

When $\Delta\theta \to 0$, we have:

$$\lim_{\Delta\theta \to 0}\left(\frac{1-e^{-\lambda\Delta\theta}}{\Delta\theta}\right) = \lambda. \tag{73.4}$$

Therefore, the desired probability $f(\theta)d(\theta)$ will be:

$$f(\theta)\,d\theta = e^{-\lambda\theta} \times \left(\lim_{\Delta\theta \to 0} \frac{1-e^{-\lambda\Delta\theta}}{\Delta\theta}\right) \times d\theta = \lambda e^{-\lambda\Delta\theta}\,d\theta. \tag{73.5}$$

The probability density of Θ is:

$$f(\theta) = \lambda e^{-\lambda\theta}, \quad \text{with} \quad \theta > 0. \tag{73.6}$$

Now let us calculate the corresponding complementary distribution function:

$$P(\theta) = \Pr(\Theta > \theta) = \int_\theta^\infty \lambda e^{-\lambda t}\,dt = e^{-\lambda\theta}, \quad \text{with} \quad \theta > 0. \tag{73.7}$$

Thus, the probability that an interval between two consecutive events will be greater than a given duration θ is equal to the probability that no event will occur in an interval θ.

This is called an exponential distribution. It must be associated with the Poisson distribution. The latter gives the probability of a number, n, of events in a given time interval τ, while the exponential distribution gives the probability that two consecutive events are separated by an interval greater than θ.

It is easy to calculate the mean and standard deviation of the exponential distribution:

$$\bar{\theta} = E(\Theta) = \int_{-\infty}^{+\infty} \theta f(\theta)\,d\theta = \int_0^\infty \theta\lambda e^{-\lambda\theta} d\theta = \frac{1}{\lambda}\int_0^\infty (\lambda\theta) e^{-\lambda\theta}\,d(\lambda\theta)$$

$= \lambda^{-1}\Gamma(2)$, (where $\Gamma(x)$ is the gamma function, i.e., Euler's second integral). 73.8

$= 1/\lambda.$

$$\sigma_\Theta^2 = \int_{-\infty}^{+\infty} \theta^2 f(\theta)\,d\theta - [E(\Theta)]^2 = \left[\int_0^\infty \theta^2\lambda e^{-\lambda\theta}\,d\theta\right] - \frac{1}{\lambda^2}$$

$$= \left[\frac{1}{\lambda^2}\int_0^\infty (\lambda\theta)^2 e^{-\lambda\theta}\,d(\lambda\theta)\right] - \frac{1}{\lambda^2} = \frac{1}{\lambda^2}\Gamma(3) - \frac{1}{\lambda^2} \tag{73.9}$$

$$= \frac{2}{\lambda^2} - \frac{1}{\lambda^2} = \frac{1}{\lambda^2}.$$

Section 74

WAITING LINE AT ONE STATION

1. General explanation.—2. Study of the permanent system.—3. Kendall's formulas.—4. Calculating the number of units in a waiting line.—5. Waiting time.—6. Transient system.

1. General explanation.

We shall now try to find the distribution of the random variable N representing the number of units in the system, which here means both in the waiting line and being serviced. We shall take the usual case in which arrivals follow Poisson's law and the service-time intervals follow the exponential law. We have, therefore, the following hypotheses:

1. The probability that a unit will enter the system during the interval Δt is infinitesimally small and of the order of Δt; it is equal to $\lambda \Delta t$, where λ is the mean number of arrivals per unit of time.

2. The probability that a unit will complete its service-time within the interval Δt is infinitesimally small, and of the order of Δt; it is equal to $\mu \Delta t$, where $1/\mu$ is the mean service-time interval.

3. The probability of more than one arrival or more than one completion of service in the interval Δt is infinitesimally small in relation to Δt, and we shall treat it as negligible.

From this point forward, we shall adopt the hypothesis that $\lambda < \mu$, or $\lambda/\mu < 1$. Under the contrary hypothesis, a stable system would be impossible. This will be demonstrated in the following calculations, but we can already conceive it intuitively: the waiting line would grow indefinitely longer with t.

It is easy to establish the linear differential equations that govern the delay phenomenon under the above hypotheses. From these equations, we shall derive $p_n(t)$ and $\bar{n}$.

The probability $p_n(t + \Delta t)$ that there will be n units ($n > 0$) in the system at time $t + \Delta t$ can be expressed as the sum of the following four independent compound probabilities:

(1) The product of the probabilities that:
- a) there are n units in the system at time t: $p_n(t)$;
- b) there is no arrival during the interval Δt: $(1 - \lambda \Delta t)$;
- c) no service is completed during the interval Δt: $(1 - \mu \Delta t)$;

(2) The product of the probabilities that:
- a) there are n+1 units in the system at time t: $p_{n+1}(t)$:
- b) there is no arrival during the interval Δt: $(1 - \lambda \Delta t)$;
- c) one service is completed during the interval Δt: $\mu \Delta t$;

(3) The product of probabilities that:
   a) there are n - 1 units in the system at time t: $p_{n-1}(t)$;
   b) there is one arrival during the interval Δt: $\lambda \Delta t$;
   c) no service is completed during the interval Δt: $(1 - \mu \Delta t)$;
(4) The product of the probabilities that:
   a) there are n units in the system at time t: $p_n(t)$;
   b) there is one arrival during the interval Δt: $\lambda \Delta t$;
   c) one service is completed during the interval Δt: $\mu \Delta t$.

The four above probabilities can be written as follows:

$$
\begin{aligned}
&(1)\ p_n(t)[1-\lambda\Delta t][1-\mu\Delta t] = p_n(t)[1-\lambda\Delta t-\mu\Delta t]+O_1(\Delta t),\\
&(2)\ p_{n+1}(t)[1-\lambda\Delta t][\mu\Delta t] = p_{n+1}(t)\,\mu\Delta t+O_2(\Delta t),\\
&(3)\ p_{n-1}(t)[\lambda\Delta t][1-\mu\Delta t] = p_{n-1}(t)\lambda\Delta t+O_3(\Delta t),\\
&(4)\ p_n(t)[\lambda\Delta t][\mu\Delta t] = O_4(\Delta t),
\end{aligned}
\qquad 74.1
$$

with $O_i(\Delta t)$, $i = 1, 2, 3, 4$, being infinitesimally small in Δt of order greater than 1 when $\Delta t \to 0$.

Adding these probabilities to form the probability $p_n(t + \Delta t)$, we obtain:

$$
\begin{aligned}
p_n(t+\Delta t) = p_n(t)\,[1-\lambda\Delta t-\mu\Delta t] &+ \\
+ p_{n+1}(t)\,\mu\Delta t &+ p_{n-1}(t)\,\lambda\Delta t + \sum_{i=1}^{4} O_i\,(\Delta t).
\end{aligned}
\qquad 74.2
$$

Or:

$$\frac{p_n(t+\Delta t)-p_n(t)}{\Delta t} = \lambda p_{n-1}(t)+\mu p_{n+1}(t)-(\lambda+\mu)p_n(t)+\frac{1}{\Delta t}\sum_{i=1}^{4}O_i(\Delta t). \qquad 74.3$$

If $\Delta t \to 0$, we obtain:

$$\frac{d}{dt}\,p_n(t) = \lambda p_{n-1}(t)+\mu p_{n+1}(t)-(\lambda+\mu)p_n(t) \qquad n > 0\,. \qquad 74.4$$

To these equations we must add the special equation corresponding to the case in which there is no unit in the system at time $t + \Delta t$. The probability that there will be no unit in the system at $t + \Delta t$ is the sum of the following two independent compound probabilities:
(1) The product of the probabilities that:
   a) there is no unit in the system at time t: $p_0(t)$;
   b) there is no arrival during the interval Δt: $1 - \lambda \Delta t$;
(2) The product of the probabilities that:
   a) there is one unit in the system at time t: $p_1(t)$;
   b) there is no arrival in the interval Δt: $1 - \lambda \Delta t$;
   c) one service is completed during the interval Δt: $\mu \Delta t$.

These two probabilities can be written:

$$\begin{aligned}&(1)\quad p_0(t).[1-\lambda\Delta t]\\&(2)\quad p_1(t)\,[1-\lambda\Delta t]\,[\mu\Delta t]=p_1(t)\,\mu\Delta t+O(\Delta t)\end{aligned} \qquad 74.5$$

where $O(\Delta t)$ is infinitesimally small in Δt of order greater than 1 when $\Delta t \to 0$.

Adding these probabilities to form the probability $p_0(t+\Delta t)$, we obtain:

$$p_0(t+\Delta t)=p_0(t)\,[1-\lambda\Delta t]+p_1(t)\,\mu\Delta t+O(\Delta t). \qquad 74.6$$

Or:

$$\frac{p_0(t+\Delta t)-p_0(t)}{\Delta t}=-\lambda p_0(t)+\mu p_1(t)+\frac{1}{\Delta t}O(\Delta t); \qquad 74.7$$

and finally:

$$\frac{d}{dt}p_0(t)=-\lambda p_0(t)+\mu p_1(t). \qquad 74.8$$

Equations (74.4) and (74.8) constitute the mathematical model of the waiting line in the case of a single station, when arrivals follow Poisson's law and service times follow an exponential law. We shall now find the $p_n(t)$ functions that constitute the solution of the differential system formed by these equations. In the specific case in which the probabilities p_n are independent of t, we say that the process is stationary and permanent:

$$p_n(t)=p_n. \qquad 74.8a$$

This case is the most important in actual practice.

2. Study of the permanent system.

If p_n is independent of t, equations (74.4) and (74.8) become:

$$\lambda p_{n-1}+\mu p_{n+1}-(\lambda+\mu)p_n=0 \qquad n>0, \qquad 74.9$$

$$-\lambda p_0+\mu p_1=0. \qquad 74.10$$

Remember the hypothesis: $\lambda/\mu<1$.

Proceeding by recurrence, and remember that, by definition, $\sum_{i=0}^{\infty} p_i=1$, we obtain:

$$\begin{aligned}p_0&=p_0,\\p_1&=(\lambda/\mu)\,p_0,\\p_2&=(\lambda/\mu)^2\,p_0,\\p_3&=(\lambda/\mu)^3\,p_0,\\&\ldots\ldots \qquad\qquad \lambda/\mu<1\\p_n&=(\lambda/\mu)^n\,p_0,\\&\ldots\ldots\end{aligned} \qquad 74.11$$

$$\sum_{n=0}^{\infty} p_n = p_0 \sum_{n=0}^{\infty} (\lambda/\mu)^n = 1. \qquad 74.12$$

But:

$$\sum_{i=0}^{\infty} \left(\frac{\lambda}{\mu}\right)^n = \frac{1}{1 - \frac{\lambda}{\mu}}; \qquad 74.13$$

since $\sum_{i=0}^{\infty} p_i = 1$ we therefore have:

$$1 = p_0 \frac{1}{1 - \frac{\lambda}{\mu}}, \qquad 74.14$$

or:

$$p_0 = 1 - \frac{\lambda}{\mu} \quad , \text{ with } \quad \frac{\lambda}{\mu} < 1. \qquad 74.15$$

Substituting (74.15) into (74.11), we find:

$$p_n = \left(\frac{\lambda}{\mu}\right)^n \left(1 - \frac{\lambda}{\mu}\right) \quad , \text{ with } \quad \frac{\lambda}{\mu} < 1. \qquad 74.16$$

The quantity $\Psi = \frac{\lambda}{\mu}$, with $0 < \Psi < 1$, is called the traffic intensity and plays a fundamental role. As the distribution (called geometrical distribution) of the probability p_n, we have:

$$p_n = \Psi^n (1 - \Psi) \quad , \text{ with } \quad 0 < \Psi < 1. \qquad 74.17$$

It is easy to show, by deriving p_n in relation to Ψ, that:

$$\max p_n \text{ corresponding to } \Psi = \frac{n}{n+1}, \qquad 74.18$$

is

$$\max p_n (\Psi) = \left(\frac{n}{n+1}\right)^n \left(\frac{1}{n+1}\right). \qquad 74.19$$

Thus, the maximum probability of finding 3 units in the system occurs when $\Psi = 3/(3+1) = 3/4$, and has the value: $\max p_3 = 0.1054$.

It is interesting to find the cumulative probability, i.e., $\Pr(N \leq n)$. We have:

$$\begin{aligned} \sum_{a=0}^{n} p_a &= \sum_{a=0}^{n} \Psi^a (1 - \Psi) = (1 - \Psi) \sum_{a=0}^{n} \Psi^a \\ &= (1 - \Psi) \left[\frac{1 - \Psi^{n+1}}{1 - \Psi}\right] = 1 - \Psi^{n+1}. \end{aligned} \qquad 74.21$$

Therefore:

$$\Pr(N \leqslant n) = 1 - \Psi^{n+1}. \qquad 74.22$$

The value of the complementary probability is:

$$\Pr(N > n) = 1 - (1 - \Psi^{n+1}) = \Psi^{n+1}. \qquad 74.23$$

We see that the probability of there being at least one unit in the system,

$$\Pr(N > 0) = \Psi, \qquad 74.24$$

is equal to the traffic intensity, which we would have found from (74.15).

Now let us calculate the average number of units in the system. By definition:

$$\bar{n} = E(N) = \sum_{n=0}^{\infty} n p_n, \qquad 74.25$$

where

$$\sum_{n=0}^{\infty} p_n = 1. \qquad 74.26$$

Now let us compute $\bar{n}$:

$$\begin{aligned}\bar{n} &= \sum_{n=0}^{\infty} n(\Psi)^n(1-\Psi) = (1-\Psi)\sum_{n=0}^{\infty} n\Psi^n \\ &= (1-\Psi)[\Psi + 2\Psi^2 + 3\Psi^3 + \ldots] = \Psi(1-\Psi)[1 + 2\Psi + 3\Psi^2 + \ldots] \\ &= \Psi(1-\Psi)\left[\frac{d}{d\Psi}(\Psi + \Psi^2 + \Psi^3 + \ldots)\right] = \Psi(1-\Psi)\frac{d}{d\Psi}\left[\frac{\Psi}{1-\Psi}\right] \\ &= \frac{\Psi}{1-\Psi}.\end{aligned} \qquad 74.27$$

Thus:

$$\bar{n} = \frac{\Psi}{1 - \Psi}. \qquad 74.28$$

3. Kendall's formulas.*

If arrivals follow the Poisson's law, while the service time distribution, Θ, is arbitrary, we use the following formula, devised by Kendall:

$$\bar{n} = \Psi + \frac{\Psi^2 + \lambda^2 \sigma_\Theta^2}{2(1 - \Psi)}. \qquad 74.30$$

---

*See: D. G. Kendall, "Some Problems in the Theory of Queues," Journal of the Royal Statistical Society, Vol. 13, No. 2 (1951), pp. 151-185.

This formula shows that the average number, $\bar{n}$, of units in the system will increase with the variance of Θ for given values of λ and μ. For given λ and μ, the minimum mean number of units in the system occurs when $\sigma_\Theta = 0$, i.e., when the service time is constant:

$$\min \bar{n} = \Psi + \frac{\Psi^2}{2(1-\Psi)}. \qquad 74.31$$

Finally, if $\sigma_\Theta^2 = 1/\mu^2$ (exponential distribution), we again find (74.28):

$$\bar{n} = \frac{\Psi}{1-\Psi}. \qquad 74.32$$

We observe in Kendall's formula (74.30) that, if the average rate of arrivals λ approaches the average rate of service μ, i.e., when $\lambda \to \mu$, the length of the line grows without limit.

We see, therefore, that for a given service-time distribution, the length of the waiting line can be reduced by a drop in the traffic intensity $\Psi = \lambda/\mu$. Obviously, this quantity is the very essence of the problem. When Ψ increases, $1 - \Psi$ decreases, which means that the solution to a waiting line problem requires a compromise between the cost of reducing the mean number of units in the system and the cost associated with the installations and personnel constituting the service.

4. Calculating the number of units in a waiting line.

We have:

$$\nu = n - 1 \qquad (\text{if } n > 0) \qquad 74.32\text{a}$$

Now we calculate $\bar{\nu}$:

$$\begin{aligned}
\bar{\nu} &= \sum_{\nu=1}^{\infty} \nu p_n = \sum_{n=2}^{\infty} (n-1)p_n \\
&= \sum_{n=2}^{\infty} np_n - \sum_{n=2}^{\infty} p_n \\
&= \sum_{n=0}^{\infty} np_n - \sum_{n=0}^{1} np_n - \sum_{n=0}^{\infty} p_n + \sum_{n=0}^{1} p_n \\
&= \bar{n} - p_1 - 1 + p_0 + p_1 \qquad 74.32\text{b} \\
&= \bar{n} - 1 + p_0 \\
\bar{\nu} &= \frac{\Psi}{1-\Psi} - (1 - p_0) \\
&= \frac{\Psi}{1-\Psi} - \Psi = \frac{\Psi^2}{1-\Psi}.
\end{aligned}$$

It will be noted that the property:

$$\frac{\bar{n}}{\mu} = \frac{\bar{\nu}}{\lambda}; \qquad 74.32c$$

is valid in this case; actually:

$$\frac{\bar{n}}{\mu} = \frac{1}{\mu}\frac{\Psi}{1-\Psi} = \frac{1}{\mu\Psi}\frac{\Psi^2}{1-\Psi} = \frac{1}{\lambda}\frac{\Psi^2}{1-\Psi} = \frac{\bar{\nu}}{\lambda}. \qquad 74.32d$$

5. Waiting time.

An important quantity to calculate is the average time spent in the waiting line. No matter what the distribution of arrivals and service times in a permanent ssystem, there cannot be, on the average, more units leaving than entered, and vice versa. The mean waiting time is governed by the rate of arrivals;* letting $\bar{t}_f$ represent the waiting time in the line, we have:

$$\bar{t}_f = \frac{\bar{\nu}}{\lambda}. \qquad 74.33$$

Letting $\bar{t}_s$ represent the average waiting time in the system:

$$\bar{t}_s = \frac{\bar{n}}{\lambda}. \qquad 74.34$$

In the case studied in this section:

$$\bar{t}_f = \frac{\bar{\nu}}{\lambda} = \frac{1}{\lambda}\frac{\Psi^2}{1-\Psi} = \frac{1}{\mu}\frac{\Psi}{1-\Psi} \qquad 74.35$$

$$\bar{t}_s = \frac{\bar{n}}{\lambda} = \frac{1}{\lambda}\frac{\Psi}{1-\Psi} = \frac{1}{\mu}\frac{1}{1-\Psi}. \qquad 74.36$$

Once again, we find:

$$\bar{t}_s - \bar{t}_f = \left(\frac{1}{\lambda} - \frac{1}{\mu}\right)\frac{\Psi}{1-\Psi} = \frac{1}{\mu} \qquad 74.37$$

which represents the average service time.

---

*The average number of arrivals in the waiting-line per unit of time is λ; the average number of units leaving the system is likewise λ. It is not surprising that this number is not equal to μ, but is smaller ($\lambda < \mu$, by hypothesis), if we remember that from time to time the station is idle.

In the case of Poisson-distributed arrivals and a service time interval having an arbitrary distribution with variance σ^2_Θ, formula (74.35) becomes:

$$\bar{t}_f = \bar{t}_s - \theta = \frac{1}{\lambda}\left[\psi + \frac{\lambda^2\sigma^2_\Theta + \psi^2}{2(1-\psi)}\right] - \bar{\theta} = \frac{1}{\lambda}\,\frac{\lambda^2\sigma^2_\Theta + \psi^2}{2(1-\Psi)}. \qquad 74.38$$

where $\bar{\theta}$ is the average service time.

If we set:

$$\sigma^2_\Theta = 1/\mu^2 \qquad 74.39$$

and

$$\bar{\theta} = 1/\mu, \qquad 74.40$$

we are lead, once again, to (74.35).

We might equally well decide to find the probability that a unit will wait in line for a period longer than a given time, w. Again we will take the case of Poisson-distributed arrivals and exponential service times.

The method of calculation will be as follows. Arbitrarily, we choose an initial instant t_0 and see what happens to a "reference" unit arriving at that instant. More precisely, we shall be computing the probability, f(w)dw, that this unit will have to wait in line for a period somewhere between w and w + dw. Let n be the number of units in the system at instant t_0 (not including the reference unit). The probability we are seeking is the sum, for all values of n, of the probabilities p(n,w)dw of the mutually exclusive events defined as follows: the number of units in the system at instant t_0 is n, and the waiting time in the line for the reference unit is between w and w + dw.

This requires the calculation of p(n,w)dw. First of all, we may note that if the service time is exponentially distributed, the times at which service intervals end are distributed according to Poisson's law as long as the station is occupied. Therefore, if a station is occupied, the probability that service will become available during the interval dt is μdt. Thus, the distribution of the number of exits (units which have just finished being served) while the station is occupied is:

$$\Pr(s) = \frac{(\mu t)^s\, e^{-\mu t}}{s!} \qquad s = 0, 1, 2, 3, \ldots \qquad 74.41$$

Let us return to our calculation. If n = 0, the reference unit will not have to wait in line at all; therefore, p(0,w) = 0 for w > 0. We shall therefore assume hereafter that n > 0.

The probability p(n,w)dw (n > 0) is formed by the product of the three following probabilities:

1. The "a priori" probability that there are n units in the system at the start of the time interval w (i.e., at instant t_0). Since we assume that the system is stationary and permanent, this probability is:

$$\Psi^n(1 - \Psi). \tag{74.42}$$

2. The conditional probability that, if the system contains n units at instant t_0, precisely s = n - 1 units are served and leave the system in the interval w, or:

$$\frac{(\mu w)^{n-1} \,.\, e^{-\mu w}}{(n-1)!}. \tag{74.43}$$

3. The conditional probability that, the foregoing two conditions being met, exactly one unit will leave the station during the interval dw, or:

$$\mu dw. \tag{74.44}$$

This probability p(n,w)dw will therefore be written:

$$p(n,w)dw = \Psi^n(1 - \Psi) \,.\, \frac{(\mu w)^{n-1}\, e^{-\mu w}}{(n-1)!} \,.\, \mu dw. \tag{74.45}$$

Thus, we have:

$$\begin{aligned} f(w)dw &= \sum_{n=1}^{\infty} p(n,w)dw = \sum_{n=1}^{\infty} \Psi^n(1 - \Psi) \,.\, \frac{(\mu w)^{n-1}\, e^{-\mu w}}{(n-1)!} \,.\, \mu dw. \\ &= (1 - \Psi)\, \Psi\, e^{-\mu w} \mu dw \sum_{n=1}^{\infty} \frac{\Psi^{n-1}(\mu w)^{n-1}}{(n-1)!} \\ &= (1 - \Psi)\, \Psi\, \mu e^{-\mu w}\, dw \sum_{h=0}^{\infty} \frac{(\Psi \mu w)^h}{h!}, \end{aligned} \tag{74.46}$$

where we have set h = n - 1. But:

$$\sum_{h=0}^{\infty} \frac{(\Psi \mu w)^h}{h!} = e^{\Psi \mu w}; \tag{74.47}$$

and thus:

$$f(w)dw = (1 - \Psi)\, \Psi\, \mu\, e^{-\mu w(1-\Psi)}\, dw. \tag{74.48}$$

The mean of this expression is given by (74.35), or:

$$i_f = \frac{\Psi}{\mu(1 - \Psi)}. \tag{74.49}$$

The probability that an arriving unit will wait for a time greater than w will therefore be:

$$p(>w) = \int_w^\infty f(t)\,dt = (1-\Psi)\,\Psi\,\mu \int_w^\infty e^{-\mu t(1-\Psi)}\,dt \qquad 74.50$$
$$= \Psi\, e^{-\mu w(1-\Psi)}.$$

Thus:

$$p(>w) = \Psi\, e^{-\mu w(1-\Psi)}, \qquad 74.51$$

which can also be written:

$$p(>w) = \frac{\lambda}{\mu}\, e^{-w(\mu-\lambda)}. \qquad 74.52$$

Specifically, the probability of not waiting is:

$$1 - p(>0) = 1 - \Psi, \qquad 74.53$$

which amounts to writing, from (74.22):

$$\Pr(n=0) = 1 - \Psi. \qquad 74.54$$

6. Transient system.

The solution of equations (74.4) and (74.8) with the initial conditions $p_0(0) = 1$, $p_n(0) = 0$, $n = 1, 2, 3, \ldots$, for a transient system is highly complicated; we show it here for the reader's information:

$$p_n(t) = e^{-(\lambda+\mu)t}\Big[\psi^{n/2} I_{-n}(2\sqrt{\lambda\mu}\,t) + \psi^{(n-1)/2} I_{n+1}(2\sqrt{\lambda\mu}\,t) + (1-\psi)\psi^n \sum_{k=n+2}^{\infty} \frac{1}{\psi^{k/2}} I_k(2\sqrt{\lambda\mu}\,t)\Big] \qquad 74.55$$

where

$$I_n(x) = j^{-n} J_n(jx), \qquad 74.56$$

is the modified Bessel function of the second kind of order n.

It can be shown* that the expression of $p_n(t)$ given by (74.55) has the asymptotic value:

$$p_n(\infty) = \psi^n (1-\psi), \qquad 74.57$$

which corresponds to the stationary and permanent state given by (74.17).

---

*See, for example: T. L. Saaty, "Resume of Useful Formulas in Queuing Theory," J.O.R.S.A., Vol. 5, No. 2 (April, 1957), pp. 161-200.

A vast amount of work has been done on waiting line phenomena in transient systems. We cannot present these special studies in this book, which must be limited to major questions; but the interested reader will find some very significant developments set forth in the reports of such work.

Section 75

BIRTH AND DEATH PROCESSES

Equations (74.4) and (74.8) constitute a specific instance of the more general equations we shall now investigate. These define what is called a birth and death process* in which both arrivals and service times are Poisson-distributed:

$$\frac{d}{dt}p_n(t) = -(\lambda_n + \mu_n)p_n(t) + \lambda_{n-1}p_{n-1}(t) + \mu_{n+1}p_{n+1}(t) \qquad n > 0 \qquad 75.1$$

$$\frac{d}{dt}p_0(t) = -\lambda_0 p_0(t) + \mu_1 p_1(t), \qquad 75.2$$

where λ_n and μ_n are functions of n.

These equations generalize many specific cases of delay (queuing) phenomena.

Earlier, we saw a particularly simple case where:

$$\lambda_n = \lambda, \qquad \mu_n = \mu, \qquad 75.3$$

the case of a waiting line at one station, which we studied in Section 74.

Let us now look at another example of the birth and death process:

$$\lambda_n = \lambda, \qquad \mu_n = n\mu. \qquad 75.4$$

This amounts to saying that the average rate of arrivals is constant, but that the average rate of service is proportional to the number of units in the system. We have the equations:

$$\frac{d}{dt}p_n(t) = -(\lambda + n\mu)p_n(t) + \lambda p_{n-1}(t) + (n+1)\mu p_{n+1}(t), \qquad 75.5$$

$$\frac{d}{dt}p_0(t) = -\lambda p_0(t) + \mu p_1(t). \qquad 75.6$$

Of course, the condition $\lambda/\mu < 1$ is no longer necessary.

---

*These are particularly important in biology.

The solution of these equations, with the conditions $p_0(0) = 1$, $p_n(0) = 0$, $n = 1, 2, 3, 4, \ldots$, is:

$$p_n(t) = \frac{e^{-\lambda/\mu\,(1-e^{-\mu t})}\left[\frac{\lambda}{\mu}(1 - e^{-\mu t})\right]^n}{n!} \qquad 75.7$$

$$n = 0, 1, 2, 3, \ldots$$

In a permanent system where $p_n = p_n(\infty)$, $n = 0, 1, 2, 3, \ldots$, we have:

$$p_n = \frac{(\lambda/\mu)^n e^{-\lambda/\mu}}{n!}, \qquad 75.8$$

which means that the situation tends toward an equilibrium governed by a Poisson distribution; then:

$$\bar{n} = \frac{\lambda}{\mu} \qquad 75.9$$

and

$$\sigma_N^2 = \frac{\lambda}{\mu}. \qquad 75.10$$

We conclude from this that the average number of units in the line is always zero if $\lambda/\mu < 1$.

Formula (75.8) can be found directly and very simply. In a permanent system, equations (75.5) and (75.6) become:

$$(n + 1)\mu\, p_{n+1} = (\lambda + n\mu)p_n - \lambda p_{n-1}, \qquad 75.11$$

$$p_1 = \frac{\lambda}{\mu} p_0. \qquad 75.12$$

Or again:

$$\begin{aligned} p_1 &= \frac{\lambda}{\mu} p_0 \\ 2\mu p_2 &= (\lambda + \mu)p_1 - \lambda p_0, \\ 3\mu p_3 &= (\lambda + 2\mu)p_2 - \lambda p_1, \\ 4\mu p_4 &= (\lambda + 3\mu)p_3 - \lambda p_2, \\ &\ldots\ldots \end{aligned} \qquad 75.13$$

hence:

$$p_n = \frac{(\lambda/\mu)^n}{n!} p_0. \qquad 75.14$$

But:

$$\sum_{n=0}^{\infty} p_n = 1; \qquad 75.15$$

therefore:

$$p_0 + p_0 \sum_{n=1}^{\infty} \frac{(\lambda/\mu)^n}{n!} = 1\,, \qquad 75.16$$

$$p_0 + p_0 (e^{\lambda/\mu} - 1) = 1 \qquad 75.17$$

$$p_0 = e^{-\lambda/\mu}, \qquad 75.18$$

and finally:

$$p_n = \frac{(\lambda/\mu)^n e^{-\lambda/\mu}}{n!}. \qquad 75.19$$

It is interesting to calculate the average number $\bar{n}(t)$ of units in the system in a transient state, which is fairly easy in the present case:

$$\bar{n}(t) = \sum_{n=0}^{\infty} n p_n(t) \qquad 75.20$$

Multiplying (75.1) and (75.2) by n, and taking the sum over n, then remembering that the sum* of $p_n(t)$ (summation over n) is equal to 1, we are led to the equation:

$$\frac{d\bar{n}}{dt} + \mu \bar{n}(t) = \lambda. \qquad 75.21$$

The solution of this equation with the hypothesis $\bar{n}(0) = 0$ is:

$$\bar{n}(t) = \frac{\lambda}{\mu}(1 - e^{-\mu t}). \qquad 75.22$$

For $t \to \infty$, we find once again:

$$\bar{n} = \bar{n}(\infty) = \frac{\lambda}{\mu}. \qquad 75.23$$

Section 76

WAITING LINE AT SEVERAL STATIONS

If the S stations that provide the service are not busy when a unit arrives, that unit is immediately served; on the contrary, if

---

*The operation $\frac{d}{dt}\Sigma = \Sigma \frac{d}{dt}$ is legitimate because $\sum_{n=0}^{\infty} np_n$ is uniformly convergent.

the S stations are busy, the unit must wait, and a waiting line is formed. If we call n the number of units in the system in the state $E_n(n \leq S)$, the units will not have to wait; in the state $E_n(n > S)$, there will be a waiting line of n - S units.

Suppose that the arrivals are governed by a Poisson distribution and that service times are exponentially distributed; let λ and μ be the corresponding rates, and $\Psi = \lambda/\mu$ the traffic intensity, which must be such that:

$$\Psi = \frac{\lambda}{\mu} < S. \qquad 76.1$$

$$\begin{aligned} \lambda_n &= \lambda, \\ \mu_n &= n\mu \qquad 0 \leqslant n < S, \\ \mu_n &= S\mu \qquad n \geqslant S. \end{aligned} \qquad 76.2$$

The equations of state are then:

$$\frac{d}{dt} p_0(t) = -\lambda p_0(t) + \mu p_1(t) \qquad 76.3$$

$$\frac{d}{dt} p_n(t) = -(\lambda + n\mu)p_n(t) + \lambda p_{n-1}(t) + (n+1)\mu p_{n+1}(t) \quad 1 \leqslant n < S \qquad 76.4$$

$$\frac{d}{dt} p_n(t) = -(\lambda + S\mu)p_n(t) + \lambda p_{n-1}(t) + S\mu p_{n+1}(t) \qquad n \geqslant S. \qquad 76.5$$

The solution of this system of equations for transient states is very complicated, and we shall not discuss it here.

Practically speaking, a permanent system (i.e., a steady state) will be achieved, in a time on the order of 3 or 4 times $1/\mu S$.

Therefore, we assume that:

$$p_n(t) = p_n = C^{te} \text{ for every } n. \qquad 76.6$$

Equations (76.3)-(76.5) then become:

$$\lambda p_0 = \mu p_1, \qquad 76.7$$

$$(\lambda + n\mu)p_n = \lambda p_{n-1} + (n+1)\mu p_{n+1} \qquad 1 \leqslant n < S, \qquad 76.8$$

$$(\lambda + S\mu)p_n = \lambda p_{n-1} + S\mu p_{n+1}. \qquad n \geqslant S. \qquad 76.9$$

From these equations we derive:

$$p_n = p_0 \frac{\Psi^n}{n!} \qquad 1 \leqslant n < S, \qquad 76.10$$

$$p_n = p_0 \frac{\Psi^n}{S!\,S^{n-S}} \qquad n \geqslant S. \qquad 76.11$$

Let us calculate p_0. We have:

$$\sum_{n=0}^{\infty} p_n = 1. \qquad 76.12$$

Therefore:

$$p_0\left[1+\frac{\Psi}{1}+\frac{\Psi^2}{2!}+\ldots+\frac{\Psi^{S-1}}{(S-1)!}+\frac{\Psi^S}{S!}\left(1+\frac{\Psi}{S}+\frac{\Psi^2}{S^2}+\frac{\Psi^3}{S^3}+\ldots\right)\right] = 1. \qquad 76.13$$

or

$$p_0\left[\left(\sum_{k=0}^{S-1}\frac{\Psi^k}{k!}\right) + \frac{\Psi^S}{S!(1-\Psi/S)}\right] = 1,$$

and

$$p_0 = \frac{1}{\dfrac{\Psi^S}{S!\,(1-\Psi/S)}+\sum_{n=0}^{S-1}\dfrac{\Psi^n}{n!}}. \qquad 76.14$$

We easily obtain:* $\lim_{S\to\infty} p_0 = e^{-\Psi}$. 76.14a

Here are some values of p_0:

	S=2	S=3	S=4	S=5	S=6	S=7	S=∞
Ψ = 1	0.333	0.363	0.367	0.367	0.367	0.367 ...	0.36788
Ψ = 2		0.111	0.130	0.134	0.135	0.135 ...	0.13534
Ψ = 3			0.037	0.046	0.049	0.049 ...	0.04978
Ψ = 4				0.013	0.016	0.017 ...	0.01831

The mean value of the number of units in the system will thus be given by:

$$\bar{n} = \sum_{n=0}^{\infty} n p_n. \qquad 76.16$$

The mean value of the number of units in line, by:

$$\bar{\nu} = \sum_{n=S+1}^{\infty} (n-S)p_n. \qquad 76.17$$

*It is not at all surprising that p_0 does not approach 1 when the number of stations becomes infinite, inasmuch as n here means the number of units waiting in line and/or being served.

And lastly, the mean number of idle stations is:

$$\bar{\varrho} = \sum_{n=0}^{S} (S - n)p_n. \tag{76.18}$$

Between these three means there exists the relationship:

$$\bar{n} = \bar{\nu} + S - \bar{\varrho} = \bar{\nu} + \Psi \qquad \text{(see 76.25)}. \tag{76.19}$$

We can give an expression of $\bar{\nu}$ which is not too complicated:

$$\bar{\nu} = \sum_{n=S+1}^{\infty} (n - S)p_n = \sum_{n=S+1}^{\infty} (n - S) \frac{\Psi^n}{S!\,S^{n-S}}\, p_0$$
$$= \frac{\Psi^{S+1}}{S.\,S!\,(1 - \Psi/S)^2}\, p_0. \tag{76.20}$$

The probability that a unit will have to wait is the sum of the probabilities p_n from $n = S$ to $n = \infty$. We shall use the notation $p(>0)$ or $\Pr(n \geq s)$.

$$p(>0) = \Pr(n \geqslant S) = \sum_{n=S}^{\infty} p_n = p_0 \frac{S^S}{S!} \sum_{n=S}^{\infty} \left(\frac{\Psi}{S}\right)^n = p_0 \frac{\Psi^S}{S!(1 - \Psi/S)}. \tag{76.21}$$

The probability of a waiting time longer than a given interval w is:

$$p(>w) = e^{-S\mu w(1-\Psi/S)}\, p(>0), \tag{76.22}$$

(This can be proven in the same manner as (74.51).)

To find the mean waiting time in line, it is sufficient to note that in a permanent system we have:

$$\bar{\nu} = \lambda\, \bar{t}_f, \tag{76.23}$$

or:

$$\bar{t}_f = \frac{\bar{\nu}}{\lambda} = \frac{\Psi^S}{S.\,S!\,\mu(1 - \Psi/S)^2}\, p_0. \tag{76.24}$$

It is possible to find a simple expression of $\bar{\varrho}$; we calculate:

$$\begin{aligned}
\varrho &= \sum_{n=0}^{S-1} (S - n)\, p_n \\
&= \sum_{n=0}^{S-1} (S - n)\, \frac{\Psi^n}{n!}\, p_0 \\
&= p_0 \sum_{n=0}^{S-1} (S - n)\, \frac{\Psi^n}{n!} \\
&= p_0 S \sum_{n=0}^{S-1} \frac{\Psi^n}{n!} - p_0 \sum_{n=0}^{S-1} n\, \frac{\Psi^n}{n!}
\end{aligned} \tag{76.25}$$

$$= p_0 S \sum_{n=0}^{S-1} \frac{\Psi^n}{n!} - p_0 \sum_{n=1}^{S-1} \frac{\Psi^n}{(n-1)!}$$

$$= p_0 S \sum_{n=0}^{S-1} \frac{\Psi^n}{n!} - p_0 \Psi \sum_{n=1}^{S-1} \frac{\Psi^{n-1}}{(n-1)!}$$

$$= p_0 S \sum_{n=0}^{S-1} \frac{\Psi^n}{n!} - p_0 \Psi \sum_{n=1}^{S} \frac{\Psi^{n-1}}{(n-1)!} + p_0 \Psi \frac{\Psi^{(S-1)}}{(S-1)!}$$

$$= p_0 S \sum_{n=0}^{S-1} \frac{\Psi^n}{n!} - p_0 \Psi \sum_{n=0}^{S-1} \frac{\Psi^n}{n!} + p_0 \frac{\Psi^S}{(S-1)!} \qquad 76.25$$

$$= p_0 (S - \Psi) \sum_{n=0}^{S-1} \frac{\Psi^n}{n!} + p_0 \frac{\Psi^S}{(S-1)!}$$

$$= p_0 \left[\left((S - \Psi) \sum_{n=0}^{S-1} \frac{\Psi^n}{n!}\right) + \frac{\Psi^S}{(S-1)!}\right]$$

$$= p_0 (S - \Psi) \left[\sum_{n=0}^{S-1} \frac{\Psi^n}{n!} + \frac{1}{(S-\Psi)} \frac{\Psi^S}{(S-1)!}\right]$$

$$= p_0 (S - \Psi) \left[\sum_{n=0}^{S-1} \frac{\Psi^n}{n!} + \frac{\Psi^S}{(1 - \Psi/S).S!}\right]$$

$$= (S - \Psi)$$

because

$$p_0 = \frac{1}{\sum_{n=0}^{S-1} \frac{\Psi^n}{n!} + \frac{\Psi^S}{(1-\Psi/S).S!}} \qquad 76.26$$

(from (76.14)).

Section 77

A SINGLE STATION AND A LIMITED NUMBER OF UNITS*

If m is the limited number of units (customers), the birth and death process will contain parameters λ_n and μ_n such that:

---

*The source considered in the case of a limited number of units (customers) has a special property: the rate of arrivals (the rate at which units emerge from the source) is proportional to the number of units in the source. This corresponds to the case, which is of the greatest practical interest, where units can be in only one of the two states, E_1 and E_2; the transition from E_1 to E_2 occurs in the station, and corresponds to an exit from the system; the transition from E_2 to E_1 occurs in a random fashion (in this case following Poisson's law) and corresponds to entry into the system. An example has been provided in Sections 29 and 30.

$$\left.\begin{aligned}\lambda_n &= m\lambda \\ \mu_n &= 0\end{aligned}\right\} n = 0, \qquad \left.\begin{aligned}\lambda_n &= (m-n)\lambda \\ \mu_n &= \mu\end{aligned}\right\} 0 < n \leqslant m. \qquad \begin{aligned}&77.1\\&77.2\end{aligned}$$

(obviously, the number n cannot be greater than m).

From this we have the equations:

$$p_0'(t) = -m\lambda p_0(t) + \mu p_1(t), \qquad 77.3$$

$$0<n<m \quad p_n'(t) = -[(m-n)\lambda+\mu]p_n(t)+(m-n+1)\lambda p_{n-1}(t)+\mu p_{n+1}(t), \qquad 77.4$$

$$p'_m(t) = -\mu p_m(t) + \lambda p_{m-1}(t). \qquad 77.5$$

In a permanent system:

$$p_n(t) = p_n = C^{te}, \ n = 0, 1, 2, 3, \dots, \qquad 77.6$$

and these equations become:

$$m\lambda p_0 = \mu p_1, \qquad 77.7$$

$$0<n<m \qquad [(m-n)\lambda+\mu]p_n=(m-n+1)\lambda p_{n-1}+\mu p_{n+1} \qquad 77.8$$

$$\lambda p_{m-1} = \mu p_m. \qquad 77.9$$

We easily derive the recurrence formula:

$$p_n = (m-n+1)\Psi p_{n-1} \qquad 0 < n < m, \qquad 77.10$$

from which we have:

$$p_n = \frac{m!\,\Psi^n}{(m-n)!}p_0 \qquad 0 < n \leqslant m. \qquad 77.11$$

We have set $\Psi = \lambda/\mu$ (traffic intensity). 77.12

As the value of p_0 we have:

$$p_0 = \frac{1}{1 + \sum_{n=1}^{m} \frac{m!\ \Psi^n}{(m-n)!}}. \qquad 77.13$$

The mean number of units in the waiting line is:

$$\bar{\nu} = \sum_{n=2}^{m}(n-1)p_n = m!p_0 \sum_{n=2}^{m} \frac{(n-1)}{(m-n)!}\Psi^n = m - \frac{1+\Psi}{\Psi}(1-p_0). \qquad 77.14$$

The mean number of units in the system is:

$$\bar{n} = \sum_{n=0}^{m} np_n = m!\ p_0 \sum_{n=0}^{m} \frac{n\,\Psi^n}{(m-n)!} = m - \frac{1}{\Psi}(1-p_0). \qquad 77.15$$

The mean value for station idleness is:

$$\bar{\varrho} = \sum_{n=0}^{1} (1 - n)p_n = p_0 . \qquad 77.16$$

The mean number of units not in the system is:

$$\overline{(m - n)} = \sum_{n=0}^{m} (m - n)p_n = \sum_{n=0}^{m} mp_n - \sum_{n=0}^{m} np_n = m - \bar{n} , \qquad 77.17$$

which is obvious.

Finally:

$$\bar{n} = \bar{\nu} + 1 - \bar{\varrho} = m - \frac{1}{\Psi}(1 - p_0), \qquad 77.18$$

from which we derive:

$$m - \bar{n} = \frac{1}{\Psi}(1 - p_0) \qquad 77.19$$

The probability of waiting any time at all is:

$$p(>0) = \sum_{n=1}^{m} p_n = 1 - p_0 . \qquad 77.20$$

The mean waiting time in the line will be readily found if it is noted that in such circumstances, under a permanent system, the average rate of arrivals is not λ but $\lambda(m - n)$, or $\lambda(m - \bar{n})$, from (77.17).

Hence:

$$\bar{\nu} = \lambda (m - \bar{n})\bar{t}_f , \qquad 77.21$$

therefore:

$$\bar{t}_f = \frac{1}{\lambda(m - \bar{n})} \sum_{n=2}^{m} (n - 1)p_n = \frac{1}{\mu}\left[\frac{m}{1 - p_0} - \frac{1 + \Psi}{\Psi}\right]. \qquad 77.22$$

The mean waiting time in the system will be:

$$\bar{t}_s = \frac{\bar{n}}{\lambda(m - \bar{n})} = \frac{1}{\mu}\left[\frac{m}{1 - p_0} - \frac{1}{\Psi}\right]. \qquad 77.23$$

Section 78

SEVERAL STATIONS AND A LIMITED NUMBER OF UNITS

If m is the limited number of units (customers) and S is the number of stations, with $m > S$ the λ_n and μ_n values of the birth and death process will be:

$$\left.\begin{matrix}\lambda_n = m\lambda \\ \mu_n = 0\end{matrix}\right\} n=0, \quad \left.\begin{matrix}\lambda_n = (m-n)\lambda \\ \mu_n = n\mu\end{matrix}\right\} 1 \leqslant n \leqslant S, \quad \left.\begin{matrix}\lambda_n = (m-n)\lambda \\ \mu_n = S\mu\end{matrix}\right\} S \leqslant n \leqslant m. \qquad 78.1$$

from which we have the equations:

$$p_0'(t) = -m\lambda p_0(t) + \mu p_1(t) \qquad 78.2$$

$$1 \leqslant n < S \quad p_n'(t) = -[(m-n)\lambda + n\mu]p_n(t) + (m-n+1)\lambda p_{n-1}(t) + (n+1)\mu p_{n+1}(t). \qquad 78.3$$

$$S \leqslant n < m \quad p_n'(t) = -[(m-n)\lambda + S\mu]p_n(t) + (m-n+1)\lambda p_{n-1}(t) + S\mu p_{n+1}(t) \qquad 78.4$$

$$p_m'(t) = -S\mu p_m(t) + \lambda p_{m-1}(t).$$

In a permanent system:

$$p_n(t) = p_n = C^{te} \qquad n = 0, 1, 2, 3, \ldots, m; \qquad 78.5$$

these equations become:

$$m\lambda p_0 = \mu p_1, \qquad 78.6$$

$$1 \leqslant n \leqslant S \quad [(m-n)\lambda + n\mu]p_n = (m-n+1)\lambda p_{n-1} + (n+1)\mu p_{n+1}, \qquad 78.7$$

$$S \leqslant n < m \quad [(m-n)\lambda + S\mu]p_n = (m-n+1)\lambda p_{n-1} + S\mu p_{n+1}, \qquad 78.8$$

$$S\mu p_m = \lambda p_{m-1}. \qquad 78.9$$

We obtain the recurrence formulas:

$$p_n = \frac{m-n+1}{n}\Psi p_{n-1}, \qquad 0 \leqslant n < S \qquad 78.10$$

$$p_n = \frac{m-n+1}{S}\Psi p_{n-1}., \qquad S \leqslant n \leqslant m \qquad 78.10a$$

where $\Psi = \dfrac{\lambda}{\mu}$.

From this we derive:

$$p_n = C_m^n \Psi^n p_0 \qquad 0 \leqslant n \leqslant S \qquad 78.11$$

where

$$C_m^n = \frac{m!}{(m-n)!\, n!}, \qquad 78.12$$

and

$$p_n = \frac{n!}{S!\, S^{n-S}} C_m^n \Psi^n p_0. \qquad S \leqslant n \leqslant m. \qquad 78.13$$

Next, we calculate the quantities $\alpha_n = p_n/p_0$ by means of the recurrence formulas (78.10) and (78.10a), and then the sum:

$$A = \underbrace{\sum_{n=1}^{S} \alpha_n}_{\substack{\text{utilizing} \\ \text{de (78.11)}}} + \underbrace{\sum_{n=S+1}^{m} \alpha_n}_{\substack{\text{utilizing} \\ \text{de (78.12)}}}. \qquad 78.14$$

From this:

$$p_0 = \frac{1}{1 + A}. \qquad 78.15$$

The mean number of units in the waiting line is:

$$\bar{\nu} = \sum_{n=S+1}^{m} (n - S) p_n = \frac{S^S p_0}{S!} \sum_{n=S+1}^{m} \frac{(n - S) n!}{S^n} C_m^n \Psi^n. \qquad 78.16$$

The mean number of units in the system is:

$$\bar{n} = \sum_{n=0}^{m} n p_n = \underbrace{\sum_{n=0}^{S} n p_n}_{\substack{\text{utilizing} \\ (78.11)}} + \underbrace{\sum_{n=S+1}^{m} n\, p_n}_{\substack{\text{utilizing} \\ (78.12)}}. \qquad 78.17$$

The mean value for station idleness is:

$$\bar{\varrho} = \sum_{n=0}^{S} (S - n) p_n. \qquad 78.18$$

The mean number of units not in the system is:

$$\overline{(m - n)} = \sum_{n=0}^{m} (m - n) p_n = m - \bar{n}. \qquad 78.19$$

Now remember (21.5):

$$\bar{n} = \bar{\nu} + S - \bar{\varrho}. \qquad 78.20$$

Finally:

$$p(>0) = \sum_{n=S}^{m} p_n, \qquad 78.21$$

and

$$\bar{t}_f = \frac{\bar{\nu}}{\lambda(m - \bar{n})} = \frac{\bar{\nu}}{\mu(S - \varrho)}. \qquad 78.22$$

Section 79

WAITING LINE WITH BINOMIAL DISTRIBUTION*

A power supply circuit supplies current to m welding stations which use this current intermittently. If a station is operating at time t, the probability that it will cease operating before $t + \Delta t$ is $\mu \Delta t$, plus negligible terms when $\Delta t \to 0$. If at time t the station is not operating, the probability that it will demand current before $t + \Delta t$ is $\lambda \Delta t$, plus negligible terms when $\Delta t \to 0$. The stations operate independently of one another.

We shall say that the system is in state E_n if n stations are using current. Hence there is a finite number of states: E_0, E_1, E_2, . . . , E_m.

If the system is in state E_n, then m - n stations are not in operation, and the probability of a further demand for current in the interval Δt is $(m - n) \lambda \Delta t$ plus negligible terms when $\Delta t \to 0$. On the other hand, the probability that one of the stations will stop is $n\mu\Delta t$, plus negligible terms etc. Thus, we have a birth and death process with:

$$\left.\begin{aligned} \lambda_n &= (m - n)\lambda \\ \mu_n &= n\mu \end{aligned}\right\} \quad 0 \leqslant n \leqslant m. \tag{79.1}$$

The equations of state are then:

$$p_0'(t) = -m\lambda p_0(t) + \mu p_1(t) \tag{79.2}$$

$$0 < n \leqslant m - 1 \qquad \begin{aligned} p_n'(t) = -[n\mu + (m-n)\lambda]p_n(t) + (n+1)\mu p_{n+1}(t) \\ + (m - n + 1)\lambda p_{n-1}(t). \end{aligned} \tag{79.3}$$

$$p_m'(t) = -m\mu p_m(t) + \lambda p_{m-1}(t). \tag{79.4}$$

In a permanent system:

$$p_n(t) = p_n = C^{te}, \qquad n = 0, 1, 2, \dots, m, \tag{79.5}$$

these equations become:

$$m\lambda p_0 = \mu p_1 \tag{79.6}$$

$$[n\mu + (m-n)\lambda]p_n = (n+1)\mu p_{n+1} + (m-n+1)\lambda p_{n-1} \qquad 0 < n \leqslant m - 1 \tag{79.7}$$

$$m\mu p_m = \lambda p_{m-1}. \tag{79.8}$$

---

*This case corresponds to the same hypotheses as the preceding one (Section 78), but this time with $S \geq m$; hence the customers never experience any delay.

It is easy to prove that the distribution of the random variable n is given by the binomial law:

$$p_n = C_m^n \left[\frac{\lambda}{\lambda+\mu}\right]^n \left[\frac{\mu}{\lambda+\mu}\right]^{m-n} , \qquad 79.9$$

or again:

$$p_n = C_m^n \left(\frac{\Psi}{1+\Psi}\right)^n \left(\frac{1}{1+\Psi}\right)^{m-n} \qquad 79.10$$

where

$$\Psi = \lambda/\mu . \qquad 79.11$$

Section 80

VARIOUS SPECIAL CASES OF DELAY (QUEUING) PHENOMENA*

1. One station: entries, Poisson; service at constant intervals.—2. One station: entries, Poisson; service, Erlang.—3. One station: entries, Poisson; service, arbitrary distribution; R lines with ordered, but not absolute, priorities.—4. One station: entries, Poisson; service, exponential; 2 lines with one having absolute priority over the other.—5. One station: entries, Poisson; service, exponential; customers impatient and chosen at random from the line.—6. One station: entries at regular intervals; service, exponential.—7. Two stations cascaded: entries, Poisson; service, exponential; First case: unlimited number of units; Second case: limited number of units.—8. Several stations in parallel: entries, Poisson; service, constant duration.—9. Several stations: entries, Poisson; service, exponential; R lines with ordered, but not absolute, priorities.—10. Infinite number of stations: entries, Poisson; service, exponential.

We shall survey briefly a number of interesting cases.

1. One station: entries, Poisson; service at constant intervals.

If the service time is constant and equal to $1/\mu$, and we set:

$$\Psi = \frac{\lambda}{\mu} : \qquad 80.1$$

we will have:

---

*See Bibliography: Ref. D-33.

$$p_n = (1 - \Psi) \sum_{k=1}^{n} (-1)^{n-k} \left[\frac{(k\Psi)^{n-k}}{(n-k)!} + \frac{(k\Psi)^{n-k-1}}{(n-k-1)!} \right], \qquad 80.2$$

$$p(>w) = \Psi \sum_{i=0}^{k} e^{-\Psi(i-\mu w)} \frac{[\Psi(i-\mu w)]^i}{i!}. \qquad 80.3$$

where k is the largest integer that is less than or equal to μw.

$$\bar{t}_f = \frac{\Psi}{2\mu(1-\Psi)} \qquad 80.4$$

2. One station: entries, Poisson; service, Erlang.

The Erlang distribution is derived from the probability density function:

$$b_k(t) = \frac{(\mu k)^k}{\Gamma(k)} e^{-\mu kt} t^{k-1}. \qquad 80.5$$

where k is a positive integer. It corresponds to the case in which, starting with Poisson-distributed arrivals, the service accepts units numbered 0, k, 2k, 3k, . . .

If k → ∞, we find once again the uniform distribution (constant intervals).* If k = 1, we find the exponential distribution.

We have:

$$p_1 = \Psi p_0, \qquad \text{où} \qquad \Psi = \lambda/\mu, \qquad 80.6$$

$$(1 + \Psi)p_n = p_{n+1} + \Psi p_{n-k}, \qquad 80.7$$

$$\bar{n} = \frac{k\Psi(1+k)}{2(1-k\Psi)}, \qquad 80.8$$

$$\bar{t}_f = \frac{\bar{n}}{\mu} = \frac{k\Psi(1+k)}{2\mu(1-k\Psi)}. \qquad 80.9$$

3. One station: Entries, Poisson; service, arbitrary distribution; R lines with ordered, but not absolute, priorities.

Consider R waiting lines, with the order of priority 1, 2, . . . , R, but without absolute priority; in other words, service for a unit in line k is not interrupted to serve a new unit appearing in line h, even though h < k.

---

*This is not paradoxical; the standard deviation decreases as k increases.

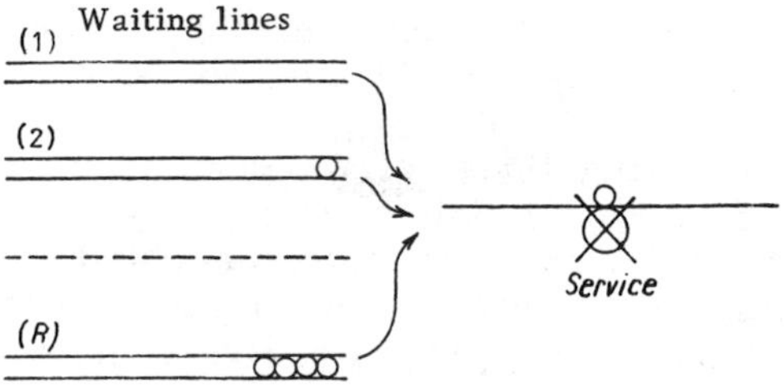

Fig. 80.1.

Let λ_k and μ_k be the average rates for line k, i.e., of the line having priority k. We set:

$$\Psi_k = \frac{\lambda_k}{\mu_k}. \tag{80.10}$$

When the service is free to accept a unit, it scans the units waiting and chooses the next unit from the highest-priority line in which there is a unit waiting.

We set:

$$\lambda = \sum_{i=1}^{R} \lambda_i \tag{80.11}$$

Let $\bar{t}_k$ be the waiting time in the k-priority line; we then have:

$$\bar{t}_k = \frac{\bar{t}_0}{(1-\Psi_{k-1})(1-\Psi_k)}, \tag{80.12}$$

where

$$\bar{t}_0 = \frac{1}{2}\lambda\int_0^\infty t^2 dF(t), \tag{80.13}$$

with:

$$F(t) = \frac{1}{\lambda}\sum_{i=1}^{R} \lambda_i F_i(t); \tag{80.14}$$

the function $F_k(t)$ represents the accumulated service-time cumulative distribution of service time for the k-priority line.

This gives us:

$$\bar{n} = \sum_{i=1}^{R} \lambda_i \bar{t}_i. \tag{80.15}$$

4. One station: entries, Poisson; service, exponential; 2 lines with one having absolute priority over the other.

Consider two waiting lines, of which one (No. 1) has priority over the other. If a type-1 unit arrives, a type-2 unit is shunted out of service to make room for the type-1 unit, while the type-2 unit returns to its line to await the later completion of its servicing.

Let λ_1, λ_2, μ_1, μ_2, be the rates of arrivals and service. We set:

$$\Psi_1 = \lambda_1/\mu_1 \tag{80.16}$$

$$\Psi_2 = \lambda_2/\mu_2 . \tag{80.17}$$

We must have:

$$\Psi_1 + \Psi_2 < 1 . \tag{80.18}$$

Use the function:

$$F(z, u) = \sum_{n_1=0}^{\infty} \sum_{n_2=0}^{\infty} p_{(n_1)(n_2)} z^{n_2} u^{n_1} \tag{80.19}$$

where $p_{(n_1)(n_2)}$ is the probability that n_1 priority-1 units are in the system at the same time as n_2 priority-2 units.

We find that:

$$F(z, u) = \left(\frac{1-\Psi_1-\Psi_2}{1-a-z\Psi_2}\right)\left(\frac{1-a}{1-a u}\right), \tag{80.20}$$

where:

$$a = \frac{1}{2\mu_1}\left[\mu_1+\lambda_1+\lambda_2(1-z)-\sqrt{[(\mu_1+\lambda_1+\lambda_2(1-z)]^2-4\lambda_1\mu_1}\right] \tag{80.21}$$

This gives us:

$$\bar{n}_1 = \left.\frac{\partial F}{\partial u}\right]_{z=u=1} = \frac{\Psi_1}{1-\Psi_1}, \tag{80.22}$$

$$\bar{n}_2 = \left.\frac{\partial F}{\partial z}\right]_{z=u=1} = \Psi_2 \left[\frac{1+\bar{n}_1 \Psi_1/\Psi_2}{1-\Psi_1-\Psi_2}\right] \tag{80.23}$$

$$\left.\frac{\partial^k}{\partial u^k} F\right]_{\substack{z=1\\u=0}} = \Psi_1^{n_1} (1-\Psi_1), \tag{80.24}$$

$$p_{(n_1)(n_2)} = \frac{1}{n_1!\,n_2!} \left.\frac{\partial^{n_1+n_2}}{\partial z^{n_2}\partial u^{n_1}} F\right]_{z=u=0} \tag{80.25}$$

5. One station: entries, Poisson; service, exponential; customers impatient and chosen at random from the line.

Consider the case in which the customers are impatient and leave the waiting line when their waiting time has exceeded T_0; furthermore, customers are chosen at random from the waiting line, instead of the first in line being served first (no queue discipline).

We have:

$$p_n = \frac{\lambda^n p_0}{\mu} \prod_{k=1}^{n} (1 - e^{-\mu T_0/k}) \qquad 80.26$$

6. One station: entries at regular intervals; service, exponential.

If the time interval between one arrival and the next is δ, that is, if:

$$\lambda = 1/\delta : \qquad 80.27$$

we have:

$$p_n = p_0(1 - p_0)^n, \qquad 80.28$$

where p_0 is the root of the transcendental equation:

$$e^{-\mu p_0 \delta} = 1 - p_0, \qquad 80.29$$

$$\bar{n} = \sum_{n=1}^{\infty} n p_n = \frac{1 - p_0}{p_0}, \qquad 80.30$$

$$\bar{t}_f = \frac{\bar{n}}{\lambda} = \frac{1}{\lambda} \frac{1 - p_0}{p_0}. \qquad 80.31$$

7. Two systems cascaded: entries, Poisson; service, exponential.

Now consider two systems in series as shown in Fig. 80.2.

Let: λ, μ_1 be the rates in the first system,
λ, μ_2 be the rates in the second system.*

---

*One should not be misled into thinking that the exits from the first system occur at a rate of μ_1; they occur at the rate of entry, λ. It is the service intervals that have a mean of $1/\mu$, and we should not forget that the service can be idle. In a permanent system, the exit rate is equal to the entry rate.

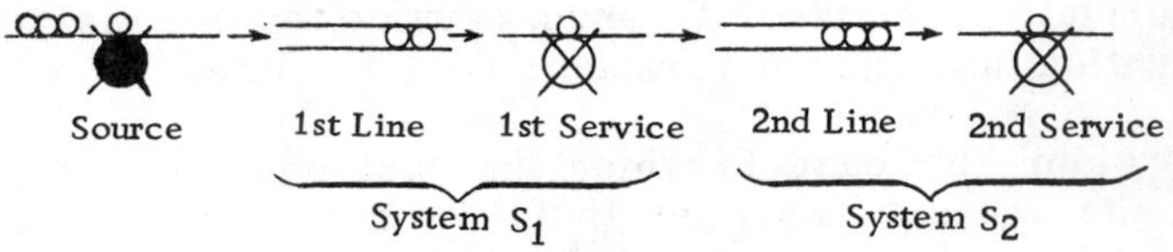

Fig. 80.2.

After going through Fig. 80.2 the first service, the units take their places in line for the second service.

We set:

$$\Psi_1 = \frac{\lambda}{\mu_1} < 1, \quad \Psi_2 = \frac{\lambda}{\mu_2} < 1. \qquad 80.32$$

First case: unlimited number of units.

		System 1	System 2	Total system
80.33 80.34 80.35	Mean number of units in the line.	$\bar{\nu}_1 = \frac{\Psi_1^2}{1-\Psi_1}$	$\bar{\nu}_2 = \frac{\Psi_2^2}{1-\Psi_2}$	$\bar{\nu} = \bar{\nu}_1 + \bar{\nu}_2$ $= \frac{\Psi_1^2}{1-\Psi_1} + \frac{\Psi_2^2}{1-\Psi_2}$
80.36 80.37 80.38	Mean number of units in the system.	$\bar{n}_1 = \frac{\Psi_1}{1-\Psi_1}$	$\bar{n}_2 = \frac{\Psi_2}{1-\Psi_2}$	$\bar{n} = \bar{n}_1 + \bar{n}_2$ $= \frac{\Psi_1}{1-\Psi_1} + \frac{\Psi_2}{1-\Psi_2}$
80.39 80·40 80.41	Mean number of units being serviced.	$\bar{j}_1 = \Psi_1$	$\bar{j}_2 = \Psi_2$	$\bar{j} = \bar{j}_1 + \bar{j}_2$ $= \Psi_1 + \Psi_2$

The probability that there are n_1 customers in system S_1, and n_2 customers in system S_2 is:

$$p(n_1, n_2) = \Psi_1^{n_1}(1 - \Psi_1) . \Psi_2^{n_2}(1 - \Psi_2). \qquad 80.42$$

The probability that there are n customers in one of the systems is:

$$p_1(n) = \Psi_1^n(1 - \Psi) \qquad 80.43$$

$$p_2(n) = \Psi_2^n(1 - \Psi). \qquad 80.44$$

Second case: limited number of units.

This will give us a diagram such as that shown in Fig. 80.3.

Let $p(n_1, n_2)$ be the probability that there are n_1 units in systems S_1, and n_2 units in System S_2:

$$p(n_1, n_2) = \Psi_1^{\,n_1} \Psi_2^{\,n_2} p(0, 0) \qquad 80.45$$

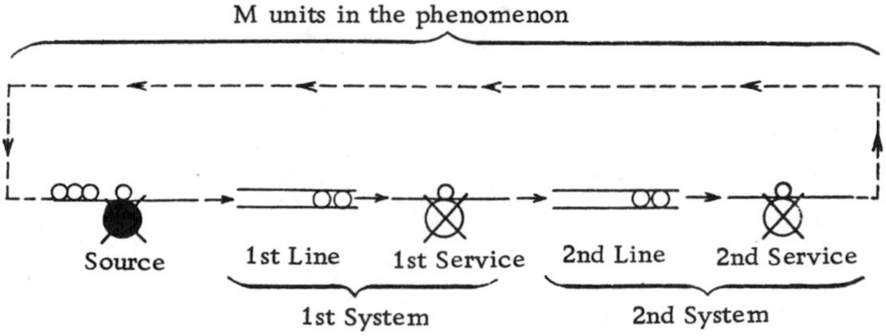

Fig. 80.3.

where:

$$p(0,0) = \frac{(\Psi_1 - \Psi_2)(1 - \Psi_1)(1 - \Psi_2)}{\Psi_1 - \Psi_2 - (\Psi_1^{M+2} - \Psi_2^{M+2}) + \Psi_1 \Psi_2 (\Psi_1^{M+1} - \Psi_2^{M+1})}. \qquad 80.46$$

$$\bar{n} = \frac{p(0,0)}{\Psi_1 - \Psi_2}\left[\frac{\Psi_1^2\{1 - (M+1)\Psi_1^M + M\Psi_1^{M+1}\}}{(1-\Psi_1)^2} - \frac{\Psi_2^2\{1 - (M+1)\Psi_2^M + M\Psi_2^{M+1}\}}{(1-\Psi_2)^2}\right], \qquad 80.47$$

$$\bar{\nu} = \left[\frac{\Psi_2^2(1 + \Psi_1)[1 - M\Psi_1^{M-1} + (M-1)\Psi_1^M]}{(1 - \Psi_1)^2} + \frac{\Psi_1^2(1 + \Psi^2)[1 - M\Psi_2^{M-1} + (M-1)\Psi_2^M]}{(1 - \Psi_2)^2}\right] +$$

$$\frac{\Psi_1\Psi_2 p(0,0)}{\Psi_1 - \Psi_2}\left[\frac{1 - (M-1)\Psi_1^{M-2} + (M-2)\Psi_1^{M-1}}{(1 - \Psi_1)^2} - \frac{1 - (M-1)\Psi_2^{M-2} + (M-2)\Psi_2^{M-1}}{(1 - \Psi_2)^2}\right] \qquad 80.48$$

$$\bar{j} = p(0,0)(\Psi_1 + \Psi_2)\frac{[(\Psi_1 + \Psi_2) - (\Psi_1^{M+1} - \Psi_2^{M+1}) + \Psi_1\Psi_2(\Psi_1^M - \Psi_2^M)]}{(1 - \Psi_1)(1 - \Psi_2)(\Psi_1 - \Psi_2)}. \qquad 80.49$$

8. Several stations in parallel: entries, Poisson; service, constant duration.

The S stations are assumed to have the same rate of service, μ. Setting:

$$\underline{\underline{\Psi}} = \lambda/\mu, \qquad 80.50$$

we have:

$$p(>0) = 1 - e^{-K} \qquad 80.51$$

where

$$K = \sum_{i=1}^{\infty} \frac{e^{-i\Psi}}{i} \sum_{j=Si}^{\infty} \frac{(i\Psi)^j}{j!} \qquad 80.52$$

$$\bar{t}_f = \sum_{i=1}^{\infty} e^{-i\Psi} \left[\sum_{j=Si}^{\infty} \frac{(i\Psi)^j}{j!} - \frac{S}{\Psi} \sum_{j=Si+1}^{\infty} \frac{(j\Psi)^j}{j!} \right] \qquad 80.53$$

(Crommelin's formulas).

For very large values of S:

$$p(>0) = 1 - p(=0) = \frac{1}{1-\Psi} \frac{(\Psi/S)e^{(S-\Psi)}}{\sqrt{2\pi S}} \qquad 80.54$$

(Pollaczek's formula).

General approximate formula:

$$\bar{t}_f = p(>0) \frac{1}{\mu(S-\Psi)} \cdot \frac{S}{S+1} \cdot \frac{1-(\Psi/S)^{S-1}}{1-(\Psi/S)^S}, \qquad 80.55$$

where

$$p(>0) = \frac{\dfrac{\Psi^S e^{-\Psi}}{S!} \cdot \dfrac{S}{S-\Psi}}{1-\left(e^{-\Psi} \sum\limits_{n=S}^{\infty} \dfrac{\Psi^n}{n!}\right) + \dfrac{\Psi^S e^{-\Psi}}{S!} \cdot \dfrac{S}{S-\Psi}}. \qquad 80.56$$

(Molina's formulas)

Fig. 80.4 is a graph of formula (80.55).

9. Several stations: entries, Poisson; service, exponential; R lines with ordered, but not absolute, priorities.

This is case 3 (Fig. 80.1) generalized for S stations. We assume here the same exponential distribution with rate μ for all stations providing the service. If:

$$\lambda = \sum_{i=1}^{R} \qquad 80.57$$

and

$$\Psi = \lambda/\mu . \tag{80.58}$$

we have:

$$\bar{t}_k = \frac{a/S\mu}{\left(1 - \frac{1}{S\mu}\sum_{i=1}^{k-1}\lambda_i\right)\left(1 - \frac{1}{S\mu}\sum_{i=1}^{k}\lambda_i\right)}, \tag{80.59}$$

where

$$a = \frac{\Psi^S}{S!\left(1 - \frac{\Psi}{S}\right)\left[\sum_{j=0}^{S-1}\frac{\Psi^j}{j!} + \sum_{j=S}^{\infty}\frac{\Psi^j}{S!S^{j-S}}\right]} \tag{80.60}$$

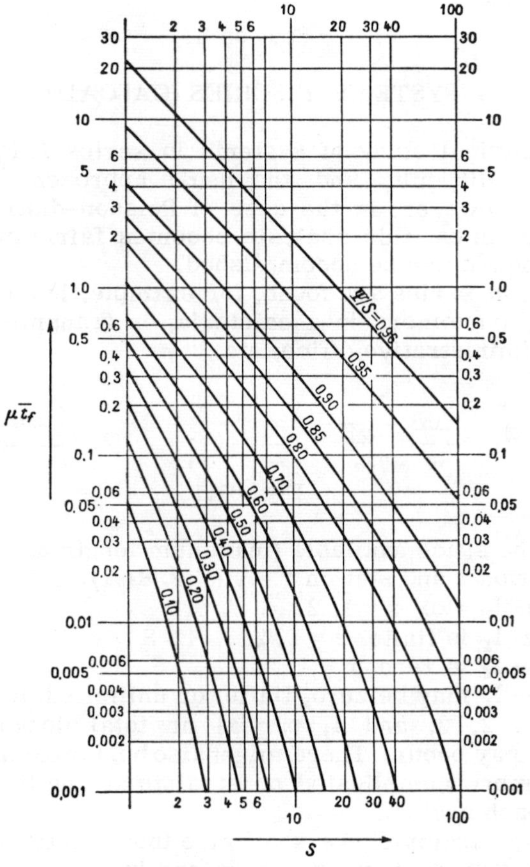

Fig. 80.4.

10. Infinite number of stations: entries, Poisson; service, exponential.

First case: unlimited number of units.

This question has already been dealt with in Section 75; see the description for (75.4). The rate of service is proportional to the number of units; this is to say that there is an infinite number of stations.

Second case: limited number of units.

This problem has already been dealt with in Section 79: Waiting Line with Binomial Distribution.

Section 81

SYSTEMS IN SERIES (CASCADE)

The analytical study of systems in series (Fig. 81.1) is generally very difficult, and the usual approach is therefore by simulation. However, in the case of Poisson-distributed arrivals and service times, this analysis becomes fairly simple; we shall show here how it can be accomplished.

Systems in series are found, for example, in an assembly line, in handling customers in a cafeteria, in transmission of papers within an administrative office, etc.

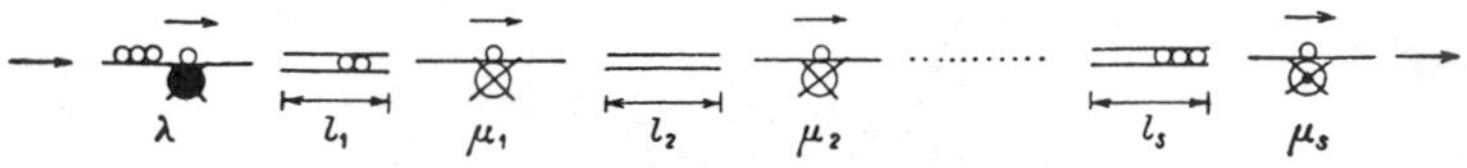

Fig. 81.1.

Call l_r the space available (maximum length of the waiting line) between station r and station r - 1 (Fig. 81.1).

1st case: $l_r = \infty$; $r = 1, 2, \ldots, S$.

2nd case: l_r is finite, $r = 1, 2, \ldots, S$

3rd case: l_r is zero, $r = 1, 2, \ldots, S$.

4th case: l_r may be zero, finite, or unlimited, depending on r.

In cases 2, 3, and 4, partial or total blockage (bottleneck) phenomena may occur. There might also be, for example, blockages caused by more complicated constraints among the conditions for entry into each system.

By way of example, we shall give the analytical description of a case with two stations in series and in which no waiting line is allowed before either of the two stations ($l_1 = 0$, $l_2 = 0$). (See ref.

D-1 (Bibliography) p. 34.) Let λ be the arrival rate, and μ the service rate in stations 1 and 2.

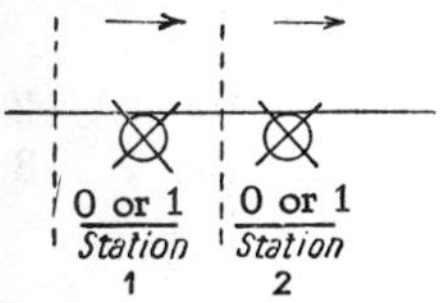

Fig. 81.2

Arrivals and service will be assumed to be Poisson-distributed, and the study will be made in the permanent system.

We shall call:

p_{00} the probability that both stations are empty;

p_{10} the probability that station 1 is busy, and 2 is empty;

p_{01} the probability that station 1 is empty, and 2 is busy;

p_{11} the probability that both stations are busy;

p_{b_1} the probability that station 2 is busy and station 1 blocked as a consequence.

We have:

$$p_{00} + p_{10} + p_{01} + p_{11} + p_{b1} = 1. \qquad 81.1$$

The equations of state will be:

$$\lambda p_{00} - \mu p_{01} = 0, \qquad 81.2$$

$$(\lambda + \mu) p_{01} - \mu p_{10} - \mu p_{b1} = 0, \qquad 81.3$$

$$\lambda p_{00} + \mu p_{11} - \mu p_{10} = 0, \qquad 81.4$$

$$\mu p_{11} - \mu p_{b1} = 0. \qquad 81.5$$

$$\lambda p_{01} - 2\mu p_{11} = 0. \qquad 81.6$$

From these we derive:

$$K_0 = 3\,\Psi^2 + 4\,\Psi + 2 \text{ where } \Psi = \frac{\lambda}{\mu}; \qquad 81.7$$

$$p_{00} = \frac{2}{K_0}, \quad p_{01} = \frac{2\Psi}{K_0}, \quad p_{10} = \frac{\Psi^2 + 2\Psi}{K_0}, \quad p_{11} = p_{b1} = \frac{\Psi^2}{K_0}. \qquad \begin{cases} 81.8 \\ 81.9 \\ 81.10 \\ 81.11 \end{cases}$$

The average number of units in the pair of two stations is:

$$\bar{n} = 1(p_{01} + p_{10}) + 2(p_{11} + p_{b1}) = \frac{5\Psi^2 + 4\Psi}{K_0} = \begin{cases} 2\Psi - \frac{3}{2}\Psi^2 & (\Psi \ll 1) \\ 1 & (\Psi = 1) \\ \frac{5}{3} - \frac{32}{45\Psi} & (\Psi \gg 1). \end{cases} \qquad 81.12$$

The average number of stations busy is:

$$\bar{j}=1(p_{01}+p_{10}+p_{b1})+2p_{11}=\frac{4\Psi^2+4\Psi}{K_0}=\begin{cases}2\Psi-2\Psi^2 & (\Psi \ll 1)\\ \frac{8}{9} & (\Psi = 1)\\ \frac{4}{3}-\frac{4}{9\Psi} & (\Psi \gg 1).\end{cases} \quad 81.13$$

The probability that a customer arrives at station 1 and cannot be served is:

$$p_{\text{refusal}}=p_{10}+p_{11}+p_{b1}=\frac{3\Psi^2+2\Psi}{K_0}=\begin{cases}\Psi-\frac{1}{2}\Psi^2 & (\Psi \ll 1)\\ \frac{5}{9} & (\Psi = 1)\\ 1-\frac{2}{3\Psi} & (\Psi \gg 1).\end{cases} \quad 81.14$$

Obviously, two stations linked in series in this way are less efficient than two stations separated by a waiting line, because of the possibility of a bottleneck.

In the work cited above (ref. D-1), Professor Morse also gives an example identical with the foregoing, but in which we have $l_1 = 0$, $l_2 = 1$ (a waiting line no longer than one unit is permissible between the two stations). The probabilities to consider then are:

$$p_{00},\ p_{01},\ p_{02},\ p_{10},\ p_{11},\ p_{12},\ p_{b2}. \quad 81.15$$

This gives us, if we set $K_1 = 4\Psi^3 + 8\Psi^2 + 9\Psi + 4$:

$$p_{00}=\frac{\Psi+4}{K_1},\ p_{01}=\frac{\Psi^2+4\Psi}{K_1},\ p_{02}=\frac{2\Psi^2}{K_1},\ p_{10}=\frac{\Psi^3+3\Psi^2+4\Psi}{K_1},$$
$$p_{11}=\frac{\Psi^3+2\Psi^2}{K_1},\qquad p_{12}=p_{b2}=\frac{\Psi^3}{K_1}. \quad \text{81.16–81.21}$$

$$\bar{n}=\frac{9\Psi^3+12\Psi^2+8\Psi}{K_1}=\begin{cases}2\Psi & (\Psi \ll 1)\\ \frac{29}{25} & (\Psi = 1)\\ \frac{9}{4} & (\Psi \gg 1)\end{cases} \quad 81.22$$

$$\bar{j}=\frac{6\Psi^3+10\Psi^2+8\Psi}{K_1}=\begin{cases}2\Psi & (\Psi \ll 1)\\ \frac{24}{25}, & (\Psi = 1)\\ \frac{3}{2} & (\Psi \gg 1)\end{cases} \quad 81.23$$

$$p_{\text{refusal}} = \frac{4\Psi^3 + 5\Psi^2 + 4\Psi}{K_1} = \begin{cases} \Psi - \Psi^2 & (\Psi \ll 1) \\ \dfrac{13}{25} & (\Psi = 1) \\ 1 - \dfrac{3}{4\Psi} & (\Psi \gg 1). \end{cases} \qquad 81.24$$

The reader can generalize this situation by imagining a waiting line that must not exceed a given number of units between stations.

Chapter **9**

Analytical study of inventory problems

Section 82

INTRODUCTION

The analysis of inventory problems in general is rather complicated and involves a large number of models. We shall limit our discussion here to a few of the most well-known models. Specifically, we shall set forth an almost general procedure for computing the optimum of the economic function for inventory problems involving discrete values. Certain problems stated in Chapter IV will be taken up again and studied for the case of continuous values. We shall examine a group of problems not dealt with at all in Part One, referring to cases where there may or may not be linear constraints; in the analysis we shall point out clearly the difficulties involved in the solution of such problems. Lastly, we shall develop an example of a linear program involving production and inventories.

Section 83

PROPORTIONAL COST PROBLEMS

1. Analysis of the third case.—2. Study of the third case when demand is a continuous random variable.—3. General analytical expression for mathematical expectation.—4. Example.—5. Numerical example.—6. Analysis of the fourth case.—7. Study of the fourth case when demand is a continuous random variable.

1. Analysis of the third case.

We shall demonstrate the method of calculating the minimum of (35.48). We write, successively:

$$\Gamma(s) = c_1 \sum_{r=0}^{s} (s - r)\,p(r) + c_2 \sum_{r=s+1}^{\infty} (r - s)\,p(r),$$

$$\Gamma(s+1) = c_1 \sum_{r=0}^{s+1} (s + 1 - r)\,p(r) + c_2 \sum_{r=s+2}^{\infty} (r - s - 1)\,p(r). \qquad 83.1$$

$$= c_1 \sum_{r=0}^{s} (s+1-r)p(r) + c_1[(s+1)-(s+1)]p(s+1)$$

$$+ c_2 \sum_{r=s+1}^{\infty} (r-s-1)\,p(r) - c_2\,[(s+1)-(s+1)]\,p(s+1) \qquad 83.2$$

$$= c_1 \sum_{r=0}^{s} (s-r)p(r) + c_1 \sum_{r=0}^{s} p(r) + c_2 \sum_{r=s+1}^{\infty} (r-s)p(r) - c_2 \sum_{r=s+1}^{\infty} p(r).$$

But:

$$\sum_{r=0}^{\infty} p(r) = 1, \qquad 83.3$$

hence:

$$\sum_{r=s+1}^{\infty} p(r) = 1 - \sum_{r=0}^{s} p(r). \qquad 83.4$$

Therefore we have:

$$\Gamma(s+1) = c_1 \sum_{r=0}^{s} (s - r)\,p(r) + c_2 \sum_{r=s+1}^{\infty} (r - s)\,p(r)$$

$$+ c_1 \sum_{r=0}^{s} p(r) - c_2 + c_2 \sum_{r=0}^{s} p(r) \qquad 83.5$$

$$= \Gamma(s) + (c_1 + c_2)\,p(r \leqslant s) - c_2,$$

where $p(r \leq s)$ is the probability of a demand less than or equal to s.

In the same way, we obtain:

$$\Gamma(s-1) = \Gamma(s) - (c_1 + c_2)\,p(r \leqslant s - 1) + c_2. \qquad 83.6$$

Suppose, now, that s_0 is such that:

$$\Gamma(s_0 - 1) > \Gamma(s_0) < \Gamma(s_0 + 1); \qquad 83.7$$

i.e. that s_0 is the stock which minimizes $\Gamma(s)$.

From equations (83.5) and (83.6) we then derive:

$$\Gamma(s+1) - \Gamma(s) > 0, \quad \text{or} \quad (c_1 + c_2)\,p(r \leqslant s) - c_2 > 0, \qquad 83.8 \quad 83.9$$

$$\Gamma(s-1) - \Gamma(s) > 0, \quad \text{or} \quad -(c_1 + c_2)\,p(r \leqslant s - 1) + c_2 > 0; \qquad 83.10 \quad 83.11$$

or again:

$$p(r \leq s-1) < \frac{c_2}{c_1+c_2} < p(r \leq s). \qquad 83.12$$

Thus, if we set:

$$\varrho = \frac{c_2}{c_1+c_2}; \qquad 83.13$$

we find precisely (35.50).

2. Study of the third case when demand is a continuous random variable.

In this case, the distribution p(r) being replaced by the probability density f(r), we have:

$$\Gamma(s) = c_1 \int_0^s (s-r) f(r) \mathrm{d}r + c_2 \int_s^\infty (r-s) f(r) \mathrm{d}r. \qquad 83.14$$

To find the minimum of $\Gamma(s)$, we determine its derivative. For this purpose, let us recall that the derivative of the integral:

$$g(m) = \int_{k_1(m)}^{k_2(m)} \varphi(m, x)\, \mathrm{d}x \qquad 83.15$$

is given by:

$$\frac{\mathrm{d}g}{\mathrm{d}m} = \int_{k_1(m)}^{k_2(m)} \frac{\partial \varphi(m,x)}{\partial m} \mathrm{d}x + \varphi[m, k_2(m)] \frac{\mathrm{d}k_2}{\mathrm{d}m} - \varphi[m, k_1(m)] \frac{\mathrm{d}k_1}{\mathrm{d}m} \qquad 83.16$$

Using this classical formula for taking the derivative under the integral sign, we obtain:

$$\begin{aligned} \frac{\mathrm{d}\Gamma}{\mathrm{d}s} &= c_1 \int_0^s f(r)\, \mathrm{d}r - c_2 \int_s^\infty f(r)\, \mathrm{d}r \\ &= c_1 F(s) - c_2 [1 - F(s)] \qquad 83.17 \\ &= (c_1 + c_2) F(s) - c_2, \end{aligned}$$

where:

$$F(s) = \int_0^s f(r)\, \mathrm{d}r = p(r \leq s). \qquad 83.18$$

Setting the derivative (83.17) equal to zero, we obtain:

$$p(r \leq s) = \frac{c_2}{c_1+c_2} = \varrho. \qquad 83.19$$

It is easy to prove that the value $s = s_0$ corresponding to (83.19) is actually a minimum:

$$\left.\frac{d^2\Gamma}{ds^2}\right|_{s=s_0} = c_1 f(s_0) + c_2 f(s_0) = (c_1 + c_2) f(s_0). \qquad 83.20$$

Since $c_1 + c_2$ is not zero and $f(s)$ is greater than 0, we then have:

$$\left.\frac{d^2\Gamma}{ds^2}\right|_{s=s_0} \geqslant 0. \qquad 83.21$$

If the unequality holds, s_0 corresponds to the minimum. If the equality holds, then $f(s_0) = 0$. But, by hypothesis, $f(r)$ is a non-negative continuous function; therefore, if $f(s_0) = 0$, then $f(s)$ is minimum for $s = s_0$, which is zero. It follows that $\Gamma(s)$ is minimum for $s = s_0$. Relation (83.19) therefore does yield a minimum; it corresponds, for the continuous case, to relation (83.12) in the case where r varies by integral values.

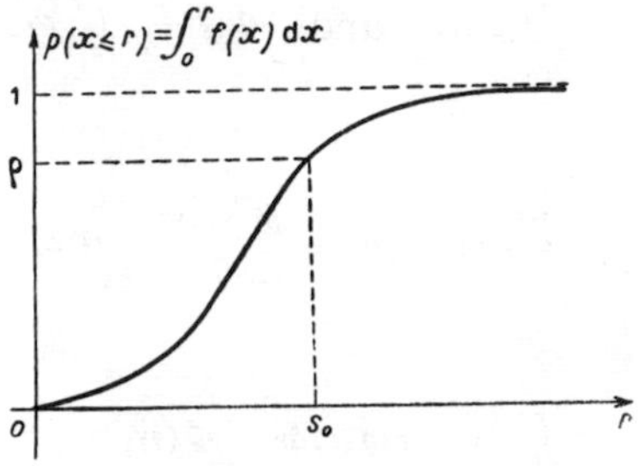

Fig. 83.1

Now let us consider the distribution $p(x \leq r)$ (Fig. 83.1). Given a shortage rate ρ, the optimum inventory level is obtained immediately, as shown in Fig. 83.1. This method is also valid for a discrete distribution.

3. General analytical expression for mathematical expectation.

Recalling the theorem of composition (Borel's theorem), let us use the Carson-Laplace transformation:

$$g(p) = p \int_0^\infty h(t)\, e^{-pt}\, dt \qquad h(t) = 0 \text{ for } t < 0. \qquad 83.22$$
$$= \mathcal{L}\, h(t)$$

This theorem is written as follows:

$$g_1(p) = \mathcal{L} h_1(t) \quad , \quad g_2(p) = \mathcal{L} h_2(t) \; ; \qquad \begin{matrix} 83.23 \\ 83.24 \end{matrix}$$

then:

$$\frac{g_1(p).g_2(p)}{p} = \mathscr{L}\int_0^t h_1(t-u)\,h_2(u)\mathrm{d}u = \mathscr{L}\int_0^t h_2(t-u)h_1(u)\mathrm{d}u. \qquad 83.25$$

Using the variable s in place of t, and the variable θ in place of p (so as not to confuse p with a probability), we write:

$$g(\theta) = \theta\int_0^\infty h(s)e^{-\theta s}\,\mathrm{d}s. \qquad 83.26$$

Using this theorem for the integral:

$$\int_0^s (s-r)f(r)\mathrm{d}r, \qquad 83.27$$

we obtain:

$$\mathscr{L}\int_0^s (s-r)f(r)\mathrm{d}r = \frac{\theta^{-1}.\mathscr{L}f(s)}{\theta} = \frac{1}{\theta^2}\mathscr{L}f(s) \qquad 83.28$$

If

$$F(s) = \int_0^s f(u)\mathrm{d}u \quad \text{and} \quad \Phi(s) = \int_0^s F(u)\mathrm{d}u \qquad \begin{matrix}83.29\\83.30\end{matrix}$$

then:

$$\mathscr{L}\int_0^s (s-r)\,f(r)\mathrm{d}r = \frac{\mathscr{L}F(s)}{\theta} = \mathscr{L}\Phi(s) \qquad 83.31$$

Thus:

$$\int_0^s (s-r)f(r)\mathrm{d}r = \Phi(s), \qquad 83.32$$

where:

$$\Phi(s) = \int_0^s \mathrm{d}\mu\int_0^\mu f(\lambda)\,\mathrm{d}\lambda\ ; \qquad 83.33$$

$\Phi(s)$ is the primitive taken over 0 to s of the primitive of f(s) taken over 0 to s. Now let us return to the expression for $\Gamma(s)$ given in (83.14):

$$\begin{aligned}\Gamma(s) &= c_1\int_0^s (s-r)\,f(r)\,\mathrm{d}r + c_2\int_0^\infty (r-s)\,f(r)\,\mathrm{d}r\\ &= c_1\int_0^s (s-r)f(r)\mathrm{d}r + c_2\int_0^\infty (r-s)f(r)\mathrm{d}r - c_2\int_0^s (r-s)f(r)\mathrm{d}r\\ &= (c_1+c_2)\int_0^s (s-r)\,f(r)\,\mathrm{d}r - c_2\int_0^\infty (s-r)\,f(r)\,\mathrm{d}r \qquad 83.34\\ &= (c_1+c_2)\int_0^s (s-r)f(r)\mathrm{d}r - c_2 s\int_0^\infty (r)\mathrm{d}r + c_2 r\int_0^\infty (r)\mathrm{d}r\\ &= (c_1+c_2)\,\Phi\,(s) - c_2\,(s-\bar{r}).\end{aligned}$$

4. Example.

Assume that the probability density function f(r) has the form:

$$f(r) = \lambda e^{-\lambda r}; \qquad 83.35$$

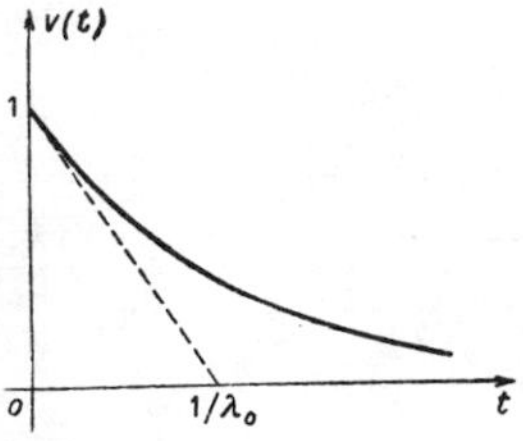

Fig. 83.2

(See Fig. 83.2.) Then:

$$F(r) = \int_0^r \lambda e^{-\lambda x}\,dx = 1 - e^{-\lambda r} \qquad 83.36$$

$$\Phi(r) = r - \frac{1}{\lambda}[1 - e^{-\lambda r}], \qquad 83.37$$

$$\begin{aligned}\Gamma(s) &= (c_1 + c_2)\left[s - \frac{1}{\lambda}(1 - e^{-\lambda s})\right] - c_2\left[s - \frac{1}{\lambda}\right] \\ &= c_1\left(s - \frac{1}{\lambda}\right) + \frac{c_1 + c_2}{\lambda}e^{-\lambda s},\end{aligned} \qquad 83.38$$

and

$$\Gamma'(s) = c_1 - (c_1 + c_2)e^{-\lambda s} \qquad 83.39$$

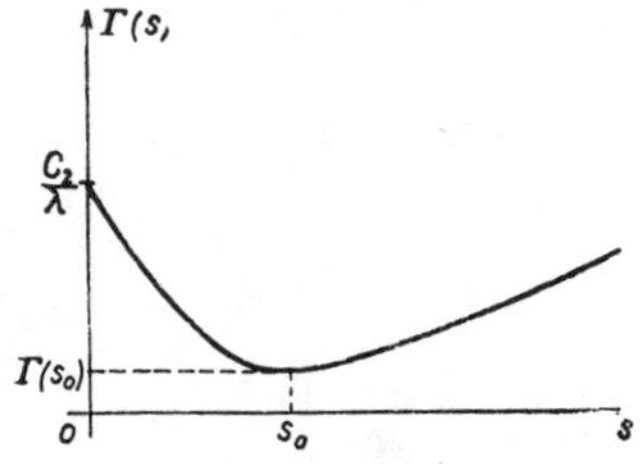

Fig. 83.3

This derived value is cancelled for:

$$\varrho = \frac{c_2}{c_1 + c_2} = 1 - e^{-\lambda s}, \qquad 83.40$$

or

$$s_0 = -\frac{1}{\lambda}\log(1 - \varrho), \qquad 83.41$$

and

$$\Gamma(s_0) = -\frac{c_1}{\lambda}\log(1 - \varrho) = \frac{c_1}{\lambda}\log\left(1 + \frac{c_2}{c_1}\right). \qquad 83.42$$

Curve $\Gamma(s)$ is represented in Fig. 83.3.

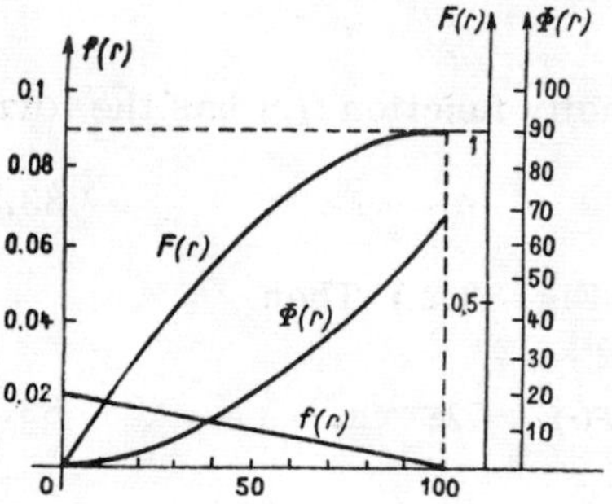

Fig. 83.4

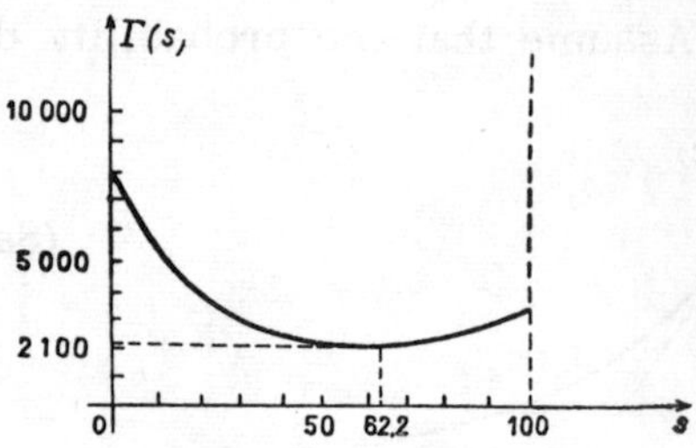

Fig. 83.5

5. Numerical example.

Let:

$$c_1 = 50 \text{ and } c_2 = 300,$$

the probability density being given by:

$$f(r) = 0.02\left(1 - \frac{r}{100}\right). \qquad 83.43$$

(Fig. 83.4)
We have:

$$F(r) = 0.02\left(r - \frac{r^2}{200}\right), \qquad 83.44$$

and

$$\Phi(r) = 0.01\left(r^2 - \frac{r^3}{300}\right), \qquad 83.45$$

the curves in Fig. 83.5.
Let us calculate $\bar{r}$:

$$\bar{r} = \int_0^{100} 0.02 r\left(1 - \frac{r}{100}\right) \mathrm{d}r = \frac{100}{3}. \qquad 83.46$$

Hence, we have:

$$\begin{aligned} \Gamma(s) &= (c_1 + c_2)\,\Phi(s) - c_2(s - \bar{r}) \\ &= 3.5\left(s^2 - \frac{s^3}{300}\right) - 300\left(s - \frac{100}{3}\right) \\ &= -\frac{3.5}{300}s^3 + 3.5\,s^2 - 300\,s + 10\,000. \end{aligned} \qquad 83.47$$

$\Gamma(s)$ is a minimum for $\Gamma'(s) = 0$ (we can also use 83.19), or:

$$7s^2 - 1{,}400\,s + 60{,}000 = 0, \qquad 83.48$$

from which:

$$s = 100 \pm 37.8. \qquad 83.49$$

Only the root less than 100 is meaningful and corresponds to a minimum.

Therefore,

$$s_0 = 62.2. \qquad 83.50$$

Corresponding to this value of s is the minimum:

$$\Gamma(62.2) = 2{,}070. \qquad 83.51$$

6. Analysis of the fourth case.

We can compute the minimum of (35.76) as follows. We write, successively:

$$\Gamma(s) = c_s \sum_{r=0}^{s}\left(s - \frac{r}{2}\right)p(r) + c_s \sum_{r=s+1}^{\infty} \frac{1}{2}\frac{s^2}{r}p(r) + c_p \sum_{r=s+1}^{\infty} \frac{1}{2}\frac{(r-s)^2}{r}p(r), \qquad 83.52$$

$$\Gamma(s+1) = c_s \sum_{r=0}^{s+1}\left(s+1-\frac{r}{2}\right)p(r) + c_s \sum_{r=s+2}^{\infty} \frac{1}{2}\frac{(s+1)^2}{r}p(r) +$$

$$c_p \sum_{r=s+2}^{\infty} \frac{1}{2}\frac{(r-s-1)^2}{r}p(r). \qquad 83.53$$

But we can write:

$$c_s \sum_{r=0}^{s+1}\left(s+1-\frac{r}{2}\right)p(r) = c_s \sum_{r=0}^{s}\left(s+1-\frac{r}{2}\right)p(r) +$$

$$c_s\left(s+1-\frac{s+1}{2}\right)p(s+1)$$

$$= c_s \sum_{r=0}^{s}\left(s-\frac{r}{2}\right)p(r) + c_s \sum_{r=0}^{s} p(r) + c_s \frac{s+1}{2}p(s+1). \qquad 83.54$$

In the same manner:

$$c_s \sum_{r=s+2}^{\infty} \frac{(s+1)^2}{2r}p(r) = c_s \sum_{r=s+1}^{\infty} \frac{s^2}{2r}p(r) +$$

$$c_s\, s \sum_{r=s+1}^{\infty} \frac{p(r)}{r} + \frac{c_s}{2} \sum_{r=s+1}^{\infty} \frac{p(r)}{r} - \frac{c_s(s+1)}{2}p(s+1), \qquad 83.55$$

and

$$c_p \sum_{r=s+2}^{\infty} \frac{(r-s-1)^2}{2r} p(r) =$$

$$c_p \sum_{r=s+1}^{\infty} \frac{(r-s)^2}{2r} p(r) - c_p \sum_{r=s+1}^{\infty} p(r) + c_p s \sum_{r=s+1}^{\infty} \frac{p(r)}{r} + \tfrac{1}{2} c_p \sum_{r=s+1}^{\infty} \frac{p(r)}{r}. \quad 83.56$$

Substituting (83.54)—(83.56) into (83.52) and (83.53), we obtain:

$$\Gamma(s+1) = \Gamma(s) + (c_s + c_p)\left[p(r \leqslant s) + (s+\tfrac{1}{2}) \sum_{r=s+1}^{\infty} \frac{p(r)}{r}\right] - c_p \quad 83.57$$

Let us set:

$$L(s) = p(r \leqslant s) + (s + \tfrac{1}{2}) \sum_{r=s+1}^{\infty} \frac{p(r)}{r}, \quad 83.58$$

then equation (83.57) will be written:

$$\Gamma(s+1) = \Gamma(s) + (c_s + c_p)\, L(s) - c_p. \quad 83.59$$

In the same manner:

$$\Gamma(s-1) = \Gamma(s) - (c_s + c_p)\, L(s-1) + c_p. \quad 83.60$$

Let us show that L(s) is a function that never decreases with s:

$$\begin{aligned} L(s+1) &= p(r \leqslant s+1) + (s+1+\tfrac{1}{2}) \sum_{r=s+2}^{\infty} \frac{p(r)}{r} \\ &= p(r \leqslant s) + p(s+1) + (s+\tfrac{1}{2}) \sum_{r=s+1}^{\infty} \frac{p(r)}{r} \\ &\quad - \frac{s+\frac{1}{2}}{s+1} p(s+1) + \sum_{r=s+1}^{\infty} \frac{p(r)}{r} - \frac{p(s+1)}{s+1} \\ &= L(s) - \tfrac{1}{2} \frac{p(s+1)}{s+1} + \sum_{r=s+1}^{\infty} \frac{p(r)}{r}; \end{aligned} \quad 83.61$$

that is:

$$L(s+1) = L(s) + \sum_{r=s+2}^{\infty} \frac{p(r)}{r} + \tfrac{1}{2} \frac{p(s+1)}{s+1}. \quad 83.62$$

But since:

$$\sum_{r=s+2}^{\infty} \frac{p(r)}{r} + \tfrac{1}{2} \frac{p(s+1)}{s+1} \geqslant 0,$$

we have:

$$L(s+1) \geqslant L(s). \tag{83.63}$$

Now we shall consider a value s_0 such that:

$$(c_s + c_p)\,L(s_0) - c_p > 0 \tag{83.64}$$

$$-(c_s + c_p)\,L(s_0 - 1) + c_p > 0. \tag{83.65}$$

For all $s' > s_0$ and $s'' < s_0$, in equations (83.64) and (83.65), respectively, are satisfied. Thus:

$$\Gamma(s'') > \Gamma(s_0) \quad \text{if} \quad s'' < s_0 \tag{83.66}$$

$$\Gamma(s') > \Gamma(s_0) \quad \text{if} \quad s' > s_0. \tag{83.67}$$

Therefore, the value of s that yields a minimum for Γ is the value, s_0, which satisfies inequalities (83.64) and (83.65), or:

$$L(s_0 - 1) < \varrho < L(s_0) \tag{83.68}$$

where

$$\varrho = \frac{c_p}{c_s + c_p}. \tag{83.69}$$

7. Study of the fourth case when demand is a continuous random variable.

In this case, with the distribution p(r) replaced by the probability density function f(r), we have:

$$\Gamma(s) = c_s \int_0^s \left(s - \frac{r}{2}\right) f(r)\,\mathrm{d}r + c_s \int_s^\infty \frac{s^2}{2r} f(r)\,\mathrm{d}r + c_p \int_s^\infty \frac{(r-s)^2}{2r} f(r)\,\mathrm{d}r. \tag{83.70}$$

Determining the derivative of Γ(s) by means of formula (83.16), we obtain:

$$\begin{aligned}\frac{\mathrm{d}\Gamma}{\mathrm{d}s} &= c_s \int_0^s f(r)\,\mathrm{d}r + c \int_s^\infty \frac{s}{r} f(r)\,\mathrm{d}r - c_p \int_s^\infty \frac{r-s}{r} f(r)\,\mathrm{d}r \\ &= (c_s + c_p)\left(\int_0^s f(r)\,\mathrm{d}r + s\int_s^\infty \frac{f(r)}{r}\,\mathrm{d}r\right) - c_p \\ &= (c_s + c_p)\left(F(s) + s\int_s^\infty \frac{f(r)}{r}\,\mathrm{d}r\right) - c_p\end{aligned} \tag{83.71}$$

where

$$F(s) = \int_0^s f(\lambda)\,\mathrm{d}\lambda = p(r \leqslant s). \tag{83.72}$$

The minimum of $\Gamma(s)$ will occur for a value $s = s_0$ such that:

$$\varrho = \frac{c_p}{c_p + c_s} = F(s) + s\int_s^\infty \frac{f(r)}{rs}\,dr. \qquad 83.73$$

Let us set:

$$M(s_0) = F(s_0) + s_0\int_{s_0}^\infty \frac{f(r)}{r}\,dr. \qquad 83.74$$

Condition (83.73) will be written:

$$\varrho = M(s_0). \qquad 83.75$$

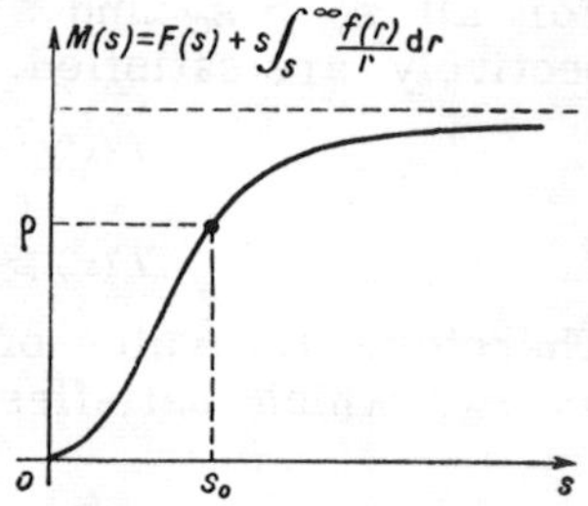

Fig. 83.6

To determine the optimum inventory level, one must first determine the curve M(s), which is done quite easily by graphical numerical calculation methods when f(r) is known.

It is possible, if the Carson-Laplace transformation is used, to obtain a fairly workable expression for computing $\Gamma(s)$. One proceeds as for the third case.

Section 84

FORMULAS FOR THE CONVOLUTIONS OF PROBABILITY DISTRIBUTIONS

Formulas (36.4) can be written in matrix form:

$$\begin{Bmatrix} p_2(0) \\ p_2(1) \\ p_2(2) \\ p_2(3) \\ \vdots \end{Bmatrix} = \begin{bmatrix} p_1(0) & 0 & 0 & 0 & \cdots \\ p_1(1) & p_1(0) & 0 & 0 & \cdots \\ p_1(2) & p_1(1) & p_1(0) & 0 & \cdots \\ p_1(3) & p_1(2) & p_1(1) & p_1(0) & \cdots \\ \vdots & \vdots & \vdots & \vdots & \ddots \end{bmatrix} \begin{Bmatrix} p_1(0) \\ p_1(1) \\ p_1(2) \\ p_1(3) \\ \vdots \end{Bmatrix} \qquad 84.1$$

Or, in abbreviated form:

$$\{P_2\} = [P_1]\,\{P_1\}. \qquad 84.2$$

In the same manner:

$$\{P_3\} = [P_1]\,\{P_2\} \qquad 84.3$$

and thus:

$$\{P_{n+1}\} = [P_1]\{P_n\} = [P_1]^n \{P_1\}. \qquad 84.4$$

Furthermore:

$$\{P_{n+1}\} = [P_n]\{P_1\}; \qquad 84.5$$

therefore, we have:

$$[P_n] = [P_1]^n. \qquad 84.6$$

This shows us how to calculate the distribution $p_n(r)$, if we know the distribution $p_1(r)$, by means of successive multiplication of the matrices.

To calculate $p_1(r)$ when $p_n(r)$ is known, one starts with equation (84.6) and uses the recurrence formulas that generalize (36.11).

In addition, we may note the formulas:

$$\begin{aligned}\Pr_{T_1+T_2}(r) &= \sum_{k=0}^{r} \Pr_{T_1}(r-k).\Pr_{T_2}(k) = \sum_{k=0}^{r} \Pr_{T_1}(k).\Pr_{T_2}(r-k) \\ &= \Pr_{T_1}(r) * \Pr_{T_2}(r) = \Pr_{T_2}(r) * \Pr_{T_1}(r).\end{aligned} \qquad 84.7$$

and for the case of continuous random variables:

$$\begin{aligned}h_{T_1+T_2}(x) &= \int_0^x h_{T_1}(x-u)\, h_{T_2}(u)\mathrm{d}u = \int_0^x h_{T_1}(u).h_{T_2}(x-u)\mathrm{d}u \\ &= h_{T_1} * h_{T_2} = h_{T_2} * h_{T_1}.\end{aligned} \qquad 84.8$$

$$h_{2T}(x) = \int_0^x h_T(x-u).h(u)\mathrm{d}u = h_T * h_T = (h_T)^{2*} \qquad 84.9$$

These formulas can be generalized as follows:

$$h_{T_1+T_2+\dots+T_n}(x) = h_{T_1} * h_{T_2} * \dots * h_{T_n}, \qquad 84.10$$

$$h_{nT}(x) = \underbrace{h_T * h_T * \quad \dots \quad * h_T}_{n \text{ times}} = [h_T(x)]^{n*} \qquad 84.11$$

Section 85

PROBLEMS INVOLVING NON-PROPORTIONAL COSTS

We shall consider the case in which there are r unit prices depending on quantity, i.e. r - 1 discontinuities.

Let us take:

$$\begin{array}{ll} c_1 & 0 < n < a_1 \\ c_2 & a_1 \leqslant n < a_2 \\ c_3 & a_2 \leqslant n < a_3 \\ \dots\dots & \dots\dots\dots\dots \\ c_r & a_{r-1} \leqslant n < \infty. \end{array} \qquad 85.1$$

We proceed as follows:

1. Calculate n_{r0}. If $n_{r0} \geq a_{r-1}$, the economic quantity is $\Gamma_r(n_{r0})$.
2. If $n_{r0} < a_{r-1}$, calculate $n_{r-1,0}$. If $n_{r-1,0} \geq a_{r-2}$ (i.e. if $a_{r-2} \leq n_{r-1,0} < a_{r-1}$), compare $\Gamma_{r-1}(n_{r-1,0})$ with $\Gamma_r(a_{r-1})$ to determine which of the quantities $n_{r-1,0}$ and a_{r-1} is the economic quantity.
3. If $n_{r-1,0} < a_{r-2}$, calculate $n_{r-2,0}$. If $n_{r-2,0} \geq a_{r-3}$, compare $\Gamma_{r-2}(n_{r-2,0})$ with $\Gamma_{r-1}(a_{r-2})$ and $\Gamma_r(a_{r-1})$ to determine economic quantity corresponding to the smallest value of Γ.
4. If $n_{r-2,0} < a_{r-3}$, calculate $n_{r-3,0}$. If $n_{r-3,0} \geq a_{r-4}$, then compare $\Gamma_{r-3}(n_{r-3,0})$ with $\Gamma_{r-2}(a_{r-3})$, $\Gamma_{r-1}(a_{r-2})$ and $\Gamma_r(a_{r-1})$; determine the economic quantity.
5. Continue in this manner up to $n_{r-j,0} \geq a_{r-(j+1)}$, $j = 0, 1, 2, \ldots, r-1$, and then compare $\Gamma_{r-j}(n_{r-j,0})$ with

$$\Gamma_{r-j+1}(a_{r-j}), \quad \Gamma_{r-j+2}(a_{r-j+1}), \ldots, \Gamma_r(a_{r-1}),$$

select the economic quantity.

The procedure will require r steps at the most.

Section 86

INVENTORIES OF SEVERAL PRODUCTS

1. General explanation.—2. Numerical example.

Now let us consider the case in which the economic function of an inventory is related to several products, each distinct from the others.

1. General explanation.

We return to the model studied in Section 35 (first case). This time, however, we shall assume that we have p different types of items. We set:

c_i = carrying cost per piece per unit of time for type i;
γ_i = setup cost per lot or order for type i;
N_i = total number of pieces of type i;
n_i = number of pieces in a lot or order for type i;
T_i = time interval between two lots or orders;
θ = length of the supply period.

Formula (35.5) will become:

$$\Gamma(n_i) = \sum_{i=1}^{p} \left(\frac{N_i \gamma_i}{n_i} + \frac{\theta c_i}{2} n_i \right). \qquad 86.1$$

If we set:

$$\Gamma_i(n_i) = \frac{N_i \gamma_i}{n_i} + \frac{\theta c_i}{2} n_i \qquad i = 1, 2, \ldots, p. \qquad 86.2$$

we will have:

$$\Gamma(n_i) = \sum_{i=1}^{p} \Gamma_i(n_i) \qquad 86.3$$

It is evident that the minimum of $\Gamma(n_i)$ occurs when the p economic functions $\Gamma_i(n_i)$ are minimized, each one separately, since these functions are independent of each other. Thus:

the minimum of $\Gamma(n_i)$ corresponds to $\partial \Gamma_i / \partial n_i = 0 \; (i = 1, 2, .., p,)$ 86.4

which is to say, referring to (35.10):

$$n_{i,0} = \sqrt{2 \frac{N_i}{\theta} \frac{\gamma_i}{c_i}} \qquad i = 1, 2, \ldots, p. \qquad 86.5$$

These formulas are obvious and can be extended to other problems that involve economic quantities.

Another example, which we shall develop more fully in Section 87, will indicate the cases in which such considerations can be of particular interest.

If the cost of inventory is a factor, one has, setting:

c_i = unit cost of raw material and labor for product i;
γ_i = all costs relating to one lot of product i;
n_i = number of units of product i in a lot;
l_i = monthly sales of product i (a known constant);
α = monthly cost of inventory, expressed as a percentage of the average value of the inventory for some period (e.g., one month).

The cost per unit product i is:

$$c_i + \frac{\gamma_i}{n_i} \qquad 86.6$$

and the cost for one month's production is:

$$l_i \left[c_i + \frac{\gamma_i}{n_i} \right]. \qquad 86.7$$

Since demand is at a constant rate, assuming that shortage costs are not considered, the mean inventory level is $1/2\, n_i$ and the inventory cost is:

$$a \frac{n_i}{2}\left[c_i + \frac{\gamma_i}{n_i}\right] \tag{86.8}$$

Finally, the total cost for all products over one time period will be:

$$\begin{aligned} \Gamma(n_i) &= \sum_{i=1}^{p} \left[l_i \left(c_i + \frac{\gamma_i}{n_i}\right) + a \frac{n_i}{2}\left(c_i + \frac{\gamma_i}{n_i}\right)\right] \\ &= \sum_{i=1}^{p} \left(l_i\, c_i + \frac{l_i \gamma_i}{n_i} + \frac{a}{2}\, n_i\, c_i + \frac{a}{2}\, \gamma_i\right). \end{aligned} \tag{86.9}$$

The economic quantities will be:

$$n_{i,o} = \sqrt{\frac{2\, l_i\, \gamma_i}{a\, c_i}} \qquad i = 1, 2, \ldots, p. \tag{86.10}$$

2. Numerical example.

Let there be two products, P_1 and P_2, for which:

$$\begin{aligned} c_1 &= 12{,}000 \text{ fr}, & \gamma_1 &= 100{,}000 \text{ fr}, & l_1 &= 200 & & \\ c_2 &= 7{,}000 \text{ fr}, & \gamma_2 &= 25{,}000 \text{ fr}, & l_2 &= 400 & a &= 0.005. \end{aligned} \tag{86.11}$$

This gives us:

$$n_{10} = 816, \qquad n_{20} = 756. \tag{86.12}$$

If Γ_1 is the total cost of product 1 and Γ_2 that of product 2:

$$\Gamma(n_{10}, n_{20}) = \Gamma_{10} + \Gamma_{20}, \tag{86.13}$$

or, in thousands of francs:

$$\begin{aligned} \Gamma(n_{10}, n_{20}) &= (200)(12) + \frac{(200)\,(100)}{816} + \frac{(0.005)\,(816)\,(12)}{2} \\ &\quad + \frac{(0.005)\,(100)}{2} + (400)\,(7) + \frac{(400)\,(25)}{756} \\ &\quad + \frac{(0.005)\,(756)\,(7)}{2} + \frac{(0.005)\,(25)}{2} \end{aligned} \tag{86.14}$$

$$= 5{,}275.74,$$

that is, 5,275,740 fr.

Note: The considerations set forth in this section would be of little or no interest if they did not serve as an introduction to the next case, in which constraints are brought in.

Section 87

INVENTORY PROBLEMS WITH RESTRICTIONS

1. General explanation.—2. Beckmann's method.—3. Nonlinear constraint.—4. The case of several constraints.

1. General explanation.

We shall now consider an economic function, $\Gamma(n_i)$, representing a total cost of the same type as (86.9). If we assign appropriate values to the coefficients K, A_i and β_1, this economic function will take the general form:

$$\Gamma(n_i) = K + \sum_{i=1}^{p} \left(\frac{A_i}{n_i} + \frac{B_i}{2} n_i \right), \qquad 87.1$$

from which we can derive:

$$n_{i,0} = \sqrt{\frac{2A_i}{B_i}}, \qquad \Gamma_0 = K + \sum_{i=1}^{p} \sqrt{2A_iB_i}. \qquad 87.2$$

$$i = 1, 2, \ldots, p. \qquad 87.3$$

For any value C of $\Gamma(n_i)$, we can imagine surfaces

$$\Gamma(n_1, n_2, \ldots, n_p) = C$$

of n_i values in p-dimensional space. These surfaces will constitute the locus of n_i values yielding the same cost, C. We shall call them Γ = constr. surfaces. In the case of only two variables, they constitute the Γ = constr. lines, as shown in Fig. 87.1. In this figure, the solid lines represent the $\Gamma(n_1, n_2) = C$ curves, and the dotted lines represent their orthogonal trajectories, showing the direction of the minimum variation of Γ in the plane n_1, n_2. The curve $\Gamma(n_i) = \Gamma_0$ is reduced to the stationary point (n_{10}, n_{20}).

Now let us consider a group of m constraints:

$$G_j(n_i) = 0 \qquad i = 1, 2, \ldots, p \quad j = 1, 2, \ldots, m. \qquad 87.4$$

These constraints will be represented by surfaces in the n_i space. If we propose to minimize $\Gamma(n_i)$ and also to satisfy the constraints

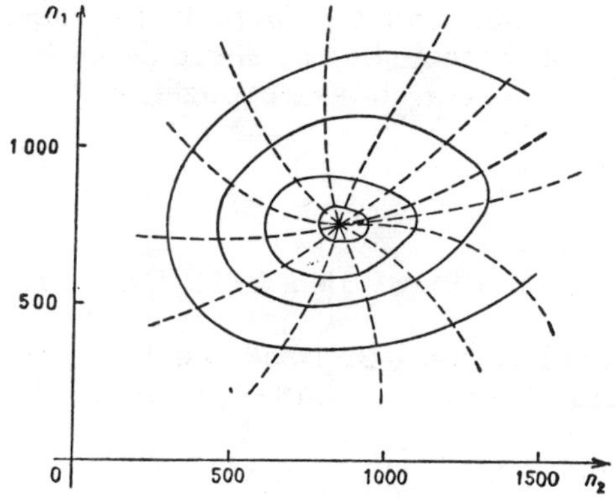

Fig. 87.1.

$G_j(n_i) = 0$, we shall be confronted with a non-linear program:

$$[\text{MIN}]\, \Gamma(n_i) \qquad n_i > 0 \quad i = 1, 2, \ldots, p \qquad 87.5$$

$$G_j(n_i) = 0 \qquad i = 1, 2, \ldots, p;\; j = 1, 2, \ldots, m. \qquad 87.6$$

which can be solved by means of Lagrangian multipliers or a variation of this method.

In cases where the constraints are stated in the form of inequations, we must add to the corresponding G function an appropriate slack variable.

The general method in the case of constraints in the form of equations can be summed up as follows.

Using functions (87.5) and (87.6), we form a new function:

$$W = \Gamma + \sum_{j=1}^{m} \lambda_j G_j = K + \sum_{i=1}^{p} \left(\frac{A_i}{n_i} + \frac{B_i}{2} n_i \right) + \sum_{i=1}^{m} \lambda_j G_j \qquad 87.7$$

where λ_j are Lagrangian multipliers.

The p equations:

$$\frac{\partial W}{\partial n_i} = 0 \qquad i = 1, 2, \ldots, p \qquad 87.8$$

added to the m equations:

$$G_j(n_i) = 0 \qquad j = 1, 2, \ldots, m. \qquad 87.9$$

will give the stationary points which we shall examine to find the one that satisfies the constraints and renders $\Gamma(n_i)$ minimum. Of course, some conditions for the numbers m, p and the functions G_j must be stated if the problem is to be meaningful.

This approach, which requires computation of all the stationary points, must be abandoned as soon as the number of n_i variables becomes very great, because the number of stationary points increases very rapidly with p. It must be admitted that there is no known "step-by-step" method for non-linear programs which would permit finding the optimum by means of an algorithm of the kind used in the simplex method for linear programs.

Let us take a few examples to show the ways in which inventory problems with constraints may appear.

Consider the problem in which the economic function is (86.1), and let us assume that, as in the numerical example (86.11), there are only two variables, n_1 and n_2.

Let us say that stocks of products 1 and 2 are limited by the available space. Let s_1 be the volume occupied by one unit of product 2. If we are concerned with a limitation of the average stock level, rather than the maximum level, we must take the quantities $1/2n_1s_1$ and $1/2n_2s_2$, instead of n_1s_1 and n_2s_2; it all depends on the manner in which the problem is stated.

Let V be the maximum total volume available; the corresponding constraint will then be written:

$$n_1 s_1 + n_2 s_2 \leqslant V. \qquad 87.10$$

This will yield the non-linear program:

$$\Gamma(n_1,n_2) = l_1 c_1 + \frac{l_1 \gamma_1}{n_1} + \frac{a}{2} n_1 c_1 + \frac{a}{2}\gamma_1 + l_2 c_2 + \frac{l_2 \gamma_2}{n_2} + \frac{a}{2} n_2 c_2 + \frac{a}{2}\gamma_2, \qquad 87.11$$

$$n_1 s_1 + n_2 s_2 \leqslant V. \qquad 87.12$$

Taking the numerical values of (86.11), and assuming that:

$$s_1 = 0.5 \text{ m}^3, \; s_2 = 3.5 \text{ m}^3, \; V = 2{,}800 \text{ m}^3 \, ; \qquad 87.13$$

we obtain:

$$\Gamma(n_1,n_2) = 5{,}200.312 + \frac{20{,}000}{n_1} + 0.03 \, n_1 + \frac{10{,}000}{n_2} + 0.0175 \, n_2 \qquad 87.14$$

(in thousands of francs.)

$$0.5 \, n_1 + 3.5 \, n_2 \leqslant 2{,}800. \qquad 87.15$$

To simplify, let us set:

$$F(n_1, n_2) = \frac{20{,}000}{n_1} + 0.03 \, n_1 + \frac{10{,}000}{n_2} + 0.0175 \, n_2 \qquad 87.16$$

$$n_1 + 7 n_2 \leqslant 5{,}600. \qquad 87.17$$

To find the smallest value of fr corresponding to values of n_1 and n_2 that satisfy the constraints imposed, we proceed as follows.

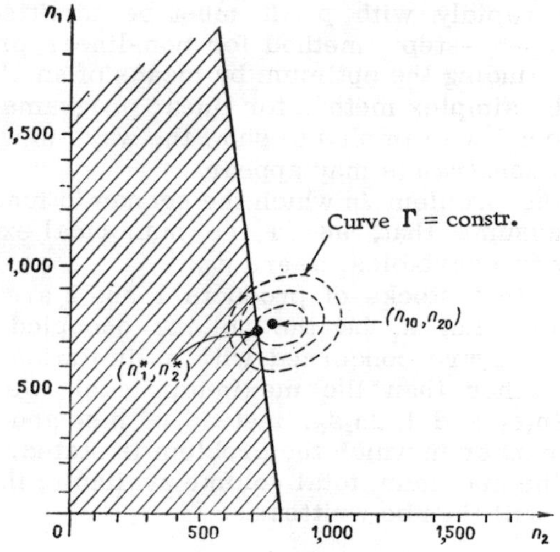

Fig. 87.2.

First, we determine the domain in which the 3 conditions:

$$n_1 \geqslant 0, \quad n_2 \geqslant 0, \quad n_1 + 7n_2 \leqslant 5{,}600, \tag{87.18}$$

are satisfied. It is the shaded region lying in the first quadrant, shown in Fig. 87.2. Next, we determine whether the point (n_{10}, n_{20}) lies in this domain. We can see that it does not:

$$816 + (7)\,(756) = 6{,}108 > 5{,}600, \tag{87.19}$$

otherwise the numbers 816 and 756 would have been the solution.

To find the optimum solution, we shall use the following special method.

2. Beckmann's method.*

Let:

$$F = \sum_{i=1}^{p} \left(\frac{l_i\,\gamma_i}{n_i} + \frac{\alpha c_i\,n_i}{2} \right), \tag{87.20}$$

*See Churchman, Ackoff and Arnoff: "Introduction to Operations Research" (Wiley, 1957); and M. Beckmann: "A Lagrangian Multiplier Rule in Linear Activities Analysis and Some of Its Applications," Cowles Commission Discussion Paper—Economics, No. 2054, 5/11/52 (unpublished).

$$\frac{1}{2}\sum_{i=1}^{p} s_i n_i \leqslant V. \qquad 87.21$$

We wish to find the minimum of F satisfying inequation (87.21), where average inventory levels are involved.

Let us take a quantity λ such that:

$$\begin{aligned} \lambda &< 0 \quad \text{for} \quad V - \tfrac{1}{2}\Sigma s_i n_i = 0 \\ \lambda &= 0 \quad \text{for} \quad V - \tfrac{1}{2}\Sigma s_i n_i > 0; \end{aligned} \qquad 87.22$$

then:

$$\lambda[V - \tfrac{1}{2}\Sigma s_i n_i] \qquad 87.23$$

is identically zero in the domain where the constraint is satisfied, and we can add it to F without changing its value in this domain. This then gives us:

$$F = \sum_{i=1}^{p}\left[\frac{A_i}{n_i} + \tfrac{1}{2} B_i n_i\right] + \lambda[V - \tfrac{1}{2}\sum_{i=1}^{p} s_i n_i] \qquad 87.24$$

where, for simplification, we have set:

$$A_i = l_i \gamma_i, \quad B_i = \alpha c_i \qquad i = 1, 2, \ldots, p, \qquad 87.25$$

Taking the derivative of (87.24), we obtain:

$$\frac{\partial F}{\partial n_i} = -\frac{A_i}{n_i^2} + \frac{B_i}{2} - \frac{\lambda s_i}{2} \qquad i = 1, 2, \ldots, p. \qquad 87.26$$

The stationary points in (87.24) will be given by:

$$\frac{\partial F}{\partial n_i} = 0 \qquad i = 1, 2, \ldots, p;$$

or

$$n_i^* = \sqrt{\frac{2A_i}{B_i - \lambda s_i}} \qquad i = 1, 2, \ldots, p. \qquad 87.27$$

The method consists of computing n_i for $\lambda = 0$, and substituting the values thus found into (87.21). If the inequation is satisfied, we have the solution we are looking for; if it is not, we assign to $(-\lambda)$ increasingly large positive values, until the n_i values obtained yield a difference $V - 1/2\Sigma s_i n_i$ equal to zero. In practice, one constructs a table giving the values of n_i and of $V - 1/2\Sigma s_i n_i$ as a function of λ, and one examines this table to find the values of n_i that satisfy the inequation.

We may note that the quantity $(-\lambda)$ is nothing more nor less than a cost assigned to the volume taken up by one unit of stock. Let us assume that the space for storage is rented at d francs per unit of volume per unit of time (a month, say). The function:

$$\Gamma(n_i) = \sum_{i=1}^{p} \left[l_i c_i + \frac{l_i \gamma_i}{n_i} + \frac{a}{2} n_i c_i + \frac{a}{2} \gamma_i + \frac{d}{2} s_i n_i \right], \tag{87.28}$$

then represents the economic function of the inventory problem; this function is a minimum for:

$$n_i = \sqrt{\frac{2A_i}{B_i + d s_i}}. \tag{87.29}$$

Let us return to the preceding numerical example:

$$\begin{aligned} &c_1 = 12{,}000, \quad \gamma_1 = 100{,}000, \quad l_1 = 200, \quad s_1 = 0.5 \\ &\qquad\qquad\qquad\qquad\qquad\qquad a = 0.005, \; V = 2{,}800. \\ &c_2 = 7{,}000, \quad \gamma_2 = 25{,}000, \quad l_2 = 400, \quad s_2 = 3.5 \end{aligned} \tag{87.30}$$

which gives us:

$$\begin{aligned} A_1 &= l_1 \gamma_1 = 20.10^6, \quad B_1 = a c_1 = 60 \\ A_2 &= l_2 \gamma_2 = 10.10^6, \quad B_2 = a c_2 = 35. \end{aligned} \tag{87.31}$$

From this, we derive the following table:

Table 87.1

$-\lambda$	$-\lambda s_1$	$-\lambda s_2$	n_1^*	n_2^*	$n_1^* + 7n_2^*$	
0	0	0	816	756	6,188	
1	0.5	3.5	813	721	5,860	
2	1	7	810	690	5,640	
						5 600
3	1.5	10.5	806	663	5,447	
5	2.5	17.5	800	617	5,119	
7	3.5	24.5	794	579	4,847	
10	5	35	784	534	4,522	

The correct value of λ is very slightly greater than 2. For $\lambda = 2$, we exceed the available volume by a few cubic meters. Taking $\lambda = 2.1$, we would obtain:

$$n_1^* = 809, \qquad n_2^* = 687. \tag{87.32}$$

The calculating of $\Gamma(n_1^*, n_2^*)$ for $\lambda = 2$ yields:

$$\Gamma(n_1^*, n_2^*) = 5{,}275{,}880 \text{ fr}. \tag{87.33}$$

In the case we are considering, where the available volume is very close to that needed for the (n_{10}, n_{20}) solution (see Fig. 87.2), there is very little difference between $\Gamma(n_{10}, n_{20})$ and $\Gamma(n_1^*, n_2^*)$.

Beckmann's method can be extended to cases in which there are any number of inequations (see below), but the computation then becomes very complicated.

3. Non-linear constraint.

Let us assume that the sole constraint has a non-linear form:

$$\gamma(n_i) \leqslant M \qquad (\text{or} \geqslant). \tag{87.34}$$

Here again, let us use Beckmann's method, introducing the parameter λ given by (87.22), and changing its sign if the inequation has the opposite sense. We write:

$$F = \sum_{i=1}^{p} \left[\frac{A_i}{n_i} + \frac{B_i}{2} n_i\right] + \lambda\,[M - \varphi(n_i)] \tag{87.35}$$

$$\frac{\partial F}{\partial n_i} = -\frac{A_i}{n_i^2} + \frac{B_i}{2} - \lambda \frac{\partial \varphi}{\partial n_i} = 0 \qquad i = 1, 2, \ldots, p. \tag{87.36}$$

In the general case, the system of equations (87.36) is very difficult to solve. Two simple cases, corresponding to important practical cases, can be solved easily:

1. $\varphi(n_i)$ is a linear form in n_i (see above);
2. $\varphi(n_i)$ is a linear form in $1/n_i$.

If φn_i is a linear form in $1/n_i$, we can transform the variables:

$$w_i = \frac{1}{n_i} \qquad i = 1, 2, \ldots, p; \tag{87.37}$$

then, instead of:

$$F = \sum_{i=1}^{p} \left[\frac{A_i}{n_i} + \frac{B_i}{2} n_i\right] \tag{87.38}$$

$$\sum_{i=1}^{p} \frac{e_i}{n_i} \leqslant T \tag{87.39}$$

where e_i are coefficients of $1/n_i$ and T is a constant, we obtain:

$$F = \sum_{i=1}^{p} \left[\frac{B_i}{2w_i} + A_i w_i\right], \tag{87.40}$$

$$\sum_{i=1}^{p} e_i w_i \leqslant T, \qquad 87.41$$

and we have again the case of a form in n_i.

Beckmann's method can also be utilized directly, as in the following example. We shall show, by means of this example, how linear constraints in $1/n_i$ can actually be considered in inventory problems.

Let us return to the expression of total cost (86.9) in the case examined in Section 86. Assume that the means available for the operations of preparing a lot (for example, set-up of machines) are limited, and that the limits cannot be exceeded. This might well occur if there are only a limited number of machine set-up men.

Assume that the time needed to prepare a lot of product i is t_i, and that the total time available per month is T; we then have a constraint:

$$\sum_{i=1}^{p} \frac{e_i}{n_i} \leqslant T \quad \text{où} \quad e_i = l_i t_i \quad i = 1, 2, \ldots, p. \qquad 87.42$$

Thus, finally:

$$F = \sum_{i=1}^{p} \left[\frac{A_i}{n_i} + \frac{B_i}{2} n_i\right] \qquad 87.43$$

$$\sum_{i=1}^{p} \frac{e_i}{n_i} \leqslant T . \qquad 87.44$$

Referring to (87.35) and (87.36), we obtain:

$$\frac{\partial F}{\partial n_i} = -\frac{A_i}{n_i^2} + \frac{B_i}{2} + \lambda \frac{e_i}{n_i^2} = 0 \qquad i = 1, 2, \ldots, p , \qquad 87.45$$

and thus:

$$n_i^* = \sqrt{\frac{2(A_i - \lambda e_i)}{B_i}} \qquad 1 = 1, 2, \ldots, p , \qquad 87.46$$

Let us illustrate this with an example. Take the data of problem (86.11), and assume that:

$$t_1 = 30\text{ h}, \quad t_2 = 10\text{ h}, \quad T = 10\text{ h} \qquad 87.47$$

which gives us:

$$e_1 = 6{,}000, \quad e_2 = 4{,}000. \qquad 87.48$$

The constraint will be written:

$$\frac{6{,}000}{n_1} + \frac{4{,}000}{n_2} \leqslant 10 . \qquad 87.49$$

The equation

$$\frac{6{,}000}{n_1} + \frac{4{,}000}{n_2} = 10 \tag{87.50}$$

is that of a hyperbola which we have shown in Fig. 87.3. It will be noted that the solution (n_{10}, n_{20}) does not satisfy inequation (87.49) and therefore lies outside the shaded area where this inequation is satisfied.

To obtain the optimum solution, we shall construct Table 87.2.

Table 87.2

$-\lambda$	$-\lambda e_1$	$-\lambda e_2$	n_1^*	n_2^*	$\frac{6{,}000}{n_1^*}$	$\frac{4{,}000}{n_2^*}$	$\frac{6{,}000}{n_1^*} + \frac{4{,}000}{n_2^*}$
0	0	0	816	756	7.35	5.29	12.64
200	$1.2\cdot10^6$	$0.8\cdot10^6$	841	785	7.13	5.10	12.23
400	$2.4\cdot10^6$	$1.6\cdot10^6$	864	814	6.95	4.91	11.86
600	$3.6\cdot10^6$	$2.4\cdot10^6$	887	842	6.75	4.75	11.51
800	$4.8\cdot10^6$	$3.2\cdot10^6$	909	868	6.60	4.61	11.21
1000	$6\cdot10^6$	$4\cdot10^6$	931	895	6.44	4.47	10.91
1200	$7.2\cdot10^6$	$4.8\cdot10^6$	953	920	6.30	4.35	10.65
1400	$8.4\cdot10^6$	$5.6\cdot10^6$	973	944	6.17	4.24	10.41
1600	$9.6\cdot10^6$	$6.4\cdot10^6$	993	968	6.04	4.13	10.17
1700	$10.2\cdot10^6$	$6.8\cdot10^6$	1003	980	5.98	4.08	10.06
1750	$10.5\cdot10^6$	$7\cdot10^6$	1009	985	5.95	4.06	10.01
1800	$10.8\cdot10^6$	$7.2\cdot10^6$	1013	991	5.92	4.04	9.96

Thus, the optimum value of $\Gamma(n_1, n_2)$, taking constraint (87.49) into account, occurs for:

$$n_1^* = 1009 \quad \text{et} \quad n_2^* = 985. \tag{87.51}$$

which gives:

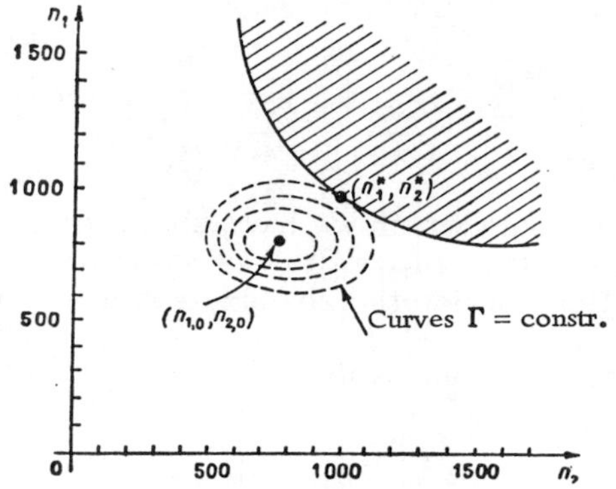

Fig. 87.3.

$$\begin{aligned}\Gamma(1009, 985) &= (200)(12{,}000) + \frac{(200)(100{,}000)}{1{,}009} \\ &+ \tfrac{1}{2}(0.005)(1{,}009)(12{,}000) + \tfrac{1}{2}(0.005)(100{,}000) \\ &+ (400)(7{,}000) + \frac{(400)(25{,}000)}{985} \\ &+ (0.005)(980)(7{,}000) + \tfrac{1}{2}(0.005)(25{,}000) \\ &= 5{,}277{,}810 \text{ fr.}\end{aligned} \qquad 87.52$$

4. Case of several constraints.

Expressions (87.34) and (87.35) can be generalized to cover the case of several constraints.

Let:

$$\varphi_j(n_i) \leqslant M_j \quad (\text{or} \geqslant) \qquad i = 1, 2, \ldots, p \quad j = 1, 2, \ldots, q, \qquad 87.53$$

$$F = \sum_{i=1}^{p} \left[\frac{A_i}{n_i} + \frac{B_i}{2} n_i\right] + \sum_{j=1}^{q} \lambda_j [M_j - \varphi_j(n_i)], \qquad 87.54$$

$$\frac{\partial F}{\partial n_i} = -\frac{A_i}{n_i^2} + \frac{B_i}{2} - \sum_{j=1}^{q} \lambda_j \frac{\partial \varphi_j}{\partial n_i} \qquad i = 1, 2, \ldots, p, \qquad 87.55$$

where all the λ_j are such that:

$$\lambda_j < 0 \qquad \text{for} \qquad M_j - \varphi_j(n_i) = 0 \qquad 87.56$$

$$\lambda = 0 \qquad \text{for} \qquad M_j - \varphi_j(n_i) > 0 \quad (\text{or} < 0 \text{ inverting } 87.56) \quad j = 1, 2, \ldots, q. \qquad 87.57$$

The application of Beckmann's method, in the general case, requires some fairly lengthy numerical computations, and hence a rather powerful electronic computer is almost a necessity.

We should like to point out here that the constraints are not necessarily compatible. In other words, several conditions may not be realizable simultaneously. (Figs. 87.4 and 87.5).

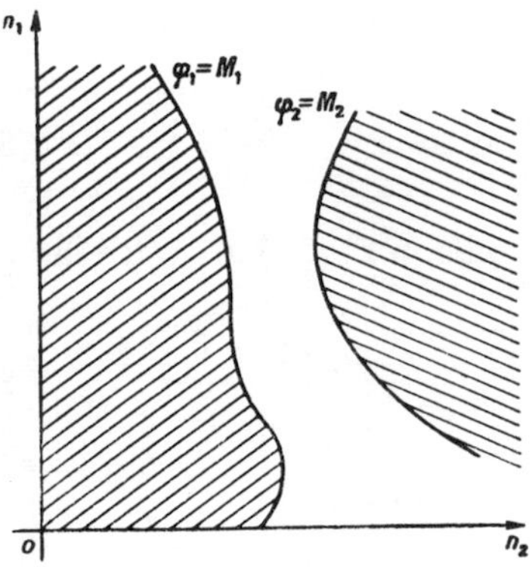

Fig. 87.4.

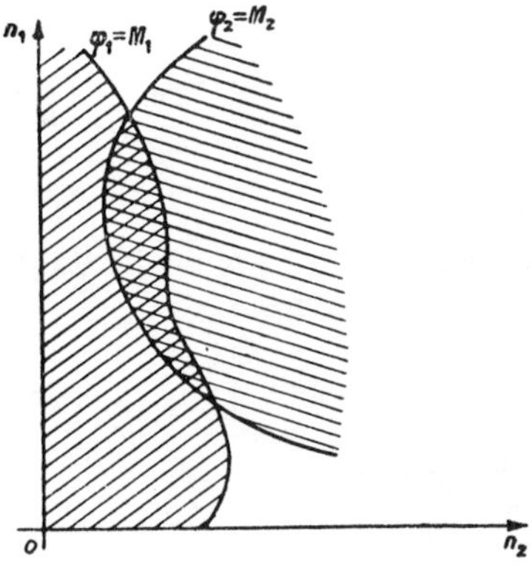

Fig. 87.5.

In a case where there are two constraints, one of them linear in n_i and the other linear in $1/n_i$, we obtain an interesting formula:

$$F = \sum_{i=1}^{p} \left[\frac{A_i}{n_i} + \frac{B_i}{2} n_i\right], \qquad 87.58$$

$$\frac{1}{2} \sum_{i=1}^{p} s_i n_i \leqslant V, \qquad 87.59$$

$$\sum_{i=1}^{p} \frac{e_i}{n_i} \leqslant T. \qquad 87.60$$

Introducing the parameters λ and μ, we have:

$$F = \sum_{i=1}^{p} \left[\frac{A_i}{n_i} + \frac{B_i}{2} n_i\right] + \lambda \left[V - \frac{1}{2} \sum_{i=1}^{p} s_i n_i\right] + \mu \left[T - \sum_{i=1}^{p} \frac{e_i}{n_i}\right], \qquad 87.61$$

$$\frac{\partial F}{\partial n_i} = -\frac{A_i}{n_i^2} + \frac{B_i}{2} - \frac{\lambda}{2} s_i + \mu \frac{e_i}{n_i^2} = 0 \quad i = 1, 2, \ldots, p. \qquad 87.62$$

$$n_i^* = \sqrt{\frac{2(A_i - \mu e_i)}{B_i - \lambda s_i}} \quad i = 1, 2, \ldots, p. \qquad 87.63$$

Let us make this concrete by taking the example we used in the case of a single linear constraint in n_i or $1/n_i$, using the following numerical data:

$$\begin{array}{llll} c_1 = 10{,}000, & \gamma_1 = 100{,}000, & l_1 = 200 & a = 0.025 \\ c_2 = 8{,}000, & \gamma_2 = 245{,}000, & l_2 = 800 & , \end{array} \qquad 87.64$$

from which we obtain:

$$n_{10} = \sqrt{\frac{2 I_1 \gamma_1}{a\, c_1}} = 400, \qquad n_{20} = \sqrt{\frac{2 I_2 \gamma_2}{a\, c_2}} = 1{,}400 \qquad \begin{matrix} 87.65 \\ 87.66 \end{matrix}$$

Let the constraints be:

$$n_1 + n_2 \leqslant 1{,}500 \qquad 87.67$$

$$\frac{8{,}000}{n_1} + \frac{4{,}000}{n_2} \leqslant 20\,. \qquad 87.68$$

The problem as posed is diagrammed in Fig. 87.6. With the notation used as before:

$$A_1 = 2 \cdot 10^7\ , \qquad B_1 = 250, \qquad s_1 = 1, \qquad e_1 = 8{,}000, \qquad 87.69$$

which gives us:

$$A_2 = 1.96 \cdot 10^8, \qquad B_2 = 200, \qquad s_2 = 1, \qquad e_2 = 4{,}000$$

$$n_1^* = \sqrt{\frac{2(2 \cdot 10^7 - 8 \cdot 10^3 \mu)}{250 - \lambda}} = 126.5 \sqrt{\frac{2{,}500 - \mu}{250 - \lambda}} \qquad 87.70$$

$$n_2^* = \sqrt{\frac{2(1.96 \cdot 10^8 - 4 \cdot 10^3 \mu)}{200 - \lambda}} = 89.4 \sqrt{\frac{49{,}000 - \mu}{200 - \lambda}}. \qquad 87.71$$

Using (87.70) and (87.71) we construct Table 87.3 for different values of λ and μ. With these values, we construct the curves μ = const. and λ = const. (Fig. 87.6). Next, we interpolate for the values of λ and μ that surround the first point of contact with the area in which the conditions are satisfied.

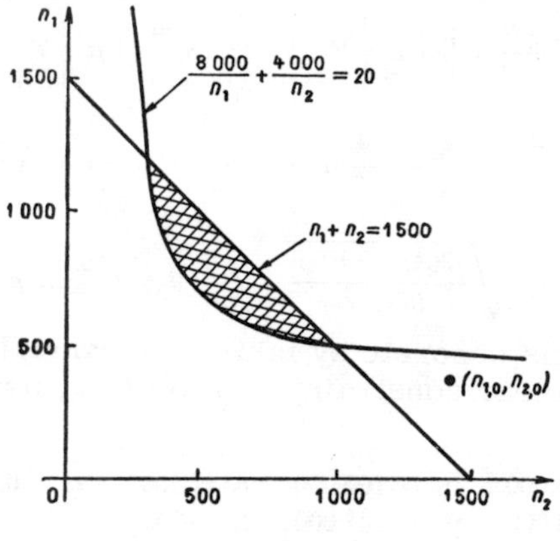

Fig. 87.6.

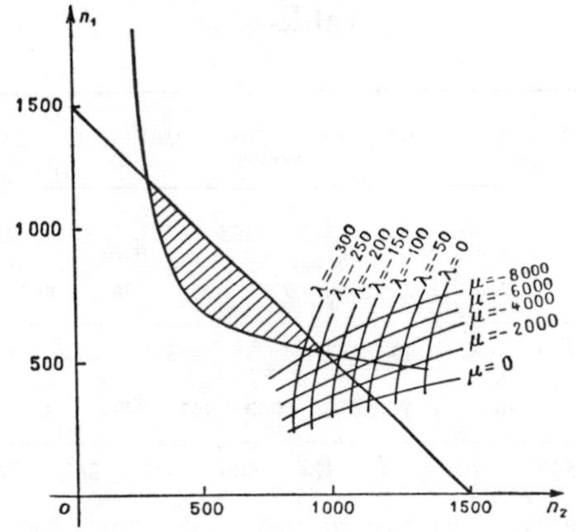

Fig. 87.7.

Another method, which is a bit longer but more acceptable in the long run if some degree of precision is demanded, consists of starting at point $P_0(n_{10}, n_{20})$ and plotting curves of constant total cost:

$$\Gamma(n_1, n_2) = K \qquad 87.72$$

For a certain value of K, a Γ = const. curve "penetrates" the area that defines the values of n_1 and n_2 for which the conditions are satisfied. We interpolate, if necessary, between two values of K.

With the data of (87.64), we obtain:

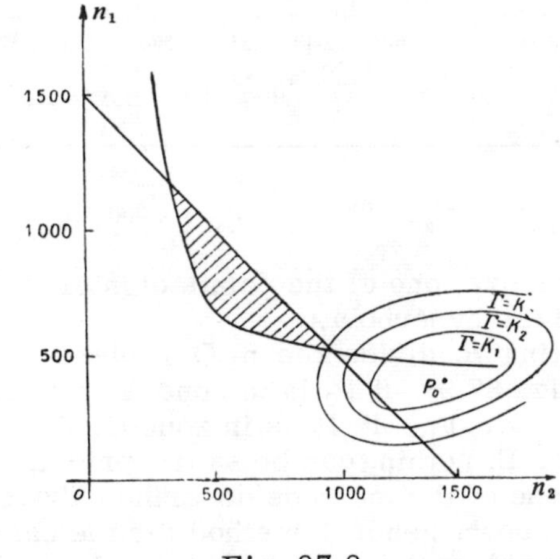

Fig. 87.8.

Table 87.3

$-\mu$ \ $-\lambda$	0	50	100	150	200	250	300	350	400	450
0	400 / 1400	365 / 1250	338 / 1142	315 / 1058	298 / 970	283 / 933	270 / 884	258 / 843	248 / 808	239 / 776
1000	474 / 1413	432 / 1265	400 / 1155	374 / 1070	353 / 1000	335 / 942	319 / 894	305 / 852	294 / 816	283 / 784
2000	537 / 1428	490 / 1276	454 / 1167	424 / 1080	400 / 1009	379 / 952	362 / 903	346 / 860	333 / 824	321 / 792
3000	593 / 1440	542 / 1290	502 / 1176	469 / 1089	442 / 1020	419 / 960	400 / 911	383 / 870	367 / 833	355 / 799
4000	645 / 1455	590 / 1304	545 / 1188	510 / 1101	480 / 1029	456 / 971	435 / 920	416 / 877	400 / 840	385 / 806
5000	693 / 1470	632 / 1315	585 / 1200	546 / 1110	516 / 1039	490 / 980	467 / 928	447 / 885	426 / 847	414 / 815
6000	738 / 1484	673 / 1327	624 / 1211	583 / 1120	550 / 1048	522 / 990	497 / 938	477 / 894	457 / 856	441 / 822
7000	780 / 1496	711 / 1340	658 / 1222	616 / 1131	582 / 1057	552 / 997	526 / 946	504 / 902	484 / 864	466 / 829
8000	820 / 1508	748 / 1350	684 / 1230	649 / 1140	611 / 1067	580 / 1003	553 / 955	529 / 910	508 / 870	491 / 836

$$n^*_{10} = 500, \qquad n^*_{20} = 1{,}000, \qquad (87.73)$$

which is, furthermore, one of the points of intersection between the straight line and the hyperbola.

It is interesting to divide the $n_1 O n_2$ plane into 5 zones, A, B, C, D, and E (Fig. 87.9). If P_0 is in zone A or B, the optimum will correspond to P^*_a or P^*_b. If P_0 is in zone C, P_0 is the optimum. If P_0 is in zone D or E, nothing can be said a priori, and we must find the optimum by one of the methods described above.

There is no known general method for the case in which there are 3 or more variables. Some work has been done which has greatly

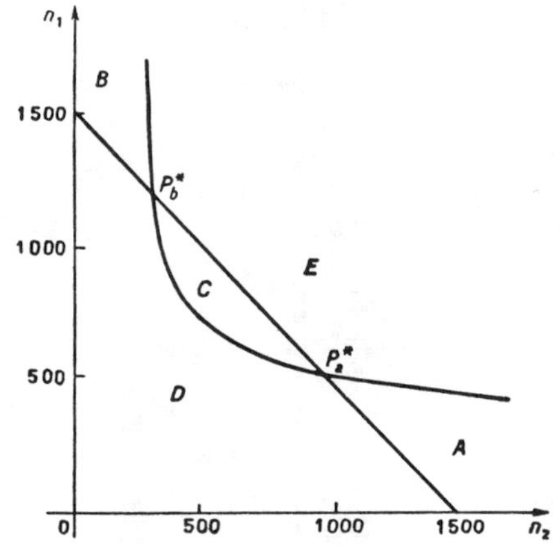

Fig. 87.9.

advanced the study of this problem.* The trial-and-error method we have used is hardly suitable when the number of variables and constraints increases.

Section 88

LINEAR PROGRAMMING OF A PRODUCTION AND INVENTORY PROBLEM

1. General explanation.—2. Case in which set-up cost is neglected.—3. Vazsonyi's "step-by-step" planning method.—4. Example.—5. Introduction of the set-up time.—6. Condition necessary for the proposed program to have a solution.

1. General explanation.

Let D(t) be the function representing the cumulative demand for a product (the solid curve in Fig. 88.1 gives an example extended over 6 months). Call P′(t) the function representing the cumulative production (the —·—·—·— curve), and P″(t) another cumulative production function (the —· ·—· ·—· ·—· ·— curve). The corresponding

*See, for example: Crockett, Bronfenbrenner and Chernoff: "Gradient Method of Maximization," Pac. Jour. Math., 5, 1955; and Kuhn and Tucker: "Non-linear Programming," Second Berkeley Symposium on Mathematical Statistics and Probability (U. of Calif. Press, 1951).

stock levels for policy P′ and policy P″ are shown in Figs. 88.2 and 88.3.

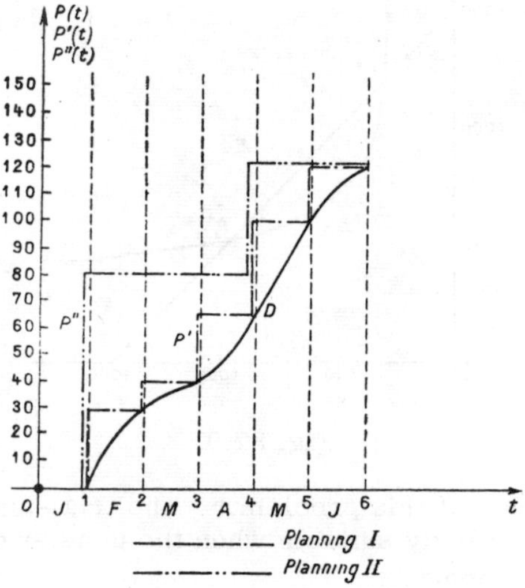

Fig. 88.1.

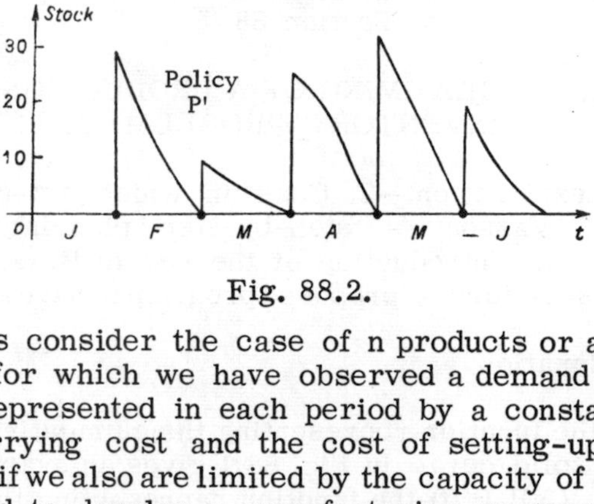

Fig. 88.2.

Now let us consider the case of n products or articles A_i (i = 1, 2, ..., n) for which we have observed a demand $d_i(t)$ which we assume is represented in each period by a constant level. If we know the carrying cost and the cost of setting-up production of a new lot, and if we also are limited by the capacity of our machines, we are forced to develop n manufacturing programs, $P_i(t)$, such that the total cost is minimum. This problem constitutes an extension of the problem of finding the economic quantities when the situation is cyclical. To start with, we shall neglect the set-up cost.

2. Case in which set-up cost is neglected.

Let T be the interval during which the inventory is studied. We break down this interval T into r equal periods of duration π_j

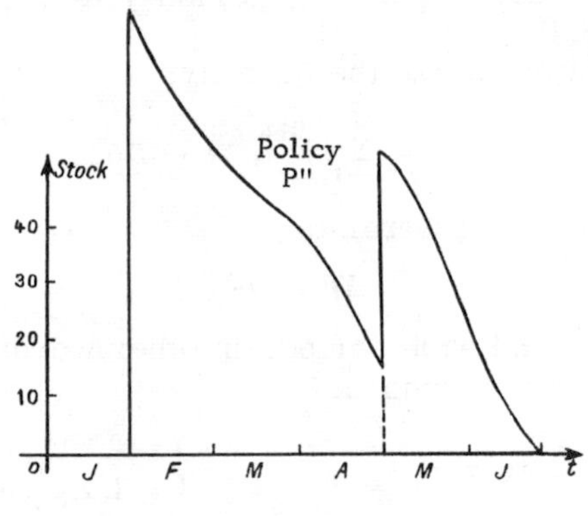

Fig. 88.3.

($j = 1, 2, \dots, r$). Let there be n articles A_i ($i = 1, 2, \dots, n$), and m machines M_k ($k = 1, 2, \dots, m$). Let us denote:

d_i^j = demand for product i in period j,
τ_{ki} = hours devoted by machine k to product i,
h_k^j = capacity (in hours) of machine k during period j,
x_i^j = output of product i during period j,
c_i = carrying cost for one unit of A_i during one period;

$$D_i^j = \sum_{\alpha=1}^{j} d_i^\alpha \quad \text{the cumulative demand for the first j periods;} \qquad 88.1$$

$$X_i^j = \sum_{\alpha=1} x_i^\alpha \quad \text{the cumulative production of product i for the first j periods.} \qquad 88.2$$

Furthermore, we shall adopt the hypothesis that the articles of any one period are all manufactured during that period, and that the order in which the M_k machines are used is immaterial.

In Fig. 88.4, we have plotted the cumulative demand in solid lines and the cumulative production in dashed lines. Then, the

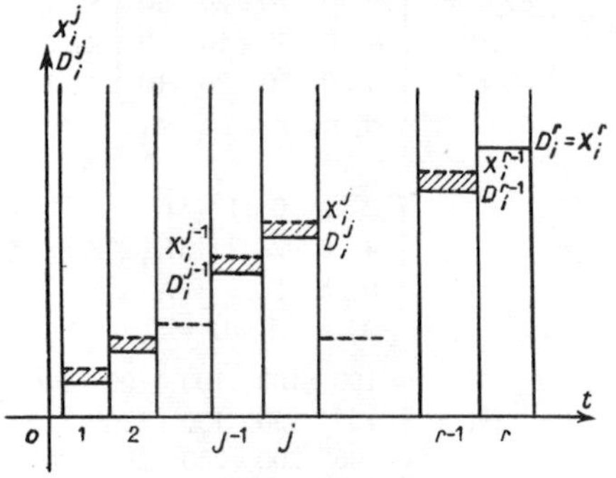

Fig. 88.4.

inventory of products A_i during period j is $(X_i^r - X_i^r)$ (the shaded areas in Fig. 88.4).

We must then minimize the quantity:

$$C = \sum_{i=1}^{n} \sum_{j=1}^{r} c_i(X_i^j - D_i^j), \qquad 88.3$$

taking account of the constraints:

$$X_i^j \geqslant D_i^j , \qquad 88.4$$

for each product and each period. In other words, we must always satisfy demand. Furthermore:

$$\sum_{i=1}^{n} \tau_{ki} x_i^j \leqslant h_k^j \qquad \begin{array}{l} j = 1, 2, \ldots, r \\ k = 1, 2, \ldots, m, \end{array} \qquad 88.5$$

a condition expressing the fact that the time needed on each machine to manufacture x_i^j products A_i (i = 1, 2, ..., n) is less than or equal to the time available on those machines. Conditions (88.3)—(88.5) can be expressed as a function of x_i^j; we must find:

$$[\text{MIN}]\ C = \sum_{i=1}^{n} \sum_{j=1}^{r} \sum_{\alpha=1}^{j} c_i\,(x_i^\alpha - d_i^\alpha), \qquad 88.6$$

$$\sum_{\alpha=1}^{j} (x_i^\alpha - d_i^\alpha) \geqslant 0 \qquad \begin{array}{l} i = 1, 2, \ldots, n \\ j = 1, 2, \ldots, r, \end{array} \qquad 88.7$$

$$\sum_{i=1}^{n} \tau_{ki} x_i^j \leqslant h_k^j \qquad \begin{array}{l} j = 1, 2, \ldots, r \\ k = 1, 2, \ldots, m. \end{array} \qquad 88.8$$

Here we have a linear program that can be solved by the simplex method.

Let us take a concrete example. Let there be 4 products, 5 periods, and 3 machines, for which we take the following matrices:

$$[d] = \begin{bmatrix} 0 & 0 & 30 & 10 & 20 \\ 0 & 0 & 10 & 20 & 30 \\ 0 & 0 & 30 & 10 & 30 \\ 0 & 0 & 10 & 20 & 10 \end{bmatrix} \begin{matrix} A_1 \\ A_2 \\ A_3, \\ A_4 \end{matrix} \qquad 88.9$$
$$\quad \pi_1 \quad \pi_2 \quad \pi_3 \quad \pi_4 \quad \pi_5$$

$$[\tau] = \begin{bmatrix} 2 & 3 & 0 & 1 \\ 4 & 0 & 2 & 2 \\ 0 & 5 & 5 & 2 \end{bmatrix} \begin{matrix} M_1 \\ M_2, \\ M_3 \end{matrix} \qquad 88.10$$
$$\quad A_1 \quad A_2 \quad A_3 \quad A_4$$

$$[h] = \begin{bmatrix} 100 & 100 & 100 & 100 & 100 \\ 150 & 150 & 150 & 150 & 150 \\ 200 & 200 & 200 & 200 & 200 \end{bmatrix} \begin{matrix} M_1 \\ M_2, \\ M_3 \end{matrix} \qquad 88.11$$
$$\quad \pi_1 \quad \pi_2 \quad \pi_3 \quad \pi_4 \quad \pi_5$$

$$[c] = \underset{A_1\ A_2\ A_3\ A_4}{[3\ \ 4\ \ 5\ \ 2]}. \tag{88.12}$$

(a special case in which the capacity of each machine is the same for all periods).

We shall then have:

$$[D] = \begin{bmatrix} 0 & 0 & 30 & 40 & 60 \\ 0 & 0 & 10 & 30 & 60 \\ 0 & 0 & 30 & 40 & 70 \\ 0 & 0 & 10 & 30 & 40 \end{bmatrix}, \tag{88.13}$$

and

$$[x] = \begin{bmatrix} x_1^1 & x_1^2 & x_1^3 & x_1^4 & x_1^5 \\ x_2^1 & x_2^2 & x_2^3 & x_2^4 & x_2^5 \\ x_3^1 & x_3^2 & x_3^3 & x_3^4 & x_3^5 \\ x_4^1 & x_4^2 & x_4^3 & x_4^4 & x_4^5 \end{bmatrix}, \tag{88.14}$$

$$[X] = \begin{bmatrix} x_1^1 & x_1^1+x_1^2 & x_1^1+x_1^2+x_1^3 & x_1^1+x_1^2+x_1^3+x_1^4 & x_1^1+x_1^2+x_1^3+x_1^4+x_1^5 \\ x_2^1 & x_2^1+x_2^2 & x_2^1+x_2^2+x_2^3 & \cdots\cdots & \cdots\cdots \\ x_3^1 & x_3^1+x_3^2 & x_3^1+x_3^2+x_3^3 & \cdots\cdots & \cdots\cdots \\ x_4^1 & x_4^1+x_4^2 & \cdots\cdots & \cdots\cdots & \cdots\cdots \end{bmatrix}. \tag{88.15}$$

$$\sum_{j=1}^{5} X_i^j \to \begin{Bmatrix} 5x_1^1+4x_1^2+3x_1^3+2x_1^4+x_1^5 \\ 5x_2^1+4x_2^2+3x_2^3+2x_2^4+x_2^5 \\ 5x_3^1+4x_3^2+3x_3^3+2x_3^4+x_3^5 \\ 5x_4^1+4x_4^2+3x_4^3+2x_4^4+x_4^5 \end{Bmatrix}, \tag{88.16}$$

$$\sum_{j=1}^{5} D_i^j \to \begin{Bmatrix} 130 \\ 100 \\ 140 \\ 80 \end{Bmatrix}, \tag{88.17}$$

$$\begin{aligned} C = {} & 15x_1^1+12x_1^2+9x_1^3+6x_1^4+3x_1^5+20x_2^1+16x_2^2+12x_2^3 \\ & +8x_2^4+4x_2^5+25x_3^1+20x_3^2+15x_3^3+10x_3^4+5x_3^5+10x_4^1 \\ & +8x_4^2+6x_4^3+4x_4^4+2x_4^5-(3)(130)-(4)(100)-(5)(140) \\ & -(2)(80). \end{aligned} \tag{88.18}$$

The constraints will be:

Group (88.7)

$$\begin{aligned} & x_1^1 \geqslant 0,\ x_1^1+x_1^2 \geqslant 0,\ x_1^1+x_1^2+x_1^3 \geqslant 30,\ x_1^1+x_1^2+x_1^3+x_1^4 \geqslant 40, \\ & \qquad x_1^1+x_1^2+x_1^3+x_1^4+x_1^5 \geqslant 60 \\ & x_2^1 \geqslant 0,\ x_2^1+x_2^2 \geqslant 0,\ x_2^1+x_2^2+x_2^3 \geqslant 10, \ldots\ldots, \ldots\ldots, \ldots\ldots, \\ & x_3^1 \geqslant 0,\ x_3^1+x_3^2 \geqslant 0,\ x_3^1+x_3^2+x_3^3 \geqslant 30,\ \ldots\ldots, \ldots\ldots, \ldots\ldots, \\ & x_4^1 \geqslant 0,\ \ldots\ldots, \ldots\ldots, \ldots\ldots, \ldots\ldots, \ldots\ldots, \ldots\ldots, \end{aligned} \tag{88.19}$$

Group (88.8)

$$\begin{aligned}
&2x_1^1+3x_2^1+0x_3^1+x_4^1\leqslant 100\\
&\quad 2x_1^2+3x_2^2+0x_3^2+x_4^2\leqslant 100\\
&\qquad 2x_1^3+3x_2^3+0x_3^3+x_4^3\leqslant 100\\
&\qquad\quad 2x_1^4+3x_2^4+0x_3^4+x_4^4\leqslant 100\\
&\qquad\qquad 2x_1^5+3x_2^5+0x_3^5+x_4^5\leqslant 100\,.
\end{aligned}$$

$$\begin{aligned}
&4x_1^1+0x_2^1+2x_3^1+2x_4^1\leqslant 150\\
&\quad\dots\dots\dots\dots\\
&\qquad\dots\dots\dots\dots\\
&\qquad\quad\dots\dots\dots\dots\\
&\qquad\qquad\dots\dots\dots\dots
\end{aligned} \qquad 88.20$$

$$\begin{aligned}
&0x_1^1+5x_2^1+5x_3^1+2x_4^1\leqslant 200\\
&\quad\dots\dots\dots\dots\\
&\qquad\dots\dots\dots\dots\\
&\qquad\quad\dots\dots\dots\dots\\
&\qquad\qquad\dots\dots\dots\dots
\end{aligned}$$

We have presented this description to bring out the volume of the computation required. Thus for this plan—with 4 products, 5 periods, and 3 machines—the linear program will contain 20 variables and 35 constraints. For n products, r periods, and m machines, there will be nr variables and (m + n)r constraints. For a plan involving 100 articles, 20 periods, and 30 machines—quantities far from unusual in some plants—there would be a system of 2,000 variables and 2,600 constraints. Such figures may well be beyond the capacities of present-day computers; at best, the cost of such calculations would use up a large part of the benefits obtained from operation at the optimum. Practically speaking, therefore, the simplex method cannot be used for solution of such problems; special planning methods must be sought that will provide at least a possible solution, if not the best. The method presented below yields such a solution.

3. Vazsonyi's "step-by-step" planning method.*

This method permits us to find a possible solution, provided such a solution exists. It has a great advantage in that it is still valid when set-up time and ordering time are taken into consideration, that is, when non-linear elements are involved in the cost function. (We shall take up this non-linear case further on.)

---

*A. Vazsonyi, "Economic Lot Size Formulas in Manufacturing," Fall Meeting of the American Society of Mechanical Engineers, Sept. 10-12, 1956, Denver, Col.

Returning to (88.3)—(88.5) and Fig. 88.4, we have:

$$C = \sum_{i=1}^{n} \sum_{j=1}^{r} c_i (X_i^j - D_i^j), \qquad 88.21$$

$$X_i^j \geq D_i^j, \qquad 88.22$$

$$\sum_{i=1}^{n} \tau_{ki} x_i^j \leq h_k^j \qquad 88.23$$

which can also be written:

$$\sum_{i=1}^{n} \tau_{ki} (X_i^j - X_i^{j-1}) \leq h_k^j. \qquad 88.24$$

Vazsonyi's method consists of first considering one of the products A_i as if it were alone and defining the optimum plan for this arbitrarily chosen product A_i, taking into account the matrix $[h]$ of the available machine times. (We shall see that the neglect of the other products in this procedure raises no difficulties.) In other words, our aim is to minimize the quantity:

$$\sum_{j=1}^{r} (X_i^j - D_i^j)$$

where i is fixed. Once this partial plan, P_i, has been determined, we deduce from it, for each period, the production time required on each machine to fill the demand for product A_i: let $[h_1]$ be the matrix of times used. The available times remaining for the other products are therefore represented by the matrix $[h'] = [h] - [h_1]$. Now we select a new product A_i among those still to be manufactured; considering it by itself, we determine the optimum plan for product A_i consistent with the matrix $[h']$ of available times. And so on for the remaining products.

Now let us see how to determine P_i, the optimum plan for product A_i considered by itself, independently of the other products. To begin with, X_i^r is known and is equal to D_i^r since the total production must equal the total demand during time T. It will therefore be natural to determine the X_i^j values "step by step," starting from the first period for which X_i^r is known and going backward in time. Furthermore, to lower the carrying costs it is obviously best to produce as much as possible (taking into account (88.23) and (88.24)) during the last periods. Therefore, with X_i^r known, we shall try to determine in succession $X_i^{r-1}, \ldots, X_i^j, X_i^{j-1}, \ldots, X_i^1$ in such a manner that the differences $(X_i^j - X_i^{j-1})$ are maximum. With X_i^r known, this amounts to saying that we shall choose X_i^{j-1} as small as possible, as can be seen in Fig. 88.4, where the shaded rectangles represent inventory. However, if X_i^{j+1} is known, taking X_i^j small is to take X_i^{j+1} large; this is possible only within certain limits, since the time available on the machines during the $(j+1)^{th}$ period is limited; moreover, we must have $X_i^j \geq D_i^j$.

Let us therefore determine X_i^{r-1}. We have:

$$X_i^r = D_i^r, \tag{88.25}$$

$$X_i^{r-1} \geqslant D_i^{r-1} \tag{88.26}$$

and

$$\tau_{ki}(X_i^r - X_i^{r-1}) \leqslant h_k^r. \tag{88.27}$$

Let:

$$X_i^{r-1} \geqslant X_i^r - \frac{h_k^r}{\tau_{ki}} \tag{88.28}$$

for any k. We shall therefore seek the minimum of h_k^r/τ_{ki} for different values of k, and (88.28) will be written:

$$X_i^{r-1} \geqslant X_i^r - \min_k \frac{h_k^r}{\tau_{ki}}. \tag{88.29}$$

Since we are looking for the smallest possible X_i^{r-1},(88.25) and (88.29) lead us to take for X_i^{r-1} the larger of the two numbers D_i^{r-1} and $(X_i^r - \min_k h_k/\tau_{ki})$, which can be written:

$$X_i^{r-1} = \max\left\{\left[X_i^r - \min_k \frac{h_k^r}{\tau_{ki}}\right], D_i^{r-1}\right\}. \tag{88.30}$$

In general, with X_i^j determined, we shall have:

$$X_i^{j-1} = \max\left\{\left[X_i^j - \min_k \frac{h_k^j}{\tau_{ki}}\right], D_i^{j-1}\right\}. \tag{88.31}$$

We have thus determined the X_i^j values defining the manufacturing program that would be optimum if A_i were the sole product. From these X_i^j, we deduce the $x_i^j = X_i^j - X_i^{j-1}$. The time used on each machine k for the chosen product A_i during each period is:

$$h_{ik}^j = \tau_{ki}\, x_i^j \quad \text{(for a certain i)}. \tag{88.32}$$

We then perform the same operation again for another product A_i, for which the matrix of available times is:

$$[h_k'^j] = [h_k^j] - [\tau_{ki}\, x^j] \quad \text{(for a certain i)}. \tag{88.33}$$

In this way a solution is obtained which, we repeat, is not necessarily the best possible.

4. Example.

Let us apply Vazsonyi's method to the example proposed earlier in (88.9)—(88.12). We shall follow the method we have just explained, using the same notations, and we shall not repeat the explanations.

To begin, let us arbitrarily consider product A_1:

$$X_1^5 = D_1^5 = 60 \qquad 88.34$$

$$X_1^4 = \max\left\{\left[60 - \min_k \frac{h_k^5}{\tau_{ki}}\right],\ 40\right\}, \qquad 88.35$$

$$\frac{h_k^5}{\tau_{k1}} = \frac{100}{2},\ \frac{150}{4},\ \frac{200}{0};\quad \min_k \frac{h_k^5}{\tau_{k1}} = 37.5, \qquad 88.36$$

$$X_1^4 = \max\{[60 - 37.5], 40\} = 40, \qquad 88.37$$

$$X_1^3 = \max\left\{\left[40 - \min_k \frac{h_k^4}{\tau_{k1}}\right],\ 30\right\}; \qquad 88.38$$

and as

$$h_k^5 = h_k^4 = h_k^3 = h_k^2 = h_k^1: \qquad 88.39$$

$$X_1^3 = \max\{[40 - 37.5],\ 30\} = 30, \qquad 88.40$$

$$X_1^2 = \max\{[30 - 37.5], 0\} = 0, \qquad 88.41$$

and obviously

$$X_1^1 = 0. \qquad 88.42$$

Hence:

$$x_1^5 = 20,\ x_1^4 = 10,\ x_1^3 = 30,\ x_1^2 = 0,\ x_1^1 = 0. \qquad 88.43$$

As

$$\{\tau_{k1}\} = \begin{Bmatrix}2\\4\\0\end{Bmatrix}, \qquad 88.44$$

we have:

$$[h_1] = \begin{bmatrix} 0 & 0 & 60 & 20 & 40 \\ 0 & 0 & 120 & 40 & 80 \\ 0 & 0 & 0 & 0 & 0 \end{bmatrix}, \qquad 88.45$$

and:

$$[h'] = [h] - [h_1] = \begin{bmatrix} 100 & 100 & 40 & 80 & 60 \\ 150 & 150 & 30 & 110 & 70 \\ 200 & 200 & 200 & 200 & 200 \end{bmatrix} \qquad 88.46$$

Let us now work on the product A_2 with the matrix $[h']$.

$$X_2^5 = 60, \qquad 88.47$$

$$X_2^4 = \max\left\{\left[60 - \min_k \frac{h'^5_k}{\tau_{k2}}\right\}, 30\right\}, \qquad 88.48$$

$$\frac{h'^5_k}{\tau_{k2}} = \frac{60}{3}, \frac{70}{0}, \frac{200}{5}; \qquad \min_k \frac{h'^5_k}{\tau_{k2}} = 20. \qquad \begin{matrix} 88.49 \\ 88.50 \end{matrix}$$

$$X_2^4 = \max\{[60 - 20], 30\} = 40, \qquad 88.51$$

$$X_2^3 = \max\left\{\left[40 - \min_k \frac{h'^4_k}{\tau_{k2}}\right], 10\right\}. \qquad 88.52$$

$$\frac{h'^4_k}{\tau_{k2}} = \frac{80}{3}, \frac{110}{0}, \frac{200}{5}; \qquad \min_k \frac{h'^4_k}{\tau_{k2}} = 26.6 \qquad 88.53$$

$$X_2^3 = \max\{[40 - 26.6], 10\} = 13.4 \quad \text{(we shall take } X_2^3 = 14). \qquad 88.54$$

$$X_2^2 = \max\left\{\left[14 - \min_k \frac{h'^3_k}{\tau_{k2}}\right], 0\right\}, \qquad 88.55$$

$$\frac{h'_k}{\tau_{k2}} = \frac{40}{3}, \frac{30}{0}, \frac{200}{5}; \qquad \min_k \frac{h'^3_k}{\tau_{k2}} = 13.3. \qquad 88.56$$

$$X_2^2 = \max\{[14 - 13.3], 0\} = 0.7 \quad \text{(we shall take } X_2^2 = 1). \qquad 88.57$$

and

$$X^1_2 = 0. \qquad 88.58$$

We then have:

$$x_2^5 = 20,\ x_2^4 = 26,\ x_2^3 = 13,\ x_2^2 = 1,\ x_2^1 = 0. \qquad 88.59$$

$$\{\tau_{k2}\} = \begin{Bmatrix} 3 \\ 0 \\ 5 \end{Bmatrix}, \qquad [h_2] = \begin{bmatrix} 0 & 3 & 39 & 78 & 60 \\ 0 & 0 & 0 & 0 & 0 \\ 0 & 5 & 65 & 130 & 100 \end{bmatrix}, \qquad 88.60$$

and

$$[h''] = [h'] - [h_2] = \begin{bmatrix} 100 & 97 & 1 & 2 & 0 \\ 150 & 150 & 30 & 110 & 70 \\ 200 & 195 & 135 & 70 & 100 \end{bmatrix} \qquad 88.62$$

Let us now work on A_3 with $[h'']$.

$$X_3^5 = 70, \qquad 88.63$$

$$X^4_3 = \max\left\{\left[70 - \min_k \frac{h_k''^5}{\tau_{k3}}\right], 40\right\}, \qquad 88.64$$

$$\frac{h_k''^5}{\tau_{k3}} = \frac{0}{0}, \frac{70}{2}, \frac{100}{5}; \qquad \min_k \frac{h_k''^5}{\tau_{k3}} = 20, \qquad 88.65$$

(the form 0/0 must not disturb the reader; the machine M_1 is not involved in the manufacture of the product A_3, and therefore cannot limit the production of A_3).

$$X^4_3 = \max\{[70 - 20], 40\} = 50, \qquad 88.66$$

$$X^3_3 = \max\left\{\left[50 - \min_k \frac{h_k''^4}{\tau_{k3}}\right], 30\right\}, \qquad 88.67$$

$$\frac{h_k''^4}{\tau_{k3}} = \frac{2}{0}, \frac{110}{2}, \frac{70}{5}; \quad \min_k \frac{h_k''^4}{\tau_{k3}} = 14. \qquad 88.68$$

$$X^3_3 = \max\{[50 - 14], 30\} = 36. \qquad 88.69$$

$$X^2_3 = \max\left\{\left[36 - \min_k \frac{h_k''^3}{\tau_{k3}}\right], 0\right\}, \qquad 88.70$$

$$\frac{h_k''^3}{\tau_{k3}} = \frac{1}{0}, \frac{30}{2}, \frac{135}{5}; \quad \min_k \frac{h_k''^3}{\tau_{k3}} = 15. \qquad 88.71$$

$$X^2_3 = \max\{[36 - 15], 0\} = 21 \qquad 88.72$$

$$X^1_3 = \max\left\{\left[21 - \min_k \frac{h_k''^2}{\tau_{k3}}\right], 0\right\} \qquad 88.73$$

$$\frac{h''^2_k}{\tau_{k3}} = \frac{97}{0}, \frac{150}{2}, \frac{195}{5}; \quad \min_k \frac{h''^2_k}{\tau_{k3}} = 39. \qquad 88.74$$

$$X^1_3 = \max\{[21 - 39], 0\} = 0; \qquad 88.75$$

we then have:

$$x^5_3 = 20,\ x^4_3 = 14,\ x^3_3 = 15,\ x^2_3 = 21,\ x^1_3 = 0. \qquad 88.76$$

$$\{\tau_{k3}\} = \begin{Bmatrix} 0 \\ 2 \\ 5 \end{Bmatrix}, \qquad [h_3] = \begin{bmatrix} 0 & 0 & 0 & 0 & 0 \\ 0 & 42 & 30 & 28 & 40 \\ 0 & 105 & 75 & 70 & 100 \end{bmatrix}, \qquad 88.77\text{–}88.79$$

$$[h'''] = [h''] - [h_3] = \begin{bmatrix} 100 & 97 & 1 & 2 & 0 \\ 150 & 108 & 0 & 82 & 30 \\ 200 & 90 & 60 & 0 & 0 \end{bmatrix} \qquad 88.80$$

Finally, we conclude with A_4:

$$X_4^5 = 40 \qquad 88.81$$

$$X_4^4 = \max\left\{\left[40 - \min_k \frac{h_k'''^5}{\tau_{k4}}\right], 30\right\} \qquad 88.82$$

$$\frac{h_k'''^5}{\tau_{k4}} = \frac{0}{1}, \frac{30}{2}, \frac{0}{2}; \quad \min_k \frac{h_k'''^5}{\tau_{k4}} = 0. \qquad 88.83$$

$$X_4^4 = \max\{[40 - 0], 30\} = 40 \qquad 88.84$$

$$X_4^3 = \max\left\{\left[40 - \min_k \frac{h_k'''^4}{\tau_{k4}},\right], 10\right\} \qquad 88.85$$

$$\frac{h_k'''^4}{\tau_{k4}} = \frac{2}{1}, \frac{82}{2}, \frac{0}{2}; \quad \min_k \frac{h_k'''^4}{\tau_{k4}} = 0, \qquad 88.86$$

$$X_4^3 = \max\{[40 - 0], 10\} = 40. \qquad 88.87$$

$$X_4^2 = \max\left\{\left[40 - \min_k \frac{h_k'''^3}{\tau_{k4}}\right], 0\right\}, \qquad 88.88$$

$$\frac{h_k'''^3}{\tau_{k4}} = \frac{1}{1}, \frac{0}{2}, \frac{60}{2}; \quad \min_k \frac{h_k'''^3}{\tau_{k4}} = 0. \qquad 88.90$$

$$X_4^2 = \max\{[40 - 0], 0\} = 40, \qquad 88.91$$

$$X_4^1 = \max\left\{\left[40 - \min_k \frac{h_k'''^2}{\tau_{k4}}\right], 0\right\}, \qquad 88.92$$

$$\frac{h_k'''^2}{\tau_{k4}} = \frac{97}{1}, \frac{108}{2}, \frac{90}{2}; \quad \min_k \frac{h_k'''^2}{\tau_{k4}} = 45. \qquad 88.93$$

$$X_4^1 = \max\{[40 - 45], 0\} = 0; \qquad 88.94$$

we then have:

$$x_4^5 = 0,\ x_4^4 = 0,\ x_4^3 = 0,\ x_4^2 = 40,\ x_4^1 = 0, \qquad 88.95$$

$$\{\tau_{k4}\} = \begin{Bmatrix} 1 \\ 2 \\ 2 \end{Bmatrix}, \quad [h_4] = \begin{bmatrix} 0 & 40 & 0 & 0 & 0 \\ 0 & 80 & 0 & 0 & 0 \\ 0 & 80 & 0 & 0 & 0 \end{bmatrix}. \qquad \begin{matrix} 88.96 \\ 88.97 \end{matrix}$$

The times not utilized will be:

$$[h''''] = [h'''] - [h_4] = \begin{bmatrix} 100 & 57 & 1 & 2 & 0 \\ 150 & 28 & 0 & 82 & 30 \\ 200 & 10 & 60 & 0 & 0 \end{bmatrix}. \qquad 88.98$$

Check.

The total time used on each machine must be:

$$\begin{aligned} \text{For } M_1 &: 2 \times 60 + 3 \times 60 + 0 \times 70 + 1 \times 40 = 340, \\ M_2 &: 4 \times 60 + 0 \times 60 + 2 \times 70 + 2 \times 40 = 460, \\ M_3 &: 0 \times 60 + 5 \times 60 + 5 \times 70 + 2 \times 40 = 730. \end{aligned} \tag{88.99}$$

These results are, in fact, obtained when the sum of elements in each row of the matrix of times utilized, $[h] - [h'''']$, is taken:

$$[h] - [h''''] = \begin{bmatrix} 0 & 43 & 99 & 98 & 100 \\ 0 & 122 & 150 & 68 & 120 \\ 0 & 190 & 140 & 200 & 200 \end{bmatrix} \begin{matrix} \rightarrow 340 \\ \rightarrow 460 \\ \rightarrow 730 \end{matrix} \tag{88.100}$$

The plan thus obtained is:

$$[x] = \begin{bmatrix} 0 & 0 & 30 & 10 & 20 \\ 0 & 1 & 13 & 26 & 20 \\ 0 & 21 & 15 & 14 & 20 \\ 0 & 40 & 0 & 0 & 0 \end{bmatrix}, \quad [X] = \begin{bmatrix} 0 & 0 & 30 & 40 & 60 \\ 0 & 1 & 14 & 40 & 60 \\ 0 & 21 & 36 & 50 & 70 \\ 0 & 40 & 40 & 40 & 40 \end{bmatrix}. \qquad \begin{matrix} 88.101 \\ 88.102 \end{matrix}$$

To calculate the carrying cost, we form:

$$[X] - [D] = \begin{bmatrix} 0 & 0 & 0 & 0 & 0 \\ 0 & 1 & 4 & 10 & 0 \\ 0 & 21 & 6 & 10 & 0 \\ 0 & 40 & 30 & 10 & 0 \end{bmatrix}, \tag{88.103}$$

from which we derive:

$$\sum_{j=1}^{5} (X_i^j - D_i^j) = \begin{Bmatrix} 0 + 0 + 0 + 0 + 0 \\ 0 + 1 + 4 + 10 + 0 \\ 0 + 21 + 6 + 10 + 0 \\ 0 + 40 + 30 + 10 + 0 \end{Bmatrix} = \begin{Bmatrix} 0 \\ 15 \\ 37 \\ 80 \end{Bmatrix}. \tag{88.104}$$

Thus, the cost C will be:

$$C = [3 \;\; 4 \;\; 5 \;\; 2] \begin{Bmatrix} 0 \\ 15 \\ 37 \\ 80 \end{Bmatrix} = 405. \tag{88.105}$$

Although this method produces only a possible solution, rather than the optimum solution, it is a convenient means of formulating a plan. In actual practice, one would compute a dozen or even a hundred different plans, from which the best (the one giving the lowest cost) can be selected.

5. Introduction of the set-up time.

To the data that have formed the program (88.3)—(88.5), we shall now add:

σ_{ki} = set-up time (machine make-ready, starting, miscellaneous delays, etc.) of machine k for product i.
$\bar{c}_{ki}$ = set-up cost of machine k for product i.

We will make the hypothesis that there is no more than one lot per period, and that the time for producing one lot cannot exceed one period. We introduce the notations $\delta(x_i^j)$ with:

$$\delta(x_i^j) = 1 \quad \text{if} \quad x_i^j > 0$$
$$= 0 \quad \text{if} \quad x_i^j = 0. \qquad 88.106$$

This function $\delta(x_i^j)$ will act always as a coefficient of σ_{ki} and of $\bar{c}_{ki}$.

Thus, we have the following non-linear program:

$$[\text{MIN}]\ C = \sum_{i=1}^{n} \sum c_i(X_i^j - D_i^j) + \sum_{i=1}^{n} \sum_{j=1}^{r} \sum_{k=1}^{m} c_{ki}\, \delta(x_i^j), \qquad 88.107$$

$$X_i^j \geqslant D_i^j, \qquad 88.108$$

$$\sum_{i=1}^{n} \tau_{ki}\, x_i^j + \sum_{i=1}^{n} \sigma_{ki}\, \delta(x_i^j) \leqslant h_k^j. \qquad 88.109$$

For such non-linear programs we cannot apply the simplex method, but we can always find a possible solution by means of Vazsonyi's method.

The general formula (88.31) becomes:

$$X_i^{j-1} = \max \left\{ \left[X_i^j - \min_k \left(\frac{h_k^j - \sigma_{ki}\, \delta(x_i^j)}{\tau_{ki}} \right) \right], D_i^{j-1} \right\}. \qquad 88.110$$

In practice, we should proceed as in the linear case, changing h_k^j to $h_k^j - \sigma_{ki}$. Actually, this procedure is correct if $\delta(x_i^j) = 1$, i.e., if $X_i^{j-1} < X_i^j$. If, in following this procedure, we were to find that $X_i^{j-1} = X_i^j$, i.e. $x^j = 0$, then we would still not have to change the result, because it shows that taking σ_{ki} into account it is impossible to have $x_i^j > 0$. Finally, therefore, we would use the formula:

$$X_i^{j-1} = \max \left\{ \left[X_i^j - \min_k \frac{h_k^j - \sigma_{ki}}{\tau_{ki}} \right], D_i^{j-1} \right\}. \qquad 88.111$$

Obviously, we must not eliminate $\delta(x_i^j)$ in the formula (88.107) for the total cost.

6. Condition necessary for the proposed program to have a solution.

Referring back to (88.22) and (88.24):

$$X_i^j \geqslant D_i^j \qquad 88.112$$

$$\sum_{i=1}^{n} \tau_{ki} (X_i^j - X_i^{j-1}) \leqslant h_k^j. \qquad 88.113$$

From (88.113) we derive, successively:

$$\sum_{i=1}^{n} \tau_{ki} (X_i^{j-1} - X_i^{j-2}) \leqslant h_k^{j-1},$$

$$\cdots\cdots\cdots\cdots\cdots\cdots$$

$$\sum_{i=1}^{n} \tau_{ki} (X_i^2 - X_i^1) \leqslant h_k^2 \qquad 88.114$$

$$\sum_{i=1}^{n} \tau_{ki} X_i^1 \leqslant h_k^1$$

Hence, taking the sum:

$$\sum_{i=1}^{n} \tau_{ki} X_i^j \leqslant h_k^1 + h_k^2 + \ldots + h_k^j. \qquad 88.115$$

Let us set:

$$H_k^j = \sum_{\alpha=1}^{j} h_k^\alpha;$$

$$\sum_{i=1}^{n} \tau_{ki} X_i^j \leqslant H_k^j. \qquad 88.116$$

Since:

$$X_i^j \geqslant D_i^j, \qquad 88.117$$

we shall necessarily have:

$$\sum_{i=1}^{n} \tau_{ki} D_i^j \leqslant H_k^j \qquad 88.118$$

for each j and each k.

In other words, every element of the matrix formed by the product $[\tau][D]$ must be less than or equal to the corresponding element of the matrix [H]. While this condition is necessary, it is obviously not sufficient.

Chapter 10

Analytical study of equipment deterioration, replacement, and maintenance problems

Section 89

INTRODUCTION

In this chapter, we shall dwell particularly on the advantages of the use of the Carson-Laplace transformation in the study of equipment deterioration, replacement, and maintenance problems. This unilateral functional transformation is particularly well adapted to the study of temporal probability distributions such as are encountered in these problems.

To this study we shall add an example of the determination of a rule for decision in non-random cases, as well as a method for calculating the Stieltjes integrals.

Section 90

REPLACEMENT OF EQUIPMENT THAT DEPRECIATES WITH AGE

1. General explanation.—2. First example: $\varphi(t)$ and $\Psi(t)$ are linear.—3. Second example: $\varphi(t)$ is exponential and $\Psi(t)$ is linear.—4. Third example: both $\varphi(t)$ and $\Psi(t)$ are exponential.

1. General explanation.

Let A_0 be the purchase-price, and:

$A_0\ \varphi(t)$ = the resale price after a certain time, t, where $\varphi(0) = 1$ and $\varphi(t)$ is a monotone decreasing function, 90.1

and

$\Psi(t)$ = the cumulative cost of repairs and maintenance, where $\Psi(0) = 0$ and $\Psi(t)$ is a monotone and increasing function. 90.2

Equipment cost for a period t is expressed as:

$$\Gamma(t) = A_0 - A_0\varphi(t) + \Psi(t); \tag{90.3}$$

and the average cost of utilization as:

$$\gamma(t) = \frac{\Gamma(t)}{t} = \frac{1}{t}\,[A_0 - A_0\varphi(t) + \Psi(t)]. \tag{90.4}$$

The minimum of $\gamma(t)$ occurs for:

$$\gamma'(t) = \frac{t\,\Gamma'(t) - \Gamma(t)}{t^2} = 0, \tag{90.5}$$

or:

$$\Gamma'(t) = \frac{\Gamma(t)}{t}, \tag{90.6}$$

or again:

$$A_0[1 - \varphi(t) + t\varphi'(t)] + \Psi(t) - t\Psi'(t) = 0 \tag{90.7}$$

As the functions $\varphi(t)$ and $\Psi(t)$ are most often given in numerical values, the optimum value of $\Gamma(t)$ is sought directly by numerical calculation. In certain simple cases, an analytical study is of value.

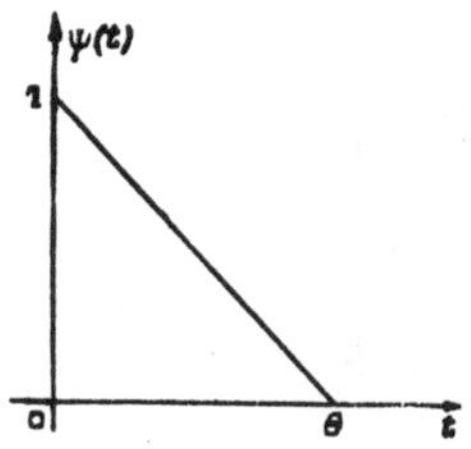

Fig. 90.1

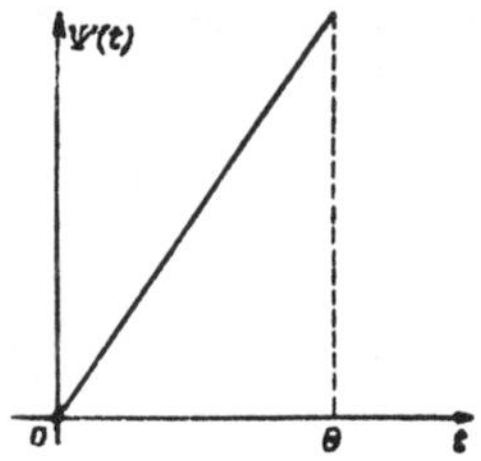

Fig. 90.2

2. First example: $\varphi(t)$ and $\Psi(t)$ are linear.

Let:

$$\varphi(t) = 1 - \frac{t}{\theta} \qquad \text{(figure 90.1)}, \tag{90.8}$$

$$\Psi(t) = kt \qquad \text{(figure 90.2)}, \tag{90.9}$$

where the functions $\varphi(t)$ and $\Psi(t)$ are taken within the interval $0 < t < \theta$.

$$\gamma(t) = \frac{1}{t}\left[A_0 - A_0\left(1 - \frac{t}{\theta}\right) + kt\right]$$

$$= \frac{1}{t}\left[A_0 \frac{t}{\theta} + kt\right] \qquad 90.10$$

$$= \frac{A_0}{\theta} + k \qquad 0 < t < \theta.$$

Thus, the average cost of utilization is constant if the two functions, $\varphi(t)$ and $\Psi(t)$, are linear.

It is interesting to interpret this conclusion. For the time of replacement to be of almost no importance or effect, it is necessary only that curves $\varphi(t)$ and $\Psi(t)$ be essentially straight lines.

3. Second example: $\varphi(t)$ is exponential and $\Psi(t)$ is linear.

$$\varphi(t) = e^{-\lambda t} \qquad \text{(figure 90.3)} \qquad 90.11$$

$$\Psi(t) = kt \qquad \text{(figure 90.2)} \qquad 90.12$$

Thus, we have:

$$\gamma(t) = \frac{1}{t}\,[A_0 - A_0\,e^{-\lambda t} + kt]. \qquad 90.13$$

Taking the derivative, we obtain:

$$\gamma'(t) = A_0\,\frac{\lambda t\ e^{-\lambda t} + e^{-\lambda t} - 1}{t^2}. \qquad 90.14$$

This derivative does not equal zero for any positive value of t, and it is easy to show that $\gamma(t)$ is monotonically decreasing;

$$\gamma'(t) = A_0\,e^{-\lambda t}\left(-\frac{\lambda^2}{2!} - \frac{\lambda^3 t}{3!} - \frac{\lambda^4 t^2}{4!} - \dots\right). \qquad 90.15$$

Hence there is no minimum, and under these conditions it is best to keep equipment in service as long as possible (Fig. 90.4).

We find:

$$\lim_{t \to \infty} \gamma(t) = k. \qquad 90.16$$

4. Third example: $\varphi(t)$ and $\Psi(t)$ are both exponential.

$$\varphi(t) = e^{-\lambda t} \qquad \text{(figure 90.5)} \qquad 90.17$$

$$\Psi(t) = k_0(e^{\mu t} - 1) \qquad \text{(figure 90.6)} \qquad 90.18$$

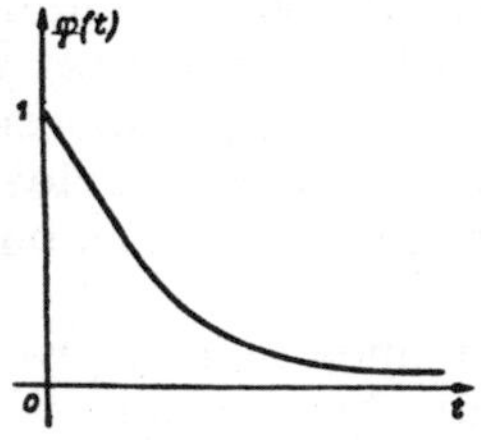

Fig. 90.3

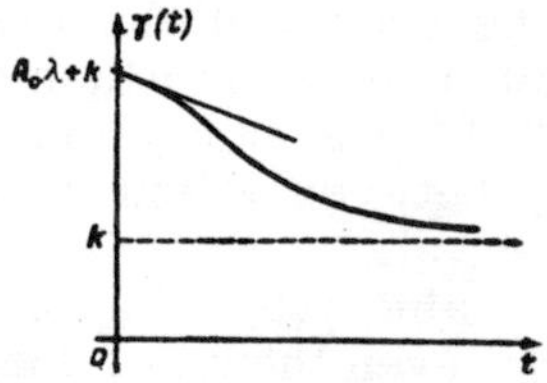

Fig. 90.4

This gives us:

$$\gamma(t) = \frac{1}{t}\,[A_0(1 - e^{-\lambda t}) + k_0(e^{\mu t} - 1)]. \qquad 90.19$$

As we shall demonstrate further on, this function, which is continuous in the interval between zero and infinity, has a minimum in that interval.

To begin, let us take a numerical example.

Suppose that we have a car whose purchase price is 700,000 francs. Assume that it is quoted in Argus (Blue Book) two years later at 350,000 francs, and that the change in its value is exponential. Furthermore, we shall adopt the hypothesis that it costs us 30,000 francs in maintenance and repairs for the first year, and 90,000 francs for the next two years together, the change being exponential.

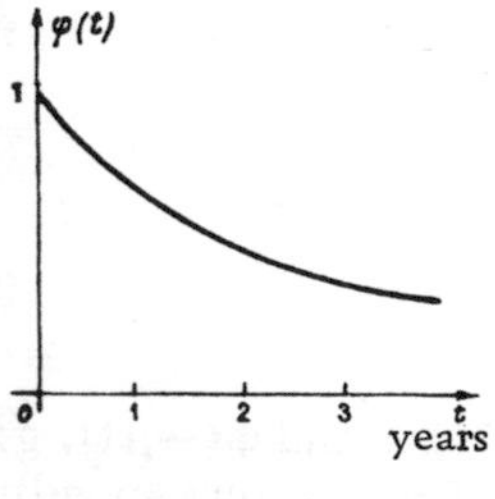

Fig. 90.5

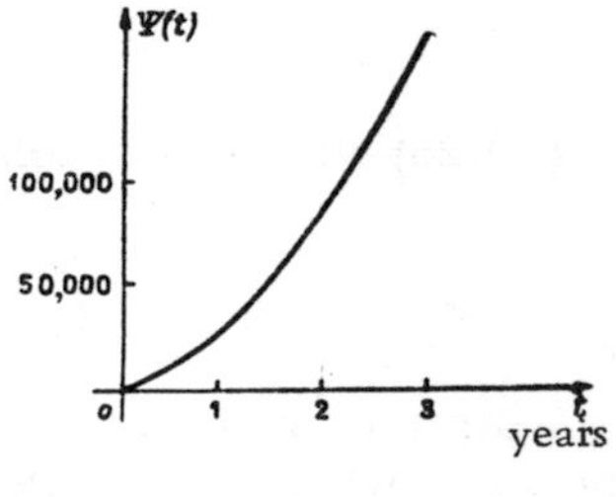

Fig. 90.6

These hypotheses give us:

$$\varphi(t) = e^{-0.34658t} \quad \text{(figure 90.5)}, \qquad 90.20$$

$$\Psi(t) = 30{,}000\,(e^{0.69315t} - 1) \quad \text{(figure 90.6)}, \qquad 90.21$$

$$\gamma(t) = \frac{1}{t}\,[700{,}000\,(1 - e^{-0.34658t}) + 30{,}000\,(e^{0.69315t} - 1)]. \qquad 90.22$$

Table 90.1 and the curve in Fig. 90.7 show the variation of $\gamma(t)$. It can be seen that the best decision is to sell the car after using it for 30 months, in which case the cost is minimum, amounting to 218,150 francs per year. It is worth noting that $\gamma(t)$ varies only slightly between 2 and 3 years, in contrast to the pattern outside that interval.

The value $\gamma(0) = A_0 \lambda + k_0 \mu = 263{,}400$ francs has no practical meaning, even though it does have theoretical significance.

We shall now deduce an interesting formula. Taking the derivative of (90.19), we obtain:

$$\gamma'(t) = \frac{(A_0\lambda\, e^{-\lambda t} + k_0\mu\, e^{\mu t})t - [A_0(1 - e^{-\lambda t}) + k_0(e^{\mu t} - 1)]}{t^2}. \qquad 90.23$$

This derivative equals zero when:

$$A_0\lambda t e^{-\lambda t} + A_0 e^{-\lambda t} - A_0 + k_0\mu t e^{\mu t} - k_0 e^{\mu t} + k_0 = 0, \qquad 90.24$$

that is:

$$A_0(\lambda t e^{-\lambda t} + e^{-\lambda t} - 1) = k_0(-\mu t e^{\mu t} + e^{\mu t} - 1), \qquad 90.25$$

or again:

$$\frac{1 - e^{-\lambda t}(1 + \lambda t)}{1 - e^{\mu t}(1 - \mu t)} = \frac{k_0}{A_0}. \qquad 90.26$$

Introducing the function:

$$\Phi(x) = 1 - e^{-x}(1 + x), \qquad 90.27$$

relation (90.26) will be written:

$$\frac{\Phi(\lambda t)}{\Phi(-\mu t)} = \frac{k_0}{A_0}. \qquad 90.28$$

It is useful to draw up a dual table of $\Phi(\lambda t)$ and $\Phi(-\mu t)$, giving $\Phi(\lambda t) | \Phi(-\mu t)$, which will indicate the time $t = t^*$ corresponding to the optimum. For the sake of convenience, we shall use the inverse of relation (90.28):

$$\frac{\Phi(-\mu t)}{\Phi(\lambda t)} = \frac{A_0}{k_0}. \qquad 90.29$$

First we construct Table 90.2, which gives the values of $\Phi(x)$ and $\Phi(-x)$ from $x = 0$ to $x = 5$. Drawing upon this table, we can construct the dual table that gives:

Table 90.1

t	$A_0 - A_0\varphi(t)$	$\Psi(t)$	$\Gamma(t)$	$\gamma(t) = \frac{1}{t}\Gamma(t)$
0.5	111,377	12,426	123,803	247,606
1	205,030	30,000	235,030	235,030
1.5	283,770	54,852	338,632	225,748
2	350,000	90,000	440,000	220,000
2.4	395,311	128,340	523,651	218,187
2.5	405,670	139,704	545,374	218,150 ←
2.6	415,716	151,884	567,600	218,307
3	452,515	210,000	662,515	220,838
4	525,000	450,000	975,000	243,750
5	576,261	930,000	1,506,261	301,252

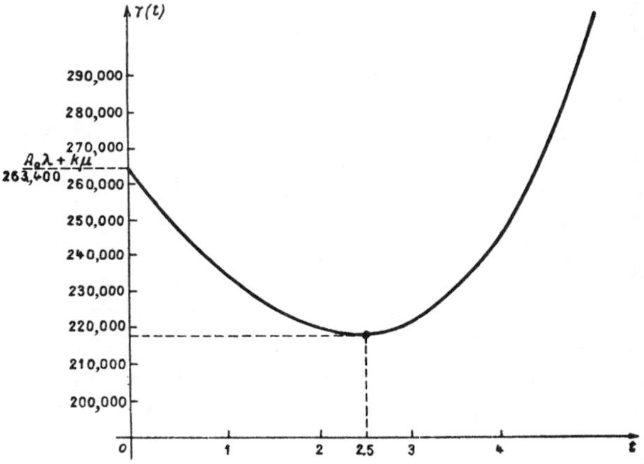

Fig. 90.7

$$\varrho = \frac{\Phi(-\mu t)}{\Phi(\lambda t)} \quad \text{for } \lambda t \text{ and } \mu t. \qquad 90.30$$

Using this table, we can then construct the graph of Fig. 90.8. In this graph, we have plotted the curves corresponding to:

$$\frac{A_0}{k_0} = 10,\ 15,\ \ldots,\ 45,\ 50. \qquad 90.31$$

Table 90.2

x	$\Phi(x)$	$\Phi(-x)$	x	$\Phi(x)$	$\Phi(-x)$	x	$\Phi(x)$	$\Phi(-x)$	x	$\Phi(x)$	$\Phi(-x)$	x	$\Phi(x)$	$\Phi(-x)$
0	0	0	1	0.264	1	2	0.594	8.38	3	0.802	41.2	4	0.909	165
0.1	0.005	0.005	1.1	0.301	1.30	2.1	0.621	9.98	3.1	0.816	47.6	4.1	0.916	188
0.2	0.018	0.023	1.2	0.337	1.66	2.2	0.646	11.8	3.2	0.829	54.9	4.2	0.922	214
0.3	0.038	0.055	1.3	0.373	2.10	2.3	0.668	14.0	3.3	0.842	63.3	4.3	0.928	244
0.4	0.062	0.106	1.4	0.409	2.62	2.4	0.690	16.5	3.4	0.853	72.9	4.4	0.933	278
0.5	0.090	0.175	1.5	0.442	3.25	2.5	0.713	19.3	3.5	0.864	83.8	4.5	0.939	316
0.6	0.124	0.273	1.6	0.475	3.97	2.6	0.733	22.5	3.6	0.874	96.2	4.6	0.944	359
0.7	0.156	0.397	1.7	0.507	4.83	2.7	0.751	26.3	3,7	0.884	110	4.7	0.948	408
0.8	0.192	0.556	1.8	0.358	5.83	2.8	0.769	30.6	3,8	0.893	127	4.8	0.952	463
0.9	0.228	0.754	1.9	0.566	7.02	2.9	0.786	35.5	3,9	0.901	144	4.9	0.957	525
												5	0.960	595

$$\lim_{x \to \infty} \Phi(x) = 1 \qquad \lim_{x \to \infty} \Phi(-x) = \infty.$$

A scale at the right of the figure gives the λ/μ ratios. Let us consider an example.

Let:

$$\lambda = 0.4, \; \mu = 0.7, \; A_0 = 1{,}050{,}000 \text{ fr}, \; k_0 = 30{,}000 \text{ fr}; \qquad 90.32$$

thus:

$$\frac{\lambda}{\mu} = \frac{0.4}{0.7} = 0.57, \qquad \frac{A_0}{k_0} = 35. \qquad 90.33$$

We draw a straight line such that $\lambda/\mu = 0.57$. At the intersection of this line and the curve $\rho = A_0/k_0 = 35$, we draw a straight line parallel to the O, λt axis, which gives us $\mu t = 2.27$. Consequently:

$$t^* = \frac{\mu t^*}{\mu} = \frac{2.27}{0.7} = \text{approximately 3 years and 3 months.} \qquad 90.34$$

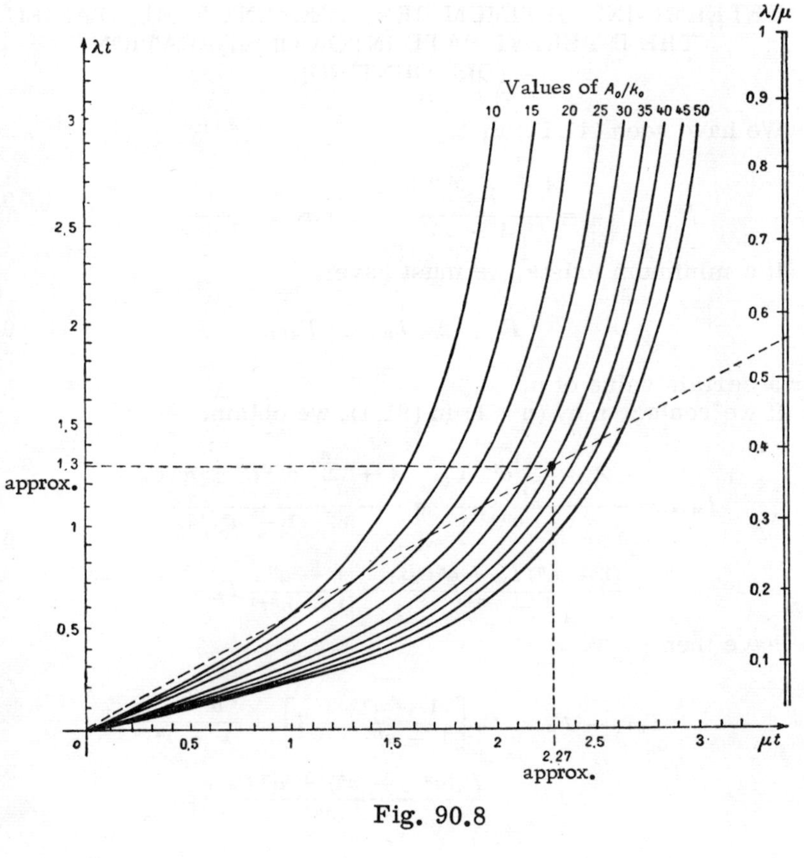

Fig. 90.8

Of course, we can refer to the other axis and still obtain the same result:

$$t^* = \frac{\lambda t^*}{\lambda} = \frac{1.3}{0.4} = \text{approximately 3 years and 3 months.} \qquad 90.35$$

This graph provides a very convenient means of finding the optimum and also facilitates discussion. For instance, if in our example the rate k_0 is twice as high, with A_0, λ, and μ unchanged, then:

$$t^* = \frac{1.5}{0.7} = \text{approximately 2 years and 2 months.} \qquad 90.36$$

The highly characteristic and representative nature of these parameters is noteworthy.

Section 91

DETERMINING OPTIMUM REPLACEMENT TIME, TAKING THE INTEREST RATE INTO CONSIDERATION (DISCOUNTING)

We have seen (41.11) that:

$$\Gamma_n = \frac{A + \sum_{i=1}^{n} \alpha^{i-1} C_i}{1 - \alpha^n}, \text{where } \alpha = \frac{1}{1+r}. \qquad 91.1$$

If a minimum exists, we must have:

$$\Gamma_{n-1} > \Gamma_n < \Gamma_{n+1}. \qquad 91.2$$

for a certain value of n.

If we replace n by (n + 1) in (91.1), we obtain:

$$\Gamma_{n+1} = \frac{A + \sum_{i=1}^{n+1} \alpha^{i-1} C_i}{1 - \alpha^{n+1}} = \frac{A + \sum_{i=1}^{n} \alpha^{i-1} C_i + \alpha^n C_{n+1}}{1 - \alpha^{n+1}}$$

$$= \frac{(1 - \alpha^n)\Gamma_n + \alpha^n C_{n+1}}{1 - \alpha^{n+1}} = \frac{1 - \alpha^n}{1 - \alpha^{n+1}} \Gamma_n + \frac{\alpha^n C_{n+1}}{1 - \alpha^{n+1}} \qquad 91.3$$

We have then:

$$\Gamma_{n+1} - \Gamma_n = \Gamma_n \left[\frac{1 - \alpha^n}{1 - \alpha^{n+1}} - 1\right] + \frac{\alpha^n C_{n+1}}{1 - \alpha^{n+1}}$$

$$= \frac{\Gamma_n(\alpha^{n+1} - \alpha^n) + \alpha^n C_{n+1}}{1 - \alpha^{n+1}}. \qquad 91.4$$

Suppose that:

$$\Gamma_{n+1} - \Gamma_n > 0, \qquad 91.5$$

or

$$\frac{\Gamma_n(\alpha^{n+1} - \alpha^n) + \alpha^n C_{n+1}}{1 - \alpha^{n+1}} > 0; \qquad 91.6$$

or again, dividing by α_n:

$$\Gamma_n(\alpha - 1) + C_{n+1} > 0. \qquad 91.7$$

Since $\alpha < 1$, we can write:

$$\frac{C_{n+1}}{1 - \alpha} > \Gamma_n. \qquad 91.8$$

Thus,

$$\Gamma_{n+1} - \Gamma_n > 0 \qquad 91.9$$

is equivalent to:

$$\frac{C_{n+1}}{(1 - \alpha)} > \Gamma_n. \qquad 91.10$$

Suppose now that:

$$\Gamma_{n-1} - \Gamma_n > 0; \qquad 91.11$$

then:

$$\Gamma_{n-1}(1 - \alpha) - C_n > 0 \qquad 91.12$$

or:

$$\frac{C_n}{1 - \alpha} < \Gamma_{n-1}. \qquad 91.13$$

Thus,

$$\Gamma_{n-1} - \Gamma_n > 0 \qquad 91.14$$

is equivalent to:

$$\frac{C_n}{1 - \alpha} < \Gamma_{n-1}. \qquad 91.14a$$

Returning to expression (91.1) for Γ_n and substituting it into (91.8), we obtain:

$$C_{n+1} > \Gamma_n(1 - a) \qquad 91.15$$

or:

$$C_{n+1} > (1 - a)\frac{A + C_1 + aC_2 + a^2C_3 + \dots + a^{n-1}C_n}{1 - a^n} \qquad 91.16$$

or again:

$$C_{n+1} > \frac{A + C_1 + aC_2 + a^2C_3 + \dots + a^{n-1}C_n}{1 + a + a^2 + \dots + a^{n-1}}. \qquad 91.17$$

Similarly, substituting (91.1) intq (91.13) and changing n to n-1, we have:

$$C_n < \Gamma_{n-1}(1 - a), \qquad 91.18$$

or:

$$C_n < (1 - a)\frac{A + C_1 + aC_2 + a^2C_3 + \dots + a^{n-2}C_{n-1}}{1 - a^{n-1}} \qquad 91.19$$

or again:

$$C_n < \frac{A + C_1 + aC_2 + a^2C_3 + \dots + a^{n-2}C_{n-1}}{1 + a + a^2 + \dots + a^{n-2}}. \qquad 91.20$$

Note that the right members of (91.17) and (91.20) are actually the weighted means of all the costs from i = 1 to i = n for (91.17), and from i =1 to i = n - 1 for (91.20). The weights are the discount factors, 1, α, α^2, α^3, . . . applied to each period.

Thus we arrive at the following rule:

"Replace when

$$C_{n+1} > \frac{A + C_1 + aC_2 + a^2C_3 + \dots + a^{n-1}C_{n-1}}{1 + a + a^2 + \dots + a^{n-1}}. \qquad 91.21$$

Section 92

RANDOM DETERIORATION, EQUIPMENT SURVIVAL, AND FAILURE RATES

1. General explanation.—2. Failure rate.—3. First example: Constant failure rate.—4. Second example: Failure rate proportional to time.—5. Operating limit.

1. General explanation.

Using the notations of Section 43, but taking the case in which the survival curve

$$\nu(t) = \frac{n(t)}{n(o)} \qquad 92.1$$

is considered as continuous (monotone decreasing), the continuous random variable T, which represents the time elapsed since entry into service, will have as its distribution function:

$$\Pr(T < t) = j(t) = 1 - \nu(t), \qquad 92.2$$

because $\nu(t)$ represents the complementary distribution:

$$\Pr(T \geqslant t) = \nu(t). \qquad 92.3$$

The probability density function of the random variable T will be called i(t):

$$\Pr(t \leqslant T < t + dt) = i(t)dt. \qquad 92.4$$

Between the functions $\nu(t)$, j(t), and i(t), the following relations exist:

$$\int_0^t i(u)\, du = j(t) = 1 - \nu(t); \qquad 92.5$$

or, in another form:

$$i(t) = \frac{d}{dt} j(t) = -\frac{d}{dt} \nu(t). \qquad 92.6$$

Note that the function i(t) can have one or more maxima.

2. Failure rate.

Let us call $\lambda(t)dt$ the conditional probability that a piece of equipment having reached age t without failure (breakdown) has a breakdown in the interval t + dt. We can write:

$$\Pr(t \leqslant T < t + dt) = \Pr(T \geqslant t).\lambda(t)dt; \qquad 92.7$$

but:

$$\Pr(t \leqslant T < t + dt) = i(t)dt = -\nu'(t)dt, \qquad 92.8$$

$$\Pr(T \geqslant t) = \nu(t). \qquad 92.9$$

Thus:

$$\lambda(t)\mathrm{d}t = -\frac{v'(t)\mathrm{d}t}{v(t)}, \quad 92.10$$

or again:

$$\lambda(t) = -\frac{v'(t)}{v(t)}. \quad 92.11$$

This quantity has been called the failure rate. Like the failure probability in the case of discrete variables, this failure rate gives a measure of the risk of breakdown.

The function $\lambda(t)$ can be constantly increasing or have one or several maxima. Clearly, it is not a probability density function.

Now we shall explore several interesting cases.

3. First example: Constant failure rate.

$$\text{Suppose that} \quad \lambda(t) = \lambda_0 = \text{const.}; \quad 92.12$$

Then:

$$\frac{v'}{v} = -\lambda_0 \quad 92.13$$

where:

$$\frac{\mathrm{d}v}{\mathrm{d}t} + \lambda_0 v = 0 \quad 92.14$$

with:

$$v(0) = 1. \quad 92.15$$

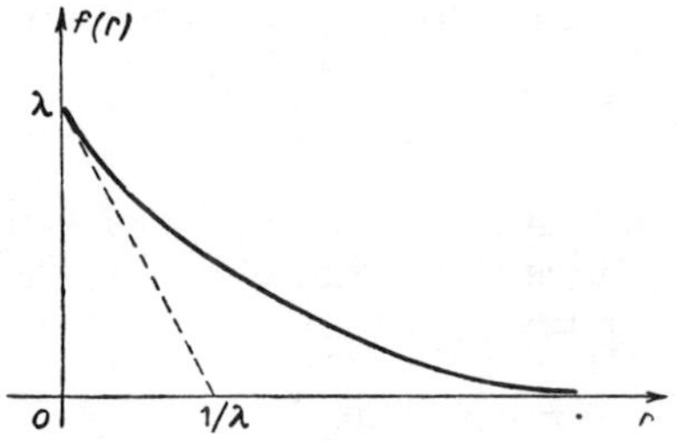

Fig. 92.1

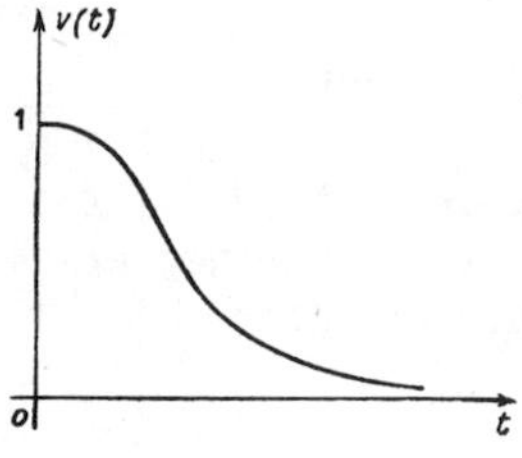

Fig. 92.2

The solution of this differential equation gives:

$$v = e^{-\lambda_0 t}. \quad 92.16$$

Thus, a constant failure rate corresponds to an exponential survival curve (Fig. 92.1).

4. Second example: Failure rate proportional to time.

Let:

$$\lambda(t) = \lambda_0 t. \qquad 92.17$$

This yields:

$$\frac{dv}{dt} + \lambda_0 t v = 0, \qquad 92.18$$

with:

$$v(0) = 1, \qquad 92.19$$

or:

$$v = e^{-\frac{1}{2}\lambda_0 t^2} \qquad 92.20$$

Thus, a failure rate proportional to time and increasing corresponds to a bell-shaped survival curve (Fig. 92.2).

5. Operating limit.

If we impose an operating limit, θ, the survival curve will be limited to the value $t = \theta$ (see Fig. 43.5); the corresponding probability density function will then be:

$$\begin{aligned} i(t) &= -v'(t) && 0 < t < \theta \\ &= q\,\delta(t-\theta) && t = \theta \\ &= 0 && t > \theta, \end{aligned} \qquad 92.21$$

where $q = \nu(\theta)$ and $\delta(t)$ is the Dirac function, such that:

$$\lim_{\varepsilon \to 0} \int_{-\varepsilon}^{+\varepsilon} \delta(t)\,dt = 1. \qquad 92.22$$

For the function $i(t)$ to actually constitute a probability density function, it is necessary that:

$$\int_0^{\infty} i(t)\,dt = 1, \qquad 92.23$$

which is achieved by the presence of an infinite probability density in $t = \theta$ and such that:

$$\lim_{\varepsilon \to 0} \int_{\theta-\varepsilon}^{\theta+\varepsilon} i\, dt = q. \qquad 92.24$$

Section 93

ANALYTICAL DETERMINATION OF THE AVERAGE AGE AT ONSET OF FAILURE

1. General explanation.—2. First example.—3. Second example.—4. General formula for calculating moments.—5. Examples.

1. General explanation.

We propose to find the mean and the standard deviation of the random variable T.

We have:

$$\bar{t} = \int_{t=0}^{t=\infty} t\, i(t) dt = - \int_{t=0}^{t=\infty} t\, dv \qquad 93.1$$

$$\overline{(t^2)} = \int_{t=0}^{t=\infty} t^2 i(t) dt = - \int_{t=0}^{t=\infty} t^2 dv \qquad 93.2$$

We shall present the calculation of these integrals in detail, to obtain some convenient formulas.*

Let us integrate by parts:

$$\bar{t} = - \int_{t=0}^{t=\infty} t\, dv = - [t v]_{t=0}^{t=\infty} + \int_{t=0}^{t=\infty} v\, dt. \qquad 93.3$$

Suppose the survival curve is such that:

$$\lim_{t \to \infty} [t\, v(t)] = 0, \qquad 93.4$$

which is the case in practice for survival curves based on real measurements. It results that:

$$\bar{t} = \int_{t=0}^{t=\infty} v(t) dt. \qquad 93.5$$

---

*We are particularly indebted to the work of M. Descamps, Ingénieur Principal de l'Air: "Prévision statistique des avaries et calcul des volants et rechanges" ("Statistical Prediction of Failures and Calculations of Flying and Replacement Aircraft"), DOCAERO, Nos. 41 and 43, November 1956 and March 1957 (Paris).

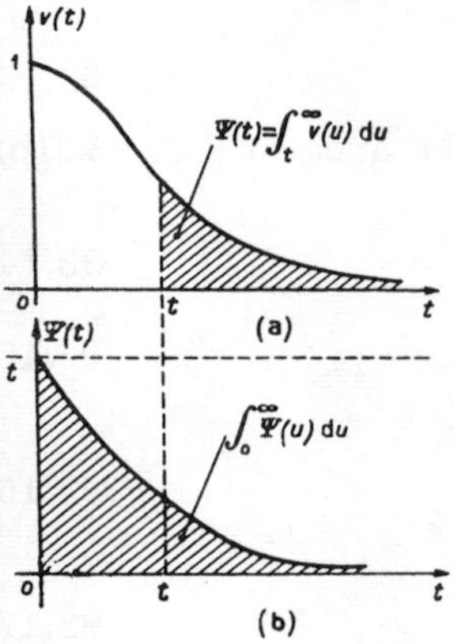

FIG. 93.1

Similarly,

$$\overline{(t^2)} = -\int_{t=0}^{t=\infty} t^2 \mathrm{d}v = -[t^2 v]_{t=0}^{t=\infty} + 2\int_{t=0}^{t=\infty} t v \mathrm{d}t. \qquad 93.6$$

Suppose also that:*

$$\lim_{t\to\infty} [t^2 v(t)] = 0; \qquad 93.7$$

then:

$$\overline{(t^2)} = 2\int_{t=0}^{t=\infty} t v \mathrm{d}t. \qquad 93.8$$

Let us set:

$$\Psi(t) = \int_t^\infty v(u)\mathrm{d}u = \int_0^\infty v(u)\mathrm{d}u - \int_0^t v(u)\mathrm{d}u = \bar{t} - \int_0^t v(u)\mathrm{d}u. \qquad 93.9$$

The function Ψ(t) can be obtained in the manner indicated in Fig. 93.1(a) and (b).

Now let us take the differential of the two members of (93.9); we obtain:

$$\mathrm{d}\Psi = -v(t)\mathrm{d}t. \qquad 93.10$$

Substituting (93.10) into (93.8):

$$\overline{(t^2)} = 2\int_{t=0}^{t=\infty} t v \mathrm{d}t = -2\int_{t=0}^{t=\infty} t \mathrm{d}\Psi = -2[t\Psi(t)]_{t=0}^{t=\infty} + 2\int_{t=0}^{t=\infty} \Psi(t)\mathrm{d}t. \qquad 93.11$$

Suppose, further, that:**

$$\lim_{t\to\infty} [t\Psi(t)] = 0; \qquad 93.12$$

---

*The survival curves take the form of $\nu(t)$ functions such that: $\lim_{t\to\infty} [e^{\alpha t}\nu(t)] = 0$, where α is a sufficiently small positive constant, which in turn implies that: $\lim_{t\to\infty} [t^n \nu(t)] = 0$, $n = 0, 1, 2, 3, \ldots$

**If $\nu(t)$ is such that $\lim_{t\to\infty} [e^{\alpha t}\nu(t)] = 0$, then

$$\lim_{t\to\infty} [e^{\alpha t}\int_0^t v(u)\mathrm{d}u] = 0.$$

then:

$$\overline{(t^2)} = 2\int_0^{\infty} \Psi(t)\mathrm{d}t . \qquad 93.13$$

Thus, $(\overline{t^2})$ is represented by twice the shaded area in Fig. 93.1(b)
If we set

$$k_1 = \bar{t} = \int_0^{\infty} \nu(t)\mathrm{d}t , \qquad 93.14$$

$$k_2 = \tfrac{1}{2}\overline{(t^2)} = \int_0^{\infty} \Psi(t)\mathrm{d}t ; \qquad 93.15$$

then:

$$\sigma_T^2 = 2k_2 - k_1^2, \qquad 93.16$$

or

$$\sigma_T = \sqrt{2k_2 - k_1^2}. \qquad 93.17$$

2. First example.

Let us return to the important special case in which $\nu(t)$ is an exponential, or:

$$\nu(t) = e^{-\lambda_0 t} ; \qquad 93.18$$

we find that:

$$\bar{t} = \int_0^{\infty} e^{-\lambda_0 t}\,\mathrm{d}t = \frac{1}{\lambda_0}, \qquad 93.19$$

$$\Psi(t) = \frac{1}{\lambda_0} - \int_0^{t} e^{-\lambda_0 t}\,\mathrm{d}u = \frac{1}{\lambda_0} + \frac{1}{\lambda_0}[e^{-\lambda_0 t} - 1] = \frac{1}{\lambda_0}e^{-\lambda_0 t}, \qquad 93.20$$

$$\overline{(t^2)} = \frac{2}{\lambda_0}\int_0^{\infty} e^{-\lambda_0 t}\,\mathrm{d}t = \frac{2}{\lambda_0^2}, \qquad 93.21$$

$$\sigma_T^2 = \frac{2}{\lambda_0^2} - \frac{1}{\lambda_0^2} = \frac{1}{\lambda_0^2}. \qquad 93.22$$

$$\sigma_T = \frac{1}{\lambda_0}. \qquad 93.23$$

Thus, in this special case, $\bar{t} = \sigma_t = 1/\lambda_0$ (a predictable result, see Section 73). The reader can verify that conditions (93.4) and (03.7) are satisfied.

3. Second example.

Suppose that $\nu(t)$ is an exponential, and that an operating limit is imposed at time $t = \theta$.

$$v(t) = e^{-\lambda_0 t} \qquad 0 \leqslant t < \theta \qquad\qquad 93.24$$
$$= 0 \qquad\qquad t > \theta.$$

We find:

$$\bar{t} = \int_0^\theta e^{-\lambda_0 t}\, dt = \frac{1 - e^{-\lambda_0 \theta}}{\lambda_0} = \frac{1-q}{\lambda_0}, \qquad 93.25$$

$$q = e^{-\lambda_0 \theta}. \qquad 93.26$$

$$\underset{(0 \leqslant t < \theta)}{\Psi(t)} = \frac{1-q}{\lambda_0} - \int_0^t e^{-\lambda_0 u} du = \frac{e^{-\lambda_0 t} - q}{\lambda_0}, \qquad 93.27$$

$$\underset{(t > \theta)}{\Psi(t)} = \frac{1-q}{\lambda_0} - \int_0^\theta e^{-\lambda_0 t}\, dt = 0 \qquad 93.28$$

$$\overline{(t^2)} = 2\int_0^\infty \Psi(t)dt = 2\int_0^\theta \frac{e^{-\lambda_0 t} - q}{\lambda_0}\, dt$$

$$= \frac{2}{\lambda_0^2}[1 - q - q\theta\lambda_0], \qquad 93.29$$

$$\sigma_T^2 = \frac{2}{\lambda_0^2}[1 - q - q\theta\lambda_0] - \frac{1}{\lambda_0^2}[1-q]^2$$

$$= \frac{1}{\lambda_0^2}[1 - 2q\theta\lambda_0 - q^2], \qquad 93.30$$

$$\sigma_T = \frac{1}{\lambda_0}\sqrt{1 - 2q\theta\lambda_0 - q^2}. \qquad 93.31$$

4. General formula for calculating moments.

To calculate the moments of the distributions h(t) such that h(t) = 0 for t < 0, which is the case here, we shall use the Carson-Laplace transformation.

One of the properties of this transformation gives:

$$\mathscr{L}\, t^n h(t) = (-1)^n s\left[\frac{d^n}{ds^n}\left(\frac{g(s)}{s}\right)\right]. \qquad 93.32$$

We have:

$$M_n = \int_0^\infty t^n h(t)dt = \lim_{t \to \infty} \int_0^t u^n h(u)du. \qquad 93.33$$

If h(t) is exponential and tends uniformly toward zero as $t \to \infty$, then we may write:

$$M_n = \lim_{t \to \infty} \int_0^t u^n h(u)du = \lim_{s \to 0} (-1)^n \frac{d^n}{ds^n}\left[\frac{g(s)}{s}\right], \qquad 93.34$$

a formula which conveniently gives all the moments.

To use this formula in calculating some of the moments of the random variable T discussed in this and preceding paragraphs, we would point out:

$$i(t) = -\frac{dv}{dt}, \qquad 93.35$$

hence:

$$I(s) = -s\,V(s) + s\,v(+0) = -s\,V(s) + s, \qquad 93.36$$

and

$$\frac{I(s)}{s} = -V(s) + 1. \qquad 93.37$$

We then have:

$$\begin{aligned} M_n &= \lim_{t \to \infty} \int_0^t u^n\, i(u)\,du = \lim_{s \to 0} (-1)^n \frac{d^n}{ds^n}\left(\frac{I(s)}{s}\right) \\ &= \lim_{s \to 0} (-1)^{n+1} \frac{d^n}{ds^n}\left[V(s)\right] \end{aligned} \qquad 93.38$$

Thus:

$$M_n = \lim_{s \to 0} (-1)^{n+1} \frac{d^n V}{ds^n}, \qquad n = 1, 2, 3, \ldots \qquad 93.39$$

5. Examples.

1. First example (already calculated; see 93.18).

Let:

$$v(t) = e^{-\lambda_0 t} \qquad 93.40$$

$$V(s) = \frac{s}{s + \lambda_0}. \qquad 93.41$$

We have:

$$M_1 = \lim_{s \to 0} \left\{(-1)^2 \frac{d}{ds}\left[\frac{s}{s + \lambda_0}\right]\right\} = \lim_{s \to 0} \frac{\lambda_0}{(s + \lambda_0)^2} = \frac{1}{\lambda_0} \qquad 93.42$$

$$M_2 = \lim_{s \to 0} \left\{(-1)^3 \frac{d^2}{ds^2}\left[\frac{s}{s + \lambda_0}\right]\right\} = \lim_{s \to 0} \frac{2\lambda_0}{(s + \lambda_0)^3} = \frac{2}{\lambda_0^2}, \qquad 93.43$$

$$M_n = \lim_{s \to 0} \left\{(-1)^{n+1} \frac{d^n}{ds^n}\left[\frac{s}{s+\lambda_0}\right]\right\} = \lim_{s \to 0} \frac{n!\,\lambda_0}{(s+\lambda_0)^{n+1}} = \frac{n!}{\lambda_0^n}. \qquad 93.44$$

2. Second example (already calculated; see 93.24).

Let:

$$\begin{aligned} v(t) &= e^{-\lambda_0 t} & 0 < t < \theta \\ &= 0 & t > \theta, \end{aligned} \qquad 93.45$$

with:

$$q = v(\theta) = e^{-\lambda_0 \theta}. \qquad 93.46$$

We have:

$$V(s) = \frac{s}{s+\lambda_0}(1 - q e^{-s\theta}). \qquad 93.47$$

$$M_1 = \lim_{s \to 0} \left\{(-1)^2 \frac{d}{ds}\left[\frac{s}{s+\lambda_0}(1 - q e^{-s\theta})\right]\right\} = \frac{1}{\lambda_0}(1-q) \qquad 93.48$$

$$M_2 = \lim_{s \to 0} \left\{(-1)^3 \frac{d^2}{ds^2}\left[\frac{s}{s+\lambda_0}(1 - q e^{-s\theta})\right]\right\} = \frac{2}{\lambda_0^2}(1 - q - q\theta\lambda_0) \qquad 93.49$$

Section 94

PROBABILITY OF A TOTAL OPERATING LIFE H FOR N IDENTICAL EQUIPMENTS

Let us consider N identical equipments, whose survival curve, $v(t)$, is known, and for which we set an operating limit of θ. What is the total number of operating hours, H, that we can hope for from these N equipments?

If $T_1, T_2, \ldots, T_N$ is the random operating life of each of these N equipments, the total number of operating hours, H, is the sum:

$$H = T_1 + T_2 + \ldots + T_N, \qquad 94.1$$

of these N independent random variables. It follows that H is a random variable itself, whose mean and variance are:

$$\bar{h} = \bar{t}_1 + \bar{t}_2 + \ldots + \bar{t}_N = N\bar{t} \qquad 94.2$$

$$\sigma_H^2 = \sigma_{T_1}^2 + \sigma_{T_2}^2 + \ldots + \sigma_{T_N}^2 = N\sigma_T^2. \qquad 94.3$$

If N is sufficiently large, then the variable H obeys a Gaussian (normal) law, no matter what the $\nu(t)$ survival function may be. Taking the reduced variable:

$$b = \frac{H - \bar{h}}{\sigma_H}, \qquad 94.4$$

we obtain:

$$Pr(|b| > t) = \frac{2}{\sqrt{2\pi}} \int_t^{\infty} e^{-u^2/2}\, du. \qquad 94.5$$

As a concrete example, let us take the value 0.1 for this probability; a table of the complementary Gaussian error function gives as the value of t:

$$t = 1.645. \qquad 94.6$$

Thus, we can write:

$$Pr\left(\left|\frac{H - \bar{h}}{\sigma_H}\right| \leqslant 1.645\right) = 0.9. \qquad 94.7$$

The parenthesis and inequality in the first member of (94.7) can be written:

$$\bar{h} - 1.645\,\sigma_H \leqslant H \leqslant \bar{h} + 1.645\,\sigma_H, \qquad 94.8$$

or:

$$N\bar{t} - 1.645\sqrt{N}\,\sigma_T \leqslant H \leqslant N\bar{t} + 1.645\sqrt{N}\,\sigma_T. \qquad 94.9$$

There is thus a probability of 0.9 that H will lie between Nt - 1.645 $\sqrt{N}\sigma_T$ and $N\bar{t}$ + 1.645 $\sqrt{N}\sigma_T$.

Let us take as a numerical example the case in which $\nu(t)$ is an exponential function with an operating limit of θ:

$$\begin{aligned} \nu(t) &= e^{-\lambda_0 t} & 0 \leqslant t < \theta \\ &= 0 & t > \theta, \end{aligned} \qquad 94.10$$

where:

$$\lambda_0 = 10^{-3} \quad \text{and} \quad \theta = 1{,}000 \text{ hours}. \qquad \begin{matrix} 94.11 \\ 94.12 \end{matrix}$$

From this we derive:

$$q = e^{-\lambda_0 \theta} = e^{-1} = 0.368, \qquad 94.13$$

$$\bar{t} = \frac{1 - q}{\lambda_0} = \frac{1 - 0.368}{10^{-3}} = 632 \text{ hours}, \qquad 94.14$$

$$\sigma_T = \frac{1}{\lambda_0}\sqrt{1 - 2q\theta\lambda_0 - q^2} = 358 \text{ hours}. \qquad 94.15$$

Assume we have 100 equipments of this type (considering 100 as a large number). For these 100 equipments:

$$\bar{h} = N\bar{t} = 63.200 \text{ hours}, \qquad 94.16$$

$$\sigma_H = \sqrt{N}\,\sigma_T = 3580 \text{ hours}. \qquad 94.17$$

The inequalities give:

$$57{,}320 \text{ hours} \leqslant H \leqslant 69{,}080 \text{ hours}. \qquad 94.18$$

All of which can be translated: the probability that the total number of operating hours before failure of these 100 equipments lies between 57,320 and 69,080 hours is 0.9.

Section 95

ANALYTICAL STUDY OF THE PROBABILITY OF CONSUMPTION

1. General explanation.—2. Example.

1. General explanation.

We shall now retrace, almost exactly, the discussion given in Section 45, but this time as applied to a continuous curve $\nu(t)$.

The probability $p_0(t)$ of zero consumption, i.e. of no replacement ($m = 0$), is obviously $\nu(t)$:

$$p_0(t) = \nu(t). \qquad 95.1$$

To calculate $p_1(t)$, we write that there is one and only one case of breakdown (or replacement at the operating limit) in the interval between 0 and t. In other words: a replacement occurs at an instant u, which lies between 0 and t; from then on, there are no more replacements between u and t. Now, the probability that there will be a breakdown (or replacement at the operating limit) between the ages u and u + du is $i(u)du$, or $-d\nu(u)$. Furthermore, the probability that the replacement equipment installed at instant u will operate without breakdown between u and t is $\nu(t-u)$. The probability that both of these conditions will be realized is:

$$i(u)\mathrm{d}u \cdot v(t-u) = v(t-u) \cdot i(u)\mathrm{d}u = -v(t-u)\mathrm{d}v(u). \qquad 95.2$$

Now, we must consider all the possibilities of breakdowns of the first equipment installed at various times, u, between 0 and t, and then take the sum of the corresponding probabilities:

$$p_1(t) = \int_0^t v(t-u)\, i(u)\, du = -\int_0^t v(t-u)\, dv(u)\,. \qquad 95.3$$

More generally, there is a recurrence formula giving $p_m(t)$ as a function of $p_{m-1}(t)$. For a consumption of m equipments in the interval between 0 and t, it is necessary and sufficient that there be a replacement (due to breakdown or the operating limit) at some instant u between 0 and t, and that, between u and t, m - 1 machines be consumed. Thus:

$$p_m(t) = \int_0^t p_{m-1}(t-u) \cdot i(u)\, du, = -\int_0^t p_{m-1}(t-u)\, dv(u)\,, \qquad 95.4$$

with:

$$p_0(t) = v(t). \qquad 95.5$$

Integrals (95.4) are Stieltjes integrals, and define a simple process constituting a Markov chain. To calculate these successive integrals, we shall use the Carson-Laplace transformation.*

Let us set:

$$\mathscr{L} p_m(t) = P_m(s), \quad \mathscr{L} v(t) = V(s), \quad \mathscr{L} i(t) = I(s) \qquad \begin{cases} 95.6 \\ 95.7 \\ 95.8 \end{cases}$$

and let us recall the covering theorem (Borel theorem).

If:

$$H_1(s) = \mathscr{L} h_1(t) \quad \text{and} \quad H_2(s) = \mathscr{L} h_2(t), \qquad \begin{matrix} 95.9 \\ 95.10 \end{matrix}$$

then:

$$\frac{H_1(s) \cdot H_2(s)}{s} = \mathscr{L} \int_0^t h_1(u) \cdot h_2(t-u)\, du = \mathscr{L} \int_0^t h_1(t-u) \cdot h_2(u)\, du\,. \qquad 95.11$$

---

*(See the footnote at the end of Section 55.) Instead of the letter p usually employed, we shall use the letter s, so as to avoid confusion with the letter p already used to represent probabilities:

$$g(s) = \mathscr{L} h(t) = s \int_0^\infty e^{-st} h(t) dt.$$

Taking the transforms of (95.4) and (95.5), we obtain:

$$P_1(s) = \frac{V(s) \cdot I(s)}{s}, \qquad P_m(s) = \frac{P_{m-1}(s) \cdot I(s)}{s}. \qquad \begin{matrix} 95.12 \\ 95.13 \end{matrix}$$

It is also necessary to calculate the transform of:

$$v(t) = 1 - \int_0^t i(t)\,dt\,; \qquad 95.14$$

which gives:

$$V(s) = 1 - \frac{I(s)}{s}. \qquad 95.15$$

Now we are able to calculate $P_2, P_3, \ldots, P_m \ldots$

$$P_0 = V$$

$$P_1 = \frac{1}{s} VI$$

$$P_2 = \frac{1}{s} P_1 I = \frac{1}{s^2} VI^2 \qquad 95.16$$

$$P_3 = \ldots\ldots = \frac{1}{s^3} VI^3$$

$$\ldots\ldots$$

$$P_m = \ldots\ldots = \frac{1}{s^m} VI^m$$

or, as a function of V only:

$$P_0 = V$$
$$P_1 = V(1 - V)$$
$$P_2 = V(1 - V)^2 \qquad 95.17$$
$$\ldots\ldots$$
$$P_m = V(1 - V)^m.$$

2. Example.

Suppose:

$$v(t) = e^{-\lambda_0 t}\,; \qquad 95.18$$

then:

$$V(s) = \frac{s}{s + \lambda_0} \qquad 95.19$$

and

$$P_m(s) = \frac{s}{s+\lambda_0}\left(1 - \frac{s}{s+\lambda_0}\right)^m$$

$$= \lambda_0^m \frac{s}{(s+\lambda_0)^{m+1}}, \qquad 95.20$$

A table of the Carson-Laplace transformation* gives:

$$p_m(t) = \frac{(\lambda_0 t)^m e^{-\lambda_0 t}}{m!}. \qquad 95.21$$

Thus, the exponential distribution $\nu(t)$ corresponds to the Poisson distribution $p_m(t)$.

For a Poisson distribution, it is well known that:

$$\bar{m}(t) = \lambda_0 t, \qquad \sigma_M^2 = \lambda_0 t. \qquad \begin{matrix} 95.22 \\ 95.23 \end{matrix}$$

Thus, the mean and the variance of consumption in the interval from 0 to t are proportional to t. The quantity λ_0 is the rate of consumption.

Now let us calculate the cumulative probabilities:

$$\underset{0\text{ to }t}{\Pr}(\leqslant m) = \sum_{r=0}^{m} p_r(t)\,; \qquad 95.24$$

hence:

$$\underset{0\text{ to }t}{\Pr}(\leqslant m) = \mathop{}_{r=0}^{m} \Pr(s)$$

$$= V[1 + (1-V) + (1-V)^2 + \ldots + (1-V)^m]$$

$$= V\left[\frac{(1-V)^{m+1} - 1}{(1-V) - 1}\right] \quad ** \qquad 95.25$$

$$= 1 - (1-V)^{m+1}.$$

---

*See, for example, D. Papin and A. Kaufmann, "Cours de Calcul Opérationnel (Transformation de Carson-Laplace)" "Course in Operational Calculus (Carson-Laplace Transformation)," Paris. Albin Michel.

**This is legitimate: the module of 1 - V is always less than 1 (see footnote ** on page 453).

Hence:

$$\Pr_{0\text{ to }t}(>m) = (1 - V)^{m+1}. \qquad 95.26$$

Returning to the case in which $\nu(t)$ is exponential:

$$\Pr(>m) = \left(1 - \frac{s}{s + \lambda_0}\right)^{m+1} = \frac{\lambda_0^{\,m+1}}{(s + \lambda_0)^{m+1}}. \qquad 95.27$$

A table of transforms gives:

$$\Pr_{0\text{ to }t}(>m) = \frac{1}{m!}\int_0^{\lambda_0 t} e^{-u}\,u^m\,du. \qquad 95.28$$

We can readily check that:

$$\Pr(>0) = \int_0^{\lambda_0 t} e^{-u}\,du = 1 - e^{-\lambda_0 t} = 1 - p_0(t). \qquad 95.29$$

We shall use a particularly convenient method* to calculate $\bar{m}(t)$ and $\sigma_m(t)$:

$$\bar{m}(t) = \sum_{m=1}^{\infty} m\,p_m(t), \qquad 95.30$$

hence:

$$\begin{aligned} \bar{M}(s) &= \sum_{m=1}^{\infty} m\,P_m(s) \\ &= \sum_{m=1}^{\infty} m\,V(1 - V)^m \\ &= V(1 - V)\sum_{m=1}^{\infty} m\,(1 - V)^{m-1}. \end{aligned} \qquad 95.31$$

Consider the identity:

$$\frac{1}{(1 - x)^2} = 1 + 2x + 3x^2 + \dots + mx^{m-1} + \dots \qquad 95.32$$

where $x < 1$; this development can be applied to (95.31), since the module** of $1 - V$ is always less than 1. This gives us:

---

*This method was developed by Ingénieur Principal Descamps (see Bibliography).

**In effect:

$$1 - V = \frac{I}{s} \quad \text{and} \quad \frac{I}{s} = \int_0^{\infty} i(t)\,e^{-st}\,dt$$

$$|I/s| \leq \int_0^{\infty} |i(t)|\cdot|e^{-st}|\,dt < \int_0^{\infty} |i(t)|\cdot|e^{-ct}|\,dt < \int_0^{\infty} |i(t)|\,dt \leq 1$$

where c = the real part of s.

$$\overline{M}(s) = V(1 - V)\cdot\frac{1}{[1 - (1 - V)]^2}, \qquad 95.33$$

or, finally:

$$\overline{M}(s) = \frac{1 - V}{V} = \frac{1}{V} - 1. \qquad 95.34$$

In the example where $\nu(t) = e^{-\lambda_0 t}$, this would yield:

$$\overline{M}(s) = \frac{1 - \dfrac{s}{s + \lambda_0}}{\dfrac{s}{s + \lambda_0}} = \frac{\lambda_0}{s}, \qquad 95.35$$

and hence:

$$\overline{m}(t) = \lambda_0 t; \qquad 95.36$$

which brings us back to (95.22).

To calculate $M^2(s)$, we proceed as follows:*

$$\overline{M^2(s)} = \sum_{m=1}^{\infty} m^2 V(1 - V)^m = V(1 - V)\sum_{m=1}^{\infty} m^2(1 - V)^{m-1} \qquad 95.37$$

Now, using these developments:

$$y(x) = x + 2x^2 + 3x^3 + \ldots + mx^m + \ldots = \frac{x}{(1 - x)^2}$$

where $0 < x < 1$, and: 95.38

$$y'(x) = 1 + 4x + 9x^2 + \ldots + m^2x^{m-1} + \ldots = \frac{1 + x}{(1 - x)^3}$$

where $0 < x < 1$; 95.39

We have:

$$\sum_{m=1}^{\infty} m^2(1 - V)^{m-1} = \frac{2 - V}{V^3}. \qquad 95.40$$

---

*We do not feel there is any possible confusion between our use of M to designate the random variable and the use of the same capital letter to indicate the Carson-Laplace transform of m.

It follows that:

$$\overline{M^2(s)} = V(1 - V)\frac{(2 - V)}{V^3} = 1 + \frac{2}{V^2} - \frac{3}{V} \qquad 95.41$$

$$\sigma_M^2 = L^{-1}[\overline{M^2(s)}] - [L^{-1}\,\overline{M(s)}]^2 . \qquad 95.42$$

Still in the example $\nu(t) = e^{-\lambda_0 t}$:

$$V = \frac{s}{s + \lambda_0}, \quad \overline{M^2(s)} = \frac{\lambda_0}{s} + 2\frac{\lambda_0^2}{s^2}, \quad \overline{M(s)} = \frac{\lambda_0}{s} \qquad \begin{cases} 95.43 \\ 95.44 \\ 95.45 \end{cases}$$

$$L^{-1}[\overline{M^2(s)}] = \lambda_0 t + \lambda_0^2 t^2 \;, \quad L^{-1}[\overline{M(s)}]^2 = \lambda_0^2 t^2. \qquad \begin{cases} 95.46 \\ 95.47 \end{cases}$$

$$\sigma_M^2 = \lambda_0 t . \qquad 95.48$$

Section 96

CASE OF ALREADY-USED EQUIPMENT

In Section 46 we established that the survival function of used equipment was:

$$\nu_a(t) = \frac{\nu(t + a)}{\nu(a)} \qquad a \geqslant 0, \qquad t \geqslant 0. \qquad 96.1$$

Let us now examine a few important special cases:

1) $\nu(t) = e^{-\lambda_0 t} \qquad t \geqslant 0,$ 96.2

then:

$$\nu(t + a) = e^{-\lambda_0 (t+a)} \quad t \geqslant 0, \qquad 96.3$$

$$\nu(a) = e^{-\lambda_0 a} \qquad 96.4$$

$$\nu_a(t) = \frac{\nu(t + a)}{\nu(a)} = \frac{e^{-\lambda_0 (t+a)}}{e^{-\lambda_0 a}} = e^{-\lambda_0 t} \qquad t \geqslant 0. \qquad 96.5$$

Thus, the conditional probability of survival in the case of exponential deterioration is equal to $\nu(t)$.

2) $\nu(t) = e^{-kt} \qquad t \geqslant 0$ 96.6

We have:

$$\nu_a(t) = e^{-2kat}\, e^{-kt^2} \qquad t \geqslant 0. \qquad 96.7$$

3)
$$v(t) = 1 - \frac{t}{k} \qquad 0 \leqslant t \leqslant k$$
$$= 0 \qquad t \geqslant k, \tag{96.8}$$

we have:

$$v_a(t) = 1 - \frac{t}{k-a} \qquad 0 \leqslant t \leqslant k - a$$
$$= 0 \qquad t \geqslant k - a. \tag{96.9}$$

4) Lastly, if the survival curve is exponential, and if an operating limit is introduced at time $\theta(\theta > a)$:

$$v(t) = e^{-\lambda_0 t} \qquad 0 \leqslant t < \theta$$
$$= 0 \qquad t > \theta; \tag{96.10}$$

then:

$$v_a(t) = e^{-\lambda_0 t} \qquad 0 \leqslant t < \theta - a$$
$$= 0 \qquad t > \theta - a. \tag{96.11}$$

To calculate the consumption probabilities, we use formulas (95.3) and (95.4), with the appropriate modifications.

If only the first equipment is initially used:

$$p_1(t) = \int_0^t v(t-u)\, i_a(u)\, du \text{, where } i_a(t) = -v'_a(t), \tag{96.12}$$

$$p_m(t) = \int_0^t p_{m-1}(t-u)\, i(u)\, du. \tag{96.13}$$

Let us pose:

$$\mathscr{L} p_m(t) = P_m(s), \quad \mathscr{L} v(t) = V(s), \quad \mathscr{L} i(t) = I(s). \tag{96.14}$$

After calculation, we have:

$$P_m = \frac{1}{s^m} V I_a I^{m-1} \tag{96.15}$$

or:

$$P_m = V(1 - V_a)(1 - V)^{m-1}. \tag{96.16}$$

If all the succeeding equipments are used to the same degree at the time they enter service:

$$p_1(t) = \int_0^t v_a(t - u)\, i_a(u)\, du\,, \qquad 96.17$$

$$p_m(t) = \int_0^t p_{m-1}(t - u) \cdot i_a(u)\, du\,, \qquad 96.18$$

and

$$P_m = \frac{1}{s^m} V_a I_a^m\,, \qquad 96.19$$

or:

$$P_m = V_a(1 - V_a)^m\,. \qquad 96.20$$

Section 97

CONSUMPTION PROBABILITY FUNCTION FOR N IDENTICAL ITEMS OF EQUIPMENT

Let there be N items of equipment having, at t = 0, the respective ages:

$$\alpha_1,\ \alpha_2,\ \ldots,\ \alpha_N\,. \qquad 97.1$$

Suppose that, from the beginning of their operating lives, the assemblies in which these items are installed have completed:

$$t_1,\ t_2,\ \ldots,\ t_N \qquad 97.2$$

hours (or any other unit of time) of service. Letting $\bar{m}^*$ represent the mean total consumption of these items of equipment, we have:

$$\bar{m}^* = \overline{m_1(t_1)} + \overline{m_2(t_2)} + \ldots + \overline{m_N(t_N)}. \qquad 97.3$$

Let us examine the special case in which the object is to predict the total consumption, $\bar{m}^*$, when the N assemblies in which the N items of equipment are installed have all completed the same number of hours of operation, while at the start of the measured times, the age distribution α_i (i = 1, 2,..., N) is defined by a function $\mu(\alpha)$ such that the number of items of equipment whose age lies between α and $\alpha + d\alpha$ is $N\mu(\alpha)d\alpha$.

Under these conditions:

$$\bar{m}^*(t) = N \int_0^\infty \bar{m}(t) \cdot \mu(a)\, da \qquad 97.4$$

and its Carson-Laplace transform will be:

$$L\bar{m}^*(t) = \overline{M}^*(s) = \frac{N}{s - I(s)} \int_0^\infty I_a(s)\,\mu(a)\,da\,. \tag{97.5}$$

This formula is very useful in computing the distribution of ages in miscellaneous equipment. (See ref. F-10 in the Bibliography.)

Section 98

METHOD OF NUMERICAL EVALUATION OF STIELTJES INTEGRALS *

Stieltjes integrals, such as:

$$f(t) = \int_0^t h(\tau)\,r'(t-\tau)\,d\tau = \int_0^t h(t-\tau)\cdot r'(\tau)\,d\tau$$

$$= \int_0^t h(t-\tau)\,dr(\tau), \tag{98.1}$$

play a fundamental role in the theory and calculations of replacement problems. The availability of a method for their numerical evaluation is thus of some importance; we suggest the following.

Let us recall Poncelet's formula for evaluating a definite integral:

$$f(ne) = \int_0^{ne} g(\tau)\,d\tau = e\{g(\tfrac{1}{2}e) + g(\tfrac{3}{2}e) + \ldots + g[(n-\tfrac{1}{2})e]\}, \tag{98.2}$$

where the interval from 0 to t has been divided into n equal parts such that ne = t (see Fig. 98.1); obviously, the precision of the calculation improves as the value of n is increased.

Setting:

$$g(\tau) = r'(t-\tau)\cdot h(\tau)\,, \tag{98.3}$$

let us use (98.2) to evaluate the integrals:

$$f(se) = \int_0^{se} g(\tau)\,d\tau\;, \tag{98.4}$$

for s = 1, 2, 3, ..., n; i.e. in the intervals e, 2e, 3e,..., ne.

---

*This method was communicated to us by Professor J. Kuntzmann, Director of the Calculation Laboratory of the University of Grenoble.

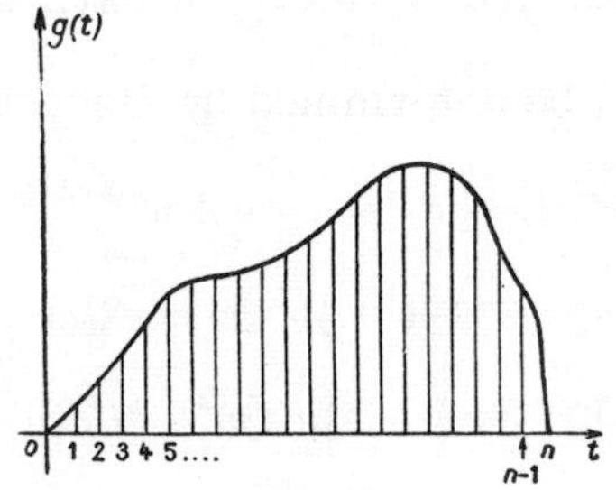

Fig. 98.1

$$s = 1,\ t = e,\ \int^{e} g(\tau)\mathrm{d}t = e\, h(\tfrac{1}{2}e)\, r'(\tfrac{1}{2}e), \tag{98.5}$$

$$s = 2,\ t = 2e,\ \int_0^{2e} g(\tau)\mathrm{d}\tau = e[h(\tfrac{1}{2}e) r'(\tfrac{3}{2}e) + h(\tfrac{3}{2}e)\, r'(\tfrac{1}{2}e)], \tag{98.6}$$

$$s = 3,\ t = 3e,\ \int_0^{3e} g(\tau)\mathrm{d}\tau = e[h(\tfrac{1}{2}e)\, r'(\tfrac{5}{2}e) + h(\tfrac{3}{2}e) r'(\tfrac{3}{2}e) + h(\tfrac{5}{2}e)\cdot r'(\tfrac{1}{2}e) \tag{98.7}$$

$$s = 4,\ t = 4e,\ \int_0^{4e} g(\tau)\mathrm{d}\tau = e[h(\tfrac{1}{2}e) r'(\tfrac{7}{2}e) + h(\tfrac{3}{2}e)\cdot r'(\tfrac{5}{2}e) + h(\tfrac{5}{2}e) r'(\tfrac{3}{2}e) + h(\tfrac{7}{2}e)\cdot r'(\tfrac{1}{2}e)], \tag{98.8}$$

$$s = n,\ t = ne,\ \int_0^{ne} g(\tau)\mathrm{d}\tau = e[h(\tfrac{1}{2}e) r'\{(n-\tfrac{1}{2})e\} + h(\tfrac{3}{2}e)\cdot r'\{(n-\tfrac{3}{2}r)e\} + \ldots + h\{(n-\tfrac{3}{2})e\}\cdot r'(\tfrac{3}{2}e) + h\{(n-\tfrac{1}{2})e\}\cdot r'(\tfrac{1}{2}e)]. \tag{98.9}$$

In certain research problems, one takes the functions f(t) and h(t) in (98.1) as given, then calculating $r'(t)$ and from this, r(t); the preceding formulas permit finding $r'(t)$ directly. We have:

$$s = 1 \quad r'(\tfrac{1}{2}e) = \frac{f(e)}{e h(\tfrac{1}{2}e)}, \tag{98.10}$$

$$s = 2 \quad r'(\tfrac{3}{2}e) = \frac{f(2e)}{e h(\tfrac{1}{2}e)} - \frac{h(\tfrac{3}{2}e)}{h(\tfrac{1}{2}e)}\, r'(\tfrac{1}{2}e) \tag{98.11}$$

$$s = 3 \quad r'(\tfrac{5}{2}e) = \frac{f(3e)}{e h(\tfrac{1}{2}e)} - \frac{h(\tfrac{3}{2}e)}{h(\tfrac{1}{2}e)}\, r'(\tfrac{3}{2}e) - \frac{h(\tfrac{5}{2}e)}{h(\tfrac{1}{2}e)}\, r'(\tfrac{1}{2}e) \tag{98.12}$$

$$s = n \quad r'[(n-\tfrac{1}{2})e] = \frac{f(ne)}{e h(\tfrac{1}{2}e)} - \frac{h(\tfrac{3}{2}e)}{h(\tfrac{1}{2}e)}\, r'[(n-\tfrac{3}{2})e] - \ldots\ldots - \frac{h[(n-\tfrac{3}{2})e]}{h(\tfrac{1}{2}e)}\, r'(\tfrac{3}{2}e) - \frac{h[(n-\tfrac{1}{2})e]}{h(\tfrac{1}{2}e)}\, r'(\tfrac{1}{2}e). \tag{98.13}$$

We have thus found the n values of $r'(t)$, which then allows us to plot the curve.

The curve $r(t)$ will be determined by discrete values as follows:

$$r(\tfrac{1}{2}e) = \tfrac{1}{2}[r'(\tfrac{1}{2}e) + r'(0)]\cdot\tfrac{1}{2}e \qquad 98.14$$

$$r(\tfrac{3}{2}e) = r(\tfrac{1}{2}e) + \tfrac{1}{2}[r'(\tfrac{3}{2}e) + r'(\tfrac{1}{2}e)]e, \qquad 98.15$$

$$r(\tfrac{5}{2}e) = r(\tfrac{3}{2}e) + \tfrac{1}{2}[r'(\tfrac{5}{2}e) + r'(\tfrac{3}{2}e)]\cdot e, \qquad 98.16$$

$$r\left((n-\tfrac{1}{2})e\right) = r\left((n-\tfrac{3}{2})\,e\right) + \tfrac{1}{2}\left[r'\left((n-\tfrac{1}{2})e\right) + r'\left((n-\tfrac{3}{2})\,e\right)\right]\cdot e. \qquad 98.17$$

The value $r'(0)$ which has not been evaluated, and which is very important, is easily obtained.

Let us recall two more theorems concerning the Carson-Laplace transformation:

If:

$$H_1(s) = \mathscr{L}\, h_1(t) \text{ and } H_2(s) = \mathscr{L}\, h_2(t), \qquad 98.18$$

$$\begin{aligned} H_1(s)\cdot H_2(s) &= \mathscr{L}\, \frac{\mathrm{d}}{\mathrm{d}t}\int_0^t h_1(u)\, h_2(t-u)\,\mathrm{d}u \\ &= \mathscr{L}\, \frac{\mathrm{d}}{\mathrm{d}t}\int_0^t h_1(t-u)\, h_2(u)\,\mathrm{d}u\,; \end{aligned} \qquad 98.19$$

otherwise:

$$\text{if } H(s) = \mathscr{L}\, h(t), \qquad 98.20$$

then:

$$\lim_{|s|\to\infty} H(s) = \lim_{t\to 0} h(t). \qquad 98.21$$

So we can write, after having posed:

$$F_1(s) = \mathscr{L} f'(t), \quad H(s) = \mathscr{L} h(t), \quad R_1(s) = \mathscr{L} r'(t) \qquad 98.22$$

$$F_1(s) = H(s)\cdot R_1(s) \quad * \qquad 98.23$$

$$\lim_{|s|\to\infty} F_1(s) = \lim_{|s|\to\infty} H(s)\cdot\lim_{|s|\to\infty} R_1(s). \qquad 98.24$$

Let us assume that

$$\lim_{t\to 0} h(t) = 1, \qquad 98.25$$

---

*The three functions, $f'(t)$, $h(t)$, and $r'(t)$ tend monotonically towards a limit when $t \to \infty$.

then:

$$\lim_{|s| \to \infty} F_1(s) = \lim_{|s| \to \infty} R_1(s); \tag{98.26}$$

or:

$$\lim_{t \to 0} f'(t) = \lim_{t \to 0} r'(t) \tag{98.27}$$

and, finally, we obtain:

$$f'(0) = r'(0), \tag{98.28}$$

which means that the curves f(t) and r(t) have the same slope at the origin.

Section 99

ANALYTICAL STUDY OF THE SUPPLY FUNCTION

1. General explanation.—2. An important special case.

1. General explanation.

Suppose that the survival function is given in the form of a continuous function, $\nu(t)$, and let us return to the description given in Section 47.

If no replacement is made:

$$n(t) = N_0\, \nu(t). \tag{99.1}$$

Let us call f(t) the utilization function. If r(u) is the number of equipments replaced up to time u, the differential:

$$r'(u)\mathrm{d}u \tag{99.2}$$

gives the number of objects replaced in the interval u to u + du. The function:

$$r'(t) \tag{99.3}$$

will be called the supply rate.

The number of equipments from this supply lot surviving at a future time t will be:

$$r'(u)\mathrm{d}u \times \nu(t - u) = r'(u)\cdot\nu(t - u)\mathrm{d}u. \tag{99.4}$$

The total number of equipments in service at time t, including those surviving from the initial lot, will be:

$$f(t) = N_0 v(t) + \int_0^t r'(u) \cdot v(t-u)\, du. \tag{99.5}$$

This equation is of a very familiar type. It is a Volterra integral equation of the second kind, having the kernel $r'(t)$. When $N_0 = 0$, this integral is said to be of the first kind.

Taking the Carson-Laplace transform of this equation, we set:

$$F(s) = \mathscr{L} f(t), \qquad V(s) = \mathscr{L} v(t), \qquad R(s) = \mathscr{L} r(t), \qquad \begin{cases} 99.6 \\ 99.7 \\ 99.8 \end{cases}$$

we have:

$$F(s) = N_0 V(s) + \frac{R'(s) \cdot V(s)}{s}, \tag{99.9}$$

where

$$R'(s) = \mathscr{L} r'(t) \quad \text{and not} \quad dR(s)/ds. \tag{99.10}$$

From (99.9) we derive:

$$R'(s) = s\, \frac{F - N_0 V}{V}. \tag{99.11}$$

We know R(s) at once, since:

$$r'(t) = \frac{dr}{dt}, \tag{99.12}$$

therefore:

$$R'(s) = sR(s) - sr(0). \tag{99.13}$$

We have:

$$r(0) = 0, \tag{99.14}$$

hence:

$$R'(s) = sR(s). \tag{99.15}$$

Let us put (99.15) into (99.9); we have

$$F = N_0 V + RV, \tag{99.16}$$

hence:

$$R = \frac{F}{V} - N_0. \tag{99.17}$$

Thus, it is possible, knowing f(t) and ν(t), to determine r′(t) and r(t) analytically.

The integral equation (99.5) can be used in another way. Suppose that we have measured f(t) and r(t); it is then possible, by means of (99.17), to obtain ν(t).

$$V = \frac{F}{N_0 + R}, \tag{99.18}$$

hence:

$$\nu(t) = \mathscr{L}^{-1} \frac{F(s)}{N_0 + R(s)}. \tag{99.19}$$

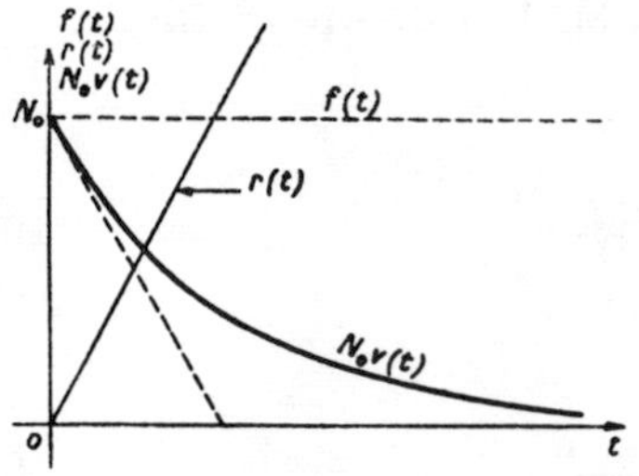

Fig. 99.1

It may be noted that the equipment survival function can be found if the utilization function (arbitrary) and the supply function (measured or known from accounting records) are known. This is an important fact, allowing us to state that the equipment survival function can be measured indirectly in this fashion.

2. An important special case.

Suppose that:

$$f(t) = 0 \quad t < 0$$
$$= N_0 \quad t \geqslant 0 \tag{99.20}$$

and

$$\nu(t) = 0 \quad t < 0$$
$$= e^{-\lambda_0 t} \quad t \geqslant 0; \tag{99.21}$$

we have:

$$F(s) = N_0, \qquad V(s) = \frac{s}{s + \lambda_0}, \tag{99.22, 99.23}$$

$$R(s) = \frac{F}{V} - N_0 = \frac{N_0}{s/(s + \lambda_0)} - N_0 = \frac{N_0 \lambda_0}{s}. \tag{99.24}$$

Therefore:

$$r(t) = N_0 \lambda_0 t \tag{99.25}$$

$$r'(t) = N_0 \lambda_0. \tag{99.26}$$

We note that in the case where f(t) is a constant, the supply rate $r'(t)/N_0$ is constant and equal to λ_0, which is the failure rate. If f(t) is constant and equal to N_0 and the supply rate is equal to λ_0, then the survival function is the exponential $\nu(t) = e^{-\lambda_0 t}$.

Numerical evaluation of the solutions of Volterra equations such as (99.5) can readily be accomplished by the method given in Section 98.

Section 100

ASYMPTOTIC VALUE OF THE MAINTENANCE RATE

If:

$$f(t) = N_0 = \text{const.}, \tag{100.1}$$

then the function R(s) can be written:

$$R(s) = N_0 \frac{1 - V}{V}, \tag{100.2}$$

or:

$$R'(s) = N_0 s \frac{1 - V}{V}. \tag{100.3}$$

The function:

$$r'(t) = \frac{dr}{dt}, \tag{100.4}$$

in the case where $f(t) = N_0 = \text{const.}$, is called the maintenance rate. We shall now show that $r'(t)$ approaches a finite limit as $t \to \infty$ and that we can thus distinguish, in the supply situation, a transitory state (or period) and a quasi-permanent state.

Let us recall the theorem:

$$\lim_{t \to \infty} h(t) = \lim_{|s| \to 0} g(s) \tag{100.5}$$

where:

$$g(s) = \mathscr{L} h(t), \tag{100.6}$$

provided that h(t) satisfies certain analytical conditions which we shall not repeat here but which are verified for $\nu(t)$ functions, which are monotonically decreasing.

We shall then write:

$$\lim_{t \to \infty} \frac{r'(t)}{N_0} = \lim_{|s| \to 0} \frac{R'(s)}{N_0} = \lim_{|s| \to 0} \left[\frac{s}{V} - s\right] = \lim_{|s| \to 0} \frac{s}{V}; \qquad 100.7$$

but:

$$\frac{V}{s} = \mathscr{L} \int_0^t v(u)\, du \qquad 100.8$$

and:

$$\lim_{|s| 0 \to} \frac{V}{s} = \lim_{|s| \to 0} \mathscr{L} \int_0^t v(u)\, du = \lim_{t \to \infty} \int_0^t v(u)\, du$$

$$= \int_0^\infty v(t)\, dt = \bar{t} \qquad 100.9$$

Thus:

$$\lim_{t \to \infty} \frac{r'(t)}{N_0} = \frac{1}{\int_0^\infty v(t) dt} = \frac{1}{\bar{t}}, \qquad 100.10$$

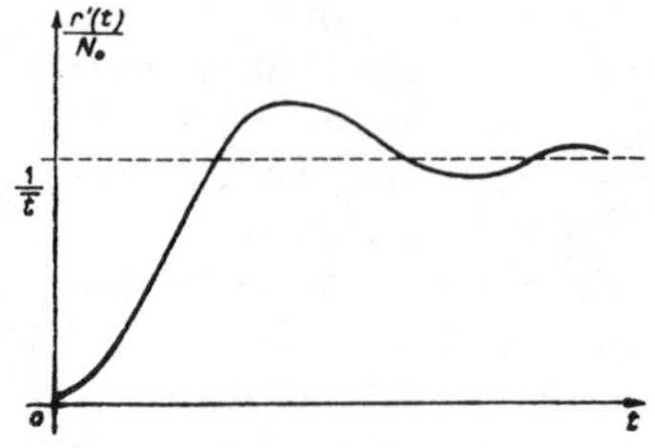

Fig. 100.1

which expresses the fact that the maintenance rate is equal, for sufficiently large values of t, to the inverse of the mean survival time. Fig. 100.1 shows the general shape of the curve representing the maintenance rate.

One may say that maintenance is in a permanent state when the maintenance rate is practically constant. It can be convenient to introduce a time, t_{perm}, after which this quasi-constant value would be considered to hold. This might be defined arbitrarily as the point at which variations are less than 1 per cent of the limit value. Generally, $t_{perm}/\bar{t}$ is very large, and it is rarely found that maintenance will be in the permanent state throughout the entire period of equipment utilization.

We may note that the results obtained by means of (100.7) can be computed directly by taking the derivative of the Volterra integral:

$$N_0 = N_0\, v(t) + \int_0^t r'(u) \cdot v(t - u)\, du. \qquad 100.11$$

Conclusion

Our aim in this book has been to present methods and models capable of solving economic management problems, never pretending that the reader can apply such methods without the exercise of reflection, analysis, and judgment on his part. No one becomes an analyst simply by having read a book; rather, this can only make one aware that problems of economic management are illuminated by truly scientific analysis.

The material we have presented must be called modest indeed when one considers the five or six thousand articles and other works already produced by a thousand or more excellent analysts working in this field. Our desire has only been to make a contribution of some usefulness. We have been concerned to keep the discussion as simple as possible, and hope we have not thereby too greatly distorted the complex aspects presented by such problems as they actually arise. But one must begin somewhere: to classify and analyze complicated phenomena one must use simple ideas and basic concepts. Through this book, the reader may have begun to crystallize some of these key ideas; his interest in operations research and his thirst for knowledge will do the rest. If the reception of the present book warrants, we shall be led to extend and complete these developments in future works.

Some will consider it inopportune or premature to have presented, for engineers and others interested directly or indirectly in economic organization and management, methods that are still in the process of evolving. But if this were true, one could never learn anything, since everything changes continually. One of the strongest attractions of operations research, as of all scientific research, is the sense of adventure and discovery—with all its false turnings and traps, but also with the satisfactions that come with one's solution of a problem, even minor and fragmentary. But today's major problems will, without doubt, be the minor problems of tomorrow.

Tables

BINOMIAL DISTRIBUTION

$$B_r = C_n^r p^r (1 - p)^{n-r}$$

The following table gives several values of B_r. To read the values of B_r corresponding to p = 0.90 or p = 0.95, for example, replace r by n - r, and refer in the table to the column q = 1 - p = 1 - 0.90 = 0.10, or q = 1 - p = 1 - 0.95 = 0.05, respectively.

n	*r*	p (or q)		
		0.05	0.10	0.50
1	0	0.950	0.900	0.500
	1	0.050	0.100	0.500
2	0	0.902	0.810	0.250
	1	0.095	0.180	0.500
	2	0.002	0.010	0.250
3	0	0.857	0.729	0.125
	1	0.135	0.243	0.375
	2	0.007	0.027	0.375
	3	0.000	0.001	0.125
4	0	0.814	0.656	0.062
	1	0.171	0.291	0.250
	2	0.013	0.048	0.375
	3	0.000	0.003	0.250
	4	0.000	0.000	0.062
5	0	0.773	0.590	0.031
	1	0.203	0.328	0.156
	2	0.021	0.072	0.312
	3	0.001	0.008	0.312
	4	0.000	0.000	0.156
	5	0.000	0.000	0.031
6	0	0.735	0.531	0.015
	1	0.232	0.354	0.093
	2	0.030	0.098	0.234
	3	0.002	0.014	0.312
	4	0.000	0.001	0.234
	5	0.000	0.000	0.093
	6	0.000	0.000	0.015
7	0	0.698	0.478	0.007
	1	0.257	0.372	0.054
	2	0.040	0.124	0.164
	3	0.003	0.023	0.273
	4	0.000	0.002	0.273
	5	0.000	0.000	0.164
	6	0.000	0.000	0.054
	7	0.000	0.000	0.007
8	0	0.663	0.430	0.003
	1	0.279	0.148	0.109
	2	0.051	0.382	0.031
	3	0.005	0.033	0.218
	4	0.000	0.004	0.273
	5	0.000	0.000	0.218
	6	0.000	0.000	0.109
	7	0.000	0.000	0.031
	8	0.000	0.000	0.003
9	0	0.630	0.387	0.002
	1	0.298	0.387	0.017
	2	0.062	0.172	0.070
	3	0.007	0.044	0.164
	4	0.000	0.007	0.246
	5	0.000	0.000	0.246
	6	0.000	0.000	0.164
	7	0.000	0.000	0.070
	8	0.000	0.000	0.017
	9	0.000	0.000	0.002
10	0	0.598	0.348	0.001
	1	0.315	0.387	0.009
	2	0.074	0.193	0.043
	3	0.010	0.057	0.117
	4	0.000	0.011	0.205
	5	—	0.001	0.246
	6	—	0.000	0.205
	7	—	—	0.117
	8	—	—	0.043
	9	—	—	0.009
	10	—	—	0.001
15	0	0.463	0.205	0.000
	1	0.365	0.343	0.000
	2	0.134	0.266	0.003
	3	0.030	0.128	0.013
	4	0.004	0.042	0.041
	5	0.000	0.010	0.091
	6	—	0.001	0.152
	7	—	0.000	0.196
	8	—	—	0.196
	9	—	—	0.152
	10	—	—	0.091
	11	—	—	0.041
	12	—	—	0.013
	13	—	—	0.003
	14	—	—	0.000
	15	—	—	0.000
20	0	0.358	0.121	0.000
	1	0.377	0.270	0.000
	2	0.188	0.285	0.000
	3	0.059	0.190	0.001
	4	0.013	0.089	0.004
	5	0.002	0.031	0.014
	6	0.000	0.008	0.037
	7	—	0.002	0.073
	8	—	0.000	0.120
	9	—	—	0.160
	10	—	—	0.176
	11	—	—	0.160
	12	—	—	0.120
	13	—	—	0.073
	14	—	—	0.037
	15	—	—	0.014
	16	—	—	0.004
	17	—	—	0.001
	18	—	—	0.000
	19	—	—	0.000
	20	—	—	0.000

COMPLEMENTARY BINOMIAL DISTRIBUTION

$$1 - P_r = \sum_{s=r}^{n} C_n^s\, p^s (1 - p)^{n-s}$$

This table gives several values of 1 - P_r. To read the values corresponding to p = 0.90 and p = 0.95, for example, subtract from 1 the quantity that is read with r replaced by n - r + 1 for the respective values: q = 1 - p = 1 - 0.90 = 0.10 and q = 1 - p = 1 - 0.95 = 0.05.

n	r	p (or q) 0.05	0.10	0.50
2	1	0.097	0.190	0.750
	2	0.002	0.010	0.250
3	1	0.142	0.271	0.875
	2	0.007	0.028	0.500
	3	0.000	0.001	0.125
4	1	0.185	0.343	0.937
	2	0.014	0.052	0.687
	3	0.000	0.003	0.312
	4	0.000	0.000	0.062
5	1	0.226	0.409	0.968
	2	0.022	0.081	0.812
	3	0.001	0.008	0.500
	4	0.000	0.000	0.187
	5	0.000	0.000	0.031
6	1	0.264	0.468	0.984
	2	0.032	0.114	0.890
	3	0.002	0.015	0.656
	4	0.000	0.001	0.343
	5	0.000	0.000	0.109
	6	0.000	0.000	0.015
7	1	0.301	0.521	0.992
	2	0.044	0.149	0.937
	3	0.003	0.025	0.773
	4	0.000	0.002	0.500
	5	0.000	0.000	0.226
	6	0.000	0.000	0.062
	7	0.000	0.000	0.007
8	1	0.336	0.569	0.996
	2	0.057	0.186	0.964
	3	0.005	0.038	0.855
	4	0.000	0.005	0.636
	5	—	0.000	0.363
	6	—	—	0.144
	7	—	—	0.035
	8	—	—	0.003
9	1	0.369	0.612	0.998
	2	0.071	0.225	0.980
	3	0.008	0.053	0.910
	4	0.000	0.008	0.746
	5	—	0.000	0.500
	6	—	—	0.253
	7	—	—	0.089
	8	—	—	0.019
	9	—	—	0.002
10	1	0.401	0.651	0.999
	2	0.086	0.263	0.989
	3	0.011	0.070	0.945
	4	0.001	0.012	0.828
	5	0.000	0.001	0.623
	6	—	0.000	0.377
	7	—	—	0.171
	8	—	—	0.054
	9	—	—	0.010
	10	—	—	0.001
15	1	0.536	0.794	1.000
	2	0.171	0.451	0.999
	3	0.036	0.184	0.996
	4	0.005	0.055	0.982
	5	0.000	0.012	0.940
	6	—	0.002	0.849
	7	—	—	0.696
	8	—	—	0.500
	9	—	—	0.303
	10	—	—	0.150
	11	—	—	0.059
	12	—	—	0.017
	13	—	—	0.003
	14	—	—	0.000
	15	—	—	0.000
20	1	0.641	0.878	1.000
	2	0.264	0.608	1.000
	3	0.075	0.323	0.999
	4	0.015	0.133	0.998
	5	0.002	0.043	0.994
	6	0.000	0.011	0.979
	7	—	0.002	0.942
	8	—	0.000	0.868
	9	—	—	0.748
	10	—	—	0.588
	11	—	—	0.411
	12	—	—	0.251
	13	—	—	0.131
	14	—	—	0.057
	15	—	—	0.020
	16	—	—	0.005
	17	—	—	0.001
	18	—	—	0.000
	19	—	—	0.000
	20	—	—	0.000

POISSON DISTRIBUTION

$$p_r = \frac{a^r}{r!} e^{-a}$$

r	a															
	0.1	0.2	0.3	0.4	0.5	0.6	0.7	0.8	0.9	1	1.5	2	2.5	3	3.5	4
0	0.904	0.818	0.740	0.670	0.606	0.548	0.496	0.449	0.406	0.367	0.223	0.135	0.082	0.049	0.030	0.018
1	0.090	0.163	0.222	0.268	0.303	0.329	0.347	0.359	0.365	0.367	0.334	0.270	0.205	0.149	0.105	0.073
2	0.004	0.016	0.033	0.053	0.075	0.098	0.121	0.143	0.164	0.183	0.251	0.270	0.256	0.224	0.185	0.146
3	0.000	0.001	0.003	0.007	0.012	0.019	0.028	0.038	0.049	0.061	0.125	0.180	0.213	0.224	0.215	0.195
4	—	0.000	0.000	0.000	0.001	0.003	0.005	0.007	0.011	0.015	0.047	0.090	0.133	0.168	0.188	0.195
5	—	—	—	—	0.000	0.000	0.000	0.001	0.002	0.003	0.014	0.036	0.066	0.100	0.132	0.156
6	—	—	—	—	—	—	—	0.000	0.000	0.000	0.003	0.012	0.027	0.050	0.077	0.104
7	—	—	—	—	—	—	—	—	—	—	0.000	0.003	0.009	0.021	0.038	0.059
8	—	—	—	—	—	—	—	—	—	—	—	0.000	0.003	0.008	0.016	0.029
9	—	—	—	—	—	—	—	—	—	—	—	—	0.000	0.002	0.006	0.013
10	—	—	—	—	—	—	—	—	—	—	—	—	—	0.000	0.002	0.005
11	—	—	—	—	—	—	—	—	—	—	—	—	—	—	0.000	0.001
12	—	—	—	—	—	—	—	—	—	—	—	—	—	—	—	0.000

POISSON DISTRIBUTION (cont'd)

r	a															
	4.5	5	5.5	6	6.5	7	7.5	8	8.5	9	9.5	10	12	14	16	18
0	0.011	0.006	0.004	0.002	0.001	0.000	0.000	0.000	0.000	0.000	—	—	—	—	—	—
1	0.050	0.033	0.022	0.014	0.009	0.006	0.004	0.002	0.001	0.001	0.000	0.000	—	—	—	—
2	0.112	0.084	0.061	0.044	0.031	0.022	0.015	0.010	0.007	0.005	0.003	0.002	0.000	—	—	—
3	0.168	0.140	0.113	0.089	0.068	0.052	0.038	0.028	0.020	0.015	0.010	0.007	0.001	0.000	—	—
4	0.189	0.175	0.155	0.133	0.111	0.091	0.072	0.057	0.044	0.033	0.025	0.018	0.005	0.001	0.000	—
5	0.170	0.175	0.171	0.160	0.145	0.127	0.109	0.091	0.075	0.060	0.048	0.037	0.012	0.003	0.001	—
6	0.128	0.146	0.157	0.160	0.157	0.149	0.136	0.122	0.106	0.091	0.076	0.063	0.025	0.008	0.002	0.000
7	0.082	0.104	0.123	0.137	0.146	0.149	0.146	0.139	0.129	0.117	0.103	0.090	0.043	0.017	0.006	0.001
8	0.046	0.065	0.084	0.103	0.118	0.130	0.137	0.139	0.137	0.131	0.123	0.112	0.065	0.030	0.012	0.004
9	0.023	0.036	0.051	0.068	0.085	0.101	0.114	0.124	0.129	0.131	0.130	0.125	0.087	0.047	0.021	0.008
10	0.010	0.018	0.028	0.041	0.055	0.071	0.085	0.099	0.110	0.118	0.123	0.125	0.104	0.066	0.034	0.015
11	0.004	0.008	0.014	0.022	0.033	0.045	0.058	0.072	0.085	0.097	0.106	0.113	0.114	0.084	0.049	0.024
12	0.001	0.003	0.006	0.011	0.017	0.026	0.036	0.048	0.060	0.072	0.084	0.094	0.114	0.098	0.066	0.036
13	0.000	0.001	0.002	0.005	0.008	0.014	0.021	0.029	0.039	0.050	0.061	0.072	0.105	0.106	0.081	0.050
14	—	0.000	0.001	0.002	0.004	0.007	0.011	0.016	0.024	0.032	0.041	0.052	0.090	0.106	0.093	0.065
15	—	—	0.000	0.000	0.001	0.003	0.005	0.009	0.013	0.019	0.026	0.034	0.072	0.098	0.099	0.078
16	—	—	—	—	0.000	0.001	0.002	0.004	0.007	0.010	0.015	0.021	0.054	0.086	0.099	0.088
17	—	—	—	—	—	0.000	0.001	0.002	0.003	0.005	0.008	0.012	0.038	0.071	0.093	0.093
18	—	—	—	—	—	—	0.000	0.000	0.001	0.002	0.004	0.007	0.025	0.055	0.083	0.093
19	—	—	—	—	—	—	—	—	0.000	0.001	0.002	0.003	0.016	0.040	0.069	0.088
20	—	—	—	—	—	—	—	—	—	0.000	0.001	0.001	0.009	0.028	0.055	0.079
21	—	—	—	—	—	—	—	—	—	—	0.000	0.000	0.005	0.019	0.042	0.068
22	—	—	—	—	—	—	—	—	—	—	—	—	0.003	0.012	0.031	0.056
23	—	—	—	—	—	—	—	—	—	—	—	—	0.001	0.007	0.021	0.043
24	—	—	—	—	—	—	—	—	—	—	—	—	0.000	0.004	0.014	0.032
25	—	—	—	—	—	—	—	—	—	—	—	—	—	0.002	0.009	0.023

COMPLEMENTARY POISSON DISTRIBUTION

$$1 - P_r = \sum_{s=r}^{\infty} \frac{a^s}{s!} e^{-a}$$

r	a: 0.1	0.2	0.3	0.4	0.5	0.6	0.7	0.8	0.9	1	1.5	2	2.5	3	3.5	4
0	1.000	1.000	1.000	1.000	1.000	1.000	1.000	1.000	1.000	1.000	1.000	1.000	1.000	1.000	1.000	1.000
1	0.095	0.181	0.259	0.329	0.393	0.451	0.503	0.550	0.593	0.632	0.776	0.864	0.917	0.950	0.969	0.981
2	0.004	0.017	0.036	0.061	0.090	0.121	0.155	0.191	0.227	0.264	0.442	0.594	0.712	0.800	0.864	0.908
3	0.000	0.001	0.003	0.007	0.014	0.023	0.034	0.047	0.062	0.080	0.191	0.323	0.456	0.576	0.679	0.761
4	—	0.000	0.000	0.000	0.001	0.003	0.005	0.009	0.013	0.019	0.065	0.142	0.242	0.352	0.463	0.566
5	—	—	—	—	0.000	0.000	0.000	0.001	0.002	0.003	0.018	0.052	0.108	0.184	0.274	0.371
6	—	—	—	—	—	—	—	0.000	0.000	0.000	0.004	0.016	0.042	0.083	0.142	0.214
7	—	—	—	—	—	—	—	—	—	—	0.000	0.004	0.014	0.033	0.065	0.110
8	—	—	—	—	—	—	—	—	—	—	—	0.001	0.004	0.011	0.026	0.051
9	—	—	—	—	—	—	—	—	—	—	—	—	0.001	0.003	0.009	0.021
10	—	—	—	—	—	—	—	—	—	—	—	—	0.000	0.001	0.003	0.008
11	—	—	—	—	—	—	—	—	—	—	—	—	—	0.000	0.001	0.002
12	—	—	—	—	—	—	—	—	—	—	—	—	—	—	0.000	0.000

COMPLEMENTARY POISSON DISTRIBUTION (cont'd)

r	a															
	4.5	5	5.5	6	6.5	7	7.5	8	8.5	9	9.5	10	12	14	16	18
0	1.000	1.000	1.000	1.000	1.000	1.000	1.000	1.000	1.000	1.000	1.000	1.000	1.000	1.000	1.000	1.000
1	0.988	0.993	0.995	0.997	0.998	0.999	0.999	0.999	0.999	0.999	0.999	1.000	1.000	1.000	1.000	1.000
2	0.938	0.959	0.973	0.982	0.988	0.992	0.995	0.997	0.998	0.998	0.999	0.999	0.999	1.000	1.000	1.000
3	0.826	0.875	0.911	0.938	0.957	0.970	0.979	0.986	0.990	0.993	0.995	0.997	0.999	0.999	1.000	1.000
4	0.657	0.735	0.798	0.848	0.888	0.918	0.940	0.957	0.969	0.978	0.985	0.989	0.997	0.999	0.999	1.000
5	0.467	0.559	0.642	0.714	0.776	0.827	0.867	0.900	0.925	0.945	0.959	0.970	0.992	0.998	0.999	0.999
6	0.297	0.384	0.471	0.554	0.631	0.699	0.758	0.808	0.850	0.884	0.911	0.932	0.979	0.994	0.998	0.999
7	0.168	0.237	0.314	0.393	0.473	0.550	0.621	0.686	0.743	0.793	0.835	0.869	0.954	0.985	0.996	0.999
8	0.086	0.133	0.190	0.256	0.327	0.401	0.475	0.547	0.614	0.676	0.731	0.779	0.910	0.968	0.990	0.997
9	0.040	0.068	0.105	0.152	0.208	0.270	0.338	0.407	0.476	0.544	0.608	0.667	0.845	0.937	0.978	0.992
10	0.017	0.031	0.053	0.083	0.122	0.169	0.223	0.283	0.347	0.412	0.478	0.542	0.757	0.890	0.956	0.984
11	0.006	0.013	0.025	0.042	0.066	0.098	0.137	0.184	0.236	0.294	0.354	0.417	0.652	0.824	0.922	0.969
12	0.002	0.005	0.011	0.020	0.033	0.053	0.079	0.111	0.151	0.197	0.248	0.303	0.538	0.740	0.873	0.945
13	0.000	0.002	0.004	0.008	0.016	0.027	0.042	0.063	0.090	0.124	0.163	0.208	0.424	0.641	0.806	0.908
14	—	0.000	0.001	0.003	0.007	0.012	0.021	0.034	0.051	0.073	0.101	0.135	0.318	0.535	0.725	0.857
15	—	—	0.000	0.001	0.003	0.005	0.010	0.017	0.027	0.041	0.060	0.083	0.228	0.429	0.632	0.791
16	—	—	—	0.000	0.001	0.002	0.004	0.008	0.013	0.022	0.033	0.048	0.155	0.330	0.533	0.713
17	—	—	—	—	0.000	0.001	0.002	0.003	0.006	0.011	0.017	0.027	0.101	0.244	0.434	0.625
18	—	—	—	—	—	0.000	0.000	0.001	0.003	0.005	0.008	0.014	0.063	0.172	0.340	0.531
19	—	—	—	—	—	—	—	0.000	0.001	0.002	0.004	0.007	0.037	0.117	0.257	0.437
20	—	—	—	—	—	—	—	—	0.000	0.001	0.002	0.003	0.021	0.076	0.187	0.349
21	—	—	—	—	—	—	—	—	—	0.000	0.000	0.001	0.011	0.047	0.131	0.269
22	—	—	—	—	—	—	—	—	—	—	—	0.000	0.006	0.028	0.089	0.200
23	—	—	—	—	—	—	—	—	—	—	—	—	0.003	0.016	0.058	0.144
24	—	—	—	—	—	—	—	—	—	—	—	—	0.001	0.009	0.036	0.101
25	—	—	—	—	—	—	—	—	—	—	—	—	0.000	0.005	0.022	0.068

PROBABILITY DENSITY OF GAUSS'S LAW

$$p(x) = \frac{1}{\sqrt{2\pi}} e^{-\frac{1}{2}x^2}$$

$\pm x$	$p(x)$	$\pm x$	$p(x)$	$\pm x$	$p(x)$	$\pm x$	$p(x)$	$\pm x$	$p(x)$
0.00	0.398	0.80	0.289	1.60	0.110	2.40	0.022	3.20	0.002
0.02	0.398	0.82	0.285	1.62	0.107	2.42	0.021	3.22	0.002
0.04	0.398	0.84	0.280	1.64	0.104	2.44	0.020	3.24	0.002
0.06	0.398	0.86	0.275	1.66	0.100	2.46	0.019	3.26	0.002
0.08	0.397	0.88	0.270	1.68	0.097	2.48	0.018	3.28	0.001
0.10	0.397	0.90	0.266	1.70	0.094	2.50	0.017	3.30	0.001
0.12	0.396	0.92	0.261	1.72	0.090	2.52	0.016	3.32	0.001
0.14	0.395	0.94	0.256	1.74	0.087	2.54	0.015	3.34	0.001
0.16	0.394	0.96	0.251	1.76	0.084	2.56	0.015	3.36	0.001
0.18	0.392	0.98	0.246	1.78	0.081	2.58	0.014	3.38	0.001
0.20	0.391	1.00	0.242	1.80	0.079	2.60	0.013	3.40	0.001
0.22	0.389	1.02	0.237	1.82	0.076	2.62	0.012	3.42	0.001
0.24	0.387	1.04	0.232	1.84	0.073	2.64	0.012	3.44	0.001
0.26	0.385	1.06	0.227	1.86	0.070	2.66	0.011	3.46	0.001
0.28	0.383	1.08	0.222	1.88	0.068	2.68	0.011	3.48	0.000
0.30	0.381	1.10	0.217	1.90	0.065	2.70	0.010	3.50	—
0.32	0.379	1.12	0.213	1.92	0.063	2.72	0.009	3.52	—
0.34	0.376	1.14	0.208	1.94	0.060	2.74	0.009	3.54	—
0.36	0.373	1.16	0.203	1.96	0.058	2.76	0.008	3.56	—
0.38	0.371	1.18	0.198	1.98	0.056	2.78	0.008	3.58	—
0.40	0.368	1.20	0.194	2.00	0.054	2.80	0.007	3.60	—
0.42	0.365	1.22	0.189	2.02	0.051	2.82	0.007	3.62	—
0.44	0.362	1.24	0.184	2.04	0.049	2.84	0.007	3.64	—
0.46	0.358	1.26	0.180	2.06	0.047	2.86	0.006	3.66	—
0.48	0.355	1.28	0.175	2.08	0.045	2.88	0.006	3.68	—
0.50	0.352	1.30	0.171	2.10	0.044	2.90	0.006	3.70	—
0.52	0.348	1.32	0.166	2.12	0.042	2.92	0.005	3.72	—
0.54	0.344	1.34	0.162	2.14	0.040	2.94	0.005	3.74	—
0.56	0.341	1.36	0.158	2.16	0.038	2.96	0.005	3.76	—
0.58	0.337	1.38	0.153	2.18	0.037	2.98	0.004	3.78	—
0.60	0.333	1.40	0.149	2.20	0.035	3.00	0.004	3.80	—
0.62	0.329	1.42	0.145	2.22	0.033	3.02	0.004	3.82	—
0.64	0.325	1.44	0.141	2.24	0.032	3.04	0.003	3.84	—
0.66	0.320	1.46	0.137	2.26	0.031	3.06	0.003	3.86	—
0.68	0.316	1.48	0.133	2.28	0.029	3.08	0.003	3.88	—
0.70	0.312	1.50	0.129	2.30	0.028	3.10	0.003	3.90	—
0.72	0.307	1.52	0.125	2.32	0.027	3.12	0.003	3.92	—
0.74	0.303	1.54	0.121	2.34	0.025	3.14	0.002	3.94	—
0.76	0.298	1.56	0.118	2.36	0.024	3.16	0.002	3.96	—
0.78	0.294	1.58	0.114	2.38	0.023	3.18	0.002	3.98	—

FUNCTION OF GAUSS'S LAW

$$P(x) = \frac{1}{\sqrt{2\pi}} \int_{-\infty}^{x} e^{-\frac{\lambda^2}{2}} \, d\lambda$$

x	$P(x)$	x	$P(x)$	x	$P(x)$	x	$P(x)$	x	$P(x)$
—3.00	0.001	—1.18	0.119	—0.38	0.352	0.42	0.663	1.22	0.888
—2.90	0.002	—1.16	0.123	—0.36	0.359	0.44	0.670	1.24	0.892
—2.80	0.003	—1.14	0.127	—0.34	0.367	0.46	0.677	1.26	0.896
—2.70	0.003	—1.12	0.131	—0.32	0.374	0.48	0.684	1.28	0.900
—2.60	0.005	—1.10	0.136	—0.30	0.382	0.50	0.691	1.30	0.903
—2.50	0.006	—1.08	0.140	—0.28	0.390	0.52	0.698	1.32	0.907
—2.40	0.008	—1.06	0.145	—0.26	0.397	0.54	0.705	1.34	0.910
—2.30	0.011	—1.04	0.149	—0.24	0.405	0.56	0.712	1.36	0.913
—2.25	0.012	—1.02	0.154	—0.22	0.413	0.58	0.719	1.38	0.916
—2.20	0.014	—1.00	0.159	—0.20	0.421	0.60	0.726	1.40	0.919
—2.15	0.016	—0.98	0.164	—0.18	0.429	0.62	0.732	1.42	0.922
—2.10	0.018	—0.96	0.169	—0.16	0.436	0.64	0.739	1.44	0.925
—2.05	0.020	—0.94	0.174	—0.14	0.444	0.66	0.745	1.46	0.928
—2.00	0.023	—0.92	0.179	—0.12	0.452	0.68	0.752	1.48	0.930
—1.95	0.026	—0.90	0.184	—0.10	0.460	0.70	0.758	1.50	0.933
—1.90	0.029	—0.88	0.189	—0.08	0.468	0.72	0.764	1.54	0.938
—1.85	0.032	—0.86	0.195	—0.06	0.476	0.74	0.770	1.58	0.943
—1.80	0.036	—0.84	0.200	—0.04	0.484	0.76	0.776	1.62	0.947
—1.75	0.040	—0.82	0.206	—0.02	0.492	0.78	0.782	1.66	0.952
—1.70	0.045	—0.80	0.212	**0**	**0.500**	0.80	0.788	1.70	0.955
—1.66	0.048	—0.78	0.218	0.02	0.508	0.82	0.794	1.75	0.960
—1.62	0.053	—0.76	0.224	0.04	0.516	0.84	0.800	1.80	0.964
—1.58	0.057	—0.74	0.230	0.06	0.524	0.86	0.805	1.85	0.968
—1.54	0.062	—0.72	0.236	0.08	0.532	0.88	0.811	1.90	0.971
—1.50	0.067	—0.70	0.242	0.10	0.540	0.90	0.816	1.95	0.974
—1.48	0.069	—0.68	0.248	0.12	0.548	0.92	0.821	2.00	0.977
—1.46	0.072	—0.66	0.255	0.14	0.556	0.94	0.826	2.05	0.980
—1.44	0.075	—0.64	0.261	0.16	0.564	0.96	0.831	2.10	0.982
—1.42	0.078	—0.62	0.268	0.18	0.571	0.98	0.836	2.15	0.984
—1.40	0.081	—0.60	0.274	0.20	0.579	1.00	0.841	2.20	0.986
—1.38	0.084	—0.58	0.281	0.22	0.587	1.02	0.846	2.25	0.988
—1.36	0.087	—0.56	0.288	0.24	0.595	1.04	0.851	2.30	0.989
—1.34	0.109	—0.54	0.295	0.26	0.603	1.06	0.855	2.40	0.992
—1.32	0.093	—0.52	0.302	0.28	0.610	1.08	0.860	2.50	0.994
—1.30	0.097	—0.50	0.309	0.30	0.618	1.10	0.864	2.60	0.995
—1.28	0.100	—0.48	0.316	0.32	0.626	1.12	0.869	2.70	0.997
—1.26	0.104	—0.46	0.323	0.34	0.633	1.14	0.873	2.80	0.997
—1.24	0.107	—0.44	0.330	0.36	0.641	1.16	0.877	2.90	0.998
—1.22	0.111	—0.42	0.337	0.38	0.648	1.18	0.881	3.00	0.999
—1.20	0.115	—0.40	0.345	0.40	0.655	1.20	0.885		

EXTRACT FROM THE TABLE OF THE PEARSON χ^2 DISTRIBUTION FUNCTION

Cumulative function $P = \int_0^{x^2} f(\lambda) \mathrm{d}\lambda$

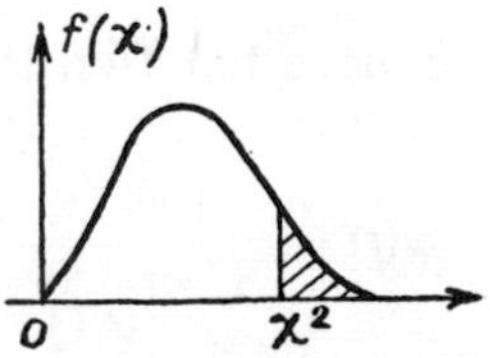

$$f(\chi^2) = \frac{(\chi^2)^{(\nu/2-1)} e^{-x^2/2}}{2^{\nu/2} \Gamma(\frac{1}{2}\nu)}$$

ν \ P	$P = 0.99$	$P = 0.95$	$P = 0.90$	$P = 0.10$	$P = 0.05$	$P = 0.01$
1	$\simeq 0$	$\simeq 0$	0.01	2.70	3.84	6.63
2	0.02	0.10	0.21	4.60	5.99	9.21
3	0.11	0.35	0.58	6.25	7.81	11.3
4	0.29	0.71	1.06	7.77	9.48	13.2
5	0.55	1.14	1.61	9.23	11.0	15.0
6	0.87	1.63	2.20	10.6	12.5	16.8
7	1.23	2.16	2.83	12.0	14.0	18.4
8	1.64	2.73	3.49	13.3	15.5	20.0
9	2.08	3.32	4.16	14.6	16.9	21.6
10	2.55	3.94	4.86	15.9	18.3	23.2
11	3.05	4.57	5.57	17.2	19.6	24.7
12	3.57	5.22	6.30	18.5	21.0	26.2
13	4.10	5.89	7.04	19.8	22.3	27.6
14	4.66	6.57	7.79	21.0	23.6	29.1
15	5.22	7.26	8.54	22.3	24.9	30.5
16	5.81	7.96	9.31	23.5	26.2	32.0
17	6.40	8.67	10.0	24.7	27.5	33.4
18	7.01	9.39	10.8	5.9	28.8	34.8
19	7.63	10.1	11.6	27.2	30.1	36.1
20	8.26	10.8	12.4	28.4	31.4	37.5
21	8.89	11.5	13.2	29.6	32.6	38.9
22	9.54	12.3	14.0	30.8	33.9	40.2
23	10.1	13.0	14.8	32.0	35.1	41.6
24	10.8	13.8	15.6	33.1	36.4	42.9
25	11.5	14.6	16.4	34.3	37.6	44.3
26	12.1	15.3	17.2	35.5	38.8	45.6
27	12.8	16.1	18.1	36.7	40.1	46.9
28	13.5	16.9	18.9	37.9	41.3	48.2
29	14.2	17.7	19.7	39.0	42.5	49.5
30	14.9	18.4	20.5	40.2	43.7	50.8

For degrees of freedom $\nu > 30$, use the formula:

$$f(\chi^2) = \sqrt{2\chi^2} - \sqrt{2\nu - 1}$$

EXTRACT FROM THE TABLE OF STUDENT'S t DISTRIBUTION FUNCTION

Cumulative function $P = 2\int_t^\infty \varphi(\lambda)d\lambda$

$$\varphi(t) = \frac{1}{\sqrt{\nu\pi}} \frac{\Gamma[\frac{1}{2}(\nu+1)]}{\Gamma(\frac{1}{2}\nu)\cdot\left(1+\frac{t^2}{\nu}\right)^{\frac{1}{2}(\nu+1)}}$$

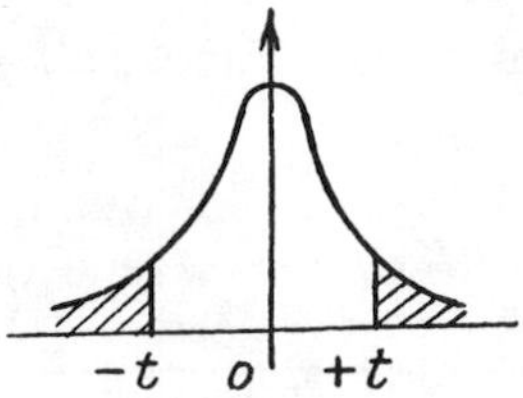

Degrees of freedom ν	$P = 0.05$	$P = 0.01$
1	12.71	63.66
2	4.30	9.93
3	3.18	5.84
4	2.78	4.60
5	2.57	4.03
6	2.45	3.71
7	2.37	3.50
8	2.31	3.36
9	2.26	3.25
10	2.23	3.17
11	2.20	3.11
12	2.18	3.06
13	2.16	3.01
14	2.15	2.98
15	2.13	2.95
16	2.12	2.9
17	2.11	2.90
18	2.10	2.88
19	2.09	2.86
20	2.09	2.85
21	2.08	2.83
22	2.07	2.82
23	2.07	2.81
24	2.06	2.80
25	2.06	2.79
26	2.06	2.78
27	2.05	2.77
28	2.05	2.76
29	2.04	2.76
30	2.04	2.75

EXTRACT FROM THE TABLE OF THE FISHER-SNEDECOR F DISTRIBUTION FUNCTION

Cumulative function $P = \int_F^\infty \varphi(\lambda)\,d\lambda$

$$\varphi(F) = \frac{\Gamma[\frac{1}{2}(\nu_1+\nu_2)]\, F^{\frac{1}{2}(\nu_1-2)}\, \nu_1^{\frac{1}{2}\nu_1}\, \nu_2^{\frac{1}{2}\nu_2}}{\Gamma(\frac{1}{2}\nu_1)\Gamma(\frac{1}{2}\nu_2)\cdot(\nu_2+\nu_1 F)^{\frac{1}{2}(\nu_1-\nu_2)}}$$

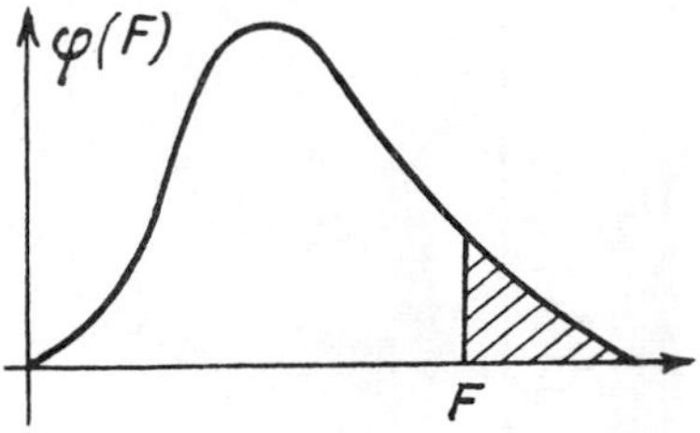

$P = 0.05$

ν_2 \ ν_1	1	2	3	4	5	10	100	∞
1	161	200	216	225	230	242	253	254
2	18.5	19.0	19.2	19.3	19.3	19.4	19.5	19.5
3	10.1	9.55	9.28	9.12	9.01	8.79	8.55	8.53
4	7.71	6.94	6.59	6.39	6.26	5.96	5.66	5.63
5	6.61	5.79	5.41	5.19	5.05	4.74	4.41	4.37
10	4.96	4.10	3.71	3.48	3.33	2.98	2.59	2.54
100	3.94	3.09	2.70	2.46	2.31	1.93	1.39	1.28
∞	3.84	3.00	2.61	2.37	2.21	1.84	1.24	1.00

$P = 0{,}01$

ν_2 \ ν_1	1	2	3	4	5	10	100	∞
1	Values greater than 1,000							
2	98.5	99.0	99.2	99.2	99.3	99.4	99.5	99.5
3	34.1	30.8	29.5	28.7	28.2	27.2	26.2	26.1
4	21.2	18.0	16.7	16.0	15.5	14.5	13.6	13.5
5	16.3	13.3	12.1	11.4	11.0	10.1	9.13	9.02
10	10.0	7.56	6.55	5.99	5.64	4.85	4.01	3.91
100	6.90	4.82	3.98	3.51	3.21	2.50	1.60	1.43
∞	6.64	4.61	3.78	3.32	3.02	2.32	1.36	1

CARSON-LAPLACE TRANSFORMATION

Table giving several transforms (*)

All h(t) functions must be considered such that: $h(t) = 0$ for $t < 0$.

$g(p)$	$h(t)$	$g(p)$	$h(t)$
1	1	$\frac{1}{\sqrt{p}}$	$2\sqrt{\frac{t}{\pi}}$
$\frac{1}{p}$	t	$p^{(-\frac{1}{2}n)}$	$\frac{2^n t^{(n-\frac{1}{2})}}{1.3.5....(2n-1)\sqrt{\pi}}$ $n = 1, 2.3, 4, \ldots$
p^{-n}	$\frac{t^n}{n!}$ $n = 1, 2, 3, 4, \ldots$	$\frac{p}{p+a}$	e^{-at}
p	$\delta(t)$ Dirac function	$\frac{1}{p+a}$	$\frac{1 - e^{-at}}{a}$
p^n	$\frac{t^{-n}}{\Gamma(1-n)}$ except for $n = 1, 2, 3, 4, \ldots$	$\frac{pa}{p^2 + a^2}$	$\sin at$
$\sqrt{p}$	$\frac{1}{\sqrt{\pi t}}$	$\frac{p^2}{p^2 + a^2}$	$\cos at$

*Taken from "Cours de Calcul Opérationnel Appliqué. Transformation de Carson-Laplace" ("Course in Applied Operational Calculus. Carson-Laplace Transformation"), by M. Denis-Papin and A. Kaufmann, (Paris: Albin-Michel, 1951). A very complete table will be found in this work.

$g(p)$	$h(t)$	$g(p)$	$h(t)$
$\dfrac{pa}{p^2 - a^2}$	$\sinh at$	$\dfrac{p(p+b)}{(p+b)^2 + a^2}$	$e^{-bt} \cos at$
$\dfrac{p^2}{p^2 - a^2}$	$\cosh at$	$\dfrac{pa}{(p+b)^2 + a^2}$	$e^{-bt} \sin at$
$\dfrac{a^2}{p^2 + a^2}$	$1 - \cos at$	$\dfrac{1}{(p+a)^2}$	$\dfrac{1}{a^2}[1 - e^{-at}(1 + at)]$
$\dfrac{a^2}{p^2 - a^2}$	$\cosh at - 1$	$\dfrac{p}{(p+a)^2}$	$t e^{-at}$
$\dfrac{1}{p(p+a)}$	$\dfrac{e^{-at}}{a^2} + \dfrac{t}{a} - \dfrac{1}{a^2}$	$\dfrac{p^2}{(p+a)^2}$	$e^{-at}(1 - at)$
$\dfrac{1}{(p+a)(p+b)}$	$\dfrac{1}{ab}\left(1 + \dfrac{be^{-at} - ae^{-bt}}{a-b}\right)$	$\dfrac{1}{p^2 + 2ap + \omega_0^2}$	$\dfrac{1}{\omega_0^2}\left[1 - \dfrac{\omega_0}{\omega} e^{-at} \sin(\omega t + \Phi)\right]$
$\dfrac{p}{(p+a)(p+b)}$	$\dfrac{e^{-bt} - e^{-at}}{a-b}$	with $\omega_0^2 > a^2$	$\omega^2 = \omega_0^2 - a^2,\ \tan\Phi = \dfrac{\omega}{a}$
$\dfrac{p^2}{(p+a)(p+b)}$	$\dfrac{ae^{-at} - be^{-bt}}{a-b}$		

$g(p)$	$h(t)$	$g(p)$	$h(t)$
$\dfrac{1}{p^2 + 2ap + \omega_0^2}$ with $\omega_0^2 < a^2$	$\dfrac{1}{\omega_0^2}\left[1 - \dfrac{\omega_0^2}{n-m}\left(\dfrac{e^{-mt}}{m} - \dfrac{e^{-nt}}{n}\right)\right]$ where $(-m)$ and $(-n)$ are the roots of $p^2 + 2ap + \omega_0^2 = 0$	$\dfrac{p^2}{p^2 + 2ap + \omega_0^2}$ with $\omega_0^2 < a^2$	$\dfrac{1}{n-m}(ne^{-nt} - me^{-mt})$ m and n defined as above.
		$\dfrac{p^2 + 2\omega_0^2}{p^2 + 4\omega_0^2}$	$\cos^2 \omega_0 t$
$\dfrac{p}{p^2 + 2ap + \omega_0^2}$ with $\omega_0^2 > a_2$	$\dfrac{e^{-at}}{\omega} \sin \omega t$ where $\omega^2 = \omega_0^2 - a^2$	$\dfrac{p^2 - 2\omega_0^2}{p^2 - 4\omega_0^2}$	$\cosh^2 \omega_0 t$
$\dfrac{p}{p^2 + 2ap + \omega_0^2}$ with $\omega_0^2 < a^2$	$\dfrac{1}{n-m}(e^{-mt} - e^{-nt})$ m and n defined as above.	$\dfrac{p}{(p+a)(p+b)(p+c)}$	$\dfrac{e^{-at}}{(b-a)(c-a)} + \dfrac{e^{-bt}}{(a-b)(c-b)} + \dfrac{e^{-ct}}{(a-c)(b-c)}$
$\dfrac{p^2}{p^2 + 2ap + \omega_0^2}$ with $\omega_0^2 > a^2$	$-\dfrac{\omega_0}{\omega} e^{-at} \sin(\omega t - \Phi)$ where $\omega^2 = \omega^2{}_0 - a^2$, $\tan\Phi = \dfrac{\omega}{a}$	$\dfrac{p}{(p+a)^3}$	$\dfrac{t^2 e^{-at}}{2}$

$g(p)$	$h(t)$
$\dfrac{p^4}{p^4+a^4}$	$\cos\dfrac{a}{\sqrt{2}}t\,\cosh\dfrac{a}{\sqrt{2}}t$
$\dfrac{p}{p^4-a^4}$	$\dfrac{1}{2a^3}(\sinh at - \sin at)$
$\dfrac{p^2}{p^4-a^4}$	$\dfrac{1}{2a^2}(\cosh at - \cos at)$
$\dfrac{p^3}{p^4-a^4}$	$\dfrac{1}{2a}(\sinh at + \sin at)$
$\dfrac{p^4}{p^4-a^4}$	$\frac{1}{2}(\cosh at + \cos at)$
$\dfrac{p(p^2-a^2)}{(p^2+a^2)^2}$	$t\cos at$
$\dfrac{p}{(p+a)^n}$	$\dfrac{t^{n-1}e^{-at}}{(n-1)!}\qquad n = 1,2,3,4,\dots$
$\dfrac{1}{(p+1)^n}$	$\dfrac{1}{(n-1)!}\displaystyle\int_0^t e^{-u}u^{n-1}\,du \qquad n = 1,2,3,4,\dots$
$\dfrac{p}{\sqrt{p^2+a^2}}$	$J_0(at)$: Zero-order Bessel function of the first kind.

$g(p)$	$h(t)$
$\dfrac{p}{p^3+a^3}$	$\dfrac{1}{3a^2}\left[e^{-at}+e^{at/2}\left(\cos\dfrac{\sqrt{3}}{2}at-\sqrt{3}\sin\dfrac{\sqrt{3}}{2}at\right)\right]$
$\dfrac{p^2}{p^3+a^3}$	$\dfrac{1}{3a}\left[-e^{-at}+e^{at/2}\left(\cos\dfrac{\sqrt{3}}{2}at+\sqrt{3}\sin\dfrac{\sqrt{3}}{2}at\right)\right]$
$\dfrac{p^3}{p^3+a^3}$	$\frac{1}{3}\left(e^{-at}+2e^{at/2}\cos\dfrac{\sqrt{3}}{2}at\right)$
$\dfrac{1}{p(p^2+b^2)}$	$\dfrac{1}{b^2}t-\dfrac{1}{b^3}\sin bt$
$\dfrac{1}{p(p^2-b^2)}$	$\dfrac{1}{b^3}\sinh bt-\dfrac{1}{b^2}t$
$\dfrac{p}{p^4+a^4}$	$\dfrac{1}{\sqrt{2}a^3}\left(\cosh\dfrac{a}{\sqrt{2}}t\sin\dfrac{a}{\sqrt{2}}t-\sinh\dfrac{a}{\sqrt{2}}t\cos\dfrac{a}{\sqrt{2}}t\right)$
$\dfrac{p^2}{p^4+a^4}$	$\dfrac{1}{a^2}\sin\dfrac{a}{\sqrt{2}}t\,\sinh\dfrac{a}{\sqrt{2}}t$
$\dfrac{p^3}{p^4+p^4}$	$\dfrac{1}{\sqrt{2}a}\left(\cos\dfrac{a}{\sqrt{2}}t\sinh\dfrac{a}{\sqrt{2}}t+\sin\dfrac{a}{\sqrt{2}}t\cosh\dfrac{a}{\sqrt{2}}t\right)$

$g(p)$	$h(t)$	$g(p)$	$h(t)$
$\dfrac{p(\sqrt{p^2+a^2}-p)^n}{\sqrt{p^2+a^2}}$	$a_n\,J_n(at)$: n-order Bessel function, where $n > -1$.	$\sqrt{p}\,e^{-a/p}$	$\dfrac{1}{\sqrt{\pi t}}\cos(2\sqrt{at})$
$\dfrac{p}{\sqrt{p^2+a^2}+p}$	$\dfrac{1}{at}J_1(at)$	$\dfrac{1}{\sqrt{p}}e^{-a/p}$	$\dfrac{1}{\sqrt{\pi a}}\sin(2\sqrt{at})$
$\dfrac{p}{(\sqrt{p^2+a^2}+p)^n}$	$\dfrac{n}{a^n t}J_n(at) \quad n > 0$	$\sqrt{p}\,e^{a/p}$	$\dfrac{1}{\sqrt{\pi t}}\cosh(2\sqrt{at})$
$\dfrac{1}{(\sqrt{p^2+a^2}+p)^n}$	$\dfrac{n}{a^n}\int_0^t \dfrac{J_n(au)}{u}\,du \quad n > 0$	$\dfrac{1}{\sqrt{p}}e^{a/p}$	$\dfrac{1}{\sqrt{\pi a}}\sinh(2\sqrt{at})$
$\dfrac{\sqrt{p^2+a^2}-p)^n}{\sqrt{p^2+a^2}}$	$a_n\int_0^t J_n(au)\,du \quad n > -1$	$e^{-a\sqrt{p}}$	$\operatorname{erfc}\dfrac{a}{2\sqrt{t}} \quad a \geqslant 0$ where erfc is the complementary function of the Gauss error function. $\operatorname{erf c}(x) = 1 - \dfrac{2}{\sqrt{2\pi}}\int_0^x e^{-\lambda^2}d\lambda$
$\dfrac{1}{\sqrt{p+a}}$	$\dfrac{1}{\sqrt{a}}\operatorname{erf}\sqrt{at}$, where erf is the Gauss error function		
$\dfrac{p}{\sqrt{p+a}}$	$\dfrac{e^{-at}}{\sqrt{\pi t}}$	$\sqrt{p}\;e^{-a\sqrt{p}}$	$\dfrac{1}{\sqrt{\pi t}}e^{-a^2/4t} \quad a \geqslant 0$
$e^{-a/p}$	$J_0(2\sqrt{at})$ (Bessel function of zero order)	$p\,e^{-a\sqrt{p}}$	$\dfrac{a}{2\sqrt{\pi t^3}}e^{-a^2/4t} \quad a \geqslant 0$

$g(p)$	$h(t)$	$g(p)$	$h(t)$
$p \arctan \frac{a}{p}$	$\frac{\sin at}{t}$	e^{-pa}	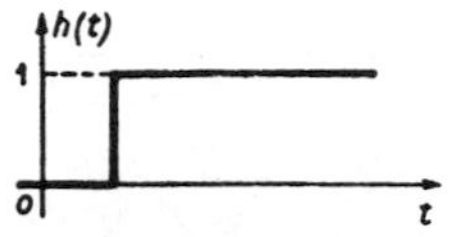
$p \log \frac{p+b}{p+a}$	$\frac{e^{-at} - e^{-bt}}{t}$		
$\log p$	$-\log t - 0,5772$	$1 - e^{-pa}$	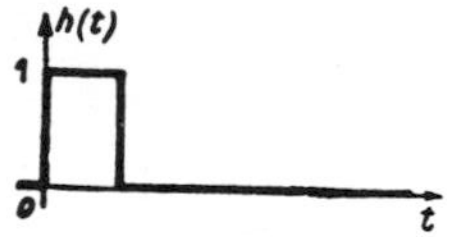
$pe^{a^2p^2} \operatorname{erf} c\,(ap)$ $a > 0$	$\frac{1}{a\sqrt{\pi}} e^{-t^2/4a^2}$		
$e^{a^2p^2} \operatorname{erf} c\,(ap)$ $a > 0$	$\operatorname{erf}\left(\frac{t}{2a}\right)$	$e^{-pa} - e^{-pb}$	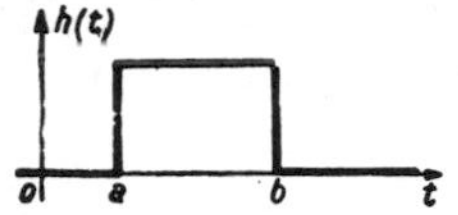
$\sqrt{p} \operatorname{erf} c(\sqrt{ap})$ $a > 0$	$= 0 \quad 0 < t < a$ $= \frac{1}{\sqrt{\pi t}} \quad a < t$	$\frac{m}{p}(1 - e^{-pa})$ $- ma\,e^{-pa}$	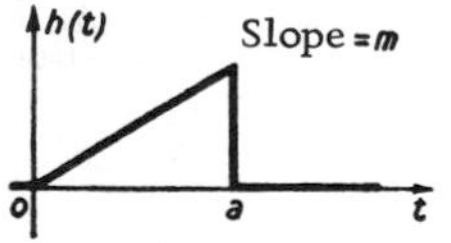
$\sqrt{p}\, e^{ap} \operatorname{erf} c \sqrt{ap}$ $a > 0$	$\frac{1}{\sqrt{\pi(t+a)}}$	$m \frac{e^{-pa}}{p}$	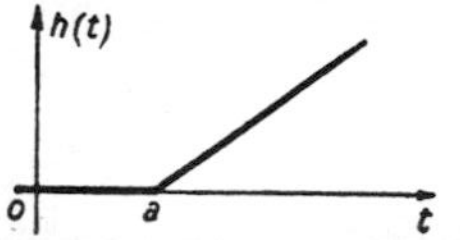

$g(p)$	$h(t)$	$g(p)$	$h(t)$
$\frac{1}{a}\,\frac{1-e^{-pa}}{p}$	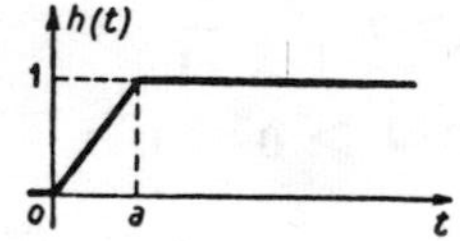	$\frac{1}{1+e^{-pa}}$	
$\frac{p\omega}{p^2+\omega^2}(1+e^{-pa})$ $=\frac{\pi}{a}$	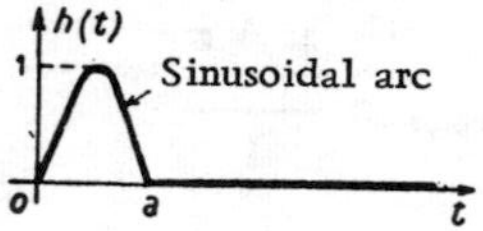	$\frac{1-e^{-pa}}{1+e^{-pa}}$	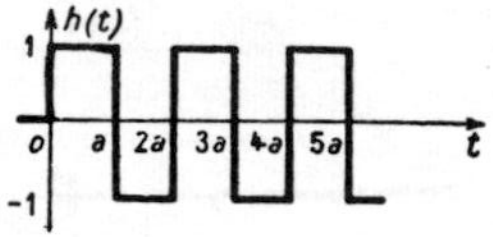
	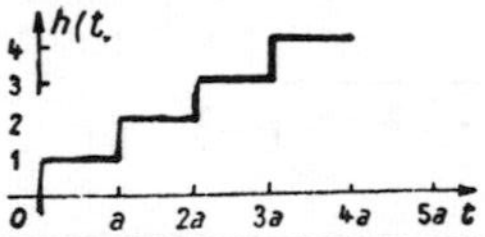	$\frac{m\tanh pa/2}{p}$	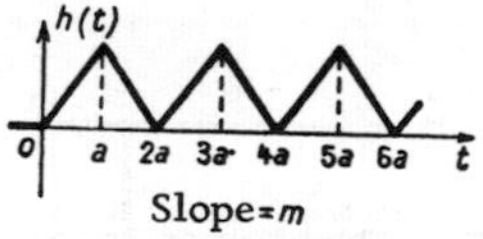

Bibliography

This bibliography provides a selection of titles chosen from among some 5,000 books, articles, and reports dealing with operations research, as surveyed in June, 1958. The size of this number points up the striking growth of interest in operations research. It may be noted that only about 100 of these titles are dated earlier than 1948.

The bibliography is divided into eight sections:

I—Basic works
II—Works on mathematics, statistics, and probability
III—Linear programming
IV—Delay (queuing) phenomena
V—Inventory problems
VI—Deterioration, replacement, maintenance
VII—Publications and reviews devoted to operations research
VIII—Works published after the preparation of this book.

The following abbreviations are used for periodicals (see section VII, below, for information concerning sources):

J.O.R.S.A.—Journal of the Operations Research Society of America.
N.R.L.Q.—Naval Research Logistics Quarterly, Office of Naval Research, Washington, D. C.
Rand Report—Report published by the Rand Corporation, Santa Monica, California.
O.R.Q.—Operational Research Quarterly.
R.R.O.—Revue de Recherche Opérationnelle ("Operations Research Review").
B.C.R.O.—Bolletino del Centro per la Ricerca Operativa ("Bulletin of the Center for Operations Research").

I—Basic Works

A-1 E. H. Bowman and R. B. Fetter—Analysis for Production Management, Richard Irwin ed., (Homewood, Ill.).
A-2 C. W. Churchman, R. L. Ackoff and E. L. Arnoff—Introduction to Operations Research, John Wiley (N.Y.) 1957.
A-3 Colin Cherry—On Human Communications, John Wiley (N.Y.) 1957.

A-4 D. B. Hertz—The Theory and Practice of Industrial Research, McGraw-Hill (N.Y.) 1950.

A-5 T. C. Koopmans—Activity Analysis of Production and Allocation, John Wiley (N.Y.) 1951.

A-6 T. C. Koopmans—3 Essays on the State of Economic Science, McGraw-Hill (N.Y.) 1957.

A-7 A. Lösch—The Economics of Location, Yale Univ. Press (New Haven) 1954.

A-8 J. F. MacCloskey and F. N. Trefethen—Operations Research for Management (Vols. I and II), Johns Hopkins Press, 1954-1956.

A-9 O. Morgenstern—Economic Activity Analysis, John Wiley (N.Y.) 1954.

A-10 P. M. Morse and G. E. Kimball—Methods of Operations Research, John Wiley (N.Y.) 1952.

A-11 J. von Neumann and O. Morgenstern—Theory of Games and Economic Behavior, Princeton Univ. Press, 1953.

A-12 R. M. Thrall, C. H. Coombs and R. L. Davis—Decision Processes, John Wiley (N.Y.) 1954.

A-13 S. Vajda—The Theory of Games and Linear Programming, Methuen, 1956.

A-14 "Proceedings of the First International Conference on Operations Research" (Oxford, 1957), The English University Press, 1958.

A-15 Colloques internationaux du Centre National de la Recherche Scientifique, Les modèles dynamiques en économétrie ("International Seminars at the National Center for Scientific Research: Dynamic Models in Econometrics")—Publications of the C.N.R.S. (Paris) 1956.

A-16 Proceedings of the Conference on "What is Operations Research Accomplishing in Industry"—Case Inst. of Technology (Cleveland) 1955.

A-17 Proceedings of the Conference on "Operations Research, Computers and Management Decisions"—Case Inst. of Technology (Cleveland) 1957.

II—Works on Mathematics, Statistics, and Probability

B-1 J. Bass—Cours de mathématiques ("Mathematics Course"), Masson (Paris) 1956.

B-2 J. Bass—Probabilités et statistiques ("Probability and Statistics"), Course given at the National Higher Institute of Aeronautics (France) 1954.

B-3 E. F. Beckenbach—Modern Mathematics for the Engineer, McGraw-Hill (N.Y.) 1956.

B-4 E. Borel, R. Deltheil and R. Huron—Probabilités, erreurs ("Probability, Error"), Armand Collin Collection (Paris) 1954.

B-5 R. S. Burington and D. C. May—Handbook of Mathematical Tables and Formulas. Handbook of Probability and Statistics with Tables. Handbook Publishers (Sandusky, Ohio) 1953.

B-6 C. E. Clark—An Introduction to Statistics, John Wiley (N.Y.) 1953.

B-7 W. G. Cochran—Sampling Techniques, John Wiley (N.Y.) 1953.

B-8 G. Darmois—Statistique et applications ("Statistics and Applications"), Armand Collin Collection (Paris) 1946.

B-9 M. Denis-Papin and A. Kaufmann—Cours de calcul matriciel appliqué ("Course in Applied Matrix Calculation"), Albin Michel (Paris) 1950.

B-10 M. Denis-Papin, R. Faure, and A. Kaufmann—Exercices de calcul matriciel appliqué ("Exercises in Applied Matrix Calculation"), Eyrolles (Paris) 1958.

B-11 J. L. Dobb—Stochastic Processes, John Wiley (N.Y.) 1953.

B-12 P. S. Dwyer—Linear Computations, John Wiley (N.Y.) 1951.

B-13 W. Feller—An Introduction to Probability Theory and Its Applications, John Wiley (N.Y.) 1950.

B-14 R. A. Fischer—Contributions to Mathematical Statistics, John Wiley (N.Y.) 1950.

B-15 T. C. Fry—Probability and Its Engineering Use, Van Nostrand (N.Y.) 1928.

B-16 H. C. Fryer—Elements of Statistics, John Wiley (N.Y.) 1954.

B-17 H. H. Goode and R. E. Machol—Systems Engineering, McGraw-Hill (N.Y.) 1957.

B-18 A. Hald—Statistical Tables and Formulas, John Wiley (N.Y.) 1952.

B-19 A. Hald—Statistical Theory with Engineering Applications, John Wiley (N. Y.) 1955.

B-20 P. G. Hoel—Introduction to Mathematical Statistics, John Wiley (N.Y.) 1954.

B-21 E. Jahnke and F. Emde—Tables of Functions, Dover Publications (N.Y.) 1945.

B-22 J. G. Kemeny, J. L. Snell and G. L. Thompson—Introduction to Finite Mathematics, Prentice-Hall (N.Y.) 1957.

B-23 M. G. Kendall—Advanced Theory of Statistics (2 volumes), Charles Griffin (London).

B-24 M. G. Kendall—Exercises in Theoretical Statistics, Charles Griffin (London).

B-25 A. G. Laurent—La méthode statistique dans l'industrie ("The Statistical Method in Industry"), Presses Universitaires de France (Paris) 1950.

B-26 M. Loève—Probability Theory, Van Nostrand (N.Y.) 1955.

B-27 W. V. Louitt—Linear Integral Equations, Dover Public. (N.Y.) 1950.

B-28 K. S. Miller—Engineering Mathematics, Rinehart and Co. (N.Y.) 1956.

B-29 L. J. Savage—The Foundations of Statistics, John Wiley (N.Y.) 1954.

B-30 L. H. C. Tippett—Technological Applications of Statistics, John Wiley (N.Y.) 1950.

B-31 L. H. C. Tippett—The Methods of Statistics, John Wiley (N.Y.) 1952.

B-32 A. Vessereau—La statistique ("Statistics"), Presses Universitaires de France (Paris) 1950.

B-33 V. Volterra—Leçons sur la théorie mathématique de la lutte pour la vie ("Lessons in the Mathematical Theory of the Struggle for Life"), Gauthier-Villars (Paris) 1931.

B-34 A. Wald—Statistical Decision Functions, John Wiley (N.Y.) 1950.

B-35 G. U. Yule and M. G. Kendall—Introduction to Theory of Statistics, Charles Griffin (London).

III—Linear Programming

1. BOOKS

C-1 A. Charnes, W. W. Cooper and A. Henderson—An Introduction to Linear Programming, John Wiley (N.Y.) 1953.

C-2 D. König—Theorie der Endlichen und Unendlichen Graphen ("Theory of Finite and Infinite Graphs"), Chelsea Publishing Company (N.Y.) 1950.

C-3 H. W. Kuhn and A. W. Tucker (ed.)—"Contribution to the Theory of Games," Annals of Mathematics Studies, Princeton Univ. Press, 1950-1953.

C-4 H. W. Kuhn and A. W. Tucker (ed.)—"Linear Inequalities and Related Systems," Annals of Mathematics Studies, Princeton Univ. Press, 1956.

C-5 A. W. Tucker (ed.)—"Linear Inequalities and Convex Polyhedral Sets," 2nd Symposium in Linear Programming, Washington, D. C., Jan. 1955.

C-6 S. Vajda—The Theory of Games and Linear Programming, Wiley (N.Y.) 1956.

2. ARTICLES

C-7 M. A. Aczel and A. H. Russel—"New Methods of Solving Linear Programs," O. R. Q., vol. 8, no. 4 (Dec. 1957), 206-219.

C-8 E. M. L. Beale—"An Alternative Method for Linear Programming," Proc. Cambridge Phil. Soc., 1954, 513-523.

C-9 R. Bellman—"On a New Iterative Algorithm for Finding the Solution of Games and Linear Programming Problems," Rand Report P-473, 1953.

C-10 R. Bellman—"On the Computational Solution of Linear Programming Problems Involving Almost Block Diagonal Matrices," Manag. Science, vol. 3 (July, 1957), 403-406.

C-11 E. H. Bowman—"Production Scheduling by the Transportation Method in Linear Programming," J.O.R.S.A., vol. 4 (August, 1956), 443-447.

C-12 E. L. Brink and J. S. De Cani—"Una soluzione analogica del problema di trasporti generalizzato con particolare applicazione alla ubicazione delle are di mercato" ("An Analogical Solution to the Generalized Problem of Transportation, with Particular Application to the Location of Market Areas"), B.C.R.O., no. 5 and 6, 45-51.

C-13 J. Carteron—"Du bon usage des programmes linéaires" ("On the Sound Usage of Linear Programs"), R.R.O., vol. 2, no. 6 (1958).

C-14 A. Charnes and C. E. Lemke—"A Modified Simplex Method for Control of Round-off Error in Linear Programming," Meeting of the Assoc. for Computing Machinery (Pittsburgh) 1952.

C-15 A. Charnes, W. W. Cooper and D. Farr—"Linear Programming and Profit Preference Scheduling for a Manufacturing Firm," J.O.R.S.A., 1953, 114-129.

C-16 A. Charnes and C. E. Lemke—"Computational Theory of Linear Programming," N.R.L.Q., no. 10 (1954).

C-17 G. B. Dantzig—"Computational Algorithm of the Revised Simplex Method," Rand Report RM-1266, 1953.

C-18 G. B. Dantzig and W. Orchard-Hays—"Alternative Algorithm for the Revised Simplex Method," Rand Report RM-1268, 1953.

C-19 G. B. Dantzig, A. Orden and P. Wolfe—"The Generalized Simplex Method for Minimizing a Linear Form under Linear Inequalities Restraints," Rand Report RM-1264, 1954.

C-20 G. B. Dantzig, W. Orchard-Hays and G. Waters—"Product-Form Tableau for Revised Simplex Method," Rand Report RM-1268A, 1954.

C-21 G. B. Dantzig, D. R. Fulkerson and S. Johnson—"Solution of a Large Scale Travelling Salesman Problem," J.O.R.S.A., 1954, 393-410.

C-22 G. B. Dantzig—"Upper Bounds, Secondary Constraints and Block Triangularity in Linear Programming," Rand Report RM-1367, 1954.

C-23 G. B. Dantzig and D. R. Fulkerson—"Minimizing the Number of Tankers to Meet a Fixed Schedule," N.R.L.Q., vol. 1, no. 3 (1954).

C-24 G. B. Dantzig—Constructive Proof of the Min-Max Theorem, Rand Report RM-1267, 1954.

C-25 G. B. Dantzig—"Linear Programming under uncertainty." Rand Report RM-1374, 1954.

C-26 G. B. Dantzig, L. R. Ford and D. R. Fulkerson—"A Primal-Dual Algorithm," Rand Report P. 778, 1954.

C-27 G. B. Dantzig—"Developments in Linear Programming," Rand Report R.M. 1281, 1954.

C-28 G. B. Dantzig and W. Orchard-Hays—"The Product Form for the Inverse in the Simplex Method," Mathematical Tables and other Aids to Computation, VII, no. 46 (April, 1954), 63-67.

C-29 G. B. Dantzig—"Recent Advances in Linear Programming," Rand Report P-662, 1955.

C-30 G. B. Dantzig—"Thoughts on Linear Programming and Automation," Manag. Science, vol. 3 (Jan., 1957), 117-130.

C-31 G. B. Dantzig—"Etat des programmes linéaires, à plusieurs étages" ("State of Linear Programs with Several Stages"), Journées de Recherche Opérationelle (Paris) Sept. 10-11, 1957.

C-32 P. S. Dwyer—"The Solution of the Hitchcock Transportation Problem with a Method of Reduced Matrices," Univ. of Michigan (Ann Arbor) Dec., 1955.

C-33 M. M. Flood—"On the Hitchcock Distribution Problem," Pacific Jour. Math., 1955, 369-386.

C-34 M. M. Flood—"The Travelling Salesman Problem," J.O.R.S.A., vol. 4 (Feb., 1956) 61.

C-35 L. R. Ford and D. R. Fulkerson—"Maximal Flow Through A Network," Rand Report RM-1400, 1954.

C-36 L. R. Ford and D. R. Fulkerson—"A Simple Algorithm for Finding Maximal Network Flows and an Application to the Hitchcock Problem," Rand Report RM-1604, and P-743, 1955.

C-37 L. R. Ford and D. R. Fulkerson—"Solving the Transportation Problem," Rand Report P-895, 1956.

C-38 R. Frisch—"Principles of Linear Programming," Memo-Univ. Inst. of Economics, Oslo, 1954.

C-39 R. Frisch—"Main Features of the Oslo Median Model," Memo-Univ. Inst. of Economics, Oslo, 1956.

C-40 R. Frisch—"Supplementary Remarks on the Oslo Median Model," Memo-Univ. Inst. of Economics, Oslo, 1956.

C-41 R. Frisch—"Generality on Planning," Memo-Univ. Inst. of Economics, Oslo, 1957.

C-42 D. R. Fulkerson and G. B. Dantzig—"The Problem of Routing Aircraft. A Mathematical Solution," Rand Report RM-1369, 1954.

C-43 D. R. Fulkerson and G. B. Dantzig—"Computation of Maximal Flows in Networks," Rand Report RM-1489, 1955.

C-44 W. W. Garvin, H. W. Crandall, J. B. John and R. A. Spellman—"Applications of Linear Programming in the Oil Industry," Manag. Science, vol. 3 (July, 1957) 407-430.

C-45 A. Gazzano and G. Pozzi—"Un metodo per i problemi di 'Linear Programming'" ("A Method for Linear Programming Problems"), B.C.R.O., no. 5 and 6, 27-44.

C-46 F. L. Hitchcock—"The Distribution of a Product from Several Sources to Numerous Localities," Jour. Math. Phys., 20 (1941) 224-250.

C-47 H. S. Houthaker—"On the Numerical Solution of the Transportation Problem," J.O.R.S.A., vol. 3 (May, 1955) 210-224.

C-48 F. E. Kindind—"Fundamentals of Linear Programming and Workshop Manual," Depart. of Industry, Univ. of Pittsburgh, 1956.

C-49 H. W. Kuhn—"The Hungarian Method for the Assignment Problem," N.R.L.Q., vol. 2, no. 1-2 (March-June, 1955), 83-98.

C-50 C. E. Lemke and A. Charnes—"Extremal Problems in Linear Inequalities," Techn. Report No. 36, Carnegie Inst. of Technology (Pittsburgh) 1953.

C-51 J. Lescault—"Programmes linéaires et calculateurs électroniques" ("Linear Programs and Electronic Computers"), R.R.O., vol. 1, no. 4 (1957).

C-52 A. S. Manne—"Notes on Parametric Linear Programming," Rand Report, P-468, 1953.

C-53 P. Massé and R. Gibrat—"Applications of Linear Programming to Investments in the Electric Power Industry," Manag. Science, vol. 3 (Jan., 1957) 149-166.

C-54 N. Orchard-Hays—"Evolution of Linear Programming Computing Techniques," Manag. Science, vol. 4 (Jan., 1958) 183-190.

C-55 A. Restelli—"La programmazione lineare applicata a problemi di distribuzione" ("Linear Programming Applied to Distribution Problems"), B.C.R.O., no. 2 (1955) 1-31.

C-56 F. V. Rhode—"Bibliography on Linear Programming," J.O.R.S.A., vol. 5, no. 1 (1957) 45-62. (List of 255 references.)

C-57 P. A. Samuelson—"Interrelations Between Linear Programming and Game Theory," Rand Report P-461, 1953.

C-58 E. Ventura—"Un exemple de recherche opérationnelle: la détermination d'un plan optimum de production d'énergie électrique par la méthode des programmes linéaires" ("An Example of Operations Research: Determining an Optimum Plan for Electrical Power Production by the Linear Program Method"), Publication of the Soc. Franc. de Recherche Opérationelle (Paris) 1955.

C-59 M. L. Vidale—"A Graphical Solution of the Transportation Problem," J.O.R.S.A., vol. 4 (April, 1956), 193-203.

C-60 H. M. Wagner—"A Two-phase Method for the Simplex Table," J.O.R.S.A., vol. 4 (August, 1956), 443-447.

C-61 H. M. Wagner—"A Comparison of the Original and Revised Simplex Methods," J.O.R.S.A., vol. 5 (June, 1957), 361-369.

C-62 H. M. Wagner—"The Simplex Method for Beginners," J.O.R.S.A., vol. 6 (March-April, 1958), 190-199.

C-63 P. Wolfe—"A Survey of the Theory of Linear Programming: Part III, Computations Methods," Meeting of Soc. for Industrial and Applied Math. (New York) 1956.

C-64 D. F. Votaw and A. Orden—"The Personnel Assignment Problem: Symposium on Linear Inequalities and Programming," Scoop-Comptroller, Hq., USAF (Washington) 1952.

C-65 B. Zimmern—"Résolution des programmes linéaires de transport par la méthode de séparation en étoile" ("Solving Linear Transport Programs by the Star Separation Method"), R.R.O., vol. 1, no. 3 (1957).

IV—Delay (Queuing) Phenomena

1. BOOKS

D-1 P. M. Morse—Queues, Inventories and Maintenance, John Wiley (N.Y.) 1958.

D-2 Massachusetts Inst. of Technology—Summer Course and Supplements on Operations Research, M.I.T. (Mass.) 1956.

2. ARTICLES

D-3 N. T. Bailey—"On Queuing Processes with Bulk Service," J.R. Stat. Soc., vol. 16 (1954), 80-87.

D-4 D. Y. Barrer—"A Waiting-line Problem Characterized by Impatient Customers and Indifferent Clerks," Third Annual Meeting of O.R.S.A., New York, June 4, 1955.

D-5 F. Benson and D. R. Cox—"The Productivity of Machines Requiring Attention at Random Intervals," J.R. Stat. Soc. vol. 13 (1951), 65-82.

D-6 G. Brigham—"On a Congestion Problem in an Aircraft Factory," J.O.R.S.A., vol. 3, no. 4 (Nov. 1955), 412-428.

D-7 P. J. Burke—"The Output of a Queuing System," J.O.R.S.A., vol. 4 (Dec., 1956), 699-704.

D-8 A. Cobham—"Priority Assignment in Waiting Line Problems," J.O.R.S.A., vol. 2, no. 1 (Feb., 1954), 70-76.

D-9 C. J. Craft—"The Role of Queuing Theory in Operations Research," Report of Price-Waterhouse and Co., New York, March, 1956.

D-10 C. D. Crommelin—"Delay Probability Formulae when the Holding Times Are Constant, P.O. Electr. Eng., J. (April, 1932), 41-50.

D-11 P. F. Dunn, C. D. Flagle and P. A. Hicks—"The Queuiac: An Electromechanical Analog for the Simulation of Waiting-Line Problems," J.O.R.S.A., vol. 4 (Dec., 1956), 648-662.

D-12 J. L. Everett—"State Probabilities in Congestion Problems Characterized by Constant Holding Times," J.O.R.S.A., vol. 5 (Nov., 1953), 279-285.

D-13 D. P. Gaver—"The Influence of Service-Times in Queuing Processes," J.O.R.S.A., vol. 2 (May, 1957), 139-149.

D-14 M. Girault—"Quelques exemples d'analyse opérationnelle des files d'attente et de stockage" ("Some Examples of Operations Analysis of Waiting-Lines and Inventory"), Colloque de Recherche Opérationelle (Aix-Marseilles) November 25-26, 1956.

D-15 J. L. Holley—"Waiting-Lines Subject to Priorities," J.O. R.S.A., vol. 3 (August, 1954), 341-343.

D-16 G. C. Hunt—"Sequential Arrays of Waiting-Lines," J.O.R.S.A., vol. 4 (Dec., 1956), 674-683.

D-17 R. R. Jackson—"Queuing Systems with Phase Type Service," O.R.Q., no. 4 (Dec., 1954), 109-120.

D-18 J. R. Jackson—"Networks of Waiting-Lines," J.O.R.S.A., vol. 5 (August, 1957), 518-521.

D-19 D. G. Kendall—"On the Role of Variable Generation Time in the Development of a Stochastic Birth Process," Biometrika, Dec., 1948, 316.

D-20 D. G. Kendall—"Stochastic Processes Occurring in the Theory of Queues and Their Analysis by the Method of the Imbedded Markov Chain," Ann. Math. Stat., no. 3 (Sept., 1953), 338-354.

D-21 D. G. Kendall—"Some Problems in the Theory of Queues," J. R. Stat. Soc., no. 2 (1951), 151-173.

D-22 E. Koenigsberg—"Queuing with Special Service," J.O.R.S.A., vol. 4 (April, 1956), 213-220.

D-23 D. V. Lindley—"The Theory of Queues with a Single Server," Proc. Cambridge Phil. Soc., April, 1952, 277-289.

D-24 G. Luchak—"The Solution of the Single-Channel Queuing Equations Characterized by a Time-Dependent Poisson-Distributed Arrival Rate and a General Class of Holding-Times," J.O.R.S.A., vol. 4 (Dec., 1956), 711-732.

D-25 T. Meisling—"Discrete-Time Queuing Theory," J.O.R.S.A., vol. 6 (Jan.-Feb., 1958), 96-105.

D-26 L. Miaskievicz—"Etude des files d'attente dans un magasin d'outillage" ("Study of Waiting Lines in a Tool Room"), R.R.O., vol. 1, no. 4 (1957).

D-27 E. C. Molina—"Applications of the Theory of Probabilities to Telephone Trunking Problems," Bell Syst. Techn. J., 1927, 461.

D-28 P. Morse—"Stochastic Properties of Waiting-Lines," J.O.R. S.A., 1955, 255-261.

D-29 P. Morse—"Application de la théorie des files d'attente à la gestion des stocks et à l'entretien des machines" ("Application of Waiting-Line Theory to Inventory Management and Machine Maintenance"), Journées de la Recherche Opérationelle (Paris), Sept. 10-11, 1957.

D-30 C. Palm—"The Distribution of Repairmen in Servicing Automatic Machines," Industritidningen Norden (Stockholm), vol. 35 (1947), 75-80, 90-94, 119-123.

D-31 F. Pollaczek—"Sur l'application de la théorie des fonctions au calcul de certain probabilités continues utilisées dans la théorie des réseaux téléphoniques" ("On the Application of the Theory of Functions to the Computation of Certain Continuous Probabilities Used in the Theory of Telephone Networks"), Annales de l'Institut Henri Poincaré, no. 1 (1946), 1.

D-32 T. E. Phipps—"Machine Repair as a Priority Waiting-Line Problem," J.O.R.S.A., vol. 4, no. 1 (Feb., 1956), 76-85.

D-33 T. L. Saaty—"Resume of Useful Formulas in Queuing Theory," J.O.R.S.A., vol. 5 (April, 1957), 161-200.

D-34 O. Swensson—"An Approach to a Class of Queuing Problems," J.O.R.S.A., vol. 6 (March-April, 1958).

D-35 E. Ventura—"Application de la théorie des files d'attente à la détermination des installations de chargement et de l'horaire de travail optima pour un port à quai minéralier unique" ("Application of Waiting-Line Theory to Determination of Optimum Loading Installations and Work Hours for a Port with a Single Ore-Loading Dock"), R.R.O., vol. 2, no. 6 (1958).

D-36 H. White and L. S. Christie—"Queuing with Premetive Priorities or with Breakdown," J.O.R.S.A., vol. 6 (Jan.-Feb., 1958), 79-95.

V—Inventory Problems

1. BOOKS

E-1 K. J. Arrow, S. Karlin and H. Scarf—Studies in the Theory of Inventory and Production, Stanford Univ. Press, 1958.

E-2 T. M. Whitin—The Theory of Inventory Management, Princeton Univ. Press, 1957.

2. ARTICLES

E-3 R. L. Ackoff—"Production and Inventory Control in a Chemical Process," J.O.R.S.A., vol. 3 (August, 1955), 319.

E-4 K. Arrow, T. Harris and J. Marschak—"Optimal Inventory Policy," Econometrica, 1951, 250-272.

E-5 T. V. V. Altwater—"The Theory of Inventory Management, A Review," N.R.L.Q., vol. 1, no. 4 (Dec., 1954).

E-6 M. Beckmann—"A Lagrangian Multipliers Rule in Linear Activity Analysis and Some of Its Applications," Cowles Comm. Discus. Paper on Economics no. 2054 (Nov., 1942) (unpublished).

E-7 C. E. Clark—"Mathematical Analysis of an Inventory Case," J.O.R.S.A., vol 5 (Oct., 1957), 627-639.

E-8 A. Dvoretsky, J. Kiefer and J. Wolfowitz—"The Inventory Problem," Econometrica, no. 20 (1952), 187-222.

E-9 A. Dvoretsky—"On the Optimal Character of the (s.S) Policy in Inventory Theory," Econometrica, no. 21 (1953), 586-596.

E-10 C. Eisenhart—"Some Inventory Problems," Nat. Bur. of Standards. Techn. of Statistical Inference (A2-2c. lecture 1), Jan., 1948.

E-11 T. Fabian and R. T. Nelson—"Production Rates and Inventories," Manag. Sc. Res. Project. no. 22, Office of Naval Research (Washington, D. C.), 1953.

E-12 G. J. Feeney—"A Basis for Strategic Decisions on Inventory Control Operations," Manag. Science, no. 1 (Oct., 1955), 69-82.

E-13 R. J. Freeman—"Ss Inventory Policy with Variable Delivery Time," Manag. Science, vol. 3 (July, 1957), 431-435.

E-14 A. G. Heyvaert and A. Hurt—"Inventory Management of Slow-Moving Parts," J.O.R.S.A., vol. 4 (Oct., 1956), 572-580.

E-15 C. C. Holt, F. Modigliani and H. A. Simon—"A Linear Decision Rule for Production and Employment Scheduling," Manag. Science, no. 1 (Oct., 1955), 1-30.

E-16 R. R. Jackson—"A Stock Model," O.R.Q., vol. 7, no. 4 (Dec., 1956), 140-142.

E-17 W. Karush—"On a Class of Minimum Cost Problems," J.O.R.S.A., vol. 4 (Jan., 1958).

E-18 B. Klein—"Direct Use of Extremal Principles in Solving Certain Optimizing Problems Involving Inequalities," J.O. R.S.A., May, 1955, 168-175.

E-19 J. Laderman, S. B. Littauer and L. Weiss—"The Inventory Problem," Jour. Amer. Stat. Ass., 1953, 717-732.

E-20 J. Lesourne—"La régulation simultanée de la production et des stocks" ("Simultaneous Regulation of Production and Inventories"), R.R.O., vol. 1, no. 2 (1957).

E-21 J. F. Magee—"Guides to Inventory Policy," Harvard Business Review, Jan., Feb., March, April, 1956.

E-22 E. S. Mills—"Expectations and Undesired Inventory," Manag. Science, vol. 4 (Oct., 1957), 105-109.

E-23 E. Naddor—"Lead Time Considerations of a Simplified Mathematical Model of Inventory," Third Meeting of O.R.S.A., New York, June, 1955.

E-24 B. Roy—"Recherche d'un programme d'approvisionnement ou de production" ("Finding a Supply or Production Program"), R.R.O., vol. 1, no. 4 (1957).

E-25 M. A. Seignerin—"Régulation de production dans une industrie à vente saisonnière" ("Production Regulation in a Seasonal Sales Industry"), R.R.O., vol. 1, no. 2 (1957).

E-26 H. A. Simon—"On the Application of Servomechanism Theory in the Study of Production Control," Econometrica, April, 1952, 247-268.

E-27 H. A. Simon—"Decision Rules for Production and Inventory Controls with Probability Forecasts of Sales," Grad. School of Industr. Adm., Carnegie Inst. of Technology, 1954.

E-28 H. A. Simon and C. C. Holt—"The Control of Inventory and Production Rates," J.O.R.S.A., 1954, 289-301.

E-29 H. A. Simon, C. C. Holt and F. Modigliani—"Controlling Inventory and Production in the Face of Uncertain Sales," Grad. School of Industr. Adm., Carnegie Inst. of Technology, 1957.

E-30 A. Vazsonyi—"Economic Lot Size Formulas in Manufacturing," Fall Meeting of the Amer. Soc. of Mechanical Eng., Denver, Sept. 10-12, 1956.

E-31 H. J. Vassian—"Application of Discrete-Variable Servo Theory to Inventory Control," J.O.R.S.A., August, 1955, 272-282.

E-32 H. R. W. Watkins—"The Cost of Rejecting Optimum Production Runs," O.R.Q., vol. 8, no. 4 (Dec., 1957), 200-205.

E-33 T. M. Whitin—"Inventory Control Research, A Survey," Manag. Science, 1954, 32-40.

E-34 T. M. Whitin—"Inventory Control and Price Theory," Manag. Science, no. 1 (1955), 61-68.

E-35 P. R. Winters—"A Trigger Decision Rule for Allocating Inventory to Production Lots and Buffers," Office of Naval Research Memo no. 48, August, 1956.

VI—Deterioration, Replacement, Maintenance

1. BOOKS

F-1 E. Grant—Principles of Engineering Economy, Ronald Press (N. Y.) 1950.

F-2 G. A. Preinreich—The Present Status of Renewal Theory, Waverly Press (Baltimore) 1940.

F-3 G. Terborgh—Dynamic Equipment Policy, McGraw-Hill (N.Y.) 1949.

2. ARTICLES

F-4 A. Alchian—"Economic Replacement Policy," Rand Report R-224, April, 1952.

F-5 R. Bellman—"Notes on the Theory of Dynamic Programming. III. Equipment Replacement Policy," Rand Report, P. 632, Jan., 1955.

F-6 D. H. Blackwell—"Extension of a Renewal Theorem," Pacific Jour. of Math., 1953, 315-332.

F-7 A. W. Brown—"A Note on the Use of Pearson Type III Function in Renewal Theory," Ann. Math. Stat., 1940, 448-453.

F-8 K. L. Chung and J. Wolfowitz—"On a Limit Theorem in Renewal Theory," Ann. Math., 55-56, (1952), 1-6.

F-9 J. C. R. Clapham—"Economic Life of Equipment," O.R.Q., vol. 8, no. 4 (Dec., 1957), 181-190.

F-10 R. Descamps—"Prevision statistique des avaries et calcul des volants et rechanges" ("Statistical Prediction of Breakdowns and Calculation of Flying and Replacement Aircraft"), Ministère de l'Air (Paris) DOCAERO No. 41 and 43, November, 1956 and March, 1957.

F-11 J. L. Doob—"Renewal Theory from the Point of View of Probability," Trans. Amer. Math. Soc., 1948, 422-438.

F-12 S. E. Dreyfus—"A Generalized Equipment Replacement Study," Rand Report P-1039, March, 1957.

F-13 B. Ebstein and M. Sobel—"Life Testing," Jour. Amer. Stat. Ass., 1953, 486-502.

F-14 D. Feller—"On the Integral Equation of Renewal Theory," Ann. Math. Stat., 1941, 243-267.

F-15 L. Goodman—"Methods of Measuring Useful Life of Equipment Under Operations Conditions," Jour. Amer. Stat. Assoc., 1953, 503-530.

F-16 S. Karlin—"On the Renewal Equation," Pac. Jour. Nath., 1955, 229-257.

F-17 M. W. Sasieni—"A Markov Chain Process in Industrial Replacement," O.R.Q., vol. 7, no. 1 (Dec., 1956).

F-18 G. G. Shellard—"Failure of Complex Equipment," J.O.R.S.A., 1953, 130-136.

F-19 V. L. Smith—"Economic Equipment Policies, An Evaluation," Manag. Science, vol. 4 (Oct., 1957), 20-37.

VII—Publications and Reviews Devoted to Operations Research

FRANCE: Revue de Recherche Opérationnelle (R.R.O.): bulletin of the Société Française de Recherche Opérationelle. Subscriptions: 27 Rue Laffite, Paris 9, France.

BELGIUM: Revue Belge de Recherche Opérationnelle et de Statistique ("Belgian Review of Operations Research and Statistics"): published by the Association Belge pour l'Application des Méthodes Scientifiques de Gestion ("Belgian Association for the Application of Scientific Management Methods"), 4 Rue Ravenstein, Brussels 1, Belgium.

U.S.A.: Operations Research: Journal of the Operations Research Society of America (J.O.R.S.A.). Subscriptions: Mr. N. E. Miller, III, Mount Royal and Guilford Avenue, Baltimore 2, Maryland.

Management Science, subscriptions: M. H. H. Cauvet, 250 North Street, White Plains, N.Y.,

GREAT BRITAIN: Operations Research Quarterly (O.R.Q.). Subscriptions: Max Davies and R. T. Eddison, 11 Park Lane, London, W. 1.

ITALY: Bolletino del Centro per la Ricerca Operativa (B.C.R.O.). Subscriptions: Centro per la Ricerca Operativa, Università, L. Bocconi, Via Sarfatti 23, Milan, Italy.

AUSTRIA: Unternehmensforschuung, Operations Research. Subscriptions: Institut für Statistik an der Universität Wien, Rathausstrasse 19/II/3, Vienna 1, Austria.

A great number of articles have appeared in reviews devoted to econometrics, industrial organization, applied mathematics, statistics, etc., and deal with matters that can be considered as relevant to the field of operations research.

VIII—Works Published After the Preparation of This Book

G-1 Dorfman, Samuelson and Solow—Linear Programming and Economic Analysis, McGraw-Hill (N.Y.) 1958.

G-2 S. I. Gass—Linear Programming: Methods and Applications, McGraw-Hill (N.Y.) 1958.

G-3 M. Girault—Initiation aux processus aléatoires ("Introduction to Random Processes"), Editions Dunod (Paris) 1959.

G-4 J. Lesourne—Technique économique et gestion industrielle ("Economic Technique and Industrial Management"), Editions Dunod (Paris) 1959.

G-5 MacCloskey and Coppinger—Recherche opérationnelle et gestion ("Operations Research and Management"), Editions Dunod (Paris) 1959.

G-6 V. Riley and S. I. Gass—Linear Programming and Associated Techniques (Bibliography on linear programming), Johns Hopkins University Press, 1958.

G-7 A. Vazsonyi—Scientific Programming in Business and Industry, John Wiley (N.Y.) 1958.

G-8 Proceedings of the First International Conference of Operations Research, publ. by J.O.R.S.A., 1958.

G-9 M. Haire—Modern Organization Theory, John Wiley (N.Y.) 1959.

G-10 Notes on Operations Research 1959, The Technology Press, M.I.T., 1959.

G-11 R. Schlaifer—Probability and Statistics for Business Decisions, McGraw-Hill (N.Y.) 1959.

G-12 P. Massé—Le Choix des Investissements ("Investment Choice"), Editions Dunod (Paris) 1959.

G-13 T. L. Saaty—Mathematical Methods of Operations Research, McGraw-Hill (N.Y.) 1959.

G-14 M. Sasieni, A. Yaspan and L. Friedman—Operations Research, Methods and Problems, John Wiley (N.Y.) 1959.

G-15 M. Spilman—Applications pratiques de la recherche opérationnelle ("Practical Applications of Operations Research"), Editions Eyrolles (Paris) 1960.

G-16 A. T. Bharucha-Reid—Elements of the Theory of Markov Processes and Their Applications, McGraw-Hill (N.Y.) 1959.

G-17 R. A. Howard—Dynamic Programming and Markov Processes, The Technology Press, M.I.T., 1960.

G-18 E. Parzen—Modern Probability Theory and Its Applications, John Wiley (N.Y.) 1960.

G-19 P. Rosenstiehl and A. Ghouila-Houri—Les choix économiques: Décisions séquentielles et simulation ("Economic Choices: Sequential Decisions and Simulation"), Editions Dunod (Paris) 1960.

G-20 R. Frisch—Maxima et Minima, Editions Dunod (Paris) 1960.

G-21 A. Kaufmann and R. Cruon—La théorie des phénomènes d'attente et ses applications ("The Theory of Delay Phenomena and Its Applications"), Editions Dunod (Paris) 1961.

Index

N

O

P

T

U

V

W

Z